2004

THE PAPERS OF JAMES C.H. ANDERSON

ACTUARIAL EDUCATION AND RESEARCH FUND
475 N. MARTINGALE ROAD
SCHAUMBURG, ILLINOIS 60173

Library of Congress Cataloging-in-Publication Data

Anderson, James C. H. (James Charles Henry), 1931-1995.
The papers of James C.H. Anderson.
p. cm.
Includes bibliographical references.
ISBN 0-938959-50-6
1. Insurance, Life. 2. Actuaries. I. Title.
HG8776.A53 1997 97-35908
368.32'01—dc21 CIP

ISBN 0-938959-50-6

Printed in the United States of America

Editor: Susan Pasini
SOA Liaison: Barbara Simmons, E.L.S., Publications Manager

Preface

Even though the voice of James Charles Henry Anderson was stilled on August 5, 1993, his vision, conviction, and intellectual courage remain an inspiration not only to the members of his profession but also to insurance and financial service executives in the U.S. and abroad.

Jim Anderson had that unique ability to see the future clearly without being overly influenced by the haze of the day. Jim was concerned that commercialism would encourage actuaries to please their employers or clients rather than to step out boldly and become instruments of change. In the actuarial profession, as in business, change is the requisite for survival.

Jim was the instrument of change in many areas where only the courageous would speak out. In 1959 he developed a new method for pricing life insurance products in the U.S., thereby challenging traditional concepts. Jim's method is the dominant one in use today for insurance product pricing. This break from tradition required vision, conviction, and courage.

Jim's vision also led to significant changes being made both in the type of products offered by life insurance companies and in the structure of their distribution systems. Indeed, Jim's vision, conviction, and courage enabled him to take the lead in the universal life revolution — a prophetic event. Others indeed made notable contributions to the universal life revolution, but it was Jim who took the brunt of the attack from those who were unwilling or lacking the courage to embrace the inevitable. In 1995, 21% of life insurance purchases in the United States was of interest-sensitive products derived from the universal life concept.

One of Jim's favorite admonitions was "Let's reexamine the premise." Indeed, this is a rational, unemotional response to intellectual challenges facing actuaries and their profession and the life insurance industry. This simple admonition encourages one to seek the truth.

Jim Anderson profoundly influenced students of the actuarial profession and the corporate executives who directed financial service activities.

One could continue at length in attribution to Jim of those concepts, visions, and pleadings for change which had a positive influence on the actuarial profession and the life insurance industry.

In the twenty-eight years during which I was associated with Jim, I knew him not only as an intellectual giant but also as a person of compassion, unselfishness, generosity, humor, sensitivity, and personal warmth. He had a profound influence on my life, and I shall always be grateful to him.

The reader's professional experience will be greatly enriched by Jim's genius, vision, conviction, and courage as revealed in this compilation of his writings.

Thomas P. Bowles, Jr.

Contents

Introduction

This book was published by the Actuarial Education and Research Fund (AERF) as part of its undertaking with regard to the implementation and administration of the James C. H. Anderson Memorial. The Memorial was established in 1995 by friends and admirers of Jim Anderson to reward excellence in his name and to foster the values that he exhibited and admired. The full statement of purpose of the Memorial follows:

> James Charles Henry Anderson was a remarkable man who made many lasting contributions not only to his profession but also to his friends and his family. He had a passion for excellence and for the truth, which he pursued relentlessly but always with a sense of humor and an appreciation of the views of others. His vision, leadership, and communication skills have had a profound influence on international financial markets, with exceptional effect in the area of insurance. He was also a constructive influence on the lives of many of the people who knew him. It is the desire of his friends and former associates to create a Memorial in his honor to foster forever the values that he exhibited and admired.
>
> The Memorial will embrace the concept of rewarding, on an international basis, achievements by individuals in fields related to financial and actuarial matters, especially those of an innovative, visionary, and iconoclastic nature.

The AERF has agreed to administer the Memorial. AERF represents seven North American actuarial organizations on a continuing basis and will coordinate with the actuarial organizations in other countries for this purpose. A Memorial fund has been created within AERF to receive and invest contributions and to make awards.

Funds will be used to:

- Commission papers or other work in actuarial or related fields identified by AERF as needing study
- Provide rewards for the best papers submitted to AERF in response to Calls for Papers on designated topics
- Provide awards for excellence of papers or for other achievements relating to financial or actuarial matters.

The following is a list of major sponsors of this project:

Neil M. Anderson
Rosalind Anderson
Richard Batty
Robert M. Beuerlein
Thomas P. & Arlene P. Bowles
William R. Britton, Jr.
Ronald M. & Kathy A. Butkiewicz
Tom & Janet Cerneka
Mike Corey/Ward Howell International, Inc.
William A. & Tannis E. Ferguson
Ardian & Anna Gill
Jeremy Goford
Patricia L. Guinn
Rodney L. & Jean S. Hale
David M. Holland
Anthony J. & Isabel D. Houghton
Irish Life of North America, Inc.
Irish Life plc
Jefferson-Pilot Corporation
Henry K. Knowlton
Ralph B. Levy and the Law Firm of King & Spalding
Liberty Life Association of Africa Limited
W. James & Barbara M. MacGinnitie
Rolph Masecar & Family
Tig Melville
Richard S. & Janet S. Miller
Randall P. Mire
Joe B. Pharr
Ralph & Minnie Sepel
Keith Skelley
J. Russell & Linda Southworth
Towers Perrin
Michael R. Tuohy
Samuel H. Turner
Jack & Edith Turnquist
Julius Vogel
David N. & Frances B. Wakely
R. Larry Warnock
Geoff Westall

Biography of James Charles Henry Anderson

Jim Anderson was born in Winnipeg, Canada, on February 14, 1931. He was a 1952 graduate of the University of Manitoba. His extraordinary abilities were evident at an early age and his strong sense of values and fairness was well formed before he entered the business world.

During his college years, Jim gathered experience with the Great West Life and Massachusetts Mutual. After graduation, he married his college sweetheart, Rosalind Milne, and joined the actuarial staff of Northwestern Mutual in Milwaukee where Roz and Jim made their first home together. In 1955 he accepted a position as Actuary of Family Fund Life in Atlanta. In 1958, he entered the consulting field in Atlanta with the firm of Bowles, Andrews and Towne.

While with Bowles, Andrews and Towne, Jim wrote a paper that was to make him famous. It was entitled "Gross Premium Calculations and Profit Measurement for Nonparticipating Insurance" and was published in the *Transactions of the Society of Actuaries* in 1959. Jim was awarded the Society's Triennial Prize for the paper. The approach presented in this paper serves as the basis for most of today's insurance pricing and appraisal work both in the United States and abroad.

In 1959, Jim became a Vice President of Georgia International Life Insurance Company. Ten years later he was elected President of Abbey International

Corporation in Atlanta, which specialized in the design and marketing of equity-linked products in several countries. For part of this time he was also Managing Director of Abbey Life in London, England.

Jim returned to consulting in Atlanta in 1972 with the firm of Bowles and Tillinghast and was named its President in 1974. The firm prospered under his leadership and grew from its two offices in Atlanta and Dallas to 28 offices in seven countries. The firm underwent several name changes over the years and finally become known as Tillinghast. During these years, Jim continued to enhance his reputation as an innovative thinker and pioneer in new products and marketing strategies. He was an early advocate of the universal life concept and became internationally renowned for his understanding of the changes taking place in the insurance industry. He curtailed some of his administrative duties with Tillinghast in 1986 and retired at the end of 1989.

During his career, Jim was a Director of at least fifteen insurance and/or financial organizations in seven countries.

It is not surprising that Jim excelled in his avocations. During his years in Winnipeg, he was a championship curler. In later years, he flew his own airplane and captained his own sailboat and yacht. He was an avid reader with remarkable retention. Although unlicensed, he was an able architect who designed and supervised the construction of two of his homes in Atlanta.

Jim was truly a giant in the insurance industry and the actuarial profession. He died on August 5, 1993 at his home in Atlanta. He was 62 years old. He was survived by his wife, Rosalind, three sons, a daughter, his sister Katherine-Mary Gibson and ten grandchildren. He will be remembered and missed by all who knew him.

Section 1
Products: Pricing, Profits, and Distribution

Gross Premium Calculations and Profit Measurement for Nonparticipating Insurance

Published in Transactions of the Society of Actuaries,
Volume XI (1959): 357–393.
Reprinted with permission from the Society of Actuaries.

Ratemaking for nonparticipating life insurance is a delightful mixture of science and art. In ratemaking, creative art begins where science leaves off. This paper will consider only the scientific aspects of ratemaking. Braver men may tamper with the mystical process which transforms actuaries into poets and calculated premiums into published rates. Final premium rates represent a blend of the sensations the actuary receives from examining the calculated rates, feeling the pulse of competition, smelling the sweet scent of low net cost, tasting the lotus of improving mortality, weighing the promise of increased new business, and hearing the distant rumble of the drums of war, epidemic, taxes and economic distress. Such activity transcends analysis:

> Weave a circle around him thrice,
> And close your eyes with holy dread,
> For he on honey-dew hath fed,
> And drunk the milk of Paradise.
>
> Coleridge

The specific purposes of this paper are:

1. To examine the relationship of gross premiums and profit margins, with particular reference to the probable effect of current developments
2. To suggest criteria for measuring contingency and profit margins and introducing these items into the calculation of premium rates

3. To discuss the types of assumptions suitable for the calculation of nonparticipating rates
4. To present the mathematical technique necessary for the determination of premiums according to the criteria and assumptions proposed
5. To develop a related technique suitable for evaluating the business in force and agency organization of a life insurance company
6. To demonstrate the practicality of the technique and to exhibit results derived by the presented method according to the proposed criteria and assumptions.

1. The Relationship of Gross Premiums and Profit Margins

Theoretical Premiums and Risk Classes

For each individual buyer of life insurance there exists a theoretical premium rate. It is uniquely defined by the following parameters:

1. the probability of collecting premiums;
2. the interest earned on accumulated funds;
3. the benefits paid on survival, death and withdrawal;
4. the expenses incurred, including taxes and reinsurance costs;
5. the charges assessed for contingencies;
6. the profit objectives adopted by the company; and
7. the basis of liabilities established for future benefits.

To the extent that this premium rate differs from the premium rate actually paid by the policyholder and to the extent that estimates of these parameters are in error, the profit objective is distorted.

A discussion of the problem of determining premium rates for any form of insurance must begin with consideration of the concept of a "risk class." By definition, a risk class is one in which all members are subject to the same probabilities of risk occurrence. To determine the theoretical premium rate for nonparticipating life insurance, it is necessary to establish risk classes for the purpose of predicting mortality rates, interest rates, expense rates, withdrawal rates, and contingency margins. For each risk, the distribution of risk classes is continuous; that is, the probability of finding any two individuals in precisely the same risk class is infinitesimal. For practical reasons this continuous distribution must be approximated by a discrete distribution, in which individuals in *similar* risk classes are treated as individuals in the *same* risk class. The width of the risk classes defined by the discrete distribution is a matter of judgment; broad classes simplify the classification problem at the expense of precision, and narrow classes improve the approximation at the expense of simplicity. Within a given class the same premium is paid by all members, but the actual profit margin is subject to substantial variation among individuals, even if classes are narrowly defined; for example, among individuals of the same nearest integral age and sex, subject to the same underwriting requirements, there are significantly different probabilities of death and hence significantly different theoretical premiums. The determination of risk classes has, therefore, an important bearing on actual profit margins.

Current Developments

The broad averaging formerly applied in defining risk classes has been superseded, to a large extent, by a more sophisticated interpretation of that term. The trend of the industry in this direction is evidenced by the now general recognition of policy size and the growing recognition of sex in rate structures for both participating and nonparticipating life insurance. However one may view these developments, there should be general agreement that rate structure refinement is a one-way street, the end of which is not yet in sight. Future developments may include:

1. a system of premium rates graded by policy size which recognizes differences attributable to the length of the premium period;
2. fractional premiums which recognize the per-collection expense, the effect of age and plan, and possibly the effect of fractional premiums on deficiency reserves;
3. nonforfeiture values which recognize the effect of policy size and sex.

Because the method of defining discrete risk classes does not affect the theoretical premium for any individual, rate refinement can be viewed as a redistribution of the margins for profit in a way which reduces fluctuations within classes.

The trend of the life insurance industry towards more refined rate structures can be interpreted as an increase in the importance of price as a factor affecting the sale of life insurance. Whether or not this sentiment originated with the buying public is immaterial; if it was created by the industry itself, it will speedily be communicated to the public through life insurance agents. The ultimate results will likely be a more informed buyer and a consequent increase in the gravitational effect of low premium rates on the distribution of life insurance sales. The importance of the distribution of profit margins obviously increases as buyers of life insurance become more informed and as the distribution of sales is more substantially influenced by pricing. Another aspect of rate refinement and buyer awareness merits observation. With a few exceptions, such as special plans available only for amounts greater than some relatively high minimum, risk classes were formerly determined by the entire industry in a relatively uniform fashion, using nearest integral age as the only criterion of classification for standard risks. Risk classes are no longer uniform from company to company. The extent of the recognition of policy size and sex varies from company to company, giving the buyer the opportunity to select against the industry as a whole by buying from a company whose classification system favors him.

Perhaps this could be said more briefly: the cost of loss leaders has increased and is still increasing. If all life insurance purchases were made on the basis of price alone, aggregate industry profits would be materially reduced and might even vanish. One way to avoid shrinking margins is through the development of more sensitive methods of measuring profits and calculating premium rates. It may also be necessary to refine continually the rate structure unless the industry adopts a uniform system of risk classification.

Control of Parameters and Rates

To what extent can a company control the factors involved in the equation which expresses the relationship between profit objectives and gross premiums? Among the expense items, commissions are subject to direct control within the limitations of section 213 of the New York Insurance Law, if applicable, and the limitations imposed by the competition for manpower. Direct control of the valuation basis may be exercised, but this is severely restricted by law in all jurisdictions of the United States and Canada and somewhat affected by competitive considerations in the United States due to the relationship of reserves and nonforfeiture values. Interest earnings, benefit payments, lapse rates, other expenses and margins for contingencies can be controlled only indirectly. The dependent variable in this equation is the gross premium, which is subject to legal limitations in Wisconsin[1] and Kansas[2] and to competitive limitations everywhere. The profit objective is therefore the only completely independent variable.

The Effect of Competition

To what extent is direct control of gross premiums limited by competitive considerations? Table 1 shows the premium rates for the whole life plan which have recently been adopted by ten prominent stock companies. This plan was selected to minimize differences attributable to cash values. Since the whole life plan is particularly sensitive to competitive considerations, the range of premium rates for any other plan would probably be much wider.

It is clear from Table 1 that competition has played a large part in the establishment of the rate patterns of these companies, especially at those points where sales volume is high. The ten companies have, in aggregate, premium rates which are quite comparable. The scale of weights used to determine the average premiums is arbitrary but in general agreement with industry averages. According to that scale, there is less than a 4% difference in the aggregate rates of the highest and lowest companies. At particular ages and for particular policy sizes, the average variation is 8%,or $1.89 per thousand. Even this narrowly defined competitive rate band is very wide in relation to the probable profit which is contemplated by these companies. The difference between adopting all of the "high" rates and all of the "low" rates is probably the difference between very comfortable profit margins and none at all.

Whenever the theoretical premium rate calculated by a particular company is outside of the competitive range, that company must choose between the following alternatives:

1. controlling one or more of the factors involved in the relation between profit objectives and premium rates;
2. revising its profit objectives;

[1]Wisconsin law specifies a maximum gross premium; this has little effect on non-participating premiums.

[2]Kansas law specifies a minimum gross premium equal to the valuation net premium on the valuation basis selected; this has a material effect on rates, especially those for large amounts, high ages, and low premium plans.

Table 1 — Nonparticipating Whole Life Premium Rates per $1,000

Age	Amount	Weight	Company A	B	C	D*	E	F	G	H†	I	J	High	Mean	Low	Range	
15	$ 3,000	.05	$14.38	$12.07	$12.05	$13.05	$12.64	$11.61	$12.57	$13.20	$11.46	$12.24	$14.38	$12.53	$11.46	$2.92	23.3%
	6,000	.02	11.38	12.07	11.22	11.80	10.64	10.77	11.41	11.70	9.80	10.99	12.07	11.18	9.80	2.27	20.3
	12,000	.01	10.53	10.57	10.38	10.78	9.89	10.36	10.82	10.95	8.96	10.37	10.95	10.36	8.96	1.99	19.2
	30,000	.01	10.08	10.07	9.88	10.40	9.64	10.11	10.47	10.50	8.46	9.99	10.50	9.96	8.46	2.04	20.5
25	3,000	.03	17.74	15.48	15.56	16.47	16.30	15.30	15.92	16.43	16.37	15.66	17.74	16.12	15.30	2.44	15.1
	6,000	.09	14.74	15.48	14.73	15.22	14.30	14.46	14.76	14.93	14.71	14.41	15.48	14.77	14.30	1.18	8.0
	12,000	.09	13.89	13.98	13.89	13.76	13.55	14.05	14.17	14.18	13.87	13.79	14.18	13.91	13.55	.63	4.5
	30,000	.04	13.44	13.48	13.39	13.38	13.30	13.80	13.82	13.73	13.37	13.41	13.82	13.51	13.30	.52	3.8
35	3,000	.03	23.45	21.25	21.26	21.95	22.10	20.82	21.15	21.30	21.98	21.26	23.45	21.65	20.82	2.63	12.1
	6,000	.09	20.45	21.25	20.43	20.70	20.10	19.98	19.99	19.80	20.32	20.01	21.25	20.30	19.80	1.45	7.1
	12,000	.12	19.60	19.75	19.59	19.07	19.35	19.57	19.40	19.05	19.48	19.39	19.75	19.43	19.05	.70	3.6
	30,000	.06	19.15	19.25	19.09	18.69	19.10	19.32	19.05	18.60	18.98	19.01	19.32	19.02	18.60	.72	3.8
45	3,000	.02	32.38	29.95	30.36	30.53	31.78	29.86	29.85	30.25	30.70	30.18	32.38	30.58	29.85	2.53	8.3
	6,000	.08	29.38	29.95	29.53	29.28	29.78	29.02	28.69	28.75	29.04	28.93	29.95	29.24	28.69	1.26	4.3
	12,000	.11	28.53	28.45	28.69	27.64	29.03	28.61	28.10	28.00	28.20	28.31	29.03	28.36	27.64	1.39	4.9
	30,000	.05	28.08	27.95	28.19	27.26	28.78	28.36	27.75	27.55	27.70	27.93	28.78	27.96	27.26	1.52	5.4
55	3,000	.01	46.77	44.36	44.60	45.62	48.84	44.09	44.65	44.25	45.36	44.48	48.84	45.30	44.09	4.75	10.5
	6,000	.02	43.77	44.36	43.77	44.37	46.84	43.25	43.49	42.75	43.70	43.23	46.84	43.95	42.75	4.09	9.3
	12,000	.02	42.92	42.86	42.93	42.33	46.09	42.84	42.90	42.00	42.86	42.61	46.09	43.03	42.00	4.09	9.5
	30,000	.01	42.47	42.36	42.43	41.95	45.84	42.59	42.55	41.55	42.36	42.23	45.84	42.63	41.55	4.29	10.1
65	3,000	.01	74.17	70.28	72.79	75.23	81.43	71.84	70.57	73.00	73.33	70.30	81.43	73.29	70.28	11.15	15.2
	6,000	.01	71.17	70.28	71.96	73.98	79.43	71.00	69.41	71.50	71.67	69.05	79.43	71.95	69.05	10.38	14.4
	12,000	.01	70.32	68.78	71.12	68.76	78.68	70.59	68.82	70.75	70.83	68.43	78.68	70.71	68.43	10.25	14.5
	30,000	.01	69.87	68.28	70.62	68.38	78.43	70.34	68.47	70.30	70.33	68.05	78.43	70.31	68.05	10.38	14.8
Weighted Average			$23.87	$23.69	$23.58	$23.50	$24.14	$23.42	$23.35	$23.36	$23.40	$23.26	$24.74	$23.56	$22.85	$1.89	8.0%
Average Index (all companies = 100.0)			101.3	100.6	100.1	99.7	102.5	99.4	99.1	99.2	99.3	98.7	102.5	100.0	98.7	3.8	3.8%

*Life Paid-up at 90 for $3,000 and $6,000, Whole Life for $12,000 and $30,000.

†Estimated waiver benefit subtracted.

3. adopting premium rates which are competitively unrealistic;
4. accepting the penalties of a loss leader.

In the case of a typical company, most of the theoretical premium rates will fall within the indicated competitive range. The competitive position of the company at particular points in the array of premium rates will then be largely determined by the distribution of profit margins adopted by the company. If there is a uniform distribution of profit throughout the rate structure, the realization of the profit objective cannot be thwarted by a shift in the distribution of sales.

Existing Methods of Expressing Profit Objectives and Calculating Gross Premiums

There is no single system for introducing profit margins into the calculation of gross premiums and, consequently, no unique scale of "uniform" profit margins. Frequently profit margins and contingency margins are introduced without specific identification. Traditionally, these margins are introduced, separately or jointly, in one or more of the following ways:

1. as a function of premium;
2. as a function of the amount of insurance;
3. as a function of a specific reserve;
4. as a redundant estimate of mortality costs;
5. as an understatement of the probable future interest rate.

With contingency margins and profit objectives expressed in such a manner, with those factors fixed which can be directly controlled, and with estimates of other factors affecting the gross premium, the calculation of theoretical premium rates can be performed in a variety of ways. The three widely known and generally accepted methods are those associated with the names of Messrs. Cammack, Hoskins, and Jenkins; each method produces satisfactory premiums from the assumptions made and the profit objectives and criteria established. One limitation shared by all three methods pertains to the establishment of profit objectives: the surplus depletion incurred at issue is recovered, together with interest at the assumed rate, and profit in excess of this interest on surplus depletion is realized, but the additional profit is not directly associated with the amount of surplus expended to produce it. The purpose of the technique to be proposed in this paper is to remove this limitation.

2. Contingency Margins and Profit Objectives

A defense of each of the traditional methods of introducing contingency and profit margins into gross premium calculations can be mustered without great difficulty, but it cannot be conclusively shown that one is superior to all others. To make a meaningful analysis of contingency margins and profit objectives, each must be considered separately.

Contingency Margins

For what purpose are contingency margins required? Fundamentally, these are charges levied to meet the cost of unpredictable events of major financial consequence for which provision has not elsewhere been made. Contingency margins are not related to funds maintained for the purpose of absorbing statistical fluctuations; that latter purpose is properly performed by the surplus account of a company issuing nonparticipating life insurance. Contingency margins are required to meet the cost of events so different from expected experience that the statistical estimates are disqualified. For example, the use of mortality estimates derived from the experience of a period free from war or epidemic makes no provision for these contingencies and a separate charge must therefore be included. Other contingencies which must be considered in establishing premium rates for nonparticipating life insurance are capital losses (as distinguished from fluctuations in the book value of assets), the long-term effect of inflation on expense rates, and increased premium and federal income taxes.

It is suggested that provision be made for contingency margins in the calculation of premium rates by some kind of estimate, however crude, of the probable impact of the given contingency. For example, the hazard of war or epidemic might be assessed as twenty-five extra deaths per thousand per century at each attained age and introduced into the calculation by adding .00025 to each mortality rate. Similarly, the contingency margin for capital losses can be introduced by an adjustment to the assumed interest rate; the adjustment might be based on the contribution, ignoring capital gains and losses, to the Mandatory Security Valuation Reserve. The dollar effect of the inflation hazard on expense rates is probably of minor consequence because the major portion of expenses are either incurred at issue or contractual. Provision for increased premium taxes can be made by an adjustment to the percentage expenses, possibly increasing by duration. The contingency of increased federal income taxes can be handled by a reappraisal of profit objectives. This list of contingencies is not exhaustive nor are the suggested methods of assessing charges unique; each represents one way to introduce the necessary charge. It is of great importance to recognize that contingency margins are *not* profit margins in the real sense despite the fact that, unless realistic reserves are established, they will emerge as such during the periods free from the occurrence of the hazards anticipated. Contingency margins are charges for real but deferred *costs.* Over a very extended period of time true profit may be realized from contingency margins, but only if charges made for contingencies prove to be redundant.

Profit Objectives

The profit objective is that introduced directly into the calculation of theoretical gross premiums. As stated in Section 1, the profit actually realized will differ from the profit objective on account of differences between the actual premium and the theoretical premium and differences between actual experience and estimated experience. Since the calculation of a theoretical gross premium is concerned only with the profit objective, these two differences need not be considered.

For what reason should profits be realized by stockholders on the sale of nonparticipating life insurance? Justification must be found in the service performed by stockholders for policyholders. Despite the dampening effect of the personal relationship between agents and prospects, life insurance sales are still subject to basic economic laws: a transaction is possible only if the lowest price at which the seller will furnish the service is less than the highest price which the buyer is prepared to pay; within this range, the actually price paid is greatly influenced by competitive considerations. Thus, the stockholders' viewpoint determines the minimum premium rate, the policyholders' viewpoint determines the maximum premium rate, and competitive considerations determine the final premium rate between these limits. In setting the profit *objective*, only the stockholders' viewpoint need be considered; the policyholders' viewpoint and competitive considerations affect only the *realization* of this objective. Two distinct profit objectives are worthy of separate consideration: the minimum *aggregate* profit which will be accepted on all business and the minimum *individual* profit which will be accepted at any particular point of the rate array. Premium rates based on the former objective will determine the average level of gross premiums and premiums based on the latter objective will determine the minimum rate which can be charged at any point. Ideally, these two objectives would be equal.

What then is the lowest aggregate and individual profit for which the stockholder is willing to perform this service and to what is it best related? A life insurance company can be viewed as a vehicle for the investment of stockholders' capital and surplus. The investment of capital must be confined to certain types of securities permitted by law, but surplus may be invested in one of three ways:

1. in tangible assets such as real estate and in stocks, bonds, mortgages and other intangible assets, subject to state regulation of life insurance company investments;
2. in absorbing the surplus drains which result from the issuance of new business in prospect of future profits on that business;
3. in expanding the agency plant by means of which additional amounts of new business will be produced, additional surplus invested and additional profit realized.

In investments of the first type, the yield is measured in relation to the amount invested and expressed as a rate which varies from one type of security to another. It is suggested that the same two criteria be applied to the measurement of profit resulting from investments of types 2 and 3 mentioned above; that is:

1. that the amount of profit be related to the amount of surplus which must be invested to acquire that profit and expressed as a yield rate on the investment; and
2. that the yield rate be associated with the degree of risk incurred on the type of investment made.

When a new policy is sold and when new agents are recruited, the surplus account of the life insurance company is depleted in virtually every case. It is proposed that the profit objective be defined by the criterion that the present value of the profits which will be received in the future be equal to the present value of the surplus depletion, with both present values based on a yield rate or yield rates which represent adequate return to the stockholders for the degree of risk incurred in expending surplus in the expectation of receiving future profits. That is, the present value of the entire series of profits and losses is zero.

The return on funds invested in an agency organization emerges in a more obscure fashion than that attributable to investment in new business. To introduce profit associated with this type of surplus investment, it is necessary to analyze the development of an agency from its date of organization for the purpose of estimating the costs incurred in that development and the volume of business which will result. Such an analysis will differ vastly from company to company. Those companies operating under the general agency system will experience different patterns of cost and return than those companies operating under a branch office system; those companies with a relatively high contractual compensation scheme will incur smaller development costs than those companies with a relatively low contractual compensation scheme. For the purpose of this analysis, it is necessary to make estimates of the following items:

1. the rate of growth of the agency, in terms of new manpower recruited;
2. turnover rates of agents;
3. average production per agent for each contract year;
4. financing costs per agent by contract year;
5. the excess of actual agency expenses over assumed agency expenses during the early years of the agency (attributable to branch manager's salary, financing of general agents, etc.); and
6. recoveries of unearned renewal commissions from terminated agents.

From these data estimates can be made of agency development costs in excess of those introduced directly into the premium rate calculation, and of the volume of production which will be realized from the agency. Table 2 traces the development of a model agency from its date of organization to its assumed date of maturity 20 years later. After the 20th year the size of the organization is assumed to be stationary and the net development outlay after that time is the excess of the financing cost for agents hired to replace ones that terminate over the amount recovered from the unearned renewal commissions of agents who

Table 2 — Model Agency Projection

Agency Year	Commission Value Produced	Financing Costs Incurred	Excess Expenses Incurred	Unearned Renewals Recovered	Net Development Outlay
1	$ 21,675	$ 5,338	$ 10,247	$ 0	$ 15,585
2	36,525	7,198	6,990	142	14,046
3	47,225	7,813	4,644	611	11,846
4	55,775	7,813	2,769	1,368	9,214
5	62,650	7,813	1,261	2,306	6,768
6	68,4000	7,813	0	3,343	4,470
7	73,375	7,813		4,438	3,385
8	77,725	7,813		5,532	2,281
9	81,625	7,813		6,652	1,161
10	85,200	7,813		7,772	41
11	88,475	7,813		8,667	– 854
12	91,525	7,813		9,421	– 1,608
13	94,450	7,813		10,076	– 2,263
14	97,275	7,813		10,720	– 2,907
15	99,925	7,813		11,353	– 3,540
16	102,525	7,813		11,680	– 3,867
17	105,050	7,813		11,809	– 3,996
18	107,550	7,813		11,809	– 3,996
19	109,975	7,813		11,809	– 3,996
20 & subs.	112,300	7,813		11,809	– 3,996

Yield Rate	Present Value of Production	Present Value of Outlay	Ratio
15%	$491,928	$46,344	9.42%
20	349,507	45,470	13.01

have previously terminated.[3] Under a fully vested agency contract this latter amount would be zero. The aggregate production of the agency is measured in terms of the present value of commissions (including contractual expense allowances) on business produced. Since commissions are the basis of determining the compensation of an agency organization, that organization will measure its own performance and effectiveness in accordance with such an index. To make the objectives of the company coincide with those of its agency organization, it is submitted that this index is the best available measure of the aggregate business activity of an agency. The suggested method could also be

[3]The evaluation of the renewal commissions on agents who have previously terminated could, instead, be included directly in the premium calculations as a modification to the commission assumptions.

applied if performance were to be measured in terms of premium volume or amount of insurance, should these indexes be deemed more appropriate. The assumptions underlying the model agency are stated below; the variations of such assumptions from company to company would be very great and it is unlikely that the illustration could be applied to any particular company.

Assumptions:

1. Four new men hired at beginning of each year
2. McConney-Guest Modified Agents Survival Table
3. Average production—$10,000 total commission value per agent, reduced to 80%, 90% and 95% in first three contract years and to 25% in year of termination
4. Financing costs to produce $4,800 stable income:
   1st Year—$1,700 per agent completing year, $850 per terminated agent
   2d Year—$1,000 per agent completing year, $500 per terminated agent
   3d Year—$500 per agent completing year, $250 per terminated agent
5. Estimated agency costs of $15,000 in 6th year, as provided in premium calculations; expenses for years 1 through 5 assumed to be $15,000; excess expenses based on ratio of production to that of year 6
6. Agents renewal commission 5% for policy years 2–10, 3% for policy years 11–15; no vesting on production of contract years 1–3, full vesting thereafter
7. Persistency and other assumptions in accordance with the standard assumptions shown in Appendix A

To provide adequate return to the stockholders for their investment, it is necessary that the value of profits generated by an agency be equal to the value of the investment made in that agency, with both present values based on a yield rate which reflects the degree of risk incurred on amounts invested in this manner. This is somewhat complicated by the fact that additional investment will be made as new business is issued, and provision must be made for adequate return on such amounts. The basic condition of the equality of the value of profits and investment can be satisfied in the following manner:

1. express the agency development costs as a percentage of commissions;
2. determine the theoretical gross premium by the criterion that the value of profits be equal to that percentage of the value of commissions.

The rate used for valuation in (1) above is the yield on surplus invested in agency development; the rate used for valuation in (2) above is the yield on surplus invested in new business. These two yield rates are independent.

3. Estimating the Parameters Which Affect Gross Premiums

With the inclusion of specific contingency margins and profit objectives, it is proposed that other assumptions necessary to calculate gross premiums be introduced on the basis of "best estimates" rather than "conservative estimates."

Five items must be established or estimated: mortality, interest, expenses, persistency, and reserves. The nature of the benefits must include a definition of the nonforfeiture values and, in the case of term insurance, the inclusion of a conversion privilege may somewhat alter the kind of mortality estimates which must be made.

A specific set of assumptions is stated in Appendix A. These assumptions have been used to determine the premium rates which are illustrated later in this paper. At this point it is appropriate only to discuss the rationale of certain of the assumptions, and the considerations affecting the choice of specific estimates.

Mortality

The technique which will be described in Section 4 uses mortality rates without the construction of intermediate functions. This allows great flexibility in the selection of mortality assumptions. It is practical to give recognition to a number of factors which have a significant effect on mortality but which are generally ignored because of the complications introduced in calculating premiums. The factors which affect mortality in some degree are: attained age, selection age, selection standards, sex, broad plan groups (such as permanent plans, term plans and possibly decreasing term plans) and amount of insurance. The extent to which each of these factors is reflected is a matter of judgment, strongly influenced by the calculation facilities available: if a computer is used, the storage space necessary to retain the mortality table or tables must not surpass the capacities of the machine. The mortality assumptions for the various risk classes can be wholly independent or can be related to one set of mortality rates by some simple formula such as:

$$q' = aq + b$$

Two items which, technically, are not mortality costs should be considered at this point. These items are contingency margins for catastrophic mortality costs and reinsurance costs. Both of these can most conveniently be included as modifications of the mortality rates, although such inclusion incorrectly affects the probability of survival. The effect of this theoretical error is very small.

Contingency margins can be introduced in the manner suggested in Section 2 by increasing each mortality rate by an amount representing the estimated cost of mortality contingencies. In the past, the impact of the war hazard was much greater on male mortality in the age range 18 through 40. To the extent that this is expected to continue, the margin for contingencies might be redistributed to increase the charges at these ages. The distribution of mortality contingency charges is subject to the judgment of each individual actuary.

Reinsurance costs can also be estimated by an adjustment to the mortality rates. Although experience refund formulas and premium rates on yearly renewable term reinsurance vary somewhat from company to company, a satisfactory approximation can be made. Typical reinsurance premium rates are quite close to the mortality rates according to the 1941 CSO Mortality Table; typical experience refund formulas return to the ceding company one half of the difference between 90% of the reinsurance premiums paid and the claim costs incurred. If k represents the proportion of the net amount at risk which is reinsured and q the expected mortality, the following relationship defines the mortality rate, q', which will approximate combined mortality and reinsurance costs:

$$q' = .55kq^{cso} + (1 - .50k)\, q.$$

In a particular case, the exact reinsurance premiums and experience refund formula could be applied to develop a better approximation.

Interest

The proposed premium calculation technique allows complete freedom in selecting interest assumptions because no intermediate functions are involved. The reliability of an estimate of future interest earnings decreases as the period to which it applies becomes more remote. This is especially significant if current interest rates are materially different from expected long-range average yields. An interest assumption varying by duration is probably the most satisfactory estimate when such a condition prevails.

Interest earnings are affected only gradually by the yield rate on new investments; the earnings of a given interval are determined by an average of yields from investment made in many prior years. An estimate of the trend of this aggregate yield can be made with reference to six items:

1. the aggregate yield on the present holdings of each risk class;
2. the estimated net new money available each year on account of each risk class;
3. the yield rate on expected maturities and sales;
4. the yield rate currently available on new investments;
5. the yield rate ultimately expected on new investments; and
6. the rate of change of the yield rate on new investments from current to ultimate levels.

The notion of risk classes for investment purposes deserves some attention. It has been customary for life insurance companies to include all policyholders in one investment risk class. Without violating any law pertaining to segregation of assets, a company might establish several risk classes to take account of major lines of business and, possibly, groups of calendar issue years.

The method of estimating future interest earnings is unaffected by the number of risk classes, although the results of one approach will usually differ from those of another. Today, the yield rate on new investments is higher than the yield on the aggregate holdings of an established company; that aggregate yield rate is higher than the long-term yield rate on which most companies are prepared to gamble. In this situation, for companies following the single risk class philosophy, the estimated interest earnings would begin at a rate equal to the aggregate yield and continue as a level or slightly increasing rate for a few years, then decline gradually for many years and approach the expected long-term yield rate. For companies establishing new issues as a risk class apart from past issues, the interest estimate would begin at a somewhat higher level, equal to the current rate available on new investments, and decline monotonically to approach the same ultimate rate.

As stated in Section 3, the hazard of capital losses can be conveniently and appropriately reflected by a reduction in the assumed interest rate. For the purpose of assessing a charge for this contingency, a single risk class is clearly indicated in the absence of special circumstances. The amount of the charge should reflect the investment policy of the company and the current distribution of assets.

Expenses

For the purpose of calculating gross premiums, estimates of future insurance expenses are usually expressed as *rates* related to premium volume, amount of insurance or number of policies. Expense rates are determined by policy year of incidence for each policy status (premium paying, paid-up, terminated by death and otherwise terminated).

Many of the expenses of a life insurance company are of an *indirect* nature, comparable to those expenses of a commercial venture which are referred to as "overhead." Such expenses are related only vaguely, if at all, to the usual indexes; it is more appropriate to express them as a function of *volume, as measured by stockholders' profit objectives*. If profit objectives are expressed as a yield on surplus investment, these expenses might be allocated as a charge against *gross* yield; this would determine *net* yield. This would treat indirect expenses in a manner analogous to the allocation of investment expenses and is probably the most precise theoretically. Practical difficulties arise for two reasons:

1. the adequacy of the expense estimate depends upon the volume of business *and* the volume of surplus invested; the latter may be difficult to control or estimate;
2. some indirect expenses are more properly related to the amount of business activity rather than total surplus investment; indirect agency expense is a suitable example.

To reduce these practical difficulties, all or part of the indirect expenses might be related to volume as measured by the present value of commissions (and, hence, profit).

The proposed method of introducing expenses allows allocation in the following ways:

1. expenses varying by policy year per policy in force, expenses per claim and expenses per other termination are used together with a stipulated policy size; for term conversions a conversion expense per policy converted is also used;
2. percentage-of-premium expenses are divided into commissions (including contractual expense allowances) and other percentage expenses, with complete flexibility by duration;
3. indirect first year expenses are introduced as a percentage of the present value of commissions; any indirect renewal expenses may either be expressed as a percentage of premium renewal expense, perhaps related to renewal commissions, or included in the first year indirect expense at discounted amount.

Indirect expenses may also be included, in whole or in part, by using a *gross* yield rate as the profit objective. In this case, the premium rate will properly reflect these expenses, but the series of annual profits will not.

The difference between the proposed method of expense allocation and the customary method is the handling of indirect expenses. Clearly, items such as advertising, general research, home office agency department, and association dues are indirect expenses; it is also clear that items such as commissions are direct expenses. For another class of expenses, the distinction is not clear because more than one philosophy can be applied. This class consists primarily of per-policy expenses. To illustrate the philosophic difference, the following example is cited:

> The issue expense of 2,000 policies of a given risk class is $140,000; if only 1,000 such policies were issued, the expense would be $90,000.

The issue expense of this company can be expressed in many ways, each representing a different mixture of the following two extremes:

1. express the issue expense as the *average cost* of $70 per policy;
2. express the issue expense as the *marginal cost* of $50 per policy and include the difference between aggregate marginal cost and total expense as an indirect expense of $40,000, which would be merged with other indirect expenses.

Evidently, the marginal cost philosophy substantially increases the importance of indirect expenses. The effect of marginal cost expense rates is especially marked for a company with a low volume of business. Theoretical premium rates for such a company will show spectacular variations for various policy sizes if the average cost philosophy is adopted. The use of marginal cost expense rates sharply reduces the effect of policy size on premium rates and produces a premium rate pattern by policy size which more closely resembles that of a large company because the expenses allocated on a per-policy basis are reduced.

One obvious objection to the use of marginal cost expense rates is the practical difficulty of determining such rates. Although this problem is outside the scope of the subject under discussion, it might be observed that marginal cost expense rates are made up of that portion of total expense which is sometimes designated as the variant. The invariant expense is immediately part of the indirect expense. Marginal cost expense rates might, therefore, be more easily and more precisely determined than average cost expense rates, since the invariant is the most awkward item to handle in an expense study.

Persistency

Any scale of probabilities of lapse can be used in the proposed method since the probabilities are introduced directly. Despite the fact that significant studies of persistency can be made on considerably smaller groups than significant studies of mortality, it is difficult to find authentic statistical data to support suspected differences in persistency among various groups or risk classes. Broad plan classes, sex, issue age, mode of payment, and amount of insurance probably have significant effects on persistency which should be recognized. Because the extent to which each of these factors affects persistency varies substantially between companies because of differences in underwriting policy, agency objectives and other factors, industry experience is not necessarily a reliable guide for a particular company. Where differences on account of any of these possible classifications are known to be significant, the differences should be recognized in estimating persistency rates for the purpose of calculating gross premiums.

It is difficult to make an accurate estimate of persistency because changes in economic conditions can produce massive shifts in probabilities. Such changes might properly be regarded as contingencies for which provisions should be made, but because the effect of such shifts is greatly different for given plans, ages and durations, it is no easy matter to introduce charges which effectively reflect the true financial impact. The use of conservative estimates of persistency is probably the only practical device for including a contingency margin.

Reserve Basis

The proposed profit objective takes account of realized profit; realized profit is profit released to surplus and available for distribution to or reinvestment by stockholders. Unless the yield rate on invested surplus is exactly equal to the assumed interest rate, the reserve basis will have a significant effect on the value of realized profit. The use of net level premium reserves rather than modified preliminary term reserves increases the amount of invested surplus at issue by an amount which probably averages $20 per $1,000 of insurance. Changes in the valuation interest rates have a less spectacular effect on invested surplus, unless deficiency reserves are involved. There is, for all practical purposes, no choice of mortality tables at this time, but this situation will be changed when the 1958 CSO Table is approved for use in all jurisdictions of the United States. In any case, the selection of a mortality table would have a relatively minor effect on the invested surplus unless, again, the question of deficiency reserves is involved.

The reserves to be used for the purpose of calculating gross premiums according to the suggested profit objective should include the deficiency reserves, if any, based on the calculated premium since this affects markedly the amount of surplus invested in the sale of a given piece of new business. At certain points in the rate array of some nonparticipating companies, deficiency reserves in excess of $100 per $1,000 are required at issue. This factor has a substantial effect on gross premiums. The proposed method takes direct account of the valuation basis and the deficiency reserves produced by the calculated premium.

4. Gross Premium Calculation Technique

Definition of Symbols:

The following items are defined by the policy benefits:

${}_tD$ = Death benefit, policy year t

${}_tS$ = Survival benefit payable to those completing policy year t

${}_tCV$ = Cash value at end of policy year t

${}_tV$ = Terminal reserve, policy year t

${}_tV'$ = Terminal reserve, policy year t, including any deficiency reserve arising from the calculated premium

${}_tTA$ = Conversion allowance, end of policy year t, in excess of cash value

T_t = Conversion cost (excess mortality) per \$1,000 converted at the end of policy year t

A = Policy size

P = Valuation net renewal premium

n = Premium payment period

m = Frequency of premium payment

The following items are yield rates; each applies to policy year t:

i_t = Interest earned on invested assets

j_t = Profit required on surplus invested in new business

The following items are expense rates and expense related items:

C_t = Commission rate, policy year t

P_t = Other percentage expenses, policy year t

E_t = Expense per policy in force at beginning of policy year t

Q = Claim expense per policy

W = Other termination expense per policy

TE = Conversion expense per policy

a = Indirect expense as a multiple of present value of commissions

b = Required present value of profit as a multiple of present value of commissions

The following items are probabilities of occurrence during policy year t among entrants of that year:

q_t = Probability of death

w_t = Probability of voluntary withdrawal, excluding conversion

c_t = Probability of conversion

The following items are calculated:

P$'$ = Calculated gross premium

${}_tB$ = Book (realized) profit, as of beginning of policy year t, based on a gross premium equal to the valuation net premium

Z = Present value at issue of book profits, ${}_tB$

X = Present value of commissions based on a gross premium equal to the valuation net premium

Y = Present value of increased profits for each \$1 increase in gross premium from P

Y' = Present value of decreased profits for each \$1 decrease in gross premium from P (algebraically positive)

Formulas

$$
\begin{aligned}
{}_tB = {}_{t-1}V &+ \frac{\mathrm{P}}{1 + \frac{m-1}{2m} \cdot i_t}\left[1 - \frac{m-1}{2m}(w_t + q_t)\right](1 - C_t - P_t) \\
&- \frac{E_t}{A} - \frac{{}_tD + Q/A}{1 + i_t/2} \cdot q_t - \frac{\frac{m+1}{2m} \cdot {}_tCV + \frac{m-1}{2m} \cdot {}_{t-1}CV + W/A}{1 + \frac{m+1}{2m} \cdot i_t} \cdot w \\
&- \frac{{}_tCV + TA_t + T_t - (E_1 - TE)/A}{1 + i_t} \cdot c_t \\
&- \frac{{}_tS}{1 + i_t}\left(1 - \frac{m-1}{m} \cdot w_t - q_t\right) - \frac{{}_tV}{1 + i_t}(1 - q_t - w_t - c_t)
\end{aligned}
$$

where $t \leq n$; where $t > n$, apply the same formula with $\mathrm{P} \equiv 0$.

$$Z = \sum_{1}^{\infty} {}_tB \, F_t$$

where $F_1 \equiv 1$ and

$$F_{t+1} = \frac{1 - q_t - w_t - c_t}{1 + j_t} \cdot F_t$$

$$X = \mathrm{P} \cdot \sum_{1}^{n} C_t F_t$$

$$Y = \sum_{1}^{n} \frac{\left[1 - \frac{m-1}{2m}(w_t + q_t)\right](1 - C_t - P_t)}{1 + \frac{m-1}{2m} \cdot i_t} \cdot F_t$$

$$Y' = Y + \sum_{1}^{n}\left[\frac{\ddot{a}_t(1 - q_t - w_t - c_t)}{1 + i_t} - \ddot{a}_{t-1}\right]F_t\,,$$

whence

$$Y' = Y + \sum_{1}^{n} \frac{\ddot{a}_t}{1 + i_t} (j_t - i_t) F_{t+1} ,$$

where $\ddot{a}_t$ represents the present value of a life annuity due for the remainder of the premium period on the valuation basis and where $\ddot{a}_0 = 0$.

Let

$$Z' = Z + (P' - P)\, Y \qquad \text{where} \qquad P' \geq P ,$$

and

$$Z' = Z + (P' - P)\, Y' \qquad \text{where} \qquad P' < P ,$$

Let

$$X' = \frac{P'}{P} \cdot X.$$

The required relationship is then:

$$Z' = (a + b)\, X' ;$$

i.e.,

$$+ (P' - P)Y = (a + b) \frac{P'}{P} \cdot X$$

or

$$P' = \frac{YP^2 - ZP}{YP - (a + b)\, X'} \qquad \text{if } P' \geq P;$$

similarly,

$$P' = \frac{Y'P^2 - ZP}{Y'P - (a + b)\, X'} \qquad \text{if } P' < P;$$

The actual book profit, ${}_tB'$, can be determined by the formula for ${}_tB$, substituting ${}_tV'$ for ${}_tV$ and P′ for P, and introducing the first year indirect expense of aX' and the results may be checked by:

$$b\, X' = \sum_{1}^{\infty} {}_tB'\, F_t$$

Description

A trial calculation is made using the valuation net premium as the test gross premium. This trial premium is then adjusted to satisfy the criterion that the present value of profit and indirect expense equal the sum of:

a — the indirect expense and

b — the required profit,

both expressed as a multiple of the present value of commissions. The use of the valuation net premium as a trial premium simplifies the problem of defining the deficiency reserve.

Comments

The calculation technique will produce a premium which exactly satisfies the condition imposed, subject only to the limitation of determining a premium rate to the nearest cent. Interest functions for fractional parts of a year are approximated by simple interest methods.

In practice, the discount function F_t becomes quite small after twenty years and the summation can be stopped at any desired duration by specifying:

$$w_r = 1 - q_r - c_r .$$

This is equivalent to the assumption that all policies surrender at the end of r years. It is also equivalent to the assumption that the difference between the reserve and cash value at duration r is equal to the then present value of profits after duration r.

If the frequency of payment is annual and if no conversion benefits are involved, numerous simplifications develop. Despite these simplifications and that of terminating the calculation prior to maturity, the arithmetic is sufficiently extensive to be practical only with a computer of the capacity of the IBM 650. The specimen calculations exhibited later were performed by such a machine.

It should be noted that for the calculation of other than annual premiums the deficiency reserve is defined as the difference between the fractional premium multiplied by the frequency of payment and the valuation net premium. In such cases, it might be appropriate to use the fractional valuation premium. Note, too, that the fractional premium is a *true* one as distinguished from the apportionable or installment type. Either could be calculated by altering the term:

$$\frac{m-1}{2m} \cdot q_t \ .$$

For apportionable premium, this would become:

$$\frac{k-1}{2k} \cdot q_t ,$$

where k is the annual number of adjustment intervals (12 for months, 52 for weeks, or 365 for days).

For installment premiums, this would become zero.

5. Determining the Aggregate Value of a Life Insurance Company

The value of a life insurance company is not adequately represented by the total of its capital and surplus. A more realistic value of an entire company must take account of its business in force and agency organization. A value of these nonledger assets is frequently needed for one or more of the following purposes:

1. determining an equitable basis of merger with another company;
2. establishing a fair price for an outright sale;
3. calculating the amount of assets to be transferred as a result of reinsuring a block of business;
4. testing the reasonableness of the offering price of an additional issue of stock;
5. demonstrating the soundness of a plan of mutualization;
6. tracing *real* earnings by taking account of changes in the aggregate *real* worth of the company.

The proposed technique for calculating gross premiums for nonparticipating life insurance suggests a method of determining the aggregate worth of a block of nonparticipating business and of an agency organization engaged in marketing this product. The suggested method operates in the following manner:

1. the worth of a block of nonparticipating business would be the present value of unrealized profits on business now in force, discounted at a rate representing adequate return to the investor on the total value; and

2. the worth of an agency organization would be the present value of profits on business expected to be produced in the future, less the present value of net development outlay.

Valuation of Business

Consider, first, the problem of evaluating a block of business in force; suppose that ${}_tB$ represents the book profit, based on the actual gross premium, realized in policy year t and ${}_kZ$ is the value of unrealized profits on business at duration k:

$$ {}_kZ = \frac{\sum_{k}^{\infty} {}_tB\, F_t}{F_k} $$

where F_t is the discount factor previously defined. By constructing a model office and calculating appropriate values of ${}_kZ$, the value of a block of business could be estimated.

This technique is superior to a gross premium valuation because future earnings can be capitalized at *any* desired yield rate. The difference between gross and net premium valuations represents the value of future profits *capitalized at the interest rate assumed* in the gross premium valuation; it is probable that this value would be viewed as excessive by the sophisticated investor, who would expect a higher return on his investment.

The values ${}_kZ$ can be developed as a by-product of the premium calculation. This is convenient for a company that wants to maintain an inventory of the value of its business in force. Specimen values are illustrated in Section 6.

Valuation of Agency Organization

To assign a value to an agency organization, two viewpoints might be taken:

1. regard present agents as a closed group and estimate future production and net development outlay on this basis; or
2. regard present organization as perpetual and estimate future production and net development outlay on this basis.

Future production must be estimated according to some index; again, it is suggested that production be measured as the discounted value of all commissions on the issue date, but other indexes might also be used. Next, an examination of current premium rates must be made to determine a relationship between the unit of production and the present value of profits at issue, discounted at a rate representing adequate return to stockholders on surplus invested in issued business. Finally, the net development outlay is estimated; this is the excess of amounts spent financing replacements for terminated agents over amounts recovered on account of unearned renewal commissions.

Let ${}^{n}P$ denote production in year n; let a denote the present value of profit at issue per unit of production; let ${}^{n}D$ denote net development outlay in year n; then H, the value of the agency organization, is given by:

$$H = \sum_{n=0}^{\infty} (a\,{}^{n}P - {}^{n}D)\, V^{n-1/2},$$

where v is the usual present value function at an interest rate, r; representing adequate return to stockholders on surplus invested in future production.

If the agency organization is viewed as perpetual and stationary then ${}^{n}P$ and ${}^{n}D$ would become constant and the following simplification can be made:

$$H = \frac{a\,{}^{n}P - {}^{n}D}{r\,v^{1/2}}$$

$$= a'\,{}^{n}P\,,$$

where

$$a' = \frac{a - {}^{n}D/{}^{n}P}{r\,v^{1/2}}.$$

This last formula offers a practical method of maintaining a current approximation to the value of an agency organization.

Although the suggested method is aimed primarily at nonparticipating life insurance, it might also be applied to the problem of valuing participating insurance. It would first be necessary to establish an estimated dividend scale or a relationship between estimated book profit and estimated dividends. Because unfavorable experience can be reflected in dividends, a more optimistic assumption regarding future experience might be warranted. Alternately, the discount rate applied to the profits might be lower than that deemed appropriate for nonparticipating insurance.

6. Exhibit of Results

Premium Calculations

Specimen premium rates were calculated by the proposed method in accordance with the assumptions stated in Appendix A. These assumptions were selected as representative of a general industry experience but apply to no specific company.

The calculated premium rates are confined to the Whole Life plan, decennial issue ages and four policy sizes. Table 3 illustrates the complete output of the calculation for age 35; the calculated items are:

1. discount factor, F_t;
2. total reserve, if a deficiency reserve is required;
3. book profit per $1,000 in force, ${}_tB$;
4. book profit per $1,000 issued;
5. present value of unrealized profits by duration;
6. indirect first year expenses per $1,000;
7. present value of book profits at issue;
8. present value of additional profit at issue per $1 additional premium;
10. calculated gross premium.

The proof of the calculation is the criterion that the indirect expense and present value of profit equal 15% and 10%, respectively, of the present value of commissions. With allowance for the limitation of determining annual book profits and the gross premium to the nearest cent, this condition is satisfied. The lapse and mortality factors shown are a result of the particular program used for these calculations; this program was designed to accommodate any multiple of a standard set of lapse and death probabilities.

The discount factors and present value of additional profit per $1 additional premium are useful for testing the effect of variations in expense assumptions; for example, commissions may be redistributed, in such a way that their present value is unchanged, and hence the premium is unchanged. Any number of approximate adjustments to the premium can be made without recalculating the book profit series. Table 4 compares the entire set of premium rates to the mean and range of the premiums of ten stock companies presented in Table 1.

Table 3 — Specimen Calculation Exhibit: Whole Life — Age 35
(*a*) Policy Amount $3,000

Issue Age	Plan Code	Policy Amount	Per-Policy Expense Initial	Per-Policy Expense Renewal	Per-Policy Expense Death	Per-Policy Expense Lapse	Level% Expense	Linton A Factor Initial	Linton A Factor Renewal
35	1	$3,000	$40.00	$4.00	$25.00	$5.00	2.0%	100%	100%

Policy Year	Discount Factor	Commission Rate	Cash Value	Terminal Reserve	Book Profit per $1,000 In Force	Book Profit per $1,000 Issued	Book Profit per $1,000 Value of
1	1.0000000	78.0%			$ –13.84	$ –13.84	$ 2.42
2	.7815913	7.5%		$ 15.69	+ 3.26	+ 2.93	20.80
3	.6379484	7.5%	$ 14.42	31.65	3.32	2.80	21.49
4	.5261243	7.5%	30.94	47.88	3.30	2.64	22.04
5	.4365185	7.5%	47.71	64.35	3.29	2.51	22.58
6	.3635630	7.5%	64.73	81.08	3.19	2.33	23.16
7	.3039355	7.5%	82.00	98.04	3.25	2.28	23.89
8	.2550706	7.5%	99.50	115.24	3.20	2.23	24.60
9	.2146585	7.5%	117.23	132.66	3.34	2.19	25.32
10	.1809608	7.5%	135.17	150.28	3.40	2.16	26.07
11	.1528128	5.0%	153.31	168.11	4.00	2.47	26.85
12	.1291241	5.0%	171.63	186.11	4.06	2.44	27.04
13	.1091716	5.0%	190.13	204.29	4.06	2.37	27.18
14	.0923525	5.0%	208.79	222.62	4.06	2.31	27.33
15	.0781616	5.0%	227.58	241.08	4.03	2.23	27.50
16	.0661784	2.0%	246.50	259.67	4.65	2.50	27.72
17	.0559944	2.0%	265.52	278.36	4.60	2.41	27.26
18	.0473420	2.0%	284.63	297.14	4.54	2.31	26.80
19	.0399954	2.0%	303.80	315.97	4.49	2.22	26.35
20	.0337606	2.0%	323.02	334.85	4.41	2.12	25.90
21	.0284713	2.0%	342.25	353.75	4.47	2.08	25.48
22	.0239862	2.0%	361.49	372.65	4.53	2.05	24.94
23	.0201847	2.0%	380.70	391.53	4.58	2.00	24.25
24	.0169644	2.0%	399.87	410.36	4.62	1.95	23.41
25	.0142383	2.0%	418.96	429.12	4.67	1.90	22.39
26	.0119325	2.0%	437.96	447.78	4.71	1.85	21.14
27	.0099836	2.0%	456.84	466.33	4.76	1.80	19.64
28	.0083382	2.0%	475.56	484.73	4.82	1.75	17.81
29	.0069507	2.0%	494.13	502.97	4.88	1.70	15.59
30	.0057820	2.0%	512.49	521.01	12.87	4.28	12.87

X_{18} Factor	X_{18} Constant	Indirect Expenses	Yield Rate	Present Value at Issue of Book Profit	Present Value at Issue of $1.00 Premium	Present Value at Issue of Commissions	Net Premium	Gross Premium
100%	.00025	$3.66	15.0%	$2.42	$4.46	$24.41	$19.88	$22.35

Table 3 — Continued
(*b*) Policy Amount $6,000

Issue Age	Plan Code	Policy Amount	Per-Policy Expense Initial	Per-Policy Expense Renewal	Per-Policy Expense Death	Per-Policy Expense Lapse	Level% Expense	Linton A Factor Initial	Linton A Factor Renewal
35	1	$6,000	$45.00	$5.00	$30.00	$6.00	2.0%	100%	100%

Policy Year	Discount Factor	Commission Rate	Cash Value	Terminal Reserve	Book Profit per $1,000 In Force	Book Profit per $1,000 Issued	Book Profit per $1,000 Value of
1	1.0000000	78.0%			$ − 8.02	$ − 8.02	$ 2.25
2	.7815913	7.5%		$ 15.69	+ 2.00	+ 1.80	13.14
3	.6379484	7.5%	$ 14.42	31.65	2.05	1.73	13.65
4	.5261243	7.5%	30.94	47.88	2.03	1.62	14.06
5	.4365185	7.5%	47.71	64.35	2.01	1.53	14.50
6	.3635630	7.5%	64.73	81.08	1.91	1.40	15.00
7	.3039355	7.5%	82.00	98.04	1.97	1.38	15.66
8	.2550706	7.5%	99.50	115.24	2.01	1.36	16.31
9	.2146585	7.5%	117.23	132.66	2.06	1.35	17.00
10	.1809608	7.5%	135.17	150.28	2.13	1.36	17.72
11	.1528128	5.0%	153.31	168.11	2.67	1.65	18.46
12	.1291241	5.0%	171.63	186.11	2.73	1.64	18.68
13	.1091716	5.0%	190.13	204.29	2.73	1.59	18.87
14	.0923525	5.0%	208.79	222.62	2.73	1.55	19.08
15	.0781616	5.0%	227.58	241.08	2.70	1.49	19.32
16	.0661784	2.0%	246.50	259.67	3.27	1.76	19.63
17	.0559944	2.0%	265.52	278.36	3.21	1.68	19.33
18	.0473420	2.0%	284.63	297.14	3.16	1.61	19.07
19	.0399954	2.0%	303.80	315.97	3.11	1.54	18.83
20	.0337606	2.0%	323.02	334.85	3.03	1.46	18.62
21	.0284713	2.0%	342.25	353.75	3.10	1.44	18.49
22	.0239862	2.0%	361.49	372.65	3.16	1.43	18.27
23	.0201847	2.0%	380.70	391.53	3.21	1.40	17.95
24	.0169644	2.0%	399.87	410.36	3.27	1.38	17.54
25	.0142383	2.0%	418.96	429.12	3.32	1.35	17.00
26	.0119325	2.0%	437.96	447.78	3.37	1.32	16.33
27	.0099836	2.0%	456.84	466.33	3.41	1.29	15.49
28	.0083382	2.0%	475.56	484.73	3.49	1.27	14.46
29	.0069507	2.0%	494.13	502.97	3.56	1.24	13.16
30	.0057820	2.0%	512.49	521.01	11.54	3.84	11.54

X_{18} Factor	X_{18} Constant	Indirect Expenses	Yield Rate	Present Value at Issue of Book Profit	Present Value at Issue of $1.00 Premium	Present Value at Issue of Commissions	Net Premium	Gross Premium
100%	.00025	$3.34	15%	$2.25	$4.46	$22.23	$19.88	$20.35

Table 3 — Continued
(*c*) Policy Amount $12,000

Issue Age	Plan Code	Policy Amount	Per-Policy Expense Initial	Per-Policy Expense Renewal	Per-Policy Expense Death	Per-Policy Expense Lapse	Level% Expense	Linton A Factor Initial	Linton A Factor Renewal
35	1	$12,000	$55.00	$7.00	$40.00	$8.00	2.0%	100%	100%

Policy Year	Discount Factor	Commission Rate	Cash Value	Terminal Reserve	Book Profit per $1,000 In Force	Book Profit per $1,000 Issued	Book Profit per $1,000 Value of
1	1.0000000	78.0%		$ 3.26	$ − 7.90	$ − 7.90	$ 2.24
2	.7815913	7.5%		18.90	+ 2.06	+ 1.85	12.97
3	.6379484	7.5%	$ 14.42	34.18	2.06	1.74	13.37
4	.5261243	7.5%	30.94	50.99	2.02	1.62	13.71
5	.4365185	7.5%	47.71	67.40	2.00	1.53	14.09
6	.3635630	7.5%	64.73	84.08	1.88	1.37	14.51
7	.3039355	7.5%	82.00	100.98	1.93	1.36	15.11
8	.2550706	7.5%	99.50	118.13	1.95	1.32	15.71
9	.2146585	7.5%	117.23	135.49	2.00	1.31	16.35
10	.1809608	7.5%	135.17	153.05	2.05	1.31	17.02
11	.1528128	5.0%	153.31	170.83	2.57	1.59	17.73
12	.1291241	5.0%	171.63	188.77	2.61	1.57	17.94
13	.1091716	5.0%	190.13	206.89	2.63	1.54	18.13
14	.0923525	5.0%	208.79	225.16	2.60	1.48	18.32
15	.0781616	5.0%	227.58	243.56	2.58	1.43	18.57
16	.0661784	2.0%	246.50	262.09	3.13	1.69	18.89
17	.0559944	2.0%	265.52	280.72	3.06	1.60	18.63
18	.0473420	2.0%	284.63	299.43	3.02	1.54	18.41
19	.0399954	2.0%	303.80	318.20	2.97	1.47	18.22
20	.0337606	2.0%	323.02	337.02	2.88	1.38	18.06
21	.0284713	2.0%	342.25	355.86	2.95	1.37	18.00
22	.0239862	2.0%	361.49	374.70	3.01	1.36	17.87
23	.0201847	2.0%	380.70	393.52	3.05	1.33	17.66
24	.0169644	2.0%	399.87	412.29	3.11	1.31	17.38
25	.0142383	2.0%	418.96	430.98	3.18	1.30	17.00
26	.0119325	2.0%	437.96	449.58	3.21	1.26	16.49
27	.0099836	2.0%	456.84	468.07	3.27	1.24	15.88
28	.0083382	2.0%	475.56	486.41	3.34	1.21	15.09
29	.0069507	2.0%	494.13	504.59	3.41	1.19	14.10
30	.0057820	2.0%	512.49	522.57	12.85	4.28	12.85

X_{18} Factor	X_{18} Constant	Indirect Expenses	Yield Rate	Present Value at Issue of Book Profit	Present Value at Issue of $1.00 Premium	Present Value at Issue of Commissions	Net Premium	Gross Premium
100%	.00025	$3.23	15%	$2.24	$13.96	$21.58	$19.88	$19.72

Table 3 — Continued
(*d*) Policy Amount $30,000

Issue Age	Plan Code	Policy Amount	Per-Policy Expense Initial	Per-Policy Expense Renewal	Per-Policy Expense Death	Per-Policy Expense Lapse	Level% Expense	Linton A Factor Initial	Linton A Factor Renewal
35	1	$30,000	$65.00	$13.00	$70.00	$14.00	2.0%	100%	100%

Policy Year	Discount Factor	Commission Rate	Cash Value	Terminal Reserve	Book Profit per $1,000 In Force	Book Profit per $1,000 Issued	Book Profit per $1,000 Value of
1	1.0000000	78.0%		$ 8.16	$ − 9.73	$ − 9.73	$ 2.09
2	.7815913	7.5%		23.72	+2.54	+2.28	15.12
3	.6379484	7.5%	$ 14.42	39.72	2.50	2.11	15.41
4	.5261243	7.5%	30.94	55.65	2.41	1.93	15.65
5	.4365185	7.5%	47.71	71.99	2.37	1.81	15.96
6	.3635630	7.5%	64.73	88.58	2.24	1.64	16.32
7	.3039355	7.5%	82.00	105.40	2.25	1.58	16.84
8	.2550706	7.5%	99.50	122.46	2.25	1.53	17.38
9	.2146585	7.5%	117.23	139.74	2.28	1.50	17.98
10	.1809608	7.5%	135.17	157.22	2.32	1.48	18.63
11	.1529128	5.0%	153.31	174.90	2.84	1.76	19.31
12	.1291241	5.0%	171.63	192.75	2.88	1.73	19.49
13	.1091716	5.0%	190.13	210.78	2.87	1.68	19.65
14	.0923525	5.0%	208.79	228.97	2.86	1.63	19.84
15	.0781616	5.0%	227.58	247.27	2.83	1.57	20.06
16	.0661784	2.0%	246.50	265.71	3.34	1.80	20.35
17	.0559944	2.0%	265.52	284.25	3.28	1.72	20.10
18	.0473420	2.0%	284.63	302.88	3.23	1.65	19.90
19	.0399954	2.0%	303.80	321.55	3.19	1.58	19.73
20	.0337606	2.0%	323.02	340.28	3.10	1.49	19.59
21	.0284713	2.0%	342.25	359.02	3.18	1.48	19.56
22	.0239862	2.0%	361.49	377.77	3.21	1.45	19.44
23	.0201847	2.0%	380.70	396.50	3.27	1.43	19.28
24	.0169644	2.0%	399.87	415.17	3.33	1.41	19.05
25	.0142383	2.0%	418.96	433.78	3.38	1.38	18.73
26	.0119325	2.0%	437.96	452.29	3.43	1.35	18.32
27	.0099836	2.0%	456.84	470.69	3.47	1.31	17.80
28	.0083382	2.0%	475.56	488.94	3.56	1.29	17.15
29	.0069507	2.0%	494.13	507.03	3.63	1.26	16.31
30	.0057820	2.0%	512.49	524.92	15.24	5.07	15.24

X_{18} Factor	X_{18} Constant	Indirect Expenses	Yield Rate	Present Value at Issue of Book Profit	Present Value at Issue of $1.00 Premium	Present Value at Issue of Commis-sions	Net Premium	Gross Premium
100%	.00025	$3.19	15%	$2.09	$13.96	$21.29	$19.88	$19.48

Table 4 — Comparison of Calculated and Typical Nonparticipating Whole Life Premium Rates

Age	Amount	Calculated Premium	Typical Nonparticipating Premiums High	Mean	Low
15	$ 3,000	$ 13.16	$ 14.38	$ 12.53	$ 11.46
	6,000	11.38	12.07	11.18	9.80
	12,000	10.39	10.95	10.36	8.96
	30,000	9.90	10.50	9.96	8.46
25	$ 3,000	$ 16.60	$ 17.74	$ 16.12	$ 15.30
	6,000	14.82	15.48	14.77	14.30
	12,000	13.82	14.18	13.91	13.55
	30,000	13.65	13.82	13.51	13.30
35	$ 3,000	$ 22.35	$ 23.45	$ 21.65	$ 20.82
	6,000	20.35	21.25	20.30	19.80
	12,000	19.72	19.75	19.43	19.05
	30,000	19.48	19.32	19.02	18.60
45	$ 3,000	$ 32.33	$ 32.38	$ 30.58	$ 29.85
	6,000	29.85	29.95	29.24	28.69
	12,000	29.37	29.03	28.36	27.64
	30,000	29.04	28.78	27.96	27.26
55	$ 3,000	$ 48.11	$ 48.84	$ 45.30	$ 44.09
	6,000	46.02	46.84	43.95	42.75
	12,000	45.34	46.09	43.03	42.00
	30,000	44.90	45.84	42.63	41.55
65	$ 3,000	$ 75.21	$ 81.43	$ 73.29	$ 70.28
	6,000	73.27	79.43	71.95	69.05
	12,000	72.25	78.68	70.71	68.43
	30,000	71.58	78.43	70.31	68.05
Weighted Average		$ 24.15	$ 24.74	$ 23.56	$ 22.85

The weighted average of the calculated premiums is 2.5% higher than the composite average of all ten companies illustrated. With three exceptions, the calculated rates are within the competitive range. The characteristics of the calculated rates are:

1. higher relative rates for smaller policies, due to the larger surplus drain at issue and the consequent increase in required profit;
2. higher relative rates at points where deficiency reserves are required, especially ages 45 and up and larger policy sizes;
3. approximate quantity discounts of $2 from $3,000 to $6,000, $.75 from $6,000 to $12,000, and $.30 from $12,000 to $30,000, compared to approximate average quantity discounts of $1.35, $.90, and $.40, respectively;

4. premium rate decreases by policy size which do not follow a reciprocal pattern — that is, the kind of pattern which could be closely approximated by a policy fee;
5. substantial variation in quantity discounts by age of issue;
6. more favorable competitive position for amounts of $6,000 and $12,000.

One general comment might be made with regard to the profit objective: the invested surplus might be regarded as "secured" by the difference between the reserve and the cash value, and the yield rate might be adjusted downward when this "security" is substantial. This would be a practical application of the suggested association of gain and risk. The adoption of such a philosophy would increase the effect of policy size on premiums, particularly at those points where deficiency reserves are required.

Value of Business

In Table 3, there is a year by year tabulation of the present value of remaining profits discounted in accordance with the assumptions made for calculating premiums for age 35. Table 5 summarizes the results at sample durations for other issue ages.

For durations above 20, the results are unreliable because of the assumption that all policies surrender after 30 years. At the young ages at issue, this assumption has a significant effect even on the 20th year values. The extent of the error could be estimated and appropriate adjustment made if a more precise value were required.

The values per $1,000 of business in force shown in Table 5 exhibit the following characteristics:

1. much smaller values on larger policies, unless deficiency reserves are involved;
2. higher values at higher ages;
3. rapid reduction in value at upper ages due to select mortality gains;
4. large and erratic variations, difficult to relate to a simple index;
5. irregular change from durations 2 to 5, consistent increase from durations 5 to 10, and stable, usually slightly increasing values from durations 10 through 20.

Table 5 — Value per $1,000 Whole Life in Force

		Value at Beginning of Policy Year				
Age	Amount	2	5	10	15	20
15	$ 3,000	$ 17.23	$ 19.21	$ 22.31	$ 24.48	$ 24.47
	6,000	10.62	12.18	14.91	17.14	17.88
	12,000	6.78	8.14	10.66	12.91	14.02
	30,000	5.44	6.63	9.02	11.26	12.61
25	$ 3,000	$ 17.87	$ 20.51	$ 24.25	$ 25.65	$ 24.52
	6,000	11.31	13.56	16.93	18.43	18.03
	12,000	7.45	9.44	12.61	14.17	14.21
	30,000	9.28	11.09	14.07	15.54	15.62
35	$ 3,000	$ 20.80	$ 22.58	$ 26.07	$ 27.50	$ 25.90
	6,000	13.14	14.50	17.72	19.32	18.62
	12,000	12.97	14.09	17.02	18.57	18.06
	30,000	15.12	15.96	18.63	20.06	19.59
45	$ 3,000	$ 27.40	$ 27.26	$ 31.38	$ 33.01	$ 30.53
	6,000	17.44	16.92	20.92	23.00	21.75
	12,000	20.27	19.35	22.90	24.77	23.49
	30,000	22.51	21.29	24.51	26.16	24.85
55	$ 3,000	$ 35.31	$ 27.83	$ 32.40	$ 35.81	$ 36.44
	6,000	33.25	25.26	29.36	32.81	34.01
	12,000	36.64	28.19	31.70	34.80	35.84
	30,000	38.78	30.00	33.10	36.00	36.92
65	$ 3,000	$ 64.84	$ 36.59	$ 43.25	$ 47.44	$ 45.22
	6,000	70.75	41.81	47.25	50.76	48.25
	12,000	73.79	44.47	49.25	52.38	49.73
	30,000	75.67	46.14	50.50	53.39	50.62

The values illustrated must be interpreted with care to avoid unwarranted conclusions. It is clear, however, that some of the broad rules-of-thumb such as "$20 per $1,000" and "one year's premium" may be dangerously crude estimates of the value of a particular block of business.

Effect of Variation of Factors

To illustrate the effect of varying certain assumptions, additional premiums were calculated with certain assumptions changed in each case. To avoid altering the indirect expense and present value of profit because of alteration of the gross premium, the amount of both items was fixed at that amount determined from the "standard" assumptions. The additional premiums are confined to age at issue 35. The following alterations were made:

1. Less Favorable Mortality: Assumed mortality was changed to 125% of the select modification of Mortality Table X_{18}, plus the catastrophe allowance of .00025; other assumptions were unchanged.
2. 100% Y.R.T. Reinsurance: The entire risk was assumed reinsured and mortality rates modified in the following way:

$$q' = .55\, q^{cso} + .50\, q^{X_{18}} \quad ;$$

   the assumed per-policy expenses were increased \$5 first year and \$1 renewal; other assumptions were unchanged.
3. Less Favorable Interest: The interest rate was assumed to be 3½% for policy year 1, declining .05% in each of the subsequent 10 years, reaching 3% in policy year 11 and remaining constant thereafter; other assumptions were unchanged.
4. Less Favorable Persistency: Linton B termination rates were assumed as probabilities of voluntary withdrawal; other assumptions were unchanged.
5. Higher Values and Reserves: 1941 CSO 2¾% minimum values and CRVM reserves were assumed; other assumptions were unchanged.
6. Monthly Payment: Monthly payment of premiums was assumed, with true monthly premiums; assumed first year and renewal per-policy expenses were increased \$3; Linton B termination rates were assumed; the deficiency reserve was determined by comparison of the total yearly premium with the valuation net premium based on monthly payment of premiums; other assumptions were unchanged.

Premium rates developed in accordance with these assumptions are shown in Table 6.

Table 6 — Effect of Variation of Certain Assumptions
Whole Life Age 35 Premium per \$1,000

Policy Size	Standard Assumptions	Less Favorable Mortality	100% Y.R.T. Reinsurance	Less Favorable Interest	Less Favorable Persistency	Higher Values and Reserves	Monthly Payment
\$ 3,000	\$22.35	\$23.06	\$25.59	\$22.66	\$23.21	\$22.78	\$25.67
6,000	20.35	21.05	23.20	20.66	20.67	20.79	22.27
12,000	19.72	20.08	22.03	19.82	19.74	20.32	20.61
30,000	19.48	19.70	21.16	19.59	19.43	20.08	20.04

The effect of increased mortality rates is surprisingly small. Where premiums are not deficient, the rate increase resulting from 25% extra mortality is less than 3-1/2%; deficient premiums increase less than 1-1/2%.

The effect of reinsurance is, on the other hand, surprisingly great. Because the illustration is quite artificial and because the assumption of 100% Y.R.T. reinsurance is unrealistic, the results require careful scrutiny if false conclusions are to be avoided. One conclusion is nevertheless evident: retention limits, whether current or projected, have an appreciable impact on premium rates and profit. The calculations suggest that the additional premium on account of reinsurance is $2.46 per $1,000 plus $2.34 per policy; both amounts are smaller if deficiency reserves are involved, since a premium increase reduces the required deficiency reserve. This statement of the effect of reinsurance can be used to determine a premium for any retention.

The increase in the premium rate due to reduced interest earnings is even smaller than the effect of higher mortality. The distribution of the changes in premium by amount is uniform, except as it is dampened by deficiency reserve requirements.

The impact of increased lapse rates is highly sensitive to policy size. The pattern of rate decreases by size becomes $2.54, $.93 and $.31 compared to "standard" differences of $2, $.63 and $.24. An astonishing property of these premiums can be observed at policy size $30,000: the premium rate per $1,000 is *lower* than the comparable standard premium. This is explained by the more rapid recovery of the deficiency reserve.

The distribution of the premium rate increases attributable to increased nonforfeiture values and reserves is opposite to that due to any of the other variations. Premium rates for larger amounts increase more than for smaller amounts because of the increase in the valuation net premium and deficiency reserve requirements.

For a policy size of $3,000, the annualized monthly premium rate is 15% above the corresponding standard premium; this increase reduces to 3% for a policy size of $30,000. The relationship between the monthly and annual premium suggested by this illustration is:

$$\frac{1}{12}P^{(12)} = .0846P + \frac{.75}{A},$$

where A represents policy size in thousands. This relationship is quite different from that traditionally used for fractional premiums. For a company using a policy fee system, it is a simple matter to include a "collection charge" and closely approach the indicated relationship.

Conclusions

The following conclusions are suggested by this analysis of gross premiums and profit objectives:

1. recent developments in the industry have made it possible, and perhaps necessary, to refine rate structures for nonparticipating insurance;
2. the suggested method of handling contingency and profit margins is one which makes sense to stockholders;
3. the proposed calculation technique allows complete flexibility in selecting assumptions without great attendant increase in the work required to determine premium rates;
4. a related technique offers a suitable basis for assigning value to a block of business or an agency organization;
5. premium rates determined by the proposed method and technique are not unrealistic competitively, given typical assumptions; there are, however, significant and systematic departures from the usual pattern;
6. direct recognition of such factors as mode of payment, retention limits, deficiency reserve requirements and other variables may suggest certain modifications or refinements of the customary rate pattern to recognize the effects of such factors upon premium rates.

APPENDIX A
SUMMARY OF STANDARD ASSUMPTIONS

Mortality

A select modification of Mortality Table X_{18} (Appendix B) with each mortality rate increased .00025 for a contingency margin of 25 extra deaths per 1,000 per century.

Interest

3.75% for policy years 1 through 5, decreasing .05% each year thereafter, reaching 3.00% in policy year 20 and remaining constant thereafter.

Dollar Expenses (per policy)

Item	Age	Policy Size			
		$3,000	$6,000	$12,000	$30,000
(*a*) First Year	15 & 25	$35	$40	$45	$60
	35	40	45	55	65
	45	50	55	65	70
	55	60	65	70	75
(*b*) Renewal Years	all	4	5	7	13
(*c*) Claim Expense	all	25	30	40	70
(*d*) Other Termination Expenses	all	5	6	8	14

Percentage Expenses

(*a*) Commissions (including expense reimbursement allowance of 30% of first year commission)

Plan	Age	Commission Rate for Policy Year			
		1	2–10	11–15	Subs.
Whole Life	all	78%	7 1/2%	5%	2%

(*b*) Other Percentage Expenses: 2% for premium taxes; all ages, policy years and policy sizes.

Indirect Expenses

First year expense equal to 15% of the present value of commissions.

Persistency

Linton A termination rates used as probabilities of voluntary withdrawal; all policies are assumed to surrender after 30 years.

Nonforfeiture Values

1941 CSO 3% minimum values.

Reserves

1941 CSO 3% CRVM reserves, including deficiency reserves.

Mode of Payment

Annual.

Profit Objectives

(*a*) Yield on surplus invested in new business: 15%.

(*b*) Present value of profit as a multiple of present value of commissions: 10%.

APPENDIX B
MORTALITY TABLE X_{18} (WITH SELECT MODIFICATION)

Mortality Table X_{18} represents the experience of fifteen large companies between policy anniversaries in 1950 and 1954, excluding policy years 1 through 5. The following select modification was prepared for use in calculating premiums for nonparticipating insurance and is based on the published intercompany experience for the same period.

Mr. Norman F. Buck has previously published a select modification of this table together with a lucid discussion of three techniques for determining select rates.[4] Because Mortality Table X_{18} was derived from a pool of experience weighted heavily toward early durations, a conservative estimate of select mortality is indicated as most appropriate for calculating gross premiums. The following table was developed in a manner similar to the second of Mr. Buck's three suggested methods: coefficients of selection were determined for policy year 1, related to the ultimate mortality rate at the same attained age, and graduated with the criterion that these coefficients increase by issue age. Coefficients for policy years 2 through 5 were determined by grading smoothly to zero at duration 6. Select mortality rates for issue ages 71 through 75 were determined by holding constant the coefficients of selection for age 70. The mortality rates for policy year 1 are very close to those shown in Mr. Buck's

[4] *TSA* IX, 28.

Mortality Table X_{18} (with Select Modification)
Mortality Rate Per 1,000

Age at Issue	Policy Year 1	Policy Year 2	Policy Year 3	Policy Year 4	Policy Year 5	Att. Age	Ultimate
0	6.33	1.00	.78	.66	.58	5	.52
1	1.00	.78	.66	.58	.52	6	.47
2	.77	.66	.58	.52	.47	7	.43
3	.65	.58	.52	.47	.43	8	.40
4	.57	.52	.46	.43	.40	9	.38
5	.51	.46	.42	.40	.38	10	.37
6	.46	.42	.39	.38	.37	11	.39
7	.41	.39	.37	.36	.39	12	.43
8	.38	.37	.36	.38	.43	13	.47
9	.36	.36	.38	.42	.47	14	.51
10	.35	.37	.42	.46	.50	15	.55
11	.37	.41	.45	.50	.54	16	.61
12	.40	.45	.49	.54	.60	17	.67
13	.44	.49	.53	.59	.66	18	.75
14	.47	.52	.58	.65	.74	19	.81
15	.51	.57	.64	.73	.80	20	.85
16	.56	.62	.71	.78	.84	21	.87
17	.61	.69	.76	.82	.85	22	.89
18	.67	.74	.80	.83	.87	23	.90
19	.72	.77	.81	.85	.88	24	.92
20	.74	.78	.82	.86	.90	25	.93
21	.75	.79	.82	.87	.90	26	.95
22	.75	.79	.83	.87	.92	27	.98
23	.75	.79	.84	.89	.95	28	1.00
24	.75	.79	.84	.91	.96	29	1.04
25	.74	.80	.86	.92	1.00	30	1.08
26	.75	.81	.87	.95	1.03	31	1.13
27	.75	.82	.90	.98	1.08	32	1.18
28	.76	.84	.92	1.02	1.12	33	1.24
29	.77	.86	.95	1.06	1.18	34	1.32
30	.78	.88	.99	1.10	1.25	35	1.41
31	.80	.91	1.02	1.17	1.33	36	1.53
32	.82	.94	1.08	1.24	1.44	37	1.68
33	.84	.98	1.14	1.33	1.57	38	1.87
34	.88	1.03	1.22	1.45	1.74	39	2.10
35	.92	1.10	1.33	1.61	1.95	40	2.36
36	.97	1.19	1.46	1.79	2.19	41	2.64
37	1.04	1.30	1.62	2.00	2.44	42	2.95
38	1.13	1.44	1.80	2.22	2.72	43	3.28
39	1.24	1.59	1.99	2.47	3.01	44	3.63
40	1.36	1.74	2.20	2.72	3.32	45	4.02
41	1.48	1.91	2.41	2.99	3.67	46	4.45
42	1.61	2.09	2.64	3.29	4.05	47	4.92
43	1.74	2.27	2.89	3.61	4.46	48	5.46
44	1.87	2.46	3.16	3.97	4.93	49	6.06
45	2.01	2.67	3.44	4.37	5.45	50	6.72
46	2.16	2.89	3.77	4.81	6.03	51	7.45
47	2.31	3.14	4.13	5.30	6.66	52	8.21
48	2.48	3.42	4.52	5.83	7.32	53	9.02
49	2.67	3.71	4.95	6.37	8.01	54	9.92

Mortality Table X_{18} — Continued

Age at Issue	Policy Year 1	Policy Year 2	Policy Year 3	Policy Year 4	Policy Year 5	Att. Age	Ultimate
50	2.86	4.02	5.38	6.95	8.78	55	10.91
51	3.05	4.33	5.83	7.58	9.62	56	12.01
52	3.24	4.65	6.32	8.27	10.56	57	13.22
53	3.43	5.00	6.85	9.03	11.58	58	14.55
54	3.62	5.37	7.43	9.86	12.70	59	15.99
55	3.82	5.76	8.06	10.77	13.91	60	17.57
56	4.02	6.19	8.74	11.74	15.23	61	19.28
57	4.23	6.63	9.47	12.79	16.66	62	21.12
58	4.44	7.10	10.24	13.92	18.18	63	23.10
59	4.64	7.59	11.07	15.12	19.82	64	25.25
60	4.83	8.10	11.93	16.40	21.59	65	27.61
61	5.11	8.70	12.91	17.83	23.55	66	30.21
62	5.39	9.33	13.96	19.38	25.71	67	33.08
63	5.66	10.00	15.10	21.09	28.08	68	36.24
64	5.93	10.71	16.34	22.96	30.70	69	39.66
65	6.21	11.48	17.70	25.01	33.51	70	43.30
66	6.65	12.44	19.28	27.29	36.55	71	47.09
67	7.11	13.48	20.98	29.70	39.70	72	51.00
68	7.61	14.59	22.78	32.21	42.94	73	55.01
69	8.13	15.76	24.63	34.78	46.26	74	59.23
70	8.66	16.95	26.52	37.41	49.75	75	63.80
71	9.42	18.36	28.60	40.28	53.59	76	68.85
72	10.20	19.80	30.80	43.38	57.83	77	74.52
73	11.00	21.32	33.18	46.82	62.60	78	80.92
74	11.85	22.97	35.80	50.67	67.97	79	87.99
75	12.76	24.79	38.75	55.03	73.91	80	95.64
						81	103.78
						82	112.32
						83	121.20
						84	130.45
						85	140.12
						86	150.27
						87	160.98
						88	172.39
						89	184.75
						90	198.38
						91	213.71
						92	231.24
						93	251.47
						94	274.90
						95	303.03
						96	343.36
						97	409.79
						98	522.62
						99	708.55
						100	1,000.00

modification; for policy years 2 through 5, the mortality rates are deliberately overstated. It is submitted that the margins in select years 2 through 5 and in the early ultimate years are sufficient to offset any understatement of true ultimate mortality.

A Critique of Traditional Life Insurance Products and Distribution Systems

Presented to the Southeastern Actuaries Club in New Orleans, Louisiana, November 18, 1976.

Early in 1975 I agreed to present a paper to the Seventh Pacific Insurance Conference at its meeting in Santa Barbara in September 1975. The paper was to be presented in that section of the program dealing with ordinary insurance products and distribution systems. Shortly thereafter, before work on the paper had even commenced, I was asked for a title which might be included in the program outline. Since I was at the time doing some research in the area of flexible contracts, I decided on the title "The Universal Life Insurance Policy." Several months later, when the paper was finished, I found that its subject was only incidentally a product concept — in fact, the paper is primarily "A Critique of Traditional Life Insurance Products and Distribution Systems," which is the title of my remarks today. The following excerpt summarizes the main arguments advanced in the paper.

> ...that it is no longer realistic to assume that the typical life insurance buyer is one who will, for an extended period of time, remain married to the same wife, work at the same job and live in the same house situated in the same city; or that the financial security needs of this typical buyer and his ability to pay for them will remain constant and can be expressed in constant nominal dollars.
>
> ...that it is not realistic for the industry to address the needs of the typical buyer with traditional permanent life insurance products requiring fixed regular premiums and providing fixed benefits, both expressed in constant nominal dollars.

> ...that the traditional life insurance industry distribution and administrative systems are excessively and unnecessarily costly and place the industry at a competitive disadvantage by comparison with other savings media.
>
> ...that the industry should respond to the needs of the contemporary market by introducing a simplified, flexible and less costly product.
>
> ...that the introduction of such a product is technically and financially feasible if a more effective distribution system can concurrently be developed.
>
> ...that the introduction of such a product would probably have a serious and adverse initial impact on the life insurance industry and its existing distribution systems.
>
> ...that, notwithstanding the foreseen difficulties, the needs and demands of the market will lead to the introduction of such a product, possibly led by companies with no commitment to traditional distribution systems, and that the eventual result will be more favorable to the life insurance industry than the only realistic alternative — an all-term industry.
>
> Obviously, these are sweeping arguments and they imply nothing less than a coming revolution within the life insurance industry. The limited scope of this paper does not permit their full development, nor does it permit adequate consideration of counter-arguments.

The paper begins with an analysis of the contemporary market environment for individual financial security products. The analysis examines, of necessity in a limited way, factors which have affected and are expected to continue to affect market conditions. Changes of a social nature, changes of an economic nature, changes relating to the industry itself and changes of a political nature are separately examined. The following is the perception of the resultant market environment:

> In summary, it is one in which family and financial circumstances can be expected to change more frequently and more extensively than in the past; a market more sophisticated and more cynical than its predecessors; a market with increased need for financial security products and increased ability to pay for them; an increasingly competitive market, particularly as related to other savings media; a market in which long-term commitments are substantially affected by inflation; a market in which life insurance companies are subject to growing financial pressures arising from consumer interests,

> unreasonable taxes, increasing maintenance expenses, and outdated legislation; a market in which further Government intervention is to be expected, along with steady pressures for increased taxation of both policyholder and shareholder earnings.

It is my firm view that the foregoing is no exaggeration and the work of professional futurists suggests that far more radical changes are in store. Those with an interest in the subject, and that should include all of us, might profit from reading or a re-reading of the more respected works in this field. For those who prefer the *Reader's Digest* approach, there is an excellent summary included in John M. Bragg's landmark paper, "The Future of the Actuarial Profession as Viewed in A.D. 1974," which appears in *TSA* XXVI. An article which appeared recently in the Atlanta *Constitution* lends some confirmation to one aspect of the foregoing perception of the contemporary market environment:

> **Both Husband, Wife in Typical Family Work**
>
> Washington (UPI) — Both husband and wife in today's "typical" American family have outside jobs, partly because of inflation's impact on income, according to the Labor department. The historic image of a breadwinner husband and homemaker wife now applies to only 34 out of 100 marriages, it said in the current issue of the Monthly Labor Review. The department said the number of employed wives has increased from 36 out of 100 in 1950 to 49 out of 100 in 1975 — a rise that has been more rapid among whites than blacks.

The paper next examines the way in which the industry today addresses the market. Overwhelmingly, the majority of financial security products sold to individuals by the life insurance industry are characterized by the requirement of regular premiums of a fixed dollar amount and providing benefits of a fixed dollar amount; most of the premium income arising from current sales relates to permanent forms of life insurance.

Are these products appropriate to the needs of the typical buyer? I think they are not. The paper includes an example of 25-year-old buyer with a young family and current annual income of $10,000. With an annual productivity gain of 2% and no inflation, he might expect an equivalent income at age 55 of $18,000. If, however, inflation is assumed to continue throughout the 30-year period at a rate of only 5%, his nominal annual income at age 55 would be $78,000. It is argued that fixed-premium, fixed-benefit, permanent life insurance does not have any relevance to this potential buyer's financial requirements over 30 years, considering only the consequences of inflation. I think that most actuaries would agree that the assumptions included in the example are quite modest and that even more radical changes in financial circumstances are more likely to occur than not.

But this is not the whole story. Our potential buyer is far more likely than not to undergo other changes that will have an even more major impact on his financial requirements over 30 years. To illustrate, consider the following proposition: Resolved that the expected number of wives of a 20-year-old unmarried male exceeds his expected number of children. Would you rather argue the affirmative or the negative? Perhaps your answer would depend upon the agreed definition of "wife"!

Together with this criticism of the inflexibility and inappropriateness of traditional products in responding to the needs of the contemporary market, the paper is also critical of the cost levels of the industry, particularly distribution costs. To my surprise, no one has challenged the expressed view that the equivalent level annual cost of the distribution system is in the range of 20% to 25% of expected premiums, and that the equivalent level annual cost of administration is in the range of 12½% to 15% of expected premiums. In other words, together with premium taxes of, say, 2½%, aggregate costs are in the range of 35% to 42½% of expected premiums.

In case there are doubters here that the figures cited are reasonably correct, I have had calculations prepared to illustrate this point (and some other points as well). For a representative set of assumptions, I have calculated a premium rate for a non-participating ordinary life policy with an issue age of 35 which turned out to be $18.54 per $1,000. Next I calculated a premium assuming expenses of zero with all other assumptions held constant; this premium was $10.89 per $1,000 indicating that 41% of the standard premium was required to meet expenses (approximately two-thirds of which are distribution expenses). Next, a premium was calculated assuming zero lapses with all other assumptions held constant; this produced a premium of $17.01 per $1,000, indicating that 8% of the premium was required to subsidize the cost of early terminations. Next, a premium was calculated with a zero rate of mortality with all other assumptions held constant; this produced a premium of $16.66 per $1,000, indicating that only 10%

of the cost of the product was required to cover death benefits. Finally, a premium rate was calculated with a zero profit with all other assumptions held constant; this produced a premium of $17.55 per $1,000, indicating that 5% of the premium was required to cover shareholders pre-tax profits.

Is it fair and reasonable that a policyholder should have 41% of his premium consumed by expenses and a further 5% consumed by profits? Are we really selling premature death benefit coverage if only 10% of the premium is required to provide the mortality cost? Is it equitable that continuing policyholders should lose 8% of their premium to subsidize terminating policyholders? In short, is this a viable product from the viewpoint of the consumer and will the consumer continue to accept these cost levels?

The second sheet of the handout is intended to illustrate quite a different point — one not covered in the paper but relevant also to the main thrust of the conclusion that the industry cannot continue its present practices indefinitely. I thought that it would be useful to compare the calculated premium rate based on representative assumptions with premium rates actually being charged in the market. Arbitrarily, I selected a group of 18 stock companies ranging in size from medium to large and tabulated their actual premium rates per $1,000 for a $20,000 ordinary life policy issued at age 35; those companies basing rates on age last birthday were appropriately adjusted to age nearest birthday. Traditional and interest adjusted net costs for 20 years were determined. The results, of which you have summaries, indicate the following conclusions:

1. Only one company, Company F, charged a premium rate as high as that produced by the standard test assumptions.
2. The average premium rate of the 18 companies is 4% less than that produced by the standard test assumptions.
3. The lowest premium rate, Company M, is 10% below the premium rate produced by the standard test assumptions.
4. One company among the 18, also Company M, has a lower 20th year cash value than that used for the standard test assumptions and the remaining 17 have higher cash values; on average, the 20th year cash values are 10% higher.
5. None of the 18 companies has either a traditional or interest adjusted cost as high as that produced by the standard test assumptions — the highest net costs among the 18 companies are nearly $1.00 per $1,000, in both cases,

below the costs indicated by the standard test assumptions and the averages of the costs are approximately $2.00 per $1,000 lower than those produced by the standard test assumptions.

Let's look more closely at the mean of these 18 companies. The average premium rate is 4% lower than the standard test assumptions. The 20th year cash value is 10% higher. The traditional net cost is $2.20 per $1,000 lower. The interest adjusted net cost is $1.66 lower. These results suggest either

1. that the representative assumptions are not representative or
2. that a large and important segment of the industry is using a pricing basis which is probably not economically sound.

Again, I ask, how long can this continue?

The paper next considers the characteristics of the product best suited to the needs and demands of the contemporary market. The primary characteristics identified are flexibility, reduced costs, simplicity and tax efficiency.

At this point "the Universal Life Insurance Policy" is described. It consists of familiar components — a flexible premium annuity with a monthly renewable term insurance rider. A specific product is described but it is not suggested that this is the only configuration or even the best configuration. The product description is specific only for the purpose of performing a test to determine whether or not it is feasible from the financial viewpoint.

Pricing and profitability tests are then performed to examine the profitability of the annuity standing alone, the competitiveness of the required term insurance premiums and the profitability of no-load conversions of existing policies with allowances for payment of standard commissions. The results of the tests indicate that the proposed product is feasible, provided the underlying assumptions are realized.

The most controversial of the assumptions, and also the most crucial, are those relating to expenses, particularly distribution costs. It is assumed that, if the product is to be distributed through a traditional agency system, the compensation of the soliciting agent will be: $100 per contract, $.50 per $1,000 initial amount of insurance and 2½% of all premiums paid. The resultant pattern of equivalent first year commission rates varies dramatically from that which is traditional to the industry. On average, the equivalent commission rate is probably in the range of 50% to 60% of the New York maximum. The same relationship would hold true for equivalent renewal commission rates. The suggested level of agent compensation is practical, in my judgment, only if a 100% increase in sales frequency is realized. It is worth noting that the average sales frequency of the industry is very low — approximately one sale per week per full-time equivalent agent.

In that one sad statistic may lie the root of the whole problem. Is it reasonable to pay an agent a full-time income for making just one sale a week? Is our product so difficult to sell that 40 hours of effort are required to effect just one sale? The paper argues, contrary to the experience of the industry, that the assumed level of distribution costs and the implied level of agent productivity can be achieved, one way or the other — if not by a traditional agency organization, then by an entirely different distribution system.

What are the implications for the life insurance industry if a product of the type proposed were successfully introduced? One obvious implication is that either the number of agents would be cut in half or the sales volume would double, or some reciprocally-related mixture of the two. Some people have suggested to me that the proposed product is a little hard on the agency organizations, which might face a 50% reduction in size. I am inclined to disagree — at least I don't believe that the agents are being singled out for special treatment. If any group is at the sharp end of this proposal, it must surely be the actuaries — after all, how many actuaries is it going to take to calculate the monthly renewable term premiums? Will actuaries even be needed for that very simple task?

Undoubtedly, the most attention getting part of the paper has been the Cannibal Life scenario. A scenario is a highly convenient literary device which offers to the author the opportunity to present outrageous ideas without requiring the support of closely reasoned arguments. Would it be stretching a point to suggest that I intended that Cannibal Life should make Missionaries of the rest of the life insurance industry (choose your own interpretation, according to personal taste)?

One aspect of the scenario I believe very firmly. It relates to the future form of our industry's distribution system. The system I envisage will be customer oriented rather than sales oriented. One arm of the sales organization, employing mass-marketing techniques not yet developed or even imagined, will be responsible for expanding the customer base. Another arm, which I believe will be composed primarily of women, will be responsible for servicing and maintaining established customer relationships. Note the emphasis on customer — it is assumed that the great majority of people will own only one life insurance policy. While this flies in the face of established industry experience, consider the position of the banking industry: Do most people maintain more than one bank account for their personal needs?

Whether or not the cannibals are really coming depends, in my view, on whether or not the industry is responsive to the winds of change which I believe have already begun to blow. Perhaps there is no way for an established agency oriented company to take the lead because the risk of losing its entire sales organization to its competitors is both real and likely. If the lead is taken by non-traditional companies, then I believe the cannibals will come.

A long accepted truism of our industry has been that our agency organizations are our most valuable assets. Is this really true? Or would it be more accurate to say that our agency organizations are our most costly assets? Based on the experience of several highly respected companies to which I have been made privy, I know that the cost of agent financing alone approaches $50,000 for each new agent who survives five years; if accumulated interest is added, together with other costs such as training and development allowances, it can be argued that the surviving agent costs $100,000. If the company developing that agent is to recover its costs, together with a reasonable rate of return on those costs, the required production level of the agent is absurdly high — which is another way of saying that it is no longer economically viable to develop new agents on the basis of current experience. Sooner or later, the process must and will be halted. What then?

How many companies represented here have examined separately the profitability of the existing business in force and that of future new business? Would you be surprised to discover that more than all of your future profits will be derived from existing business and that future business, viewed separately, might project perpetual losses if an adequate return on capital invested in new business is factored into the calculations? Can you imagine what the projection would look like if you further subdivided future new business between that which will be produced by your existing agents and that which will be produced by agents you have not yet hired? How long can this situation continue?

Obviously, this is a big subject to which justice cannot be done either in a brief talk such as this or even in a paper such as "The Universal Life Insurance Policy." I realize that the views I have outlined have been presented in a one-sided manner — partly for effect and partly because of limitations on content. Perhaps in the ensuing discussion some of you will make a case for alternatives. It is my personal view that the only realistic alternative is that of an industry offering only term products and specialty products and services aimed almost exclusively at the upper 10% to 20% of the market as a whole; it takes little imagination to foresee that the consequences of this alternative would be even more severe and even more destructive to the industry than the type of change suggested in the paper.

When I presented this paper to the Pacific Insurance Conference last year, I expected to encounter a certain amount of Maginot Line thinking from members of the audience; some, I imagined, would at least want my buttons and epaulets, if not my head, for articulating such heresy. To my surprise, the reaction was quite mild and more sympathetic than I expected. In subsequent discussions and correspondence with representatives of at least 50 companies, I have not encountered even one outright scoffer. This persuades me that the industry itself is conscious also of the winds of change to which I made earlier reference. Perhaps it also signals a readiness to contemplate revolutionary change in a traditional industry.

Before opening the floor for questions, discussion and comment, let me close by answering your first question even before it is asked. The question: Is Cannibal Life a client of Tillinghast? The answer: There have been a few applicants for the role but none has yet accepted.

Future Profit Outlook for Nonparticipating Life Insurance

Published in the RECORD OF THE SOCIETY OF ACTUARIES *Vol. 5, No. 1 (1979): 1–21. Reprinted with permission from the Society of Actuaries.*

The historic trends in profitability of Nonparticipating Life Insurance can be viewed in two ways — prospectively and retrospectively.

The prospective view relates to the *intended* profitability at the date of original pricing. The retrospective view relates to the *actual* profitability of the business as experience develops. Both views are significant in terms of evaluating the future. Viewed in a 20-year prospective, from 1959 to 1979, it is my opinion that the prospective and retrospective trends in profitability of nonparticipating life insurance have moved in opposite directions — prospectively I believe the trend has been downward and retrospectively I believe the trend has been upward. In other words, I believe we have priced for progressively less profitability and obtained progressively more.

By coincidence, the paper which I wrote on the subject of pricing and profit measurement for nonparticipating life insurance was published exactly twenty years ago. The paper includes a "Summary of Standard Assumptions" and an exhibit of results based thereon which may afford some clues as to what the prospective and retrospective profitability of business issued at that time was and has been. The profit criterion stated in the standard assumptions was that the present value at issue of future profits, discounted at 15%, be equal to 10% of the present value of commissions. The other assumptions were typical of the era and represented reasonable best estimates with specific contingency margins. The results produced weighted average premium rates for ordinary life at various ages and amounts which were 2 1/2% higher than the mean of actual premium rates then charged by ten prominent stock companies. If the same exercise were repeated today (I did repeat it in another context approximately two years ago) I believe that the premium rates required by a calculation based upon realistic assumptions in today's environment with the same profit criterion would produce a set of rates approximately 9% higher than the mean of those now available in the marketplace. This comparison convinces me that the trend in profitability, viewed prospectively at the date of issue, has been downward and substantially so. The change can be seen most dramatically in the pricing of term insurance.

The retrospective position is quite different. Looking again at the calculations included in the 1959 paper, I note that the calculated premium rate at age 35 for a $12,000 policy produced an interest adjusted cost (based on 5%) in excess of $10 per thousand. Today, on a policy amount of $25,000 (the inflation adjusted equivalent of $12,000 twenty years ago), it would typically be less than $6 per thousand. Clearly, from a retrospective viewpoint, the historic trend in profitability of nonparticipating life insurance has been upwards.

It is of interest to examine why there has been this historic upward trend in retrospective profitability. The program outline suggests mortality, expense, and investment income as causative factors, and I am sure the other panelists will address these factors. I intend to direct my remarks to factors not included in the list.

The first of these is lapse rates. From the *Life Insurance Fact Book* (1978 Edition), it can be seen that voluntary termination rates have increased significantly. For the period 1960 through 1977 (the closest available comparison to the 20-year period used above), lapse rates on policies in force less than two years have increased from 14.5% to 19.5%, an increase of 34%, and lapse rates on policies in force for more than two years from 3.7% to 4.7%, an increase of 27%. Of course, these statistics include both participating and nonparticipating business. If nonparticipating business were analyzed by itself, I would expect that the increase in lapse rates would be even more dramatic. This increase has eroded profitability from the retrospective view.

The second factor not mentioned in the outline is the cost of capital. In the 1959 paper, the cost of capital was assessed at a rate of 15% per annum in the standard assumptions. My recollections of practices at that time suggest that most companies regarded such a yield on invested surplus as high and perhaps a more representative figure for 1959 would be 12 1/2%. Today, most calculations which I see are done at 15%. Accordingly, I think it is reasonable to assume that the cost of capital represents another unfavorable factor affecting the trend of both prospective and retrospective profitability, but one which is consistent with the movement in interest rates.

The third factor not included in the list is federal income taxes. In the 1959 paper and in pricing techniques used at that time, federal income tax was provided for (if at all) through a relatively minor adjustment of assumed interest rates since the implications of the Life Insurance Company Income Tax Act were not at that time clear. Even after the enactment of the tax legislation which is still largely in effect, the effective tax rate borne by profits on nonparticipating insurance was relatively modest — in general, taxable gain from operations exceeded taxable investment income and only half of the excess was subject to current tax, and this was further mitigated by the use of exact or approximate net level reserve bases for tax purposes and by available special deductions arising on nonparticipating life insurance. Today, taxable investment income attributable to nonparticipating life insurance often exceeds taxable gain from operations and the full rate of corporation tax then applies, though still mitigated by the net level reserve election; now more often, special deductions are not available in full to reduce taxes.

What do these observed trends suggest for the future? Obviously, it would be foolish to suggest with any conviction that history will repeat itself; but perhaps it would be even more foolish to suggest that it will not. The continuation of some trends seems clear. Improvements in mortality seem even more likely today than ever before although the significance of this factor is much diminished because the expected improvement is acting upon a much lower base. Inflation also seems likely to continue and its significance may be greater than in prior years since it appears that most of the benefits of scale and mechanization have already been realized; in the past, those benefits have substantially offset the effects of inflation upon unit maintenance expenses. It would require a brave forecaster to predict that the trend of increasing lapse rates will reverse, but the outlook for new business may be better than the outlook for old because of the now permissible use of higher interest rates in the determination of minimum cash values.

Turning to trends less clear, the most difficult of the factors to predict is the future course of interest rates. For the purpose of pricing nonparticipating life insurance under today's circumstances, I generally suggest to clients the use of a declining series of assumed interest rates consistent with the assumption that new money rates on risk-free investments will decline from 9% today to an ultimate level of 6% in ten years. I do not pretend that this is a likely (let alone the most likely) assumption. Perhaps the most likely scenario is a level or increasing series of interest rates, but I would not bet my company (or a client's) on such an assumption.

My views on the need for changes in the products offered by the industry and the methods used to distribute them have already been widely stated in this and other forums, and I will not this afternoon do more than to repeat my confidence in those views and to note that one company, based in California, has recently introduced radically revised products and is in a position to mobilize a different and powerful distribution system. Could this be the harbinger of things to come?

Finally, the prospect for nonparticipating life insurance in an inflationary environment clearly must diminish though the diminution relates, more properly in my view, to the prospects for *permanent* life insurance and participating life insurance is only marginally better off in this respect. More flexible product design, lower distribution costs, and higher valuation interest rates would improve the prospects for permanent life insurance of both types.

Products, Pricing and Profitability in the 1980s

Presented to the Life Office Management Association (LOMA) Inflation Conference, Northwestern University, April 2, 1980. Reprinted with permission from LOMA.

Several years ago, Alvin Toffler wrote a challenging book entitled *Future Shock.* As those of you who have read the book know, his thesis did not relate to a shock predicted to arrive at some future date. Instead, he suggested that mankind and his institutions were being subjected to shock, here and now, caused by an on-rushing future driven by an accelerating rate of change. In other words, future shock is analogous to electric shock with the shock being caused by the accelerating rate of change instead of by the electricity.

I think Mr. Toffler's thesis is particularly applicable to the life insurance industry of the 1980s, its products, pricing and profitability, and this is the fundamental idea I intend to develop today.

For the past four years, in various forums, I have expressed concerns relating to the future direction of the life insurance industry. In summary, I believe that the industry has entered a period of significant change from which it *cannot* emerge unchanged. I observe:

- change in the social, economic and political environment in which it operates;
- change in the financial needs of the public it serves;
- change in the types of products it should be selling;
- change in the needed distribution of expense and profit margins; and

- change in the distribution systems required to sell the new products to the new market in this new environment.

The views I have expressed before and will express again today are not popular ones within the life insurance industry — particularly within the traditional sector of the industry. This is hardly surprising and it is important to recognize why: the basic products and the distribution systems of the industry, which I am suggesting must be changed, have remained essentially unchanged since the early years of this century when legislation that largely shaped the industry was enacted in New York following the Armstrong investigation of 1905. It is also important to recognize that the industry has over an extended period of time been well served by its methods, which have built a large, successful and, as related to stock companies, profitable industry.

Notwithstanding this long and successful record, it is my firm belief that the industry must identify and address some significant new problems created by the contemporary environment; it is also my contention that, if the industry does not take steps now to determine its own future, another future, considerably more menacing, will be thrust upon it:

- by further large-scale government intrusion into the financial security market;
- by forces in the marketplace which already exist; or
- by new forces in the marketplace, probably of a renegade nature.

The Contemporary Environment

The thesis I have outlined begins with the premise that the contemporary environment is changing rapidly. Let us briefly examine that premise.

First, there is change of a social nature:

- Change in attitudes towards marriage and the family, manifested by an increase in the number of single and divorced persons and a decrease in the number of children in the average family.
- Change in social attitudes which play an important role in motivating people to provide for their own and their families' financial security, evidenced by a decline in self-reliance and increased dependence on employer-sponsored and government-sponsored financial security programs. In short, the entitlement ethic rather than the work ethic.

- Change in public confidence in institutions ranging from government to oil companies and — yes — even financial companies, which must depreciate the value attached to long-term contractural money promises — the kind that life insurance policies provide.
- Change in the general level of education of the public at large accompanied, arguably, by an associated increase in their ability to evaluate critically the insurance industry, its products and their costs.

Taken as a whole, the traditional marketing strategy of the life insurance industry still rests, to an important extent, on the implicit assumptions that the market consists of a stable family comprising a breadwinner husband, a homemaker wife, and two dependent children. How does this assumption square with today's realities?

Consider this U. S. Labor Department release dated March 8, 1977:

> The concept of a family where the husband is the only breadwinner, the wife is a homemaker..., and there are two children may be a useful one for many illustrative purposes, but it does not represent the typical American family of the mid-1970s. Among husband-wife families in 1975, only seven out of 100 fit this description.

Although the foregoing quotation is faithful to the Labor Department release, the excerpt is misleading in that it refers to families with *exactly* two children. There are approximately 47 million husband-wife families in the United States of which only 14 million are families where the husband is the only earner; 9 million such families consist of three or more persons, and it is these 9 million families, 19% of all of the husband-wife families, that fit the classical pattern. Although these facts are startling enough, it should also be noted that husband-wife families account for only two-thirds of the adult population of the country. This is 1975 information and the trends indicated have probably carried further already. Clearly, the stereotype of the 1950s no longer applies and is no longer even close to representative.

Second, there is change of an economic nature:

- Change in family income levels, a major contributor to which is the growing economic importance of working women and the associated trend towards two-income families; clearly, the typical family today can afford and needs more financial security products than ever before.

- Change in the economic environment represented by the accelerated rate of inflation accompanied by unprecedentedly high levels of interest rates, both of which impact the motivation to save and the choice of savings vehicle. For the life insurance industry, the choice is manifesting itself in major increases in policy loan utilization and significant increases in surrenders.
- Change represented by the much increased complexity and interdependence of worldwide economic activities, with increased risks of instability and economic dislocation accompanied by shortages and scarcity of basic resources. The best example of this is the worldwide energy crisis, the effects of which have probably only begun to be felt.

These changes of an economic nature suggest that an expanded but less stable market for financial security products exists but that its needs and wants, particularly with respect to savings products, are different from those of earlier years.

Third, there is change of a political nature:

- Government-sponsored benefits have changed dramatically in both scale and scope and now include built-in adjustments that ensure that increases will continue for the foreseeable future; government has become the principal purveyor of financial security products — the "life insurance in force" of the social security system (if it could be calculated) probably exceeds $3 trillion, about 20% more than the sum of private life insurance of all types in the United States. This estimate may prove to be absurdly conservative when viewed with hind sight from the perspective of, say, 1990.
- Consumer and environmental interests of an organized nature represent major new political forces which have already altered national priorities and threaten directly to affect the life insurance industry.
- In the past decade, it is clear that the traditional gap between political and economic logic has widened, adding fuel to the fires of inflation and increasing the appetite of government for taxation from sources that are not politically sensitive — for example, the life insurance industry.

These changes, too, affect the life insurance market. The expansion of social insurance benefits raises real questions as to whether or not there is a substantial need for private life insurance at the lower end of the income spectrum. The Federal Trade Commission, although it denies it, has clearly mounted an attack on the life insurance industry; its recent report on the individual ordinary insurance business, though laced with deliberate distortions to sensationalize its findings, cannot easily be dismissed and has disturbing implications for permanent life insurance generally and for nonparticipating permanent life insurance in particular.

These then are the changes which I perceive have had, are having, and will have significant impact on the life insurance industry. But is there any evidence that the impact is already being felt? I believe there is. Consider:

1. Although private savings continue to expand, the life insurance industry is consistently losing its share of the private savings market; the loss of market share is more noticeable if policy loans are regarded as withdrawn savings rather than assets. From 1960 to 1970, the ordinary life insurance reserves of all U. S. companies, net of policy loans, increased from $54 billion to $84 billion, a compound annual increase of 4.5%, roughly equal to the rate of inflation for that period. From 1970 to 1978, the net "savings" increased from $84 billion to $127 billion, a compound annual growth rate of 5%; from 1970 to 1978, the average inflation rate was probably 8% and, in constant dollars, the *absolute* industry participation in the savings market *declined* by 18%. The *relative* participation declined still more.
2. Since 1951, lapse rates on both old and new policies have increased steadily, over the 27-year period from 1951 to 1978, lapse rates more than doubled. Lapse rates on policies less than two years old increased steadily from 1951 to 1970 and have remained stable since that date. Lapse rates on policies more than two years old increased from 1951 to 1960 and remained stable until 1972; since that date, there has been an ominous and steady increase which probably signals increased replacement activity.
3. Sales of term insurance of all types represent a steadily increasing proportion of new business. Sales of annuity business, carrying much lower distribution costs than traditional life insurance products, have soared. Sales of permanent insurance have declined relatively and absolutely (in constant dollars), particularly in the family market.
4. A recent McKenzie study disclosed that until approximately ten years ago market shares within the life insurance industry were relatively insensitive to competitive position. Since then, market shares have shifted noticeably

in the direction of the most competitive companies. Until recently, it has been thought that demand within the life insurance industry was relatively inelastic — largely due to inexact methods of price comparison and to the dampening effect on price competition of the personal relationship between the agent and the prospect. The evidence, while not conclusive, strongly suggests that weaker competitors will suffer a further loss of market share to stronger competitors and that the trend in this direction is likely to gather strength.

This evidence suggests that the public is turning more to other savings media and less to life insurance, that the industry is being subjected to a raid on its accumulated assets (at a time when its fixed interest investments stand at an unprecedented discount in the marketplace); that sales of the type of business which provides the majority of its income and, particularly, the income of its distribution system are declining in constant dollar terms; and that life insurance is now a more price-sensitive product.

The Permanent Life Insurance Dilemma

The thrust of the FTC report is that permanent life insurance is a bad buy by comparison with the purchase of term insurance combined with a separate savings fund. Thus far, the industry's response has been a stonewall denial of the FTC's conclusion, a rejection of the FTC's proposed cost comparison methodology, and savage criticism of the FTC's analysis and motives. But the forces behind the efforts of the FTC and others to discredit the industry and its products cannot, in my view, be deflected by public relations alone.

I once appeared on a panel at the Conference of Actuaries in Public Practice with another actuary who began his discussion of current trends in product development with the following statement:

> Buy term and invest the difference is good advice. And that's because the difference is too big.

The outrage of the industry at the obvious distortions and manipulations included in the FTC report is clearly justified. But that's not to say that the basic conclusion of the report — that permanent life insurance is a poor savings buy — is incorrect. Moreover, the FTC has proposed a cost disclosure system which would permit a comparison of unlike policies — term versus permanent, for example. Conceivably, the industry could survive a massive shift to term insurance (this has happened in several other countries) but its distribution system could not, at least not in its present form.

Consider the characteristics of traditional permanent life insurance products in the context of the contemporary environment. These products are characterized over an extended time period by the requirement of regular premiums on a fixed dollar amount and provide benefits also of a fixed dollar amount. Are these products appropriate to the needs of the typical buyer under today's conditions?

Consider the effects of inflation. Even at a rate of only 5%, long-term money promises depreciate in value approximately 40% every ten years. At 10%, the depreciation is 61% and at 15% the depreciation is 75%. Ten years is not a long time in the context of a permanent life insurance policy. In an inflationary environment, even at inflation rates which appear modest by today's standards, fixed-premium/fixed-benefit permanent life insurance has questionable relevance to a typical buyer's financial requirements over the extended period of time necessary to justify the purchase of permanent insurance instead of term insurance. In fact, ordinary life insurance today is *not* level premium/ level benefit life insurance — it is decreasing premium/decreasing benefit life insurance in real terms, and this is the crux of some of the industry's economic problems.

The implications are clear: the financial security needs of a typical buyer under today's circumstances are not likely to be well served by permanent life insurance of the traditional type. Yet the industry and particularly its distribution systems are heavily dependent on this one product. Herein lies the principal dilemma facing the industry. Should it soldier on and experience a slow and painful decline? Should it shift to term insurance products? Or should it invent new forms of permanent life insurance with greater flexibility and improved costs?

The Permanent vs. Term Dilemma

Included in the legislation which grew out of the Armstrong investigation of 1905 was Section 213 of the New York Insurance Code. This section deals with the regulation of commission rates and certain other expenses, and it has effectively dictated the pattern of commission rates and other expenses for the entire life insurance industry.

At the time the legislation was passed, its framers decided that the highest commission rates should be paid on the longest form of term insurance. In the environment of the early twentieth century, when mortality rates were very much higher than they are today, it was proper to consider an ordinary life policy as the longest form of term insurance and this type of contract has since carried the highest commission rate of any form of life insurance.

The improvement in mortality since the early twentieth century has altered the nature of an ordinary life policy. Today, only 10–15% of the premium on an ordinary life insurance policy is required to pay the death benefit costs; in other words, if all mortality rates dropped to zero up to age 100 and if the rate of mortality at age 100 were 100%, the premium on an ordinary life policy could be reduced by only 10–15%. By contrast, 45–55% of the total premium is required to accumulate the cash values provided in the policy or to pay dividends to policyholders. Clearly, under today's conditions, an ordinary life policy is first and foremost a savings product and secondarily a protection product and the ratio of the two types of benefits is on the order of 3 or 4 to 1. Seventy-five years ago, the proportion of the premium on an ordinary life policy required to pay death benefits was about 30% to 40% with correspondingly less to provide savings benefits. In other words, the product has changed but the pattern of commissions and other expenses has not.

When a permanent insurance policy is regarded primarily as a savings product, it is clear that the expense levels associated with the product (driven mainly by sales commissions and related costs) are very high by comparison with competing savings products, which operate on benefit-to-cost ratios ranging from 90–100%.

A life insurance product designed primarily to provide protection benefits can support much lower benefit-to-cost ratios. For example, benefit-to-cost ratios in the range of 40–60% can be found in individual health insurance and certain personal casualty insurance lines. In all probability, the industry as a whole is underpricing its term insurance products and overpricing its permanent insurance products, largely because of the commission pattern dictated by Section 213.

Viewed in this light, it is easy to see why the industry is alarmed by the suggestion by the FTC that a cost comparison method be adopted which would permit the comparison of the costs of unlike products — particularly term versus permanent. For the distribution system as it exists today and at prevailing commission rates to survive a shift to an all-term mode would require an increase in the aggregate premium on each year's sales on the order of 20% and this would probably mean the aggregate face amount on each year's sales would need to increase five-fold. On an industry-wide basis, this is an unachievable result.

The Par vs. Nonpar Dilemma

There is a subsidiary argument involving the relative viability of participating and nonparticipating permanent life insurance.

The Standard Nonforfeiture Law dictates the limitations within which cash values of permanent life insurance policies must be fixed. The law imposes a maximum interest rate, currently 5.5% in most jurisdictions, which may be used in the calculation of cash values. Since the cash value of all ordinary life policies must be $1,000 per $1,000 face amount at age 100, where the statutory mortality table expires, the choice of interest rate determines how rapidly the cash value must be accumulated to $1,000 — a high interest rate accumulates less in the early years and more in the later years than a low interest rate. If interest rates available in the marketplace are reasonably close to the rate being used for the accumulation of cash values, there are no material distortions between law and reality. But under today's conditions, with interest yields on government securities in excess of 12%, the distortions are substantial. The cost of accumulating unrealistically high cash values in the short-to-intermediate years of a policy causes a higher premium to be charged to support those cash values; but in the intermediate-to-later years of a policy, the premium is far too high.

With participating insurance, this distortion is dealt with through the dividend scale. But with nonparticipating insurance, there is a dilemma. If the pricing basis is appropriate for, say, the first twenty years, it is inappropriate thereafter or vice versa.

Some industry observers have been pointing to this problem for several years. Mr. E. J. Moorhead, a past President of the Society of Actuaries and also of the American Academy of Actuaries, was one of the first to speak out on this subject. More recently, a senior official of the Lincoln National Life Insurance Company has stated publicly that nonparticipating permanent life insurance did not feature importantly in that company's future marketing plans. Clearly, these products, in today's environment, belong on the endangered species list.

The Distribution System Dilemma

Approximately two-thirds of the expenses of a typical life insurance company are associated with its distribution system. If major changes are to be made in the benefit-to-cost ratio of permanent life insurance products, it follows that significant changes must be made in the expenses associated with the distribution system. In this connection, it is worth noting that the average sales frequency of the industry is very low — less than one sale per week per full-time equivalent agent. In that one sad statistic may lie the root of the whole problem. It may also be the germ of a solution.

The Insurance Institute of London *Report of the Advance Study Group (No. 27)* includes the following quotation from the records of one United Kingdom company:

> The Committee having considered Proper Measures for enlarging the Insurance of this Office, have thought convenient to Appoint Persons of Reputation and substance in the chief Towns and Cities to Distribute Policies and receive all Quarterages and to allow such persons One Shilling in the Pound as an Equivallent for their Trouble.

That statement reasonably describes the marketing strategy being followed today by companies distributing their wares through personal producing general agents. Yet it was recorded in December, 1720 — 259 years ago! It is possible that such a person-to-person marketing strategy could still be the best available today? When a typical Sunday press run of the New York Times far surpasses the entire printed word as it existed in 1720? When commercial radio is well into its second half century? When commercial television has been generally available for approximately 30 years? And when a computer terminal no costlier nor less portable than a 1960 desk top calculator can access powerful computers over an ordinary telephone line?

Two years ago I participated in a debate sponsored by the Society of Actuaries which addressed the following question: Resolved, that the life insurance industry as conducted today is in its terminal state. As you might have already guessed, I argued the affirmative side of the question. One of the statements I made in the course of my presentation was that the cost of "manufacturing" from scratch a full-time established agent is in the vicinity of $100,000 (to the nearest $100,000). At the time, the statement stirred up a certain amount of controversy. As it turns out, time may have vindicated my critics. Today, I would say that the cost of manufacturing from scratch a full-time established agent may have reached $200,000 (to the nearest $100,000)!

If this sounds like an extract from *Alice in Wonderland*, let me assure you that the only thing Charles Lutwidge Dodgson (alias Lewis Carroll) and I have in common is that we're both mathematicians. The figures cited are disturbingly real and they are consistent with the experience of a number of companies to whose affairs I am privy. Skeptics should consult LIMRA who have a number of more precise examples. Even if the other problems I have already alluded to do not exist, there is a very serious problem connected with the capital costs required to maintain existing agency organizations. If a company developing new agents is to recover its costs, together with a reasonable rate of return on its costs, the required productivity of that agent is absurdly high — which is another way of saying that it is no longer economically viable to develop new agents on the basis of current experience. Many, if not most, companies have, in fact, abandoned efforts to develop new agents in favor of proselytization. While this may permit the string to be played out a little longer for some companies, it is obviously a dead-end strategy for the industry as a whole.

The Replacement Dilemma

The spectre of large-scale replacement of existing business in force is no illusion. Whether this takes the form of an outright raid on accumulated cash values or a systematic exploitation of policy loan provisions, the result would be the same. Particularly after the events of the last five months, the industry as a whole is holding fixed income securities on which there is substantial market depreciation, but there are outstanding policy contracts containing guaranteed cash and loan values which afford little protection from market depreciation in the event of a major call on those guarantees. In these circumstances, the danger of a raid is real, and many would argue that the raid is already in progress and accelerating. Recently, products specifically designed as replacement vehicles have been introduced by a few companies and many more are on the drawing board. The activities of these companies must further exacerbate an already serious situation.

For the reasons noted earlier, nonparticipating insurance is more vulnerable than participating insurance to such a raid because higher interest rates (the cause of the market depreciation) are not reflected in higher current dividends. I would predict that within the next few years some companies, to protect their business in force, are going to extend enhanced benefits to holders of their nonparticipating policies; the implications for shareholders and directors, including the potential for litigation, are not pleasant to contemplate. But the alternative is even more unpleasant.

The Alternative Futures of the Life Insurance Industry

In other forums, I have written and spoken about the alternative futures of the life insurance industry. To spice up the presentations (and to permit the introduction of somewhat outrageous ideas), I have used the device of a scenario to outline each of the various possibilities. Time does not permit my repeating them here today, but the titles of the scenarios and a capsule description may give you the general flavor:

1. *Business (Almost) As Usual*, a self-descriptive title;
2. *Big Brother Arrives*, which postulates a major incursion by government into the financial security business;
3. *Götterdämmerung*, which postulates a significant asset raid by competitors;
4. *Doomsday*, which postulates an all-term industry with only part-time agents; and
5. *Revolution*, which postulates a redirection of the products and distribution systems of the industry.

I believe that, for the reasons already discussed, Scenario (1), *Business (Almost) as Usual*, is an unrealistic expectation. Scenarios (2), (3) and (4) represent the possibilities I foresee if the industry continues on its traditional path; each leads to a slightly different form of disaster. Today I would like to concentrate on Scenario (5), *Revolution.*

Products in the 1980s

First of all, let me say that I believe that the marketplace (meaning the ultimate consumer, not the agent) is going to demand an overhaul of the permanent insurance products offered by the industry. As I see it, the overhaul will require the introduction of far more flexible and more cost-effective products which are responsive to changing financial needs caused by inflation and other factors. Second, let me say that I believe that to accomplish the necessary product change, it will also be necessary to alter the expense structure of the distribution system if not its composition. These changes will not easily be made because at the point of adopting a new product/distribution philosophy, a company must face the prospect that it may lose its entire agency organization to its competitors; to most companies, their agency organizations *are* their customers.

Is there any magic which might make such a fundamental change easier to implement? I do not know whether or not there is but I think I can point to where some might be found:

1. The development of a product design which would reduce the federal income tax burden borne by investment earnings of policyholders would substantially increase the attraction of life insurance as a savings medium.
2. An increase in the productivity of the existing distribution system would revolutionize the economics of the industry, particularly the cost of developing and maintaining the existing distribution system; if sales frequency could be increased from less than one per week to, say, two per week, the industry's basic economics would be transformed.
3. The introduction of products designed so that inflation works for the company instead of against the company would also revolutionize the economics of the industry; products with escalating coverage *and* premiums, designed to keep pace with inflation, are feasible and do produce the desired result.

Let me turn now to a specific question: How might a specific company — your company, for instance — address the problems I have discussed today?

What is required, in my opinion, is a substantial redistribution of commissions and expense margins. First, commissions and expense margins on the protection element should be increased and, on the savings element, reduced. Second, commission rates and other expense margins should vary substantially according to the size of the sale; with the advent of negotiated commission rates on stock exchange transactions, the life insurance industry is left alone as one which does not recognize to a meaningful degree the principle of cheaper by the dozen. So much for theory.

A practical approach to achieving the desired redistribution of commissions and margins is through the introduction of a new product, probably one aimed at the upper end of the market, without disturbing existing products. Moreover, if the new product were designed in such a way as to afford much increased flexibility to the buyer and if the new product were designed with an eye towards minimizing the burden of federal income taxes imposed on policyholder investment earnings, such a product would relate more meaningfully to the market needs and would have added appeal. If the new product were introduced as an alternative to existing products rather than a substitute for them, this would permit a low risk test of the viability of achieving increased productivity through the introduction of a more attractive product. This must be achieved, in my opinion, if current agency distribution methods are to continue.

A year ago, a California company introduced a product of the kind I have in mind. Essentially, the product is a combination of a savings account and a term insurance rider. It includes explicit loadings and commissions which match. Loadings and commissions grade steeply by policy size since the largest single element is a one-time, flat charge per policy. Patterns of coverage and premium payments are completely flexible. Interest is credited on the savings account at a rate at least competitive with leading participating products. The result is a highly competitive product. I would predict that this product will be the prototype for many similar products which follow; in fact, this is a low-risk prediction because we, as a firm, are involved in the design of such products for a number of our clients.

One footnote that may be of interest to a number of companies represented here: A stock company with no participating business may be able to design excess interest products in such a way that they are able to pay an investment return based on their own pretax yield; mutual companies, on the other hand, will find it extremely difficult to achieve the same result and may be limited to paying an investment return based on their own *after* tax yield. If this is the result, it follows that many mutual companies will organize stock life insurance subsidiaries to market such products. A few already have.

Pricing and Profitability in the 1980s

My vision of the products of the 1980s moots a number of pricing issues that apply to traditional products. This is because the design contemplated matches quite closely each element of cost with a corresponding element of loading. Moreover, the design is pseudo-participating with respect to the investment element.

Addressing more generally the subject of pricing and profitability in the 1980s, I see the following important issues:

1. The protection element of life insurance is its distinguishing feature. Why is the industry charging so little for it? The real threat to the future of industry may well be its own cheap ART products.
2. Mortality rates seem destined further to improve. Perhaps this will rebuild needed margins on term products. For permanent products (except at older ages) this will not be an important factor. It does suggest that current underwriting classifications may be too refined.
3. Guaranteeing or even predicting the future level of interest rates in the new economic environment involves unacceptably high risks for most products. This suggests that participating and pseudo-participating products will become more common.
4. Federal income taxes may well represent one-third of the total tax and expense burden on permanent life insurance products. Ways must be found to mitigate this burden.
5. High interest rates *increase* the effective expense charge because initial expenses require a larger amortization charge in subsequent years.

6. Inflation of maintenance expenses needs explicit recognition in the current environment.
7. The industry has chronically underestimated lapse rates. Flexible product designs will require separate recognition of premium suspensions and surrenders.
8. Particularly in stock companies but also in mutuals, the required return on the investment in new business must increase. For stock companies, an after tax return of at least 15% is required to meet shareholder expectations. For mutual companies, an after tax return equal to the desired rate of growth of new business is required to finance expansion; unless the company is willing to shrink in constant dollar terms, the growth rate must at least equal the rate of inflation.

Conclusion

Not unexpectedly, there are those within the industry that would prefer that the perceived problems and possibilities which are the subject of this talk not be discussed — at least not publicly discussed. Four years ago, or even two years ago, a suppression of these perceptions and possibilities, arguably, might have postponed the onset of some of the predicted problems. Today, in my opinion, there can be no argument; I say this because I believe that the lions are already loose and there is no way to cage them up.

Periods of change are two-sided coins. On one side in bold-faced type is stamped "PROBLEMS"; on the other is stamped "OPPORTUNITIES." I expect to see in the coming decade a significant realignment of market shares in the life insurance industry. While there may be more losers than winners, I am convinced that there will be winners and that some will win big.

Products of the 1980s: Liquidity, Profitability and Other Considerations

Presented to the Life Office Management Association (LOMA) Conference on Planning for Liquidity and Profitability, Boston, Massachusetts, January 28, 1982. Reprinted with permission from LOMA.

Throughout the 20th century, and particularly during the past three decades, the leading individual life insurance product of the industry has been whole life, contributing more than two-thirds of the income derived from individual business and even higher percentages of profits and, most significantly, income to its distribution system. Clearly, this product is under attack and is loosing favor. Critics include consumer advocates, the Federal Trade Commission, views from the academic community and even voices from within the life insurance industry itself. This month, one company (not a major one) announced the withdrawal from its portfolio of all whole life products in favor of a combination product which ties together term insurance and a deferred annuity. Another company has advertised this theme for more than a year. In response, wagons are being circled in various quarters. For this particular match-up, I am inclined to take the points and bet on the Indians — even though it didn't work last Sunday!

The decline in the popularity of whole life is evident from the statistics. Sales of term insurance have expanded steadily at the expense of whole life, and annuity sales have boomed along with an upsurge of a variety of nontraditional products, notably universal life. Clearly, these trends will continue, and it is more likely than not that they will accelerate, notwithstanding major efforts to reverse the tide — something tried earlier by King Canute!

What does this suggest that the products of the 1980s will be? In the view of this observer, five products seem likely to account for most of the business that will be sold in the 1980s; in fact, they already do, but their market shares seem likely to change substantially:

1. First, universal life in approximately its current form is likely to attract an increasing share of the market. Offered in 1981 by perhaps 50 companies, only a few of which are large, and offered only for a fraction of the year by most of the companies, universal life probably attracted a total market share of between 1% and 2%, measured by annualized premiums for 1981. The current sales rate of universal life is estimated to be attracting a market share of 3% to 4% and most of the companies offering the product find that it represents about half of all individual sales. The impending introduction of this product by several major companies suggests that the market share in 1982 will rise sharply, perhaps to a level of 10% for the year as a whole. By year-end 1982, the then current market share might approach 15%.
2. Second, variable life insurance in both its current form as well as the expected variable version of universal life, an idea being actively pursued by a substantial number of companies, including some major ones, is likely to be a growing factor in the market. In 1981, variable life insurance probably attracted a market share of between 2% and 3%, even though it was offered by only three companies, two of which are quite large. Variable life insurance in its current form is not expected to be offered by a significant number of additional companies in the near future, but the variable form of universal life may make its appearance by the beginning of 1983 and seems destined, ultimately, to become the dominant form of variable life products. In 1982 the market share of variable life insurance will probably increase but seems unlikely to surpass 5%.
3. Third, sales of term insurance seem destined to continue to grow. In 1981 it is estimated that term insurance accounted for more than 20% of new premium income, notwithstanding the progressive move towards one-year renewable term and the continuing reductions in premium rates. Meaningful statistics regarding the relative sales of various types of insurance may never be seen again due to the introduction of hybrid forms of term insurance masquerading as modified premium whole life insurance.

4. Whole life insurance — yes, good old whole life — will still be with us. In 1981 it is estimated that whole life insurance accounted for at least 65% of new individual life premium income, and even though that proportion continues to decline, it remains an overwhelming majority and is likely to continue as such. I expect the decline in whole life to continue and to accelerate, but there is one major market to which it will remain well suited and that is the minimum deposit market. If universal and variable life are aimed at the market among those who wish a combined insurance and savings program and if term insurance is aimed at the market among those who prefer to buy term and invest the difference elsewhere, whole life can be aimed at the market among those who prefer to buy permanent and borrow the difference!
5. Annuities, both qualified and nonqualified, have exhibited booming sales, but the statistics are difficult to interpret because of massive amounts of single premium annuities sold through stockbrokers. The Economic Recovery Tax Act of 1980 has opened a major new market for the sale of Individual Retirement Accounts, and this seems likely to insure an increased participation in the annuity market by companies operating through traditional distribution systems.

These then are the main individual products I foresee the industry offering in the 1980s. Let me now review with respect to each such issues as liquidity, profitability and taxation — the latter from the viewpoint of both the policyholder and the issuing company.

Universal Life

Because of the visibility of the investment component of universal life, many experts involved with this product anticipate an increased need for liquidity in investments matching the accruing liabilities on universal life. They expect, for example, that the availability of partial withdrawal (as an alternative to policy loans) will generate an abnormal amount of turnover by comparison with traditional forms of life insurance. Accordingly, most companies issuing universal life are investing the assets matching the reserves on a relatively short-term basis, primarily in maturities of one year or less. So far, this investment strategy has been an easy one to follow because, throughout the period of time that universal life has been available, we have experienced an inverted yield curve. The real test of nerve and character will come when the yield curve reverts to its normal shape.

I do not disagree with those who believe that universal life may create liquidity demands which dictate that investments be made in short maturities. I fail to see, however, that there is as much difference as is alleged between universal life and traditional products in this respect. Considering that more than 25% of individual life insurance reserves have been borrowed by policyholders, it is clear that traditional products, too, are subject to heavy demands on liquidity. The difference is that this was not recognized as a likely possibility until quite recently.

I have often been asked what will happen when the yield curve reverts to its normal shape and long-term interest rates exceed short-term interest rates. Sadly, I have replied that I suppose that the industry will make the same dumb mistake again!

Turning from liquidity to profitability, universal life in its present form is quite profitable primarily because of the much reduced front-end surplus strains associated with the lower levels of commissions. Most companies have attempted to match reasonably closely sources of revenue and costs. Generally, loadings do not cover the full amount of expenses, and there is a loss on this element of revenue and cost. The pricing of most universal life products on the market today anticipates an investment spread of between 1% and 2% and this flows directly through to profits. In general, the cost of insurance rates are expressed on an aggregate basis although one company has introduced select and ultimate cost of insurance rates; the level of cost of insurance rates is higher than the most competitive ART rates, even though ART rates must cover both mortality and expenses. As a result, there are substantial profits implicit in the cost of insurance rates, particularly during the period of select mortality.

Some people anticipate that the transparency of universal life will lead to competitive pressures not unlike those seen today in the term market. In the long run, I expect that they are correct, but the current emphasis is not on the comparison between universal life products but is instead on the comparison between universal life products and traditional products. In addition, the development of universal life appears to be proceeding in two directions —

one is the development of consumer oriented products with commissions and loads that reduce as the size of the sale increases, and the other is the development of products with relatively high loads intended to support something close to the traditional levels of agent compensation. It remains to be seen which of the forms will become the dominant one, and we may see elements of reverse price competition caused by commission competition.

It is the viewpoint of this observer that questions of policyholder taxation with respect to universal life are a settled matter. The Hutton ruling, while it applies only to a single policyholder, is very broad and clear in its discussion of the issues. I believe that universal life will continue to be treated for tax purposes in the policyholders' hands like any other life insurance policy. Questions such as the possibility of paying a million dollar single premium under a policy providing only $25,000 of insurance risk are, in my view, red herrings planted by those who would prefer to arrest the development of universal life — the IRS might well deny life insurance treatment where the product was abused on this basis, but surely it would not deny that treatment to all universal life products simply because somebody might so abuse the product. Other questions such as the current taxation of interest credited under universal life or the possibility that interest credited might be deemed to have been constructively received because it can be withdrawn without penalty, are also in my view red herrings. Formal opinions have been given on each of these issues by more than one responsible law firm.

Issues involving company taxation are quite another matter, and I intended to deal with these later collectively rather than on a product-by-product basis.

Variable Life

Variable life in its present form and the expected variable version of universal life neatly solve all liquidity problems by transferring the market value risk to policyholders. In the United Kingdom, where variable life insurance is well established and represents a large proportion of the market, this practice has been in place for many years and has worked well. In fact, even on traditional products in the U.K., the market value risk is substantially in the hands of the policyholders because most policies do not contain guaranteed surrender and loan values; instead, these values are calculated on the basis of current circumstances and, effectively, a market value adjustment is made. Assuming that the recent period of instability in interest rates will be with us for some years to come, ultimately variable life insurance may be the only acceptable alternative to managing our investment portfolios as if we were money market funds. Recognition is overdue that the standard nonforfeiture law is a dangerous piece of legislation from the viewpoint of policyholders. This law should be repealed, but as long as it is in effect, variable life insurance is the only solution to liquidity problems that does not distort investment policies.

The profitability of variable life insurance is difficult to measure at this stage. Two of the three companies offering the product are mutuals. Substantial development expenses have been incurred. Perhaps it is a reasonable generalization to expect that variable life insurance in its present form might exhibit profit characteristics similar to that of traditional participating business. Certainly, there are no limitations on charges that would mandate lower profit levels on this product.

The profitability of the variable version of universal life is easier to predict. Development costs should be substantially less than for the existing form of variable life insurance; administrative complications should also be fewer. If the asset charge is similar to the intended spread on current forms of universal life, a reasonable assumption, profit margins should also be similar.

From the viewpoint of the policyholder, the tax position of variable life insurance appears to be no different than that of traditional life insurance except that the policyholder effectively is charged with any capital gains taxes paid by the company on realizations within the separate account.

Term Insurance

With term insurance products, issues of liquidity are moot and policyholder tax questions are clear. The issue worth discussing is profitability.

Traditionally, term insurance products sold by the life insurance industry have been highly profitable. Deficiency reserve requirements tended to keep premium rates higher than market forces would. Due to the effect of select mortality gains, profit emergence has been early. Mortality improvement, which has been substantial during the past 15 years, has increased profit levels above original expectations. In general, level term insurance has been much more profitable than decreasing term insurance. So much for the past. What about the future?

History offers little help in forecasting the profitability of today's term insurance products. The advent of annually renewable term insurance as the dominant product, the introduction of separate rates for smokers and non-smokers, the introduction of select and ultimate rates (leading to re-entry term, in one company or another) and the introduction of term insurance masquerading as modified premium whole life, all raise substantial questions which relate to the profitability of this business. In addition to exotic questions raised by the foregoing considerations, there is also the simpler matter of intensified price competition.

The problem which is new and potentially very serious is the possibility under current forms of term insurance that the policyholder will engage in extensive anti-selection, giving rise to a mortality experience unlike that which might be suggested by any prior statistics. Frankly, I am highly skeptical as to the ultimate pre-tax profitability of the business being sold today — particularly given the intensity of current price competition.

On the bright side, the introduction of modified premium whole life policies might give rise to highly favorable tax consequences that could be important enough to convert a pre-tax loss to an after-tax gain! The issue relates to the company tax position and the effect of the 818(c)(2) election.

Whole Life

The liquidity implications of whole life are well known to us all and have already been extensively discussed this morning. Where whole life is used as a minimum deposit plan, it becomes term insurance for all practical purposes, mooting questions of liquidity.

Profitability is another matter. Unfortunately, many companies' entry into minimum deposit business was field inspired rather than home office lead. The result was that the same products were used for minimum deposit as were used for traditional sales, leading to substantial inequities between classes of policyholders, particularly when interest rates increased to a level far above policy loan interest rates. Minimum deposit can and should be a viable and profitable product, but it is best to design a product specifically for minimum deposit use and to price it accordingly. It is even possible to design a minimum deposit plan which imitates whole life insurance rather than term insurance.

Policyholder tax questions on whole life would appear to be well established although it is conceivable that the deductability of policy loan interest could at some stage be eliminated.

Annuities

It is my firm view, and one that is shared by most if not all of my associates, that there are extremely menacing liquidity problems associated with annuities, particularly single premium deferred annuities sold by stockbrokers, usually in large denominations. The combination of long term investment guarantees plus cash on demand principal guarantees is a liability which cannot be matched by any orthodox investment. Of course, one possibility is to invest the assets in a deferred annuity issued by a competitor, thus passing the risk to him! This extremely serious potential problem, if it became actual, could threaten not only the solvency of a number of companies, but could have a domino effect on the entire industry, not just those companies issuing such products.

Is there a solution? Considering that something like $20 billion of premiums have gone into deferred annuities through stockbrokers, the potential problem is very large and beyond the limits of what can be solved in any conventional way.

Companies issuing deferred annuities in large volumes are reporting substantial earnings on a GAAP basis, indicating that these products are very profitable, all provided that nothing goes seriously awry. If the unexpected but possible should happen, in the form of a run on the bank, past profits would be wiped out and staggering losses would be incurred.

Other types of annuities, such as qualified plans and IRAs, seem destined to be low margin products because they will be offered in competition with banks, savings and loan associations and mutual fund sponsors. The secret of profitability in these areas must be found in the ability to hold down distribution expenses and to streamline administrative procedures.

Except for the more exotic forms of wraparound annuities and so forth, the taxation of annuities appears to be well established from the policyholder's point of view. If variable annuities are involved, the same question arises with respect to capital gains taxes as was discussed with respect to variable life insurance.

Company Tax Issues

The Life Insurance Company Income Tax Act of 1959 is rapidly coming unglued and is in need of a thorough overhaul. Efforts by the American Council of Life Insurers to put together a tax reform package acceptable to each of the several main constituencies of the industry continue. In my view, the proposal is looking more and more like a letter to Santa Claus and less and less like a piece of legislation that Congress will pass, particularly in the current environment of large government deficits, commitments to reductions in direct taxation and a consequent increase in the appetite of government for tax revenue from sources that are not politically sensitive — for example, the life insurance industry.

The burning issue is the taxation, within life insurance companies, of policyholders' investment earnings. Under current law, the tax rate effectively borne by policyholders' investment earnings is high and rising and the possible throughput of investment return is uncompetitive with other savings vehicles. The future of the industry as a participant in the savings market depends upon the industry's ability to find ways, legislative or other, to solve this problem. The current techniques involve:

1. Issuing policies where the premium actually charged is less than that stated in the policy, without characterizing the difference as a policyholder dividend;
2. Issuing life insurance policies or annuities on which excess interest above that guaranteed at the inception is credited at a rate determined from time to time, without characterizing the excess interest as a policyholder dividend; and
3. Engaging in reinsurance transactions which separate the taxable investment income generated by policyholder reserves from dividends payable to policyholders, permitting the latter to be deducted for tax purposes.

Clearly, all of this is not going to continue forever and some change in the whole basis of taxation of the life insurance industry and its policyholders is on its way. Current efforts by the ACLI to inspire reform is impeded by the substantially different interests of its various constituencies, and it appears doubtful to me, particularly in the current political environment, that a politically acceptable package will emerge.

It is instructive to note what has recently happened in Canada. On November 12, 1981 the Minister of Finance presented his budget to Parliament and included in it is a provision which provides for the taxation of policyholders and annuitants, every three years, on the gain on permanent life insurance policies and annuities issued after November 12th. Details of the plan are still unsettled, but it is clear that in calculating the gain there is to be included as part of the gain the value of the effective insurance coverage. This is not the first time that the Canadian Government has attempted to reach for the investment earnings of policyholders as a source of tax revenues. The threat to the industry is unmistakable, and a slide by the industry into an all term mode seems quite likely; in this context, it is worth noting that term insurance already accounts for a larger proportion of the market in Canada than it does in the United States.

What brought this situation about in Canada? My view is that it came about because the industry has never paid any substantial amount of tax and most of what has been paid came from Canadian branches of foreign companies, many of which could offset their Canadian tax liabilities against those assessed in the country in which they were incorporated. Had the industry come forward with a clear and fair proposal for taxation, I think it likely that the events of last November would not have taken place. Could the same thing happen in the United States?

With more than a little trepidation, let me suggest to you a basis for taxing the life insurance industry and its policyholders that I think would be fair and equitable. It would place stocks and mutuals on a level playing field, would be completely neutral as to the form of product design and would raise about the same amount of revenue contemplated at least in the early work by the ACLI on its tax package. Moreover, I think it is politically acceptable because its thesis would be to tax life insurance companies and their policyholders just like any other financial institutions and their customers, levelling another playing field.

The tax would consist of two parts. Part one would be the policyholders' tax and it would be paid by the company on behalf of its policyholders and treated as a tax deduction, just like an excise tax, for purposes of determining the company's taxable income. Policyholders would be taxed, collectively through the company, on their aggregate gain — all benefits paid, including dividends, plus increases in reserves (or cash values) minus premiums paid. Algebraically, this policyholders' taxable income is equal to policyholders' investment earnings minus total expenses, minus company profits; interestingly, this is precisely the basis of taxation of life insurance companies in the United Kingdom. To this taxable income should be applied a composite tax rate representing the average of all policyholders; in the case of the All-Savers' Certificates, the imputed composite tax rate was 30%. The total policyholders' taxable income would not be a large number. Gains on surrender and maturity would no longer attract tax in the policyholders' hands. Certain classes of business, such as qualified plans, health insurance and so forth would necessarily be excluded.

The company would then be taxed as if it were a casualty insurance company. All dividends would be deductible (levelling the playing field for participating and pseudo-participating products), tax-exempt investment income would be excluded in full and dividends received would be subject to the full 85% exclusion (levelling the playing field for life insurance companies and other financial institutions).

Now where is the catch? Perhaps the most important of the negative issues would be the treatment of policyholders' surplus and the 818 (c)(2) election. Since time and courage are running out at much the same pace, I shall leave these thorny matters for you to ponder.

Section 2
Unit Linked, Variable, and Adjustable Products

Unit Linked Insurance

Published as a White Paper in July 1971 and submitted to the U.K. Committee on Property Bonds and Equity Linked Life Assurance. Reprinted with permission from Abbey Life Assurance Company Limited, London, England.

Abbey Life

Abbey Life Assurance Company Limited
Head Office: Abbey Life House
1-3 St. Paul's Churchyard
London EC4M 8AR
Telephone: 01–248 9111 Telex: 886417

July, 1971

The Chairman and Members of the Committee on
Property Bonds and Equity Linked Life Assurance

Sir Hilary, Miss Roberts, Gentlemen:

We submit herewith for your consideration this Evidence, which reflects the views of Abbey Life on the subject of your enquiry. We shall be pleased to comply with your further requests for additional information or to provide such other assistance as you may require.

Respectfully submitted on behalf of
ABBEY LIFE ASSURANCE COMPANY LIMITED

James C.H. Anderson
Managing Director

TABLE OF CONTENTS

SUMMARY AND CONCLUSIONS

The terms of reference of the Committee relate specifically to unit-linked life assurance. The issues involved are, however, related to the life assurance industry generally and may relate also to the "savings" industry in a wider sense. This submission of evidence takes a wide view of the scope of the enquiry.

The importance of the life assurance industry to the United Kingdom economy is manifest. The unit-linked sector of the industry is already an important part of the whole and its growth is expected to continue to lead that of the industry. The healthy development of the industry, particularly the unit-linked sector, is not unrelated to the freedom from restrictive regulation. A close analysis of conventional and unit-linked life assurance schemes reveals that there is much in common between them.

Since 1870 there has been legislation regulating insurance companies. Contemporary legislation is embodied in the Insurance Companies Act 1958, as amended and extended by Part II of the Companies Act 1967. This legislation provided general requirements as to the control of entry into the insurance business, its subsequent general conduct, accounting requirements and solvency margins under the supervision of the Department of Trade and Industry. The Prevention of Fraud (Investments) Act of 1958 has never been applied, and was not intended to apply, to life assurance contracts of any type, although it contains ambiguities which admit the argument that the Act should so apply; this argument has equal force with respect to both unit-linked and conventional "with profits" life assurance contracts. The nature of the unit trust industry, which is regulated by the Act, differs in several fundamental respects from that of the life assurance industry and legislation applicable to one industry is not appropriate to the other. The favorable record of the life assurance industry might be attributed as much to long-standing tradition as to existing legislation, which may contain serious potential weaknesses in three areas: asset management, marketing methods and solvency requirements.

The life assurance industry in the several overseas countries discussed is much more extensively regulated than in the United Kingdom. Regulation in the areas of asset management, valuation of liabilities, solvency requirements and unauthorized reinsurance are general. Practices in the area of policy approval, marketing methods and company examination are mixed. Except in the United States, unit-linked contracts with guarantees are considered to be life assurance policies and are regulated as such. Except in The Netherlands and South Africa, there are some features of regulation applicable only to unit-linked contracts. There is no evidence to support the view that policyholders in those more extensively regulated countries have received greater protection than their counterparts in the United Kingdom. There is evidence which suggests that the cost of certain forms of assurance has been increased unnecessarily as a by-product of certain regulatory practices. There is also evidence which suggests that the healthy development of an important industry has been impeded by restrictive regulation, notably in the area of unit-linked contracts.

The absence of present regulations governing asset management is, for all practical purposes, total, and there is no distinction between assets underlying conventional life assurance and unit-linked life assurance. The extensive freedom of action permitted exposes policyholders to flagrant abuse although the industry record shows that asset management in the past has been responsible. Regulation dealing with misapplication of assets is general in other countries and similar legislation could well be introduced in the United Kingdom. Regulation designed to limit the mismanagement of assets is extremely difficult to formulate without adopting arbitrary and inhibiting standards which can lead to unexpected and unreasonable results. Publicly expressed concerns regarding the potential problems of valuing the assets underlying unit-linked funds, liquidity and asset-type seem exaggerated.

The marketing function is central to the life assurance industry and is largely responsible for its successful development. The traditional method of selling in the United Kingdom is the agency system, which has evolved in its most modern form into direct selling by full-time professional salesmen. The principal contemporary marketing methods of the industry are direct selling, broker selling, general agency selling and non-agency selling, which are used in several combinations by various companies. The prevailing levels of commission rates are fairly uniform throughout the industry, due in large measure to the commission agreement of the Life Offices Association. Existing marketing methods are subject to several criticisms, generally directed towards their susceptibility to abuse. Abbey Life, together with all companies in the industry and some companies in related industries, have a vested interest in any proposals which might lead to changes in existing marketing methods. The general criticism of direct selling seems, upon examination, to be misdirected. Likewise, criticism of the application of life assurance marketing methods to unit-linked life assurance seems, upon examination, to be unwarranted. Criticism of present commission levels seems, upon examination, to be based on inaccurate information, and proposals to regulate future commission levels are unwarranted. A licensing system for those selling life assurance may be desirable, but not all of the intended objectives of such a system seem practical. Likewise, proposals to regulate advertising copy and sales literature may have considerable merit. Criticism of agent or broker malpractice seems, upon examination in the light of the experience of Abbey Life, exaggerated.

The existing legislation appears to be inadequate insofar as it does not permit the DTI to maintain an effective watching brief upon the solvency of life assurance companies. Particular weaknesses can be found in the areas of the comprehensiveness of information disclosed, the minimum margins of solvency and capital requirements.

There is considerable scope for self-regulation by the industry or by its member companies in the areas that do not lend themselves to explicit legislation. It is common practice that unit-linked companies regularly disclose the nature and activities of their unit-funds. Codes of conduct have been devised for this purpose by groups of companies and these will be further improved and extended in the future. Abbey Life itself is considering the incorporation of a regular certificate by an independent party in its annual reports.

Accordingly, based on these considerations, Abbey Life concludes:

- that the unit-linked sector of the life assurance industry cannot be fairly examined in isolation and therefore the scope of the enquiry should include the life assurance industry generally and might also include the "savings" industry in a wider sense;
- that freedom from restrictive regulation has fostered the successful growth and development of an industry of major importance to the United Kingdom economy and a continuation of this long-standing tradition is in the public interest;
- that unit-linked life assurance differs in form rather than principle from conventional life assurance and, consequently, there should continue to be parity of regulation applicable to both sectors of the life assurance industry;

- that the Prevention of Fraud (Investments) Act 1958 is not applicable to life assurance contracts, whether unit-linked or conventional, although the Act contains ambiguities which ought to be resolved;
- that the style of regulation applicable to unit trust management companies is not appropriate to the life assurance industry, which is already as extensively if less explicitly regulated;
- that the successful record of the life assurance industry justifies a continuation of the style of existing regulation, which need not be fundamentally redrawn, although consideration should be given to strengthening existing legislation in the areas of asset management, marketing methods and solvency requirements;
- that the experience of countries with detailed and comprehensive regulation of the life assurance industry affords no conclusive argument favouring the adoption of such an approach over the approach traditional in the United Kingdom;
- that serious consideration be given to the enactment of legislation intended to prevent the flagrant misapplication, as distinct from mismanagement of assets and to require companies to fully disclose the manner in which their assets have been invested;
- that the marketing methods prevailing in the life assurance industry are effective and ethical and should not, therefore, be fundamentally altered;
- that the already high standards observed by the industry in its marketing activities might be further improved and potential for future abuse might be diminished by the introduction of a licensing system for all persons selling life assurance and by the adoption of regulations dealing with advertising and sales literature;
- that existing legislation should be strengthened by the introduction of further reporting requirements and minimum margins of solvency, and that concurrently minimum capital requirements be increased to £250,000 and the application of the 1967 Companies Act be extended to cover all life assurance companies;
- that there are important aspects of the activities of life assurance companies which do not readily lend themselves to explicit regulation and that self-regulation, either on an industry or company basis, and disclosure can be an effective substitute, and indeed the industry, particularly the unit-linked sector thereof, as evidenced by recent actions, has indicated its intention to further this process.

CHAPTER I
SCOPE OF THE ENQUIRY

This Chapter examines the terms of reference of the Committee and the scope of its enquiry and this evidence.

1. Terms of reference

In February 1971, the Secretary of State for Trade and Industry announced the formation of a Departmental Committee, under the chairmanship of Sir Hilary Scott, with the following terms of reference:

> To consider the working of the Insurance Companies Acts 1958-67, and of the Prevention of Fraud (Investments) Act 1958, insofar as the latter is relevant, in the light of life assurance schemes involving the issue of equity-linked policies, unit-linked policies, property bonds and similar schemes and to advise on the adequacy of the protection afforded by these Acts to policyholders in these schemes.

2. Scope of the enquiry

The above-mentioned legislation provides the framework within which the whole life assurance market operates. It is necessary, therefore, in considering regulations affecting life assurance schemes which are unit-linked, to consider also the application of such regulations to the life assurance industry generally. In this connection the Financial Times Survey of Unit-linked Insurance on 26th May 1971 commented upon the terms of reference as follows:

> The reasons for confining the scrutiny (of the Committee) to just this form of assurance and not, say, including conventional "with profits" contracts from the traditional life offices, have not been made clear.

The concept of the unit-linking of life assurance policies is generally styled, for reasons of convenience, upon the unit trust industry. Unit trust management companies are regulated by the Prevention of Fraud (Investments) Act 1958 and the schedules thereto, and supervised by the Department of Trade and Industry. Analogies between unit-linked life assurance and unit trusts are frequently drawn. Life assurance companies and unit trusts are, however, only two of many movements making up the "savings" industry and Abbey Life is of the opinion that it would be desirable in formulating their conclusions that the Committee consider the consequential implications flowing therefrom for the "savings" industry in a wider sense.

3. Scope of this evidence

The Secretary to the Committee has communicated the wish of the Committee to receive written evidence from Abbey Life and we have therefore given deep consideration to the issues involved and this submission of evidence, which takes a wide view of the scope of the enquiry, is the result. We welcome the formation of the Committee and we recognise that an opportunity is now presented to appraise and, if necessary, to strengthen and clarify the existing legislation.

4. Summary and conclusions

The terms of reference of the Committee relate specifically to unit-linked life assurance. The issues involved are, however, related to the life assurance industry generally and may relate also to the "savings" industry in a wider sense. This submission of evidence takes a wide view of the scope of the enquiry. Accordingly, based on these considerations, Abbey Life concludes:

- that the unit-linked sector of the life assurance industry cannot be fairly examined in isolation and therefore the scope of the enquiry should include the life assurance industry generally and might also include the "savings" industry in a wider sense.

CHAPTER II
THE LIFE ASSURANCE INDUSTRY IN THE UNITED KINGDOM

This Chapter outlines the relative importance of the life assurance industry in the wider context of the United Kingdom economy, surveys the prevailing regulatory environment, and describes conventional and unit-linked life assurance schemes.

1. The role of life assurance in the United Kingdom economy

In the introduction to its 1968 pamphlet on *The Insurance Industry in Britain* the Central Office of Information said:

> In addition to the cover afforded, one branch of insurance, namely, life assurance, is an essential element in the economic system in that

it provides a means of contractual saving for a large proportion of the population.

According to information contained in the March 1971 edition of the Bank of England Quarterly Bulletin the nominal and book value of the assets of life assurance companies at the end of 1969 amounted to £12,741 millions, having increased by some £4,470 millions during the previous six years. For comparison the total of current and deposit accounts in the banking sector at the same date was £27,493 millions of which the deposit banks accounted for some £11,789 millions. Although the bases of valuation are not consistent, the relative size of other types of financial institutions at the same date can be gathered from the following information extracted from the same source:

	Holding of assets at 31.12.69 (£m.)
General Insurance Companies	1,460
Pension Funds	7,383
Property Unit Trusts	119
Investment Trust Companies	4,902
Unit Trusts	1,344
Building Societies	9,336
Trustee Savings Banks (Investment Accounts)	1,296
National Savings Banks (Investment Accounts)	226
Finance Houses	1,141
Special Finance Agencies	358

The importance of life assurance companies as a factor in the "savings" market is thus evident. The use made of these funds is equally relevant and it is clear from the information below that the channeling of consumer savings by life assurance companies into investments, both public and private, provides a substantial element in the financing of new capital investment. The information (Bank of England Quarterly Bulletin, June 1971) includes that relating to general insurance companies but these can represent only a minor proportion of the whole.

	Holding of assets at 31.3.70 (£m.)	Net acquisition of assets 1969 (£m.)
U.K. Government	3,198	107
U.K. Local Authority	426	–20
Company Fixed Interest	1,750	118
Company Ordinary	4,600	148
Loans and Mortgages	N/A	201
Land, Property, Ground Rents	N/A	186

It is clear that the assets of life assurance companies are widely spread. The industry is one of few investing primarily on a long-term basis and this feature is also evident from the above information.

According to the same source, the gross capital issues in 1969 amounted to £1,248 millions and the net domestic capital issues in 1969 (allowing for redemptions and excluding international issues) amounted to £684 millions. The proportion of these issues taken up by life assurance companies is thus seen to be substantial.

The net acquisition of assets by insurance companies in 1969 which totalled £740 millions should be viewed in the context of the total of personal savings (defined as total disposable income less consumer expenditure) in 1969 which amounted to £2,474 millions, according to the C.S.O. Monthly Digest of Statistics.

Information on the proportion of the U.K. population who carry life assurance, and hence contribute to the flow of funds described above, is inexact. Clearly the proportion is substantial, although below that of some other countries. The Life Offices Association figures suggest that the number of life assurance policies in existence at the end of 1970 was approximately 14 millions and new business in 1970 amounted to £156 millions of annual premiums and £146 millions of single premiums (including annuity considerations). It can be estimated that assets under management at the end of 1970 were £13,500 millions.

No reliable statistics are available on the size of the unit-linked market but it is estimated that the number of policies in existence at the end of 1970 was at least 500,000 and in 1970 perhaps £25 millions of new annual premiums and perhaps £40 millions of new single premiums were linked to units in one way or another. At the end of 1970 assets under management probably approached £200 millions. Abbey Life is the dominant company in this sector of the life assurance market. The number of its unit-linked policies in existence at the end of 1970 was 150,000, new unit-linked annual premiums in 1970 were nearly £5 millions and new unit-linked single premiums in 1970 were nearly £22 millions. At the end of 1970 assets under management totalled £100 millions, of which £93 millions derived from unit-linked business.

The statistics and estimates cited demonstrate the disproportionately high growth of the unit-linked sector of the life assurance industry. This sector now represents approximately 15% of all new annual premium business and approximately 30% of new single premium business (substantially more, in both cases, if industrial branch and group business is eliminated) but only 2% of total assets accumulated, a measure of "old" business. It is the view of Abbey Life that in 1971 and later years the market share of the unit-linked sector is likely to increase, without fundamental changes in the regulatory environment.

2. The regulatory environment

The growth and development of life assurance in the United Kingdom since the late eighteenth century has been against the background of minimal legislation in contrast to the development of the same industry in North America and Continental Europe. *The Financial Times* survey referred to previously commented:

> The United Kingdom life assurance industry can justifiably claim to being the best in the world, thanks probably to the fact that it is not encumbered by superfluous rules.

Such legislation as has been introduced from time to time has been concerned with the minimum capital requirements of a company operating in this field and with the subsequent reporting requirements both to the public and to the Department of Trade and Industry (the DTI). It should be mentioned and perhaps stressed, that the important role played by the actuarial profession, which has been recognised by Governments since the earliest days of life assurance, has meant that the financial affairs of the industry have been in the hands of a responsible body of men, to whom all parties concerned could look for performance of the long-term contractual elements of the business.

There is no doubt that the absence of restrictive legislation is responsible for much of the past healthy development of an industry of major importance to the United Kingdom economy. However, we recognise that the time has now arrived for a comprehensive survey of the adequacy of existing legislation, due partially to the vigorous growth of unit-linked schemes and partially to the associated increase in the number of recently formed companies. The experience in the United Kingdom and the corresponding experience overseas (described in Chapter IV) indicates clearly the particular susceptibility of the unit-linked sector of the industry to restrictive legislation. This sector of the industry has achieved a position of importance in only three major markets — the United Kingdom, the Netherlands, and South Africa. These same countries treat conventional and unit-linked business as sectors of one industry for regulatory purposes.

3. Conventional life assurance schemes

Up until the late nineteen-fifties the principal types of endowment and whole-life assurance policies were "non-profit" or "with-profit." The distinction between these two types is well known:

1. The non-profit type is one in which the policyholder benefits are defined in sterling terms at the outset of the policy, subject only to payment of premiums as due and the information upon which the policy has been underwritten being given in good faith;
2. The with-profit type incorporates an additional regular premium, which permits the policyholder to participate in the profits of the life assurance company and hence, if experience is favourable, the additional profits paid as bonuses will exceed the additional premiums. The policyholder benefits, other than the minimum guaranteed sum assured, are not defined in sterling terms at the outset of the policy, but are assessed regularly (usually once a year) and a bonus declared (which typically attaches to and increases the minimum guaranteed sum assured). The basis of this assessment is the profitability of the company, although the mechanism is largely obscure to members of the public.

The with-profit type is more comparable to unit-linked schemes.

Traditionally the bonus declarations are kept at a reasonable level (perhaps increasing slightly) it being felt that a reduction in the level of bonuses would place a company at a competitive disadvantage. For this reason the bonuses represent what the actuary of the company feels the company can maintain *on a long-term basis* and do not accurately reflect the emerging profits of the company. In this connection it should be remembered that the largest single element of profit has arisen, and is likely to continue to arise, from the company's investment portfolio. These profits particularly are not reflected as they emerge. Hence different generations of policyholders are not necessarily treated equitably as between each other. Both types of conventional life assurance schemes provide benefits in the event of non-payment of premiums. Sometimes these benefits are expressed as a guaranteed cash or paid-up value, but often the benefits are at the discretion of the company.

4. Unit-linked life assurance schemes

In describing the evolution of the unit-linked concept we find it difficult to better the words of G. L. Melville (in a paper entitled "The Unit-Linked Approach to Life Insurance," submitted to the Institute of Actuaries in April 1970) who, after defining a conventional life assurance premium as consisting of an "insurance" element and a "savings" element and after referring to what is effectively an investment guarantee on the "savings" element represented by the guaranteed sum assured and accrued bonuses, goes on:

> In effect, intending unit-linked policyholders are saying to the life office involved: "We don't want your guarantees on investment. We don't want either you or your Actuary to have to be bothered about the future of interest rates, nor about future capital appreciation (or depreciation), nor about short-term fluctuations in the market, in making your decisions about premium rates or surplus distribution. We just want you to credit the 'savings elements' of the premiums we pay to your unit fund (or funds), invest those to the best of your ability, tell us exactly what you are doing and why, and give us exactly our share of whatever happens, good or bad, as determined in the market place. We want you to concentrate your thoughts on investment management rather than on its subsequent distribution."

The simplest unit-linked policies attempted to provide an answer to the specific request. The investment distributions were no longer at the option of the company, but were exactly defined by means of the unit-linking. The "insurance" element and the "savings" element were also defined, with typically a sterling sum assured which was not variable after the outset of the policy, other than as defined in the policy document, paid for by the "insurance" element and the "savings" element was specifically allocated to a unit-fund. After some years duration the build-up of the savings element would overtake the sterling sum assured and the excess thus achieved would replace the effect of the surplus distribution under a conventional scheme.

Unit-funds which are used for the purpose are sometimes unit trusts, sometimes general investment portfolios and sometimes particular portfolios based upon sectors of the investment market, e.g., equities, property, etc. The type of investment chosen is normally that which would typically appear in the investment portfolio of a life office writing only conventional schemes. It should be remembered that the policyholder does not acquire any better title to a share in the assets making up the unit-fund than he would have under a conventional scheme. The allocation is descriptive only and the mechanics, drawn largely from unit-trust precedent, are selected as a matter of convenience.

The fundamental concept underlying unit-linked life assurance schemes has been refined in several ways and a wide variety of schemes is now generally available in the United Kingdom. The following excerpt from the introduction to the *Equity Linked Life Assurance Tables* published (1970) by Stone & Cox (Publications) Ltd., represents a general review of this sector of the industry and the types of schemes currently available.

> An equity linked life assurance is a contract under which the benefit at the maturity date is directly related to the value at that date of equity investments, as compared with the value of the proportionate part of those same investments at the date each premium was paid. In practice, in the United Kingdom anyway, the sum assured on death will be expressed partly in money terms or will be subject to a guaranteed minimum in money terms, so every equity linked assurance policy is to a minor extent a compromise with traditional assurances expressed throughout in money terms. Some are compromises to much more than a minor extent and the line that separates the equity linked from the with-profits life policy is indistinct at times. In this manual we have included all life assurance plans where a substantial part of the benefit payable will vary directly with the results of investment in equities (i.e., ordinary shares and/or property) over the term of the policy. Our ultimate line of demarcation is that any plan entitled to be included in our Ordinary Branch Life Assurance Tables is *ipso facto* not eligible for inclusion in Equity Linked Life Assurance Tables.
>
> The first equity linked contract offered by a life office in Britain was a deferred annuity, approvable under S.22 of the Finance Act, 1956, which was introduced by the London and Manchester early in 1957. It was linked to a unit trust: Investment Trust Units. The first

equity linked life assurance contract was the "Equitas" endowment policy issued by the London and Edinburgh in the Autumn of 1957. This was also linked to a unit trust. It was some years before the idea was taken up by the general body of offices, but a number of developments in the late 'sixties were favourable: the continuance of inflation, increased competition for savings from unit trusts, and the fact that the wholesale revision of the terms for allowance of tax on life assurance premiums embodied in the Finance Act 1968 did nothing to detract from the value of unit-trust linked policies as long as they provided the minimum sum assured on death specified in that Act.

The unit trust groups were among the first to follow London and Edinburgh with a variant on that company's plan; then came the traditional life offices, first the smaller ones and then the larger, in a trickle that became a flood so that by the end of the 'sixties there were over 70 offices offering plans.

The plans are in great variety and the degree to which they are compromises with traditional life assurance contracts varies enormously. It is possible, however, to categorise them into types, although the differences tend to blur. These types are:

(1) A stated amount out of each premium is deemed to be invested in units of a unit trust or of an internal equity fund. The sum paid at maturity (by survival) is the greater of the value at the maturity date of the total number of units deemed to have been purchased over the term of the policy, and a guaranteed amount that may be the total of the premiums paid.

(2) A stated amount of each premium is deemed to be invested in units and the sum paid at maturity is the value of these units at the maturity date plus the value of additional units allocated out of the distributions on them made by the trust. There may also be a guaranteed minimum at maturity.

(3) A proportionate part of the guaranteed minimum sum assured is deemed to be invested in units as each premium is paid. The total invested may thus exceed the total premiums paid, but income distributions are retained by the company. The sum payable at maturity will be the value at maturity date of the units.

(4) A stated amount out of each premium is deemed to be invested in units; the sum paid at maturity is the value of the units at the maturity date and, in addition, a bonus is paid. This bonus may depend only on the distributions that have been made on the units by the unit trust or it may depend on the overall profitability of this class of policy.

> (5) Part of the premium is used to purchase in one contract a conventional with- or without-profit assurance and part an equity linked assurance on one of the lines described above.
>
> A further and broader sub-division is between those offices' plans which are directly linked to the value of units of a unit trust and those which are linked to units of an internal fund. For convenience, we have described above the various types of equity linked contract in their endowment assurance form, with premiums payable annually or at shorter intervals. But many plans are available in whole life form on just the same lines and there are also single premium policies or "bonds."

Cash values for unit-linked life assurance schemes are sometimes explicitly derived from the unit allocations or, as in the case of conventional life assurance schemes, are sometimes determined at the discretion of the company. In general, explicit cash value bases are more common for unit-linked schemes than for conventional schemes. Details of the range of unit-linked products offered by Abbey Life have already been made available to the Committee.

5. Summary and Conclusions

The importance of the life assurance industry to the United Kingdom economy is manifest. The unit-linked sector of the industry is already an important part of the whole and its growth is expected to continue to lead that of the industry. The healthy development of the industry, particularly the unit-linked sector, is not unrelated to the freedom from restrictive regulation. A close analysis of conventional and unit-linked life assurance schemes reveals that there is much in common between them. Accordingly, based on these considerations, Abbey Life concludes:

- that freedom from restrictive regulation has fostered the successful growth and development of an industry of major importance to the United Kingdom economy and a continuation of this long-standing tradition is in the public interest.
- that unit-linked life assurance differs in form rather than principle from conventional life assurance and, consequently, there should continue to be parity of regulation applicable to both sectors of the life assurance industry.

CHAPTER III
EXISTING LAWS AND REGULATIONS IN THE UNITED KINGDOM

This Chapter examines contemporary legislation and regulation and its historical background as related to the life assurance industry in the United Kingdom, contrasting the position with that applicable to the unit trust industry.

1. Historical background

In addition to the Companies Act 1948 which had general application to all companies, there has been since 1870 legislation regulating insurance companies and other bodies carrying on insurance business. The general object of the legislation has been the protection of the public following the increase in the number of insurance companies during the nineteenth century, particularly as the Companies legislation protected the members by limited liability. Moreover, these companies by their nature controlled large funds subscribed by the public and had to meet perhaps considerable future liabilities.

The Life Assurance Companies Act 1870 required all new life assurance companies to deposit £20,000 (of which the modern equivalent is perhaps £250,000) into court and enacted special provisions upon the amalgamation and winding up of companies. The Employers Liability Insurance Companies Act 1907 dealt with this branch of insurance in the same way.

The Assurance Companies Act 1909 replaced the 1870 and 1907 Acts and furthermore applied the principle of control begun by the 1870 Act in relation to life assurance to fire, accident insurance and bond investment business. Motor insurance business was added by S 42 (1) of the Road Traffic Act 1930, aircraft insurance business by S 20 Air Navigation Act 1936, and marine and transit insurance by the Assurance Companies Act 1948.

2. Contemporary legislation — general background

The present law is to be found in the Insurance Companies Act 1958 (the 1958 Act), as amended and extended by Part II of the Companies Act 1967 (the 1967 Act). The effect of the Acts is to apply more stringent provisions to insurance companies and to other insurers to ensure their solvency and the

DTI has been given extensive powers to prevent unauthorised insurers from carrying on business, to obtain information from insurers as to their business and to take proceedings to wind up companies who fail to meet the required solvency margins. In short, the DTI now has the powers to investigate any life assurance company and to supervise and make recommendations which, if not complied with, could lead to the winding up of the company. It is worthy of note that Part II of the 1967 Act followed the failure of several non-life assurance companies. In this century no life assurance company has failed to the detriment of its policyholders. The major question is whether the relevant Acts and the manner of their administration, taken together with civil remedies, are sufficient to protect policyholders.

3. Definition

S 59(6) of the 1967 Act applies the 1958 Act to "ordinary long-term insurance business" which is defined to include life insurance, the issue of annuities, accident insurance and endowment insurance.

4. Control of entry into insurance business and its general conduct

DTI authorization S2 1958 Act and SS60-69 1967 Act.

The general principle set out in the 1967 Act is that insurance companies who were carrying on business of a particular class immediately before 3rd November 1966 are authorised to continue to do so provided such business was not being carried on in contravention of S 2(1) of the 1958 Act which provided for a minimum paid-up share capital of £50,000. Any existing company which wishes to extend its business to include new classes and new companies must obtain authorisation from the DTI and before this authorisation can be given it must comply with certain requirements of SS62-67 of the 1967 Act:

a. *Initial/Capital & Solvency Margin (S.62 1967Act)*
   i. The paid-up share capital of the company must not be less than £100,000.
   ii. If the company is carrying on (whether within or outside Great Britain) "general business" (i.e., insurance of the types specified in S 59 of the 1967 Act, not being "long-term" business) and has completed its first

financial year, the value of its assets must exceed its liabilities by the amount set out below:

Case	Relevant Amount
Premium income in last financial year not exceeding £250,000	£50,000
Premium in that year £250,000-£2,500,000	1 /5th of the premium income that year
Premium income in that year over £2,500,000	Aggregate of £500,000 and 1/10th of the amount by which the premium income in that year exceeded £2,500,000

iii. In any other case its assets less liabilities must amount to not less than £50,000.

Moreover, S 13 of the 1958 Act and SS 79 and 80 of the 1967 Acts provide that if the above margins as to general business are not maintained, the company can be compulsorily wound up in accordance with S 222 Companies Act 1948 or if the DTI believe that there is a risk of the company becoming insolvent they may impose additional requirements on the company (see below).

b. *Securing that risks are capable of being borne (S 63 1967 Act)*

The DTI must be satisfied that as regards each class of risk against which the company insures, "adequate arrangements are in force or will be made for reinsurance" of those risks or "that it is justifiable not to make" such arrangements.

c. *Preventing unfit persons from being associated with insurance companies (S 64 1967 Act)*

The DTI cannot issue an authorisation if it appears to them than an officer of the company or of "a body corporate of which it is a subsidiary or a person in accordance with whose directions or instructions the directors of the company or of a body corporate of which it is a subsidiary are accustomed to act or a person who has one-third voting control at any general meeting of the aforesaid companies "is not a fit and proper person to be associated with the company".

In addition, S 82 obliges the company to notify the DTI of any changes in the officers or control of the company and of any body corporate of which it is a subsidiary.

d. *Additional requirements with respect to initial conduct of business (S 65 (1) 1967 Act)*
Where the DTI issue an authorisation they can as a condition precedent thereto impose any of the following additional requirements:

i. that the company shall not make investments of a specified class or that it shall realise such investments held (perhaps within a limited time).
ii. that assets of the company to an amount not less than its "domestic liabilities" be maintained in the United Kingdom. "Domestic liability" means S 65(9) liability arising under a contract made in the United Kingdom or under an insurance contract made elsewhere where the premium(s) are payable in the United Kingdom.
iii. that documents of title to assets (free of any mortgage or charge) and to a value of whichever is the greater of a specified proportion of its domestic liabilities or £50,000 be deposited with a person approved by the DTI. Notice of this deposit will be registered with the Registrar of Companies and therefore open to public inspection. By S 66, the DTI must give its written consent to the withdrawal of such documents of title and if the company creates any mortgage or charge over the assets whilst the deposit requirement is in force such mortgage or charge will be void against a liquidator or creditor of the company.
iv. that the company shall at specified times or intervals furnish such information as the DTI require about specified matters.

These requirements may continue for a maximum period of five years, although the DTI may dispense with any requirement before that time.

e. *Revocation of authorization on company's ceasing to carry on business (S 69 1967 Act)*
The DTI may revoke any authorisation given if the company ceases to carry on insurance business within Great Britain or does not commence such insurance business within one year of such authorization being granted.

5. Restriction on the conduct of business

Having obtained authorisation the DTI still holds a watching brief over the activities of insurance companies. These powers of the DTI come into operation if they are not satisfied as to the solvency of the company or with the way it is carrying on business. For example: S 68 of the 1967 Act gives the DTI power in certain circumstances to restrict the conduct of any class of insurance business, even where authorization has been given under S 61 of the 1967 Act to carry on that class of business. These restrictions are enumerated in S 68(1) of the 1967 Act and effectively prevent the Company from entering any further contracts or varying any existing contracts. The circumstances referred to are:

a. the company has failed to satisfy any obligation of the 1958 or 1967 Acts.
b. where the company is carrying on general business and the DTI is not satisfied that the company is able to pay its debts or where it is not carrying on general business the DTI is not satisfied that its assets exceed its liabilities.
c. the DTI is not satisfied that adequate arrangements have been made or that it is not justifiable not to make such arrangements.
d. if an "unfit" person becomes an officer of the company or of any body corporate of which it is a subsidiary.
e. if the company, when applying for authorisation furnishes misleading or inaccurate information.

Before exercising this power the DTI must serve written notice on the company stating that they are considering exercising this power and specifying the grounds on which they are considering exercising the power and inviting the company within one month to make representations as to why the power should not be exercised.

6. Accounting requirements

a. *Separation of funds relating to certain classes of business (S 3 1958 Act, as amended by Schedule 5 of the 1967 Act)*

   Where the company carries on together with other business either ordinary long term insurance business or industrial insurance business or carries on, with or without other business ordinary long term insurance business and industrial insurance business, the receipts from that class or each of these classes of insurance business shall be entered into a separate account and shall form a separate "insurance fund" with an appropriate name. The DTI may by order apply this to different classes of insurance business. In the event of a winding up, each separate fund is for the benefit of the policyholders of the class in question and the policyholders whose claims arise in connection with the business of that class are preferred to all other creditors.

b. *Preparation of annual accounts and balance sheets (S4 1958 Act as substituted by S71 1967 Act)*

Every insurance company must prepare each year a revenue account for the year, a balance sheet as at the end of the year and a profit and loss account for the year and the DTI are given power to issue regulations dealing with the contents of such accounts. The present regulations are contained in the Insurance Companies (Accounts and Forms) Reg. 1408 of 1968.

The DTI may modify the requirements of the regulations on the application of any company if special circumstances exist.

c. *Periodic investigation by an actuary (S5 1958 Act as amended by S78 1967 Act)*

Every insurance company which carries on "ordinary long-term insurance business" or industrial assurance business shall at least once every three years cause an investigation to be made of its financial condition, including a valuation of its liabilities, by an actuary.

Where such an investigation has been made with a view to distributing profits of the results being made public, the company must publish an abstract of the actuary's report.

d. *Statement of business by insurance companies*

The DTI may by regulation prescribe that companies carrying on certain classes of insurance business shall issue annual statements of the business of that class in the form prescribed by the regulations.

The form of such a report may be modified in relation to a particular company in special circumstances.

e. *Deposit of accounts with the DTI (S8 1958 Act as amended by S75 1967 Act)*

Within six months of the close of business to which such accounts, etc. relate, the company must deposit with the DTI four copies of the company's accounts, balance sheet and the report of the affairs of the company submitted to the shareholders. One copy of the documents must be signed by the secretary or manager if any and by at least two directors.

f. *Audit of accounts (S9 1958 Act as substituted by S72 1967 Act)*

The accounts and balance sheet of every company must be audited in the manner prescribed by regulations made by the DTI and by auditors described therein.

g. *Powers of DTI and Industrial Assurance Commissioner to alter insurance companies' financial years (S73 1967 Act)*

The DTI may extend or shorten the duration of any financial year of an insurance company.

7. Solvency and winding up

a. *Margin of solvency for general business (S13 1958 Act as amended by S79 1967 Act)*

b. *Provisions for securing that a company's solvency is maintained (S80 1967 Act)*
   If it appears to the DTI that the business of an insurance company is being so conducted that there is a risk of the company being insolvent, the DTI may impose any of the following restrictions:
   i. that the company shall not make investments of a specified class and shall realise investments of that class.
   ii. that assets of the company to an amount not less than its domestic liabilities be maintained in the United Kingdom (see S65 above).
   iii. that documents of title to assets be deposited with a person approved by the DTI (see S65 above).
   iv. that the company takes all necessary steps to secure that the premiums received by it during a specified period shall not exceed a specified amount.
   v. that the company shall at specified times or intervals furnish such information as the DTI require about specified matters. Any of the above restrictions may be rescinded by the DTI if it appears that it is no longer necessary for the restriction to continue in force.

c. *Investigation by DTI of company of doubtful solvency (S14 1958 Act)*
   The DTI may by notice in writing require the company to furnish to the DTI such explanations, information, accounts, balance sheets, etc. as they consider necessary for determining whether the company is insolvent and may further require that such explanations, etc. be signed by such directors and officers of the company as the DTI specifies and be certified as correct by an auditor or actuary approved by the DTI.

   If the company fails to comply with the requirements of the notice the DTI may by notice in writing served on the company state that they propose to appoint one or more inspectors to investigate the affairs of the company.

d. *Policyholders and DTI's power to petition for winding up of an insurance company (S15 1958 Act as amended by S81 of the 1967 Act)*

The Court may order the winding up of an insurance company in the same way as any other company under the Companies Acts 1948 to 1967. In addition, the Court may, if a prima facie case is made out and subject to security for costs being given, order the winding up of an insurance company on the petition of ten or more policyholders owning policies of an aggregate value of not less than £10,000. The leave of the Court must be obtained before the petition is presented.

The DTI may present a petition (without leave of the Court) for the winding up of an insurance company on the grounds:

i. that the company is unable to pay its debts within the meaning of SS222 and 223 of the Companies Act 1948. If the DTI shows that the company was insolvent at the end of the accounting period last before the petition was presented, there is a rebuttable presumption that the company continues to be unable to pay its debts.
ii. that the company has failed to satisfy certain obligations imposed upon it by the 1958 Act (as amended) e.g., as to its accounts, periodic investigations by an actuary, deposit of accounts with the DTI.
iii. that the company has failed to keep proper books of account in accordance with S147, Companies Act 1948.

In lieu of making a winding up order the court may order, in the case of a company which has been proved to be unable to pay its debts, that the company reduce the amount of its contracts (S.18 1958 Act).

8. Prevention of Fraud (Investments) Act 1958 — Life Assurance Companies

The Act was designed to prevent dealings in securities except by persons who are licensed under or exempted, whether specifically or generally, from its provisions. The Act, then, defines those persons who are entitled to deal in securities and also, of necessity, defines securities. As a necessary corollary to the above, the Act has a second purpose which is to prevent the fraudulent inducing of persons to invest money. In this latter context, the two areas which have most significance are advertising and direct sales. The Act has never been applied to life assurance contracts of any type.

Possible ambiguities are contained essentially in S14 and S26 of the Act, and it might be useful to recapitulate the essential content of these two sections.

S14 of the Act makes it an offense for a person to distribute or cause to be distributed or to have in his possession for the purpose of distribution, circulars inviting persons or giving information which would lead the recipients:

a. to enter into or offer to enter into:
   i. any agreement for, or with a view to, acquiring, disposing of, subscribing for or underwriting *securities;*
   ii. *any agreement*, the purpose or pretended purpose of which is *to secure a profit* to any of the parties from the yield of *securities or by reference to fluctuations in the value of securities;* or
b. to take part or offer to take part in any arrangements *with respect to property other than securities*, being arrangements the purpose or effect, or pretended purpose or effect, of which is to enable persons taking part in the arrangement (whether by becoming owners of the property or any part of the property or otherwise) *to participate in or receive profits* or income alleged to arise or to be *likely to arise from the acquisition*, holding, management or *disposal of such property*, or sums to be paid or alleged to be likely to be paid out of such profits or income; or
c. to enter into or offer to enter into an agreement, the purpose or pretended purpose of which is to secure a profit to any of the parties by reference to fluctuations in the value of any *property other than securities.*

Any person guilty of an offense under S14 is liable to imprisonment for up to two years and/or a fine of £500 if tried on indictment and six months and/or a fine of £100 if tried summarily. In addition, all offending documents may be seized.

In S26 securities are defined as follows:

i. shares or debentures, or rights or interests (described whether as units or otherwise) in any shares or debentures, or
ii. securities of the Government of the United Kingdom or of Northern Ireland or the Government of any country or territory outside the United Kingdom or
iii. rights (whether actual or contingent) in respect of money lent to, or deposited with, any industrial and provident society or building society,

> and includes rights and interests (described whether as units or otherwise) which may be acquired under any unit trust consisting of such securities as are mentioned in this definition.

In our view neither conventional nor unit-linked schemes fall within the definition of *securities*. However, Section 14 (b) and (c) refer to *property other than securities* and it is possible that assurance policies fall within this wider definition.

Hence it is important to consider further the possible construction to be placed upon "circulars" in relation to "property other than securities". In our view it is possible that publicity literature containing application forms for single life assurance policies and newspapers and other advertisements with application coupons could, in strict legal theory, be construed as circulars as defined in the Act; moreover on that construction it is arguable that all other publicity material, sales aids and advertisements which are circulated could conceivably also be so construed.

One has to look at the intention of the Prevention of Fraud (Investments) Act 1958 to establish its intended scope and to correctly interpret what might otherwise be ambiguities in the wording.

The opening sections of the Act cover "provisions for regulating the business of dealing with securities". The sections covered by this portion of the Act are nos. 1-9. These sections refer to the imposition of a licensing restriction in dealing with securities and the means and formalities relating thereto.

The second portion of the Act deals with "provisions as to industrial and provident societies, building societies and unit trusts". Section 12 (i) in fact reads inter alia as follows:

> The DTI may appoint one or more competent inspectors to investigate and report on the administration of any unit trust scheme, if it appears to the DTI:
> a. that it is in the interests of unitholders so to do, and
> b. that the matter is one of public concern.

It is significant to note that no mention is made of life assurance companies; quite correctly, as they, of course, are regulated by statutes elsewhere referred to herein.

The third portion of the Act deals with "General Provisions for the Prevention of Fraud" and these are covered by the very pertinent sections 13 and 14.

The remainder of the Act deals with exemptions (S15-17), "Supplementary provisions" (S18-25), and "Interpretation" which is essentially embodied in S26. Sections 27-29 of the Act are formal only.

Looking specifically at the opening sections of the Act, we note that S2 states that S1 shall not apply to the doing of anything by or on behalf of:

a. a member of any recognised stock exchange or recognised association of dealers in securities, or
b. the Bank of England, any statutory corporation or municipal corporation, any exempted dealer or any industrial and provident society or building society, or
c. any persons acting in the capacity of manager or trustee under an authorised unit trust scheme.

This part of the Act has been referred to as showing that a licensing system for "servants or agents" is not a new concept in the securities field. Incidentally all Abbey Life salesmen have attached to their agency contract an addendum dealing with the Act which makes it quite clear that this Company conscientiously ensures that no possibility of misunderstanding by our sales force could occur.

It is the unmistakable intention of the Act to control unauthorised dealing in securities, and to eliminate possible loopholes. To achieve this end recourse has been had to wording, extending the definitions applicable to securities. It is this extension that is most unfortunate in the context of life assurance selling and as has been previously stated herein, is not congruent with the intention of the Act, even assuming that the unit-linked assurance is more susceptible to misinterpretation because of the overt reference to unit-linking in the policies.

It should be remembered that the life assurance industry is effectively controlled by the Insurance Companies Act of 1958 and the Companies Act of 1967. We understand this view has been maintained by the Department of Trade and Industry, in applying the Act, and in correspondence with the Life Offices Association.

It is pertinent to mention that the Prevention of Fraud (Investments) Act was approved in mid-1958 which was less than a year after the first application for a unit-linked policy of assurance introduced by London & Edinburgh

Insurance Co. towards the end of 1957. There could be little doubt that the drafting of the Act took no cognisance of with-profit life assurance policies and even more clearly, no cognisance of unit-linked policies of assurance.

Our contention is that the industry should not be placed in the position of having to rely on interpretations by the DTI or to find legal argument as to the construction of terminology of the Act. It is desirable that the Act be amended specifically so as to exclude its operation from the marketing of all life assurance policies.

9. Prevention of Fraud (Investments) Acts 1958 — Unit Trust Management Companies

The prevention of Fraud (Investments) Act 1958 extensively regulates the unit trust management companies as to:

1. The establishment of an authorised unit trust operation.
2. The promotion thereof.
3. The lodging of the assets with a trust corporation and the duties thereof.
4. Regular reporting to unitholders.
5. Investment portfolio and investment dealing.
6. Management charges.
7. Calculation of unit bid and offer prices.
8. Issuance and cancellation of units.
9. Borrowings.

The Committee will no doubt be receiving evidence from officials of the DTI on the operation of the Prevention of Fraud (Investments) Act 1958 as regards unit trust operations. The extent and explicitness of the regulations are self-evident; indeed in some respects the Jenkins Committee formed the view that the regulations were unnecessarily restrictive. However, in Abbey Life's view the fundamental reasons for the requirement of explicit legislation are based upon the following factors, none of which have any relevance to the life assurance business:

1. The separation of the unit trust management company from the assets comprising the property of the unitholders.
2. The addition to the framework of a trust corporation whose purpose is to hold the assets on behalf of the body of unitholders and to generally look after their interests. The presence of this additional party requires a detailed definition of

the responsibilities of the various parties involved in an authorized unit trust operation in order to clarify what would otherwise be a confusing situation.

3. The acquisition by a unitholder of units in an authorised unit trust fund is essentially no different in purpose to the acquisition of any other quoted investment. Acquisitions of this type are notably short-term operations in the sense that there are no guarantees attached to the value at any future date of the investment thus acquired and the unitholder must therefore retain the initiative as to when the investment should be sold. In this respect, therefore, there is a clear-cut distinction between the relationship of a unit trust scheme with its unitholders and the relationship of a life assurance company with its policyholders, where the contractual characteristic is of a long-term nature.

We contend that the style of regulation applicable to unit trust management companies would not be appropriate to the life assurance industry, and our argument is based upon the different natures of the industry. Likewise, the application of regulation of life assurance companies would not be appropriate to the unit trust industry.

10. Adequacy of existing legislation

The Committee has been asked to consider the adequacy of the protection afforded by existing legislation to policyholders in unit-linked schemes. Abbey Life contends that the protection afforded by existing legislation applies equally to conventional life assurance schemes and suggests that its adequacy be considered with respect to policyholders generally.

The record of the life assurance industry both recently and over many years supports the view that it has served its policyholders well and responsibly. The absence during this century, of insolvency, the infrequency of scandal, the efficiency of operation and the effectiveness of investment policy are widely recognised and acclaimed. Judged by this evidence alone, existing legislation might be considered adequate to protect policyholders' interests. Such a conclusion overlooks, however, the influence of another force upon the industry — that of long-standing tradition. Indeed, it is arguable that the "hidden agenda" of this enquiry is to determine whether or not recently established offices, which have tended to concentrate their efforts in the unit-linked sector of the market, can be relied upon to continue this tradition of honourable behaviour.

An objective analysis of the applicable legislation itself, without reference to the record of the industry, reveals serious potential weaknesses in three areas, which deserve consideration:

1. asset management;
2. marketing methods; and
3. solvency requirements.

Succeeding chapters will deal with each of these areas.

11. Summary and conclusions

Since 1870 there has been legislation regulating insurance companies. Contemporary legislation is embodied in the Insurance Companies Act 1958, as amended and extended by Part II of the Companies Act 1967. This legislation provided general requirements as to the control of entry into the insurance business, its subsequent general conduct, accounting requirements and solvency margins under the supervision of the Department of Trade and Industry. The Prevention of Fraud (Investments) Act of 1958 has never been applied, and was not intended to apply, to life assurance contracts of any type, although it contains ambiguities which admit the argument that the Act should so apply; this argument has equal force with respect to both unit-linked and conventional "with profits" life assurance contracts. The nature of the unit trust industry, which is regulated by the 1958 Act, differs in several fundamental respects from that of the life assurance industry and legislation applicable to one industry is not appropriate to the other. The favourable record of the life assurance industry might be attributed as much to long-standing tradition as to existing legislation, which may contain serious potential weaknesses in three areas: asset management, marketing methods and solvency requirements.

Accordingly, based on these considerations, Abbey Life concludes:

- that the Prevention of Fraud (Investments) Act 1958 is not applicable to life assurance contracts, whether unit-linked or conventional, although the Act contains ambiguities which ought to be resolved;
- that the style of regulation applicable to unit trust management companies is not appropriate to the life assurance industry, which is already as extensively if less explicitly regulated;

- that the successful record of the life assurance industry justifies a continuation of the style of existing regulation, which need not be fundamentally redrawn, although consideration should be given to strengthening existing legislation in the areas of asset management, marketing methods and solvency requirements.

CHAPTER IV
OVERSEAS REGULATORY POSITION

This Chapter surveys legislation and regulation affecting the life assurance industry overseas contrasted, where appropriate, with the corresponding position of the unit trust industry.

1. General

The regulatory position of the life assurance industry in general, and the unit-linked sector of the industry in particular, varies considerably from country to country. It may be of value to review regulatory practices elsewhere and their consequences so that the Committee may formulate an informed opinion as to the advisability of proposing that similar practices be adopted in the United Kingdom. In this connection, it should be noted that Abbey Life is associated with life assurance, general assurance and unit trust companies operating in many different countries and a number of its executives have active experience in the management of several of these companies.

2. United States of America

The life and general insurance industries in the United States have been extensively regulated for many years. From the outset, regulation of insurance companies has been conducted by each of the fifty states and the District of Columbia. In a landmark decision (1944) the Supreme Court held that insurance was "interstate commerce" and as such was subject to regulation by the Federal Government. Soon thereafter the Congress of the United States passed Public Law No. 15 which consented to the continuing regulation of the industry by the individual states but held out the possibility of Federal regulation in the future. So far, this has not transpired. By contrast, the securities industry, of which the mutual fund (unit trust) industry is a part, is regulated by both the Federal Government and the governments of the several states. The principal statutes are the Securities Act of 1933, the Federal Securities Exchange Act of 1934, and the Federal Investment Company Act of 1940. State regulation is usually referred to by the all-encompassing term "blue sky laws".

Regulation of the life assurance industry is detailed and comprehensive. In practice, the results produced are not always reasonable. Applicable regulations may be considered in the following broad groups:

a. *Asset management*

Life assurance companies are restricted in their choice of investments by limitations on the types of assets which may be purchased, the total proportion which may be invested in a single holding, the total proportion which may be held in ordinary shares, preference shares and property. Certain investments, such as loans to directors or affiliates, are prohibited. Other investments, such as ownership of subsidiary companies, are prohibited in some states but may be allowed in others with the special consent of the Insurance Commissioners. For practical purposes, nearly all states follow valuation guidelines laid down by the National Association of Insurance Commissioners and each year this organization publishes authorised values for individually named securities. There are equally detailed rules governing the valuation of assets such as mortgage loans, collateral loans and property. Assets of doubtful value, or failing to meet certain criteria are considered as "non-admitted" and are carried at zero value.

Annually each life assurance company is required to include in its annual statement a complete list of its investment portfolio together with a list of all purchases and sales, including such details as price and vendor or purchaser.

b. *Valuation of liabilities*

The Standard Valuation Law, drafted originally by the Guerton Committee of the National Association of Insurance Commissioners in the early 1940s, has now been adopted, in some cases with modifications, by all states. This Law specifies the minimum standard for reserves by a detailed definition of the permitted valuation method, the applicable mortality table and the maximum permitted interest rate. The valuation standard embodied in this Law produces a statutory liability which, under today's conditions, would be judged to be unreasonably conservative by most actuaries and others; there is ample evidence to support this view — a recent example is the ongoing study of life assurance accounting practices undertaken by the American Institute of Certified Public Accountants: this study was initiated because, in the view of the accounting profession, statutory accounting practices inadequately reflected the real financial progress of companies thereby making informed judgments by shareholders difficult if not impossible.

Companies are also required to establish a Mandatory Securities Valuation Reserve. This reserve, shown as a liability in the statements, is accumulated year by year by applying a given percentage, ranging from 1/20% to 1% of assets in various categories; all capital gains are credited to the reserve and all capital losses are debited to the reserve. The intention is to provide an additional margin of safety against possible decreases in the market value of assets.

c. *Solvency requirements*

A new life assurance company, when established, is required to have a specified minimum capital together with an amount of capital surplus (share premium account). The minimum capital is generally fixed by law. The minimum surplus is also fixed by law but the Insurance Commissioner usually has the discretion to require a larger amount of surplus and may have the discretion to require a larger amount of capital. The minimum capital and surplus vary significantly from state to state. In certain states, either by law or regulation, the minimum capital is often as high as $1 million and the minimum initial surplus as high as $2 millions; a more typical requirement might be $500,000 capital and $500,000 surplus. A notable exception is Arizona, where life assurance companies with limited authority may be established with as little as $25,000 capital and $12,500 surplus (in fact there are several hundred such companies but none operates in the public domain). A life assurance company is required to maintain its capital unimpaired — that is, once the surplus of the company is exhausted and while the capital account remains substantially intact the company is subject to being placed in receivership.

d. *Approval of policies*

In practically all states (a notable exception is California) policy forms must be submitted to the insurance departments for prior approval. In general, there are statutory provisions governing the content of policy contracts which take the form of specification of required clauses and prohibited clauses. For example, it is required that policy contracts include a provision of thirty days' grace for the payment, without penalty, of an overdue premium. It is prohibited to include any provision which would negate the payment of the death benefit for any cause whatsoever, except that statutes generally allow the exclusion of suicide for a limited period. Among the required provisions are: an incontestability clause, a non-forfeiture benefit in the event of lapse which must meet minimum cash value requirements as specified in the Standard Nonforfeiture Act.

e. *Marketing methods*

It is generally required that anyone soliciting life assurance hold a license granted by the Insurance Department of the state in which such business activity is conducted. All states have such licensing requirements which vary in detail from state to state. A license may be granted with respect to only one line of business (e.g., life assurance) or may apply to all classes of insurance; certain states have limited licenses which permit the holder to solicit only a certain class of business (for example, employees of banks and hire purchase companies are frequently licensed to solicit credit life and accident and health insurance from customers). Most states have provision for non-resident licenses, which permit a resident of one state to conduct an insurance business in another. It is not generally required that an individual holding a license be engaged full time in the insurance business. To obtain a license an agent or broker is required to submit personal information and to take a test designed to demonstrate his knowledge of the business. In most states certain individuals, such as convicted felons, are prohibited from holding a license and in a few states the regulation takes a more parochial form, sometimes requiring that only United States citizens may hold a license. Licensing does have the advantage of excluding individuals with a poor record from engaging in the business and the threat of withdrawing a license, which is fairly frequently exercised, does tend to maintain higher standards of ethics than might otherwise obtain. One feature of the licensing system, the knowledge test, is so superficial that it ought not to be regarded as contributing significantly to improved standards.

There are also requirements dealing with the form and content of sales literature and advertising but these are almost always applicable to the accident and sickness business rather than to the field of life assurance. Along with the licensing requirements, there are two notable prohibited practices, "twisting" and "rebating". Twisting refers to switching a policyholder from one policy to another. Where this happens it is incumbent upon the agent to demonstrate that the switch was in the policyholder's interests and his is the burden of proof. The penalty for violation is almost invariable loss of license and often the company which is party to the switch is required to make restitution. Rebating, meaning the sharing of commissions with an unlicensed person, is strictly prohibited and punishable by loss of license.

f. *Expense limitations*

The State of New York is unique in imposing limitations on the expenses of life assurance companies. The detailed provisions of the New York expense limitations are included in Section 213 of the New York Insurance Code. Limitations are imposed on each of the following aspects of the company's operations:

i. a direct limit on first year commissions;
ii. a direct limit on the commuted value of first year and renewal commissions;
iii. an aggregate limitation on total field expenses, and
iv. for mutual companies only, a limitation on total expenses. Although the expense limitation statute has been enacted only by the State of New York it is extraterritorial in effect and operative upon all companies licensed to transact business in the State of New York with respect to their operations throughout the United States of America. The effect of this statute has been to produce a division within the industry between New York operating and non-New York operating companies with a differential in commission rates — the former companies are limited to a first year commission of 55% of the first year's premium and the latter companies might offer an average first year commission of 65%. There are no demonstrable differences in overall premium levels as between New York operating companies and non-New York operating companies.

g. *Unauthorised reinsurance*

Amounts due from unauthorised reinsurance are non-admitted assets, and no credit is allowed for reserves held by unauthorised reinsurers unless such reserves are deposited with the ceding company or a trustee.

The effects of these regulations upon the life assurance industry in the United States have been mixed. The limitations on asset management generally present no difficulties except to those companies which aspire to diversify into other lines of business: for example, a life assurance company wishing to establish a companion company to operate in the general insurance field. Since ownership of a subsidiary continues to be somewhat restricted (and also because there are tax disadvantages) more and more insurance companies of both types are reorganising their corporate structure so that they themselves become subsidiaries of holding companies established for the purpose.

It is interesting to note that in certain states, notably New York, there are strenuous attempts under way to extend the authority of the Insurance Department to such an extent as to permit the regulation of these holding companies. The detailed manner in which liabilities must be calculated undoubtedly provides a comfortable margin of solvency for most companies but an undesirable by-product has been that certain forms of life assurance and annuities are excessively costly; companies would be willing to sell many contracts at lower prices if they were not obliged to establish unreasonably high reserves. Perhaps the best example of this is the single premium annuity business which, as a result of the unattractive yields offered by assurance companies, has become of diminishing importance.

Because of the legislation dealing with the valuation of assets and liabilities life assurance companies generally incur significant losses for perhaps ten years after formation. Therefore, the required initial capital and surplus levels of even those states with the highest requirements seem reasonable; experience suggests that even these figures may be inadequate. The requirement to maintain the capital account unimpaired also provides some measure of protection because, where the system operates well, a receiver can be appointed before the situation becomes desperate. In practice, few companies in the United States have been placed in receivership due to a gradual erosion of their net worth. More often, the outcome has been a last-minute amalgamation with another company, or the assumption of all outstanding business by another company, or receivership has happened suddenly due to a flagrant mismanagement of assets. Only in the latter cases have policyholders suffered.

The requirement of prior approval of policy contracts is administratively burdensome and because there is no universal set of standards applicable in all states it is sometimes necessary to offer different policy forms in different states. If all of the relevant statutes were repealed, it seems unlikely that there would be much change in the form or content of life assurance contracts. The minimum non-forfeiture value requirements, specifically the minimum cash value requirement, tend to drive up the price of certain products in much the same way as the minimum reserve requirement; a specific example would be single premium life assurance, which is practically unknown in the United States.

Agent licensing requirements have probably had a beneficial effect mainly because of the possibility of sanction by withdrawal of license.

Expense limitation statutes represent an extensive incursion into the affairs of the life assurance industry which is distinctly contrary to the traditions prevailing in the industry in the United Kingdom. In the United States, the expense limitations of the State of New York are a subject of much controversy within the industry. There is little doubt that these statutes favour the competitive position of non-New York operating companies. Many companies operate through subsidiary companies in the State of New York and thereby escape the provisions of the New York code with respect to their operations elsewhere. The expense limitation laws, particularly as related to commissions, have also provoked in some instances illegal practices such as under-the-table payment of commissions.

Regulation of the life assurance industry in the United States also requires periodic examination of each life office by representatives of the state insurance departments. Companies are examined every three years and the examination procedure is similar to that of a company audit, but also examiners will review policyholder files to determine whether or not company practices towards policyholders have been fair and reasonable. These examinations are met at the expense of the company and the examiners' reports are matters of public information. Consider next the counterpart of unit-linked life assurance in the United States. The earliest form of such contract was introduced approximately fifteen years ago and is called the variable annuity. The concept involved the payment of premiums by the policyholder into a unitised account, invested in ordinary shares, until the retirement date and thereafter a variable pension would be paid with the amount of each payment being adjusted as dictated by total investment performance. Such a contract could only be offered at that time in a limited number of jurisdictions, two of which were the District of Columbia and Arkansas. One of the earliest companies in this field was the Variable Annuity Life Insurance Company organized in Washington, D.C. in 1955. Soon after the introduction of the variable annuity contract a legal dispute ensued between the Securities and Exchange Commission and the Variable Annuity Life Insurance Company. The point at issue was whether a variable annuity contract was a contract of life assurance (such term to include annuities) or, alternatively, a security. The case was heard in the District Court, appealed to the U.S. Court of Appeals and appealed again to the Supreme Court of the United States. The final verdict (5 assenting and 4 dissenting), held that the variable annuity was a security and as such was subject to all of the relevant statutes dealing with securities. The several insurance departments involved insisted that they also maintained jurisdiction and consequently the variable annuity business has since been subject to dual regulation.

The consequences of this decision were that companies selling variable annuities were subject to the following additional requirements:

(i) A limitation on charges identical to that governing mutual funds (companies have partially circumvented this feature of the regulation by including a "risk charge" in addition to the expense charges permitted to mutual funds);

(ii) The requirement that an agent or broker be licensed as a securities salesman, a process requiring a considerable degree of education and training;

(iii) Strict limitation on advertising and sales materials, including prior approval;

(iv) The preparation and distribution of a prospectus analogous to that which would apply in the case of a public offering of securities;

(v) Further restrictions on asset management which, while not a substantive addition to the existing life assurance regulation on the subject, constitutes a further administrative burden; and

(vi) Further requirements as to reporting to the Securities and Exchange Commission.

Enabling legislation to permit the sale of variable annuities and other unit-linked contracts has now been passed in most if not all jurisdictions. The key feature of the legislation was the legal separation of the assets of the life assurance company into what are called "separate accounts". The assets of each separate account are held only for the benefit of the policyholders with contracts linked to that account and cannot, for example, be applied to pay claims arising from other classes of business. Although variable annuities are now available throughout the country, experience has shown that the sale of these contracts is quite limited and confined, usually, to special groups — a notable example is that the majority of the variable annuities have been sold to teachers under the special tax benefits of the Teachers Retirement Act. The reason for this is quite plain — because of the limitations on charges it is not possible to offer commission rates high enough to permit an effective salesman offering variable annuities on an individual basis to earn a reasonable living from his efforts. The limitations on charges, meaning a limitation on commissions, have been derived essentially from the securities industry and are appropriate only where sales are made in very large denominations. Where, on the other hand, sales are made in amounts such as $25 (£10) per month, a much higher level of commission would be necessary to adequately compensate for the sales effort involved. Efforts are now under way to persuade Congress to enact legislation exempting unit-linked assurance and annuities from most of the securities regulations. Recent editions of the *Transactions of the Society of Actuaries* have included papers prepared by members reflecting their views and those of their respective companies, including some of the most important, on the subject and describing the proposals being advanced by them. It is widely expected that regulation will be relaxed to a significant extent in the not too distant future.

One feature of the life assurance industry in the United States has troubled informed observers for many years. While the face amount of life assurance in force continues to grow, though the recent rate is rather lower than 10% per annum, whereas earlier rates were higher than 10% per annum, the growth of assets of the life assurance industry, which measures its importance in the savings field, has slowed dramatically. In 1970 the assets of the life assurance industry, as reported in the *Life Insurance Fact Book*, increased by 5.1%. If allowance is made for the increase in policy loans which took place during the year the net increase in assets was 4.3%. The latter comparison seems more reasonable since a policy loan is analogous to a withdrawal of savings. It is the view of many people that life assurance can compete in the savings market in an inflationary climate only if it is able to bring to that market a form of savings which affords protection against the results of inflation. Moreover, the distribution methods of the life assurance industry are designed to tap the vast bulk of the population for whom a periodic savings plan of modest size is best suited, and the distribution force of the industry can only be brought to bear on this market if commissions can be maintained at levels necessary to adequately compensate salesmen. Thus, it can be argued that the application of extensive regulation has inhibited the healthy growth of the industry.

3. Canada

The regulation of the life assurance industry in Canada is generally similar to that which prevails in the United States and this section will deal only with the significant differences.

Most life assurance companies in Canada are licensed by the Superintendent of Insurance appointed by the Federal Government under the provisions of the Canadian and British Insurance Companies Act. A few companies (Abbey Life Insurance Company of Canada is one) have been established under the laws of one of the several provinces. In general, a company holding a Federal license can usually obtain without difficulty a license to transact business in each of the ten provinces. A provincially incorporated company may or may not be able to obtain a license to operate in provinces other than that of incorporation and, in practice, the provinces of Manitoba, Nova Scotia, Prince Edward Island and Newfoundland will only license federally registered companies.

Except for those few companies not registered federally, the industry is subject to dual regulation by Federal and provincial departments of insurance. The Federal Department concentrates on the supervision of the financial affairs of the company; the several provincial departments concentrate on items such as agent licensing, policyholder complaints and matters of a purely local nature. The Uniform Life Insurance Act applies in all provinces except Quebec, where applicable legislation is much more in harmony with French legal traditions.

Accordingly, in Canada there is much less difficulty in conforming to varying regulations from jurisdiction to jurisdiction than is the case in the United States.

The securities industry in Canada is regulated at the provincial level and the Ontario Securities Commission is the most important of the several regulatory bodies active in this field.

Regulation of the life assurance industry in Canada is less detailed but as comprehensive as in the United States. Supervisory officials are generally allowed wider discretion and fewer matters are the subject of legislation. Regulation has generally been enlightened and consequently the results produced have been more reasonable than in the United States. Applicable regulation may be contrasted with that of the United States as follows:

a. *Asset management*

Regulation in this area is quite comparable to that applicable in the United States although there are differences in detail. Reporting practices are practically identical.

b. *Valuation of liabilities*

The method of determining actuarial liabilities for life assurance contracts is specified by law and is similar to that in use in the United States although the standard is slightly more stringent. The choice of mortality tables and interest rates is a matter of discretion on the part of the Superintendent of Insurance. At the present time the same mortality table and interest rate in use in the United States is also used by most Canadian companies although a more liberal basis is allowed for single premium annuities. This has made the annuity business in Canada much more popular and annuity rates available in Canada are more favourable than those available in the United States.

c. *Solvency requirements*

A federally registered company is required to have and maintain a minimum capital of $500,000 and, at the date of licensing, the Superintendent of Insurance has the discretion to require surplus funds of such amount as he deems necessary. In practice, it is doubtful that a new company would be registered unless its total capital and surplus funds were $1 million and it is likely that larger capital funds would be required. It is possible to organise provincial companies with smaller amounts of capital, but such companies form a relatively minor segment of the market.

d. *Approval of policies*

Prior approval of policy forms is not required but the Uniform Life Insurance Act and its counterpart in Quebec contain provisions governing the content of policy contracts. Contracts not conforming to the requirements are interpreted by the courts as conforming nonetheless. A noticeable difference between Canada and the United States is the absence in Canada of any requirement for minimum non-forfeiture benefits in the event of lapse. The result is that Canadian companies have more latitude in selecting cash value bases. This has resulted in lower premium rates in Canada on certain forms of life assurance, notably non-profit whole life.

e. *Marketing methods*

There is practically no difference between Canadian and United States practice. An important distinction between Canada and the United States is the requirement that a license to solicit life assurance may only be held by a person who is engaged full time in the insurance business. Moreover, agents are generally licensed to solicit business for only one company and an exemption is required to sell a policy issued by another company.

f. *Expense limits*

These are not applicable in Canada.

g. *Unauthorised Reinsurance*

The practice is the same as in the United States.

The practice of examination of life offices by representatives of the Department of Insurance is practically the same in Canada as in the United States. The unit-linked sector of the life assurance industry in Canada has developed more than in the United States. The first unit-linked contracts to be offered in Canada were introduced by companies, both Canadian and British, also operating in the United Kingdom. Two of the early companies in this field were the Norwich Union and the Confederation Life. Canadian law had already provided for the establishment of "separate accounts", very similar to the corresponding legislation in the United States, including the important element of legal separation of assets. At the outset, equity linked contracts received scant attention from regulatory officials. In 1968, at a conference of Federal and provincial insurance superintendents, this subject received considerable attention and the outcome was the promulgation of common guidelines governing unit-linked contracts. The guidelines included the following main features:

i. Requirements as to disclosure of charges and mechanics, taking the form of the requirement of prior approval of sales material and policy forms.

ii. Limitations applicable to contracts including minimum guarantees. Companies were required either to establish double reserves on such contracts (that is, one reserve in the separate account of the unit-linked part of the contract, and a separate reserve allowing no off-set for the whole of the benefits guaranteed in the general fund of the company) or to subject their separate account in combination with the general funds of the company to the limitations imposed on total investments in ordinary shares. The effect of this upon established companies with substantial total assets was negligible but the effect upon companies seeking to specialise in unit-linked business was to make it impossible for them to offer competitive guarantees.

iii. The manner in which reserves for various benefits, including maturity value guarantees, were to be determined.

Initially, the securities departments of the various provinces were content to regard unit-linked contracts as life assurance policies or annuity contracts not subject to their jurisdiction. Later, there has been litigation on the subject (in Manitoba) and the position now is that contracts including substantial guarantees are regarded as life assurance contracts, while those that do not contain substantial guarantees are regarded as securities. The former category of contracts is exempt from security regulations. The latter category is subject to regulations by both the Department of Insurance and the Securities Department.

Abbey Life Insurance Company of Canada is one of a few companies offering a contract which is subject to dual regulation. A prospectus concerning this contract has been filed with and approved by the Ontario Securities Department and copies have been provided to the Committee.

Regulations governing unit-linked contracts in Canada are again under review and significant modifications are expected. It seems reasonable to predict that the attitudes of the various departments of insurance are likely to lean towards more liberal regulations which will permit the general inclusion of guarantees with the probable outcome being the exemption of these contracts from existing securities legislation. This trend corresponds closely to that discussed in connection with the position in the United States. For many years, Canadians have owned more life assurance, as a proportion of their national income, than the residents of any other country. The ratio to national income most recently reported for the year 1970 was 200% which may be contrasted with a ratio of 100% applicable in the United Kingdom. The growth of assets of life assurance companies in Canada has slowed in recent years though the tendency has been much less marked than in the United States. It is too early to assess whether or not the introduction of unit-linked life assurance contracts will significantly affect this trend.

4. The Netherlands

The regulation of the life assurance industry in The Netherlands is more comparable to that prevailing in the United Kingdom than to that prevailing in North America or in Europe. Since unit-linked life assurance contracts have never been considered as securities in The Netherlands no comments are included regarding regulations applicable in the securities industry in that country.

Life assurance companies are subject to regulation by the Verzekeringskamer (Insurance Chamber). In theory the Verzekeringskamer has little real authority over the industry but in practice its right to publish "advices" gives it very considerable influence. The specific areas of regulation are as follows:

a. *Asset management*

There is practically no legislation operative in this area. However, the Verzekeringskamer reviews in detail the investments of each company and would be likely to publicly express its disapproval of or lack of confidence in a company mismanaging its investment portfolio. The practice of valuation of assets is fairly flexible: generally, fixed interest securities are valued at cost; other investments are valued at market, although sometimes a lower figure is used.

b. *Valuation of liabilities*

There are no statutory regulations governing valuation of liabilities. Nevertheless, the right of the Verzekeringskamer to publish contrary views tends to produce a standardised method of valuation. In general, the minimum standard for reserves is the Zillmer method of modified preliminary term valuation with an initial allowance of not more than 2% of the sum assured, a population mortality table and an interest rate not in excess of 4%. Considering the conditions now prevailing in The Netherlands, this valuation method is highly conservative.

c. *Solvency requirements*

The statutory requirements for minimum capital in The Netherlands are absurdly low at fl.100,000 (£11,667). As a practical matter, a license would not be granted by the Verzekeringskamer to a company which did not have a substantially larger initial capital. Abbey Leven Nederland, N. V. was organized in 1966 with an initial capital of fl.2 million (£233,333) and the capital of this company has since been increased to fl.4 million (£466,667). It is not customary for a company to have contributed surplus at the outset.

d. *Approval of policies*

Policy forms must be submitted to the Verzekeringskamer within fourteen days after their introduction to the market. Policy provisions are dictated more by practice than by statute. Once again, the authority of the Verzekeringskamer to dictate terms to the companies is limited, but the right of publication is an important deterrent to practices not in the public interest.

e. *Marketing methods*

It is required that anyone soliciting life or general insurance either holds a license granted by the Sociaal Economische Raad (Council for Social and Economic Affairs) or is an employee of an individual or a firm which is licensed. The licensing requirement is all-inclusive and, by contrast to the situation in North America, the knowledge test which must be passed is quite comprehensive. There are four registers of licensed agents, denominated A, B, C and D. A new applicant is given a D license, for which requirements are very minimal. This license is valid for not more than one year, at the end of which the agent must successfully complete the requirements for a C license, which is permanent. The A and B licenses represent more advanced status. Licenses are valid for the solicitation of all forms of insurance. The alternative to licensing is salaried employment by a licensed individual or firm. It is now required that unlicensed salesmen be paid a salary of not less than fl.750 (£87·50) per month. Such salesmen may either be employed directly by the life office or may be employed by a broker, bank or other organization having a licensed agent as a principal employee.

f. *Expense limitations*

As in Canada, this is not applicable in The Netherlands.

g. *Unauthorised reinsurance*

This is not specifically regulated, but discretionary powers apply.

h. *Other regulations*

The basis of premium rates charged by a company is also subject to review by the Verzekeringskamer and the same position regarding publication of "advises" prevails. In general, the thrust of the interest of the Verzekeringskamer is to ensure that premium rates are not too low and there is no known case of objection to premium rates which were held to be too high. This philosophy towards premium rates is visible elsewhere in the industry. The Nederlandse Vereniging ter Bevodering van Levensverzekeringen (Netherlands Union of Life Assurance Companies), an organisation similar to the LOA in the United Kingdom, requires that its members observe a uniform set of minimum premium rates and in practice all member companies charge practically the same rates.

The unit-linked life assurance contract was in fact invented in The Netherlands some seventeen years ago and was first brought into the market by the N.V. Levensverzekering Maatschappij de Waerdije. The early equity linked contracts were tied in most cases to internal funds maintained by the companies and units in these funds are generally referred to as "fractions". Partly because these contracts were introduced on the basis of level commissions, whereas traditional forms of life assurance sold in The Netherlands provide substantial initial commissions (higher than those prevailing in the United Kingdom) and partly because of the unfortunate experience of the stock market in The Netherlands during the early 'sixties, these contracts did not at the outset capture a large share of the market. In 1967 Abbey Leven Nederland, N.V. introduced to the Netherlands market an equity linked contract of similar form to that sold by Abbey Life in the United Kingdom. This contract provided commission rates comparable to traditional forms of life assurance. Many companies operating in The Netherlands have now introduced similar contracts and the unit-linked business now accounts for perhaps 15% of the ordinary life business in that country.

Life assurance companies are examined not less frequently than every tenth year by the Verzekeringskamer.

5. South Africa

Legislation regulating insurance business has been in force since pre-Union days but most of the present regulations stem from the Insurance Act 1943. This Act created machinery to regulate the arrangement and functions of insurers mainly for the protection of the public. It provides that insurers have to be registered and imposes various conditions on registration. The regulations are largely administered by the Registrar of Insurance who performs a function similar to the DTI in the United Kingdom. An annual report on his activities under the Act is issued by the Registrar. There is no legislation relating specifically to unit-linked life assurance although unit-linked policies are widespread. The legislation regulating unit trusts (which includes a provision similar to S.14 of the United Kingdoms Prevention of Fraud (Investments) Act 1958) is not thought to apply to unit-linked life assurance business although the Registrar and the Life Offices Association are at present having informal discussions on the point.

a. *Asset management*

When an insurer wishes to commence any class of insurance business he must furnish the Registrar with a statement of how the business will be carried on and this must give details of the principles which will be applied in investing the funds. The Registrar may refuse registration if he is not satisfied that it will be in the public interest. The auditors and valuers appointed by the insurer are subject to approval by the Registrar. The auditors are obliged to report to the Registrar if nothing is done by the insurer about their recommendations. Insurers may not borrow money or give guarantees without the Registrar's consent. Detailed annual reports relating to the assets have to be submitted to the Registrar. In relation to South African business, assets held must be of the type listed in the third schedule to the 1943 Act (which includes any stocks and shares of any South African company). Assets must be valued in accordance with the detailed provisions of Section 15 of the Act.

b. *Valuation of liabilities*

Schedule II of the 1943 Act provides the minimum basis for calculating liabilities in respect of life policies and specifies the applicable mortality tables. Interest rates are limited to between 4% and 5% depending on the type of policy. A detailed statement of liabilities must be furnished to the Registrar every three years.

c. *Solvency requirements*

There is no minimum capital requirement for life assurance companies but there are provisions requiring deposit of R 100,000 (£58,125) with the Treasury in cash or authorised securities. The level of these deposits must usually be maintained but they may be returned in certain circumstances, e.g., to insurers of long standing. There are also provisions requiring the insurer to hold adequate assets. The rules differ slightly between domestic and foreign insurers. A domestic insurer must hold assets (in addition to his deposits) having an aggregate value of not less than the amount of his net liabilities in respect of each class of business and such assets as are held in respect of South African business must be of specified (South African) types.

d. *Approval of policies*

There is no specific regulation relating to any provisions which must be included in the policies.

e. *Marketing Methods*

There are no provisions requiring licensing of agents or representatives of insurance companies. The only relevant provisions are that no inducements may be offered to persuade persons to enter life assurance contracts and that only cash or cheques payable on the date of issue may be accepted in payment of premiums (this is intended to prevent persons effecting assurance beyond their ability to pay).

f. *Expense limitations*

This is not applicable in South Africa.

g. *Unauthorized reinsurance*

No information is available on this subject.

h. *Other regulations*

The Registrar may refuse registration if the direct or indirect control of the insurer's affairs may, in the opinion of the Registrar, react to the detriment of the policyholder. There are also related provisions concerning amalgamations, takeovers and acquisition of business. Breach of the insurer's obligations relating to deposits, accounts and statements of liabilities or assets may result in the Registrar prohibiting the insurer from issuing any further policies. Other breaches may result in criminal prosecution.

We have been advised by the Office of the Registrar of Insurance in Pretoria, South Africa, that it is the generally held view that the legislation affecting life assurance companies and that affecting unit trusts do not encroach upon one another. Furthermore, the percentage of annual premium life assurance business which now comprises unit-linked life assurance is of "significant proportions" although this has not been quantified. It was added that because of the tax advantages of life assurance over conventional forms of investment, the assumption is that there have been substantial increases in savings type policies of assurance.

6. Other countries

In Australia the regulatory position might reasonably be compared in extent to that prevailing in Canada. One aspect of the industry in Australia is, however, worthy of note. The Insurance Commissioner in that country published in 1969 a set of regulations dealing with unit-linked business. One feature of the legislation is the requirement that contracts be linked only to internal funds. Another feature is the imposition of a limitation on charges, and consequently commissions. The result has been that unit-linked life assurance contracts are not yet generally available in the Australian market.

Elsewhere in Europe, there are other variations in approach to regulation. The long-term aim of the EEC to harmonise insurance regulation has, thus far, made little progress. In Germany, the life assurance industry is regulated to an extent which practically compels companies to operate on terms appropriate to mutual companies. The introduction of a new form of contract, such as the unit-linked contract, would require extensive and detailed prior review by regulatory officials. Thus far no such contracts have been introduced. In France and Belgium, premium rates are uniform throughout the industry and are established by regulatory authorities; also in these countries policy forms and sales literature are subject to prior approval. In France, only 20% of the business of a life office can be unit linked; in practice, few companies offer such contracts. In Belgium, unit-linked policies are not available. Generally, throughout the European Economic Community (excepting the Netherlands) valuation methods and bases are prescribed.

7. Summary and conclusions

The life assurance industry in the several overseas countries discussed is much more extensively regulated than in the United Kingdom. Regulation in the areas of asset management, valuation of liabilities, solvency requirements and unauthorised reinsurance are general. Practices in the area of policy approval, marketing methods and company examination are mixed. Except in the United States, unit-linked contracts with guarantees are considered to be life assurance policies and are regulated as such. Except in The Netherlands and South Africa, there are some features of regulation applicable only to unit-linked contracts. There is no evidence to support the view that policyholders in those more extensively regulated countries have received greater protection than their counterparts in the United Kingdom. There is evidence which suggests that the cost of certain forms of assurance has been increased unnecessarily as a by-product of certain regulatory practices. There is also evidence which suggests that the healthy development of an important industry has been impeded by restrictive regulation, notably in the area of unit-linked contracts.

Accordingly, based on these considerations, Abbey Life concludes:

> That the experience of countries with detailed and comprehensive regulation of the life assurance industry affords no conclusive argument favouring the adoption of such an approach over the approach traditional in the United Kingdom.

CHAPTER V
THE REGULATION OF ASSET MANAGEMENT

This Chapter examines the various dangers inherent in the absence of present regulation dealing with asset management and evaluates the merits of explicit regulation.

1. Absence of present regulation

Except for the required Certificates to the Annual Accounts, expressing opinions as to the value of the assets shown on the Balance Sheet, the assets of a life assurance company may be dealt with by its management in precisely the same manner as those of any company. Moreover, it is not generally required that the company disclose how its assets have been dealt with.

This extensive freedom is unique among countries with an advanced life assurance industry. It should be noted that similar freedom is enjoyed by other United Kingdom financial institutions. It should also be noted that this freedom has not often been flagrantly abused; the absence of disclosure makes it impossible to be more positive than this.

Although the terms of reference of the Committee are confined to the protection of policyholders under unit-linked life assurance schemes, the absence of present regulation raises major issues of industry-wide concern. To illustrate, should a life office be allowed to invest policyholders' funds, whether arising from conventional or unit-linked schemes in any of the following ways:

(i) In a loan (conceivably of its entire assets) to an associated company?
(ii) To mount a takeover bid?
(iii) To manipulate markets (whether or not for the advantage of policyholders)?

Not only is it legal at the moment to do each of these things but moreover the manner in which these can be done would not necessarily lead to their disclosure.

In most other countries which have advanced life assurance markets most of these actions by life assurance companies are prohibited. It is therefore not without precedent elsewhere that consideration be given to the introduction of appropriate legislation to control such of these practices as seem undesirable.

If asset management by life assurance companies is to be explicitly regulated in the United Kingdom, first priority must be given to the prohibition of flagrant *misapplication* of assets. By comparison, the protection to be gained by regulation aimed at limiting the permitted extent of *mismanagement* of assets appears less urgent. As stated earlier, Abbey Life is of the view that parity of regulation should continue to prevail between the conventional and unit-linked sectors, of the industry, a conclusion which has particular application to the subject of asset management.

2. Misapplication of assets

a. *Dealings with associates*

It is difficult to distinguish between transactions involving associates which represent orthodox investments and those where the investment judgment has been influenced by the identity of the other party involved. For this reason both types of transaction are open to criticism on the grounds that an "arms-length" transaction has not taken place.

There are undoubtedly occasions when the range of contact of the associate is so extensive that he is in a position to bring forward possible investment acquisitions of a high quality which would not otherwise be available. On the other hand the situation could be abused and prohibitions, controls or the requirement of disclosure may be desirable.

On balance, therefore, we feel that it is in the best long term interests of policyholders if transactions involving an associate as a principal are avoided except in the case of internal transfers between parts of a company's life fund. In the latter case we should prefer the acquisition price to be certified by an independent party.

The definition of what is an "associate" must be fairly wide, but would exclude minority and non-controlling interests. It would certainly include associates both of the company and its directors and its principal officers. Instances can arise where the associate is in a position to benefit indirectly (by way of commission or otherwise) from a transaction which would otherwise be perfectly acceptable. We would regard this type of involvement by an associate as unobjectionable, but we feel that it is an item of relevance to policyholders, and therefore the basis and amounts of any financial advantage thus gained should be regularly disclosed to them.

b. *Concentration of economic control*

Is it in the public interest to allow a life assurance company or any other financial institution to use the accumulated savings of its policyholders or customers to acquire control of an industrial company, such as a brewery or shipping line or even a property company? In most countries this practice is controlled by placing strict limitations upon the ownership of subsidiary companies and the acquisition of controlling interests.

c. *Market manipulations*

There is also a danger that the accumulated savings (referred to above) could be used as part of an associated operation to profit other parties. A practical example might be the purchase of shares by an associate followed by a major purchase of the same shares by the institution thus raising the price. This obviously undesirable practice is regulated in certain other countries though the regulations have proved difficult to police.

d. *Reassurance*

There is a general principle that companies should carry adequate reassurance compatible with their ability to underwrite the prime risks that they accept and that they should use reassurers of adequate standing and reputation. This principle is not an issue relevant to asset management except insofar as the potential exists for an unscrupulous operator to remove the assets of his company into an associated, and perhaps foreign based, reassurance company where the investment traditions and principles may not be of the same high standard as currently obtain in the United Kingdom. This removal of assets can be effected by the stratagem of reassurance. If there is to be regulation to prevent the misapplication of assets, controls on unauthorised reassurance would be required. In this connection we would consider that adequate trusteeship of the assets by the reassurer for the account of the company would be a sufficient safeguard against abuse.

3. Mismanagement of assets

a. *Mismatching leading to possible insolvency*

Life assurance companies invest their reserves in assets which, together with future premium income, must produce sufficient revenue to provide for future expenses and policy benefits.

In general it is impossible to achieve a perfect match between assets and liabilities with respect to the incidence of future income and outgo since it is impossible to predict accurately the amount and type of new business, the behaviour of investment markets and the rate at which policyholders will withdraw or die. Like other financial institutions, life assurance companies provide for the guarantees they make to individuals partly by accumulating a fund of suitable assets and partly by providing capital to absorb unpredictable and unmanageable fluctuations. Serious mismatching, whether with respect to duration, kind (equity, property, fixed interest, etc.) or currency carries with it the risk of serious loss or insolvency. "With profits" business, whether conventional or equity linked, provides an additional margin in this respect since future premiums will be substantially higher than is necessary to cover the probable level of claims. Past profits do not provide such a margin insofar as they have already been converted into guaranteed benefits in the form of bonuses.

There is one type of matching which is practically exact. A unit linked policy calls for a reserve of which the major part can be expressed in units, and which can be matched by an asset of the same number of units.

Apart from the question of a "with profits" element and of the variety of sterling (i.e. non-unit) guarantees which may be provided at death or maturity, unit-linked policies are essentially of two types:

i. Those which are essentially a combination of two separate contracts, with an explicit split of each premium between an amount which is to be considered invested in units and an amount which is intended to provide life assurance and non-unit guarantees. The unit part is analogous to a unit trust investment, with dividends being reinvested in further units, and may be reserved for by holding an equal number of units. Some annual and monthly premium plans and practically all single premium plans are of this type.
ii. Contracts whose essential principle is the same as that of the traditional endowment assurance policy, but for which benefits are expressed in a different currency, namely units, instead of pounds. Investment income is not reflected directly in the benefits as for contracts in class (i). For convenience premiums usually remain constant in sterling terms and to provide additional protection minimum guarantees at death and sometimes at maturity are also so expressed. For this class of policy the major part of the reserve is again expressed in units and may be matched by a holding of units. In this case it is not necessary to reserve for the full amount payable at maturity in respect of premiums already paid, but only for a proportion which with reinvested income will accumulate to the full benefit of maturity. This method of reserving and matching is generally referred to as "actuarial funding". Exactly the same principles apply as to the determination of reserves for conventional policies. It is necessary to make an assumption as to the level of future investment income and it is important to note that yields on equity shares and property, expressed as

a percentage of market values, have for a great many years displayed considerable stability, certainly by comparison with yields on long and short term fixed interest securities.

Matching the main liability on unit-linked policies is thus significantly more precise and certain than is the case for conventional business. It is still necessary to establish a small sterling reserve to allow for premiums being fixed in sterling (this may be negative in the policy's early years if allowance is made for initial expenses) and for guaranteed amounts payable at death. The question of a reserve for sterling maturity guarantees is more complex however; this reserve should be matched by investments whose performance is relatively independent of that of the relevant unit. Departures from actuarial funding are normally referred to as under or overfunding and may be justifiable within reasonable limits according to the disposition of the company's other assets and liabilities. For example, a company entitled to receive future annual management charges expressed as a percentage of the value of a growing unit fund will profit disproportionately according to the level of capital gains achieved and can more easily absorb any loss due to underfunding which arises from such gains.

Shadow funding involves matching unit liabilities of one type with unit assets of another type and may be tolerable so long as there is not too great a disparity between the types of unit involved or between the risk of potential loss and the company's other resources. Significant underfunding in order to finance the expense of acquiring new business or for investment in fixed interest securities would represent serious mismatching and involve the risk of insolvency if unit prices were to rise substantially.

b. *Gearing leading to possible insolvency*

Borrowings by life assurance companies in the past have generally been for the purpose of the development of their businesses and have been seen as an infrequent alternative to the subscription of new equity capital. Borrowings of this type have not often proved necessary because the development of with-profits policies has meant that additional capital has effectively been available from this source. With-profits policyholders can be said to have drawn some advantage therefrom, and undoubtedly would expect to do so if the new business thus acquired turned out to be profitable.

In contrast "gearing", as used in the heading of this paragraph, is borrowing for the purpose of enhancing investment performance, it being accepted that additional risks are embraced thereby. However, excessive gearing has dangers for the solvency of a life assurance company whose contracts are written in terms of a guarantee because the volatility of the assets is increased in direct proportion to the amount of gearing. In the context of unit-linking, undefined gearing can be criticised for the reason that it is not always clear for whose benefit the gearing has been introduced. The presence of gearing can be used, by managements who base their annual charges upon the gross assets involved, as a means of increasing the absolute amount of management charges thus taken. Abbey Life is not against gearing as such provided that it is not excessive. We do feel however that disclosure of company policy as regards gearing is essential and that managements should never put themselves in the invidious position of taking increased charges as a result of gearing which they have instigated.

c. *Non-diversification leading to possible insolvency*

The concentration of the investment portfolio of a life assurance company in a small number of large investment holdings could in certain circumstances lead to the insolvency of the life assurance company concerned. United Kingdom life assurance companies have a long and successful record of investment which has been based upon the twin principles of maximising investment return and of a wide spread of investment by investment type, by company and by geographical location. This achievement has been as beneficial to the economy as it has been to the contributing policyholders. The introduction of unit-linking has no major implication for this investment aspect except that the portfolio spread of an individual life assurance company may be changed as the element of selection moves in some degree to the policyholder.

The practical application of the principles of life office investment has resulted in a position where it would be unusual, indeed perhaps unprecedented, for the portfolio to be invested as to more than 10% in any one investment unless that investment itself effectively provides a further degree of spread (e.g. an investment or unit trust). We doubt whether formal legislation is required, the effect of which would be to make this sensible practice statutory.

4. Other considerations

a. *Liquidity*

It is a general principle of life office investment that the liquid resources of the company should be adequate at all times to meet claims and maturities as they occur, with only minor and occasional recourse to bank borrowing. Liquidity for these purposes is usually no great problem in the industry, reflecting the substantial inflow of new and renewal premiums and investment income on existing assets. To date, this experience has been paralleled in the unit-linked sector of the market, but questions have been raised in connection with single premium policies as to the possibility that liquidity levels should be explicitly raised to a level above what would be normal for the industry as a whole.

This question is only answerable if one considers the many interlocking parts, and the following comments are, we feel, relevant, although not listed necessarily in order of importance:

i. A single premium life assurance policy is intended to be a relatively long term asset, and hence in the hands of the policyholder, an illiquid one. It could be compared directly with a term deposit where the return offered is higher than on a demand deposit, because the financial intermediary is able to make better use of the funds so deposited. The withdrawal facilities commonly written into single premium policies are a concession which are not intended to cover the circumstances of a simultaneous and full scale withdrawal by all policyholders, and they are not seen by policyholders as any more than that. Withdrawal rates on the Abbey Equity Bond Fund and Abbey Property Bond Fund have always been low, in the order of 3%-4% per annum.

ii. The liquidity of a unit-linked fund has to be judged against this principle and is additionally a function of:

(a) The proportion of single premium liabilities (or more properly the exposure to withdrawal) against which the total assets of the unit-fund are held.

(b) The relative liquidity of the assets already in the portfolio (e.g. real property, shares in unquoted Companies or shares in quoted Companies in which dealings take place only infrequently) and an informed opinion about the time scale which would be required for the disposal of these assets to take place.

(c) The terms of the policy document which may or may not permit the assurance company to defer payment of withdrawals for up to a specified period.

(d) The size of the unit-fund and the number of policyholders who are involved.

(e) The cash flow from other sources and whether or not this is predictable (e.g., the existence of annual premium policies linked to the fund clearly provides an element of predictable future cash flow).

(f) The extent of resources outside the unit-fund which could either comprise the other resources of the company or some other credit facilities of which advantage might be taken.

(g) The extent of any forward commitments (e.g., property development).

In the view of Abbey Life, the liquidity issue is not the problem which some commentators have suggested. The interests of policyholders are not necessarily best served by the stipulation of a minimum liquidity percentage (which in the case of property bonds it has been suggested should be a high one), and that they are better served by the preservation of maximum investment freedom.

As a matter of interest the liquidity of the Abbey Property Bond Fund has never been less than 10% but it would be our judgment that taking account of all the circumstances, this level is more than adequate.

b. *Valuation*

The particular nature of unit-linked assurance necessitates the continuing valuation of the assets comprising the unit fund. This necessity arises not only because the unit price is an integral feature of the unit-link, but because the form of the policy requires that equity be continuously preserved as between different policyholders, including those who are becoming new policyholders. The unit price calculation usually follows the DTI regulations for unit trusts, so that the process can be traced back to the asset valuation with no difficulty. The valuation of the assets is, however, a question which has received some public attention in recent years, although some of the commentary has, in our view, been ill considered.

Valuation should be examined as to two distinct types of assets:

i. *Quoted*

Prices of Stock Exchange securities are usually taken out at a particular time for all the investments in a portfolio (although it should be noted that in the hour or so that this process might take, some of the earlier prices noted might have altered) on either a "cheapest offer" or a "best bid" basis. These market quotations have relevance only to the number of shares in which the jobber is prepared to trade on those bases, and do not have any particular relevance to the price at which a trade might have been arranged for the number of shares in the portfolio in question. However, this procedure is justified on the basis that only the marginal movement in the number of units in issue is financially affected and therefore, provided this marginal number is relatively insignificant, then the cardinal objective of equity is achieved. It should be pointed out, however, that the calculation of the unit price is not completed until some hours after the prices are taken out of the market, and moreover that the unit price then calculated is held steady for (typically) one day or a week, by which time the prices of the underlying assets may have changed materially. Once again, it should be stressed therefore that the valuation process and the unit price calculation process are believed to be the best way of achieving the objective of equity.

ii. *Unquoted*

Unquoted shares or other investments (such as real property) are not represented by an "offer" and a "bid" price, and hence this distinction falls away. The usual basis is therefore an estimate of the price at which an "arms-length" transaction would take place between a willing buyer and a willing seller. In our view unquoted investments (other than real property) are extremely difficult to value, there being firstly the problem of what the valuation would be if the investments were quoted and secondly, the difficulty of assessing what discount should be applied to this presumed "market valuation" in order to allow for there being no quotation and perhaps a minority interest as well. We understand, for example, that the Inland Revenue usually apply a discount of the order of 35% to allow for these factors. For this reason we would be reluctant to include investments of this type in our unit-funds, and we would suggest that a percentage limitation might be appropriate.

Turning to *real property* the valuation of which is in fact the issue most discussed, we recognise that a real difficulty can arise from differing valuations which can come from different professional valuers with the same brief. In our experience, the variations which arise are accentuated if only one property investment is processed, whereas we find that ready agreement on the valuation of a portfolio consisting of a large number of properties (say over 25) is forthcoming. Reflecting the public concern on the issue of real property valuations we feel that it is worthwhile setting out the basis of property valuation as we understand it. This is seen as a logical and systematic process, the variables in which are few and the assumptions leading to the choice of variable can be adequately checked against the market place. The consciousness of the property bond companies to the real concern over the valuation issue led to the general practice of engaging the services of two valuers, independent of one another, and one at least being independent of the company. The agreement on value which must result from this practice has gone a long way to satisfy previous skepticism of the reality of the valuation process. We would therefore conclude that the generally accepted methods of property valuation are at least as effective in achieving the objective of equity between policyholders as the methods used for the valuation of Stock Exchange securities and hence the major difficulties have fallen away.

For the interest of the Committee, detailed reference is made to the Abbey Property Bond Fund so that the practical application of the process can be seen in operation.

The values supplied are determined on a willing buyer/willing seller basis, and make no allowance whatever for any costs which either party would incur. This evaluation is performed monthly for all properties by Hambros Bank (our property managers) and Richard Ellis (our independent valuers) and an agreed valuation is supplied to Abbey Life. Aside from the principles which are involved in this evaluation, the following general rules are followed:

i. Mortgages on properties (and we have four such mortgages) are valued at par, irrespective of term and coupon.

ii. Uncompleted property developments are valued at cost, irrespective of stage of development, or progress in lettings, unless in the strong opinion of the valuers this basis would be inappropriate.
iii. Valuations ignore accruals of rent completely, this item being brought in at a later stage.
iv. All properties are physically inspected by both parties once a year.

The valuation principles, although apparently shrouded in some mystery, are in fact quite straightforward. These can be itemised in a number of steps, each of which has to be taken in respect of each property investment.

i. The valuer moves forward to the next rent review date. He looks at the remaining terms and conditions of the existing lease from that date forward. He estimates the rental which would be negotiated at that date, on the basis of the information known now. He specifically ignores any inflation of rents in market place which might take place between now and the next rent review date. This rental is commonly known as the rental value.
ii. The valuer judges the appropriate yield at which this rental value should be capitalised (assuming the property is freehold). This yield, as is the rental value is a function (inter alia) of the location of the property, the quality of the covenant, the terms of the lease, the type of property and observable yield basis inherent in recent property transactions in the market place.
iii. The valuer calculates the difference between the rental value and the current rents and capitalises this in an annuity-certain at a chosen rate of interest for the period of years up to the next rent review date.
iv. The valuer discounts the capitalised value obtained in (ii) back from the next rent review date to the present valuation date, again at a chosen rate of interest.
v. The valuer makes the appropriate allowance for any ground rents, service expenses, etc., which bear upon the Fund.
vi. The value obtained is thus (iv) – (iii) – (v) = (vi).
vii. Leasehold properties are treated on a comparable basis.

c. *Asset type*

We understand that the Committee is considering the special issue of whether the range of asset type which can constitute a unit-link should be curtailed. Particularly relevant for consideration would be assets which are illiquid and non-income producing such as antique furniture and so forth. We cannot foresee that life assurance companies would wish to promote unit-linked policies of such a type nor that such policies would be readily accepted by the public. In these circumstances therefore, we would not consider that any legislation is necessary.

5. Summary and conclusions

The absence of present regulations governing asset management is, for all practical purposes, total, and there is no distinction between assets underlying conventional life assurance and unit-linked life assurance. The extensive freedom of action permitted exposes policyholders to flagrant abuse although the industry record shows that asset management in the past has been responsible. Regulation dealing with *misapplication* of assets is general in other countries and similar legislation could well be introduced in the United Kingdom. Regulation designed to limit the *mismanagement* of assets is extremely difficult to formulate without adopting arbitrary and inhibiting standards which can lead to unexpected and unreasonable results. Publicly expressed concerns regarding the potential problems of valuing the assets underlying unit-linked funds, liquidity and asset-type seem exaggerated.

Accordingly, based on these considerations, Abbey Life concludes:

> that serious consideration be given to the enactment of legislation intended to prevent the flagrant misapplication, as distinct from mismanagement of assets, and to require companies to fully disclose the manner in which their assets have been invested.

CHAPTER VI
THE REGULATION OF MARKETING METHODS

This Chapter describes existing marketing methods, examines alleged abuses therein and evaluates the merits and likely consequences of various proposals which have been advanced to curtail such abuses by extending regulation to this aspect of the industry.

1. The role of marketing in the life assurance industry

Amid the sound and fury of argument over marketing methods prevailing in the industry too little has been said about the importance of this function to the industry, to the economy and to Society at large. *Without new business*, a life assurance company becomes a liquidating institution. *Without an increasing volume* of new business the capability of the industry to generate capital for long-term investment will not keep pace with the growing capital requirements of the United Kingdom economy. *Without an expanded market thrust* the socially desirable objective of wider ownership of life assurance will not be met. Thus, it can be seen that the marketing function is not a "necessary evil" to be endured and restricted but is instead both essential *and desirable* and should instead be fostered *and encouraged.*

The successful development of the life assurance industry in the United Kingdom would not have taken place without the concurrent development of progressively more effective marketing methods. Throughout the history of the industry the trend towards more energetic techniques has been unmistakable.

The Insurance Institute of London *Report of the Advanced Study Group (No. 27)* showed that historically an increased use of agents has been the method by which business has increased. In December, 1720 one company recorded:

> The Committee having considered Proper Measures for enlarging the Insurances of this Office, have thought convenient to Appoint Persons of Reputation and substance in the Chief Towns and Cities to Distribute Policies and receive all Quaterages and to allow such persons One Shilling in the Pound as an Equivalent for their Trouble.

In its early development the agents were appointed for their local influence and were therefore appointed from solicitors, bankers and land agents.

Nevertheless, at first the growth of the agency system was slow and the paper states:

> . . . even as late as 1848, it appears that some companies employed no agents, relying on personal recommendations of proprietors and local directors, but in the face of increasing competition, it was found impossible to get sufficient business by these methods.

It is likewise revealing to examine the period of great growth of the insurance industry between 1870 and 1914. In his book *The Royal Exchange Assurance: A History of British Insurance 1720-1970* Barry Supple, when referring to the impact of competition and the growth of insurance companies during period 1870-1914 said (page 284):

> In fact, . . . for both the industry in general and the Royal Exchange Assurance in particular, one of the most critical responses to new market problems and opportunities lay in the adaptation of organisation and the application of effort. It was, in fact the increasingly energetic search for business itself, and the inevitable effect of that search on the agency network of most offices which created the 20th century insurance industry. The reason for this was simple: insurance, if it was to expand, had *to be sold* [his italics], and the effective point at which business was done was, therefore, the contact between agent and policyholder. The magic of personal influence in the words of a President of the Institute of Actuaries, meant that "the Head Office manufactures the article, but has to look to its middleman to get orders". Whatever else was important, an effective and vigorous agency network was indispensable to growth.

Even at that time "... some managers were saddened to note the contrast between the 'stately negotiations' and 'strict enquiries' of previous years and the increased reliance upon salesmen and intensive competition for business 'but this sort of intensity was unavoidable if the industry was to grow' ...".

It appears to Abbey Life that these comments are equally applicable to the growth of the industry in the 1960's and its continued development today. If the industry is to continue to grow and play its part in the economy of the country, the use of an agency sales force is necessary. It is useful to trace the development of the agency system in the United Kingdom if only to illustrate the fact that it is not a new concept, but is a traditional manner of marketing life assurance. It appears that the newer offices are facing criticism for converting an inefficient and outmoded agency system into an efficient and modern sales force. This is perhaps because at the same time advanced products are being marketed with considerable success.

Abbey Life holds the view that the full-time professional agent selling assurance direct to the public is to be welcomed and is a logical development leading to a further growth in the industry, and hence the long term financial protection of persons who would otherwise remain uninsured and without savings.

The October 1969 edition of *Focus*, the magazine of the Consumer Council, in a survey of 990 people showed that 54% had no Whole Life Policy and 59% had no Endowment Assurance. The report welcomed the increasing reliance upon full-time "salesmen" as leading to the giving of better advice to the consumer, and, we would add, ensuring that the benefits offered by life assurance ownership were extended to a greater proportion of the uninsured or non-saving population.

2. Existing marketing methods

The principal marketing methods which have evolved may be classified into groups as follows:

1. *Direct selling*, a term generally applied to those methods involving agents whose allegiance runs primarily to one company, which may be further classified into sub-groups:
   a. where the agent is a company employee;
   b. where the agent is required to be engaged full-time as an agent; and
   c. where neither of the above sub-groups applies.
2. *Broker selling*, a term generally applied to those methods involving an independent intermediary, which may be further classified into sub-groups:
   a. where the intermediary is a professional insurance broker and is expected to complete the sale without extensive reliance on company representatives; and
   b. where the intermediary is a part-time insurance broker, a solicitor, accountant, stockbroker, etc., whose function is often limited to providing an introduction from which the sale is completed by company representatives.
3. *General agency selling*, a term generally applied to methods involving the appointment of a general agent, to whom is delegated responsibility for the appointment of agents and/or brokers of any of the categories described above.
4. *Non-agency selling*, a term generally applied to methods involving no intermediary, of which the main sub-groups are:
   a. advertising with proposal forms attached, or advertising to solicit persons interested in receiving sales literature accompanied by a proposal form; and
   b. direct mailing of sales literature accompanied by a proposal form.

These several methods are frequently identified with certain types of companies: method (1) (a) is used for industrial branch business by practically all companies; method (1) (b) is usually identified with Dominion offices, which are probably responsible for its introduction and development in the United Kingdom; method (1) (c) is used deliberately by only a few offices and is more often an unintended result of method (1) (b); method (2) is usually identified with the established offices and a majority of conventional business is sold in this manner; method (3) is used rarely, usually by a newly established office seeking to develop business quickly through a sales outlet already in existence; method (4) is most often used to market products thought to have sufficient appeal to "sell themselves", such as single premium bonds. In practice, the lines between the various methods are often blurred, and most companies use a combination of methods.

It may be relevant to note that unit trust management companies use method (4) only.

This description of marketing methods would be incomplete without reference to prevailing commission practices. Universally, commissions are paid by the company rather than by the buyer. All methods are influenced by these practices, although in the case of methods (1) (a) and (4), the effect is indirect — caused by the necessity to keep costs within the overall margins available for selling expenses. The commission practices of LOA member companies are practically uniform: on annual premium business the initial commission is 2% of the sum assured and the renewal commission 2 1/2% of the premium, with reduced commissions on pension business; on single premium business the commission is 3% of the premium, with reduced commissions on several classes of business; commissions are not paid in advance of receipt of the associated premium ("indemnity terms"). Technically, the commission agreement of the LOA limits commissions only for "broker selling", and "direct selling" is exempt. In practice, except in the area of commission advances, the necessity to keep costs within the overall margins available for sales expenses compels member companies using both methods to adopt similar commission practices for each. Companies not bound by the LOA agreement are free to deviate from these practices and frequently do. Nevertheless, there is considerable uniformity of commission practices throughout the industry.

3. Criticism of existing methods

The marketing methods of the life assurance industry are the subject of much controversy and considerable criticism, both within the industry and outside it. So vehemently are their causes argued by detractors and defenders alike that the fundamental objectives, which must be common ground to both camps, are obscured if not consumed in the debate. Moreover, substantial commercial interests would be involved if existing marketing methods were changed by legislation, particularly if the effects were disproportionately distributed. In this mixed atmosphere of legitimate concern, emotional argument and self-serving prejudice, it is difficult to identify exactly the main criticisms and the proposed remedies. The following list is intended to cover those most frequently voiced:

1. that direct selling lends itself particularly to abuse and should, therefore, be subjected to restrictions not applied to other methods of marketing;
2. that the marketing of unit-linked life assurance products by whatever method lends itself particularly to abuse and should, therefore, be subject to restrictions not applied to other types of products;
3. that commission levels on all types of life assurance are, or are in danger of, becoming too high and should, therefore, be regulated;
4. that all persons selling life assurance occupy a position of trust susceptible to abuse and should, therefore, be licensed;
5. that advertising copy and sales literature is, or is in danger of, becoming misleading and should, therefore, be restricted;
6. that civil remedies do not adequately protect policyholders from agent malpractice and should, therefore, be reinforced with specific legislation.

4. Declaration of interest

Before examining the validity of these criticisms as related to the actual experience of Abbey Life it seems appropriate to begin with an outline of the marketing methods of this Company and an indication of the extent to which it would be affected by each of the suggested changes in regulatory practices.

Abbey Life markets its products by methods (1) (b), (2) (a) and (b) and (4) (a) and (b), as set forth below (figures cited are current):

1. b. The Agency Organisation of nearly 1,000 men and women (10% are employed managers and 90% are self-employed agents) is responsible for 80% of the annual premium production and 35% of the single premium production. This is probably the largest and certainly the most productive "direct-selling" organisation in the industry (excluding industrial branch). The Company requirement that all agents be "full-time" is probably 90% effective.

2. a. The Broker Organisation of approximately 1,000 professional insurance brokers serviced by more than 30 employed managers and consultants is responsible for 20% of the annual premium production and 40% of the single premium production.

   b. Part-time insurance brokers and solicitors, accountants, stockbrokers etc. are recognised by the Company as agents only for single premium business and 5% of such business is sold in this way; certain of the Company's agents and brokers rebate an introductory commission to such sources on all business produced jointly.

4. a. Newspaper advertising, with coupons attached, is directly responsible for 15% of the single premium production and indirectly responsible for an undetermined proportion of business received through other channels. In 1971, the Company expects to expend approximately £400,000 on advertising of this type — perhaps twice as much as any other company in this market.

   b. Direct enquiries, some arising from direct mail and some from other sources, are responsible for 5% of the single premium production.

The following additional information bears upon the marketing methods of Abbey Life:

1. Although the Company is not a member of the LOA its basic commission practices are generally in line with the LOA members' agreement. The Company does, however, depart from the agreement in three respects: by offering indemnity terms in unusual circumstances, by offering "standard" commissions (as opposed to "reduced" commissions) on pension business and by offering a volume expense allowance on all business, thus passing on

to brokers and agents the expense savings of business received in substantial volume from a single source.

2. Approximately 90% of the annual and single premium business expected to be sold in 1971 will be unit-linked, 80% property-linked and 10% equity-linked.

Abbey Life would be affected in various ways if marketing methods were restricted as suggested:

1. A complete or partial embargo on direct selling would have extremely serious and disproportionate consequences for Abbey Life; restrictions on certain aspects of direct selling might or might not be serious, depending upon the nature and extent of such restrictions.
2. A complete or partial embargo on the sale of unit-linked life assurance or restrictions on certain aspects thereof would be at least as serious and disproportionate.
3. Regulation of commission rates at present industry levels would represent to Abbey Life no particular embarrassment as its commission rates are in line with the industry generally; regulation of commission rates at levels lower than present industry levels would adversely affect Abbey Life, but not disproportionately; any regulation of commission levels may have undesirable and unforeseen consequences to Abbey Life and the industry generally.
4. Any imaginable system of licensing (particularly an embargo on part-time agents) would have, probably, less effect upon Abbey Life than upon any other major company because (except in the case of single premium business) the Company does not intend to grant agencies to anyone, agent or broker, not engaged full-time in the insurance business. Abbey Life is confident that its agents and brokers would, with rare exceptions, qualify easily under any likely licensing scheme.
5. Any reasonable requirements for prior approval of advertising copy or sales literature, though administratively burdensome, would not adversely affect Abbey Life. Indeed, such a practice would probably lead to a standardisation of such items as projected rates of investment return, which could be helpful to companies such as Abbey Life by eliminating the competitive escalation of assumptions and projected benefits which takes place from time to time in the industry. A more general restriction or embargo on

advertising would affect Abbey Life as the leading industry advertiser, but because the Company is already established and has a large distribution system the effect would not be as disproportionate as might be expected.

6. Any imaginable sanctions on agent or broker malpractice would have, probably, little or no effect upon Abbey Life because sanctions already imposed by Company practice are superior or equivalent to any likely to be imposed by regulation.

5. Direct selling

Criticism of direct selling is usually supported by arguments dealing with potential problems arising from the appointment of unqualified and ill-trained agents, exacerbated by the incentive afforded by commissions towards mis-selling and over-selling. These potential problems are indeed present in the system, but it is the contention of Abbey Life that the criticism is one which should more properly be directed towards the system as a whole, rather than towards direct selling only.

In fact it can be argued that direct selling methods are less susceptible to abuse than other methods. The Advanced Study Group commented:

> Those offices employing a full-time agency staff can reasonably give close attention to educating them in insurance matters. Sometimes a school is run for this purpose; often meetings are arranged with specialists to address them. Local officials give much of their time to training their agents, though in many cases the training is in salesmanship rather than technique. House magazines carry on the work supplemented by booklets prepared specially to teach the agency staff how to prospect for and canvass for the various classes of business.

Moreover, the costs incurred to train and finance new agents by those companies operating through direct sales forces are a powerful inducement towards proper selection in the first place.

Abbey Life accepts its responsibility to select representatives with care and to establish a reasonable level of competence before allowing new agents to approach members of the public. All representatives must qualify for a fidelity bond before their appointment is confirmed. Agents are trained in methods of salesmanship to equip them with the sales skills and product knowledge which are the essential tools of their job. The practical application of this objective takes a number of different forms and it is recognised that the responsibility is a continuous one which the Company is constantly attempting to fulfill.

To meet this need the Company maintains a Development and Training department. The first requirement of "training the trainers" is provided through management development courses and study groups conducted on a continuous basis. These courses are held in Head Office for members of branch management who in turn train agents in the respective branches also on a continuous basis in groups and where necessary individually. Field supervision is included as part of a new agent's training under the guidance of an experienced member of branch management.

A new agent is trained to a minimum standard as regards salesmanship and the particular range of policies which he is to be allowed to sell. Before he is permitted to engage in any actual selling he must satisfy his Branch Manager that he has attained these minimum standards. There is no formal written examination that he must first pass, although the Company is actively considering the introduction of such an examination. After a suitable period new agents attend courses for evaluation of knowledge and introduction to more advanced studies.

The Company issues regular field bulletins designed to circularise information of an immediate nature and to draw attention to those aspects which may need special attention. In addition senior executives of the Company and specialists in particular fields regularly visit branches, the purpose of which visits is at least in part of furtherance of the educational process.

Criticism is often misdirected towards direct selling which might more appropriately be levelled against part-time agents of all types (including brokers, solicitors, accountants, stockbrokers, etc.). This issue will be considered later in connection with the question of licensing.

Another argument sometimes advanced to support criticism of direct selling is the lack of independence (and, arguably, objectivity) of an agent who represents, primarily or exclusively, only one company. The observation is an accurate one, but the implied conclusion is moot — not every sales outlet must offer all available products to produce a freely competitive market, and the life assurance industry is far more competitive than most.

In favour of the unimpeded continuation of direct selling methods there are these substantial further arguments:

1. the principal alternative marketing method, broker selling, is not as effective in reaching the broadest population groups below the upper third of the economic pyramid;
2. there is no evidence (certainly, Abbey Life has none) to suggest that direct selling methods, properly managed, are more expensive than other methods;
3. to single out direct selling methods for separate restriction would require a careful definition of such methods, which are difficult if not impossible to distinguish from certain variations of other methods;
4. there is no precedent elsewhere for restrictions upon direct selling methods not applicable to other methods and one country, Canada, has legislation, the force of which requires the use of direct selling as opposed to other methods.

6. Unit-linked life assurance

Criticism of marketing unit-linked life assurance by whatever method rests on the following arguments:

1. that such products are more susceptible to misrepresentation than conventional life assurance products; and
2. that the marketing of such products should be circumscribed in like manner to the unit trust industry because both products are subject to similar abuse.

The similarity between unit-linked life assurance and conventional "with profits" endowments has already been described. The scope for misrepresentation of the former rests primarily on the use of unreasonably high projected rates of growth, whereas the scope for misrepresentation of the latter rests on the use of unreasonably high projected bonus rates, leading in both cases to unreasonably high projected final benefits. As a practical matter, projections are in both cases provided by the life offices, and sales representatives, whether agents or brokers, are instructed to use only these projected values. The question is whether or not the unit-linked product lends itself more to abuse than the conventional product. On the one hand, it could be argued that a company is free to select whatever growth rate it chooses to illustrate, even one which it considers to be unreasonably high, and provided the assumption is clearly stated the company enjoys the competitive advantage of the resultant projections; this practice, it can be argued, is misleading because few buyers are sufficiently sophisticated to be able to evaluate the reasonableness of the projected rate of growth. On the other hand, it could be argued that the company is free to select whatever assumptions it chooses as to future investment rates, mortality rates and expenses and project the resultant bonus scale on such a basis even if it is unreasonably optimistic; this practice, it can be argued, is misleading because intending policyholders have neither the information nor the experience necessary to evaluate the validity of the resultant projections. Thus, it would appear that there is no convincing argument to support the view that one product is necessarily more susceptible to misrepresentation than the other and both rely, in the final analysis, upon the integrity of the office involved.

There is, however, precedent elsewhere for limiting assumed rates of growth in such illustrations. Canadian practice requires that companies offering unit-linked life assurance schemes illustrate maturity values in one of two ways:

1. using a projected growth rate of 71/2%; or
2. using two rates of growth, which must be 5% and 10%.

The adoption of such a practice in the United Kingdom with respect to unit-linked life assurance would present no serious difficulties to the industry and many offices would welcome such a limitation. It should be noted, however, that equitable and effective regulation in this area would be notably difficult to draft for several reasons:

1. the tax positions of various companies are quite different and within companies there are also differences in tax rates on various funds, all of which must significantly influence the illustrated rates of growth;
2. charges are not standardised among companies and a fair comparison between companies would require that growth rates be adjusted to take account of these differences;
3. certain products available on the market pass reinvested income along to the policyholder whereas other products do not, another difference which ought to be reflected in projected rates.

The corresponding Canadian regulation ignores these various distinctions and it could therefore be argued that the regulation is achieving the exact opposite of the intended purpose — companies wishing to misrepresent their products can do so, with official sanction, by designing the products to maximise the advantages available under the arbitrary rules.

It might also be argued, with considerable validity, that different companies ought to be able to illustrate different growth rates if there is a convincing reason to support the view that their investment performance is likely in the future to deviate significantly from the average.

It is also argued that unit-linked life assurance lends itself to misrepresentation because the charges are not always explicit and are subject to possible manipulation by the company. But in this instance the scope for abuse is even greater in conventional life assurance products where charges are not stated explicitly at all.

In this evidence, Abbey Life has already expressed the view that regulation applicable to the unit trust industry is inappropriate for application en bloc to the life assurance industry, whether unit-linked or conventional. In this context, a more limited possibility is being explored — the application of unit trust marketing methods, wholly or partially, to unit-linked life assurance but not to conventional life assurance. The principal limitations involved in unit trust marketing methods are:

1. a complete embargo on all direct selling and broker selling;
2. limitations on charges;
3. restrictions on advertising copy and sales literature.

The application of these restrictions to unit-linked life assurance would completely undermine such business to the serious detriment of the industry. An embargo on selling through agents of any type would alone be sufficient to achieve that effect. Three separate arguments can be advanced against such a proposal, any one of which is sufficient.

First, it can be argued that the distinction between unit-linked and conventional life assurance is not sufficiently clear to warrant such a radical difference in regulation. An embargo on selling through agents applied to the whole industry is inconceivable. Limitations on charges, the equivalent of which is upper limits on premium rates, would be completely contrary to the traditions of the industry in the United Kingdom and, paradoxically, in other countries where premiums are regulated it is more customary to impose *lower* limits.

Restrictions on advertising copy and sales literature, though administratively burdensome to both the industry and government, would probably not adversely affect the industry.

The second argument, applicable only if the distinction between unit-linked and conventional life assurance is judged to be sufficiently clear to warrant differences in regulation, is that these are not the appropriate regulations. Unit-linked life assurance contracts afford minimum guarantees not found in the unit trust industry and the companies offering these contracts are subject to existing life assurance regulations whereas unit trust management companies are not. With these additional protective features it is reasonable to expect that more liberal regulation of marketing methods would apply to unit-linked life assurance.

The third argument, applicable only if no distinction is found between unit-linked life assurance and unit trusts, is that these are not the appropriate regulations for *either* industry. It is the view of Abbey Life that the restrictions imposed upon marketing methods in the unit trust industry are unnecessarily and unreasonably limiting. The similar views expressed by the Jenkins Committee have already been referred to in Chapter III. In overseas markets there is no embargo on selling through agents, although a license is sometimes required, and limitations on charges are either significantly higher or nonexistent; restrictions on advertising copy and sales literature are sometimes more extensive and sometimes less extensive than those applicable in the United Kingdom.

7. Commission

The argument for regulation is generally that the prospect of a commission war can best be thereby avoided. Commissions have never been regulated in the United Kingdom and therefore no evidence exists which can be used to measure the impact on the industry which such regulations might have. Voluntary commission agreements have been attempted with varying degrees of success, although there has generally been some minor freedom of manoeuvre for individual signatories. However, the main point to be noted here is that the established life companies do not in the main benefit from a general raising of commission levels because the absolute amount of assurance business available is not capable of a sufficient upward movement as a result of the increased impetus which would be given to their marketing forces to compensate them for the increased overheads which they would have to meet. This point leads therefore to the theory that commission levels are self-regulating due to the essential similarity of policies issued by the companies involved and that profit levels cannot be reduced below what is generally available for the industry for an extended period of time.

One argument against regulation is that companies should have flexibility to raise their commission levels if they so wish or if their other overheads so permit. (Flagrantly high commissions are a different matter since they raise the prospect of insolvency, but in our experience the financial intermediaries who make up the principal outlet for this type of business are sufficiently wary to steer clear of business upon which commissions of this order are paid.) The deliberate payment of above average commissions by new companies, or by established companies upon new lines of business which they wish to promote, can be a means of assisting the healthy development of the industry as a whole. The cost of this deliberate extra expense is containable and would be viewed in the financial sense as a promotional expense.

Another argument against regulation is that commission rates in the United Kingdom are not excessive. A comparison with commissions prevailing in North America is inexact because the manner of expression is differently based, but it is significant to note that several Canadian companies use essentially the same commission structure for the operations in the United Kingdom, Canada and the United States. Commission rates prevailing in Continental Europe are expressed in the same manner as in the United Kingdom and are distinctly higher — by 25% or more.

It should be clearly stated that commission rates on unit-linked life assurance are not significantly different from those applicable to conventional life assurance, but where distinctions exist the commission rates offered by a given company on unit-linked business are more often lower than higher.

It is sometimes argued that commission levels should be disclosed to policyholders or intending policyholders. The terms upon which an assurance company is prepared to issue business are primarily based upon what in its opinion constitutes a competitive product. The gross income which the assurance company expects to receive from a policy over its lifetime will be required to meet issuing expenses, renewal expenses, mortality costs, reserve allocations and a profit margin. The distinction as between these various components is an internal matter within the deliberations of an individual company. The solvency aspect is covered by the regular reporting requirements of the DTI.

Commission levels are therefore directly a function of (inter alia) administration expenses and profit objectives. Disclosure of commission payments would carry an implied stigma on those companies which were prepared to pay a higher level of commission even though this decision might well have been based upon an extremely cost effective administration system and perhaps a significantly lower-than-average profit objective.

8. Licensing

A licensing system for those selling life assurance has been suggested in many quarters without any clear indication of what such a system should seek to achieve and without identification of what such a system should consist.

Some proponents have suggested that a licensing system should apply only to direct selling, or only to unit-linked life assurance. In the view of Abbey Life, for the reasons set forth in preceding sections, there is no justification for such distinctions. It has also been suggested that a general licensing system be adopted but with exemptions for members of certain professions or occupational groups. In the view of Abbey Life a licensing system, if it be adopted at all, should have universal application to all those selling any form of life assurance or receiving commissions therefrom in any way. This would require associated legislation prohibiting the rebating of commissions to unlicensed parties.

The possible objectives of a licensing system with universal application are:

1. to improve standards of knowledge among those selling life assurance;
2. to improve ethical standards within the industry; and
3. to improve the professional standing of those selling life assurance by the elimination of part-time agents.

A licensing system involving an extensive knowledge test (modelled, perhaps, on the Dutch system) would have widespread repercussions throughout the industry because many persons who have acted as part-time agents, in some cases for many years, might not qualify. Any less extensive knowledge test (modelled, perhaps, on the North American system) would, based on experience elsewhere, do little to improve standards of knowledge among those selling life assurance. The choice, therefore, would appear to be between an extensive test of knowledge or none at all, the latter appearing to be the more practical.

There are three distinct benefits to be gained from a licensing system, whether or not a knowledge test is involved:

1. applicants with obviously unsatisfactory reputations can be denied a license at the outset;
2. the "rogue" salesmen, having been identified as such, could thereafter be banned from further activities in the business; and
3. the threat of a cancellation of license would deter from malpractice those who might otherwise be tempted.

These benefits would, it is clear, improve ethical standards within the industry.

A licensing system requiring that agents engage "full time" in the business (not easily defined) does not seem appropriate for the United Kingdom market, although the case against the use of part-time agents has been argued from time to time. Plymen and Pullen commented in 1968:

> In our view the time has come for the traditional offices to make drastic changes in their branch and agency organisation. It may well become necessary for these offices to choose between two alternative methods, and concentrate their sales efforts on either the professional broker or the full-time staff salesman dealing direct with the public. Either of these methods appear to be distinctly more efficient than the present hybrid system, which involves much overlapping of responsibilities and services. Neither of them admits of the continued employment of the part-time amateur agent.

Referring to the use of part-time agents, the October 1969 edition of *Focus* commented that contrary to the consumer's belief, the advice of his bank manager is not always impartial. They and accountants, solicitors, estate agents and others become part-time agents for insurance companies and receive commission for business they introduce. *Focus* remarks:

> they are almost sure to be tied to one or two companies. Unfortunately, the bulk of consumers rely on these tied intermediaries for guidance, believing no doubt that their bank manager or

> solicitor is selecting from the whole industry whereas he is pushing his own company's wares.

It seems likely that, if the life assurance industry were being constructed today ab initio that the part-time agent would not be involved. Any suggestion, however, that the use of part-time agents be abandoned now should in our view be supported by powerful evidence to quantify the damage to the consumer which results therefrom. If this can be adequately demonstrated and should the subsequent decision be that part-time agents be no longer permitted, then this should be industry-wide and made effective by the introduction of a ban on the rebating of commission by full-time to part-time agents.

This analysis suggests that the only practical licensing system is one of universal application, involving no knowledge test and permitting part-time agents. Such a system could be reasonably expected to improve ethical standards, but it is not possible to quantify the improvement. Against this must be weighed the cost of administering such a system.

It is worth noting that many of these same considerations apply equally to the non-life sector of the insurance industry.

9. Advertising and sales literature

Advertising copy and sales literature used by life assurance companies are sometimes criticised on the grounds that they are or may become misleading and should, therefore, be regulated.

Without denying that there exists scope for abuse, Abbey Life is of the view that little or no such abuse has actually occurred.

Before proceeding to describe the practices of Abbey Life it seems advisable to point out that advertising is a significant and beneficial factor in overall marketing methods. The Advanced Study Group, previously referred to, commented:

> Publicity, wisely employed, can be a driving and persuasive force which can not only foster favourable public opinion of insurance enterprises generally, but also assist in the work of selling to the public the insurance cover it needs. A radical overhaul and extension of publicity methods might well give the insurance industry that prominence which it deserves.

Abbey Life supports this viewpoint. The Committee will have seen already that we consider advertising to be a separate element in our overall marketing thrust. We consider also that advertising is an essential factor in the growth of new companies and is helpful in the promotion of new types of policy.

However, financial advertising has been long recognised as containing a potential for abuse. Company prospectuses have been and are carefully controlled by the Stock Exchange. Unit trust advertising has to be shown to the trustees of the unit trust. Requests for deposit funds for banking houses are controlled by the issue of licenses. The newspaper organisations have their own advertising standards authority. Some property bond companies subscribe to an informal "code of conduct" which prohibits some features of advertisements which are thought to be undesirable. There is no doubt that a higher standard of financial advertising has been the result of all this effort. Whether there should be a central authority for the control of assurance advertising is an open question, but we should prefer this not to be the case, as in what little lessons can be learnt from the unit trust precedent suggest that the depth of control does not have a particularly inhibiting impact, although the presence of a trustee is no doubt sufficiently salutary to prevent the worst kind of abuse.

The advertising used by Abbey Life typically takes two distinct forms:

1. *coupon sale*, the effect of which can be that the intending policyholder returns a completed application form and a cheque for the premium due as a result of which the policy will be issued immediately subject only to satisfactory answers being provided as to the health of the applicant;
2. *lead advertising*, the effect of which can be that the intending policyholder returns a coupon indicating interest in one of our policies as a result of which either further details will be sent to him or alternatively an appointment will be made for him to see one of our agents.

Occasionally an insurance broker may advertise one of our products on an incognito basis.

Examples of our recent advertising have been separately provided for the general interest of the Committee.

The overriding considerations in the construction of our individual advertisements, aside from the requirement to make them eye-catching and readable, are to put a full and fair view of the product on offer and to make use of the maximum amount of relevant factual information that is available whilst keeping the use of generalisations to a minimum.

The "full and fair" view is necessary because the advertisement may lead to a policy sale without further contact with the applicant and, therefore, there is a considerable wealth of detail included in all advertisements of this type. "Relevant factual information" is of the kind "The Abbey Property Bond Fund offer price increased by 10.5% in the latest year" and would be supported by, for example, only displaying photographs of properties already in the portfolio. The "generalisations" are restricted to optional statements of the type "experts agree that property is a good investment" and mandatory statements of the type "the value of your units can go up or down".

Identical considerations apply to sales literature, which has broader industry implications since many companies do not advertise extensively but all companies use some form of sales literature.

Should this aspect of the industry be regulated? Undeniably, some benefits would accrue. It should be remembered that the industry is already subject to considerable self-restraint in that competitors are quick to object to each other's advertising and sales literature. The financial press also is a strong influence. The cost of a system of regulation should also be considered and weighed against the benefits likely to be derived.

10. Malpractice

(a) Misrepresentation/policyholder complaints

Misrepresentation by salesmen generally can be identified as of three types:

1. fraudulent
2. innocent, due perhaps to accidental omission
3. misconception by the policyholder where no errors of types (1) or (2) are present.

In addition, one should mention "pressure selling" where the policyholder is fully aware of the nature of the policy but nonetheless would have preferred not to have entered into the contract.

Abbey Life attempts to eliminate the occurrence of any of these types of misrepresentation but it has to be recognised that examples do occur — such as type (3) — over which it has no control.

In cases where, notwithstanding every effort on our part, a justifiable grievance does arise, we give immediate redress to the policyholder. If the circumstances warrant such action we apply suitable disciplinary measures to the agent involved.

As a part of the process to keep misrepresentation to a minimum we have taken or take the following action:

1. all agents are "bonded" and satisfactory references taken out;
2. we leave the sales literature and accompanying illustrative material with the prospect for his consideration and for his future reference;
3. before policy issue, we dispatch to each applicant an acknowledgement letter which spells out the details of the policy for which he has applied;
4. the subsequent acceptance letter is similarly worded;
5. in assessing the obligations of the Company we do not restrict our vision to the policy document but take into account also the sales literature and other material which were presented to the applicant at the point of sale.

An index from which the sensitivity of this issue can be gauged would be an analysis of the volume of complaints actually received by the industry from its policyholders. For the period July 1969 to October 1970 Abbey Life has analysed the record of complaints received from its policyholders (insofar as the policies were sold by its agency force) and an analysis of this data is included later in this section. The experience of the Company since this date has not been specifically different from that obtained from this data, although the number of policies issued has grown. The later information cannot be supplied to the Committee for the reason that for the months of November and December 1970 the register was unfortunately not completed.

Abbey Life maintains a section within its Sales Department consisting of a few but highly experienced number of officers which section is known internally as the Agency Service Section.

The main functions of this section are:

1. to investigate complaints referred to the Agency Department concerning the activities of any agent throughout the country;

2. to carry out selective investigations into the activities of individual agents where this is felt necessary;
3. to assist with spot checks of business produced by the agency force as a whole at selected intervals.
4. to maintain and promote the good image of the Company in the eyes of the general public with particular regard to existing policyholders and to the agency field force.

The administrative work necessary to carry out the above functions of this section involves:

1. interviewing complainants, policyholders and agents and producing written reports detailing the results of investigations;
2. making decisions concerning the most satisfactory method of resolving complaints and initiating appropriate interdepartmental action to implement them;
3. maintaining records of complaints and producing periodical reports of trends and activities for senior management;
4. maintaining close liaison with Head Office departments to resolve individual complaints;
5. maintaining close and regular contact with branch management, keeping them informed of our activities that are concerned with their respective branches;
6. from time to time visiting branches and attending branch meetings giving talks to agents about the nature of the agency service function. The aim is to inform the agents so that they are encouraged to avoid the main stream of agency failures which we have found from experience, e.g., misrepresentation, late policy delivery, early surrenders, etc.

The nature of most complaints dealt with falls into two broad categories:

1. *complaints generally involving "service" activities*

   Total for above period: 306

   Within this category are included the following more specific types of complaints:

   Head office administrative errors

   Branch/agent administrative errors

   Inadequate understanding of policies

   Changes of circumstance

Delays in arranging medicals
Non-delivery/slow delivery of policies
Delays in sending (Not Proceeded With) refund cheques
Unit allocation enquiries
Inadequate servicing of policyholders by agents
Objections to "cold canvass" sales approach

2. *complaints involving alleged misrepresentation/dishonest activities*
Total for above period: 292
Within this category are included the following more specific types of complaints:
Low cash surrender values (C.S.V.)
Low C.S.V. with specific allegations of misrepresentation
Policies sold on a "deferred house purchase" basis or with guarantees of future mortgage facilities
Switch selling
Misappropriation of cash paid in respect of single premium
Overselling
General allegations of misrepresentation/unethical conduct. During the period under review the complaints above which number 598, of which 306 relate to administrative shortcomings, resulted in a close scrutiny of the affairs of some 37 agents. Of this number 31 are no longer in the service of the Company.

In order to retain perspective on this matter it is germane to note that the number of policies applied for during this period (as a result of the activities of the Agency Department) were in excess of 53,000. In addition some of the complaints undoubtedly arose in relation to policies issued in previous periods, so that the complaints involving alleged misrepresentation or dishonest activities were related to considerably less than 1% of our business activity.

In our view the data suggests that the incidence of misrepresentation is not high enough to represent a source of over-concern, although the Company is continually striving to reduce its impact. It should of course be remembered that the data contains cases of *alleged* misrepresentation where none in fact took place but it is impossible to quantify the the proportion which such cases might constitute. Nonetheless, we expect that an improvement will naturally result from the continuance of the effective training programmes which the Company has in hand.

(b) Switch selling

This practice is essentially that of persuading a policyholder to surrender or cease premium payments on an existing policy in order subsequently to take out a new policy either with the same or a different company in circumstances where it is demonstrably not to the advantage of the policyholder. The financial advantage to the salesman involved is the introductory commission payable by the Company upon the new policy taken out.

This practice is deplored throughout the industry but there is no evidence as to the extent of this malpractice. It is not illegal in the United Kingdom, other than to the extent that it involves exposure to the Theft Act and we know of no successful prosecution. To our knowledge, most companies take some positive steps to try to prevent instances of this type occurring in the conduct of their own businesses. In some other countries the practice is illegal, although notably difficult to enforce.

Abbey Life has recently formulated its own policy in respect of Switch Selling, with the intent of defusing any potential problem rather than having to act as a result of serious evidence of its frequency.

This policy is as follows :

1. This practice is absolutely prohibited.
2. Any agent found to be transgressing (proof will not be easy) will face instant dismissal.
3. where an agent leaves to join the service of another company, we are prepared to release details to his new employer of any policies (for which he was responsible for the sale) which are subsequently terminated. We would expect this information to be supplied to us on a reciprocal basis.

Beyond this we cannot see any further steps that we can take which would add further to the effectiveness of our control. We doubt whether legislation would be viable and in any event the extent of this malpractice may be so limited that legislation might not be the best way of handling the issue.

11. Summary and conclusions

The marketing function is central to the life assurance industry and is largely responsible for its successful development. The traditional method of selling in the United Kingdom is the agency system, which has evolved in its most modern form into direct selling by full-time professional salesmen. The principal contemporary marketing methods of the industry are direct selling, broker selling, general agency selling and nonagency selling, which are used in several combinations by various companies. The prevailing levels of commission rates are fairly uniform throughout the industry, due in large measure to the commission agreement of the Life Offices Association. Existing marketing methods are subject to several criticisms, generally directed towards their susceptibility to abuse. Abbey Life, together with all companies in the industry and some companies in related industries, have a vested interest in any proposals which might lead to changes in existing marketing methods. The general criticism of direct selling seems, upon examination, to be misdirected. Likewise criticism of the application of life assurance marketing methods to unit-linked life assurance seems, upon examination, to be unwarranted. Criticism of present commission levels seems, upon examination, to be based on inaccurate information, and proposals to regulate future commission levels are unwarranted. A licensing system for those selling life assurance may be desirable, but not all of the intended objectives of such a system seem practical. Likewise, proposals to regulate advertising copy and sales literature may have considerable merit. Criticism of agent or broker malpractice seems, upon examination in the light of the experience of Abbey Life, exaggerated.

Accordingly, based on these considerations, Abbey Life concludes:

> that the marketing methods prevailing in the life assurance industry are effective and ethical and should not, therefore, be fundamentally altered.
>
> that the already high standards observed by the industry in its marketing activities might be further improved and potential for future abuse might be diminished by the introduction of a licensing system for all persons selling life assurance and by the adoption of regulations dealing with advertising and sales literature.

CHAPTER VII
THE REGULATION OF SOLVENCY REQUIREMENTS AND RELATED MATTERS

This Chapter examines the adequacy of legislation dealing with solvency requirements and related matters.

1. Weakness of existing legislation

Any effective set of regulations should enable the DTI to make an independent and informed judgement as to the financial condition of a life assurance company and should give it adequate powers to protect policyholders from the consequences of impending insolvency. The existing legislation may be criticised in this respect in two ways:

a. companies are not required to supply the DTI with sufficient information to enable it adequately to appraise the financial condition of the company;
b. companies are not required to maintain intact the minimum paid-up share capital nor are they required to maintain a specified margin of solvency.

2. Financial reporting

Detailed information relating to the liabilities of a life assurance company is required to be included in the schedules regularly supplied to the DTI, but there is no corresponding requirement in relation to the assets. Thus the solvency of a life assurance company cannot actually be determined by the DTI. We would therefore suggest that it would be appropriate to expand the schedules to cover the assets in as detailed a manner as the liabilities, so that the DTI may more effectively exercise its power under existing legislation.

3. Minimum capital requirements

The present minimum capital requirement of £100,000 is, to say the least, modest and it has already been observed that the modern equivalent of the initial capital required under the terms of the Life Assurance Companies Act 1870 is perhaps £250,000. We make the specific recommendation that the minimum paid-up share capital of life assurance companies should be increased to £250,000. We also recommend that there be a requirement to maintain a continuing margin of solvency of £250,000 and that the DTI be given necessary authority to intervene where the margin of solvency drops below this level. Our reasons for these recommendations, which are hardly likely to prove an embarrassment to the companies already in existence, are:

1. the proposed minimum bears a realistic relationship to the minimum paid-up share capital thought to be necessary in the nineteenth century;
2. additional capital consistent with the extent of the likely "start-up" costs would thus be required for the formation of a new life assurance operation;
3. even at this level the capital requirement is modest by comparison with other countries (e.g., in Australia the figure is Australian $2 million).

It must be recognised that in the absence of detailed and comprehensive regulations dealing with the valuation of both assets and liabilities, the quantification of the actual margin of solvency may be a matter of disagreement and dispute.

4. Other matters

The powers of the DTI to adequately maintain a watching brief over the activities of life assurance companies is more extensive in the case of companies formed after 3rd November 1966; because of the provisions of the 1967 Companies Act.

We recommend that the relevant provisions of this Act should be extended to cover all life assurance companies.

5. Summary and conclusions

The existing legislation appears to be inadequate insofar as it does not permit the DTI to maintain an effective watching brief upon the solvency of life assurance companies. Particular weaknesses can be found in the areas of the comprehensiveness of information disclosed, the minimum margins of solvency and capital requirements.

Accordingly, based on these considerations, Abbey Life concludes:

> that existing legislation should be strengthened by the introduction of further reporting requirements and minimum margins of solvency, and that concurrently minimum capital requirements be increased to £250,000 and the application of the provisions of the

1967 Companies Act relating to the powers of the DTI to maintain a watching brief on solvency be extended to cover all life assurance companies.

CHAPTER VIII
THE ROLE OF SELF-REGULATION AND DISCLOSURE

This Chapter examines the role of self-regulation and disclosure in those areas of the life assurance industry which do not lend themselves to explicit legislation and examines the feasibility of extending this practice as a substitute for further legislation.

1. Introduction

Throughout this evidence we have indicated certain aspects of the life assurance industry where we feel that further legislation would be appropriate. We have also indicated aspects where in our judgment further legislation would not be appropriate but nonetheless consideration should be given and indeed has been given by the industry to controlling abuses which may arise in these areas.

It is our view that these additional controls can be provided by the industry operating as it does in a competitive atmosphere and we shall indicate in this chapter some attempts by the industry at self-regulation of this type and demonstrate that the lead has in almost all cases been taken by the unit-linked sector of the market even though the subject matter has almost always been relevant to conventional life assurance as it has been to unit-linked life assurance. The one exception of which we are aware is the necessity of the unit-linked companies to adequately describe the unit fund on a regular basis.

2. Industry associations

The life assurance industry associations are the Life Offices Association and the Industrial Life Offices Association. In Scotland the parallel organisation is the Associated Scottish Life Offices. The objects of these associations include the advancement of the business and the protection of the interests of insurance or assurance by consultation and combined action upon questions appertaining to the interests common to the companies involved and by co-operation with any association having similar objectives.

By number, the majority of companies writing unit-linked assurance schemes do not belong to the above mentioned industry associations and Abbey Life itself is not a member. From time to time attempts have been made to create an industry-wide association (the principal stumbling block is the LOA commission agreement) or alternatively an association of companies mainly engaged in the unit-linked sector of the market. In 1970 there was a proposal that a new association, provisionally called the Equity-linked and Property-linked Association be formed, the membership of which would be open to companies engaged in the unit-linked sector of the market and the objectives would be similar to those of the LOA. This proposal has aroused considerable interest but the formation of the association has not yet been proceeded with. The ability of associations of this type to regulate the industry is not high because the ultimate sanction upon an individual member (expulsion from membership) has not proved an effective deterrent. However, the purpose of the LOA is not principally one of regulation (except in the specific area of commissions) and its effectiveness need not therefore be judged against this criterion.

3. Matters for self-regulation

In our view there is considerable scope for industry self-regulation and indeed company self-regulation, in the areas of management of assets, conflicts of interest, pecuniary advantage and standards of behaviour. The type of self-regulation involved is either an industry-wide agreement that certain practices be controlled or prohibited or else a stated company position to that effect, coupled with a requirement that disclosure of all the relevant factors be made on a regular basis.

4. Disclosure and unit-linked life assurance

There is one particular facet of a unit-linked life assurance policy which requires a degree of disclosure to *policyholders* over and above that which is appropriate for a conventional life assurance policy and in addition to the increased disclosure which we have recommended earlier for all life assurance schemes. This unique feature arises from the particular nature of the policy which is that the policyholder or intending policyholder has entered or will enter into his contract on the basis of a sales presentation in which a range of investment assumptions may have been incorporated (leading to a range of potential benefits) and the policyholder is therefore entitled to expect regular reporting on the reasonableness of the initial assumptions in the light of the achieved investment performance.

5. Attempts at self-regulation

The subject matter which has been included in the attempts by groups of companies, mostly in the unit-linked sector of the market, to introduce self-regulation can be broadly categorized as follows:

a. *Items having specific reference to unit-linked contracts:*

  i. *Investment material:* evaluation of unit price performance, analysis of investment income and capital appreciation, identity of investment managers, valuation procedures, investment policy (e.g., attitude to property development, etc.) and changes therein, commentary on investment markets and outlook, liquidity, evidence of existence and ownership of stated securities and a full analysis of the portfolio (sufficient to allow a full and fair appraisal by policyholders or intending policyholders) are all items which would be covered by this heading.

  ii. *Conflicts of interest:* dealings by the company in units of the unit-fund, equitable issuance of new units and cancellation of old units and equitable valuation practices are typical items which would be covered by this heading.

  iii. *Financial benefit: management charges:* a full report on the accrual and extraction of proper management charges as defined in the policy or some other binding document is essential.

b. *Items having an industry-wide significance*

  i. *Marketing standards:* modern codes of conduct include a full description of the standards to which an agent/broker should comply.

  ii. *Conflicts of interest:* acquisitions from or investments in associates or sales to associates, are either expressly forbidden or controlled with adequate requirements for disclosure.

iii. *Financial benefit:* pecuniary advantages arising from direct or indirect involvement with the unit-fund or arising in an otherwise relevant manner, such as commissions or brokerage payable to associates out of the unit-fund, have to be disclosed.

6. Industry codes of conduct

The discussions mentioned earlier led to the first industry code published in July 1970 by a number of unit-linked companies. This had to do with the items described in the section above on disclosure and specifically sought to limit the possibility that conflicts of interest would arise. The Committee will no doubt have copies of this industry code which was entitled "A Code of Conduct". The use of the description industry code is perhaps misleading because although it can probably be described as a code it was certainly not industry-wide and indeed the relatively small number of signatories did not legally undertake to comply with its conditions. However, the signatories represented a material proportion (perhaps a major proportion) of the unit-linked business being issued at that time and Abbey Life was amongst their number. Arising partly out of the resolution that a new industry association be formed to which the unit-linked life assurance companies could apply for membership, and partly out of a resolution by the Steering Committee of that embryo organisation (to which Abbey Life belongs) that, although they were not yet in a position to proceed with the establishment of an association, nonetheless their grouping represented a major part of the unit-linked business currently being written, a new attempt at the formulation of a satisfactory industry code has been made. This new code is contained in the evidence submitted by the Steering Committee of the proposed Equity-linked and Property-linked Association (in the drafting of which Abbey Life played a part) and we have the permission of the Chairman of the Steering Committee to make reference to it.

The most notable feature of this new code is that, besides including and indeed improving upon the Code of Conduct published in July 1970, for the first time specific reference is made to the marketing of unit-linked assurance policies and the formulation of an ethical code of marketing standards has been attempted.

The Committee will note, however, that in spite of our reference to the involvement of Abbey Life in the formulation of this new code nonetheless

Abbey Life does not appear amongst the names of the various signatories to that submission of evidence. The reasons for this are various and do not reflect adversely upon the standards laid down in that new Code of Conduct. Principally we feel that the proposed Association has not yet received the broad support of the major companies engaged in the issuance of unit-linked business and hence it would not be proper at this stage to proceed with the establishment of a formal association. Following from this, and coupled with our judgement of the likelihood that member companies would in any event wish to provide the Committee with individual submissions of evidence, we doubted the wisdom of a combined submission of evidence of this type. Indeed we understand that the letter accompanying the Steering Committee submission of evidence indicates that a degree of compromise has been involved and that member companies are free to demonstrate any issues where their views are at variance with those agreed as being the majority opinion when they are considering their own submission of evidence to the Committee. For these reasons, and only partially because we believe the terms of the code could be further improved did we express to the Steering Committee our preference for not being named as a signatory. One aspect of all codes formulated this far, which has been causing us concern, is that, in the absence of any Industry Association (pre-supposing the effectiveness which such a body could introduce), there is a notable lack of any enforceability or indeed independent reporting. These codes do not generally receive wide publicity nor are they legally a part of the contractual relationship of the company with its policyholder. The industry, including the conventional offices, have given much consideration to this matter and we understand that the majority opinion is heavily against the concept of "trusteeship." In this matter we have deliberated at length amongst ourselves and with our contacts in the industry and feel as a result that the balance of argument is against a formal relationship of this type (which can broadly be described as a parallel to the position of a trustee of a unit trust fund). We have touched on this subject earlier in our submission of evidence and we have already noted the relevant factors.

Notwithstanding our rejection of the "trustee" concept we are not altogether confident that the industry codes of conduct have reached the stage of development that they eventually will and we have therefore continued to explore and shall continue to explore the possibility of incorporating an element of enforceability and a degree of independent reporting.

7. Future development

The development of industry agreements and the lack of any industry authority which can regulate them has led Abbey Life to explore the possibility of enforceable self-regulation as perhaps providing the best solution to questions of the type mentioned and we are becoming increasingly convinced that in the present circumstances this objective is the one to be pursued.

The most promising avenue to explore in the search for enforceability, both for reasons of convenience and realism, would appear to be the possible expansion of the non-statutory functions performed by the Auditors of the unit fund (which are at present confined to a Report upon some only of the financial aspects of the operations of the unit fund) to include, so far as their professional organisations will permit, all of the aspects of the operations of the unit fund which fall into this category.

We are presently engaged in discussions with our own Auditors with a view to seeing precisely what additional non-statutory functions they might realistically be able to perform and hence in what manner the Auditors' Certificate which appears in the Annual Reports of our unit funds might be made more comprehensive.

At this stage in our discussions it seems likely that there will be some items that cannot be covered. These will probably include:

a. Marketing.
b. Aggrieved policyholder redress.

However, it seems to us that the possible extra involvement by the Auditors will prove to have a distinctly measurable impact. Items on which they seem likely to be able to give a certificate include:

a. Report on conflicts of interest.
b. Equity of unit price calculation methods and consistency thereof with policy or other documentation.
c. Dealings in units of the unit fund by the Company.
d. Formulation of the necessary (and increased) amount of financial information to be included in the Annual Report.

In addition, and as a beneficial by-product, the increased exposure of the Auditors to the affairs of the Company and their awareness of the Company's standards will make them both well-suited and well-placed to provide the Company with any comments on an informal basis which they feel to be appropriate and which have relevance to the wider aspects of the Company's behaviour upon which they are not formally required to comment.

8. Summary and conclusions

There is considerable scope for self-regulation by the industry or by its member companies in the areas that do not lend themselves to explicit legislation. It is common practice that unit-linked companies regularly disclose the nature and activities of their unit funds. Codes of conduct have been devised for this purpose by groups of companies and these will be further improved and extended in the future. Abbey Life itself is considering the incorporation of a regular certificate by an independent party in its annual reports.

Accordingly, based upon these considerations, Abbey Life concludes:

> that there are important aspects of the activities of life assurance companies which do not readily lend themselves to explicit regulation and that self-regulation, either on an industry or company basis, and disclosure can be an effective substitute, and indeed the industry, particularly the unit-linked sector thereof, as evidenced by recent actions, has indicated its intention to further this process.

Securities and Exchange Commission Proceedings on Variable Life Insurance

Testimony given on May 3, 1972.

Mr. Chairman, Gentlemen:

Variable life insurance was introduced in 1956 in The Netherlands and has developed extensively in several countries, notably the United Kingdom, during the past sixteen years. Because I have been personally involved in these developments in several countries I have been asked by a major client of my firm to offer this testimony on a subject which is of interest to practically all of our 100 life insurance company clients.

1. The Development of Variable Life Insurance in Other Countries

a. Types of Products

The earliest form of variable life insurance (frequently called unit linked life insurance) was introduced in The Netherlands in 1956 by the Maatschappij van Levensverzekering op Basis van Belegging in Aandelen de Waerdye. The type of contract introduced by that company was identical in all respects to a traditional life insurance contract except that all sums, instead of being expressed in terms of Dutch currency, were expressed in terms of "fractions," the name given to units of an internal fund maintained by the company and invested in ordinary shares. Similar products were soon introduced by other companies in The Netherlands but after an initial period of considerable interest these products failed to capture a major share of the Dutch life insurance market, an event for which there were two primary reasons: (1) the commission rates offered on these products were significantly lower than commissions offered on corresponding products of a traditional type; (2) since the products provided that all amounts were expressed in units, the required premium fluctuated in accordance with changes in the value of the units.

The major development of variable life insurance soon transferred to the United Kingdom where the earliest products were introduced in 1957 by the London & Manchester Assurance Company Limited and by the London & Edinburgh Life Insurance Company Limited. Two immediate changes in the original products were made in the United Kingdom—the adoption of commission rates comparable to those applicable to corresponding conventional products, and the introduction of plans which provided for variable benefits but fixed premiums. A few years later it became the general practice to offer a guaranteed minimum death benefit and, later still, many companies introduced guaranteed minimum maturity values and a few companies introduced guaranteed minimum surrender values.

Variable life insurance appeared next in the Republic of South Africa and in Canada and developments in these countries have been much influenced by the experience of companies operating in the U. K. as well as in these countries. The fundamental concept underlying variable life insurance has been described by G. L. Melville, B.A., F.I.A., A.S.A., in a paper entitled "The Unit Linked Approach to Life Insurance" submitted to the Institute of Actuaries of Australia and New Zealand in September, 1969 and to the Institute of Actuaries of Great Britain in April, 1970. In Mr. Melville's view, the unit linked approach introduces a new method of surplus distribution to the life insurance industry.

This fundamental concept has now been refined in several ways and a wide variety of schemes is now generally available, particularly in the U. K. The introduction to the *Equity Linked Life Assurance Tables* published by Stone & Cox (Publications) Ltd. (published 1970) states: "In practice, in the U. K. anyway, the sum assured on death will be expressed partially in money terms or will be subject to a guaranteed minimum in money terms, so every equity linked assurance policy is to a minor extent a compromise with traditional assurance expressed throughout in money terms. Some are compromises to much more than a minor extent and the line that separates the equity linked from the with profits life policy is indistinct at times." This quotation is included to indicate that in the U. K. at least variable life insurance is widely regarded as generally comparable to with profits (participating) life insurance.

For nearly ten years after the introduction of the first variable life insurance contracts, the form of the policies offered was practically always comparable either to endowment policies or to deferred annuities. In 1965 variable life insurance policies of a single premium whole life type were introduced in the U. K. market. More recently, plans designed to provide higher life insurance protection, comparable perhaps to whole life policies, have been introduced.

All of the foregoing types of contracts are available with a variety of investment links. Originally, most variable life insurance policies were linked to an external unit trust (mutual fund), usually but not always managed by interests closely identified with the underwriting life insurance company. With the advent of single premium policies in 1965 it became more common to link the policies to an internal fund and this is now the most common investment vehicle. Originally, most internal funds were invested in ordinary shares and were generally comparable to unit trusts. Soon thereafter, several companies established funds invested in real property and still later funds invested in a mixture of equities and real property and sometimes fixed interest securities were introduced.

Two aspects of the variable life insurance as offered in the United Kingdom are worth special mention. Firstly, the internal funds are not "separate accounts" as that term is understood in the United States; the internal fund is descriptive only and the holder of a variable life insurance policy does not acquire any better title to a share in the assets making up the unit fund than he would have under the conventional scheme or, indeed, than a holder of a conventional policy issued by the same company. Secondly, the investment performance of the unit fund is a means of defining the liability of the life insurance company, which has no obligation actually to invest in the unit fund and may choose to invest differently and underwrite the investment risk involved for its own account.

In The Netherlands and in South Africa the commonest form of variable life insurance policies is also of the endowment type whereas in Canada the commonest form is of the deferred annuity type. These variations relate primarily to differences in tax treatment of life insurance policies and annuity contracts but it is noteworthy that both forms are ones which emphasize the savings element as opposed to the protection element.

b. Marketing Methods

In all countries where variable life insurance policies are available they are sold by the same marketing methods as conventional life insurance policies. There are, however, differences in emphasis, notably in the United Kingdom where companies specializing in the sale of variable life insurance have tended to adopt more aggressive marketing techniques than competitive companies. Also in the United Kingdom non-agency selling, a term generally applied to marketing methods involving no intermediaries, have assumed greater prominence in connection with variable life insurance which is extensively advertised, with application forms attached to the advertisement, and is also sold by direct mailing of sales literature accompanied by an application form.

The marketing methods of the life insurance industry have been the subject of much controversy and considerable criticism both within the industry and outside it. The considerable success of variable life insurance in the U. K., which has led to the adoption of more aggressive marketing techniques by several companies, has focused public, press and Government attention on the marketing methods of the industry and has given rise to several criticisms. Upon examination these criticisms would appear at least to be exaggerated or at most to be entirely misdirected.

c. Market Acceptance

The market acceptance of variable life insurance has been exceedingly good. To quote Mr. Melville, "In each country the position is the same — a remarkably favorable response from the public, particularly in the last few years, causing urgent reassessment of previously held views, sometimes, unfortunately, most widely and eloquently recorded!"

The Life Offices' Association in the U. K., together with the Associated Scottish Life Offices and the Linked Life Assurance Group have undertaken to compile statistics concerning linked life assurance and annuity business in the U. K. These statistics show the rapid development in the sale of variable life insurance and annuities during the period 1961-1970. New annual premiums are shown as increasing from a negligible amount prior to 1963 to more than $65 million in 1970 and I would estimate that when the figures for 1971 are compiled they will indicate total sales of $90 million of annual premiums. Single premium sales have increased even more spectacularly from a negligible amount prior to 1965 to $140 million for the year 1970 and when statistics for the year 1971 are compiled I expect that the total sales of single premium policies for that year will exceed $300 million. At the end of 1970 the number of variable life insurance and annuity policies of all types stood at 950,000 and I expect that statistics will show this to be 1,300,000 policies at the end of 1971.

These statistics indicate that variable life insurance now represents more than 25% of industry sales of annual premium policies and, conceivably, the 1971 statistics will show considerably more than 25%; variable life insurance policies represent more than 50% of all single premium policies sold and the 1971 statistics will surely show that this figure has advanced considerably above 50%.

Variable life insurance in The Netherlands has not achieved as great a market acceptance as in the U. K. but the growth is nevertheless noteworthy. For 1969 the total premiums for variable life insurance (both new and renewal premiums) was $11 million and the total for 1970 was $16 million. The latter figure probably represents approximately 5% of the individual ordinary premium income in The Netherlands for that year, but, measured by new business, variable life insurance probably is responsible for 10% to 15% of all individual ordinary business in The Netherlands.

Statistics on the sale of variable life insurance in Canada are sketchy but a report of a June, 1971 discussion at a meeting of the Canadian Institute of Actuaries includes an estimate that 10% to 20% of new individual ordinary products are of the variable type. I would personally incline towards the lower end of this range. Authoritative information concerning the acceptance of variable life insurance in South Africa is not available but a representative of the Office of the Registrar of Insurance in Pretoria, South Africa, estimates that the percentage of annual premium life assurance business of this type is now of "significant proportion".

2. The Future Role of Variable Life Insurance

a. Consumer Needs

The case to support the social desirability of life insurance often has been made. One of the most persuasive of the arguments in support of this thesis is afforded by the laws of most western countries (notable exceptions are the United States and Canada) which encourage the purchase of life insurance by offering a variety of tax concessions to individuals who do so.

The 1971 *Life Insurance Fact Book* states:

> People buy life insurance for a variety of reasons, but the main one is to provide financial protection for their families in case they themselves should die prematurely. A man creates or adds to his estate immediately when he buys a life insurance policy, and he protects the future of that estate as he maintains his policy over the years.

The same source also indicates the kind of life insurance policies Americans are buying; more than 50% of the amount of individual ordinary life insurance purchased in 1970 related to "permanent" plans of insurance — ones providing for the accumulation of substantial amounts of savings. Statistics are not shown on the basis of premium income but it is reasonable to assume that about 80% of the new premium income related to these same kinds of policies.

Although the main reason for buying life insurance is to provide financial protection in the event of premature death, the fact remains that the investment results achieved on the savings accumulation which is inherent can substantially affect the cost of that protection or the amount of protection which is ultimately afforded. If the means can be found to permit policyholders' funds to be invested more effectively, considerable benefits arise — policyholders will enjoy the same benefits for a lower price or greater benefits for the same price, and it is likely (as indicated by the experience in other countries) that a more attractive return per dollar of premium will induce a larger number of people to provide for their own and their family's security through this form of long term, systematic savings. Both of these developments have occurred in the U. K. since the widespread introduction of variable life insurance.

I believe, and I think that most observers believe, that the American public has become in recent years more conscious of the impact of inflation upon their savings and more convinced that continuing inflation is probable. This same phenomenon occurred approximately 20 years ago in Europe and may account for the earlier interest in that part of the world in forms of accumulating capital which afforded some offset to the effect of future inflation. According to the 1971 edition of *Best's Insurance Reports* the net yield of the life insurance industry as a whole was 5.3% in 1970 and 5.12% in 1969. Considering the corresponding inflation rates for these two periods the "real rate of interest" was zero or less, and if it is assumed that the policyholder will bear some tax on his so-called "gain" his real rate of return after taxes is indeed negative. Under these circumstances it is not surprising that there has been a trend for many years away from permanent forms of life insurance, which include a substantial savings accumulation, towards term insurance, where the savings element is negligible. This trend shows up unmistakably in the statistics. During 1955 the assets of the United States life insurance companies (net of policy loans) increased by approximately $5 billion, 30% of the total income received that year; during 1970 the assets of the industry increased by approximately $8 billion, only 16% of the total income received that year.

b. The Economics of Variable Life Insurance

The earliest experience with variable life insurance in The Netherlands represented an attempt to market variable life insurance on a significantly different economic basis from conventional life insurance. This attempt was unsuccessful. In all countries where these products are successful, the economics from an expense standpoint are essentially the same as those applicable to conventional life insurance.

This result should not particularly be surprising since the economics of all forms of life insurance, variable or conventional, must be essentially similar if the marketing methods employed are the same. Only if a significantly different amount of sales effort is required to produce a given volume can there be any major change in the established economics of the business.

It is important to note that the economics of the life insurance industry are geared to serving the needs of a customer who typically spends $300 per year, or more likely $25 per month, on a life insurance policy. Necessarily the economics of the business require that a significant portion of each premium (particularly the early premiums) be used to cover the substantial costs incurred in the sale and issuance of the contract. The economics of the security business, on the other hand, are designed to cover the situation of an investor who might typically make a lump sum purchase involving $5,000 and a much smaller portion is required to cover the related expenses. It is desirable that life insurance protection be available to a broad sector of the public at a reasonable cost but this result, I submit, is not likely to be achieved by the adoption of unrealistic limitations on the expenses which may be charged against premiums paid by policyholders regardless of which type of policy they buy, variable or conventional. Experience shows that it is no simple task to persuade an individual to set aside a substantial portion of his current income to make provision for future financial needs for his family or himself. As long as this remains true, as seems likely, the expenses associated with the provision of life insurance protection are likely to remain relatively high by comparison with other savings media. The introduction of variable life insurance may affect the economics of the industry to a limited extent; this will happen provided such products are more attractive to potential buyers than conventional products thus making it possible to secure a larger volume of business with the same effort. If this happens, I believe that competitive forces can be relied upon to reduce the cost of life insurance protection since there are few industries where free competition is as widespread as in the life insurance industry.

c. The Significance to the National Economy

Recognition of the importance of the life insurance industry in the national economy is widespread throughout the western world. This recognition is reflected in the strenuous and spreading attempts by Governments of many countries to insure that their life insurance industries will operate in a manner suitable to the national interest. In some cases, such as India, this has taken the form of nationalization of the industry; in other cases, including Canada,

Japan and South Africa, this has taken the form of enacting legislation to limit foreign ownership of life insurance companies operating in those countries; in numerous other cases this has taken the form of adopting administrative restraints with the same effect. This worldwide concern for the control of the life insurance industry in various countries is a striking example of the importance attached to the industry by government.

One does not have to look far for the explanation of this attitude. Statistics are readily available to demonstrate the role of the life insurance industry in the capital markets of most western countries. But the importance of the industry is even greater than would appear from the simple comparisons involving total assets, or the acquisitions of capital issues during any given period: the industry is one of few which enjoys a reliable net cash inflow, even during periods of severe economic adversity, and this permits the industry to invest its funds primarily on a long term basis.

It's predictable that if the life insurance industry were permitted to enter the variable life insurance market on a reasonable basis, the flow of funds to the industry would probably increase, and might increase substantially. This has certainly been the result in the United Kingdom and most informed observers have predicted a similar trend in other such countries where these products can be sold. It is also probable that the sale of variable life insurance products would produce a consistent flow of funds rather than the fluctuating ebb and flow which occur in other savings media where short term savings and investment objectives prevail. These developments must have a positive effect on the national economy and, perhaps, on security markets.

Opponents of variable life insurance have sometimes argued that widespread sales of such a product would fundamentally alter traditional capital flows by redirecting funds from debt to equity investments. This argument may have some validity but I would like to point out that it usually rests on the assumption that the savings accumulation under variable life insurance policies will be invested primarily or exclusively in common stocks. Recent trends in the United Kingdom indicate a movement of public favor towards funds invested in real property or funds invested in a mixture of common stocks, real property and fixed interest securities.

3. Regulation of Variable Insurance in Other Countries

a. Insurance Regulation versus Securities Regulation, the Significance of Guarantees

In the U. K., The Netherlands, and South Africa variable life insurance is regulated as life insurance and is not subject to securities regulation. In general, the regulation of the life insurance industry in the U. K. is minimal and companies enjoy more or less complete freedom to market such products as they wish at such prices as they see fit and to invest the resulting funds without restriction. Responsibility for enforcing the relevant legislation applicable to life insurance companies is in the hands of the Department of Trade and Industry which has extensive powers to prevent unauthorized insurers from carrying on business, to obtain information from insurers as to their position and to undertake proceedings to wind up companies failing to meet required solvency margins.

The regulatory position in The Netherlands is similar to that of the U. K. except that the Verzekeringskamer (Insurance Chamber) is much more active in its supervision of the industry and although in theory it has little real authority, in practice its right to publish "advices" gives it very considerable influence.

In Canada, the various securities commissions have taken the view that variable life insurance is a security but agreement has been reached to exempt certain classes of variable life insurance policies from the applicable securities regulations provided the policies are in accordance with agreed guidelines. The key distinction in the question of guarantees — the Ontario Securities Commission, for example, will exempt variable life insurance policies from their jurisdiction if there is a minimum maturity guarantee of 75% of the premiums paid and a minimum death benefit guarantee of 100% of the premiums paid. This distinction between guaranteed and non-guaranteed contracts may be directly relevant to the U. S. It is also noteworthy that the Superintendent of Insurance of Canada has promulgated guidelines dealing with variable life insurance contracts which tend to limit the extent to which companies can include guarantees in their contracts. The contrast in regulatory approach between the Securities Commissions and the Department of Insurance is one which recurs in other jurisdictions — one regulatory agency tending to promote guarantees, the other to limit them.

b. Disclosure Requirements and Practices

Sales literature is not subject to screening in either the U. K. or The Netherlands and companies are free to act as they see fit. The same applies to advertising. In practice, flagrant violations would probably be brought to the attention of regulatory authorities and steps would likely be taken to prevent a repetition of objectionable practices. As a practical matter, there have been no such complaints to the best of my knowledge.

In the U. K. the industry itself has attempted to develop a self-regulating code of conduct dealing with sales material and advertising and this appears to have gained widespread acceptance by the industry, the public and the press.

In Canada, variable life insurance policies not exempt from the securities regulation may be sold only when accompanied by a prospectus approved by the Securities Commission. Exempt contracts may be sold only on the basis of an information circular, the contents of which are similar to a prospectus, which must be approved by the provincial Insurance Department following prior review by the Canadian Life Insurance Association.

c. Limitations on Charges

In the U. K., The Netherlands, Canada and South Africa no limitations on charges are imposed either by law or by regulation. In fact, in The Netherlands the situation is rather the reverse as the Verzekeringskamer is more concerned about the adequacy of premium rates than about the amount charged to the policyholder and would object to rates considered to be too low.

In one instance, Australia, a limitation on charges for variable life insurance has been imposed by the Insurance Commissioner which results in available margins for expenses which are considerably lower than those applicable to conventional life insurance. Although the guidelines were promulgated in Australia more than two years ago it is significant to note that not one company has introduced an individual variable life insurance product despite widespread interest within the industry. Very approximately, the limitations on charges included in the Australian guidelines are 40% of the amount provided for charges on conventional life insurance.

d. Agent Licensing

In the United Kingdom there is no requirement that an agent or broker selling life insurance be licensed. By contrast, unit trusts (mutual funds) may not be sold through intermediaries other than stockbrokers. In The Netherlands and in Canada there is a system of agent licensing similar to that prevalent in the U. S. except that a license authorizes an agent to sell both variable life insurance and conventional life insurance. In The Netherlands mutual fund salesmen need not be licensed; the position in Canada is similar to that in the United States.

e. Recent Developments in the United Kingdom

In February, 1971 the Secretary of State for Trade and Industry announced the formation of a departmental committee, under the chairmanship of Sir Hilary Scott, with the following terms of reference:

> To consider the working of the Insurance Companies Acts 1958-67, and of the Prevention of Fraud (Investments) Act 1958, insofar as the latter is relevant, in the light of life assurance schemes involving the issue of equity-linked polices, unit linked policies, property bonds and similar schemes and to advise on the adequacy of the protection afforded by these Acts to policyholders in these schemes.

This Committee, which has become generally known as the Scott Committee, has sought and received written evidence from interested parties, including individual life insurance companies, industry associations, prominent individuals, professional bodies and the London Stock Exchange. The scope of its inquiry would appear to be limited to questions involving variable life insurance and, particularly, the possible application of the basic legislation of the securities business to this type of life insurance. Many commentators have advanced the view, with which I agree, that the scope of the inquiry is too limited; in this connection, the *Financial Times* on May 26, 1971, commented on the terms of reference as follows:

> The reasons for confining the scrutiny (of the Committee) to just this form of assurance and not, say, including conventional 'with profits' contracts from the traditional life offices, have not been made clear.

Many of the viewpoints which have been advanced have received widespread publicity and, judging by these reports, there is a considerable difference of opinion as to what the Committee should recommend. At this stage it is impossible to forecast what the findings and recommendations of the Committee will be.

4. Recommendations for Regulation of Variable Life Insurance in the United States

From my experience with variable life insurance in other countries I am convinced that the success or failure of that business in the United States is dependent directly upon the regulatory environment. I am convinced that public acceptance would be high, as it has been in other countries, provided that reasonably simple products can be brought to the market, sold by the methods traditional to the industry on the basis of realistic economics which recognize that the great majority of potential buyers need and can only afford a periodic premium of a relatively modest amount. I am also convinced that variable life insurance is a desirable product from the viewpoint of both the potential buyer and society in general.

Given these convictions, I am anxious that the regulatory climate for these products be one which will foster their development. In my opinion, the essential requirements are as follows:

a. That variable life insurance not be subject to substantial regulation by both Federal securities legislation and State insurance legislation. Although such products bear a relationship to both the securities and the life insurance industries, the nature of the products and the consumer needs which are to be served relate more closely to the life insurance industry and it would seem appropriate, therefore, that this be the major prevailing regulation. This result can probably be achieved through the extension of exemptions from aspects of the Federal securities legislation as proposed by the ALC-LIAA.

b. That the emphasis of regulation be placed upon disclosure requirements rather than upon direct limitation of charges. This is also consistent with the ALC-LIAA proposal.

c. That considerable latitude be allowed in the design of variable life insurance products qualifying for exemption. In particular, the inclusion of minimum guarantees upon death, maturity and possibly surrender are constructive additions to these products and might reasonably be the basis upon which exemptions are granted. In this connection, the proposal of the ALC-LIAA suggests that the design of products be further limited and would exclude policies of the endowment type, and also of the single premium type, the two most popular forms in those countries which now permit the sale of variable life insurance.

The ALC-LIAA petition would seem to afford a reasonable basis for a beginning of the variable life insurance in the United States and I would urge the adoption of this proposal by the Commission.

The Universal Life Insurance Policy

Published in EMPHASIS *in November 1975. Reprinted with permission from Tillinghast - A Towers Perrin Company.*

Editor's note: This issue of EMPHASIS *breaks with tradition, since it represents not the collective view of the staff of Tillinghast & Company but the outlook of an individual staff member. James C. H. Anderson, president of the firm, presented the paper from which this article is taken before the Seventh Pacific Insurance Conference in September 1975. Mr. Anderson's approach is provocative, and his perceptions may be controversial to some; but, in the current climate of concern over the future of the life insurance industry's traditional products and distribution systems, they deserve careful consideration. Here, then, is one man's blueprint for a "universal" life insurance policy — for what the author calls "a fully flexible alternative to conventional life insurance contracts, designed to meet the needs and demands of the life insurance market in 1975 and beyond."*

Purpose and Scope

The purpose of this paper is not to present a revolutionary new concept; instead, it is to reexamine a familiar concept in the light of new market circumstances and to consider the consequences to the life insurance industry if the concept were adopted.

In summary, this paper advances the following arguments:

. . . that it is no longer realistic to assume that the typical life insurance buyer is one who will, for an extended period of time, remain married to the same wife, work at the same job and live in the same house situated in the same city; or that the financial security needs of this typical buyer and his ability to pay for them will remain constant and can be expressed in constant nominal dollars.

. . . that it is not realistic for the industry to address the needs of the typical buyer with traditional permanent life insurance products requiring fixed regular premiums and providing fixed benefits, both expressed in constant nominal dollars.

. . . that the traditional life insurance industry distribution and administrative systems are excessively and unnecessarily costly and place the industry at a competitive disadvantage by comparison with other savings media.

. . . that the industry should respond to the needs of the contemporary market by introducing a simplified, flexible and less costly product.

. . . that the introduction of such a product is technically and financially feasible if a more effective distribution system can concurrently be developed.

. . . that the introduction of such a product would probably have a serious and adverse initial impact on the life insurance industry and its existing distribution systems.

. . . that, notwithstanding the foreseen difficulties, the needs and demands of the market will lead to the introduction of such a product, possibly led by companies with no commitment to traditional distribution systems, and that the eventual result will be more favorable to the life insurance industry than the only realistic alternative — an all-term industry.

Obviously, these are sweeping arguments and they imply nothing less than a coming revolution within the life insurance industry. The limited scope of this paper does not permit their full development, nor does it permit adequate consideration of counterarguments. This paper is intended to apply to the individual financial security market and general environment of the United States; its application to other countries of the Pacific Rim is limited, sometimes significantly, by differences in the environment.

The Market in 1975 and Beyond

What are the important differences between contemporary market conditions and those of the past? Much could be said on the subject of changed and changing market conditions; so much, in fact, that it is essential to limit this review to an identification of those continuing changes most likely to impact the life insurance industry, its products and its distribution systems.

First, there are the changes of a social nature. Changes in attitudes toward marriage and the family are perhaps the most fundamental of these. These changes are manifested in an increase in the number of single and divorced persons and a decrease in the number of children in the average family. Frequent change of employment, often accompanied by relocation, also is a characteristic of contemporary society. Changes are apparent in social attitudes which play an important role in motivating people to provide for their own and their families' financial security: evidence of a decline in the desire for self-reliance can be seen in the increasing dependence upon employer-sponsored and Government-sponsored financial security programs. Changes are also apparent in public confidence in institutions ranging from Government to financial companies which must depreciate the value attached to long-term contractual promises such as life insurance policies. Notable changes have occurred in the general level of education of the public at large (accompanied, arguably, by an associated increase in their ability to evaluate critically the insurance industry, its products and their cost).

Second, there are the changes of an economic nature. Perhaps the most important of these is the significant increase in family income levels, contributed to by the growing economic importance of working women and the associated trend toward two income families; clearly, the typical family today can afford and needs more financial security products than ever before. Major changes are also apparent in the much higher interest rates prevalent today and in the accelerated rate of inflation, both of which impact the motivation to save and the choice of savings vehicle. Finally, there is the much increased complexity and interdependence of all economic activities, with increased risk of instability and economic dislocation, an example of which is the present high level of unemployment.

Third, there are the changes relating to the industry itself. Competition for savings among various financial institutions has intensified. The recent and continuing experience of the life insurance industry with increasing policy loans and the recent experience of the thrift institutions with disintermediation have raised new problems in the area of investment management for both kinds of institutions, and have adversely affected their competitive position in the savings market. Except on tax-qualified products, life insurance companies are at a competitive disadvantage because the progressively increasing tax burden on investment earnings is effectively borne by policyholders; unless legislative relief is obtained, this trend will accelerate as the 10-for-1 rule is applied to progressively wider differentials between earned and valuation rates.

Outdated legislation relating to minimum reserves and nonforfeiture values has also limited the extent to which higher interest rates can be reflected in lower premiums on non-participating life insurance. Maintenance expenses, which have remained stable for many years despite inflationary pressures, are now rising significantly as the rate of inflation has over-taken economies of scale and computerization; if present trends continue, as seems likely, this will become a major industry problem.

Fourth, there are the changes of a political nature. Government-sponsored benefits have increased dramatically in both scale and scope and now include built-in inflation adjustments which ensure that the increases will continue for the foreseeable future. Consumer and environmental interests of an organized nature represent a major new political force which has already altered national priorities and now threatens directly to affect the life insurance industry. The traditional gap between political and economic logic is widening. One major consequence of these political changes is increased levels of taxation — particularly Social Security, state and local taxes.

How, then, can the resultant market environment in 1975 and beyond be described? In summary, it is one in which family and financial circumstances can be expected to change more frequently and more extensively than in the past; a market more sophisticated and more cynical than its predecessors; a market with increased need for financial security products and increased ability to pay for them; an increasingly competitive market, particularly as related to other savings media; a market in which long-term commitments are substantially affected by inflation; a market in which life insurance companies are subject to growing financial pressures arising from consumer interests, unreasonable taxes, increasing maintenance expenses, and outdated legislation; a market in which further Government intervention is to be expected, along with steady pressures for increased taxation of both policyholder and shareholder earnings.

Traditional Products and Distribution

Having reviewed the factors affecting the contemporary life insurance market, it is appropriate next to examine the way in which the industry today addresses the market.

Overwhelmingly, the majority of financial security products sold to individuals by the life insurance industry are of the traditional type, characterized by the requirement of regular premiums of a fixed dollar amount and providing benefits of a fixed dollar amount. Most of the premium income arising from current sales will relate to permanent forms of life insurance. With few exceptions, these products are not responsive to changing circumstances. The multiplicity of plans, issue ages, rate tables, dividend scales, and nonforfeiture values create a vast array of unique cells, each a stereotype, which lends itself only tortuously to change by conversion to another stereotype with similar characteristics. Limited flexibility is afforded, but rather clumsily, by such features as premium and policy loans, nonforfeiture options, conversion rights and various optional attached benefits. Although policies offering increasing or decreasing benefits and policies requiring increasing or decreasing premiums are available, these are merely additional stereotypes which attempt to anticipate future financial needs and ability to pay, generally unsuccessfully. Too often, flexibility is expensively achieved by lapsing one stereotyped policy which has outlived its usefulness, sometimes replacing it with another stereotype which also will outlive its usefulness.

Considering the implications of inflation alone, it is clear that permanent life insurance products requiring fixed-dollar premiums and providing fixed dollar benefits are of limited value. Examine the case of a 25-year-old buyer with a young and growing family and an annual income of $10,000. Assuming only an annual productivity gain of 2%, he might expect an equivalent income at age 55 of $18,000; but if inflation should continue throughout that period at a rate of only 5%, his nominal annual income at age 55 would be $78,000. Does fixed-premium, fixed benefit, permanent life insurance have any relevance to this potential buyer's financial requirements over 30 years, even disregarding the major consequences of changing family circumstances, unemployment, or substantially greater increases in real earnings (all of which are more likely to occur than not)?

The life insurance industry markets its traditional products through its traditional distribution systems. The composition of these systems generally includes the soliciting agent, managers or general agents and supporting field staff. Although it is not easy to distinguish between full-time and part-time agents, it is clear that the sales frequency is quite low: probably on the order of 50 sales per year by the full-time equivalent agent of minimum acceptable standards. It is also clear that the costs of these distribution systems are quite high: for a typical mixture of individual business, a cost of 100% of first-year premiums and 7 1/2% of renewal premiums would probably be representative of the experience of medium-to-large companies; many companies experience higher rates. Depending upon the assumed persistency experience and the rate of interest used to redistribute first-year costs, the equivalent level annual cost of the distribution system is in the range of 20% to 25% of expected premiums.

Traditional life insurance products and distribution systems are also expensive to administer. On average, for medium-to-large companies, head office acquisition and overhead expenses of 50% of first-year premiums and maintenance expenses of 5% of all premiums would be representative, with an equivalent level annual cost in the range of 12 1/2% to 15% of expected premiums. Moreover, most policyholders own more than one policy and incur multiple maintenance costs.

Although the cost levels cited may be arguable and will vary, perhaps significantly, from company to company, the indicated equivalent level cost is in the range of 32 1/2% to 40% of expected premiums, to which must be added at least 21/2 % to cover premium taxes, resulting in aggregate costs in the range of 35% to 42 1/2% of expected premiums.

Although such an expense level, or even a higher level, is probably acceptable on the protection element of the premium, it compares most unfavorably with cost levels incurred by competing savings media unless substantial tax advantages not available on competing media are afforded to the policyholder as an offset to these costs.

One form of traditional life insurance warrants special mention: term insurance. Although term products are also stereotypes, they afford greater flexibility than permanent forms, at least for those who remain insurable; and cost levels are acceptable even to those who terminate early. Notwithstanding powerful counter-incentives afforded by typical commission scales, term insurance continues to capture an increasing share of the life insurance market.

It should be noted that not all of the products offered by the life insurance industry require regular fixed-dollar premiums and provide fixed-dollar benefits, nor are all types of products subject to the cost levels cited above. The Minnesota Mutual Life Insurance Company has for three years been marketing a type of "life-cycle" policy which it calls "Adjustable Life." The Minnesota Mutual plan is one which permits an adjustment of premium levels through a variation in the mix of term-type and permanent-type coverage. The face amount of the policy can also be increased or decreased but, once established, premiums and benefits remain fixed until another change is made. Another type of contract which has recently acquired considerable prominence is the flexible premium annuity which is used in the sale of tax-sheltered annuities and individual retirement accounts. These are generally simple accumulation plans which afford complete flexibility in the amount and interval of premium payment. Most variable annuities are a form of flexible premium annuity where the accumulation is based on the investment results of a unitized separate account. A few companies have introduced policies which contain cost-of-living adjustments, but these have not met with widespread success due, perhaps, to the conservative pricing bases which underlie them. With the exception of flexible premium annuities, which provide substantially lower commissions, these new products continue to be sold through the traditional distribution systems at traditional cost levels.

In summary, the industry response to the needs of the contemporary life insurance market has thus far involved no fundamental change in its traditional products and distribution systems, which are not well suited to the market's characteristics. Considering the cost levels involved in the distribution and the administration of these products, it appears unlikely that the industry can expect to maintain its share of the savings market; and a continued diminution of its market share seems more likely than not. Thus far, the industry response to the need for more flexible products has been quite limited; what new products have been introduced continue to be distributed and administered in the traditional manner.

Ideal Product Characteristics

Given the foregoing perception of the contemporary life insurance market, what are the characteristics of the product best suited to the needs and demands of that market?

The overriding need is for *flexibility*. At a minimum, the buyer should have the right to maintain his insurance protection intact, notwithstanding inflation. Ideally, he should be able to adjust his insurance protection upward or downward at any time, subject to reasonable conditions and without unreasonable cost or penalty. He should be able to make premium payments at his convenience, including the right to make lump-sum payments and to suspend payments, even for extended periods of time.

The next most important requirement is for substantial cost reductions as related to the savings element of the contract. To achieve this, a significant increase in the effectiveness of the distribution system is required, together with a major simplification of the product and the required administrative systems.

To increase the investment return on the savings element to competitive levels, to reduce federal income taxes levied on policyholder accumulations and to avoid problems arising from unreasonable requirements relating to nonforfeiture values and reserves, the ideal contract should be of the accumulation type. It should provide a guaranteed investment return limited to the statutory valuation interest rate, with a provision for payment of excess interest on a basis taxable to the policyholder and deductible without limit by the company. Thus, the form of contract indicated for the savings element resembles a flexible premium annuity with taxable excess interest credits (this may also afford premium tax savings in states which have lower tax rates for annuities).

The ideal contract must provide reasonable short-term benefits, even if payment is suspended in year one. For early suspensions, it is probably not practical to provide cash benefits, but extension of coverage probably is practical.

The ideal contract must realistically recognize economies of scale, but without attendant complications. This inevitably leads to the corollary that very small contracts cannot economically be sold on a compatible basis.

In summary, the characteristics of the ideal contract for the contemporary market are flexibility, reduced cost, simplicity and tax efficiency.

The Universal Life Insurance Policy

A specific product design possessing the characteristics described in the foregoing section is offered for purposes of discussion.

General Description: A flexible-premium annuity with a monthly renewable term insurance rider.

Loadings: Payments to the annuity are subject to a deduction ("load") of 10% of the first $5,000 of accumulative premium and 5% of excess amounts, plus applicable premium taxes. Maximum renewal term life premiums are equal to valuation net premiums (life and disability) to avoid deficiency reserves; the company's current rates (presumably lower) would actually be charged. For the first month the term premium is $1.00 per $1,000 greater.

Initial Premium: Minimum initial premium is $250 plus $1.00 per $1,000 initial amount of term life insurance.

Renewal Premiums: Subsequent premiums for the annuity may be paid at any time, subject to a minimum of $100. Regular payments by preauthorized check are subject to a minimum of $25. Term insurance premiums are paid only by withdrawal from the annuity fund.

Accumulation Basis: Annuity payments (less load and applicable premium taxes) are accumulated at a guaranteed interest rate of 4% (where equal to the maximum valuation interest rate) on amounts in excess of $250 (interest earned on the first $250 or less offsets maintenance expenses); excess interest is paid at the discretion of the company and is reported as such for tax purposes (thus permitting payment of gross interest).

Renewal Dating: Term life insurance will renew on a calendar-month basis with a pro-rata premium (plus $1.00 per $1,000) payable for the first calendar month.

Surrender Charge: A surrender charge of 5% of the amount by which the cumulative payments are less than $5,000 will apply.

Loans and Withdrawals: Policy loans are not available; a partial withdrawal may be made, but not less than $250 must remain in the annuity account.

Amounts of Insurance: Level amounts of term life insurance will apply prior to age 65, with automatic indexation available (CPI-based); at and after age 65, term life benefit reduces 1/35th of the level amount annually (indexing continues) and expires at age 100. Amounts of insurance may be decreased or, subject to evidence of insurability and a charge of $1.00 per $1,000 additional insurance, increased at any time.

Nonforfeiture Benefits: None; contract terminates 30 days after annuity fund is exhausted (this is to satisfy grace-period requirements).

Waiver of Premium: Term insurance premium is waived during total and permanent disability commencing prior to age 65 (three-month waiting period).

Multiple Lives: Term riders covering dependents are available on the same terms and may later be transferred to another annuity contract without evidence of insurability.

Existing Policies: Existing term and permanent policies may be converted without evidence of insurability by applying cash values to the annuity contract and effecting term life insurance for the net amount at risk under all contracts. Cash values so applied are subject to no load and are included in the accumulative premium to determine subsequent loads. Term insurance is issued at renewal premium rates.

Annual Statements: Policyholders will be furnished an annual statement on a calendar-year basis.

The foregoing is only one approach to the design of a contract with the desired characteristics. There is ample scope for variations in the form of the term life insurance, the loading pattern, the accumulation process, the availability of optional benefits and other features. It should be noted that the suggested design can provide any conceivable pattern of premium payment and coverage and thus can replace all other products. Hence, the Universal Life Insurance Policy.

It appears that the Universal Life Insurance Policy could be sold under existing regulation, although minor changes might be necessary in the suggested surrender charges on smaller policies to meet minimum cash value requirements in some states. There are also several unresolved questions relating to reserve requirements on flexible-premium contracts, and questions might arise as to the proper treatment of the proposed contract for purposes of determining applicable state premium taxes and federal income taxes. None of these regulatory uncertainties appears to be a major impediment to the introduction of the proposed contract.

Financial Considerations

Is the Universal Life Insurance Policy feasible from a financial viewpoint? To answer this question, pricing and profitability tests have been performed. They indicate that the answer is affirmative.

The pricing and profitability tests examine three cases: the profitability of the annuity standing alone; the competitiveness of the required term insurance premiums; and the profitability of no-load conversions of existing policies with allowance for payment of standard commissions. The results of the tests indicate that the proposed product is feasible, provided the company retains a 1% interest margin and provided the other underlying assumptions are realized. Several of the assumptions relate to areas where little or no experience exists or where the nature of the product is expected to alter typical experience; these deserve particular attention.

The assumed average premium is $500 for the first year; although this is higher than experienced on typical life insurance sales, the nature of the product and the minimum initial premium of $250 would tend to encourage higher premiums. In subsequent years, for those who do not suspend payment, it is assumed that premiums increase at a rate of 5% annually.

The assumed net suspension rates are comparable to the lapse rates which might be expected on life insurance business of reasonably good quality. The nature of the product, particularly the aspect of voluntary premium payment, might lead to higher suspension rates, especially in the early policy years; against this must be weighed the effect of resumed payments on previously suspended policies, which could lead to a near-zero net suspension rate in later policy years. It is also assumed that 50% of current net suspensions and 10% of previously suspended policies are surrendered each year and that partial withdrawals are equal to investment earnings credited. Although industry experience with other flexible premium contracts may not be closely comparable, judged by that standard the assumed suspension rates are rather optimistic and the assumed surrender and partial withdrawal rates are somewhat pessimistic.

Probably the most crucial of the assumptions are those relating to expenses. Maintenance expenses are assumed to be offset by investment earnings on the first $250 of accumulated funds; this allowance is comparable to maintenance expenses incurred on traditional life insurance products, and is probably adequate; the added cost of monthly premium accounting and annual statements to policyholders is offset by simplified accounting and the absence of premium notices. Initial processing and issue expenses are assumed to be $50 per policy, which is comparable to industry experience. Underwriting expenses are assumed to be offset by select mortality savings, which is probably an adequate, if simplistic, assumption. The controversial expense assumptions are those relating to distribution and overhead costs.

If the product is to be distributed through a traditional agency system, it is assumed that compensation to the soliciting agent is $100 per contract, 50¢ per $1,000 initial amount of insurance and 2-1/2% of all premiums paid. For various first-year premiums and amounts of insurance, this translates into the following equivalent first-year commission rates:

First-Year Premium	Initial Amount of Insurance	First-Year Commission	Commission Rate
$ 300	$ -0-	$107.50	35.8%
	30,000	122.50	40.8
500	-0-	112.50	22.5
	50,000	137.50	27.5
1,000	-0-	125.00	12.5
	100,000	175.00	17.5
1,500	-0-	137.50	9.2
	150,000	212.50	14.2

Clearly, these commission rates are very low in comparison with rates on traditional life insurance products, particularly for larger premiums. The suggested level of soliciting agent compensation is practical only if sales frequency increases substantially (an increase of 100% is probably required to maintain agent earnings at traditional levels).

Other sales and overhead expenses are assumed to be 100% of total agents' compensation. This is quite close to current industry experience, if other sales and overhead expenses are expressed as a function of agents' compensation. To the extent that such expenses relate to the management of the agency organization, as seems reasonable, the relationship between such expenses and aggregate agent compensation should not be significantly affected by the assumed increase in sales frequency.

Although the appropriateness of various of the assumptions may be argued, the central issue relates to the assumed level of distribution costs and the implication that agent productivity can be increased as required to maintain current income levels. Alternatively, the product might be distributed in an entirely different manner (for example, by a bank) at the cost levels suggested. Considering the distribution costs of other financial security products, such as mutual funds and savings accounts, it appears more likely than not that the suggested cost levels can be achieved, one way or the other. It is recognized that existing agency organizations would strongly resist the proposed compensation basis; this suggests that an entirely new distribution system might be required and, if that is the case, suggests also that companies sponsored by non-traditional interests are more likely to accept the suggested concept than are established life insurance companies with substantial financial (and emotional) commitments to their existing distribution systems.

In summary, the financial viability of the proposed product is primarily dependent upon the development of a distribution system which is much more efficient than traditional life insurance distribution systems. The balance of evidence, largely the experience of other industries, suggests that the development of such a distribution system at the cost levels assumed is practical.

Implications for the Industry

What would be the impact on the life insurance industry of the successful introduction of the Universal Life Insurance Policy? What practical considerations would affect the manner of introduction of such a product and its likely success? How would the industry respond? To suggest answers to these questions, the following scenario is offered:

Cannibal Life is a medium-size stock life insurance company owned by a powerful non-financial company. Its management and that of its parent company are aggressive and non-traditional; its agency organization is traditional and commission-oriented.

At the urging of its parent company, Cannibal Life decides to adopt a completely new marketing strategy designed to achieve major market penetration. It decides to withdraw all currently issued life insurance plans and to offer only the Universal Life Insurance Policy, notwithstanding the risk of losing its entire agency organization. It decides that it will make a conversion offer to all existing policyholders. Furthermore, it decides to take the unprecedented step of offering to convert, without evidence of insurability, life insurance policies issued by other companies on the same terms as are being offered to its own policyholders. Although a no-load offer is to be made both to its own policyholders and to policyholders of other companies, Cannibal Life intends to pay commissions on such conversions at the usual rates. Existing policyholders are to be notified that they can consolidate all of their life insurance policies with all companies into one Universal Life Insurance Policy. Cannibal Life intends to support its marketing strategy through an aggressive public relations and advertising program, particularly including efforts to enlist the sympathy of activist consumer groups; this is a vital aspect of the marketing strategy, as will later appear.

The new marketing strategy is unveiled to the agency organization and launched with great public fanfare. Company representatives call press conferences and appear with consumer activists on television interview programs; their comments regarding traditional life insurance products are not kind. Notwithstanding the radical reduction in commission rates, the agency organization is enthusiastic because of the income opportunities afforded by the conversion program and the confidence generated by widespread publicity. The conversion program is highly successful and Cannibal Life's expectation that business in force would increase by 100% within one year is surpassed; on average, each of its own policy-holders converts one additional policy issued by another company and many policyholders of other companies also convert their policies. Although the profitability of the new contract is significantly lower than that of existing business, Cannibal Life is able to increase its aggregate GAAP earnings on the increased volume of business (previously capitalized acquisition expenses are charged off as an extraordinary item). Its agency organization also prospers and grows. Large statutory losses are incurred, but these are absorbed by tax recoveries and by a substantial infusion of capital from the parent company.

Cannibal Life realizes that the conversion program is not a permanent source of new business. As a follow-up strategy, Cannibal Life decides to mount a major effort to capture a large share of the juvenile market by offering a special variation of the

Universal Life Insurance Policy specifically tailored to the needs of this market. The sales program promotes the product as "The Only Life Insurance Policy Your Child Will Ever Need." Because premiums on the juvenile plan are relatively low and commissions are relatively high, the reception by the agency organization is again enthusiastic and the customer base of Cannibal Life is greatly expanded, thus ensuring a future flow of business. Cannibal Life also decides to mass-market its new contract through employers and associations and, for this purpose, undertakes to develop a specialized agency organization which, in the long term, becomes its principal source of new customers. Eventually, its original agency organization will be disbanded and replaced by a new service-oriented organization designed to maintain its established customer relationships; this organization will be composed primarily of women. The new marketing strategy is a huge success, and Cannibal Life becomes a market leader in the individual insurance business.

The activities of Cannibal Life do not go unnoticed. Through regulatory agencies, life insurance industry and agent associations attempt to block Cannibal Life's conversion program, but these efforts are unsuccessful due largely to the public outcry by activist consumer groups. A temporary injunction is obtained against Cannibal Life, but the request for a permanent injunction is denied; in its opinion, the Court observes, "To grant the relief sought would be tantamount to accepting the view that a class action suit on behalf of mousetrap makers against the maker of a better mousetrap is valid." The Court decision receives the attention of the national media, including network television. Cannibal Life receives large numbers of applications for employment from agents of other companies, many of whom are hired. Conversions of other companies' policies increase dramatically.

The activities of Cannibal Life also attract the attention of four national retail organizations, all of which are already engaged in financial service businesses; these companies decide to introduce similar products and to market them on a non-agency basis through retail outlets. Similar action, based on a direct mail approach, is taken by the sponsors of two nationally recognized credit cards. Several life insurance companies of various sizes, including one sponsored by a credit union association, adopt a marketing strategy similar to that of Cannibal Life. All of these ventures are reasonably successful.

The impact upon the rest of the life insurance industry is now quite severe. A major decline in sales is experienced, accompanied by a substantial loss of agency manpower;

leading to a further decline in sales. Surrenders increase to the extent of causing a negative cash flow. Investment losses are incurred on the liquidation of investments to meet cash flow requirements; to minimize investment losses, higher-yielding assets are sold and portfolio investment returns decline. The loss of sales and business in force and the reduced investment returns cause an expense and earnings crisis which is temporarily masked by large surrender profits under statutory accounting. Most stock life insurance companies report GAAP losses due to the writeoff of unrecoverable deferred acquisition expenses. Mutual companies are forced to reduce dividends. Life insurance company share prices fall precipitously. Due to the decrease in business and the associated reversal of the effect of certain tax elections, most companies incur substantially increased federal income taxes on current income and some companies are subject to Phase III taxes on prior years' income previously deferred. Some companies decide to suspend writing business to avoid insolvency and there are numerous consolidations within the industry involving both stock and mutual companies.

Eventually, the surviving companies also introduce similar products and adopt similar marketing strategies. Gradually, stability returns to the industry, but market shares within the industry are substantially and permanently rearranged and the distribution systems are fundamentally altered. Following a period of adjustment, industry penetration of the individual savings market increases to record levels.

Is this scenario a real possibility? Are the Cannibals really coming? And does the story really have a happy ending? It is right to be skeptical of both Doomsday talk and happy endings; but not always right. Consider what has happened in the mutual fund industry within the past 10 years: how many retail funds of yesteryear are dealer or no-load funds today? Can similarly revolutionary changes happen in the life insurance industry? And happen as quickly?

No industry, regardless of how well entrenched, is invulnerable to basic economic forces; it must offer a product or service that the public needs or wants, at a price the public is prepared to pay. The life insurance industry offers a unique product that the public needs and wants and for which it is prepared to pay current prices and, arguably, even higher prices. The product is term life insurance, whether sold alone or in combination with a savings plan. Unfortunately, the majority of the income of the life insurance industry (and especially that of its distribution system) arises from amounts paid for life insurance policies over and above an appropriate price for the term life insurance provided (i.e., the savings element). Thus, the industry is primarily dependent for its income on its role in the savings business and there it has no product monopoly and a seriously disadvantageous competitive position. Of course, this problem is not new but, due to changes in the market environment, notably the increase in inflation rates and in public awareness, the problem is now more widely recognized. These are the circumstances that argue for revolutionary change.

Evaluation and Conclusions

If revolution is to come, should it be welcomed or resisted? Will it damage an established industry to the point of no repair, or will it forestall the even more destructive evolution which has been in progress for many years? It is the view of the author that the life insurance industry either will remain in the individual savings market on a sensible economic basis, or will be forced to withdraw from the individual savings market altogether and confine its activities to underwriting term insurance and a limited number of other specialized products. The case for the first alternative has already been argued; the case for the second can be argued simply by pointing to established trends and to the examples of various countries where endemic inflation has led to the practical disappearance of all permanent life insurance, accompanied by severe changes in industry economics. Given only these two alternatives, it seems clear that the less destructive and more promising is the first, leading to the conclusion that the revolution should be welcomed.

Given this conclusion, it remains to be seen who the Cannibals and their victims will be. As the scenario suggests, those who are prepared to lead the revolution are likely to emerge from it in a greatly strengthened position, while the last to follow will suffer the most and may even not survive.

As stated at the outset, this paper is intended to apply to the individual financial security market and general environment of the United States. Its application to other countries would be affected by differences in industry economics, regulation, taxation and other factors. Particularly in those countries where life insurance enjoys special tax concessions are the differences likely to be significant.

Acknowledgements

Many persons have contributed to the ideas and views assembled in this paper. The basic concepts underlying the Universal Life Insurance Policy have been advanced before by many others. The most striking example that has come to the author's attention was a presentation made several years ago by G. R. Dinney, F.S.A., F.C.I.A., to the Canadian Institute of Actuaries, entitled *A Descent into the Maelstrom of the Insurance Future*, which argued many of the same views and even included a description of a product entitled "Universal Life Plan."

Adjustable Products

Presented to the Executive Workshop sponsored by American United Life, Hot Springs, Virginia, October 20, 1980. Reprinted with permission from American United Life Insurance Company.

Three years ago, I participated in a debate sponsored by the Society of Actuaries which addressed the question: Resolved, that the life insurance industry as conducted today is in its terminal state. My assignment was to argue the affirmative side of that question. My opponent was my good friend, E. J. Moorhead, a past president of the Society of Actuaries and the American Academy of Actuaries, and in the course of his presentation, he labeled me the Casandra of the industry. It has been my custom in introducing presentations such as that I will make this morning to assure the audience that I would live up to my reputation, because the speech would be the same and only the title has been changed to conform to the program.

Unfortunately, that ploy is no longer feasible because the last time I gave the speech, to an inflation conference sponsored by LOMA, the sponsor saw fit to reprint my speech in its own publication, making it necessary for me to write a new one.

The views with which I have identified myself during the past several years in various forums can be summarized as follows. I believe that the industry has entered a period of significant change from which it *cannot* emerge unchanged. I observe:

- change in the social, economic and political environment in which it operates;
- change in the financial needs of the public it serves;

- change in the types of products it should be selling;
- change in the needed distribution of expense and profit margins; and, in all probability,
- change in the distribution systems required to sell at acceptable costs the new products to the new market in this new environment.

The views I have expressed before and will express again today are not popular ones within the life insurance industry — particularly within the traditional sector of the industry. This is hardly surprising and it is important to recognize why: the basic products and the distribution systems of the industry, which I am suggesting must be changed, have remained essentially unchanged since the early years of this century when legislation that largely shaped the industry was enacted in New York following the Armstrong Investigation of 1905. The industry has over an extended period of time been well served by its methods, which have built a large, successful and, as related to stock companies, profitable industry.

Notwithstanding this long and successful record, and notwithstanding our emotional attachment to the products and distribution systems which have produced this result, it is my firm belief that the industry must identify and address some significant new problems created by the contemporary environment; it is also my contention that, if the industry does not take steps now to determine its own future, another future, considerably more menacing, will be thrust upon it by government or by competitive and economic forces.

The Contemporary Environment

The thesis I have outlined begins with the premise that the contemporary environment is changing rapidly. Let us briefly examine that premise.

First, there is change of a social nature:

- Change in attitudes towards marriage and the family, manifested by an increase in the number of single and divorced persons and a decrease in the number of children in the average family. Earlier this year, one phenomenon of social change received official recognition by an agency of the United States government. (Slide 1) You will all recognize this slide as a reproduction of the title page of the census form mailed to some 80 million households last March. Now let us look inside the form. (Slide 2) I direct your

Slide 1

1980 Census of the United States

A message from the Director, Bureau of the Census . . .

We must, from time to time, take stock of ourselves as a people if our Nation is to meet successfully the many national and local challenges we face. This is the purpose of the 1980 census.

The essential need for a population census was recognized almost 200 years ago when our Constitution was written. As provided by article I, the first census was conducted in 1790 and one has been taken every 10 years since then.

The law under which the census is taken protects the confidentiality of your answers. For the next 72 years — or until April 1, 2052 — only sworn census workers have access to the individual records, and no one else may see them.

Your answers, when combined with the answers from other people, will provide the statistical figures needed by public and private groups, schools, business and industry, and Federal, State, and local governments across the country. These figures will help all sectors of American Society understand how our population and housing are changing in this way, we can deal more effectively with today's problems and work toward a better future for all of us.

The census is a vitally important national activity. Please do your part by filling out this census form accurately and completely. If you mail it back promptly in the enclosed postage-paid envelope, it will save the expense and inconvenience of a census taker having to visit you.

Thank you for your cooperation.

Slide 2

Page 2

→ *ALSO ANSWER THE HOUSING Q*

Here are the QUESTIONS ↓ / **These are the columns for ANSWERS** → *Please fill one column for each person listed in Question 1.*	**PERSON in column 1** Last name First name — Middle initial	**PERSON in column 2** Last name First name — Middle ini
2. How is this person related to the person in column 1? *Fill one circle.* *If "Other relative" of person in column 1, give exact relationship, such as mother-in-law, niece, grandson, etc.*	*START in this column with the household member (or one of the members) in whose name the home is owned or rented. If there is no such person, start in this column with any adult household member.*	If relative of person in column 1: ○ Husband/wife ○ Father/mother ○ Son/daughter ○ Other relative – ○ Brother/sister If not related to person in column 1: ○ Roomer, boarder ○ Other nonrelativ ○ Partner, roommate ○ Paid employee
3. Sex *Fill one circle.*	Male ■ ○ Female	Male ■ Female
4. Is this person — *Fill one circle.*	○ White ○ Asian Indian ○ Black or Negro ○ Hawaiian ○ Japanese ○ Guamanian ○ Chinese ○ Samoan ■ ○ Filipino ○ Eskimo ○ Korean ○ Aleut ○ Vietnamese ○ Other — *Specify* ○ Indian (Amer.) *Print tribe*	○ White Asian Indian ○ Black or Negro Hawaiian ○ Japanese Guamanian ○ Chinese Samoan ■ ○ Filipino Eskimo ○ Korean Aleut ○ Vietnamese Other — *Specify* ○ Indian (Amer.) *Print tribe*
5. Age, and month and year of birth *a. Print age at last birthday.* *b. Print month and fill one circle.* *c. Print year in the spaces, and fill one circle below each number.*	a. Age at last birthday c. Year of birth: 1 _ _ _ 1 ● ; 8 ○ 9 ○ ; 0–9 ○ ; 0–9 ○ b. Month of birth ■ ○ Jan.—Mar. ○ Apr.—June ○ July—Sept. ○ Oct.—Dec.	a. Age at last birthday c. Year of birth: 1 _ _ _ 1 ● ; 8 ○ 9 ○ ; 0–9 ○ ; 0–9 ○ b. Month of birth ■ ○ Jan.—Mar. ○ Apr.—June ○ July—Sept. ○ Oct.—Dec.
6. Marital status *Fill one circle.*	○ Now married ○ Separated ○ Widowed ○ Never married ○ Divorced	○ Now married ○ Separated ○ Widowed ○ Never married ○ Divorced
7. Is this person of Spanish/Hispanic origin or descent? *Fill one circle.*	○ No (not Spanish/Hispanic) ○ Yes, Mexican, Mexican-Amer., Chicano ○ Yes, Puerto Rican ○ Yes, Cuban ■ ○ Yes, other Spanish/Hispanic	○ No (not Spanish/Hispanic) ○ Yes, Mexican, Mexican-Amer., Chicano ○ Yes, Puerto Rican ○ Yes, Cuban ■ ○ Yes, other Spanish/Hispanic
	CENSUS USE ONLY A. ○ I ○ N ○ ○	*CENSUS USE ONLY* A. ○ I ○ N ○ ○

attention to column 2 of this slide, specifically the area which describes the relationship of the person in column 2 to the person in column 1 and even more specifically to the category "Partner, Roommate." Charles Osgood, who conducts the morning talk show on CBS Radio, called attention to this official recognition of informal living relationships that contrast with the traditional family concept but was dissatisfied with the term "Partner, Roommate" as not being sufficiently descriptive. He suggested that the English language was inadequate and needed a new word to describe this newly accepted type of relationship. His suggestion for the word was "POSSLQ". (Slide 3) Mr. Osgood went further by offering the following addition to the poetic literature of the English language:

"Roses are Red,
Violets are Blue,
Will you be my POSSLQ?"

Returning now to change of a social nature:

- Change in social attitudes which play an important role in motivating people to provide for their own and their families' financial security, evidenced by a decline in self-reliance and increased dependence on employer-sponsored and government-sponsored financial security programs. In short, the work ethic replaced by the entitlement ethic.
- Change in public confidence in institutions ranging from government to oil companies and — yes — even financial companies, which surely depreciate the value attached to long-term contractural money promises — the kind that traditional life insurance policies provide.
- Change in the general level of education of the public at large accompanied, arguably, by an associated

Slide 3

POSSLQ

PERSON OF
OPPOSITE
SEX
SHARING
LIVING
QUARTERS

increase in their ability to evaluate critically the insurance industry and its products.

Second, there is change of an economic nature:

- Change in family income levels, a major contributor to which is the growing economic importance of working women and the associated trend towards two-income families, which now outnumber single-income families among husband/wife families. It is clear that the typical family today — the two-income family — can afford and needs more financial security products than ever before. But do the products of yesteryear and today address appropriately this market?
- Change in the general economic environment represented by the accelerated rate of inflation accompanied by unprecedentedly high levels of interest rates, both of which impact the motivation to save and the choice of savings vehicle. For the life insurance industry, the choice is manifesting itself in several ways — by major increases in policy loan utilization, by significant increases in surrenders, and by a continuing drift (or is it becoming a slide?) towards term insurance and away from permanent insurance. In keeping with the thesis that every dark cloud must have a silver lining, take heart from the following remark by Senator Allan Cranston of California: "Inflation is not all bad. After all, it has made it possible for every American to live in a more expensive neighborhood without actually moving."
- Change represented by the much increased complexity and interdependence of worldwide economic activities, with increased risks of instability and economic dislocation accompanied by shortages and scarcity of basic resources. The leading example of this today is the worldwide energy crisis, the effects of which have probably only begun to be felt.

These changes of an economic nature suggest that an expanded but less stable market for financial security products exists but that the needs and wants of that market, particularly with respect to savings products, are different from those of earlier years.

Third, there is change of a political nature:

- Government-sponsored benefits have changed dramatically in both scale and scope and now include built-in adjustments that ensure continuing increases for the foreseeable future; government has become the principal purveyor of financial security products — the "life insurance in force" of the social security system (if it could be calculated) probably exceeds $3 trillion, about 20% more than the sum of private life insurance of all types in the United States. And this estimate may prove to be absurdly conservative when viewed with hindsight from the perspective of, say, 1990.

- Consumer and environmental interests of an organized nature represent major new political forces which have already altered national priorities and now threaten directly the life insurance industry.

These changes, too, affect the life insurance market, its wants and its needs. The expansion of social insurance benefits raises real questions as to whether or not there is a substantial need for private life insurance at the lower end of the income spectrum, an issue of major importance to those companies operating in the home service sector of the industry. The Federal Trade Commission, although it denies it, has clearly mounted an attack on the life insurance industry; its recent report on the individual ordinary insurance business, though laced with deliberate distortions to sensationalize its findings, cannot be deflected by public relations alone and has disturbing implications for traditional permanent life insurance generally and for nonparticipating permanent life insurance in particular.

These, then, are the changes which I perceive have had, are having, and will have significant impact on the market for individual private life insurance and the types of products needed to address that market. Is there any evidence that the impact is already being felt? I believe there is. Consider:

- Although private savings continue to expand, the life insurance industry is consistently losing its share of the private savings market. The loss of market share is more noticeable if policy loans are regarded as withdrawn savings rather than assets. From 1960 to 1970, the ordinary life insurance reserves of all U. S. companies, net of policy loans, increased from $54 billion to $84 billion, a compound annual increase of 4.5%, roughly equal to the rate of inflation for that period. From 1970 to 1978, the net "savings" increased from $84 billion to $127 billion, a compound annual growth rate of 5% during a period when the average inflation rate was approximately 8%. In other words, in constant dollars, the *absolute* industry participation in the savings market *declined* by 18% and the *relative* participating declined still more.

- Since 1951 lapse rates on both old and new policies have increased steadily; over the 28-year period from 1951 to 1979, lapse rates more than doubled. Lapse rates on policies more than two years old increased from 1951 to 1960, remaining stable thereafter until 1972; since that date, there has been an ominous and steady increase which probably signals increased replacement activity.
- Sales of term insurance of all types represent a steadily increasing proportion of new business. Sales of annuity business, carrying much lower expense margins than traditional life insurance products, have soared. Sales of permanent insurance have declined (in constant dollars) both absolutely and relatively, particularly in the family market.
- In an address to the American Council of Life Insurance in early 1979, Richard Neuschel of McKinsey & Company, presented the results of a study which indicated that, until approximately ten years ago, market shares within the life insurance industry were relatively insensitive to competitive position. Since then, however, market shares have shifted noticeably in the direction of the most competitive companies.

This evidence suggests that the public is turning more to other savings media and less to traditional forms of permanent life insurance; that the industry is being subjected to a raid on its accumulated assets at a time when its fixed interest investments stand at an unprecedented discount in the marketplace; that sales of the traditional forms of permanent life insurance, which provide the majority of the income of the industry and, particularly, the income of its distribution system, are declining in constant dollar terms; and that life insurance is now a more price-sensitive product. In summary, the evidence confirms that the contemporary environment is impacting the life insurance industry in important ways and will continue to do so.

The Product Dilemma

In the fifth century B.C., over 2400 years ago, Socrates admonished us: "The first step in knowing the truth is to call a thing by its right name."

In the spirit of Socrates' admonition, let us examine the mainstay products of the life insurance industry — traditional permanent life insurance products, mainly ordinary life. Is ordinary life a product well suited to the wants and needs of today's typical buyer to meet his or her financial security requirements? I say no and I think that Socrates would agree. Instead, I say that ordinary life is a product well suited to the wants and needs of the life insurance industry in order to make possible a continuation of its traditional methods of doing business. I recognize that these are fighting words within the life insurance industry, and I say them only because I believe that they are true.

The inflexibility of permanent life insurance is manifest. Consider just the effects of inflation. Even at a rate of *only* 5%, long-term money promises depreciate in value approximately 40% every ten years. At 10%, the depreciation is 61% and at 15%, the depreciation is 75%. Ten years is not a long time in the context of a permanent life insurance policy. In an inflationary environment, permanent life insurance has little relevance to a typical buyer's financial requirements over the extended period of time necessary to justify the purchase of permanent insurance instead of term insurance. In fact, ordinary life insurance today is *not* level premium/level benefit life insurance — it is decreasing premium/decreasing benefit life insurance in constant dollar terms and this is the crux of some of the industry's economic problems.

But inflation is only part of the story. Modern life styles which include geographic mobility, job mobility and even marital mobility mean frequent change in financial security requirements. The inflexibility of permanent life insurance does not lend itself well to the realities of today's marketplace.

A second problem is expense tolerance. The distribution of commission and other expense margins across the product spectrum of the industry has been effectively dictated since the early years of this century by Section 213 of the New York Insurance Code. At the time the legislation was passed, its framers decided that the highest commission rates and expense margins should apply to the longest form of term insurance, which they considered ordinary life to be. In the environment of the early twentieth century, when mortality rates were very much higher than they are today, this was a proper characterization. However, the improvement in mortality since the early twentieth century has altered the nature of an ordinary life policy but not its name. Today, only 10% to 15% of the premium on an orthodox ordinary life insurance policy is required to pay the death benefit costs; in other words, if all mortality rates dropped to zero up to age 100 and if the rate of mortality at age 100 were

100%, the premium on an ordinary life policy could be reduced by only 10% to 15%. By contrast, 45% to 55% of the premium is required to accumulate the cash values or to pay dividends to policyholders. Clearly, under today's conditions, an ordinary life policy is first and foremost a savings product and secondarily a protection product and the ratio of the two types of benefits is on the order of 3-4 to 1. Seventy-five years ago, the proportion of the premium on an ordinary life policy required to pay death benefits was two or three times as large with correspondingly less required to provide savings benefits. This has altered the expense tolerance of the industry's main product.

When a permanent insurance policy is regarded primarily as a savings product, it is clear that the expense tolerance of the product is much reduced — competing savings products operate on a benefit-to-cost ratio ranging from 90% to 100% of the amount saved. The benefit-to-cost ratio of permanent life insurance is only 60% to 70%. On the other hand, a life insurance product designed primarily to provide protection benefits has a much higher expense tolerance — benefit-to-cost ratios in the range of 40% to 60% can be found on individual health insurance products and certain personal casualty insurance products.

In summary, I believe the market is saying that it will no longer tolerate the expense levels inherent in traditional permanent life insurance products, and they are voting their preference by buying more and more term insurance.

The third problem with traditional permanent life insurance products relates to the investment risks associated with the products: the policy loan problem, the possibility of massive replacements and the particular dilemma associated with nonparticipating permanent life insurance. These risks are inherent in the nature of the product and the regulations governing it which cause the product to be priced conservatively and, thus, to appear to be more expensive.

The fourth problem associated with traditional permanent life insurance is the difficulty of achieving an adequate investment through-put to policyholders. The mechanics of the Life Insurance Company Federal Income Tax Act effectively limit the investment return that can be paid to policyholders on participating products. Nonforfeiture legislation effectively limits the investment return that can be paid on nonparticipating products. In an environment of high interest rates, the difference between what can be earned on alternative savings and what can be paid on permanent life insurance becomes substantial.

These four problems — the need for flexibility, expense tolerance, the investment risks and investment through-put — require, in my view, a different approach to the design of life insurance products. If the industry persists in defending its traditional products with their relatively high expense margins in order to maintain its existing distribution systems, I believe the marketplace will thwart the strategy by increasing its already high preference for term products and that the result will be a disintegration of the distribution system of the industry leading to a disintegration of the industry as we know it today. The alternative is to design products in such a way that some or all of the four problems I have discussed are addressed rationally.

Adjustable Products

Some companies have introduced products which do address some or all of the problem areas. Almost all of the products I will discuss this morning address the issue of flexibility and some of them address certain of the other problems.

Three of the seven products I will discuss are well known and have been with us for many years. Variable annuities, which have been offered for more than 25 years, address all of the problems: there is flexibility of premium payment and benefit payout; the expense tolerance is low but this is recognized in the pricing basis; the investment risks are entirely in the hands of the policyholder; and the investment through-put is unaffected by the company's tax position and by nonforfeiture legislation. Variable annuities have traditionally been thought of as linked to common stock funds and their popularity has ebbed and flowed with the tides of the stock market. A variable annuity linked to a fixed dollar fund or to a money market fund might present an attractive product in today's financial environment.

Flexible premium annuities and single premium deferred annuities have gained in popularity dramatically in the past several years. They afford flexibility and have been priced realistically to their expense tolerance. However, particularly with respect to single premium deferred annuities, it is arguable that the investment risks assumed by the issuing company are unacceptably high. There are also serious tax questions receiving current attention which relate to the issue of whether or not excess interest payments can be deducted as a policy benefit rather than treated as a policy dividend, subject to limitation of deductibility.

Annually renewable term insurance is another familiar product which affords great flexibility, particularly if it is inflation indexed. Since it is entirely a protection product, its expense tolerance is quite high and the issues of investment risks and investment through-put do not arise. For reasons already discussed, the industry cannot become dependent upon ART as its major product line.

Let me turn now to four more recent product innovations, most of which afford some measure of flexibility in one way or another and some of which address the other problems.

The first is Adjustable Life, a product introduced about ten years ago by Minnesota Mutual and now offered by Bankers Life, College Life and University Life. This product affords flexibility in that the buyer, within wide limits, can change the amount of the benefit or the amount of the premium payment. Automatic indexing of benefits is offered. Either type of change results in a change of the plan of insurance. However, once the amount and premium have been determined, they remain unchanged until the date of the next adjustment. Adjustable Life was designed to preserve the traditional pattern of commission and expense margins and, therefore, has the same inherent problems with expense tolerance as is present with traditional permanent life insurance. Likewise, Adjustable Life does not alter the nature of the investment risks assumed by the company nor does it address the limitations on investment through-put inherent in traditional forms of permanent life insurance. I understand that Adjustable Life has been approved in all jurisdictions except Mississippi and Montana. The pioneering of the product is largely complete. One formidable barrier remains, particularly to a small and medium company: the cost of developing the systems required to administer Adjustable Life are reportedly very large.

Indeterminate premium products have increased enormously in market share in recent years. They are accepted in most jurisdictions. These are non-participating traditional products which provide that the company may, from time to time, change the premium it is charging up to a maximum level specified in the contract. This affords a limited degree of flexibility but to the company and not the buyer. If this product is designed with the lowest permissible levels of cash values, as is usually the case, it becomes more protection oriented, increasing its expense tolerance. The issue of investment risk is addressed in part by the ability of the company to increase the premium if interest rates should decline. There is a significant Federal Income Tax question associated with this product: is the difference between the maximum premium and the premium actually charged a dividend to policyholders? If the answer is yes, the same limitation on investment through-put applies as for traditional products.

Two specific designs of indeterminate premium products are worth noting. Life of Virginia has marketed such a product for several years under the name "Econoflex." This product provides for a redetermination of the premium every three years and the formula for redetermination is included in the policy, driven by an index of yields on long-term government bonds. More recently, United Benefit Life Insurance Company has introduced a policy which includes a complete premium formula based on current interest rates, mortality rates and expense rates. In both cases, the objective is to remove discretion from the company in the redetermination of premiums, strengthening the argument that the premium reduction is not a dividend.

In 1972, variable life insurance was thought to be one of the major products of the future. The product afforded no flexibility in terms of premiums or benefits and the policyholder had no alternative other than to take any superior investment performance in the form of additional insurance. As the product has in fact evolved, its expense tolerance is probably no different from that of traditional permanent life insurance although commission and expense margins are actually somewhat lower. The investment risk is largely in the hands of the policyholder and the policy loan problem is automatically solved. The investment through-put depends on the performance of the assets in which the separate account is invested. The way in which the company will be taxed on variable life insurance remains to be determined but it appears most likely that it will be taxed in the same way as orthodox products. For several years, Equitable Variable Life Insurance Company was the only company offering this product.

Two other companies have recently introduced or will soon introduce such products, reportedly with a choice of investment alternatives.

Perhaps the most recent of the products to appear on the scene are those variously described as Universal Life, Completelife, the Economist or the Challenger. These products provide for total flexibility in the amount of protection and the amount and frequency of premium payment. Essentially, this product represents "unbundled" life insurance with separately identified savings and protection components. The mechanics are relatively straightforward. The buyer selects an amount of insurance and usually has the choice of a level total amount or a level amount plus the accumulated cash value; all amounts of insurance can be varied at any time (with evidence) and there is available an automatic option to index the amount to the CPI (without evidence). Premiums are completely flexible, including stop-and-go and lump sums. When each premium is paid, a load is deducted (usually a level percentage of each premium — say 7-1/2% — plus a flat one-time charge per contract — say $250). The premium less the loan is accumulated in a reserve fund which earns interest at a guaranteed interest rate and which is credited with excess interest at a rate determined from time to time. The cost of term insurance is deducted from the fund either monthly or annually. This product represents the ultimate in flexibility. The expense tolerance of the product is limited by its unbundled design and the loads are substantially different from traditional life insurance products. Note that the expense charge varies substantially according to the size of the sale. Basic commissions are generally about one-half the load plus a normal type ART commission on the term insurance charges, sometimes expressed as a function of the amount of insurance. The investment risk is changed in only one respect — excess interest is based on the net cash value after deducting policy loans; accordingly, the product involves the direct recognition of policyholder borrowing. The same tax issues arise on this product as is present in the case of flexible premium annuities — is the excess interest a dividend to policyholders?

These, then, are the offerings of some segments of the industry as alternatives to traditional life insurance products. What will their future be? Among the current offerings, I would identify Universal Life as the product most likely to succeed. But success will require two changes:

1. A favorable resolution of the excess interest/dividend tax issue is needed if the product is to compete successfully with alternative savings media. External indexing may provide the answer or changes in the 1959 tax law may also afford relief.
2. In order to market Universal Life in something like its present form, I believe it is necessary to alter the expense structure of the distribution system if not its composition.

The Distribution System Dilemma

Approximately two-thirds of the expenses of a typical life insurance company are associated with its distribution system. If major changes are to be made in the benefit-to-cost ratio of savings-type life insurance products, it follows that significant changes must be made in the expenses associated with the distribution system. Yet, the distribution system of the industry is today under severe pressure because of generally declining agent income levels. The pressure from the distribution system itself is for increased commissions at a time when the industry's principal products are under intense price pressure caused by consumer preference. How can these two opposing forces be squared? The only possible answer is increased productivity.

The present distribution system of the life insurance industry is made up of approximately 250,000 agents who derive more than half of their income from the sale of life insurance and approximately 250,000 agents who derive less than half their income from the sale of life insurance. The average sales frequency of the industry is very low — less than one sale per week per full-time equivalent agent. Therein lies the inherent inefficiency of the present distribution system and that is the statistic that must be changed. The alternative is an implosion of the existing life insurance distribution system and it will happen regardless of whether we increase commissions on existing product lines or reduce them — the former will cause increased consumer rejection of the industry's high-margin permanent products and the latter will drive agents from the industry because they cannot survive financially. Productivity is the only answer and I believe that it is most likely to be achieved by substantial improvement of the product — both its design and its cost.

At the beginning of this presentation, I made reference to the debate sponsored by the Society of Actuaries three years ago. One of the statements I made in the course of my presentation at that time was that the cost of "manufacturing" from scratch a full-time established agent was in the vicinity of \$100,000 (to the nearest \$100,000). At the time, the statement stirred up a certain amount of controversy. As it turns out, time may have vindicated my critics. Today, I would say that the cost of manufacturing from scratch a full-time established agent has probably reached \$200,000 (to the nearest \$100,000)! Let me assure you that either statistic, take your pick, is as real as it is disturbing. Skeptics should consult LIMRA for more precise examples. Obviously, there is a very serious problem connected with the capital costs required to maintain existing agency organizations. If a company developing new agents is to recover its development costs, together with a reasonable rate of return on those costs, the required productivity of its agents is absurdly high — which is another way of saying that it is no longer economically viable to develop new agents on the basis of the current experience of most companies. Many companies, if not most, have, in fact, abandoned efforts to develop new agents in favor of proselytization. How much longer will a small group of companies (mainly mutual companies licensed in New York) be willing to finance the development of sales manpower for the entire industry?

Is an agentless future likely? My answer is "probably not" although I think it is conceivable. Just as a reminder of how quickly things can change, let me show you a few illustrations.

(Slide 4)

"Neath the spreading chestnut tree
The village smithy stands
The smith a powerful man is he
With broad and sinewy hands."

As an indication of just how prevalent the blacksmith was in our society once, consider the number of people you know named Smith! In 1870, the then President of the United States asked his Secretary of Transportation for a prognosis of the transportation needs of the northeastern United States 50 years later, in 1920. The Secretary's report began with the prediction that by

1920 the northeast United States would be covered with three feet of horse manure. And where is the blacksmith today? Or even in 1920?

(Slide 5)

Mr. Oxenham vs. Safeway.

(Slide 6)

When was the last time you received an honest-to-God telegram delivered to your door? Do you remember how much a part of the scene was the telegraph boy back in the early 1940s? Do you recall the World War II movies in which this character became an instant sociologist while delivering the bad news of a lost soldier to parents or wives?

(Slide 7)

Will the home service agent go the way of the milk man?

(Slide 8)

And how about the elevator operator? I asked our Communications people for a buxom model, but I didn't expect science fiction!

(Slide 9)

Here is an example considerably closer to home — the mutual fund salesman. From the glamour business of the middle-to-late 1960s to the no-load funds of the early 1970s required only five years and what were the causes? Dissatisfaction on the part of the consumer with the product offered plus a change in regulation. Could the same thing happen with respect to the life insurance industry? In 5 years?

The Distribution System of 1990

I believe that by 1990 life insurance will be distributed by three major types of distribution systems.

Slide 4

Slide 5

Slide 6

Slide 7

Slide 8

Slide 9

The first is the traditional full-time agent who, I believe, will be serving almost exclusively sophisticated markets, particularly markets in which tax considerations are of major importance. I believe, however, that the number of full-time life insurance agents of this type will be reduced from their present number of 250,000 to approximately 25,000 to 50,000. It is probable that 90% of these survivors are already in the business. Single company representation may diminish. Fee for service may become an important factor in their compensation. I believe they will continue to produce approximately 50% of the new business.

The second type of distribution system I envisage could be described as a multi-product distribution system. In other words, life insurance will be sold as a product ancillary to other products. The multi-line agent is an obvious example and State Farm may be a good prototype. Stockbrokers are another example and E. F. Hutton may be another type.

The third type of distribution system falls under the umbrella term "mass marketing." Perhaps someone other than USAA Life will find a way to sell quality life insurance products via media or mail. I also see employer-sponsored selling through salary savings as an important marketing outlet for the future. It is noteworthy that several companies which have developed or are developing Universal Life products intend to make a major marketing thrust in the salary savings market.

Some of you may be wondering, what happened to the home service agents? Or what happened to all those PPGAs? I believe that many of them will become multi-product agents, but I see their importance as a distribution outlet for the industry to be much diminished.

Conclusion

Periods of change are two-sided coins. On one side in bold-faced type is stamped "PROBLEMS"; on the other is stamped "OPPORTUNITIES." If a picture is worth a thousand words, let me save some time by illustrating. (Slide 10) "PROBLEMS." (Slide 11) "OPPORTUNITIES."

Now let me tell you a story which offers an alternative interpretation of these slides. The story concerns two girl ostriches who were running together across the veldt in South Africa and were being chased by two boy ostriches, who were gradually gaining. One of the girl ostriches said to the other, "I'm getting nervous; let's hide." So they stuck their heads in the sand. (Slide 10) Whereupon the two boy ostriches stopped and one turned to the other and said, "Hey! Where did they go?" (Slide 11) This is an illustration of what happens when problems are mixed with opportunities!

I expect to see in the coming decade a significant change in the products offered to the public by the life insurance industry and I expect also to see a significant change in the way in which those products are distributed. I further expect to see additional consolidations of companies within the life insurance industry, including some mutual companies. All of this will, I believe, lead to a significant realignment of market shares. While there may be more losers than winners, I am convinced that there will be winners and that some will win big.

Slide 10

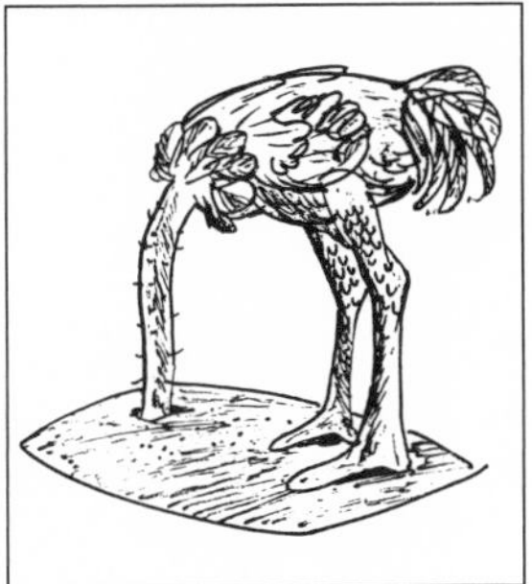

Slide 11

Variable Universal Life

Presented at a Variable Universal Life Seminar on April 18, 1985. Reprinted with permission from Tillinghast - A Towers Perrin Company.

Well, this afternoon I've had to throw away my usual talk because I thought that it was appropriate to try to stay at least somewhere close to the subject of the seminar which is Variable Universal Life. My typical talk consists more of sketching background rather than foreground, and I'm going to do a little of that this afternoon, too. But I will try to stay fairly close to the issues involved in variable universal life. And I started by asking myself a question — Why are you here? Why are each of you in attendance at this seminar? Well, of course, there's the statutory reason, and that's staying abreast of what is a new, a changing, and an interesting development in the industry, but I think you had some specific questions in mind about variable universal life. Here are some of the questions that I think you want answered in the course of today and tomorrow.

First of all, you want to know whether this thing really is a better mousetrap. Is it really a better mousetrap or is it just some faddish gimmick that might be around for awhile and then is going to fade away? In addition to that, I think you want to know whether it will actually catch some mice. And, finally, I think you have a third question, and that is whether or not you can put it all together. Now, this reminds me of an experience that I've gone through a few times and I'll bet you that nearly everyone in this room has, too, particularly if they have children. The setting is Christmas Eve and you've gone toy shopping at Sears, and you've bought something innocent looking that says in small type, "some assembly required." Well, the question is pertinent to variable universal life. Can we put it all together? Some assembly is indeed required. What you're leading up to, I think, is the question: Is this suitable for your particular company? Let me talk about these questions and along the way, a few other subjects.

First, is it a better mousetrap? My answer is that it is. I think technically variable universal life is a superior product and that the concept is essentially sound, and here's why I reached that conclusion. For the buyer, variable universal life like other forms of variable products do allow investment flexibility that is not present in other products, and the way in which the investment flexibility works because with flexibility will probably come two things. One is a higher rate of return, and the other is greater fluctuations in value. With this flexibility the way it works is that the rate of accumulation of values is what changes if the investment experience fluctuates. In other words, the accumulating cash values of these products are the expansion tank that are able to absorb the fluctuations in value that are inherent with products invested in equities, and equities would, of course, include things other than common stocks. Now, because of this flexibility and because of the disadvantage, the fluctuations in value can legitimately be absorbed by cash value accumulations as the expansion tank. In the long run, the results to the buyer ought to be better than would be achieved through a restricted investment policy, so the buyer because he is able to take the opportunity of a flexible investment medium is likely, by high odds, to come out better in the long run. The long run I would define as 10 years or more.

I've done some work on equity investments. The probability is about 80% that an equity investment will surpass the results from some other kind of investment, a fixed interest type investment, 80% probability over about a 10-year period. How about the seller? Is it a better mousetrap for him? Well, I think the answer there, too, is yes, and the reason primarily is because finally, the assets and the liabilities that he has are going to roughly match; that is, they will match given certain restrictions on the product design. This industry in the last 10 years had some education about mismatched assets and liabilities, and I would predict that we haven't learned our final lesson about this and that some time over the next 10 years we're going to enter the postgraduate level. So I think it's a better mousetrap.

Now, will it catch mice? Well, this has to be a matter of considerable speculation. There are, however, a few signals that can be used to guide us. The overseas experience with variable products suggests that the answer is yes, that the buyer, in fact, will respond to this kind of product and to the basic presentation of the product which is this is an opportunity to earn an enhanced rate of return because of a flexibility of offers. This experience is particularly clear in the United Kingdom, it's clear also in South Africa where this product has been very important in the market place, and in the room is the former managing director of one of the major South African companies that knows even more about this than we do. The experience elsewhere is more mixed but nevertheless, it's generally favorable, generally favorable where the regulatory environment has not been inhospitable. Will it catch mice? Well, the inflation psychology is an important factor in the answer to that question. If the general public were to come to believe that inflation was a thing of the past, my guess is that they would move back in the direction of fixed dollar guarantees. So inflation psychology is important to the success of this product from the viewpoint of whether or not the buyer will like it and appreciate it. Along with this, the historically low yields that are associated with life insurance in this country are also a motivating factor. That's a factor that is likely to lead people in the direction of products like variable life.

The third element is the visibility of the return to the buyer. This is one of the appeals of variable products, that the buyer actually has some concept of what is happening to his investment in his contract, and visibility is very important in the attractiveness and appeal of these products. If you look in the *Financial Times*, there's published there a listing of unit trusts — they are the equivalent of mutual funds — there's published also a listing of insurance bonds and related products. These are really the insurance companies internal indices to which their variable products are linked, and it's rather remarkable the insurance listings are now longer than the mutual fund listings, and this is the kind of visibility and prominence that these products have had in the UK at least.

Buyer understanding is another big plus. And here they particularly favor the variable universal design versus earlier designs. What was wrong with earlier designs? Well, apart from the fact that no one but actuaries understood them, they had one other flaw, and that is basically they did not give the buyer what the buyer wanted, what he was seeking when he opted to purchase variable life insurance, and what he is seeking is cash value response to investment results. The earlier products gave amount of insurance response to investment results to a greater degree than cash value response. The U.S. experience is pretty limited. That which exists suggests that under the right sort of circumstances these products will receive a welcome reception in the U.S. market. To the best of my knowledge, there are only about five companies that are active in a significant way in the variable life market generally and those have had reasonably good results as I would measure them. It's noteworthy that most of these companies are selling the older style of variable life, and I would predict that the newer style will have an even better response.

In passing, one thing to keep in mind about variable products of all kinds when you start addressing the question, will they catch mice, is the need for investment alternatives. I can tell you without any doubt or any qualification that there are fashions in investments that are just as powerful as fashions in the clothing industry. There are times when equity investments simply cannot be sold in the retail market. There are times when real estate investments simply cannot be sold in the retail market, and so forth. So if variable life is going to become a main product line for a company and if that company has a lot of fixed expense and plant and equipment ready to process business and if they want to avoid having their business suddenly stopped because it's out of fashion, they'd better have available investment alternatives to meet whatever the desire of the market place is at the moment.

We turn to the assembly problem. First of all, I'd like to welcome you all to the securities business because that's what you're in if you're going to offer variable life products. The securities business will lead you directly into a confrontation with federal versus state regulation, and federal regulation will be the prevailing discipline that your operations will be subject to when you become an operator in the securities business. Well, this means that you've got to get to know King Kong. It's often said that the difference between federal and state regulation in the insurance business is analogous to the difference between whether you'd like to deal with fifty monkeys or one gorilla. Well, it may not be quite that simple, and the analogies may not be exactly appropriate, but nevertheless, the dealings that you will have at the federal level are significantly different from those which you may be used to in dealing with regulators at the state level.

While I'm on the subject of federal regulation, let me ask you a question. Do you think there's an FDIC in your future? I think there is, and I think that some time within the next few years, we're going to get to a stage where there will be a general outcry within the insurance industry to provide exactly that kind of coverage. I think that developments that are going on in the thrift industry are developments we may see in the banking industry, developments which unhappily we're witnessing in the insurance industry that are testing the efficacy of state guarantee arrangements. All of these, in my opinion, are going to lead us into some kind of federal guarantee for financial products of all kinds including insurance. So I think there's an FDIC in your future, and if that's true, you're going to be involved with federal regulation anyway.

The cost of all this is not going to be inconsequential. I would not hazard a dollar guess here as to what the entry price might be to the variable universal life business. I'll leave that to some of my associates this afternoon and tomorrow to address. Now is this product for you? Well, before I try to answer that, let me begin by telling you what the product revolution is all about. We've heard a lot of talk about the product revolution in the life insurance industry which most people say started about 5 or 6 years ago. Well, the product revolution — if you look back through the history of the life insurance business, going back say 200 years which is about as far as you can go — if you look back, you can see that there have been various product revolutions at different times. For example, the first of them was the invention of level premium life insurance. Another was the invention of endowment policies. There was the product revolution that accompanied the introduction of income tax, and so on and so forth. Now, each of these product revolutions — each one of them — has simply been the prelude to a distribution revolution, and so in my mind, what the product revolution is all about is that it's a prelude to a distribution revolution. Now, given that we live in a world that is gradually being deregulated, this distribution revolution is going to take place in the context of the financial services revolution, so that the product revolution is really a distribution revolution in disguise, and the distribution revolution is not going to happen in the life insurance industry. It's going to happen in the financial services industry. When this happens, there's going to be the collision of two fundamental and different business strategies. The collision is going to be between the distribution driven strategy that has long prevailed in the insurance industry, the distribution driven strategy. That means you behave as if your agents are your customers versus the consumer driven strategy which applies in the most important of the other financial services which is banking, so the financial services revolution is going to represent a collision of these two fundamentally different business strategies.

Let me talk next about what competition is all about. I'll eventually get around to the question, Is this for you? Competition is conducted basically according to one of three strategic plans. The first of them is price competition. And the textbooks on economics tell us what pure price competition will lead to. Pure price competition in a completely free market, if it ever exists, will eventually lead to a price level where prices are equal to cost — price level where prices are equal to cost. Now, included in that cost will be a cost of capital, so there will still be a profit margin left, but the profit margin will basically be the cost of the capital employed. That will eventually happen in a completely free market where the driving competitive force is price.

We talk next about the second strategy, and that's the quality strategy. And here, the purveyors of products and we could be talking about cans of peas because this discussion has very general application — what the purveyors are trying to do is they're trying to differentiate their product as having a higher quality than the products of their competitors. Well, how does that apply to the products of this industry? Well, it might apply, for example, to the issue of how sound financially the issuing company might be. That might be one quality differentiation. Of course, that would disappear with an FDIC. There's another brand differentiation that has direct application to variable products of all kinds, and that is investment performance. And variable universal or other forms of variable products have inherent in them the potential for brand identification or quality, and investment performance is the essence of this.

The third competitive strategy is essentially the idea of monopoly. What you try to do is become the only player in the market, and as it relates to the insurance industry, this has always taken the form of distributing products through controlled distribution outlets. Somewhere or other, somebody forgot why they were doing this. I think that most of us are generally aware that companies with controlled distribution outlets in this business also happen to be among the price leaders. Now, that's all wrong. The raison d'etre of a controlled distribution system is so you can charge more. That's the reason you have controlled distribution outlets, and I think somewhere along the line, that point has been missed. It hasn't been missed, for example, by Avon. That's why Avon sells its products the way that they do.

So these are the basic strategic choices that you can face. Now how does variable universal life or other registered products fit into all this? Well, basically, registered products can support the quality strategy because of the investment differentiation, and they can also support the monopoly strategy because of the restrictions on dual company representation. In other words, they are conducive to the concept of a controlled distribution system which is what monopoly is all about. It's to control the distribution outlets. So registered products are conducive to these two strategies. But it's important to note that gross margins, because these are regulated products, are likely to be controlled, and what that means is that they are likely to become standard. So where are we left? We're left with a situation where this is a product that lends itself to brand identification. Notice Northwestern Mutual's advertisements for their variable life products where the prohibitions on dual representation or restrictions on dual representation are conducive to a controlled distribution system enhanced to a pseudo monopoly. Now, the economics, because prices are likely to become standard, are going to be dependent on your costs, but basically, it is likely that people in this market place are all going to have the same margins because they're going to be controlled and their profits are going to be a direct function of their costs. So that's what variable products are all about, and variable universal is a particular example of it.

Now, I'd like to add a footnote to all of this which I'm doing anytime I have an exposure to people who are opinion molders in the life insurance business these days, and that is I would like to take a minute to talk to you about tax reform. The general issue of tax reform is quite fundamental, and it goes far beyond the narrow commercial interests in which all of us are involved, whether we be consulting actuaries or whether we be involved in the sale of insurance products. This is something that involves this entire country, and in many respects, it involves issues that get as fundamental as the question of free enterprise on trial. I don't think that it's necessary to belabor the point that some kind of tax reform is needed. And moreover, this issue is becoming sufficiently hot politically that tax reform looks as though it's inevitably going to come, and it's really an argument about what kind of tax reform. So, in my opinion, tax reform is real, and it's likely to become law, to some degree at least, this year. Now, where does life insurance fit into all this? Well, tax reform is really not so fundamentally a discussion about who pays how much tax. If the tax reformers take a dollar off my tax bill and let Tommy pay it, for example, and Tommy and I may have personal opinions as to whether that's a good or a bad idea, but fundamentally, nothing happens. Fundamentally, nothing happens. It's a question of a dollar out of his pocket or a dollar out of my pocket.

Now, this is the politically hot part of tax reform. But the real importance of tax reform is what it's going to do to product prices and values. It's not a question of who pays what taxes, and that's just a zero summary distribution game. The real question is what it's going to do to the prices of certain products and their relative appeal. For example, if you dissect the price you would pay to buy the Ritz-Carlton Hotel here in Buckhead and if you decided that your economic analysis suggested to you that the right price was $75 million, sounds like about the right number, you would find that you're paying $15 million for the tax benefits and $60 million for this brick and mortar that you see around you — paying $15 million for the tax benefits. It's clear that tax reform is going to change the value of real estate investments, and that's why the real estate lobby is so excited. It's going to alter the pattern of construction in this country. There's going to be less building. Eventually, it's going to lead to higher rents and prices will get right back on track again. Eventually, that's going to happen.

Now, I use real estate because in my opinion, it's in the forefront of tax reform. The more relevant points to all of you in the context of your involvement with the life insurance industry is what tax reform is going to do to the tax avoidance business. And it's clear that tax advice businesses are in trouble and that tax shelter businesses are in trouble. If the tax reformers succeed in doing nothing but reducing the marginal tax rate from 50% to 35%, if they succeed in doing nothing else, the value of all tax shelters has just fallen by 30%, and therefore, this is going to change the perceived value of any tax shelter. The sharpest stand of all of this is going to be the position of the people who are in the business of marketing tax shelters. Because it's their economics that are going to change even more dramatically. They are able to operate today on a basis where they are offering this tax shelter benefit for which people will arguably pay, and it's clear that they will now pay 30% less for it. So, that's where the sharp end of the action is.

Now, how about life insurance? Well, life insurance is a tax preference in many respects. However, some of these respects are illusory rather than real because there's some very big offsets to what the Treasury has proposed that are consistent with their idea of the level playing field. For instance, the Treasury plan does not contemplate that the policyholders will get any offset for the expenses they incur by buying this tax shelter called life insurance, and it's pretty clear that if you buy any other kind of investment, you would get an offset for expenses. Well, surprise, surprise, this does rather dramatic things. You see the FDC was basically right. When the FDC said the yield to policyholders is only 2%, they were basically right, and if all you did was tax that 2%, there wouldn't be much tax paid at all as you can work out for yourselves. The tax bill would be something like $1.5 billion, which is less than the industry's current bill is going to be. So the expense offset is the big issue, and those who want to talk about level playing fields and hence, tax inside buildups of life insurance, that actually wouldn't be too bad if there was an expense offset to it. It would give us exactly the same tax system as operates in the United Kingdom, for example. Another offset is the surrender and maturity offset. If you're going to tax the inside buildup, presumably the proceeds of insurance policies payable on surrender and maturity become tax-free. So that's a big offset. There are arguments that there are worthwhile social purposes served by this kind of product. When it used to pay death benefits so the step-up in basis on death may be something that can be salvaged on social arguments.

But there's one aspect of tax shelter in the life insurance industry that I think is very much at risk, and that is the whole idea of minimum deposit. I think that any fair minded people looking at the scene and trying to come up with a responsible tax reform plan would likely conclude that minimum deposit is an abusive tax shelter. My advice to the industry would be, don't ally yourselves with the real estate lobby, the tax shelter lobby, the oil and gas lobby, and so forth because I think you're going to lose.

My advice would be your argument is good on the merits. Support the idea of tax reform and point out how the level playing field in fact should be defined, and I think the industry has some good arguments on that score.

Now, in conclusion, I think variable universal life is going to fit the needs of most companies, and I would identify those companies that particularly want to continue or prolong their traditional business strategies as being especially suited for this kind of product, mainly because it will tend to support the traditional distribution system in the industry notwithstanding differences in compensation. I'd also like to observe that this product might conceivably become the chassis for all future products. Virtually any kind of product can be manufactured on a variable universal life chassis. It's not necessary to make the investment element variable and of course the universal mechanics permit complete flexibility in the death benefits that are provided.

Section 3
Life Insurance Industry: Past, Present, and Future

Debate, "Resolved . . . The Life Insurance Business, as Transacted Today, Is in Its Terminal Stages."

Published in the Record of the Society of Actuaries* *Vol. 3, No. 1 (March–April 1977): 1–14. Reprinted with permission from the Society of Actuaries.*

MR. JAMES C. H. ANDERSON: Eighteen months ago, I presented a paper to the Seventh Pacific Insurance Conference with the innocuous title "The Universal Life Insurance Policy." Because the title of the paper antedated its writing by several months, it did not adequately describe the content. In fact, the paper could more appropriately have been titled "A Critique of Traditional Life Insurance Products and Distribution Systems," a title which I have since used in subsequent discussions of the paper before various actuarial clubs and life insurance industry groups. The following excerpt summarizes the main arguments advanced:

> . . . that it is no longer realistic to assume that the typical life insurance buyer is one who will, for an extended period of time, remain married to the same wife, work at the same job and live in the same house situated in the same city; or that the financial security needs of this typical buyer and his ability to pay for them will remain constant and can be expressed in constant nominal dollars.
>
> . . . that it is not realistic for the industry to address the needs of the typical buyer with traditional permanent life insurance products

* Besides James C. H. Anderson, these people participated in this debate: as Moderator: Ardian C. Gill. As Panelists: James C. H. Anderson, Dr. Davis W. Gregg, CLU (not a member of the Society, is President of the American College, Bryn Mawr, Pennsylvania), and E. J. Moorhead.

requiring fixed regular premiums and providing fixed benefits, both expressed in constant nominal dollars.

. . . that the traditional life insurance industry distribution and administrative systems are excessively and unnecessarily costly and place the industry at a competitive disadvantage by comparison with other savings media.

. . . that the industry should respond to the needs of the contemporary market by introducing a simplified, flexible and less costly product.

. . . that the introduction of such a product is technically and financially feasible if a more effective distribution system can concurrently be developed.

. . . that the introduction of such a product would probably have a serious and adverse initial impact on the life insurance industry and its existing distribution systems.

. . . that, notwithstanding the foreseen difficulties, the needs and demands of the market will lead to the introduction of such a product, possibly led by companies with no commitment to traditional distribution systems, and that the eventual result will be more favorable to the life insurance industry than the only realistic alternative — an all term industry.

Obviously, these are sweeping arguments and they imply nothing less than a coming revolution with the life insurance industry. The limited scope of this paper does not permit their full development, nor does it permit adequate consideration of counter-arguments.

The life insurance industry is not a homogeneous business. In fact, a broad interpretation of the subject of this debate would require a separate examination of the number of sub-businesses. I intend, however, to concentrate my attention on the individual ordinary life insurance business, which still represents the backbone of the industry, and to examine the health of this sector of the industry by addressing the following five questions: (1) Does the industry really understand the contemporary environment for individual financial security products? (2) Are traditional life insurance products, notably permanent insurance, appropriate to the needs of the typical buyer under today's market conditions? (3) Are traditional life insurance products economically viable from the viewpoint of either the buyer or the industry? (4) Is the industry seriously vulnerable to a concerted raid on its accumulated assets mounted either from within the industry or from outside it? (5) Why are the shares of many publicly quoted life insurance companies selling at discounts of 50% or more from their underlying values?

Does the industry really understand the contemporary environment for individual financial security products?

I submit that the marketing strategy of the life insurance industry taken as a whole still rests, to an important extent, on the implicit assumption that the average American family consists of a breadwinner husband, a homemaker wife and (on average) two dependent children. Is this perception even approximately true today?

The following article which appears last year in the Atlanta Constitution suggests that that is not the case:

> BOTH HUSBAND, WIFE IN TYPICAL FAMILY WORK
>
> WASHINGTON (UPI) - Both husband and wife in today's "typical" American family have outside jobs, partly because of inflation's impact on income, according to the Labor department.
>
> The historic image of a breadwinner husband and homemaker wife now applies to only 34 out of 100 marriages, it said in the current issue of the Monthly Labor Review.

More recently, in a Labor Department release dated March 8, 1977, there appears the following startling (and also misleading) statement which was reported on national television a few weeks ago: "The concept of a family where the husband is the only breadwinner, the wife is a homemaker. . . , and there are two children may be a useful one for many illustrative purposes, but it does not represent the typical American family of the mid-1970s. Among husband-wife families in 1975, only seven out of 100 fit this description."

Although the foregoing quotation is faithful to the Labor Department release, the excerpt is misleading when the facts included in the tables which accompanied the release are examined closely. There are approximately 47 million husband-wife families in the United States of which only 14 million are families where the husband is the only earner; five million families have no earners; two million have one earner other than the husband; 20 million have two earners; and seven million have three or more earners. Of those 14 million families where the husband is the only earner, nine million such families consist of three or more persons and it will be these nine million families, 19% of all of the husband-wife families, who would fit the classical pattern. Although these facts are startling enough, bear in mind that husband-wife families account for only two-thirds of the adult population of the country.

Other fundamental changes in the market environment are, for this audience self-evident and I will only enumerate them:

1. Government is rapidly becoming the principal purveyor of financial security products — I estimate that the life insurance in force of the Social Security system alone is at least two trillion dollars, roughly equal to the life insurance in force of all types in the United States.
2. Most people believe that we are in an era where we may expect, for an extended period of time, higher rates of inflation than we are accustomed to; inflation must undermine the value of all long term promises, particularly money promises such as life insurance policies provide.

To what extent can the industry reasonably claim that it has modified its products, its delivery systems and its own economics in response to these changed circumstances? Moreover, the work of professional futurists suggests that the changes in store for us in the immediate future are far more radical than those which I believe are already shaking the foundations of this industry. Those with an interest in futurism, and that should include us all, might profit from a reading or a rereading of the more respected works in this field. For those who prefer a course of condensed reading, there is an excellent summary included in John M. Bragg's landmark paper, "The Future of the Actuarial Profession as Viewed in A.D. 1974," which appears in *TSA* XXVI.

Are traditional life insurance products, notably permanent insurance, appropriate to the needs of the typical buyer under today's market conditions?

Overwhelmingly, the majority of financial security products sold to individuals by the life insurance industry are characterized by the requirement of regular premiums on a fixed dollar amount and provide benefits also of a fixed dollar amount; most of the premium income of the industry and the commission income of its distribution systems arising from current sales relate to permanent, cash value forms of life insurance.

Are these the products appropriate to the needs of the typical buyer under today's market conditions? Consider the case of a 25-year-old buyer with a young family and a current annual income of $10,000. With an annual productivity gain of 2% and no inflation, he might expect an equivalent income at age 55 of $18,000. If, however, inflation is assumed to continue throughout the 30-year period at a rate of only 5%, his nominal annual income at age 55 would be $78,000. If this buyer purchased a $10,000 policy at age 25, its value in constant dollars would be only $2,300, 30 years later. I do not believe that fixed premium, fixed benefit, permanent, cash value life insurance has any relevance to this potential buyer's financial requirements over 30 years, considering only the consequences of inflation. I believe that most actuaries would agree that the assumptions underlying the illustration are quite modest and that even more radical changes in the financial circumstances of such an individual are more likely to occur than not.

But this is not the whole story, or even half of it. Our potential buyer is far more likely than not to undergo nonfinancial changes that will have an even more major impact on his financial requirements over 30 years. Since our format this morning is that of a debate, consider the following proposition: Resolved, that the expected number of wives of a 20-year-old unmarried male exceeds his expected number of children. Would you rather argue the affirmative or the negative case for this proposition?

Are traditional life insurance products economically viable from the viewpoint of either the buyer or the industry?

In the interest of determining the profile of a typical premium rate for permanent, cash value life insurance, I have made some calculations dealing with a nonparticipating and a participating ordinary life policy issued at age 35. The calculations were based on what I believe to be optimistic but representative sets of assumptions, comparable to those I have observed being used by well managed medium and large companies. After calculating a standard premium rate for both the nonparticipating and participating forms, I successively reduced each of the various assumptions to zero with all other assumptions held constant and calculated premium rates to determine how much of the premium was attributable to each of the assumptions. The results indicated that the amount of the standard premium required to meet expenses was quite high — 41% of the total for the nonparticipating form and 30% for the participating form. (This difference, incidentally, relates not to differences in the assumed level of expenses but to differences in the cost of capital required to finance new business by the shareholder-owned and policyholder-owned companies.) The cost of lapses was 8% for the nonparticipating and 4% for the participating form. The cost of death benefits was 10% of the total for the nonparticipating form and 14% for the participating form. Profits represented 5% for the nonparticipating form and surplus contributions 2% for the participating form. Cash value accumulations and policyholder dividends accounted for 36% of the nonparticipating premium and 50% of the participating premium.

Is it fair and reasonable that a nonparticipating policyholder should have 41% of his premium consumed by expenses, 8% by premature lapses and 5% by shareholder profits — a total of 54%? Is it fair and reasonable that a participating policyholder should have 30% of this premium consumed by expenses, 4% by premature lapses and 2% by surplus contributions — a total of 36%? I would reiterate that the differences in the profiles of the nonparticipating and participating premium rates are attributable to differences in the cost of capital required to finance new business and not to differences in expense levels.

It is often argued that an ordinary life insurance policy must be viewed in its entirety as a contract providing protection against premature death. But are we really selling premature death benefit coverage when only 10% of the premium is required to provide the mortality cost for the nonparticipating policy and only 14% for the participating policy? In short, is this a viable product from the viewpoint of the consumer and will the consumer continue to accept these cost levels, particularly when competing savings products are available at substantial lower cost levels which can be supported by term insurance products that the industry is prepared to offer quite cheaply?

Socrates admonished us that the first step in knowing the truth is to call a thing by its right name. I am suggesting that the buyer of our wares, given the facts, would not choose a flattering name for either of these products.

It is also instructive to compare the relative competitive position of these representative premium rates with prices available in the marketplace. A comparison with nonparticipating products offered by 18 medium- to large-sized companies indicates that their average traditional net cost is \$2.20 per thousand lower than the representative calculation, 12% of premium; the interest adjusted cost is \$1.66 per thousand lower, 9% of premium. A similar comparison of the participating product shows a traditional net cost \$1.93 per thousand less than that of the representative product, 9% of premium; the average interest adjusted cost is \$.49 per thousand less, 2% of premium. These results suggest either:

1. That the representative assumptions are not representative, a possibility which I reject, or
2. that a large and important segment of the industry is using a pricing basis which is probably not economically sound.

How many companies represented here have examined separately the profitability of their existing business in force and that of their future new business? Would it surprise you to discover that *more than all* of your future profits will be derived from existing business and that future business, viewed separately, might project perpetual losses if an adequate return on the capital invested in new business is factored into the calculations? Can you imagine what the projection would look like if future new business were further subdivided into that which will be produced by your existing agents and that which will be produced by agents you have not yet hired? Since approximately two-thirds of the expenses of a typical life insurance company are associated with the distribution system, it follows that a critical examination of expense levels quickly focuses on this area of operation. In this connection, it is worth noting that the average sales frequency of the industry is very low — approximately one sale per week per full time equivalent agent.

In that one sad statistic may lie the root of the whole problem. Is it reasonable to pay an agent a full time income for making just one sale a week? Is our product so difficult to sell that 40 hours of effort are required to effect just one sale? Is it not possible that a more attractively priced product could be sold twice as easily and that the present distribution system might effect twice as many sales with a 50% reduction in unit distribution costs?

Ours is an industry particularly susceptible to its own cant, in my view. I have heard my friend and associate, Tom Bowles, refer to our "velvet rut."

Let's start with *"Life insurance has to be sold."* The Insurance Institute of London *Report of the Advance Study Group (No. 27)* includes the following quotation from the records of one United Kingdom company: "The Committee having considered Proper Measures for enlarging the Insurance of this Office, have thought convenient to Appoint Persons of Reputation and substance in the Chief Towns and Cities to Distribute Policies and receive all Quarterages and to allow such persons One Shilling in the Pound as an Equivalent for their Trouble."

That statement reasonably describes the marketing strategy still being followed by companies distributing their wares through personal producing general agents. Yet it was recorded in December 1720 — 257 years ago! Is it possible that such a marketing strategy could still be the best available today when a typical Sunday press run of the *New York Times* far surpasses the entire printed word as it existed in 1720? When commercial radio is well into its second half century? When commercial television has been generally available for approximately 30 years? And when a computer terminal no costlier nor less portable than a 1960 desk top calculator can access powerful computers over an ordinary telephone line?

I am reminded of a conversation I had a few years ago with a representative of Coutts Bank, a venerable if somewhat old fashioned financial institution, where striped pants and frock coats are still very much in vogue. He said to me, "Mr. Anderson, it would be a mistake for you to think of us as a 19th century institution — we are an 18th century institution." Is it possible that this observation has some relevance to our own venerable distribution system?

It's also instructive to observe the recent growth of savings bank life insurance, particularly in New York. From 1970 to 1975, life insurance in force increased at a compound rate of 14% per annum and sales increased at a compound rate of 17% per annum; both rates substantially surpassed those of the life insurance industry.

Another long accepted truism of our industry is this: *Our agency organizations are our most valuable assets.* Is this really true? Or do we mean that our agency organizations are our most costly assets? Based on the experience of several highly respected companies to which I have been made privy, I know that the cost of "manufacturing" from scratch a full time established agent is in the vicinity of $100,000. I judge this figure to be right, at least to the nearest $100,000! If the company developing that agent is to recover its costs, together with a reasonable rate of return on its costs, the required productivity of the agent is absurdly high — which is another way of saying that it is no longer economically viable to develop new agents on the basis of current experience.

In summary, it is my contention that we are distributing a product which is economically unattractive to the buyer and economically unsound from the industry viewpoint. This unsatisfactory state of affairs is attributable, in my view, to unreasonably high expenses, notably distribution costs, to an unfavorable Federal income tax position and to high termination rates. To make matters worse, it is my judgment that the trends in each of these areas suggest a worsening position — most companies are experiencing increasing expense rates, the Federal income tax burden of the industry as a whole is increasing disapportionately year by year, and the *Life Insurance Fact Book* shows clearly a 25-year trend of increasing lapses (from 1951 to 1975 voluntary termination rates on new policies, on old policies and on both groups combined have increased by more than 100%).

Is the industry seriously vulnerable to a concerted raid on its accumulated assets mounted either from within the industry or from outside it?

I believe that the spectre of large scale replacement of existing business in force is no illusion. Whether this takes the form of an outright raid on accumulated cash values or a systematic exploitation of policy loan provisions, the result would be the same. The industry, as a whole, is holding fixed income securities on which there is a substantial market depreciation but its outstanding policy contracts contain guaranteed cash values and guaranteed policy loan facilities which afford the industry no protection from market depreciation. In these circumstances, the danger of a raid is real and some might even argue that the raid is already in progress and has been for a number of years.

Why are the shares of many publicly quoted life insurance companies selling at discounts of 50% or more from their underlying values?

Those who have been involved in the business of evaluating life insurance companies for purchase, sale, merger or other purpose will agree, I believe, with the discount cited. In fact, some whole companies have recently sold at substantial premiums over their quoted market values. What does this signal?

I believe that it signals that the investment community is conscious of some of the industry problems which I have discussed in this presentation. In particular, I believe that investors are dissatisfied with the return on capital. It also means that many companies are worth more dead than alive, a phrase for which I am indebted to Mel Gold. The implications for stock life insurance companies are quite disturbing: particularly for overcapitalized stock life insurance companies, there exists the opportunity for a nonfinancial company in another industry to purchase the life insurance company at a discount and redeploy its capital funds elsewhere. The public interest may also be involved if a substantial portion of the industry should fall into the hands of nonfinancial companies with different attitudes towards acceptable levels of risk and responsibility as well as profits.

Other lines of business

I've concentrated in this presentation on the individual ordinary life insurance business. It is appropriate, in addition, to note that all is not necessarily well in other lines of business which make up the industry.

The home service branch of the industry suffers from even more unsatisfactory benefit to cost ratios than the ordinary branch. Surely it must be recognized that this line of business is vulnerable to the attention of politicians and consumerists alike.

Both the individual and group health insurance lines of business have experienced an extended period of unsatisfactory financial results and a major proportion of these lines of business is vulnerable to a national health insurance program.

Credit insurance is a line of business which is also vulnerable to state regulatory intervention.

Summary

In summary, I see an industry in a state of actual or impending crisis. But to address more directly the subject of this debate and to present a more believable argument that fundamental change is imminent, it is necessary for me to suggest who will administer the coup-de-grâce to some of our more cherished practices and how it will be administered. In this context, I would suggest that you bear in mind that while civil libertarians, courts and juries may be reluctant to administer capital punishment on an individual basis, I detect no comparable squeamishness on the part of creditors of corporations.

My preferred scenario is that the industry itself — hopefully, lead by the actuarial profession — will recognize its own problems and shortcomings and initiate changes from within. Are we as actuaries living up to our professional responsibilities if we do not communicate forcefully our concerns for the future of the industry — both for the companies which comprise it and for the policyholders it serves? If change is to come in this way, I would predict that it would take the form of a radical change in our products, our price structure and our distribution systems. It is worth noting that precisely such changes in products, price structure and distribution systems have, in the past, lead to major rearrangements of industry market shares.

If change is to be imposed upon the industry from outside, it might take any of several forms. Massive intervention by government, either by the imposition of wide-ranging regulations or by a further takeover of many of the industry's functions, might be considered as the "Big Bang" alternative which leaves behind only a pile of rubble to be picked over; to some extent this is what happened to the mutual fund industry's retail operations some years ago. An aggressive program mounted by renegade companies or by competitors from other savings media, perhaps supported by consumerists, leading to a concerted raid on asset accumulations might be described as the "Götterdämmerung" alternative. These are but two among many such possibilities.

Failing all else, it's my view that the industry will experience a gradual and painful self destruction caused by a "Doomsday" machine which has already been manufactured and has been running for several years. The "Doomsday" machine is our own cheap term insurance products which we freely make available to all who wish to construct their own insurance cum investment program. The present economics of our business requires that the industry maintain a substantial stake in the savings market. Since we have a product monopoly on life insurance products, it is a mistake for us to make that product freely available at very low prices to those who wish to channel their savings into other media.

Conclusion

When I began to write and speak about these problems some 18 months ago, I expected to encounter a considerable amount of Maginot Line thinking from actuaries and other persons involved in the life insurance industry. Some, I imagine, would at least want my buttons, my epaulets and my sword (if not my head) for articulating such heresy. To my surprise, the reaction has been quite mild and significantly more sympathetic than I expected. This persuades me that the industry itself is already conscious of the problems which I have discussed in this presentation. Let me express the hope that it also signals a readiness to contemplate revolutionary change and that my preferred future may become a reality.

MR. E. J. MOORHEAD: Mr. Anderson is confusing terminal illness with the normal trials and tribulations that are good for us. I disagree that the business now being issued will not pay its way because the reverse can be demonstrated simply by the proposition that actuaries are conservative and what they are doing is conservative and what they are doing is going to turn out all right in the long run for everybody except the policyholders.

Years ago, when I worked for what was then the Life Insurance Agency Management Association, we used to teach in the Agency Management School the belief that just so long as men loved their wives and children, just that long will life insurance endure. I have since changed my view on that. I now say just so long as presumably well-educated people thoughtfully accept the typical explanation of why life insurance gives you good value for the dollar, just so long will life insurance endure, and that is a long time. We do not yet have a public that has reached the highly tuned state of spending aversion to life insurance that Mr. Anderson has portrayed.

The major parts of our differences are in identifying the problems that do exist and considering the time that is available to do something about them. Whole life insurance as it is provided today by the most efficient of the life insurance companies does justify buyer acceptance and will continue to do the job fairly well. The problem is that the spectrum of prices and to some degree the spectrum of quality of those products is broader than is desirable in an era of greater consumer enlightment. The problem is not that there are not products on the market that justify the trust and use of the buying public. The answer therefore is not to sweep away what we have today and replace it by something else, although innovations that supplement the basic life insurance policies are very much to be desired and are in fact taking place. We *must* demonstrate to those who are looking at us that competition with its desirable features as envisaged two centuries ago by Adam Smith does exist and does cause life insurance companies in their own self interest to provide products that are as close as possible to matching the best that are available in the market today.

The following shortcomings urgently need your attention. First, we must consider whether whole life insurance on the nonparticipating system is really feasible in the volatile economic, demographic, and social conditions that exist today. The actuary calculating a nonparticipating premium is faced with a more painful dilemma than has ever been the case in the actuarial profession before. He is in the position of believing one thing and making his calculations on a different set of assumptions. He believes in general that interest rates will stay up; he makes his calculations on the assumption that interest rates will remain at present levels during the time when the reserve is so small that it does not make any difference what assumption he uses, and that they will decline at the time when the value of the policy increases to the point when the interest element is significant. The answer is the abandonment of nonparticipating insurance except on low investment element short-term policies.

Second, urgent attention must be devoted to active promotion by actuaries of more enlightened policy approval systems in the state insurance departments. At the present time, policies are being designed for the purpose of either quoting or evading easy comparison with other policies. That is not a problem, as some believe, which can be solved by laying vast numbers of figures in front of the consumer but is a problem which must be faced at the regulatory level. It will have to be faced by the formation in the insurance departments of central offices adequately staffed with people who understand this subject and who are prepared to go to battle on the question of whether a particular pattern of cash values and endowment benefits and dividends does serve the interest of the public or whether it is there for a less appropriate purpose.

Finally, both company actuaries and, of more importance, consulting actuaries need to approach the matter of calculation of premiums, cash values and dividends from a different angle than has been traditional in the business these many years. The procedure is to make the calculation on the assumptions that seem to fit the operating factors in the company and then take a look to see whether they are competitive. It will be more and more necessary as buyer enlightenment increases and as pressures for regulation become stronger that actuaries tackle the competitive questions first, and then instruct and work with the management of their company to see whether they can live within those competitive factors. We are doing the whole job backwards. If you feel that this set of processes to which I have referred is a good set of processes, and if you feel that you have a choice between doing some of these things now or eventually, my only warning is that eventually may not be soon enough.

MR. ANDERSON: Another long accepted truism of our industry is that . . . "our agency organizations are our most valuable assets." Is this really true? Perhaps we mean our agency organizations are our most costly assets. The cost of manufacturing from scratch an established agent is in the vicinity of $100,000. This figure I would judge to be right to the nearest $100,000. If the company developing that agent is to recover its cost together with a reasonable rate of return on its costs, the required productivity of the agent is absurdly high — which is another way of saying that it is no longer economically viable to develop new agents on the basis of current experience. Is that a viable ongoing operation? The reason why the equivalent level expense turns out to be 41% for nonparticipating and 30% for participating may be puzzling. The difference between those two figures is really the difference between the fact that policyholders traditionally receive rates of return preferable to that which can be earned on bonds and stocks and then discounted for tax; let's say 6%. Shareholders need to have a return of approximately 15% on the investment in the life insurance company in order to be competitive with other investments, so the 11% difference is largely attributable to required rates of return on the use of the shareholders capital. Mr. Moorhead has suggested a new procedure for establishing premium rates and at first I was not sure whether he was going to suggest that we raise them to cover what our expenses actually are or lower them down to where our expenses should actually be. I am sympathetic with the latter point of view.

DR. DAVIS W. GREGG: There is a lack of passion in what has been expressed and if the actuary can prove that he is passionate in his beliefs, I would feel better. The proposition that has been debated is that *individual* life insurance as transacted today is in its terminal stages. We should put this in a proper framework as to whether we are talking about the more limited area of individual life insurance or the broader area of the life insurance industry.

MR. ARDIAN C. GILL: Mr. Moorhead first called upon the requirement of love to sustain the industry and then said, "No, he rejects that." It depends on the gullibility of the public. An agent of my company once explained that to me in a slightly different way. He said the three sweetest words in the English language are not "I love you," but "check is enclosed."

Mr. Moorhead, I understand you to say that you want to mutualize the stock companies, or at least the whole life product and raise the price of term. Whatever happened to the marketplace forces and the forces of free enterprise? Are we headed as one of Mr. Anderson's scenarios suggests, toward government as our saviour? Are we going to be like the airlines where we require regulation to keep us in business?

MR. MOORHEAD: The complexities of the life insurance business are too great for the marketplace forces to operate in the classic economic fashion. It is the public ignorance that is preventing marketplace forces from working as they should. I am not suggesting that there is *no* competition. I am suggesting that the spectrum of prices suggests that there is insufficient price competition. The competition tends to be rather muted and tends to be competition for agents rather than competition in the quality and pricing of our product. A great deal is said in the training of life insurance agents that give them a false and unduly rosy picture of the way in which life insurance functions. That was one of the reasons for the development of the interest adjusted method. We were working with a system that encouraged the belief that permanent life insurance doesn't cost anything, which is not the case.

MR. ANDERSON: We are behaving in the normal economic pattern if you make the one assumption that the client of the industry is the agent and not the policyholder. If you make that assumption, then the general behavior pattern becomes a lot closer to the classical one.

The industry's pattern of commission rates is substantially influenced by the New York legislation. What would the profile of a typical premium rate have looked like circa 1905? If the arithmetic has been done in more or less the way I demonstrated in my opening remarks, the mortality costs at that time would have represented a more substantial portion of the premium than it does today.

Perhaps the framers of the legislation that has governed our commission pattern for the last 70 years or so actually intended that the top commission rate should be paid on the longest form of term insurance. Around the beginning of this century, whole life insurance was really closer to term insurance than it was to anything else. The whole life products as a result of changes in mortality rates have drifted into the savings end of the spectrum. We have not adjusted our commissions accordingly.

DR. GREGG: The institution of life insurance serves basic human needs and wants for financial security. There is ample evidence that these needs and wants are increasing. People in our society are better able to pay for them. There is a second dimension that is essentially economic but it is totally broad. The institution of life insurance fills an increasingly significant role in an area. If the economic pie in our society is going to grow in a manner such that everyone can be better off, we have to have capital formation. The life insurance institution has a unique opportunity to make a continuing contribution in this particular way. This contribution should be understood by all. We have to build and renew our economic plant. Long-term capital source is quite important.

We must examine marketing on the one-to-one basis in life insurance, warts and all, if it's going to be improved in the future. There is only one way that one can provide individual life insurance in the way that it should be provided to the American individual, family and business. There is only one way to do it, someone has to knock on the door and talk to people and persuade them to think about the future.

MR. ANDERSON: It is instructive to observe the recent growth of savings bank life insurance particularly in New York. From 1970 to 1975, life insurance in force increased at a compound rate of 14% per annum. Sales increased at a compound rate of 17% per annum. Both rates substantially surpassed those of the life insurance industry.

While life insurance still has to be sold, it does not necessarily have to be sold on the one-on-one basis leading up to what Dr. Gregg wants to describe as the critical encounter. We have a population today that is far better educated than any prior population that this country or any other country has ever had. Life insurance is not a novelty. It is something that people are familiar with. The process of selling life insurance 30 or 40 years ago was a very different process than it is today. There is hope for the use of the technology that has become available to us which has been ignored for the past 257 years. The agency system as we know it today, has a future, but its future lies in operating far more efficiently. It is madness that we have the equivalent of 500,000 life insurance agents in this country. The latest statistics suggest that there are 250,000 who get at least one-half of their income from life insurance and 250,000 who get less than one-half of their income from life insurance.

Assuming a 75%/25% mix, this works out to 250,000 full time equivalent agents. The distribution of our products does not require that much manpower. There was a time when we had thousands of elevator operators. What has happened to them? Technology has replaced people. It has replaced people in all industries.

MR. GILL: Mr. Gregg said the public is better able to pay for our product. It seems he is talking only about the upper and middle classes or about businesses. Is the industry now competing principally for the so-called sophisticated markets and ignoring the real mass market for individual life insurance in terms of numbers of people to be insured?

MR. MOORHEAD: There is a substantial argument that there is too much concentration on the affluent area of the business but that is understood by the marketing officers. They have to deal with it in two ways; first through their actuaries with the product that they offer and second, by trying to make sure that field people who can effectively handle the middle income market do not divert themselves by digging for gold in the affluent market and then eventually drop out of the business because that is not for them. The problem exists, but it is recognized and there is a good chance that it will be dealt with.

To the extent that the life insurance business does completely move away from a market, the government coverage will simply take over and life insurance business has that option. We can, if we wish, vacate more and let the government take over. It is not entirely a matter of whether the company would like to have that business. There is also a question of social responsibility. At what dividing point is it in the interest of the public that government coverage be the major provider, the "one-on-one" limited to a smaller part? The competitive element of trying to get bigger and bigger and bigger may interfere with the social responsibility element in that whole matter. It needs to be worked on.

DR. GREGG: If the expansionist group prevails in our society and the government schemes, whether Social Security, welfare, or whatever continue to expand, then we have examples around the world as to what will happen. Ninety percent of the American public is more fearful of big government than of big business. Therefore, the opportunity of the life insurance business in the financial security area is immense if we respond.

MR. MOORHEAD: The question is to what extent that attitude on the part of the public is fostered by a lack of understanding of just how life insurance works. Their eyes may be closed to some of the difficulties of the private enterprise side of this. That 90% may change as the public becomes more knowledgeable.

DR. GREGG: If the "Big Bang" is the enemy, then a lot of things are going to change in this country beyond life insurance. The Götterdämmerung concept is a dangerous one. We saw what happened to private pensions when we turned our back on the field. The banks did quite well. The "Doomsday" scenario is the most risky element that Mr. Anderson has alerted us to, the concept that erosion is going to take place. Life insurance management has gone beyond the point where the opinion of the intellectual in the company is regarded to be of small import.

MR. GILL: A ratio of increase in policy loans to increase in premiums of three to one is respectable today. A ratio of increase in policy loans to increase in reserves of 30% or more is respectable. Is this not, in itself a raid on our assets? Are we not depending upon investment income for capital formation? Are we going to end up as flow-throughs to our policyholders and vitiate our role in the area of capital formation?

MR. ANDERSON: We are prisoners of our own statutory balance sheets and think that policy loans are assets. That is nonsense. Policy loans are not assets at all and have nothing to do with capital formation. It is just a peculiarity of the way that we keep books that makes us think that they are assets. If we were a normal kind of savings institution, they would be under the label of partial redemptions or partial withdrawals. If we look at our real results in terms of how we have managed to stay in the savings markets, those real results are a lot worse than the aggregate assets suggest.

The industry must stay in the savings business, otherwise its economics are going to be destroyed in a way worse than anything else we have discussed. That "Doomsday" scenario is the worst of all the scenarios. The only way we can stay in the savings market is to sharpen up our savings products and make them competitive with other savings products. Basing an industry of this size on public gullibility is a completely unsound premise.

MR. GILL: If each of you were to be appointed consultant to the entire life insurance industry, and recognizing that the essence of planning is to get the job done, what is the first step that you would recommend the industry take?

MR. ANDERSON: It would be an overhaul of the form of our permanent insurance products to make them more flexible and responsive accompanied by a radical overhaul of our field compensation system. Generally speaking, an overhaul would increase commission rates moderately to slightly on term insurance and reduce them radically on permanent forms.

MR. MOORHEAD: The first step the industry has to take is to recognize the things that we have debated. These are all controversial questions and we cannot deal with them as if we are sheep without a bellwether. There is bound to be a controversial element in anything that enlightens the public to these differences and gives them a more intelligent basis for choice than they have at the present time.

As long as we are committed institutionally to unity, we are unlikely to be able to take the first necessary step. It must be up to the heads and the actuaries of the companies which are providing products that do stand up well. It must be up to them to start to announce more steadily and more clearly that these differences do exist and that there is a reason for the public to turn to attractively priced types of products without fear of being shortchanged in quality or service.

DR. GREGG: The first step is to listen to what Mr. Anderson has said very carefully. Are we an insurance institution or are we something beyond an insurance institution as a financial security institution? What is our role in savings? This has been an ambivalence that has existed in this industry over several decades. It is a tragedy for the American public.

We must talk about life insurance as a savings institution in order to strengthen the quality of life in this nation in which we live. We can do things that others cannot do and we must be competitive and creative.

The Alternative Futures of the Life Insurance Industry

Presented to the Life Office Management Association (LOMA) Investment Seminar at Rockford College, Rockford, Illinois, June 13, 1978. Reprinted with permission from LOMA.

FRIENDS, ROMANS, COUNTRYMEN,
Lend me your ears
I come to bury Caesar not to praise him.

So, according to William Shakespeare, on the Ides of March, 2,021 years ago, spoke Mark Antony at the funeral of Julius Caesar.

My purpose this morning is somewhat different. I come not to bury the life insurance industry; neither do I come to praise it.

Introduction

For the past three years, in various forums, I have expressed concerns relating to the future of the life insurance industry. In summary, I believe that the industry has entered a period of significant change:

- Change in the marketplace we serve
- Change in the economic environment in which we operate
- Change in the financial security needs of the public
- Change in the types of products we should be selling
- Change in the distribution systems needed to sell the new products to the new market under these new circumstances.

The views I have expressed and will express again this morning are not popular ones. Nevertheless, it is my firm belief that if we are to have a voice in determining the future of the industry, we must identify and address some significant problems; it is also my contention that if we do not take steps now to determine our own future, another future, considerably more menacing, will be thrust upon us:

- By further large-scale government incursion into the financial security markets;
- By forces of the marketplace; or
- By competition, either of a progressive or renegade nature.

The Current State of the Industry

A consideration of the alternative futures of the life insurance industry must begin with an appraisal of the current state of the industry. For the purpose of this appraisal, it is instructive to consider the viewpoint of investors in publicly quoted life insurance companies' shares.

During the past five years, Tillinghast, Nelson & Warren, Inc. has been asked to make independent appraisals of approximately 100 life insurance companies. The purposes of the appraisals were varied — purchase and sale, merger, reorganization, rehabilitation and management information. In general, our assignment was to determine a value which represented a fair price for an arm's length transaction between a willing buyer and a willing seller, uninfluenced by temporary or aberrational market conditions, with neither party being under any immediate obligation to consummate a transaction.

The methodology used to make such an appraisal is widely accepted within the actuarial profession in the United States. Briefly, the method consists of an evaluation of three separate components:

1. the adjusted statutory net worth;
2. value of business in force; and
3. value of future new business.

As often as not, the value of this third component is negative, indicating that new business is not profitable enough to justify its acquisition costs.

Without exception, the appraised value of every publicly quoted life insurance company appraised by TN&W since 1972 has substantially exceeded the aggregate market value of its outstanding shares, often by 100% or more. What does this signal?

One obvious possible answer is that this phenomenon does not apply only to the life insurance industry and that share prices generally are lower than a rational appraisal would suggest. Nevertheless, the magnitude of the differential between appraised values and market values (comparable to an "appraised value" of 1700 for the Dow Jones Industrial Average) suggests that there are special problems which relate to the life insurance industry. I believe that financial analysts and investors are concerned by some or all of the following problems and potential problems of the industry:

1. that the industry does not appropriately address the contemporary environment for individual financial security products;
2. that traditional life insurance products, notably permanent insurance, are not appropriate to the needs of the typical buyer;
3. that traditional life insurance products are not economically viable from the viewpoint of either the buyer or the industry;
4. that the traditional life insurance distribution system is contracting because it is financially unsound; and
5. that the industry is seriously vulnerable to a concerted raid on its accumulated assets.

The Contemporary Environment

Taken as a whole, the marketing strategy of the life insurance industry still rests, to an important extent, on the implicit assumption that the average American family consists of a breadwinner husband, a homemaker wife, and (on average) two dependent children. Is this perception even approximately true today?

In the U. S. Labor Department release dated March 8, 1977, there appears the following startling (and also misleading) statement which was reported on national television at that time:

> The concept of a family where the husband is the only breadwinner, the wife is a homemaker..., and there are two children may be a useful one for many illustrative purposes, but it does not represent the typical American family of the mid-1970s. Among husband-wife families in 1975, only seven out of 100 fit this description.

Although the foregoing quotation is faithful to the Labor Department release, the excerpt is misleading in that it refers to families with exactly two children. There are approximately 47 million husband-wife families in the United States of which only 14 million are families where the husband is the only earner; 9 million such families consist of three or more persons, and it is these 9 million families, 19% of all of the husband-wife families, that fit the classical pattern. Although these facts are startling enough, it should also be noted that husband-wife families account for only two-thirds of the adult population of the country.

Other fundamental changes in the market environment are self-evident and need only be enumerated:

1. Government has become the principal purveyor of financial security products; the "life insurance in force" of the Social Security System alone exceeds two trillion dollars, an amount greater than the private life insurance in force of all types in the United States.
2. Most observers expect, for an extended period of time, higher rates of inflation than have prevailed in the past; inflation must undermine the value of all long-term money promises such as life insurance policies provide.
3. Although private savings continue to expand, the life insurance industry is consistently losing its share of the private savings market; the loss of market share is particularly noticeable if policy loans are regarded as withdrawn savings.
4. Since 1951, lapse rates on both old and new policies have increased steadily; over the 25-year period 1951–76, the aggregate increase exceeds 100%.
5. Sales of term insurance of all types and permanent insurance which qualifies for tax concessions represent an increasing proportion of new business; sales of permanent insurance in the family market are declining relatively.

The Appropriateness of Permanent Life Insurance Products

Overwhelmingly, the majority of financial security products sold to individuals by the life insurance industry are characterized by the requirement of regular premiums of a fixed dollar amount and provide benefits also of a fixed dollar amount; most of the premium income of the industry and the commission income of its distribution systems relate to permanent forms of life insurance, which are particularly inflexible.

Are these products appropriate to the needs of the typical buyer under today's market conditions? Considering only the effects of inflation, at a rate of only 5%, long-term money promises to depreciate in value approximately 40% every 10 years. In such an environment, fixed premium/fixed benefit, permanent life insurance has little relevance to a typical buyer's financial requirements over the extended period of time necessary to justify the purchase of permanent insurance instead of term insurance. Moreover, a typical buyer is far more likely than not, under conditions prevailing in society today, to experience other changes that will have an even more significant impact on his probable financial requirements than the effects of inflation. To illustrate, consider the following proposition: Resolved, that the expected number of wives of a 20-year old unmarried male exceeds his expected number of children. On which side of that argument does the advantage lie?

The Viability of Permanent Life Insurance Products

In the interest of determining the profile of a typical premium rate for permanent life insurance, I have made calculations for a nonparticipating ordinary life policy issued at age 35. After determining a standard premium rate on the basis of assumptions representative of those used by well-managed medium-to-large stock companies, additional hypothetical premium rates were calculated by successively reducing each of the various assumptions to zero with all other assumptions held constant. By comparing the additional premiums with the standard premium, it is possible to determine how much of the standard premium is attributable to each of the assumptions.

The results indicate that 41% of the standard premium is required to meet expenses, 8% to meet the cost of premature lapses, 10% to meet the cost of death benefits, 5% for shareholder pre-tax profits and the remaining 36% to accumulate cash values. The aggregate cost of benefits represents only 54% of the total premium.

Such a low benefit-to-cost ratio might be supportable for a product primarily intended to provide protection benefits; comparable ratios, for example, can be found in individual health insurance and some personal casualty insurance lines. But the profile also suggests that the ordinary life product is primarily a savings vehicle and competing savings vehicles operate on benefit-to-cost ratios ranging from 90% to 100%.

In short, is this a viable *savings* product from the viewpoint of the consumer and will the consumer continue to accept these cost levels, particularly when competing savings products are available at substantially lower cost levels which can be packaged with term insurance products that the industry is prepared to offer quite cheaply?

It is also instructive to compare the relative competitive position of the standard premium rate with prices available in the marketplace. A comparison with nonparticipating products offered by 18 medium-to-large size companies indicates that the average interest adjusted cost of those companies is $1.66 per $1,000 lower than the standard premium rate, a difference of 9%. This comparison suggests either:

1. that the "representative" assumptions are not representative; or
2. that a large and important segment of the industry is using a pricing basis which is probably unsound.

The Viability of Existing Distribution Systems

Since approximately two-thirds of the expenses of a typical life insurance company are associated with its distribution system, it follows that a critical examination of expense levels quickly focuses on this area of operation. In this connection, it is worth noting that the average sales frequency of the industry is very low — less than one sale per week per full-time equivalent agent. In that one sad statistic may lie the root of the whole problem. It may also be the germ of a solution.

The Insurance Institute of London *Report of the Advance Study Group (No. 27)* includes the following quotation from the records of one United Kingdom company:

> The Committee having considered Proper Measures for enlarging the Insurance of this Office, have thought convenient to Appoint Persons of Reputation and substance in the Chief Towns and Cities to Distribute Policies and receive all Quarterages and to allow such persons One Shilling in the Pound as an Equivalent for their Trouble.

That statement reasonably describes the marketing strategy being followed today by companies distributing their wares through personal producing general agents. Yet it was recorded in December 1720 — 257 years ago! Is it possible that such a marketing strategy could still be the best available today when a typical Sunday press run of the *New York Times* far surpasses the entire printed word as it existed in 1720? When commercial radio is well into its second half century? When commercial television has been generally available for approximately 30 years? And when a computer terminal no costlier nor less portable than a 1960 desk top calculator can access powerful computers over an ordinary telephone line?

It's also instructive to observe the recent growth of savings bank life insurance, particularly in New York. From 1970 to 1975, life insurance in force increased at a compound rate of 14% per annum and sales increased at a compound rate of 17% per annum; both growth rates substantially surpassed those of the life insurance industry. Perhaps the truism, *life insurance has to be sold*, implying *sold in the traditional way*, is not as true as it used to be.

Another long accepted truism of the industry is this: *Our agency organizations are our most valuable assets.* Is this really true? Or should it read: Our agency organizations are our most *costly* assets? The experience of several highly respected companies to which I am privy suggests that the cost of "manufacturing" from scratch a full-time established agent is in the vicinity of $100,000 (to the nearest $100,000). If the company developing that agent is to recover its costs, together with a reasonable rate of return on its costs, the required productivity of the agent is absurdly high — which is another way of saying that it is no longer economically viable to develop new agents on the basis of current experience. Many companies have, in fact, abandoned efforts to develop agents in favor of proselytization. Obviously, this is a dead-end strategy for the industry as a whole.

Vulnerability to a Concerted Raid on Assets

The spectre of large-scale replacement of existing business in force is no illusion. Whether this takes the form of an outright raid on accumulated cash values or a systematic exploitation of policy loan provisions, the result would be the same. The industry, as a whole, is holding fixed income securities on which there is a substantial market depreciation, but its outstanding policy contracts contain guaranteed cash value and guaranteed policy loan facilities which afford the industry no protection from market depreciation. In these circumstances, the danger of a raid is real, and some might even argue that the raid is already in progress.

It should be noted that nonparticipating insurance is more vulnerable than participating insurance because higher interest rates (the cause of the market depreciation) are not reflected in higher dividends.

Alternative Futures

What are the alternative futures of the life insurance industry? To stimulate more than to instruct, this question will be addressed by presenting a series of five scenarios. To add an Orwellian touch, each of the scenarios has a setting in 1984.

The scenarios share a common background:

- The decline of the traditional family as the basic unit of society has continued. The birth rate, which dropped below the zero population growth level in the early 1970s, has gradually increased and stabilized at approximately the ZPG rate. The generation gap has not closed.
- A coin telephone call now costs 25¢. The rate of inflation, while still high, is down from the dizzying heights of earlier years, and 5% inflation is now considered an acceptable target. The widely followed prime interest rate, after touching 12%, has receded to 8% as inflation subsided. Talk of an impending energy crisis continues, but its expected arrival has been postponed several times.
- Supersonic travel is now fairly routine, following the introduction of the more efficient extended-range Concorde II and the success of the Russian-built supersonic transport, dubbed Concordski. American aircraft makers are racing to catch up with a rocket powered model which will fly at altitudes that make supersonic overland travel practical.
- The United States is preparing for what looks like a hotly contested presidential election, with the Republicans bent on recapturing the White House on the basis of the pragmatic policy: "If you can't beat them, join them."

- In general, although old problems remain unsolved, these are peaceful and prosperous years. It may be that the eighties will be judged by historians as the decade of toleration.
- In this environment, the life insurance industry continues to operate, but how? The following scenarios are intended to suggest various possibilities.

Scenario 1 — Business (Almost) as Usual

In defiance of all the prophesies, the life insurance industry continues to flourish and grow. The industry continues to receive the majority of its income from traditional permanent insurance products notwithstanding the continuing rise in term insurance sales and the introduction of various "open track" policies carrying significantly lower commissions. The industry continues to distribute its wares through the agency system, despite a continuing decline in the number of full-time agents and the development of a scattering of non-agency distribution methods. Most agents now make extensive use of computer terminals as a point-of-sale aid. Recently, there has been a decrease in sales by number of policies.

The number of freestanding stock life insurance companies has reduced and life insurance company shares continue to sell at substantial discounts from their intrinsic values, leading to a continuation of the trend for non-financial companies to acquire life insurance companies. Fears relating to the possible underpricing of individual life insurance products from the mid-1970s onwards have proven to be unfounded: High interest rates and substantially improved mortality have resulted in higher than expected earnings and dividends.

While prophesies of doom continue, the prophets themselves, notably one aging actuary in Atlanta, have largely been discredited.

Scenario 2 — Big Brother Arrives

The date is Friday, June 29. In its race towards the summer recess for the July 4 holiday and the ensuing national conventions, Congress has just put the finishing touches on what will probably be the biggest watermelon cutting in history — the Financial Security Act of 1984. Together with existing legislation, the new Act provides cradle to grave coverage on a heretofore unimagined scale.

Social Security benefits have been increased well beyond the subsistence level, and the coverage is now universal. A feature of the new Act is a variable retirement age with a corresponding adjustment of retirement benefits. This feature, together with the expansion of benefits, gives the program many of the aspects of private pension plans.

Previous legislation mandating national health insurance has been scrapped in favor of a government-sponsored plan.

A spokesman for the American Council of Life Insurance bitterly observed, "This Act marks the end of private health insurance and may be the beginning of the end of private medical care, private pension plans, and private savings."

Scenario 3 — Götterdämmerung

The date is Friday, April 15. The place is the office of the treasurer of the Preservation Mutual Life Insurance Company. The cash report for the week shows that the cash outflow for benefits, expenses, surrenders and policy loans, partly due to the income tax deadline, has reached 300% of total cash inflow. As usual, many of the surrendering policies are assigned to Cannibal Life. Preservation Mutual has experienced negative cash flow for four consecutive years and has already sold all investments realizable without incurring capital losses. Since long-term interest rates are now in excess of 10%, the company has a substantial unrealized depreciation on its remaining portfolio of bonds and mortgages. To avoid recognizing losses, it has incurred substantial bank debt on which the interest differential is significantly adverse.

The office is conspicuously empty. Two years ago, the investment department was disbanded since the company had no funds to invest. The sales department has also been disbanded since the company ceased writing new business to protect its solvency.

Scenario 4 — Doomsday

The date is Thursday, December 30. Since New Year's Day falls on Saturday, this is the last business day of the year. The vice president for sales is reviewing results for 1984. He notes that business is up 10% over the previous year, measured by face amounts of insurance. Companywide sales have reached $1 billion for the first time in history, a milestone which gives satisfaction to all. Aggregate new premium income, however, is only $5 million, a decline of 50% over the previous five years.

A review of the sales results indicates that the company did business with 2,000 brokers during the past year, each producing an average of 10 sales for a total of $2,500 of premium income and $1,000 of commission. Ninety-eight percent of new business was term insurance.

Scenario 5— Revolution

The scene is the employees' lounge of the Acme Manufacturing Company. In a semi-darkened room, a group of employees is watching a television screen on which a videotape presentation is playing. The film explains how proper planning using the right tools can provide a means of achieving personal financial goals. The film illustrates how a computer can assist in identifying the right tools to achieve particular goals.

At the end of the presentation, the audience is invited to make use of self-operated computer terminals along the wall of the lounge to identify which tools are best suited to help achieve their individual goals. Personal advisors, they are told, are available to help with the operation of the computer terminal and to help interpret the results.

The company sponsoring this personal financial planning seminar is a member of a financial complex offering a wide range of financial services including innovative life insurance contracts which provide complete flexibility to meet changing circumstances. Its sales representatives are salaried employees. The 1,000-man sales organization provides national coverage. For the year 1984, the company expects to sell more than 200,000 policies with a face amount in excess of $10 billion along with a substantial volume of other financial security products.

In addition to its sales organization, the company maintains a large service organization which communicates regularly with customers. The system is customer oriented, not sales oriented. It is composed primarily of women.

Controlling Destiny

What probability should be attached to each of these scenarios? More importantly, what can be done to influence the future direction of the industry?

Is *Business (Almost) As Usual* a realistic expectation for the future and, if not, what will the future be? If major change is coming, will the change be imposed externally, perhaps by government *(Big Brother Arrives)* or by renegade companies and competitors from other savings media *(Götterdämmerung)*? Or, will change come by default, leading to an all-term industry completely different in nature from the existing industry *(Doomsday)*? Or, will the industry itself take affirmative action to control its own destiny *(Revolution)*?

If the appraisal of the current state of the industry is realistic, *Business (Almost) As Usual* is not a reasonable hypothesis for the future. Accordingly, the industry must, if it wishes to control its own destiny, take positive steps to correct the fundamental problems addressed in this discussion. The following is a suggested list of Action Assignments:

1. Premium rates for term insurance should be increased to make it less attractive to package these products with other savings media; commission rates for term insurance should also be increased to the highest levels offered on any products.
2. Premium rates for permanent insurance should be reduced (or dividends increased) and cash value structures appropriately modified so that the marginal cost associated with the savings element of these products becomes competitive with other savings media; this implies a radical reduction of commission rates on permanent insurance and a probable elimination of the front-end load associated with the savings element of these products.
3. New products, affording much increased flexibility, should be developed; this will be much more easily accomplished if commissions on the savings element are reduced.
4. To the extent that agency distribution methods are expected to continue, it follows that productivity must be substantially increased from present levels to support the income expectations of agents; this will require sophisticated marketing support.
5. The industry should lobby for modifications in the present federal income tax legislation, which imposes a large and growing burden on the investment earnings of policyholders; the industry should also lobby for an elimination of premium taxes, at least to the extent that they apply to savings accumulations.

6. The industry should abandon its dependence on artificial tax avoidance, such as minimum deposit, and concentrate on serving more efficiently the family market of the mainstream population; to have realistic expectations of success in lobbying for a reduction in taxes, it will probably be necessary to sacrifice some existing tax concessions.
7. The industry should concentrate on conserving its existing business and, perhaps more importantly, its existing customer base; the truism of the future may be: *Our customers are our most valuable assets;* conservation efforts may include the need to pay voluntarily "interest profits" on nonparticipating policies, a practice adopted several years ago in the Netherlands.

I'm not suggesting that it will be easy to implement any of the foregoing Action Assignments. How, for example, can one company take the lead in increasing term insurance premiums without losing a substantial portion of its market share? Nevertheless, solutions must be found. Perhaps a form of Adjustable Life, hopefully simpler than the existing forms, will be the key to the restructuring of the relative costs of term and permanent insurance, and perhaps some variation of this product will afford the necessary increase in flexibility. Perhaps such a product, supported by point-of-sale computer terminals, will lead to the necessary increase in agent productivity. Perhaps such products can be designed to mitigate the effect of federal income taxes on investment earnings of policyholders.

I'm not suggesting that Adjustable Life is the all encompassing panacea, the long sought Holy Grail — obviously it does not address several of the problems and there may be other and better solutions.

I am, however, expressing the view that the most likely and the most attractive solution to various of the problems noted will be found in a new product form.

Conclusion

Not unexpectedly, there are those within the industry who would prefer that the perceived problems and possibilities which are the subject of this paper not be discussed — at least not publicly discussed. Admittedly, there are risks in open discussion; expectations may thereby become self-justifying and events may be precipitated. On the other hand, an absence of open discussion increases the risks associated with inaction. Which is the larger danger?

In conclusion, I am guardedly optimistic that the industry can and will resolve its problems and realize its possibilities. My attitude is well expressed in the following quotation which appeared some years ago in an American news magazine: "I think I see light at the end of the tunnel. I hope it's not a locomotive."

Product Design in an Inflationary Era — The Four Horsemen

Presented at the Tenth Pacific Insurance Conference, Manila, Philippines, October 25–30, 1981.

In its journey through modern history, the life insurance industry in the United States has been stalked by Four Horsemen; and in recent years, the hunters have been gaining on their prey. The stalkers are not Conquest, Slaughter, Famine and Death, the Four Horsemen of the Apocalypse described by St. John the Divine. Nor are they Crowley, Layden, Miller, and Stuldreher of Notre Dame backfield fame, as named by Grantland Rice. These four horsemen are Taxation, Expenses, Replacement, and Inflation.

Taxation, like Conquest, rides the white horse; Expenses, like Slaughter, rides the red; Replacement, like Famine, the black; and their leader, Inflation, rides Death's pale horse.

Who is this pale rider, Inflation, and how has he enlisted his lieutenants? Taxation of life insurance companies, driven relentlessly higher by high interest rates driven in turn by inflation, threatens the industry's ability to provide acceptable rates of return to its policyholders. Expenses, directly driven ever higher by inflation, threaten the ability of the industry to compete in the savings market; most importantly, agents' incomes are failing to keep pace with inflation, a trend which if continued threatens to implode the existing distribution system of the industry. Replacement, too, is fostered by inflation — whether it involves the replacement of one policy with another, the replacement of a policy with something else, or the replacement of real assets with policy loans.

Who is this pale rider, Inflation? Clearly, inflation is an economic phenomenon, but that is not to say that it is purely an economic problem. Inflation today is strongly reinforced by elements of both the social and political environment in the United States (and elsewhere). Social forces, which might be characterized as the entitlement ethic replacing the work ethic, lead to inflationary pressures driven by unrealistic expectations. Political forces, which might be characterized as the re-election ethic replacing the responsibility ethic, use inflation to bridge the gap between economic logic and political logic.

The foregoing introduction is extravagant, and deliberately so — to dramatize the point that these Four Horsemen literally threaten the survival of the main branch of the life insurance industry in the United States, the individual life business.

Fundamental Causes

What are the fundamental causes of inflation? The author prefers the view that inflation is primarily rooted in today's social environment — in elements of human behavior such as personal greed and unreasonable expectations — and that the economic and political aspects of inflation are exacerbating factors rather than the root cause of the problem. This suggests that inflation is an affliction which will not be cured easily, particularly in a democratic society which is governed by popular opinion.

It is instructive to note that, in recent memory, virtually every government elected in every democratic country in the world has pledged to restrain or control inflation; but hardly any, if any, has actually succeeded. Indeed, in many countries, the debate as to whether inflation will continue at a double-digit level has been replaced by the debate as to whether the first of the digits will continue to be a "1."

The inescapable conclusion is that the life insurance industry, whose very survival is threatened by inflation and the forces which it drives, must adapt to the likelihood that the conditions recently experienced on the economic, social, and political scenes will continue for the foreseeable future. For this the life insurance industry must prepare.

A Time for Change

This industry, in the United States, is one in which the basic products and the basic distribution systems have remained essentially unchanged since the early years of this century, when legislation that largely shaped the industry was enacted in New York State following the Armstrong Investigation of 1905. The industry, over an extended period of time, has been well served by its traditional methods — methods which have built a large, successful, and, in the case of stock companies, profitable industry indeed.

The time for change has now arrived; arguably, it is overdue. In fact, it is this observer's belief that the life insurance industry in the United States has already entered a period of significant change from which it cannot possibly emerge unaltered. The signs are evident:

- change in the social, economic, and political environment in which the industry operates;
- change in the financial needs of the public which it serves;
- change in the types of products it should be selling;
- change in the needed distribution of expense and profit margins; and, in all probability,
- change in the distribution systems required to sell at acceptable costs the new products to the new market in this new environment.

There is evidence that the impact of these forces of change already is being felt:

1. As is widely recognized, the importance of life insurance as an individual savings vehicle declined relatively during the 1970s. But more ominous, and less well known, is the fact that the industry's *absolute* participation in the savings market declined also, by approximately 20% (in terms of constant dollars).
2. Lapse rates on both old and new policies have increased steadily. In 1979, lapse rates on old policies increased dramatically — an unwelcome signal of increased replacement activity — and in 1980 the increase accelerated.
3. Sales of term insurance of all types are continuing to increase, as are sales of annuity products, both at the expense of traditional permanent life insurance.

4. Money market funds have burgeoned in recent months, helped no doubt by the favorable attitude of the Administration. The funds' assets increased by some 50% in the first three months of 1981, following more than a dozen consecutive weeks of sizable gains.

Space does not permit a detailed review of the social, economic, and political forces which this writer believes have wrought these changes. For the past several years, the author has written and spoken at some length about these gathering forces of change. The intended message might reasonably be summed up in this fashion:

> The first rule of survival is as follows: When one is standing in the middle of a railroad track and hears a locomotive whistle, one does not turn one's back on the locomotive.

By their attendance at various functions and their recent attention to this message of change, others in the industry have led the author to conclude that they accept at least the possibility (and perhaps even the likelihood) that the thesis is correct: that the time for change has arrived.

The Taxation Dilemma

The reader is probably familiar with the acceleration of United States federal income taxes on policyholder investment earnings caused by high interest rates, a most extreme example of "bracket creep." If this problem is not solved, and if interest rates continue at high levels, the consequences are clear: The industry will be driven from the individual savings business. How can the industry respond?

One response is legislative. The American Council of Life Insurance is preparing a plan of tax relief for the industry, but will that plan succeed? It involves several proposals which substantially reduce taxes, at the suggested sacrifice of benefits already subject to challenge; a favorable exchange, to be sure. But are harder sacrifices — ones which may fall disproportionately on various sectors of the industry — needed to achieve acceptability?

A second response is in the area of product design. Many of the nontraditional life insurance and annuity products recently introduced are intended to eliminate or mitigate the tax borne by policyholder investment earnings.

A third response is the amendment of existing policies to vary the reserve basis and benefits. Two mutual companies recently have implemented such a program; more are planned. For stock companies, this is an uncomfortable alternative, but one which may become necessary to counter the threat of inflation.

The Product Dilemma

More than 2,400 years ago, Socrates admonished that, "The first step in knowing the truth is to call a thing by its right name." Much later, Shakespeare caused Polonius to counsel, "This above all, to thine own self be true; and it must follow as the night the day, thou canst not then be false to any man."

In the spirit of these wise words, a fateful question: Are traditional permanent life insurance products well suited to the wants and needs of today's typical buyer in the United States? The author answers, "No," and believes that both Socrates and Polonius would agree. What traditional life products are well suited to are the wants and needs of the life insurance industry and its distribution system as a means of preserving a cherished way of doing business. These are fighting words within the industry, and the author is well aware of that; they are stated here because the author is convinced that they are true.

In summary: A growing sector of today's market is saying that it will no longer tolerate the inflexibility, the low investment returns, and the high expense levels which are inherent in traditional permanent life insurance products — and it is voting its clear preference by buying more and more term insurance, more and more annuities, more and more nontraditional products. Significantly, each of these trends in product preference threatens to impact agents' earnings adversely.

The Distribution Dilemma

Roughly two-thirds of the expenses of a typical life insurance company are associated with its distribution system. If major changes are to be made in the benefit-to-cost ratio of savings-type life insurance products, it follows that significant changes must be made in the expenses associated with distribution. Yet, today the distribution system of the industry is under severe pressure because of generally declining agent income levels. The pressure from the distribution system itself is for increased compensation at a time when the industry's principal products are under intense price pressure caused by consumer preference. How can these two opposing forces be squared? The only possible answer, in the author's view, is through increased productivity.

The present distribution system of the nation's life insurance industry is made up of approximately 500,000 agents, of whom about half derive the majority of their income from the sale of life insurance and about half do not. The average sale frequency of the industry is very low: less than one sale per week per full-time equivalent agent. Therein lies the inherent inefficiency of the present distribution system, and that is the statistic that must be changed. The alternative is an implosion of the existing life insurance distribution system, and that will happen regardless of increases in or inattention to the commissions paid on existing product lines. Increasing the commissions will cause additional consumer rejection of the industry's high-margin permanent products; leaving them as they are will simply serve to drive more agents from the industry, because they cannot survive financially on existing commission levels on existing products. Productivity is the only answer, and it is most likely to be achieved by substantial improvement of the product — both its design and its cost and even at the expense of traditional commission rates.

Throughout this observer's 30 years in the life insurance industry, the distribution system has been one of the givens. The question of marketing strategy typically has been addressed in this way: "We know how we are going to sell the product; so let's decide what product we (or our agents) want to sell." Today, for the first time in memory, a significant number of companies are reversing this thrust. Some are even saying something like this: "What products does the market want and need? Let's design them, and then decide how they should be distributed."

Is an agentless future a likelihood in the United States? Probably not, in the author's opinion, but it is not inconceivable. Witness the substantial demise of such once-common occupations as blacksmith, telegraph delivery-person, milkman, elevator operator, and, quite recently, the retail mutual fund salesman. In the case of the latter, consumer dissatisfaction with the product plus hostile regulation destroyed a career category in five years. Could the same thing happen with respect to the life insurance industry? In five years?

The Replacement Dilemma

Of all the threats to the industry, the most lethal is that of widespread replacement — policies replaced by other policies or by something else, or real assets replaced by policy loans.

The impending expiry of Regulation Q, which limits interest rates that can be paid by banks and savings and loan associations on passbook accounts, probably will increase further the level of public awareness of interest rates and will foster a further increase in replacements.

Notwithstanding the ominous and steady increase in voluntary termination rates on policies more than two years old (3.9% in 1970, 4.5% in 1975, 5.1% in 1979, and perhaps 6% in 1980), the most serious replacement threat seems to be that of policy loan utilization. In terms of magnitude, consider the relationship of policy loans to ordinary insurance reserves on an industrywide basis: In 1960, only 8.9% of ordinary reserves were represented by policy loans; by 1970, that figure had climbed to 16.1%; by 1978 it was 19.2%; and in 1979, 21.0%. By the time the 1980 figures are assembled, the portion of ordinary reserves lent to policyholders may well have reached 25%. And the experience of the past decade may be only a foretaste of things to come. Considering the nature of the outstanding guarantees, which will be around for another half-century, can anything be done?

Clearly, to prevent the recurrence of the problem on the business being sold today, major reform (or even repeal) of the Standard Nonforfeiture Law is needed. But what about existing business? A few years ago, one company succeeded in amending about a third of its existing policies, raising the loan interest rate from 5% or 6% to 8%. But who today, with the prime rate around 20%, would be brave enough to remind policyholders of the availability of loans at 5% or 6%? This is a solution which makes sense only in a very different economic climate.

There may, however, be another solution; one involving taxation, which was discussed earlier. If policyholders were denied a tax deduction for interest on a policy loan (effectively adding interest paid to the cost of the contract, the problem might be largely solved. Moreover, the case for a higher rate of tax-free inside buildup would be strengthened. And, finally, the Treasury would recapture some revenue lost in concessions to the industry. (This situation currently exists in Canada.)

It is recognized that this proposal would be resisted vehemently by industry leaders; it already has been so resisted, in fact. But the suggestion has merit, and should be considered carefully — so, and more so, should the alternatives.

Perhaps it will be necessary, before the industry can accept such strong medicine, for a substantial company to get into major difficulties because of the replacement problem. In the words of Abba Eban, former Israeli foreign minister: “In the end, men and nations will do the reasonable thing, but only after they have exhausted all of the other alternatives.”

Products and Distribution in 1990

The dominant products of the life insurance industry in 1990, this observer believes, will not be the traditional forms of permanent life insurance. Instead, a future is foreseen in which the sale of open-tract products with greatly increased flexibility and (one hopes) greater tax effectiveness will predominate, along with the continued sale of large volumes of term insurance.

A glimpse of what may be in store is in the news already, in the form of a large number of nontraditional life and annuity products of various types. These products are generally aimed at breaking out of the straightjacket imposed on the throughput of investment returns to policyholders, either by altering the way in which policyholder earnings are taxed within the life insurance companies or by sidestepping the limitations on investment returns imposed by the Standard Nonforfeiture Law. Included in the list are nonparticipating products with nonguaranteed premium rates, products on which excess interest is credited on policyholder cash values, annually renewable term insurance policies parading as modified premium whole life policies, and single premium life and annuity products which are strikingly similar to certificates of deposit. Particularly in 1981, the product which has attracted most attention is the Universal Life insurance policy. This flexible premium adjustable whole life policy is designed to address each of the major issues which threaten the life insurance industry in the United States. The possibility of such a product was alluded to by Mr. George R. Dinney in a 1971 address to the Canadian Institute of Actuaries. The product was described in detail in a paper presented to the Seventh Pacific Insurance Conference by this author in 1975. Universal Life is now offered by approximately 25 companies, and it is confidently expected that the number will pass 100 early in 1982. The introduction of this product has attracted an unusual amount of attention from the media, with articles appearing in the *Wall Street Journal*, the *New York Times*, *Time* magazine, *Changing Times*, and *Money* magazine; all of these articles have been quite favorable.

Venturing again into prognostication, this writer believes that the products of 1990 will be distributed by three major types of distribution systems:

1. The traditional full-time agency, serving almost exclusively sophisticated markets, particularly those in which tax questions are of major importance. The outlook here is for the number of these full-time life insurance specialists to drop from 250,000 to somewhere between 25,000 and 50,000. This manpower reduction is not as radical as it might appear; the disappearance of a substantial proportion of today's home-service agents, the disappearance of those who will leave the industry during the next year in any case, and a reduction in the number of new recruits would be sufficient to achieve more than half of the anticipated reduction. Despite diminished numbers, this segment of the distribution force might produce approximately half of the new business written in 1990.
2. The multi-product agent, offering life insurance as a product ancillary to other products such as property-casualty insurance and investment vehicles. The prototypes for this kind of distribution system might be State Farm, Nationwide, E.F. Hutton, Bache, and Merrill Lynch.
3. Mass marketing distribution systems, including selling via mail or media and selling on a quasi-group basis with employer sponsorship. To the best of the author's knowledge, very few companies have succeeded in selling quality products via media, mail, or telephone; one such company is USAA Life, the affiliate of United Services Automobile Association. Many companies now are evidencing interest in entering the salary savings market with products designed specifically for that market; interestingly, some of

these companies are in the home-service business, and see the salary savings business as a continuation of the home-service business with the venue shifted from the home to the place of employment.

It would be natural to wonder, at this point, what has happened to all the home-service agents — not to mention the PPGAs. In all seriousness, this observer is suggesting that most of them will no longer be deriving the majority of their income from the life insurance business in 1990. Many of them will simply leave the business altogether; others will become multi-product agents.

The vision seen in the author's crystal ball does, indeed, represent radical change. But it does not lead to an agentless future, and it could lead to a healthier life insurance industry. The other likely alternatives are even more radical.

Alternative Futures

The author has written and spoken about the alternative futures of the life insurance industry in the United States, including a paper presented to the Eighth Pacific Insurance Conference. To spice up the presentation (and to permit the introduction of somewhat outrageous ideas), a scenario has been utilized as a device to outline each of the various possibilities. Space considerations preclude the repetition of the scenarios themselves, but a title and a severely encapsuled description of each may give the reader the general flavor:

1. Business (Almost) As Usual — the title is self-descriptive;
2. Big Brother Arrives — government intrudes further, in a major way, into the financial security business;
3. Götterdämmerung — renegade competitors stage a significant raid on assets;
4. Doomsday — in which there survives only an all-term insurance industry with only part-time agents; and
5. Revolution — the products and the distribution systems of the industry take off in new directions.

For reasons already discussed, the author considers Scenario 1 to be an unrealistic and nostalgic expectation. Scenarios 2, 3, and 4 are possibilities if the industry continues undeterred on its traditional path; each leads to a slightly different form of ultimate disaster. Scenario 5 is the most favorable alternative future for the industry, but it has a chance of arriving only if the industry takes the initiative to determine its own direction, rather than having a course thrust upon it by market forces already at work.

Obverse and Reverse

It has often been noted that periods of change are two-sided coins. On one side is cleanly struck, in bold relief, the legend "PROBLEMS"; on the reverse is writ "OPPORTUNITIES."

In the coming decade, the author expects to see a significant change in the products offered to the public by the life insurance industry, as well as a significant change in the way in which those products are distributed (and administered). The Product Revolution is here. The opening lines of *A Tale of Two Cities*, Dickens' classic novel of the French Revolution, come to mind: "It was the best of times, it was the worst of times." The Product Revolution may provide one, or both, or neither — but none can deny that it has spawned the most interesting of times! Perhaps this time each will keep his head!

There will be new products, and there will be additional consolidations of companies, including some mutual companies. Together, these factors will lead to a significant realignment of market shares. And, while there may be more losers than there are winners in this most interesting of times, there will be winners — and some will win big.

The Changing Financial Services Scene

Published in EMPHASIS *in December 1984. Reprinted with permission from Tillinghast - A Towers Perrin Company.*

A major transformation of the financial service industries in the United States is in progress. Unlike earlier periods of change, which affected particular industries within the group, this period of change is affecting all industries more or less simultaneously and in interrelated ways. The likely outcome is change of a magnitude previously unimagined, abounding with pitfalls for the unwary and opportunities for the visionary.

Consolidation

Much has been written and more said concerning the widely anticipated move towards consolidated financial services. What has until recently been mainly speculation is now fact, which has decimated the rank of the skeptics and their confidence in the "Business as Usual" scenario.

A discussion of the consolidation of financial services properly begins with an examination of the position of the banking industry, the spider that controls the payments web. The future role of banks, which largely will be dictated by regulation, is the most important unanswered question relating to the consolidation of financial services. The aspirations of major banks to extend their activities into other financial services are clear. Approximately a year ago, the then chairman of CitiCorp, Walter Wriston, spoke to the American Council of Life Insurance, choosing as his title, "A String Bag and the Right Stuff." His first observation was that, even in London, where shoppers traditionally used a string bag to carry their purchases from specialty shops, the supermarket has arrived, and he argued that the forces responsible for that change would lead to the consolidation of financial services in the United States. Next, he challenged the thesis implicit in U.S. regulations that banks do not have the "Right Stuff" to engage in certain financial businesses. His speech represented a clear warning to the insurance industry that strenuous efforts will be made to eliminate the prohibitions which now inhibit the expansion of banks into other financial businesses, notably insurance.

Notwithstanding inhibiting regulations, banks are expanding — into each other's previously protected territory and into other financial businesses. Examples are easy to find:

1. Through nonbank banks, many banking organizations have succeeded in expanding their activities geographically.
2. Regional banking agreements among several states, such as in New England and in the Southeast, are leading to interstate mergers of full service banking organizations.
3. Certain large banks, notably CitiBank, are using extensive media advertising to promote the concept that it only takes a telephone to do business with them no matter where the customer lives.
4. Through the rescue of failed banking and near-banking institutions, many banks have been able to circumvent restrictions on interstate acquisitions.
5. Many banks have extended their activities in the consumer finance business through acquisition.
6. Bank credit cards are everywhere, and their use now includes "instant loan" or overdraft facilities.
7. Various large banks have become major competitors in the issuance of travelers checks, which is a close approximation to the authority to print money.
8. Banks now offer discount brokerage facilities to their customers on securities transactions.
9. Banks are extending their traditional activity as intermediaries and underwriters of credit insurance into other insurance lines, albeit on a limited basis.
10. Overseas, U.S. banks are beginning to engage more extensively in the insurance business, both as distributors and as underwriters.

Other financial institutions, including those primarily engaged in the insurance industry, are also expanding their services, including incursions into the near-banking business through nonbank banks and cash-management accounts. Cross acquisitions have occurred within the insurance industry involving life/health and property/liability insurers. Securities firms have featured prominently in the activities, both as acquirers and as acquirees; and practically all national securities firms now have an ownership affiliation with an insurance company. Residential real estate brokerage, exclusively a local mom-and-pop business since anyone can remember, has been included in consolidation activities and several national organizations and networks have emerged. Also active have been financial conglomerates, such as American Express, and retailers, such as Sears, that were already involved in the insurance business. New and expanded areas of service have emerged, such as the underwriting of financial guarantees.

Nonfinancial enterprises have also been expanding into financial businesses. The list includes a diverse cross section of American industry: oil companies, automobile manufacturers, chemical companies, publishers, steel makers, transportation companies, farm equipment companies, tobacco companies, forest product companies, business equipment companies, railroads, consumer products companies, broadcasters and various industrial conglomerates.

In summary, the questions remaining now relate to how far, how soon, and in what direction consolidation will proceed.

A Look At One of the Causes: Brown Pasture

To begin with an analogy that has been used by others before, the motivation for diversification into financial services either by companies already engaged in other such businesses or by companies in unrelated businesses is not necessarily because the grass on the other side of the fence looks so green — much of the motivation has to do with the realization that the grass on this side of the fence is turning brown. In other words, a substantial part of the motivation for diversification is related to troubles within the traditional businesses of those who seek to diversify. This has particular application to retail financial service business of various kinds.

The economic history of the world since the beginning of the industrial revolution is a long tale featuring the advance of technological power at the expense of people power. Essentially, the story is that of man's discovery that machines can perform certain work much better and much more cheaply than people. Concurrently, the use of people has become progressively more expensive. In the wake of progress, many traditional occupations have been left behind — the blacksmith, the neighborhood grocer, the telegraph delivery boy, the milkman, the elevator operator and the family farmer, to mention only a few.

It is worth reviewing how technological change and market forces have affected various of the principal financial service industries and those of the aspirants to enter such businesses:

1. Banking. Traditionally, this customer-oriented business has provided low cost financial services to the retail market. Recently, the economics of the banking industry have been strained by an overexpanded branch network, involving too much brick and mortar and too many people, and the removal of limitations on interest rates which may be paid to smaller depositors. This has fostered a cost and margin squeeze within an industry whose previous margins were protected by regulation. These conditions have led to a search by the banking industry for additional and alternative products (to support the existing system) and for alternative systems (to lower costs). Interest in diversification is a manifestation of the first strategy, while automated teller machines, "800" numbers and plastic bank cards are a manifestation of the second.
2. Life Insurance. Traditionally, this has been a distribution-oriented, high-cost financial service business, conducted on a basis that has been very people intensive. Within the industry's distribution system, a financial crisis has arisen caused by declining agent incomes relative to other occupations and by rapidly increasing capital costs required to maintain the distribution system. This has resulted in an industrywide search for additional and alternative products (to support the existing distribution system) and alternative distribution systems (to reduce distribution costs) and has led many companies to seek the answer through the acquisition of companies engaged in other financial service businesses.

3. Casualty and Health Insurance. Traditionally, these have been risk-oriented, price-regulated financial service businesses with important social implications. In the casualty insurance business, a perceived overcapacity problem has existed and has fostered a price war which began in 1978 and continues today. High inflation and overheated medical costs during the 1970s fostered a financial crisis among health insurers and government programs; government has protected itself to a degree by cost shifting to the private sector, exacerbating the problems of medical cost insurers. Ignoring the operative economics, some insurance regulators and other public officials have insisted that insurance, particularly automobile and health insurance, should be "affordable," no matter what it actually costs. the response of the industry to these conditions has been a search for more stable sources of profits (to counteract underwriting volatility) and for preferred market sectors (contrary to the wishes of many regulators and other public officials). The first strategy has promoted interest on the part of casualty and health insurers to diversify.
4. Securities. Until ten years ago when stock exchange commissions were deregulated, this was a distribution-oriented financial service business, conducted on a basis that was people intensive and involved a high degree of cross-subsidization between larger and smaller customers. Deregulation of stock exchange commissions altered the economics of the business, introducing price competition both among traditional firms and with newly emergent discount brokers. An important subset of the securities industry is the mutual fund industry. Earlier restrictions on front-end loads for mutual funds resulted in the virtual disappearance of many retail mutual fund sales organizations and the reorganization of many funds on a no-load basis. The business has also experienced severe cycles associated with the popularity of stock market investments. The response of the industry has been to reduce dramatically the size of its distribution system, to mechanize its back office operations (both aimed at reducing costs) and to add significant new product lines, including special insurance products such as term life insurance and single premium deferred annuities (to stabilize and increase income). Major consolidation has occurred within the industry and several national and regional securities firms have been acquired by other

financial institutions; many of the remaining independent firms have entered other branches of the financial service business, notably insurance.

5. Nonfinancial Businesses. Reasons for the interest on the part of nonfinancial companies to diversify into financial services businesses are as varied as the companies that have taken or are considering this action. Some are seeking strategically to redeploy their assets from traditional businesses with lower growth potential into an industry perceived as having substantial growth potential. Some are seeking a "parking place" for excess capital funds, in some cases windfall earnings. Among industrial organizations, it is the general perception that the financial service industries, particularly insurance, offer opportunities to introduce management techniques which are believed to be superior to those of present competitors within those industries. At least in some cases, there also exist possible tax synergies between industrial organizations with large amounts of taxable income and financial services businesses which may afford the opportunity to shelter that income from current taxation. Tax aspects have featured prominently in the diversification and acquisition activities of nonfinancial businesses.

While the motivations to diversify and to consolidate financial service businesses are diverse, "brown pasture" has been one of the important elements.

A Second Cause: Deregulation

Recent deregulation of financial businesses has been a force which, some might argue, caused the diversification into and consolidation within the financial service industries; that deregulation has accelerated the trends is beyond argument.

Deregulation within financial service industries has taken many forms, intended and unintended. The phase-out of Regulation Q, which limited interest rates that banks and thrift institutions could pay to small depositors, has had a major impact on expense and profit margins of banks and near-banks; banks have expended into certain other businesses because of the wider powers gradually given to them by bank regulators; thrift institutions have been allowed to move into areas of service previously reserved for banks; the invention or discovery of money market funds, cash management accounts and so forth represented an entry by nonbanks into the traditional banking business on an unregulated basis, permitting them to "cherry pick" profitable market sectors; the exploitation of the exemptions enjoyed by nonbank banks has effectively circumvented the intent of existing, geographically restrictive banking legislation; and, importantly, since 1980 there has been a noticeable change in government attitude towards concentration of business enterprises — implied acceptance of the thesis that big is not necessarily bad.

The impact of deregulation upon any industry previously protected either from price competition or from the inclusion by new competitors into established territory can be observed in the airline industry. There, deregulation has resulted in overexpansion by some carriers to their sorrow and cut-throat price competition by low-cost competitors that threatens established carriers which, during the regulated era, tended to become high-cost providers of services. The race to reduce costs to enable established airlines to compete with leaner new competitors is apparent; press reports of wage concessions by airline employees have become a routine item of business news. Similar pressures can be expected with respect to all retail financial services as a result of the deregulation of the financial services industry.

While the established trend can be expected to continue, the widely publicized difficulties of Continental Illinois and the possibility of major defaults on international loans could arrest the deregulation of the banking industry and its expansion into other financial services.

The Search for Green Pasture

The individual life insurance industry has become practically everyone's favorite target in the search for green pasture. Essentially, this industry is perceived as competitively "soft" for these reasons:

1. Its high cost, inefficient distribution system is well known and viewed as an opportunity by many "outsiders."
2. Historically, its products have provided high margins for expenses and profits, largely or partly because price competition has been blunted by a complex product.
3. The industry is perceived to be a captive of its own distribution system and, therefore, poorly positioned to compete through alternative distribution systems which many potential new competitors are confident will soon emerge.

4. The industry is vulnerable to a raid on its existing business because it seeks to recover from its somewhat uncooperative existing policyholders (whose cash values are demand deposits) the large unrealized losses on its investment portfolios.

To what extent are these perceptions held by many outside the life insurance industry accurate? The facts are not really in dispute; the disagreement relates primarily to whether or not alternative products or alternative distribution systems can succeed in achieving material cost savings and can also produce a significant level of sales. History supports the skeptics; yet the recent evidence supporting the view that alternative products and alternative distribution systems can succeed is mounting. So-called interest-sensitive products, notably universal life, may represent more than 50% of industry sales in 1985; while efforts to launch alternative distribution systems remain experimental, it appears that one or more is likely to succeed in a major way; and the expected emergence of banks as a major force in the distribution of life insurance products may affect the industry in a substantial way — banks could conceivably become the major distribution system for individual insurance products.

In a deregulated environment, with increased price competition from alternative products and alternative distribution systems, the traditional high-cost distribution driven strategy of the industry is in trouble. Arguably, that strategy must be replaced by a customer-driven strategy, emphasizing better value products and more efficient distribution systems, either of the traditional type or of some new alternative type. These concepts will not receive willing acceptance by those now engaged in the distribution of life insurance products in the traditional way.

Fortunately, the life insurance industry today is better positioned to cope with its new environment than it has been for at least a decade — a decade during which its problems have been building. Although mutual life insurance companies are not entirely happy with the outcome, the recently enacted basis of taxation of life insurance companies and their policyholders has altered the slope of the competitive playing field in a manner which favors the products of the life insurance industry; previously, their goal was at the downhill end of the field and today it stands on somewhat higher ground than the goals of the competing teams. Expenses remain the single most serious problem, and the industry has not yet addressed the need for the quantum reduction which is necessary if it is to compete in a consumer-oriented environment; this will involve major structural change in the way the industry does business and will have substantial impact on its distribution system. Replacement continues as a lethal threat but is less menacing than before, partly because much of its force is already spent, partly because of increases in the values of securities portfolios and partly because the industry has redeployed its assets to some degree; the industry still needs to face the fact that its unrealized portfolio losses are real and then concentrate on progressing from the current position rather than trying to recover from unwilling policyholders what has already been lost. Even the destructive effects of inflation have abated, partly because the rate of inflation has declined (perhaps only temporarily) and partly because the industry has produced flexible new products that are more responsive to the effects of inflation.

In summary, while the outsiders' views of the industry is substantially correct, the current position of the life insurance industry is stronger than it has been for many years. The major remaining problem is the expense of distributing individual life insurance products in the traditional way. The companies most likely to succeed will be those that are first effectively to address this difficult problem.

Other Targets

Other targets for diversification and expansion within or into the financial services industries are viewed much less uniformly by potential aspirants and acquirors.

The banking industry, because it offers a service for which the customer need is continuous, is seen as the best way to "lock-in" a customer base. In addition, banking is still regarded by many as the premier industry within the group. The leading disadvantage is the formidable and inhibiting regulation to which the industry is subject, much of which extends to associated companies.

The casualty and health insurance industries are attractive to some, particularly to those seeking to add a "demand product" to support the income of another distribution system. These businesses are also attractive to innovators who believe that financial results can be improved through new products, improved distribution or better management techniques; group auto insurance, product wholesaling through fee-paid consultant-intermediaries and selective underwriting illustrate the concepts. The primary disadvantages are the volatility of underwriting results and the possibility that submarginal pricing will continue indefinitely, mainly due to social and regulatory pressures.

The securities industry is very diverse, including retail and wholesale distribution, investment management and investment banking. This non-homogenous industry offers several opportunities for synergy with other financial services involving products, distribution, client base and investment skills; probably for this reason, this industry is already substantially integrated with other financial services.

The Financial Service Industries of the 1990s

The key to success in the consolidated retail market for financial services in the 1990s will most likely be efficient customer access.

With respect to many financial services (insurance is one), customers have only a periodic need for a particular service. With respect to others (banking is one), customers have a continuing need for that service. One of the compelling reasons for the consolidation of financial services is the economies which would flow if customer contact could be maintained on a more frequent or continuing basis rather than on an infrequent basis. It is well known, for example, that prospecting is the most time-consuming aspect of the job of a life insurance agent; prospecting really consists of identifying those among the universe of potential customers who need the particular service offered now. If customer access were achieved through an intermediary prepared to address various financial service needs of a potential customer instead of just one, the frequency of finding a customer needing some service now would obviously increase. The "downtime" now spent in the search for immediate customers would reduce, and the system would become more efficient. This principle applies to most financial services where the need for service is periodic.

Efficient customer access in the future will surely require major support from a powerful computer-based customer information system. A total system, capable of handling all financial services, does not exist today. The development of such a system, which obviously is a massive undertaking, will surely occur. If such a system is to be developed within the industry, it is clear that only the largest organization will be able to afford the development costs. Groups may form to share development costs. Alternatively, systems may be developed outside the industry, intended to be sold to many users; impetus for this may come, for example, from manufacturers of computer equipment.

How will the customer interface of the future actually function? Many who believe that consolidated financial services will predominate foresee the emergence of a new occupation, a Financial Account Executive; skeptics believe that this new occupation will be too demanding but they may overlook the point that the number of people need not be particularly large — a cadre of only 225,000, for example, would be required to cover the entire U.S. population if each serviced only 1,000 persons — men, women and children at every economic level. As a practical matter, fewer than 100,000 may be required.

Some believe that location selling and servicing will become the norm in the financial services industry and point to the Sears Financial Network, Kroger Financial Centers and branch banks as likely prototypes; in this context, it should be noted that personal casualty lines are likely to be the dominant product.

Others imagine that location selling will diminish rather than increase; they visualize a world of banks without branches, increasingly reliant on media advertising, utilizing plastic cards and teller machines and riding the crest of the electronic revolution, with home computers everywhere connected with telephone lines or cable television.

Still others expect that customer interface will take place to an increasing extent at the place of employment, extending the concept of employee benefits to include many new employee services, both financial and nonfinancial.

In addition to efficient customer access, imaginative customer service will still be important, particularly in the tax-driven individual and wholesale markets for financial services. Here may be found the opportunity for specialist "boutiques," which may be distributors, product wholesalers or various combinations. Those who follow this road are likely to succeed by finding ways to use financial services to solve other problems, such as corporate and personal tax avoidance and deferment. These specialists, providing imaginative customer service, will seek to optimize benefit/cost ratios by designing programs to optimize tax, cash flow and cost considerations for the benefit of buyers; examples include tax-efficient executive compensation plans, health care financing programs designed to achieve cost containment and risk management activities in the casualty insurance field.

As part of this foreseen development, it can be predicted that fee-for-service and negotiated commissions may largely displace traditional commissions as the method of compensating intermediaries and advisors who provide these services; the recent Florida Appeals Court decision, striking down Florida's anti-rebating law, may signal the beginning of an era of negotiated commissions, which are essentially the same as fees. To an increasing degree, these sophisticated intermediaries will be professional advisors rather than commissioned salesmen.

These trends are quite similar to developments which took place 30 years ago in the group insurance and group annuity field, 10 years ago in the securities business and which are currently emerging in commercial casualty lines. Signs are appearing of the beginning of this development in the individual life insurance marketplace. The other half of the the fee-for-service trend will be the availability of product wholesalers prepared to offer net rate quotations and no-load products. In the employee benefits field, such products have been available for years, and they are making their appearance in commercial casualty lines and in special areas of the individual life insurance market.

Three Potential Power Bases

A vision of the future consolidated financial services industry of the 1990s would be incomplete without identifying the likely players and their respective missions.

Established banks represent one likely power base. These banks, because of their existing branch networks, are committed to the broad retail market. Their fundamental choice will be between expanding the services they offer and expanding the market sectors, geographics or otherwise, that they serve. A major consolidation among the existing 15,000 banks is an easy forecast to make but the question remains whether that consolidation will take place on a local basis, a regional basis or a national basis. Future regulation will largely dictate the general pattern.

Because banks are required to maintain minimum ratios of capital to deposits, they face increasing capital needs because their aggregate deposits expand in parallel with economic activity. Banks will be strained to finance normal expansion from retained earnings, leaving little, nothing or less than nothing to finance external growth. As long as bank shares have quoted market prices at or below their book values, raising capital through new issues of stock will remain an unappealing alternative. Accordingly, capital is likely to be a scarce resource.

Some banks, whether because they are excluded from geographic expansion or for other reasons, may play successfully the renegade strategy and develop national bank networks without branches; CitiBank appears already to be testing this strategy.

Because of their unique position in the payments system, banks are likely to occupy a central place in the consolidation of financial services, subject to whatever regulatory restraints remain.

What about established insurers? Clearly, they must either abandon the broad retail market or change in a fundamental way their method of doing business. Their basic choice will be between the expanded financial services strategy and the boutique strategy. If the first strategy is adopted, it will probably be necessary to provide some aspects of banking services, either through a nonbank bank, through an alliance with one or more existing banks, through the development of a bank without branches, or through outright purchase of or consolidation with a bank. If the second strategy is adopted, a choice will be required between a captive distribution strategy and a product wholesale strategy. Inevitably, there will be a continued meltdown of the number of independent insurance companies. Mutual companies, with no access to security markets for equity capital, face important capital constraints; for this reason and also because there may be significant tax advantages, the demutualization of several major insurers should be expected.

The third potential power base is customer oriented — organizations with access to large numbers of potential customers for financial services. Retailers, such as Sears, are already active in the financial service field, as are stockbrokers, such as Merrill Lynch. Other organizations, such as American Express, have large customer bases and a desirable clientele. To be effective, such organizations need a customer base which is both large and of high quality.

In the end, the stock market may decide who the survivors will be. If the consolidation of financial services occurs through mergers and acquisitions, it is clear that cash cannot be the only currency of exchange — the aggregate amount of the available capital is not adequate to finance a large number of cash acquisitions. Accordingly, stock is likely to be the medium of exchange in many transactions and it is more or less certain that the industries and companies which enjoy the highest price/earnings and market/book ratios are likely to be the survivors.

What Does It All Mean . . . to the Current Players?

The current purveyors of financial services, notably life insurance companies, face a dilemma not unlike that of Hamlet:

> To be, or not to be: that is the question:
> Whether 'tis nobler in the mind to suffer
> The slings and arrows of outrageous fortune,
> Or to take arms against a sea of troubles . . .

To these organizations, the choices are not easy ones; the alternatives include:

1. The Strategy of Minimum Change: remain in the same basic business and seek to improve but not alter its fundamentals (products and distribution systems). This strategy is likely to limit growth because it will work best in a highly selective market sector. Because the strategy will appeal to established management, preferred market sectors are likely to be crowded and competitive.
2. The Diversification and Acquisition Strategy: seek to serve all major financial service needs of the retail, middle-market by diversification, most likely through merger or acquisition. This strategy is likely to require very large capital resources and important new management skills. Competition can be expected from powerful organizations with large capital resources and large customer bases.
3. The Boutique Strategy: seek to serve selective market sectors on the basis of superior product or product application methodology, either as a wholesaler, a distributor or both. This strategy places a high premium on continuing superiority of management skills.

4. The Renegade Strategy: seek to serve selective market sectors on an unconventional basis, exploiting weaknesses of existing products and/or distribution systems. This strategy can be very effective on a short-term basis for those with no vested interest in the status-quo; a longer-term followup plan is required.
5. The Reverse-Acquisition Strategy: seek to be acquired on favorable terms by another organization. This strategy, which is likely to be unpopular with established management, may be the preferred alternative for organizations with no clearly defined competitive strengths and limited capital resources.

. . . to the Consumers?

To the consumers of financial services, the future offers the promise of better service or lower cost but, in the broad retail market, consumers are likely to be required to pay their own way in a sector of the marketplace that has increasingly become a loser. Much can be learned from the breakup of AT&T and its likely impact on personal telephone costs as existing cross-subsidies among customer of various types disappear; striking similarities exist in the financial services industries, notably in the banking sector, where larger retail customers have traditionally subsidized smaller ones.

. . . to the Intermediaries?

To financial service intermediaries, especially insurance agents, the new environment is likely to bring the greatest change. If they are to function effectively, their range of product knowledge and expertise must expand. Point-of-sale computer aides will likely be routine in the very near future. Fees and salaries will partially displace commissions as the primary method of compensation. Increased results will be required to support the same income. In the life insurance industry, the number of full-time intermediaries will continue to shrink, perhaps from 200,000 to 50,000. In contrast, the number of multi-line agents and part-time agents is likely to increase, perhaps from 300,000 to 400,000. Stockbrokers and insurance agents may become members of the same occupational group.

. . . to the Investors?

What does the future hold for investors in financial service industries? In all sectors, there is likely to be a major rearrangement of market shares with sharply revised earnings expectations. Entrenched competitors may be dislodged from their positions. Some renegades will succeed spectacularly. Merger and acquisition activity will increase, and it will be better to own the shares of the acquiree rather than the acquirer.

The investor can expect some big winners and some big losers. The big winners are most likely to be found among companies with superior fundamentals, particularly those with low unit expenses, and among companies with a captive customer base. The big losers are most likely to be found among companies that seek to defend an untenable, entrenched market position because they are committed to their existing way of doing business, and among companies that are not adequately capitalized for the strategic plans undertaken.

Conclusion

Will we recognize the financial service industries of the 1990s? Will today's familiar names be as familiar tomorrow? To the extent that the future may be foreseen today, signs point to a largely consolidated industry dominated by fewer than 100 organizations, all giants by today's standards, dwarfing all but the largest of the existing major insurance groups. Their names will be familiar ones, perhaps more so in contexts other than insurance. Besides these giants, there will also remain a larger number of specialty organizations, serving specific needs of various market sectors; their names will also be mainly familiar but a few newcomers will be included. Other now familiar names will not be found in the new environment; many will have disappeared into larger groups. Clearly, opportunities for the visionary exist, but clear vision, strong nerves and an enterprising spirit will be required to capitalize on those opportunities.

Let the Real Revolution Begin...

Published in BROKER WORLD, *June 1985: 8, 14–16.*
Reprinted with permission from BROKER WORLD.

Since 1980 or thereabouts, the marketing sector of the life insurance industry in the United States has been preoccupied by a product revolution which has manifested itself in more than one way. Products introduced during the five-year period may even represent a majority of individual sales by the industry in 1985. The new products include annually renewable term, indeterminate premium products and universal life, first in its fixed interest and now in its variable form.

What does all this mean and where will it lead? Are we at the beginning, the middle or the end of the cycle? Where can one look for answers to these questions?

The Lessons of History

We study history for its inspiration and its guidance for the future, based on the familiar theory that history often repeats itself. In search of an answer to where today's product revolution is likely to lead, we begin by examining the past.

The late 20th century life insurance industry of the United States is the result of a shaping and reshaping process which began more than 200 years ago. Many of the important events can be identified as direct outgrowths of earlier product revolutions, five of which, including the present one, are worth revisiting.

The first product revolution was the invention of level premium (permanent) life insurance, which occurred over 200 years ago. This development, pioneered by the Old Equitable in the United Kingdom, signaled the beginning of the modern life insurance industry. Several major consequences still visible today flowed directly from this event:

- It separated the life and general insurance industries, which have since traveled down largely independent paths.
- The technical nature of the new product created the actuarial profession and resulted in extensive government regulation of the industry.
- The new product was one with high expense tolerance and, in particular, high *initial* expense tolerance because, at first, there were no nonforfeiture values.
- From its introduction emerged the agency system, initially composed of part-time agents compensated on a commission basis.

The second product revolution saw the introduction first of endowment policies and then of cash surrender values, changes which occurred over 100 years ago in the United Kingdom and in North America. Again, there were major direct consequences:

- The new product transformed the industry into an important branch of the individual savings business by providing benefits available to the buyer himself, greatly widening the appeal and the market for life insurance products.
- The first professional agency system, a branch office network established by the Scottish Widows Fund, emerged in the United Kingdom.

The third product revolution occurred at intervals during the past 50 years in response to the widespread introduction of significant income and estate taxes and associated pension legislation. Because this change occurred over an extended period, the consequences were similarly spread out but still connected:

- To an important and progressively increasing degree, in various countries, life insurance became a tax planning and tax avoidance business.
- Life insurance distribution systems took on many of the characteristics of a professional advisory service and the financial planner emerged.

The fourth product revolution was "unit linking" or "variable life insurance," which began 30 years ago in the Netherlands but which has had the greatest impact thus far in the United Kingdom and South Africa. Until recently, this revolution largely bypassed the United States where it was inhibited by regulation. In those countries where it was permitted to flourish, the direct consequences are clear:

- Life insurance became an important branch of the retail investment business, further widening its appeal and greatly increasing its glamour.
- Full-time agency organizations, with primary company representation, expanded dramatically.
- Many companies were successful in the development of a brand identification based upon the perceived investment merit of the funds underlying their products.
- A major rearrangement of market shares occurred, generally favoring newer companies, some of which became major institutions in a very short period of time.

The fifth product revolution was unbundling, made possible from a marketing viewpoint by the development of small, cheap and portable computers; this product revolution is the one currently in progress in the United States which may now be combined with the more or less simultaneous introduction of widespread unit linking. The consequences are not yet entirely clear, but the product characteristics likely to influence the ensuing change are clear:

- In a departure from the characteristics of the original life insurance products, the new product is one with low expense tolerance, due primarily to its transparency.
- The new product is characterized by the absence of meaningful guarantees, particularly when combined with unit linking.
- While the associated distribution revolution has only begun, the low expense tolerance of the new products will intensify the already serious pressure on distribution cost levels.

Each previous product revolution has been followed by a distribution revolution; this one is not likely to be an exception.

The Impending Distribution Revolution

Due mainly to the relatively high expense tolerance of traditional life insurance products, the life insurance industry virtually since its inception has pursued a fundamental business strategy which can be described as "distribution driven." In other words, the behavior of the industry is rational only if the underlying assumption is that the industry views its distribution system, not its policyholders, as its real customers. Over extended periods of time, it is clear that the companies which have experienced the most rapid growth have been those with the most aggressive and the most agent-oriented philosophies; superior product from the policyholder's viewpoint has represented only a secondary factor in the success of companies, measured by their growth.

Much of this may now be changing. In addition to reductions in the expense tolerance of the industry's products, another important new factor has appeared on the scene — the likelihood of materially increased competition from outside the life insurance industry, important segments of which have traditionally pursued a price-oriented marketing strategy which can be described as "consumer driven." When competition was exclusively among life insurance companies, all competing on the basis of the same strategy and similar price levels, the dominant competitive factor was the battle for distribution outlets and the bias was strongly towards aggressive marketing and higher commissions, even at the expense of product price. If the competitive scene now or soon includes important participants prepared to compete at a very different price level, using different distribution systems, the traditional distribution driven strategy of the life insurance industry is in trouble.

Future Distribution Systems

In the future, quite possibly in the very near future, distribution systems for life insurance products seem likely to become far less homogeneous than they are today. What are the leading distribution systems of the future likely to be?

Traditional life insurance distribution systems will surely survive and will continue for many years as the single most important outlet for life insurance products. The independent entrepreneur acting as a distributor of life insurance products, whether classified as agent or broker, seems likely to continue to serve, as he has always done, the sophisticated end of the marketplace. Yet there will be important changes.

Arguably, his wares must expand to include a variety of financial products because increasingly his customers will be wooed by others who will claim the ability to meet a broad range of needs on some convenient basis.

Another likely change is a movement away from traditional commission compensation and towards a salary plus incentive or fee-based alternative compensation system. There is an elementary economic reason which supports such a change: commissions systems are intended to charge for services according to *value* delivered, whereas salary and fee systems are intended to charge more according to the *cost* of delivery; in a consumer driven, price oriented marketplace, there will be a tendency towards cost based pricing and away from value based pricing.

There is also an important further argument which favors a fee-based compensation system for financial intermediaries which has nothing to do with the product or distribution revolutions now in progress. To the extent that tax planning is likely to feature importantly in the activities of financial intermediaries, their products will be sensitive to the tax benefits they provide. It is axiomatic that an expense should not be internal to a tax shelter if the expense paid externally qualifies as a further tax deduction. This is a powerful argument favoring fees on tax-oriented business. The customary (and boring) way this is often said is that tax-deductible fees can reduce the cost by 50%; the other (and more exciting) way to say the same thing is that fees can be at twice the level of commissions!

New distribution systems which still employ intermediaries but are quite different from existing distribution systems are likely to emerge in the relatively near future. Their common theme will be the concept of improving cost efficiency by eliminating the necessity for prospecting. The possibilities range from location selling, such as a financial services desk in a branch bank or retail establishment, to selling among employees of a sponsoring employer or customers of a sponsoring financial or consumer service organization. These systems would aim to replace many intermediaries with few intermediaries and the compensation basis would be very different from that which is traditional for the life insurance industry today.

Systems which do not involve intermediaries in the conventional sense are also likely to appear. These would include mass marketing programs which rely on media and mail, telemarketing and so forth. Some of the more outrageous possibilities may seem like excerpts from Jules Verne. In many cases, the success of such distribution systems depends on the ability to transplant the distribution system of a different business into the life insurance business. Can the techniques for selling Ginsu knives be adapted to selling life insurance and other financial products? Most of these efforts can be expected to fail, but not all of them.

How to Get Ready

From the viewpoint of the distributor of life insurance products, the real revolution is only now beginning. How can he or she prepare for the coming revolution? Some suggestions:

- The producer should seek ways to lock in his existing customer base and seek ways to expand it. Insurance companies, banks and others will be striving for exactly the same objective, even at the expense of the intermediary. Each participant will be trying to stake out as protected territory a controlled customer base and will attempt to make it as difficult as possible for any competitor to encroach upon his territory. If the independent intermediary is to be an important participant in the future, it will be because he alone is seen as having access to a defined customer base. Part of the process of protecting the customer base is to minimize the opportunity for encroachment by others by providing the widest practical range of services.
- The independent intermediary must be prepared for a world in which his compensation may no longer be exclusively or even primarily based upon scale commissions. Negotiated commissions and fees are a likely development in the immediate future and signs of this change are already apparent in the recent Florida Appeals Court decision concerning rebating and in scattered signs of the appearance of no-load products in the individual life insurance business. Plans for this change should be formulated now and should include decisions as to the appropriate fee levels which will be charged and advice as to the circumstances under which fees and commissions may legally be charged.
- In addition to his customer base, the strength of the independent intermediary rests importantly on his abilities and motivation as an individual

entrepreneur. The distribution of life insurance and allied products is not an activity easily supervised and life insurance companies and other participants in the financial services business will be reluctant to move towards some of the fixed cost distribution alternatives, such as those involving salaried representatives; except for those engaged in location selling, few have the skills and personnel necessary adequately to supervise a noncommission distribution system. If the independent intermediary is prepared to price his services at a level at which he will not be driven out of the marketplace by consumer-oriented competitors, he still will occupy an important position in the future distribution of life insurance and related products.

- Will the independent intermediary of the future be tied more or less to a primary company than he is today? With a few notable exceptions, the existing distribution system seems more likely than not to move towards multicompany representation and away from single or primary company representation. In competing for the business of independent intermediaries, insurance companies are likely to expand their salaried staffs and other activities supporting such intermediaries to better secure the continuing services of such intermediaries.
- The future role of the independent entrepreneur as a distribution of financial products will stress “advising” rather than “selling.” The premium value of product knowledge is likely to increase at the expense of selling skills. Most distributors will find SEC registration is a necessity.

And now let the real revolution begin!

How We Got Where We Are Today and Where Do We Go from Here?

Presented to the Annual Meeting of the Life Insurance Marketing and Research Association (LIMRA), New Orleans, Louisiana, October 27, 1986. Reprinted with permission from LIMRA International.

I stand here, an aging prophet, come to your meeting to speak his prophecies! I have taken the liberty of expanding the published title of these remarks, "How We Got Where We Are Today" by appending to it, "And Where Do We Go from Here?"

The Perils of Prophecy

About ten years ago, a good friend of mine hung on me a sobriquet which has since stuck; he called me The Cassandra of the Industry, and perhaps it has stuck because I have embraced it. Most of you, my learned friends, have some idea of who Cassandra was. You probably know her best for her pessimistic but accurate forecast of the doom that awaited her nation, Troy, in its war with Greece. But as Paul Harvey would say, "Now, let me tell you the rest of the story."

Cassandra was the daughter of the last king of Troy. During the Trojan War, she became the object of the hot passion of Apollo, the Greek God. He courted her, but alas, without success. Cassandra rejected all of his advances. Finally, in desperation, he offered a straight deal: he would endow her with the gift of prophecy in return for her personal favors. Cassandra accepted his gift and then defaulted on her end of the bargain. This so enraged Apollo that he then imposed upon her the curse that, while her prophecies would always be true, they would never be believed.

Prophecy is a tricky business. It's possible, for example, for a prophecy to misfire, like this one: Not long ago one of my colleagues read to me a passage in which a very convincing case was made for the imminent demise of the Home Service business. The case was somewhat less convincing when he told me that it was an excerpt from the report of the Armstrong Investigation and was written in 1905!

Then there is the problem of understatement, like the morning that Noah got up, looked at the sky and said, "It sure looks like rain."

Over the weekend on the Associated Press Wire there appeared a story that reported another pitfall for prophecy: it can also be just plain embarrassing. The story related to a confession made in the last few days by the publisher of the *Daily News* of Springfield, Massachusetts. He admitted, 57 years afterwards, that his paper's report of the result of one of the World Series Games played in 1929 was not correct. The game was between the Chicago Cubs and the Philadelphia Athletics, and it was played at Shibe Park. Going into the last half of the 9th inning, the Cubs had a two run lead which had stood for five innings. The *Daily News* was determined to score a beat on its rival, the *Evening Union*, and without waiting for the results of the bottom half of the ninth inning, a pressman was told to punch zero in the box score, and roll the presses. Needless to say, the result turned out to be different from that which was reported! The Athletics came alive in the bottom of the ninth inning and scored three runs to win the game. Fortunately, some cautious heads prevailed and the circulation manager was told to stand in the alleyway, blocking the loaded trucks until confirmation of the score was received. On that day in 1929, the *Daily News* did not reach the news stands!

I have had my share of hits and misses in the prophecy business. If I hadn't, I wouldn't be here this morning. If there had been no hits, your organizing committee would not have invited me, and if there had been no misses, I'm sure that my schedule would have been much too busy to accommodate their invitation. Perhaps the best known hit was made in 1975 when I wrote a piece about a hypothetical company with the name Cannibal Life; and perhaps the most embarrassing miss was in 1980 when I confidently predicted that there would soon be no more than 50,000 full time life insurance agents in this business.

Three Questions

But enough of prologue. Hopefully, it has relaxed you a bit, but more to the point, hopefully it has accustomed me to these rather imposing surroundings!

This morning I would like to begin by looking backward rather than forward — to begin by focusing on yesterday, seeking understanding of the problems of today which are the opportunities of tomorrow. I propose to address three questions. Let me tell you first what they are:

- The first question is this: how and why did the basic business strategy of the industry work so well for so long?
- The second: How and why did that strategy falter beginning around 1970?
- And the final question: What new or old business strategies are likely to succeed today and in the future?

The Glory Years

My three questions could be discussed under descriptive headings, each representing a different era. The first might be called the Glory Years. How and why did the basic business strategy of the industry work so well for so long?

In my view, it worked well and it worked long because there existed a stable social contract within this industry. The social contract involved three participants: the consumer, the agents, and the companies which comprise the industry. Important provisions of the social contract related to the consumers and the agents who served them, and other provisions related to the relations between the agents and the industry that provided their products. Let's look at how the social contract was supported by each of the participants.

Consumer Acceptance

The first leg was consumer acceptance. The consumer in those days was tolerant of the industry's high cost products and, in particular, was tolerant of its high front-end loads. The loads on the products that were available in those years were quite similar to those that apply to today's products.

In addition, the consumer was tolerant of relatively low investment returns in those Glory Years prior to 1970. The investment returns that were offered on the products of those years were lower relatively than are offered on today's products. Now, I don't just mean that interest rates have increased since 1970;

I mean that, adjusting for the fact that interest levels have changed, the rates of return offered then were lower relative to those being offered now.

The third aspect of consumer acceptance was that life insurance pricing was not well understood and price comparisons within the life insurance industry were inherently soft. Comparisons dealt with such things as projected net cost, or assumed dividend scales, or dividend histories, or entry premium levels and so forth. There was no clearcut, conclusive basis of price comparison available. And finally, in those days, competing alternative products were not seen by the consumer as comparable to life insurance products and the real competition was internal to the life insurance industry, not between the life insurance industry and other sub-industries in the financial business.

So much for consumer acceptance, the first leg supporting the social contract.

Agent Loyalty

The second leg was agent loyalty. In those days single company representation was the norm, and what that meant was that an agent sold the products of his primary company regardless of whether they were good or bad. He sold all of their products. Moreover, in those days there was a general acceptance within the industry and within the ranks of agents that the commission cartel was a normal part of life. That commission cartel was, of course, based on Section 213 of the New York Insurance Code. So, agent loyalty — the second leg of the social contract; essentially, it depended on single company representation and acceptance of a commission cartel.

Industry Support

The third leg was support within the industry and by individual companies for this social contract. It was manifested in many different ways. Agents and general agents were protected by a variety of practices. Most companies had rules which prohibited any "house" business; anti-rebating statutes were supported strongly; some companies granted exclusive territories to their agents or general agents; and, for most companies, there was no such thing as a personal producing general agent. Companies in the industry also supported the social contract by offering products which had built into their prices very high margins. Those margins were conservative because in those days actuaries tended to act that way when pricing products; and, in addition, gently rising interest rates and steadily improving mortality provided even higher margins than were programmed in to begin with.

A Stable Social Contract

So in summary, in these Glory Years there was a stable social contract among the three parties and it worked. There were only a few renegade companies in the life insurance industry and none of these gained an important market share. There was no real external competition from other types of companies also active in the savings market. And, in general, the life insurance business exhibited the characteristics of a growth industry. These were the Glory Years.

The Troubled Years

I come now to the troubled years. The question: How and why did that strategy falter, beginning around 1970? Walt Zultowski has already given you some of the reasons in his address this morning. I believe, as he does, that there were important forces of change at work that became clear sometime around 1970.

Consumer Revolt

First of all, the consumer revolted. His actions are manifest if one looks at the sales statistics of the industry itself. There was an unmistakable shift, beginning around 1970, towards low-margin and low-commission products, mainly term insurance and annuities. Deregulation was one important force of change and this was manifested by an increase in extra-industry competition, mainly from the banking sector and from securities products. Another force was sharply rising interest rates, which tended to foster new money products and which presented the opportunity for wholesale replacement of existing business by renegade agents and new competitors. And finally, high inflation diminished both the value and the relevance of the traditional products that the industry sold. These were the forces which influenced the action of the consumer, and this caused the social contract to collapse.

Agent Response

What was the agent's response to the consumer revolt? The agent, of course, was the first to know that the consumer had changed his habits. The change showed up in his next paycheck! The agent response, importantly, was to seek commission increases to offset the effects of the income reduction that agents sustained because of the consumer reaction to the new forces. Among the things that occurred was that replacement became a respectable part of the business — and also supported the income needs of agents.

Industry Response

What did the industry and individual companies do? What was their response? Weaker competitors abandoned the whole idea of single company representation in favor of the concept of personal producing general agents. They did this to improve their cost levels which had become unacceptably high. Stronger competitors and their own general agents then experienced increased costs because of the out-brokerage of business by agents who previously were loyal, primary producers. These are the agents who became PPGAs of other companies, on the side. This lead the weakest among the strong companies also to move to the PPGA strategy, and it reinforced that trend.

Next, commission competition ensued at these new and higher PPGA levels, and the commission competition negated the initial cost advantage of the change from the high fixed-cost system of exclusive agents to the high variable-cost system of PPGAs. The end result was that cost levels of all types of companies increased. Out-brokerage came out of the closet and became endemic. With nonexclusive agents, industry competition became price sensitive product-by-product, and price visibility increased with the offering of unbundled products, leading to a lowering of the margins which cover expenses and provide profits.

A Broken Contract

In the end, higher costs, higher lapse rates and reduced pricing margins has resulted in large and unsustainable new business subsidies for most companies, including most large companies. The industry is now experiencing labor cost problems not unlike those of the airline business, the steel industry and automobile manufacturers. Due to the new competitive price and commission environment, the social contract has been broken and abandoned by most agents and by most companies. The industry, as a result, is locked into a price war on a product-by-product basis that most companies cannot long sustain. Industry consolidation, which is already evident, will soon reduce the number of mainstream competitors quite dramatically. A business that has long been distribution driven is now also financially driven, and the business now exhibits the characteristics of a mature or stagnant business. These were the Troubled Years.

The Opportunity Years

I come now to the Opportunity Years, and my question is, "What new or old business strategies are likely to succeed today and in the future?"

Strategy vs. Tactics

First of all, let me comment about the difference between strategy and tactics. Strategy deals essentially with business fundamentals. Strategic questions, when asked, go to the root fundamentals of any business. Tactics arise after the basic strategy has been established. In the old days, the Glory Years, the strategy of this industry was practically uniform from company to company, and it was practically unchanged over long periods of time. Therefore, in those years, the planning focus of this industry was primarily tactical. The basic strategy issue had already been settled — each company had already decided to operate in the particular way which we have come to call traditional.

Today I would suggest to you that most companies — by which I mean all but a hundred or fewer — most companies require a new strategic initiative. Yesterday's strategy simply will not work under today's conditions. Strategic planning is now essential for success and even for survival, and for the smallest of the companies represented here, strategic planning is particularly important to their future survival and success.

This industry has limited experience with real strategic planning which affords little assistance. The industry must, therefore, look to other industries and their experience for guidance in strategic planning.

Strategic Options

Let me now discuss the strategic options that are available to companies under today's circumstances. A discussion of strategic options is not unlike the problem one faces in trying to describe to a complete newcomer a deck of playing cards. You probably have the experience of describing a deck of playing cards to novices — perhaps to children. I want you to think back on how you went about explaining it. Did you begin to turn the cards over one by one and say, "This is the three of clubs; this is the seven of diamonds; this is the jack of hearts; this is the queen of spades; this is the king of clubs; etc."? No, that's not the way you did it at all. What you did was to explain that there were four suits in the deck and that the deck contained 13 cards in each suit. You named the suits; you showed the symbol of the suits; you explained that two of them were red and that two of them were black; you hoped that it would not be necessary to explain what the cards marked with the numbers two through ten were; and then you concentrated on explaining jacks, queens, kings, and aces. That's how you described a deck of playing cards.

A similar problem arises in trying to describe strategic options, except that there are far more than 52 involved! So it is necessary to talk about them in groups, in suits if you like, or according to colors or rank. Using this technique of grouping, let me first go through the types of strategic options that are available to companies in this industry. They fall into four groups.

Continued Independence

Each of us and probably each of the companies with which we are associated have an important element of ego and, in looking at strategic options, we gravitate first to those options that are aimed at continued independence and success — that is the first group. Continued independence and success depends on a sustainable competitive viability, and that viability must be based on one of two things: it can be based on superior cost fundamentals, or it can be based on price and commission competitive avoidance. Both of these will be discussed in just a few minutes. At this point I would like only to say that acquisitions, both financially-driven and strategically-driven, may be a major feature of either of these two options. These are the only two ways of sustainable competitive viability and achieving continued independence and success.

Mergers of Equals

The second group of strategic options falls under the heading of Mergers of Equals; these also can be either financially driven or strategically driven. I have always used a rule of thumb to describe what is meant by a merger of equals. In my experience, a merger between two parties is not a merger of equals if either party is more than twice as big as the other. It may still not be a merger of equals if that requirement is satisfied, but it certainly will not be if the requirement is not satisfied. (Some of you know I speak from considerable personal and recent experience of this, since the firm with which I am associated has just experienced a nonequal merger itself!) Usually, a dominant partner will emerge from a merger of equals, even if the two-to-one ratio is satisfied. The cynics will say that there is no such thing as a merger of equals, but I am not quite that pessimistic. That's the second option — a merger of equals.

Dressing-Up for Sale

The third option is to dress up the company for sale or acquisition by another party. Let me tell you that this often is the best strategic alternative, unattractive though it may seem from an emotional viewpoint. Golden parachutes can be very effective in cushioning the ego fall that is often involved for management! This is one of the reasons why this choice often represents the best alternative! Under this option, a company consciously decides to dress itself up for sale or acquisition by another. It is important that management take charge of this process. This result should not happen by accident. It should happen as a result of a conscious decision because only in that way is it likely that the result can be optimized, that the terms offered can be made most attractive. In connection with the undertaking of dressing-up for sale or acquisition, I would suggest to you that outside professional assistance is probably worth its cost, knowing that I speak from a position of vested interest.

The Last Alternative

The last alternative is the one you don't want to hear about. The last alternative is slow and painful decline, and this I would suggest to you is the worst alternative. The trouble is it is also the default scenario. This is what will happen, I confidently predict, if a conscious (and rational) choice among the other alternatives is not made. The most usual result of this default alternative is that a sale or an acquisition then occurs on unfavorable terms.

Four Choices

So these are the four families of strategic options. Reviewing them for you: continued independence and success, based either on superior cost fundamentals or competitive avoidance; a merger of equals; a dress-up for sale or acquisition; and finally, slow painful decline. I know that the option that interests you most is the first and I would like to spend a few minutes discussing the strategic options which are based on superior cost fundamentals and then I will deal with the options based on competitive avoidance.

Superior Cost Fundamentals

First of all, let's understand what the objective of the superior cost strategy is. The objective of this strategy is to compete on the basis of low prices or high commissions, and to support that by having superior cost fundamentals in other respects. Notice, low prices or high commissions. In our complex business, prices and commissions are interchangeably and inversely connected. If this strategy to compete on the basis of low prices or high commissions is to be broadly based — in other words, if it is to cover many product lines, large sectors of the market place and so forth — you should understand that critical mass is very large. My personal estimate is that to compete in the broad middle market on the basis of superior cost fundamentals, a company requires individual new premium income of at least $100 million. Without that volume, it cannot in my view realistically aspire to compete on superior fundamentals in the broad market place. It can, however, aspire to compete as a specialist company. It can decide that it is only going to do one thing or a few things, and it is going to do that one thing or few things better than anyone else. It therefore expects to achieve superior cost fundamentals in its selected niche. This is a realistic idea, but you should understand that the concept of traditional, primary company agency distribution system is inconsistent with this idea; you cannot expect agents to represent your company primarily and then restrict them to a narrow product line or market.

One of the problems with this strategy of superior cost fundamentals is that the commitment to maintaining these fundamentals is permanent, and this position is difficult to maintain. The sensitive factors, in rough order of their importance, are as follows: the first is expenses, the second is investment return, the third is persistency, and the fourth, a distant fourth, is mortality experience. It should also be noted that the life insurance industry is not well positioned to compete on cost fundamentals with external competition from other industries, such as the banking industry or the investment industry, that come from a different historical position. In some future scenarios, superior cost fundamentals become even more difficult to maintain.

Competitive Avoidance

Let me now discuss the other possible strategic option intended to provide continued independence and success. This is the strategic option that is based on competitive avoidance. For most companies, this is the only realistic choice. Once again, let's review the objective. The objective is to compete on the basis of higher than the best prices, or lower than typical commissions, and to support that position by offering differentiated products or services, or by establishing a captive market or a captive distribution system. I repeat, the objective is to compete on the basis of high prices or low commissions, and to support this by differentiation of product or service, or by establishing a captive market or a captive distribution system.

In our business, the product is money for future delivery and product differentiation is very difficult to achieve. There are also no meaningful patents, copyrights, or whatever, in this industry; therefore, any product differentiation that is successful is likely soon to be imitated, and the action of the imitators will probably undercut the success of the strategy. You can see this if you look at the experience of the companies that first introduced universal life.

Experience in other fields suggests, however, that product differentiation, if soundly conceived, will work. The public will indeed accept premium prices for premium benefits. Public acceptance is particularly noticeable when the premium benefits offered are aimed at their convenience, their prestige, their self-confidence or providing personal service.

Some Examples

Let me give you some examples. Several years ago, many of you in this room received a mailing from the American Express Company which offered you the opportunity to carry a platinum American Express card. Some of you who received that mailing may have lacked in self-confidence because the unimpressive chap in front of you in the checkout line the last time you were at a hotel had a green card just like yours. You may have felt the urge to accept the offer to acquire a platinum card. It cost you about $200 a year. The benefits you received were not really worth $200, but it did provide you with the opportunity to impress the cashier the next time you checked out of the hotel! On the first mailing, I am told that 50,000 people accepted the offer of the platinum card and almost $10 million dropped to the bottom line of the American Express Company's travel division! Self-confidence for sale at $200.00 per year!

Another example is a Southern department store which also decided to offer a special charge card, their gold card. One of my associates asked what benefits people received by taking the gold card and paying for it when they could have a normal card free. It was explained to him that when the gold card holders came into the store they were given a free cup of coffee, they had a special place to go in the store and they got free gift wrapping — all of which didn't really add up to enough to make the price worthwhile. But the retailer went on to say, "But what they really like is what we call the 'gold gush'." Now, the gold gush works like this: when a customer comes in with a gold card the salespeople are trained to call to the sales person at the next cash register and say, "Look — I've got a gold card customer!" And the other sales person is trained to come over and says, "My, my — A gold card!" By this time all of the other customers are gathered around to see what all the fuss is about. They call this the "gold gush," and they train their sales personnel to do personal attention for sale at $35.00 per year!

Not long ago I did a favor for some friends in Atlanta, and they thoughtfully gave me a memento. It was a glass paperweight, shaped like an oversized emerald, very nicely made. If K-mart sold them, I expect that they would offer them for about $1.50 each. However, this one had product differentiation. If you set this glass paperweight on the desk, without turning it over, you could read through the prism on the top of the paperweight what was stamped upside down on the bottom. What was stamped there was "Tiffany & Company." Now, I am sure that that particular paperweight did not cost

$1.50, and I am also sure that the difference in price had nothing to do with the cost of stamping the bottom. This is an example of what people will pay for prestige benefits. I am very fond of my paperweight!

Many of you traveled here to New Orleans in the front half of the airplane. So would I have, but the plane happened to be full! First class air travel is another example of a premium benefit for which the public will pay a substantial premium price.

Realistic Possibilities

Now, all of these are fairly exotic examples. What are some realistic possibilities for the life insurance industry? One of them is superior sales support; that's taking the view that your product is the sales support that you give your intermediaries. Another is such things as exotic conventions, and no doubt that has something to do with some of the guests in attendance at this meeting! A third is investment performance, a real potential differentiator between life insurance products.

When I was with Abbey Life a number of years ago, a company engaged primarily in the variable life insurance business, we had a fairly aggressive advertising program. At that time our investment manager was Hambros Bank. Hambros Bank had an outstanding image and reputation, but some of our agents weren't quite satisfied with the actual investment performance. They sometimes amused themselves by writing mock headlines for our advertising copy. One of them was "Let Hambros Bank show you how to make a small fortune" and the subtitle said "First you start with a large fortune." So, it is perceived investment performance that counts, not actual investment performance.

Another of the realistic possibilities, one that is in fact used with considerable success by some companies, might unkindly be described as brainwashing one's own agents.

The strategy of competitive avoidance might be targeted on the consumer or might more likely be targeted on the intermediary. But remember, the objective is to achieve higher prices or to pay lower commissions. The objective is to achieve higher prices or to pay lower commissions so that average levels of cost can be supported, so that it's not necessary to have superior cost fundamentals.

Captive Markets and Distribution

Another way of achieving the same result is through a captive market. This is a rarity, but it features very prominently in the strategy of banks that are interested in widening their involvement in financial service businesses.

Reluctantly, I had the pleasure of speaking to a group of people from one of the Lutheran Fraternals and, in the course of that discussion, I made the observation that they have something that is pretty close to a captive market, which is very, very rare in my experience in this industry. In fact, the only example of a captive market that readily comes to mind is the United States Automobile Association. It was also very interesting to note that both the fraternal and the USAA have a somewhat similar problem — their membership isn't expanding fast enough. I said to the Lutherans, "Now, their problem could be solved with a small war; but your problem is going to take a second Reformation!"

Likewise, captive distribution is another effective method of competitive avoidance. That, in fact, was the strategy of this industry in the Glory Years, but today this is also quite rare and some cynics have said, "Ah yes, captive distribution — raising the question 'Who is the captive?'"

Another Perspective

The strategies for survival and success, like the deck of playing cards, can be grouped in a different way. Let me briefly mention four strategies for survival and success viewed from another perspective. The most interesting thing about this is that there are four and only four. Three are aimed at cost fundamentals and one is aimed at margins. Here they are:

- The first, improve cost fundamentals, primarily by attacking expenses.
- The second: improve unit costs by expanding sales while holding expenses where they are.
- The third: increase margins by raising prices or lowering commissions.
- And the fourth: increase investment returns.

Raising prices is something that few of us in this industry have any experience with. Those involved in the health insurance business have had some experience with price increases, but those whose experience is entirely in the individual life insurance business and who have only been in the business since 1945 have only seen prices going continuously downward. In other businesses, it is a major strategy.

So, there they are. Four and only four: improve cost fundamentals, spread overhead, raise prices, increase investment return. Now, reasonably, you might say well that's all theory.

Saving Chrysler

Well, it's not quite all theory. Who is America's best known business executive? Think about that for a moment. I'll wager that practically everyone in this audience mentally answered, Lee Iacocca, and I think justifiably so. He is a legendary success, and is widely credited with saving Chrysler. How did he do it? Well, would you believe that he had four programs. Let me tell you about them.

First, although his public relations department doesn't broadcast this one, he reduced the employment level at Chrysler by between 40,000 and 50,000 people. That sounds to me like a program to improve cost fundamentals, and it was probably his leading achievement. He downsized Chrysler.

Second, do you remember the television commercials, and there has been another round of them just within the last week, where Iacoca said, "If you can find a better car, buy it!" That program was very successful, and I would predict that the current one is going to be successful, too. Sales at Chrysler did indeed increase, and this permitted them to spread overhead.

Third, who introduced the mini-van? I recently have had the personal experience of purchasing a van, and in exploring the possibilities I discovered that a full size van and a mini-van cost the same amount of money. Perhaps I am old-fashioned: I think that the cost of those two products is somewhat connected to their weight and size, and I conclude that the profit margin on mini-vans is considerably higher than the profit margin on full sized vans. Who introduced mini-vans? Chrysler did. And who reintroduced the American built convertible? Chrysler did.

Fourth, Chrysler had a program to refinance it's debt. Now, Chrysler is a borrower and not an investor; this program was the borrower's counterpart to increasing investment return.

There you have it. The four programs of Chrysler, corresponding precisely to the four suggested strategies for survival and success.

Acquisitions and Mergers

What about acquisitions? Acquisitions can support either of the two methods of achieving independent survival and success. These acquisitions can either be financially driven, where the object is to improve the bottom line, or they can be strategically driven, where the object is to enter another line of business or territory or whatever. I have already mentioned that mergers of equals are a rare breed. But what about being acquired? The forces of consolidation in this industry are very strong.

Already they extend throughout the industry, and soon they will increase between this industry and other financial businesses, eventually including banks.

If your company should decide that it's best strategy was to be acquired, how do you go about it? Basically, you identify the potential acquirers by role reversal. You pretend that you are an acquirer looking for a company like your own, and you attempt to back into the characteristics of such a potential acquirer. There may be some tax benefits available to mutual life insurance companies in a merger with each other, or in being acquired; these might finance golden parachutes at no cost to policyholders. Prices currently prevailing in the market place are still high for life insurance companies, and financial markets are generally favorable today towards an acquisition. Banks may one day be important new buyers of insurance companies, but this is not likely to be a major force until the 1990s.

Conclusion

In summary, the favorable economic environment of the last five years has strengthened the capital base of the industry, which now stands at an all time high in real terms. This has allowed the industry to preserve its existing distribution system, and it has given the industry time to adapt to the new realities. These are the Opportunity Years, but they will not last forever. Adverse economic developments, unfavorable tax changes or further deregulation of banks could suddenly lead to a crisis environment in which radical change could be imposed quickly by market forces. For example, look at the massive consolidation that has occurred within the airline industry in 1986 alone.

I think that among the things that it takes to succeed in today's environment is conviction. The conviction that business as usual is not a realistic plan, and that "do nothing" is a high risk option. I have a strong personal affinity for those companies that are willing to dare to be different, and I think that a disproportionate number of them will wind up in the winners' circle. The Glory Years are gone for good. A new and different future beacons, and the strong will greet it with confidence. These are the Opportunity Years.

This aging prophet thanks you for your invitation.

The Dawn of the Third Millennium

Published in Actuarial Futures, *No. 8 (October 20, 1987): 1–4. Reprinted with permission from the Society of Actuaries.*

Futurism — that's the process whereby sight is lost of both the forest and the trees. Let me read to you a brief excerpt from the *Encyclopedia Brittanica*. It has to do with tulips:

> Demand for new varieties soon exceeded supplies and prices for individual tulip bulbs rose to unwarranted heights. By about 1610 [This is approximately 50 years after tulips were introduced in Europe.] a single bulb of a new variety was acceptable as a dowry for a bride. In one case, a flourishing brewery in France was exchanged for a single bulb of the variety "tulip brasserie." But it was in Holland that the craze reached its height during the period 1633 to 1637. This created such extraordinary speculation that a national scandal and economic disaster was brought on the country. Homes, estates and industries were mortgaged so that bulbs could be bought for resale at higher prices. Sales and resales were made many times over without the bulbs ever leaving the ground or the flowers ever being seen by the buyer. The boom crashed in the spring of 1637.

Why do we forecast the future? I believe there are three reasons we undertake to do this. First, we are attempting to exploit anticipated opportunities. And next, we intend to defend against unforeseen threats. Finally, in some rare cases, we attempt to forecast the future in order to influence the direction of events, and it's that third purpose to which I am going to turn most of my attention.

The methods of futurism are probably well known to all of you. There are really three ways in which we attempt to forecast the future. The simplest is by mere extrapolation of observed trends. This is the conventional wisdom of futurism, and it is widely practiced in areas such as budgeting and so forth. Usually, these kinds of forecasts are right, but only in the short term. They're always wrong when trends reverse.

A second method is through the anticipation of secondary consequences of observed trends. These generally are based on deductive reasoning. They're often right in terms of the forecast for the intermediate term future, and they don't necessarily depend on a continuation of the underlying trend. For example, certain population forecasts can be made with considerable confidence even if trends and birth rates and death rates should suddenly alter. These kinds of forecasts, however, are susceptible to error if new factors alter the cause and effect relationships which form the basis of the forecast.

The final method is to identify fundamental relationships which eventually lead to trend reversal. Some of the soothsayers on Wall Street might, for example, have applied that kind of technique to accurately predict that when stock prices get to be lighter than air, that sooner or later they do come crashing down. I used the title "The Third Millennium Dawning" for these remarks, and it gives me an opportunity to have a little fun. My first question is, "When does the third millennium in fact dawn?" Will it happen on Saturday, January 1st in the year 2000, or will it happen on Monday, January 1st in the year 2001? Basically this issue pits the odometer type mentality of the public against the mathematical purity of people like ourselves. We're aware that those calendar designers were generally nonnumeric people, and they did not have the foresight to install a year 0 in our calendar which illogically progresses directly from year minus one to year plus one.

My suspicion is that in the end, the odometer mentality is going to win, and I suggest a simple test to you. Have you ever, when driving your automobile, noticed that your odometer was approaching 999.9 and made it a point to observe it roll to the next round thousand. I think you have. Have you ever watched after it rolled to the thousand for it to roll to 001? I'll bet the answer is no. So I suggest that on Saturday, January 1st, the year 2000, we join the public in celebrating the arrival of the third millennium because it's going to have the more obvious aspects. Our checkbooks for example are all going to be obsolete because they will have the "19 blank" printed in them which no longer is appropriate.

Now, the arrival of the third millennium, and the juxtaposition of the two dates I've just mentioned, allows me to make passing reference to another rare phenomenon. In the course of making reference to this, I get the opportunity to use a rarely used word. The word is "bisextile." And I would wager that this word is known only to a small fraction of this audience — conceivably to a fraction as small as zero. Let me tell you about bisextile. In 46 B.C., or if you prefer, minus 46, Julius Ceasar approved a change in the calendar. And the approval of the change in the calendar involved the insertion of a day into the month of February on a periodic basis. The word bisextile is a reference to leap year. It's reference to the Latin expression, "bisextus dias" which refers to the doubling of February 28. When this change in the calendar was adopted, they did not precisely estimate the number of leap years that it would be necessary to have in order to maintain the correct speed of the world around the sun measured in days. This gave the first approximation of the speed of the earth at 365.25 days per year. That didn't, in fact, correspond to the actual time that it takes the earth to orbit the sun, and at a later stage, there was inserted the so-called century exception which said that a year that is a century year will not be a leap year. That altered the approximation to 365.24 days. Finally, that was not deemed to be sufficiently accurate either and the second exception was introduced. The second exception is that a century year divisible by 400 is a leap year. So the year 2000 will be a bisextile year and that will be another rare event.

Now let me try to place in context the kind of geopolitical world we are likely to have on our hands in the year 2000. It seems to me that we are approximately an equal distance from the year 2000 as measured from today as we were to a date in 1985 when a paper was published that included a scenario referred to by the title, Cannibal Life. So if you will think backwards to that event, it gives you a kind of time frame within which we are speaking. There's one fact about the future that I think we can rely on. Sometime during the summer of 1987, we were told that there became 5 billion passengers aboard spaceship earth. It's clear that by the year 2000, there will be more than six billion passengers on spaceship earth. What is not perhaps so clear is that 90% of those additional passengers are going to be from the lesser developed countries of the world. I've come across an entertaining forward written by Lawrence Seigel in the 1982 edition of a publication called *Stocks, Bonds, Bills and Inflation*, by Ibbotson & Sinquefield. There are a couple of passages in here which I think are relevant to this fact about the population of spaceship earth. Mr. Seigel says that squirrels horde: knowing that they must have food in the winter, they willingly forego present consumption in exchange for further consumption in exchange for future consumption. Within an individual squirrel's lifetime, the animal makes numerous trades between the present and the future. Yet, squirrels do not build wealth over time. The offspring of particularly industrious squirrels do not find their lives made richer by their parents' past efforts. Squirrels as a species are not better off than they were a hundred years ago. So clearly, holding or storage is not a sufficient condition for building wealth.

Ants, which incidentally are organically far less complex than squirrels, not only horde, but they build structures, anthills, which may last longer than an individual ant. Thus, ants transfer wealth intergenerationally. Young ants may find themselves born into a well constructed anthill. Since an ant may not live to reap the fruit of his own labour, we regard ants as investors and not just hoarders. Yet, unlike that of humans, the per capita wealth of ants does not grow steadily over time. Each generation of ants is not really better off than its predecessors.

Humans can influence outcomes in three ways. First, man can identify good and bad uses for capital and then select the good ones. Second, man can change the environment in a way favorable to the desired outcome. Third and most importantly, man can change himself.

Why then do human economies have secular growth while ant economies do not? The reason is that ants most probably multiply in a Malthusian fashion expanding their population to consume any attained economic growth. Humans sometimes react to growth by limiting their populations. I'm suggesting of course that there may be some similarity to what is likely to happen in the lesser developed countries of the world and what happens in ant economies where the population expands such that resources are always expended to the fullest at subsistence. I'm suggesting to you that the developed and lesser developed countries over the remaining 12 years, between now and 2000, are going to experience economies that diverge in terms of success, and that they may eventually experience a divergence in their civilizations.

What are some of the implications of all this? First, the implications for the lesser developed countries are that they face problems, such as the urbanization of these large and growing populations. They face problems in the area of housing, transportation, jobs, security and pollution. The subsistence needs of these countries include several expected items and one perhaps unexpected item. My list includes food, shelter, medicine, energy, education, and the surprising one is munitions. Undoubtedly there are going to be tremendous immigration pressures arising between the lesser and more developed countries of the world. We're likely to see in these increasingly crowded countries, a tendency towards totalitarianism, political instability, religious fanaticism, terrorism, provocation, and possibly nuclear proliferation. In other words, it all sounds very familiar. It sounds like what's going on in Iran today.

The implications for the developing countries also are serious. These countries are likely to experience tremendous aging of their populations, and some, like Germany and Switzerland, are actually forecasting significant population losses. These counties are going to, however, experience an increase in their per capita wealth. There will be stresses on the social conscience of the more developed countries and in particular, there will be stresses in choosing between domestic and international priorities. In general, these countries are going to have to decide whether to practice a form of neocolonialism or whether to mount Marshall Plan II. In summary, the context of the future that I foresee within the countries in which we live is an outlook for prosperity with considerable stress.

Now let's move closer to home. Let's talk for a minute about the users of actuarial services circa the year 2000. I've identified three users of actuarial services, beginning first with insurers. I would tell you that I expect insurers will no longer be the largest users of actuaries in the year 2000. Mainly, I foresee insurance companies becoming parts of large consolidated financial, and perhaps financial and industrial, groups resembling what might be described as the new zibetsu. In these enlarged groups, I foresee that there will be no clear senior role for actuaries as such, as actuaries are now trained. Instead, I see as was mentioned yesterday during a panel discussion, other individuals taking on senior responsibilities in these kinds of expanded organizations. I would predict that actuaries who are involved in areas of health and casualty insurance are likely to experience considerable gain in the importance of what they do as contrasted to those who are active in the field of life insurance.

The second user of actuarial services is retirement plan sponsors. Here, too, I foresee considerable change. I see that the whole process of retirement plan sponsorship will become a part of a wider set of issues — the wider set of issues being labor costs and human resource issues. These are compartmentalized solutions that we have been accustomed to in the past. Solutions, for example, that separate employee benefits from direct compensation will be less appropriate in the world I foresee in the future. Finally, among the users of actuarial services, I would mention the consulting firms. By the year 2000, the consulting firms may in fact employ significantly more than 50 percent of the actuaries in North America. A couple of weeks ago, I attended the meeting of the Conference of Actuaries in Public practice, and using the preregistration list that was published in their program, was able to classify the individuals in attendance at that meeting into one of three categories. In the first category were individuals who were involved in a monoline actuarial firm, an actuary or single practitioners. This is a firm, in other words, in which there was only one area of practice — perhaps the employee benefits field, perhaps the casualty field, or whatever. The second group consisted of multiline actuarial firms which practiced in more than one actuarial field and where the firms were controlled by actuaries. The third category was those who were involved in mixed professional practices that were not controlled by actuaries. I won't go into all of the statistics, but there's one very striking one. Category three, the mixed professional practice not controlled by actuaries, represented 54% of the people who were preregistered to attend that meeting. What I am leading up to, of course, is the issue that was discussed yesterday, the future of the actuary. Harking back to what I said at the very outset, it's my belief that the future of the actuary is something that we can control. I think that the future of the actuary is entirely within the bounds of being dictated by the current profession, but we're going to have to face some decisions. One is whether we are going to continue to be traditional specialists in a field, which I think is going to decline in a period as short as the next 12 years, or are we going to become problem solvers who act on a larger stage? To me, I think that not only is the choice ours to make, but the choice is very clear. I think this profession must move towards becoming problem solvers acting on a larger stage. I have several times made the suggestion that life contingencies may no longer remain part of the core curriculum of the actuarial profession, and it's something that I sincerely believe. I think that we have got to separate ourselves from the narrow specialties on which this profession has been built for so many years. The future is within our control provided we make appropriate modifications to our educational process, our training process, and our qualification process. It's on the last of those three that I want to focus.

If my suggested future for the actuarial profession becomes a reality, we as actuaries are going to become less bound than we are today by a common specialty. We are going to be practicing it in a wide variety of fields. Some will be completely outside the scope of the profession. For example, some of us may have the title "actuary" in a bank. Meyer Melnikoff, one of the leading figures in our profession for many years, became a member of Goldman-Sachs after he retired from the insurance industry. He used the title actuary at Goldman-Sachs. That may be a signal of the future.

This need for a common bond, I think, must be reflected by a stronger organizational definition of who is an actuary. In the U.S., the situation is very different from what it is here in Canada. In Canada, it is clear. If you ask the question, "Who is an actuary?", there is a clear answer. The answer is a Fellow of the Canadian Institute of Actuaries. There are similarly clear answers in the United Kingdom and in Australia. But in the United States, there is no clear answer to that question no matter what the membership of the Society of Actuaries may think. The international focus of the Society of Actuaries and the international focus of the Casualty Actuarial Society may in fact actually impede a solution to this problem, which is basically a United States problem. The American Academy of Actuaries, but not the Society of Actuaries, nor the Casualty Actuarial Society, has come to terms with the enrolled actuaries in the United States, but has not come to terms with the American Society of Pension Actuaries. I don't think that we are going to have a widely accepted organizational definition until these competing bodies are put into a single organization.

The Future of the Life Insurance Industry

Presented to a Joint Meeting of the Actuaries Club of the Southwest and the Southeastern Actuaries Club, New Orleans, Louisiana, November 19, 1987.

As I stand here this morning, I can't help but think first of my long-standing personal relationship with these two major regional actuarial clubs. I would like to acknowledge the major contribution the two clubs have made, both to the profession and to the life insurance industry in the regions that they serve. I've enjoyed participating from time-to-time in these occasional joint meetings, and they seem always to be held here on contested turf in Louisiana! It is no wonder that both clubs claim this state as a part of their territory because it gives them the opportunity to meet in this exceptional city.

As I arrived here last evening, I couldn't help but think back to the first time I attended a meeting of the Southeastern Actuaries Club. It was in 1956; the meeting took place in this city; it took place in this hotel, which was then called the Roosevelt. To be candid, it really was my first introduction to life in the fast lane. I learned, for example, that no matter what your heart desired, it was for sale here in New Orleans! I remember, too, flying here with a group of other people from Atlanta. We flew on a Delta DC-7 which was a state-of-the-art airplane at the time; the flight took two hours. Going back we were a little more adventurous and flew on an airplane called a Vickers Viscount which was operated by Capital Airlines, which took only an hour and a half.

Also, at that meeting I recall joining a group of people who gathered at Pat O'Brien's. The group was hosted by the staff members of Bowles, Andrews and Towne and included a number of clients of that firm. At the time, I was one of the clients. I will never forget the conversation between Bill Brown of BAT and Roy Barnes, a client. Roy Barnes was complaining bitterly about the level of BAT's charges. Finally, Bill Brown took up the point and said: "Roy, you ought to understand that we have two levels of charges in our firm. We have a low rate and a high rate, and you always pay the high rate." Mr. Barnes was very incensed by this and demanded an explanation. The explanation was: "The low rate is charged when we are talking and the high rate is charged when we are listening." For those of you who are clients of our firm, I would warn you that we also observe the same rule!

My last appearance on the program of the Southeastern Actuaries Club was in 1980 at Kiawah. It was even earlier when I appeared last on the program of the Southwestern Club at a meeting at the Shamrock Hilton in Houston. I am delighted to have the opportunity to be with you again today.

The future has become my business in recent years. That is perhaps less surprising than it may sound. That's because vision has become a key factor in strategic planning. And strategic planning has become a key factor in the life insurance industry. The future of the life insurance industry, we must recognize, is an issue which is subordinate to some broader issues.

Three Issues

Today's agenda consists of three of these broader issues, and I intend to address each of them. The first issue is the geopolitical and geo-economic context of the future; I pick the year 2000 A.D. as a benchmark of that future because it will mark the borderline not only between an old century and a new one but between the second millennium and the third millennium. Any business, any activity, is necessarily a function of the context in which it exists. If we're going to address the future of the industry, we must first address the future of the world at large. The second issue is the forces of change which are affecting not only the life insurance industry but also related financial service businesses. The third issue is the implications of all of this for the life insurance industry generally as well as for the types of companies that are representative of those that exist in the Southwest and the Southeast.

The Third Millennium

What is the third millennium going to be like? What kind of world are we going to live in some 13 years from now? I begin by apologizing for what I am about to do to a fellow mathematician. His name is Charles Ludwig Dodgson and his alias is Lewis Carroll. I parody his famous verse from "Alice":

"The time has come," the Walrus said,
"Peer through the clouded lens
At squirrels and nuts,
At ants and hills,
At Homo Sapiens."

Now, what is this piece of doggerel all about? It is a take-off on the preface to the 1982 publication by Ibbotson & Sinquefield with the dazzling title, *Stocks, Bonds, Bills and Inflation.* The preface was written by Lawrence V. Seigel, and I think it is a revealing commentary on how the economies of man and nature work. Mr. Seigel points out that squirrels save. Squirrels are very good savers; they make endless choices in the course of their lives between savings and consumption. Yet, the offspring of particularly industrious squirrels do not find their lives made richer by their parents' past efforts; squirrels as a species are not better off then they were a hundred years ago. Why is that? That is because squirrels, while they save, do not invest. Ants, on the other hand, are not only savers but they are also investors. They build structures called anthills. And through the building of these structures, they become investors. They are able to achieve an intergenerational transfer of wealth. It is possible for some lucky ant to be born in a particularly well-constructed anthill. Despite the fact that ants are not only savers but investors as well, the average 20th century ant is no better off than the average 19th century ant. Why is that? That is because the population of ants always expands to consume all of the available resources. Therefore, the per capita ant wealth never increases. It is left to man alone to achieve this phenomenon called economic progress. Man alone is able not only to save and invest; man has the unique capacity to increase per capita wealth. Man alone has the ability to influence the events that surround him and particularly to control population growth.

In looking to the future, it seems to me we can learn a great deal from an examination of one statistic. Last summer we were told that the five billionth passenger had boarded Spaceship Earth. We know from our professional experience that it can be reliably predicted that before the year 2000 there will be 6 billion passengers aboard Spaceship Earth. One fact that gives us insight into the shape of the future is the knowledge that 90% of those additional 1 billion passengers will come from the less developed countries of Spaceship Earth.

Let me give you some economic comparisons that I think shed a lot of light on this. The figures that I am going to cite are in terms of gross national product per capita for the year 1985 and are in U.S. dollars. The developed countries of the world, with about two-thirds of a billion people, had a per capita GNP of about $12,000. The Soviet and Eastern European countries of the world, with about a third of a billion people, had an average per capita GNP of $2,000. The less developed countries of the world, with a population of four billion, had an average per capita GNP of $300. The world average was less than $2,000. Now let's project this forward to the year 2000 using reasonably conservative estimates. We're still in constant 1985 dollars and we're not including any adjustment for what may take place in foreign exchange rates. It is reasonable to assume that by the year 2000 the developed countries of the world will have about 700 million people and their GNP per capita will be about $18,000. That is an increase of 50% in GNP per capita. The Soviet and Eastern Bloc countries will have about 400 million people, and their per capita income will increase to around $3,500. That is an increase of 75%. The lesser developed countries of the world will have 4.9 billion people, and it is likely that their per capita GNP won't be higher than $330, a 10% increase. Now why is that? Primarily it is because of the ant-like phenomenon of increasing population, which explains the relevance of my earlier remarks.

Implications

What are the implications of all of this? What does this tell us about the kind of world we're going to live in? From the viewpoint of the developed countries, which concern most of us here, it is clear that the world of the future involves one where income or asset-based wealth is going to increase quite substantially. In particular, asset-based wealth is going to expand even more substantially than income-based wealth. It is also clear that contrary to the trends of the last, say, fifty years, there is going to be a significant increase in the common interests between the Eastern and Western Bloc nations and a growing gulf between both groups and the Third World. It is also clear that there are going to be major increases in the frustration level within the lesser developed countries. This is going to lead to governments that are dominated by totalitarianism; it is going to lead to widespread religious fanaticism; it is going to lead to terrorism; it is going to mean that among the subsistence needs of these countries you would list not only food, clothing, shelter, energy and so forth, but also munitions. In other words, the future of these countries looks all too uncomfortably like present-day Iran. We are going to see in this world tremendous increases in immigration pressures, and there will be incentives for the developed countries of the world to yield somewhat to these immigration pressures because of their aging populations. One foresees within the developed countries of the world a great strain on our social conscience. We're going to have to choose between domestic and international priorities in terms of our social conscience. Basically, in the end we are going to have to decide whether to embark on a program of neo-colonialism or a second Marshall Plan on the grandest of scales.

In summary, the world of our future looks like one in which there will be a tremendous increase in asset-based prosperity in the developed countries and a tremendous increase in international stress vis-à-vis the Third World.

Globalization of Financial Markets

Among the other features of this geopolitical, geo-economic context of the future, is the globalization of world financial markets. One month ago today, we learned something about the globalization of world financial markets. Suddenly, on October 19, 1987, the fairy tale of Hans Christian Anderson came true. All at once that day, in all the markets of the world except one, it was discovered that the Emperor didn't have any clothes.

Let me tell you that I think there's still a second chapter to come in this saga. The Mikado doesn't have any clothes either! But investors in the Japanese stock market have not yet awakened to that reality. Let me tell you a few things that are happening in Tokyo today that lead me to this conclusion. First of all, the stock market in Tokyo is the world's largest and that alone ought to be warning enough. Second, the market capitalization of one company listed on the Tokyo exchange, Nippon Telephone, exceeds the value of the entire West German stock market! The company sells at a price earnings ratio of over 250! If that is not exciting enough for you, you can buy Japan Airlines at a price earnings ratio of 450!

So, I think that we have another chapter yet to unfold in the globalized world financial market and all of this should be a warning to us. Globalization of world financial markets is here to stay and with it will run increased stress, increased volatility and, for those in the business of being financial intermediaries, increased importance will attach to their capital resources.

Forces of Change in the Financial Service Business

So much for the larger picture. Let me now narrow the focus and talk about the financial service businesses generally and the life insurance business more particularly. Let's start with some of the forces of change that are at work in these businesses. I'll give you only a sample this morning of several of these forces of change. There are actually quite a few others.

It seems to me that the first and most important of the forces of change that we have witnessed in our recent careers is the behavior of the consumer of financial services. It is clear that the consumer today is much more sophisticated than the consumer of, say, fifteen years ago. This sophistication on the part of the financial service consumer is showing up in the greatly increased sensitivity to price. In the life insurance business, this price sensitivity is reflected in the statistics which track the distribution of sales in the industry. From 1970 onward, there was a noticeable and consistent rise in the public preference for term insurance products and for annuities. Both of those preferences were motivated by the consumer sophistication and increased sensitivity to price. Basically, the consumer was selecting against high margin products of the industry. Consumer sophistication is something that I don't believe is going to lessen. I don't think there is any way to de-sophisticate the consumer. This is one case where, when the lions get loose, there is no caging them up again.

The second notable force of change is deregulation. Deregulation also affects the pricing of financial service products. It affects pricing indirectly because it changes the entry barriers; it fosters competition that was not present before.

Traditionally, financial service businesses have always been regulated along lines dictated by technical specialty. In other words, life insurance companies were regulated in a way that dealt with their technical specialty, their technical reserve requirements, etc. Similarly, general insurance companies were regulated in a way that related to their own technical specialty, and banks were regulated in a different way that related to their own technical specialty. The move towards deregulation is bringing with it a somewhat more rational approach to the regulation of financial service businesses. The tendency, I think, is toward market-based regulation. A recent example of this has happened in the United Kingdom; a bill called the Financial Services Act will go into effect sometime next year. The Financial Services Act deals not with life insurance but with all personal financial products; the Act contains regulation as to sales methods, commission rates, etc., and it is not unique to a particular branch of the financial services industry. I think that it is the kind of regulation we are likely to see in the future. Individual financial products will be regulated one way and commercial financial products will be regulated another way. This deregulation has created for the first time important cross-industry competition. This cross-industry competition is important to the life insurance industry for reasons I'll explain in a moment. The best example of this is the dismantling of Regulation Q and the discovery that a money market mutual fund can be used to simulate an unregulated bank. That single discovery probably had more to do with what has happened in the individual financial service market than any other single event in recent years.

The reason it is so important is that different branches of the individual financial service business have very different economics. Let me illustrate the extent of the difference. Let's suppose that all branches of the individual financial service business operated using the parlance of the mutual fund industry. In other words, all branches talk in terms of load and each uses that kind of language in order to market its products. If life insurance companies all operated on a level-load basis, what do you suppose the level load would be? My calculations suggest that the level load is somewhere between 30% and 40% of each and every premium. I'm not talking about the part of the premium required to provide the insurance coverage benefits, I'm talking only about the part of the premium intended to cover expenses.

What would the banking industry look like if it had such a load on its products? What sort of level load would you apply to certificates of deposit? Once again, my calculations suggest to me that the equivalent level load which is implicit in the interest rate spreads that are a part of the banking business would be between 10% and 15%. In mutual funds, the implicit load is between 5% and 10%. You can see that financial products issued by these previously separate businesses have very different economics. Therefore, cross-industry competition is going to become one of the dominant forces of the future of the life insurance business.

The third force of change is technology. This has transformed some parts of the financial service business and probably those changes will continue into the future. The automated teller machines, of course, have had a tremendous impact on the way in which banks do business. The telephones we use every day, if you can figure out how to use them, do amazing things. Microcomputers have made possible the current generation of life insurance products; unbundling would have been quite impractical without them.

Another force of change has been taxation. In the United States, changes in tax law having direct impact on our business have become an annual event. From 1981 to 1986 we have had six consecutive years with major tax legislation affecting either the life insurance industry or its products or the buyers of its products.

All of these forces of change are not spent. They are likely to continue into the future and, in particular, I think one of them is likely to be very important. I foresee that banks will eventually be allowed to compete quite openly in the insurance industry and vice versa. What are the implications of all of this for the life insurance industry? What is it that the life insurance industry does? One focus of our business activity is on income protection. We provide income protection against events such as premature death, disability and retirement. How does each of these basic businesses look today and how will it look in the future?

The Basic Business Activities

The business of protecting income against premature death probably has a secure future. The competition in that business is entirely within the life insurance industry. There are no competitors from outside the industry that are going to become involved in that kind of business. They will have to join the industry in order to provide that kind of service. What's on the horizon affecting this class of business is, of course, AIDS. Depending on what one foresees as the future course of that deadly disease, one might imagine circumstances under which it might be very difficult to conduct an individual private life insurance business. But with that exception, that end of the business looks secure. The disability business also looks secure. The competition there is more or less entirely intra-industry. There may be some self-insurance type competition, but generally speaking, the disability business looks reasonably secure for the future, and indeed, it looks underserved.

It is in the retirement savings business that the industry faces major new external competition. That is because of the relatively adverse economics that I mentioned just a few minutes ago. When the retirement savings business is expressed on an equivalent level-load basis, it is clear that the life insurance industry is operating at the high cost end of that business.

Another business activity in which the industry is involved is health-care financing. The group branch of the health-care financing business has tended, particularly in recent years, to shift its focus to the issue of cost containment. For the individual side, risk selection and risk management appear to be the dominant factors. In these businesses, external competition is likely to be fairly modest. It may come from HMOs and, conceivably, it may come from government.

So the basic businesses that make up the life insurance industry appear to have a reasonably secure future with the exception of external competition in the retirement savings field. This means that external price-based competition is the main threat to the industry and that that threat is going to focus primarily on the retirement savings end of the business which really is the largest sector of this industry. The industry is going to have to respond to quite severe economic pressures, economic pressures to change its pricing to correspond more closely with competing products. These pressures are going to be felt particularly by the distribution system of the industry. Besides distribution, the industry is going to have to face up to other cost initiatives. Companies are going to either have to strive to achieve lower cost levels through economies of scale or they are going to have to achieve it through narrowing the field of activities in which they engage and thereby becoming, if you like, large companies in a small market. This is what you might call economies of scale in small packages.

Future competition is likely to come from banks operating on a consumer-driven basis. The likely competition from banks will be in terms of their ability directly to access a customer base. Their appeal is likely to be price-based aimed at the consumer, whereas in contrast the insurance industry strategy has usually been distribution-based and not customer-based. In all this, the threat of loss of tax advantages for life insurance products is likely to be crucial. I estimate that the current tax laws give life insurance products a cost advantage of approximately 10% of each and every premium. The preservation of this advantage is vital if the current economics of the industry are going to be even approximately preserved.

Future for the Smaller Companies in the South

I want to get a little more specific for this audience in particular. In general, this region of the country is made up of life insurance companies that are relatively small. There are relatively fewer mutual life insurance companies in this part of the country than in other sections. What does the future look like for companies of this type?

Most of the companies in this region have pursued for many years a business strategy based on high commissions and high margins. This strategy is vulnerable to the kind of competitive threats that I have described. Another strategy that has been pursued by companies in this region has featured agent relationship building. With the general collapse of single company representation, this strategy is not as effective as it used to be. The smaller size of the companies in this region, in my view, demands that they focus their business strategies on particular market sectors or on particular product lines.

I think that the viability of competing on an across-the-board basis with all comers has diminished. I think that consolidation among companies in this region is more or less inevitable and that there will be two kinds of consolidations: financially driven consolidations within the industry aimed at increasing economies of scale and strategically driven consolidations with another financial service company aimed at adding product lines that can be offered through existing distribution systems. Joint ventures may be a strategy that suits the companies in this region better than it does those in other parts of the country. The purpose of joint ventures generally is to access somebody else's customers or to access somebody else's distribution system. Joint ventures between insurance companies and banks in this region are a quite practical possibility. There are many home service companies in the Southeast and Southwest. These companies, in defiance of all the forecasts that go back more than 80 years, are enjoying a renaissance in recent years. This renaissance illustrates the power of truly captive distribution systems and the ability of captive distribution systems to offset the price sensitivity that we see in the marketplace. AIDS is going to be a problem that will have to be dealt with, but in this part of the country it may be a less serious problem than elsewhere, with some exceptions. Cities such as Houston, Miami, New Orleans and to a lesser extent cities like Dallas and Atlanta do have serious problems. But the region as a whole may be in a favored position with respect to that particular issue.

Summary

In summary, I foresee that the world in which we are going to be operating in the future will be one which, from the perspective of the developed countries, will feature great prosperity and great stress. I see that market forces are changing the shape of financial institutions in this country. I expect that those changes will continue. The life insurance industry is looking at a growing but changing market. The increase in asset-based wealth, for example, is going to create a huge market in the future for single premium business, assuming no change in tax structure.

The survival of the life insurance industry as a business is reasonably well secure, but the survival of the life insurance industry as a separate and independent industry is not necessarily assured. Life insurance may simply become one branch of a wider financial service business in the future. Survival in this new environment demands either low cost or differentiation of products, service or distribution system.

Integrated Resources Success

Presented to a Joint Meeting of the Actuaries Club of the Southwest and Southeastern Actuaries Club, Dallas, Texas, January 1988.

Jim Anderson: Good morning, ladies and gentlemen. I'm sorry that I can't see you but I assume that you're all there. Taking a queue from William Shakespeare who suggested to us that the past is prologue to the future, I'd like to spend this few minutes this morning looking at where the life insurance industry has been, where it is today and where it's probably going. Since 1970, the life insurance business has changed more than in any period of its history in North America. What's even more remarkable is that the industry has changed twice during that period since 1970. Between 1970 and 1979, the changes were almost all for the worse and threatened the very existence of the industry. In 1980 onwards, the changes were for the better, redefining the role and purpose of the life insurance industry. And this process of fundamental change is continuing.

Let me turn the clock back to what I have sometimes referred to as the glory years of the life insurance industry prior to 1970. Let's look at how the industry conducted its affairs during those years. At that time, the general public viewed life insurance products as differentiated from alternate financial products, and the competition in those years was entirely within the life insurance industry. Price comparisons by the public were then not well understood, and the products of the industry generally tended to be non-price sensitive. The industry in those years was entirely distribution driven. The competitive focus was on building relationships within the field organizations. Single company representation was the norm for practically the whole industry. There existed a commission cartel and according to the theory of gains, there existed the usual coalition that one finds in three-player games. The basic rule of three-player games is that two of the players will form a coalition against a third. During those pre-1970 years, the established coalition was the distributor and the insurance companies in coalition against the consumer.

Costs during this period escalated to progressively higher levels. In the environment of an expanding market, the winners were those companies that spent money to expand their business. These were the conditions that existed up until 1970.

Now, let me come to the first period of dramatic change which took place during the years 1970 to 1979. It began with a consumer revolt, and the consumer revolt showed up in the sales statistics of the industry. The sales and public preference clearly shifted to low margin products like term insurance and annuities. Whole life sales declined quite steeply. This shift in public preference or this consumer revolt, if you like, had a very adverse impact on intermediaries, and they then reacted. The result of their reaction was a breakdown in the single company representation within the industry, and in its place emerged the independent distributor often called a personal producing general agent. The social contract which had been stable for many years within the life insurance industry collapsed, and in addition, the coalition in the three-player game changed. Basically, the new coalition was the distributor and the consumer versus the industry.

At the same time during these years, there were many external forces that were quite adverse to the industry. High rates of inflation diminished the appeal of traditional life insurance products, rising interest rates caused tremendous losses on investment portfolios, a tax breakdown occurred that affected the investment throughput on life insurance products. All these were interconnected, all these were very adverse. By the end of the 1970s, the industry was truly threatened. This capital base had been eroded, most companies were looking at unrealized losses on their investment portfolios that were about three times their capital funds. The industry had survived in those years on tax avoidance products primarily, the most important of which was minimum deposit. You know minimum deposit is that plan where there are paper premiums, there are paper loans, there are paper cash values, and the only thing real in the whole transaction is the commission dollars that they're paid and their tax deductions.

Now, let's move to 1980, the years of the favorable developments. The industry responded beginning about 1980 with a product modernization. Interest sensitive products were developed first by a few companies and then became the industry norm. These interest sensitive products were designed in a way to make them more tax-effective, to bypass the proxy tax that the insurance industry was paying on its policyholders investment earnings. These products were also unbundled and flexible and more responsive to the new circumstances of high inflation that it undercut the appeal of traditional products. In these products, costs were very visible, that one of the consequences of that was a move to lower rates of commissions. All of this led to a reversal of the sales trend which up to then were pointed in the direction of an all term industry. These products also spawned a widespread replacement activity within the industry, and while this widespread replacement has had much criticism, it should be recognized that this actually was a temporary salvation for the distribution system of the industry. It was the commission earnings that were generated by the replacement programs that kept many people in this business.

The financial market recovery restored the capital base of the industry, and during the 1980s there were taxation changes that were generally favorable. It was established in the revised method of taxing life insurance companies that gross interest rates could be payable to policyholders on all types of products. The Tax Reform Act eroded other tax preferences and enhanced the appeal of certain life insurance products. One negative in tax reform was the disappearance, for all practical purposes, of leveraged life insurance products. Minimum deposit today has virtually disappeared. Single premium products emerged in these same years. This is not just a phenomenon observable in the United States; it's a worldwide phenomenon and no doubt it relates to the fact that we are, today, experiencing a maturing market, and this market is one in which, to an increasing extent, affluence is defined in terms of assets rather than income. Single premium products are important to the industry because the economics of those products have always been more competitive with other forms of investment.

What next? Well, first of all, let me say that I do not expect any return to yesteryear. Life insurance products have never been of better value than they are today. Policyholders receive the benefit of gross interest throughput on their investments. The products offer a tax deferral and possibly even tax avoidance, depending on what happens at the end. Mortality costs are lower than they have ever been. The industry has improved its expenses although they are still at a relatively high level on periodic premium business when compared to other forms of investment.

In summary, life insurance is a suitable investment today for a conservative investor with predictable needs. The industry, however, remains under pressure. The margins of the industry have been reduced, the industry has faced higher costs due to increased expenditure on research and development, the systems required to administer the new generation of products. One of the consequences of this is that critical mass within the industry has changed, and today it requires a much larger company to be viable than it did, say 15 years ago. Thus, we can then look forward to continuing consolidation within the life insurance industry. Taxation now plays an important and a positive role in the life insurance business.

What, you may wonder, is the outlook for further change in tax law? There are four kinds of possible change that might take place in the taxation of life insurance products. One that I think is decidedly unlikely is a direct taxation on the inside buildup within these products. In other words, a direct taxation of policyholders. It's conceivable, however, that some kind of proxy tax imposed on the life insurance industry but really borne by policyholders investment earnings might reappear. This was the form of taxation that applied up to 1984. This kind of tax change would likely impose a rather modest tax on the inside buildup, but it would also likely be retroactive in its effect. I think that a return to a proxy tax is also unlikely but not as unlikely as a direct tax on inside buildup.

A third approach would be to alter the definition of a qualifying policy so as to exclude certain more extreme forms of single premium business from the current tax preferences. This is one change I do expect; I do not expect to see it be retroactive. And finally, there is some discussion in Congress today about a change in the practice of allowing a step-up in basis on death for assets of all types. In other words, someone holding a portfolio of appreciated securities, the estate of that person does not have to pay capital gains tax at death. It is this same provision that permits life insurance policies to escape taxation upon death, and it is conceivable that life insurance might be included in any change in the rules on step-up and basis at death. This, of course, would be retroactive in effect. One of the most remarkable things is that I sit here this morning, actually participating in a panel where life insurance is considered an investment. This is a far cry from yesteryear.

Question and Answers Session:

Commentator: I want to go back to life insurance for a second, an area that I think is sensitive but is on a lot of peoples' minds. Jim, you concluded by saying how special it felt to be at an investment conference, and we're glad to have the insurance industry at an investment conference. Certainly, there is tremendous advantage to investing through the insurance vehicles. Let's talk a little bit about the AIDS and the risk of AIDS — the impact that you believe it will have in terms of how insurance companies change underwriting requirements.

Jim Anderson: Well, first, Jay, let me make a reference to a paper that was published by two actuaries last August. The actuaries are Michael Cowell and Walter Hoskins of State Mutual Life. In this paper, they attempted to quantify the probable financial impact of AIDS on the life insurance industry. And their conclusions were rather startling. They estimated that AIDS would cost the industry $50 billion on the policies that are already in force, and they projected that a further cost of some $40 billion would be incurred on policies that haven't yet been written. These are cost levels between now and the end of the century. Now, let me hasten to add that there's a great deal of speculation in these numbers. One can look at the work that these two people did and can say well, that looks too conservative or that looks too optimistic, but the pluses and the minuses are fairly evenly balanced. What is very clear is that these estimates could be wrong by a wide margin in either direction. So the problem is a serious one, and it's a problem that, from my personal research with the Centers for Disease Control in Atlanta, I don't believe is going to go away. I don't think we are going to see either a vaccine or a cure for this disease between now and the end of the century. Insurers have already taken some actions. Practically all of them have withdrawn from the District of Columbia, for example, and fortunately, what I see on the regulatory scene suggests that the regulators' attitude towards the insurance industry and its handling of AIDS is shifting again. Initially, the industry looked like a very convenient group onto which to dump this problem, but I think the regulators are waking up to the reality that the solvency of these institutions may be at stake and are backing off from their initial position. My guess is that within a very short period of time, it's going to be very pricey for males in the age range of 20–50 to buy low-cost term insurance. I think we are going to see an impact on term insurance rates as the first and most obvious signal of industry response.

Commentator: You mentioned in your comments a little bit about pending tax legislation and some of the concerns. I think that is an area where a great deal of questions are asked, so I'd like to go back to that and ask you to review that with us one more time. Inside buildup — everyone seems to feel very comfortable. Beyond that, there are some fears.

Jim Anderson: Beyond that, there are some concerns. I think it's more or less inconceivable that we would see a situation where each of us on our individual tax returns would enter an item into our taxable income called "Gain on Life Insurance Policies." I just don't think we're going to see that. From the early 1920s until 1984, the industry, through its corporate tax, paid a proxy tax on behalf of the policyholders. It was actually a proxy tax that was levied on policyholder investment earnings and it resulted in a reduction in the rates that the industry could credit. It's conceivable that that sort of thing could come back. If it did as a practical matter, it would have to be retroactive because there's no way, if you're going to levy it on the companies, to split type A business from type B business, so it would be an across-the-board thing, but the tax rate would probably be very modest.

Commentator: Generally, you mean you do continue to see pretty clear sailing ahead?

Jim Anderson: Orthodox type business, yes. I think the significant danger is some kind of special taxation aimed at single premium business. It probably will, may be addressed by altering the definition of what is a qualifying policy, and forcing more life insurance in the transaction.

Consolidation in the Life and Health Insurance Industry — Who Is Left? Economic & Financial Overview of the Shakeout

Presented to the American Bar Association Annual Meeting, TORT and Insurance Practice Section Panel, August 10, 1988, Toronto, Ontario, Canada. Reprinted with permission from the American Bar Association.

Since 1970 or thereabouts, the life and health insurance industry in the United States has been buffeted by major changes, and the industry has since been conducting a fire fight to contain the impact of those changes and, in many cases, to attempt to preserve or prolong its traditional way of conducting business.

Among the driving forces of change are:

- Consumer rejection of high margin products, which affected more directly and immediately the industry's agents rather than the companies.
- The ensuing breakdown of the social contract between the industry and its agents.
- Unprecedentedly high rates of inflation which affected the perceived value of long-term fixed-dollar, fixed-premium contracts.
- Unprecedented volatility of financial markets, especially fixed-income markets.
- Actual and de facto deregulation.
- Changes in taxation.
- Dramatic escalation of health care costs and the associated drive by government to shift those costs from the public to the private sector.
- AIDS.

The impact of these forces upon the life and health insurance industry already has been quite profound and has led to a transformation of the way in which many companies, but not all, conduct their businesses. Arguably the period of change is still in its early stages. One likely possibility is that this still widely fragmented industry will now undergo a further and more dramatic period of rationalization and consolidation from which will emerge fewer and larger competitors; many of those will be allied with other kinds of financial institutions, both domestic and international.

The future outlook for the life and health insurance industry is not conclusively optimistic nor pessimistic, except for those who regard change as inherently threatening. Both opportunities and problems abound. The surest element is change.

Consumer Rejection

Beginning around 1970, industry statistics showed clearly that consumers were opting in progressively increasing numbers for term insurance and annuity products rather than permanent life insurance products. The most dramatic consequence of this shift related to its impact on the commission earnings of agents because the industry's traditional commission pattern was quite different with respect to the two groups of products. This consumer response represented an acceleration of a long established trend, the origins of which might be traced to the days when "buy term and invest the difference" was the platform of many retail mutual fund organizations.

The impact upon the income of the industry's agents was immediate and, by 1970, had become acute. The companies which comprised the industry were less immediately and less dramatically affected because these relatively low commission products actually provided reasonably good operating margins for the companies.

Perhaps the most significant effect upon the companies was the financial viability of their efforts to maintain and develop their semi-exclusive distribution systems. As agent incomes came under pressure, the failure rate of agents increased and the required subsidy to support new agents increased. As a result, only the most efficient companies could afford to continue to bear the fixed expenses associated with the maintenance and development of their traditional semi-exclusive distribution systems.

Breakdown of the Social Contract

Prior to 1970 or thereabouts, most agents of life and health insurance companies accepted the implied social contract which required that they represented their primary company more or less exclusively, selling its products, good and bad, to their established customers. In effect, each successful agent operated his own semi-monopoly and each company, through its captive distribution system, did the same.

The increasing consumer awareness of the relative value of different kinds of individual life and health insurance contracts and the resulting impact of their collective behavior on the income of agents provoked a breakdown in this long-established social contract. Established agents negotiated to receive higher commissions on their personal production, mainly at the expense of general agents (who were essential to the agency development process) but also at the expense of the companies. Many companies were willing to pay higher commissions to established agents, who then were called Personal Producing General Agents; in effect, companies accepted higher variable costs in exchange for a reduction in their fixed costs, which had become unacceptably high. First the weaker companies adopted this strategy and, temporarily, it was successful. Its very success caused the cost fundamentals of more efficient companies to deteriorate and, progressively, they were drawn into adopting the same strategy. Eventually, commission rates escalated as competition for these now semi-independent established agents intensified. One ultimate result was an increase in distribution costs for practically all companies, which eroded the industry's margins which were already under pressure from consumer rejection. Another result was participation by the semi-independent agent which increased price competition within an industry previously protected from such a competitive force.

High Inflation

Traditional life insurance products offer long-term, fixed-dollar benefits, supported by fixed-dollar premiums. As rates of inflation increased during the

1970s and the early 1980s, the perceived value of the future benefits depreciated substantially.

At the same time, a social revolution was in progress in much of the western world. This social revolution featured new family patterns, such as serial marriage and remarriage, new and informal family structures, frequent changes of employment, fewer children, frequent changes of residence, the trend towards two income families, a crisis of confidence in established institutions of all kinds and other changes which meant that long-term financial responsibilities and needs could not be predicted, frequently underwent significant change and could not be entrusted to established institutions. These factors, in combination with the unprecedented high rates of inflation, tended to depreciate the value of long-term fixed-dollar promises and tended also to shorten the investment horizon of savers.

All of these changes operated to reinforce the consumer preference for financial products which afforded more immediate benefit guarantees than were provided by traditional life insurance products. The "Now Generation" became an active force in the financial marketplace.

One response by the life insurance industry was the introduction, on an isolated basis in early 1979 and on a widespread basis in 1983, of "unbundled products" such as universal life and its various derivatives. These products now represent a significant proportion of the industry's sales — perhaps 50% if one includes universal life and all other "interest-sensitive" products. The result was to increase the visibility of the high expenses and low yields offered by the industry, exposing it to greater extra-industry competition.

Volatility of Financial Markets

The decade of the 1970s was characterized by volatility in financial markets which had not been observed for many years. The most unusual feature was the behavior of the bond and mortgage markets, driven by rising interest rates. Since most life insurance companies in the United States invest about 90% of their total assets in fixed-income debt securities, the impact on the value of their investment portfolios was quite dramatic. By the spring of 1982, most companies had experienced a depreciation of 30% in the value of their investment portfolios.

The dramatic rise of interest rates created two opportunities for consumers to disintermediate against the life insurance industry. The first and most important was the opportunity to exercise the policy loan provisions of their existing policies which generally guaranteed the right to borrow money at interest rates of 5%, 6% or 8%, depending upon the era of those policies. Many policyholders, particularly the sophisticated ones, holding policies of large amounts, exercised their rights. The second opportunity was to exchange old policies for new ones, often issued by newer or more aggressive companies who had little to lose from the turnover of existing business and were eager to receive cash to invest at then current high rates of interest. This process was accelerated by agents who generally earned a new "sales" commission on these transactions.

During the middle 1970s, a handful of companies — many new, many small and mainly with limited capital funds — began to promote the sale of single premium deferred annuities which offered attractive rates of return (based on the new money investment rates). An amazing volume of this business was sold, primarily as a tax-deferred investment and primarily by stockbrokers. In effect, these contracts offered a guaranteed investment return combined with a "put," something few other issuers of securities would have been willing to offer. As interest rates increased, it became possible for holders of these contracts to roll-over an old low-yield annuity into a new higher yielding annuity, also generating commissions for the stockbroker involved as intermediary. Among the companies prominent in this marketplace were certain subsidiaries of Baldwin-United Corporation, which filed for reorganization. Others sustained large but less widely recognized losses on this business; some of the issuing companies survived; a few spectacularly succeeded, either through good luck or good management of their investment portfolios.

A few companies also experienced a different kind of disintermediation relating to their group pension business. Some of these companies entered into contracts which gave the contract holder certain cash out rights or renewal rights which exposed the companies involved to major losses in the event interest rates moved materially in one direction or the other. Some companies have now established very large reserves for losses under these contracts.

In the spring of 1982, the combined effects of these various types of disintermediation had reached crisis levels. Many companies had negotiated standby lines of credit with major banks. Some wonder what might have happened had it been necessary for a significant number of companies simultaneously to have drawn upon these lines of credit, often issued by the same bank to different companies.

Deregulation

Perhaps the most important element of deregulation was enacted by no legislature nor approved by any administrative body. It was the discovery that a mutual fund which invested in short-term, low-risk, fixed-interest obligations and which allowed its customers to write checks or drafts against their accounts, could operate as an unregulated bank with zero capital requirements. The most prominent organization successfully to promote this concept was Merrill-Lynch, but there were many imitators and Merrill-Lynch may not, in fact, have been the originator.

The effect of this upon the banking and thrift industries and upon the life insurance industry was quite profound and accelerated dramatically the disintermediation already in progress. In a period of less than five years, the assets of money market funds were double those that the life insurance industry had accumulated on its individual life insurance products in its history of more than 150 years.

The impact on the banking and thrift industries was arguably more severe and led to the dismantling by the Federal Reserve Board of Regulation Q, which had limited the interest rates that banks and thrifts could pay to retail depositors. It also allowed banks and thrifts to establish their own equivalent of money market funds. Thus, banks and thrifts became more significant competitors in the retirement savings market.

In effect, the economics of retail banking and savings institutions were transformed in a very short period of time. One consequence of this transformation was an increased effort on the part of banking and thrift organizations to find other sources of income to support the deteriorated economics of their retail business. In part, they have been successful and now offer discount brokerage services, securities underwriting and limited insurance services. Most observers believe that the remaining restrictions on activities by banks will eventually be dismantled and that they will become competitive factors in the insurance business and particularly in the life insurance business.

The potential consequence of cross-industry competition between the life and health insurance companies and other financial companies, such as banks, is quite significant. Life insurance companies clearly are the highest cost provider of individual financial services. On an equivalent level load basis, representative costs are 30% and higher. Banks and thrifts, if their "spreads" are translated into loads, operate on an equivalent level load basis of 10% to 15%. Investment companies operate on an equivalent level load basis of less than 10%. Thus, life insurance companies operating on a traditional basis would need to persuade their buyers that the personalized services offered, primarily by their agents, had a value equivalent to these cost differentials. Otherwise, they would be faced with the very difficult task of restructuring their own economics on a basis which would permit them to be cost competitive.

Taxation

The Life Insurance Income Tax Act of 1959 was an arcane labyrinth which attempted, in the context of a single tax law, to impose taxes on the shareholders of life insurance companies and a proxy tax on some of the investment earnings of policyholders. The law produced strange and inconsistent results. Sometimes shareholders paid taxes on policyholders' earnings and sometimes policyholders paid taxes on shareholders' earnings.

The rise in interest rates which occurred during the 1970s caused a breakdown in this strange law. As interest rates increased, earnings attributed to policyholders increased correspondingly, but the law not only recognized this, it also imposed a progressively increasing rate of proxy tax on these increased earnings. This threatened the entire competitive position of the life insurance industry on products which provide an important element of savings accumulation (as opposed to insurance).

Wonderful and often successful products were designed to address this serious problem, including term insurance plans that were called permanent insurance plans and permanent insurance plans that were called term insurance plans! Never had the industry experienced such a proliferation in its products and the associated administrative costs were very high because existing systems were often inadequate to cope with these new products.

The industry also devised ingenious reinsurance schemes under which companies taxed on the basis of investment earnings transferred their earnings to companies taxed on the basis of profits. Perhaps as a result of these ingenious arrangements, Congress finally acted to reform the basis on which life insurance companies are taxed and today the operative law is quite favorable to life insurance products. Stock and mutual companies can now pass through gross rates of interest to policyholders without being subject to any proxy tax; but mutual life insurance companies must now pay a tax on their accumulated surplus, arguably to equalize the position of mutual companies to that of stock companies on the theory that the policyholders of mutual companies stand in the same position as shareholders, whose earnings are taxed at the corporate level.

Changes in personal taxation have also had a significant impact on the industry. The enactment of the unlimited marital deduction and the general reduction of estate tax rates have diminished the need for life insurance to provide for the payment of estate taxes. The general reduction in personal income tax rates, especially on high incomes, has diminished the tax benefit associated with the tax-free inside build-up of life insurance products. And the limitations on the deductibility of policy loan interest have eliminated much of the market for so-called "minimum deposit" or "borrow-all" products which were particularly lucrative from the viewpoint of agents because they received permanent insurance commissions for the sale of what were essentially term insurance products.

From the viewpoint of life insurance corporate tax, today's environment is quite favorable for stock companies and moderately favorable for mutual companies. From the viewpoint of changes in personal taxation, the industry has lost a significant potential market in the area of estate taxes and tax avoidance schemes, although it can be argued that the industry has benefited from the fact that the same tax changes have had even greater impact on other tax avoidance schemes.

Health Care Costs

The cost of health care in the United States is today measured at 10% of Gross National Product! The escalation of these costs is undoubtedly related to the widespread perspective, among those privately insured and those covered by government programs, that these benefits are "free"!

Contributing to the rising cost of health care are factors such as the increasing level of professional accountability of health care providers, which has increased quite dramatically the cost of medical malpractice insurance which has been transmitted more or less directly to the end consumer — ostensibly the individual recipients of the health care but, in financial terms, to those who insure or guarantee these benefits. The standards of public accountability for the quality of health care have not only contributed to costs in terms of medical malpractice insurance; this threat has also resulted in ultra-conservatism in the way in which doctors, hospitals and other professionals conduct their practice — it has led to more x-rays, more tests, more laboratory work and significantly more cost. One can only speculate as to the extent of these forces upon overall medical costs, but it is obvious that the extent is considerable.

These effects have impacted both the public and private sectors of the health care financing system in the United States. The unexpected rise in costs has created a response in the public sector, faced with other financial problems, which have included various efforts to transfer these increasing costs into the private sector, mainly to employer financed health care schemes. As a result, the cost escalation in the private sector has been even more rapid than the overall experience and insurers and other financiers of health care costs have consistently experienced financial difficulties, not anticipating in their premium rates or capitation charges the extent to which their future costs would increase.

Many health insurance companies have experienced large losses, primarily on group health insurance, during the last 10 to 15 years.

Today, the competitive focus of group health insurance (the primary segment of the health insurance industry) has shifted from competitive comparisons based on distribution and administrative expenses towards methods to contain costs emanating from the health care industry. This shift has caused a substantial upward change in the level of critical mass required to compete successfully in the industry because it implies the need for an extensive claims settlement network which includes detailed knowledge of local conditions, sophisticated information support and sufficient volumes of business to allow the establishment of preferred provider facilities to capture the benefits of "volume buying" of medical care services.

It is noteworthy that two major life and health insurance companies, Transamerica Occidental and New England Life, have withdrawn from the group life and health insurance market during the last two years, suggesting that the many other players smaller than they may face issues of critical mass, whether or not those problems are recognized.

The individual branch of the health insurance industry has fared better, probably because most of the contracts issued have limitations on benefits that have operated to neutralize somewhat the impact of cost inflation.

AIDS

This menace as it relates to the life and health insurance industry, according to responsible estimates, ranges in severity from significant to catastrophic.

The ranges of the estimates of the financial impact of this plague during the rest of this century upon the industry extend from $50 billion to $100 billion — to the nearest $50 billion! The various estimates involve a high degree of speculation, but they do not represent, in the view of many outspoken members of the actuarial profession, a deliberate effort either to magnify or to diminish the potential problem. It exists, but it cannot confidently be quantified at this stage.

The data supporting the estimates has tended to experience dramatic fluctuations. For example, within the last month, health authorities in New York have reduced by 50% their estimate of the extent of the HIV infection in that city. On the other hand, estimates of the extent of likely spread into the heterosexual community vary wildly — perhaps in a ratio of as much as 10 to 1.

Even the most optimistic of the estimates predicts a substantial impact on the life insurance industry and much of this relates to business that has already been issued and is beyond recall.

From the viewpoint of the future viability of the life and health insurance industry, it is essential that the industry retain effective means of selecting risks. The social consequence of this will be the denial of insurance coverage to some members of society; the social consequence of mandating that no such selection take place may be to destroy the entire concept of voluntary insurance. This legal issue is one in which members of the American Bar Association are likely to be involved for many years, either as litigators or as legislators.

The Outlook

The life and health insurance industry in the United States is not a tranquil business. The forces at work are powerful and their impact cannot be predicted with a high degree of certainty. There are both hopeful and disturbing signs.

On the positive side, the industry does enjoy preferential tax treatment for its products, arguably more for stock companies than for mutual companies. This preferential treatment of its products is not an unreasonable situation. The industry does provide a valuable social service. The benefits provided in many cases substitute for what otherwise would be a call on the public treasury. The industry has improved its economics, less on the distribution side than on the administrative side, and it may yet find a way to correct the imbalance of control which has shifted dramatically towards the distributors since 1970, thus allowing a reduction in its very high distribution costs. The industry does have the only effective "high-touch" distribution system among its current and likely future competitors.

One new and notable product line from the life insurance industry is its investment products which are well suited to an aging society with progressively more people who are asset rich rather than income rich. Further rationalization within the industry is likely to increase the gains in efficiency which already are quite significant.

On the negative side, this extensively fragmented industry does face continuing problems with respect to critical mass. Perhaps half, probably more than half, of the nonfocused current competitors are not viable because they are not large enough to sustain a reasonable competitive position. This is easiest to see in the individual life insurance business, but some think that the problem is even more widespread in the group insurance business.

One major future development, which is not conclusively positive or negative, relates to the likely consolidation that will occur not only within the life and health industry but within the financial service industries generally. In this context, capital funds assume a much increased importance. The life and health industry is probably better capitalized than the banking industry and is clearly much better capitalized than the thrift industry. The capital position of the investment industry is very mixed; this industry has largely already consolidated with some of the other businesses. Capital funds for stock life and health insurance companies can be augmented by future stock issues but capital funds of mutual life insurance companies are severely restricted.

New competitors will enter the life and health insurance industry, most likely by the acquisition of existing companies. These new competitors may bring the possibility of improved economics to the business, placing pressure on the free standing competitors which remain. Among the most likely organizations to enter the market are major foreign financial companies (notably Japanese life insurers), consumer based organizations (retailers and credit card issuers), industrial organizations (most likely to blunder into the business thinking that it is easier than their own business), other domestic financial institutions (particularly banks, once they are finished with their own industry consolidation) and multiline insurers (to whom the life and health insurance industry may represent a true marginal line of business).

All of these potential developments argue for even more substantial change than has already taken place in an industry recently disturbed from its traditional ways after 150 years.

Lessons from Hamlet

Presented at a meeting of the Committee on Seminars of the Life Insurance Council of New York City, New York, September 7, 1988.

The English speaking world has been fascinated by William Shakespeare for now nearly four hundred years; this fascination relates not only to the marvel of his language but also to the timelessness of his many themes. Let me begin today by reading an often quoted and familiar excerpt from his play, *Hamlet, Prince of Denmark:*

> To be or not to be, that is the question:
> Whether tis nobler in the mind to suffer
> The slings and arrows of outrageous fortune
> Or to take arms against a sea of troubles
> And by opposing end them.

Let me remind you of the Prince's dilemma and his fatal error. He had two choices. He could accept passively the murder of his father by his mother and her lover and their usurpation of his father's throne; or he could choose the path of vengeance and recovery of that throne. His indecision and procrastination precipitated the ultimate tragedy.

It seems clear to me that smaller and medium-sized life insurance companies in 1988 face a similar dilemma; so, too, do many undistinguished large companies. Their choices are these: either to continue along their familiar path, which, for most, as I will explain, leads eventually to oblivion, or to embark in new and unfamiliar directions, which lead to destinations that cannot be forecast with confidence. The lesson of Hamlet is clear: indecision and procrastination can be deadly. The decision will not become easier with the passage of time and, meanwhile, resources are being expended and, for stock companies, investors are losing patience. Events may overtake the ability of management to make conscious decisions; as with Hamlet, the result may be tragedy.

"The slings and arrows of outrageous fortune"

Now let me speak to you about "the slings and arrows of outrageous fortune" that all companies represented in this room have experienced in recent years. I would say that it all began about 1970. Prior to that time, how did small and medium-sized companies compete successfully within the life insurance industry? Many did. How did undistinguished larger companies compete successfully? Many did.

At that time the focus of the entire industry was on building relationships with and expanding their "captive" distribution systems. At that time, agent loyalty was very high. And, moreover, there existed within the industry an informal commission cartel. That informal commission cartel was accepted by practically all agents. Another feature of those years was that the general agent was an important personage in the distribution systems of most life insurance companies. General agents at that time performed a vital function, and the position of the general agent had some clear meaning to it. Agents accepted this arrangement, too. They were generally loyal to their general agents.

Also, at that time, consumers generally didn't recognize that other financial products were possible substitutes for cash value life insurance. Despite all the talk about buy term and invest the difference, which began in those times, very little actually happened. Permanent life insurance was seen by the public as being different from other financial products. This meant that price competition affecting life insurance, which wasn't well understood by the public, was essentially intra-industry price competition. It was not competition between life insurance companies and some other businesses offering a different financial product. This was very important, because life insurance companies were then and are today the highest cost providers in the whole spectrum of the individual financial service industry. They have a manpower-intensive distribution system which contributes primarily to this high cost phenomenon. Competition in those days was confined exclusively to competition among high cost providers of financial services. There were no low cost providers involved in the competitive equation at that time.

And finally, in those years, interest rates were relatively low and lapse rates were also relatively low, both of which reduced the cost of amortizing front-end expenses, which have long characterized the economics of the industry. To explain, let me use an analogy. If you place a mortgage on your home at 5% interest, your monthly payment is lower than if the interest rate is 10%. The same thing applies to the amortization of front-end expenses. If either interest rates or lapse rates rise, the annual amount that must be set aside each year to amortize front-end expenses is increased as a percent of the premium. This acts to increase the price charged the consumer. In the years since 1970 the movement of interest rates and lapse rates has increased the effective cost of a amortizing front-end expenses enormously. This is more true for stock than mutual companies because their costs of capital are very different.

The Old Order Changeth

What changed about 1970 to alter all of this? The margins to cover fixed expenses and to provide profits are clearly much lower today than they were in, say, 1970. In addition, over the last several years we have seen a period of unprecedented frequency of change in product design. These frequent changes in product design required the development of costly systems to provide sales and administrative support for these products. These costly systems have had the effect of increasing the fixed costs of the industry. This increase has been even more noticeable considering that today the shelf life of administrative systems is much shorter than it used to be.

These systems must today be written off over periods of three to five years. They don't last ten years anymore. The effects of increasing interest and lapse rates that I explained a moment ago were another part of the phenomenon of change.

One major consequence of these changes is that the required level of new business to cover fixed costs with reduced margins increased dramatically — partly because the fixed costs have increased but more importantly because the available margins have shrunk. My very off-hand estimate is that in 1970 a well-managed small to medium-sized company could be viable if it sold approximately 5,000 individual policies a year. Today, my observation is that it takes about 25,000 individual policy sales to achieve viability for companies operating in the middle of the market, broadly addressing Mr. and Mrs. America. A big change in "critical mass" has occurred.

It is worth noting that critical mass exists for each separate line of business, for each separate product line, for each separate market sector addressed and for each type of distribution system. In some cases, lines of business, products, market sectors and distribution systems may be mutually supportive, but the narrower the focus the lower the overall critical mass is likely to be.

Why did margins shrink?

The consumer became more sophisticated and more demanding. This is noticeable, if you look at statistics in the Life Insurance Fact Book which show the extent to which the consumer opted to buy low-margin products. This trend became pronounced around 1970. The shift took the form of dramatic increases in the sales of term insurance and annuities, two of the lowest margin products from the viewpoint of the life insurance industry and particularly its distribution system. It was also noticeable somewhat later that a major shift to alternative financial products began; this showed up dramatically in the rapid growth and development of money market funds beginning around 1975. Margins also shrank because agent loyalty collapsed for all but a few companies and all but a few general agents. Thus, both price and commission competition intensified.

Moreover, traditional life insurance, in the highly inflationary environment of the 1970s, lost much of its appeal from the viewpoint of the buying public. Finally, actual and de facto deregulation, which centered on the banking business, fostered major new competition which for the first time came from outside the life insurance industry. In some cases, this pitted low-cost competitors against high-cost competitors and dramatic changes occurred in the disposition of the consumer savings dollar.

How did margins shrink?

What form did the shrinking of margins take? Did we wake up one Monday morning and discover that margins had shrunk? And, if so, what changed?

Initially the shrinkage took the form of commission increases. (Remember, I'm talking about margins available to cover fixed expense and to provide profits.) This happened as weaker competitors abandoned their efforts to maintain a captive distribution system in favor of personal producing general agents. In effect, what they did was to trade higher variable costs in order to reduce their fixed costs. This initially successful practice then spread to stronger competitors and commission rates escalated industry wide. These newly independent personal producing general agents by their actions reinforced the consumer demand for better value, thus causing prices to decline in absolute terms. The increase in interest rates and the consumer and agent behavior increasing replacement activity fostered an unanticipated increase in lapse rates. These factors exacerbated the increase in cost of amortizing front-end expenses quite dramatically. Term and unbundled products became the order of the day and focused attention on the elements of pricing which fostered intra-industry price competition as well as the new extra-industry price competition.

And, finally, artificial tax benefits, mainly based on the late lamented IRS Section 8.18(c), were factored into the prices in various products of the industry and became part of the pricing structure of the industry. When that tax benefit was lost, companies were reluctant to increase prices to their necessary levels. I believe we still have some vestiges of those 8.18(c) pricing actions built into our prices today.

Other Lines of Business

I have been focusing on individual life insurance. Now I will mention some other lines of business.

The group insurance business used to focus competitively on the element called retention. A number of years ago, the focus of competition was on this company's retention vs. that company's retention in what was basically a cost-plus business. This is no longer true today. Today the focus of competition is on a different issue. Today, the plan sponsor says, "Which competitor will do the best job of holding my *costs* down, which is more important to me than the amount of their *retention?* Which carrier can do the better job of containing the medical costs that are going to be incurred under my cost-plus type medical plan?" This has created a competitive situation within the group insurance business where skill at cost control has become the fundamental competitive issue, requiring extensive networks, information and detailed knowledge of the practices of medical providers in each of the geographic areas in which companies operate.

It is significant that Transamerica Occidental decided that $800 million of group life and health premium was not enough to achieve critical mass in this climate. They sold their businesses to a company with a larger volume of group insurance business. More recently, New England Life has done the same. So, in the group line, too, we have this phenomenon of critical mass having increased dramatically. Some of my colleagues believe that the change in the group arena have been even greater than those in the individual life insurance arena. I won't argue that, but it is worth noting that such an opinion is held by some knowledgeable observers.

One line in which the life insurance industry has learned to compete successfully with other providers is the area of group pensions. I am speaking specifically about deposit-administration type contracts, investment-only type contracts and guaranteed investment contracts. Basically, pension plan sponsors have a misconception about these contracts which favors the industry. I have observed this misconception within the investment committee that oversees the management of the Towers Perrin pension fund. The misconception is that a GIC is meaningfully guaranteed, whereas, an IBM debenture is not meaningfully guaranteed. This gives the industry a creditworthy standing which exceeds that which is real. Students of management science call this a "Factor Cost" advantage. It permits life insurance companies, in effect, to offer GICs in the marketplace at yields of a quasi-government security. I offend some of my associates at Towers Perrin when I refer to our GIC investments as our "junk bond" portfolio. If Standard & Poor's were doing the ratings I believe this is pretty close to what the ratings would indicate.

The group pension line has an interesting psychological competitive advantage because the public thinks that this industry's credit is actually better than it is. This is an advantage that a number of companies have exploited over the last fifteen years. If you look at the financial results of large mutuals, for example, it is no contest as to which large mutual company has done the best financially. It is Principal Mutual, formerly the Bankers Life of Iowa. If you look for the reasons, you will find that Principal Mutual has made a lot of money in the group pension business over the years.

Another line of business where "the slings and arrows of outrageous fortune" have not been quite as painful is the individual health insurance business. I still see in that business margins that are essentially similar to what they were many years ago. One of the problems of that business is that it is clearly a business in which the smart get richer and the dumb get poorer at a very rapid rate! It is an expertise-based business, and one into which amateurs ought not to blunder.

"To take up arms against a sea of troubles"

Let's now talk about Hamlet's other alternative — "to take up arms against a sea of troubles." Just exactly how should companies like yours go about operating in this environment where long-standing and serious problems exist? What you should be seeking to do is to establish a sustainable competitive advantage for your company which supports an acceptable rate of return on the capital employed, where acceptability is measured by the expectations of your investors, be they shareholders or policyholders.

Time does not permit me to talk about all of the kinds of competitive advantages that might exist but I'll mention a few from which you can extrapolate.

The most powerful competitive advantage and the easiest to exploit clearly is a cost advantage. This may be based on low expenses, high investment yields, low mortality costs or low lapse rates. If you establish a cost advantage, how do you compete? You compete successfully either with low prices or high commissions. But, practically, to achieve a cost advantage as a broad-market competitor requires very large scale. However, there is one other way and that is with narrow focus. Your company may not reasonably aspire to compete in terms of scale with a company such as Prudential or State Farm. But, if you select a narrow specialty to operate within, it is quite conceivable that your company can be larger than even the largest company within that narrow specialty. The narrower the specialty, the smaller you can be and still be the biggest in that particular field. What this does is bring the advantage of economies of scale that are normally associated with size, but it brings it in small packages. So, as a practical matter, to establish a cost advantage, you either have to be very large or very specialized. In boxing terms, the advantage of scale can be thought of as the right cross, a knockout punch; the most effective counter punch is the left jab, focus.

Let's look at another possible competitive advantage. Suppose the advantage is to be based on differentiation, either a differentiation in product or in service, which supports higher price realization.

Let me show you a differentiated product. For those of you who have forgotten, in this era of anti-smoking, this is a cigarette lighter and this lighter is made by Dunhill. It might surprise you to learn that it cost me $200. Now for $200 I could have bought a lifetime supply of matches, or a lifetime supply of throw-away lighters. I am sure most of you think that it is pretty silly to spend $200 on a cigarette lighter. But, you have not heard the whole story.

This lighter is like the heroine of a Victorian novel. About once a year she gets afflicted by "the vapors" and, when this happens, this lighter must be sent to a lighter spa in New York to take the treatment. It takes about a month and it costs about $25. I can buy another lifetime supply of matches or throw-aways with that $25 a year. But, you still have not heard the whole story.

The rest of the story, as Paul Harvey would say, is that I find it so inconvenient when this lighter is at the lighter spa in New York, that I own two of them!

Dunhill does not have a cost advantage and does not know how to manufacture lighters cheaply, and they certainly don't know how to market cheap lighters. But, they are very successful. Why? It is because they have a product differentiation that allows them to realize higher prices. That is their basic business strategy, and it works.

Differentiation is one of the ways in which companies can compete successfully without a cost advantage. The way they compete is to charge higher prices for a more appealing product, and this permits them to succeed despite their above-average costs.

In your business, where the product is, in the end, money, the ultimate commodity, it is very difficult to achieve a product based differentiation. The few companies that do establish a product-based differentiation usually find it does not last. There are no patents in this business, and it is too easy to imitate success. You might achieve a first entrant advantage that will last, perhaps, a year or two. That is about how long the earliest entrants had in the case of Universal Life, reentry term and other recent product innovations.

A service-based differentiation is more viable because it's more difficult to imitate. It is worth noting that focus can support this approach as well. If your advantage is to know more about say, pension products than any other company, including the largest in the industry, you have an advantage that is very difficult to imitate. It is one that you can expect to maintain over a long period of time.

The third type of advantage that I want to illustrate is a preferred-access advantage. This means access to semicaptive customers or semicaptive distributors. The object of this advantage, if you have it, is to compete successfully with either higher prices or lower commissions. A distribution-based preferred access advantage is very fragile because the distributors are in control of the ultimate customers and that is the point of vulnerability. A customer-based advantage is stronger, but even this must be defended in an environment of consolidating financial services where everyone's customer is becoming everyone else's customer.

These are examples of competitive advantage: cost-based, differentiation-based, preferred-access-based. There are limiting factors and other problems in all of this. It is not an easy matter for a small to medium-size company or an undistinguished large company to establish a competitive advantage. First of all, capital resources must be adequate to carry out the plan undertaken. I have seen far too many $10 million programs undertaken with $5 million budgets. It just does not work. It is necessary also to have in place the right management skills. Either they must exist or they must be obtained to support the selected strategy. Let me illustrate with a theatre-of-the-absurd story.

Suppose that we are the owners of the New York Knicks. We notice that our fan attendance is dropping off and our business is threatening to fail. We also notice that the New York Rangers are doing quite well. We decide that the right strategy for the New York Knicks is to become a hockey team! We convince ourselves that our basketball players are all good athletes. Patrick Ewing, we say, will become the next Wayne Gretzky. We buy a couple of dozen pairs of size fourteen skates and a few dozen hockey sticks and the other necessary equipment. We hold a team meeting and announce that we are now going to play hockey. What do you think are the chances of that strategy working?

If you and your company decide on some grand new strategy and then expect the in-place players to implement that strategy, the chances are very high that your chance of success will be about the same as that of the New York Knicks becoming a successful hockey team!

The time scale required to achieve success must also match your investors' expectations. There is no point in embarking on a ten-year plan if your investors are going to run out of patience in five years. This is analogous to embarking on a $10 million plan with a $5 million budget.

And, finally, if the plan involves some material change in what you are currently doing, which I am strongly suggesting to you it will, and if you are embarking on a new path leading to a destination that cannot be predicted with confidence, it is likely that you will have some potentially valuable existing structures which are not relevant to your new strategy; these must be divested on some optimum basis. These may be lines of business, these may be personnel, these may be a lot of things, these may even be your whole distribution system.

"Thus conscience does make cowards of us all"

Later in Hamlet's soliloquy there is the line — "Thus conscience does make cowards of us all." One of the problems with the kinds of decisions that many or most of you or maybe even all of you face is that these necessary decisions are personally uncomfortable. They involve a choice between two betrayals. You can betray your existing employees, agents and values which have no place in the new strategy. Or, you can betray the owners of your enterprise. It is this dilemma that caused Hamlet to dither and his indecision and procrastination is what precipitated the ultimate tragedy.

I suggest to you that you must find a competitive advantage. If no competitive advantage exists today in your company, then you must build it or buy it or you should exit. Do not scorn the third alternative. If you decide to exit, you are still in control of the process; you can choose the terms on which you exit. I would predict that if you do not consciously do one of these things — build it, buy it or exit — what is likely to happen is that you will lose control of events and your company will then become the object of somebody else's interest on their terms and not on your terms. And if this happens, Hamlet has some final advice for us — his dying words, "The rest is silence."

Section 4
Investments, Taxation, and Demutualization

Investment Outlook: The 1970s

Published in Emphasis, *October 1, 1972. Reprinted with permission from Tillinghast - A Towers Perrin Company.*

The decade of the 1970s promises to be a turbulent one from the investment viewpoint and, perhaps, from other viewpoints also. From the vantage point of 1972, we have already seen enough events to ensure that this prediction will come true. First, let us explore several basic developments which seem likely to have the greatest influence on the investment outlook for the coming years:

World Trade

In the quarter-century which has elapsed since the end of World War II, world trade has expanded dramatically. There is hardly a developed country in the world today which could claim that its domestic economy is not influenced to a major extent by developments on the international trading scene. The nation which might come closest to making this claim is the United States; but such a claim, which might have been appropriate 20 years ago, is not appropriate today. During those 20 years, we have witnessed the emergence of two nations — first West Germany, and then Japan — as major industrial powers which have demonstrated their capabilities to compete successfully in sectors of the world market which traditionally had been dominated by American products.

The upsurge of world trade and the emergence of new competitive forces in the international marketplace have a significance which extends to all sectors of the American economy, and which influences even the social and political affairs of this country. The reasons are quite straightforward: Once a country is extensively involved in international trade, its wage rates, interest rates, method of taxation, policy on inflation, and numerous other items can no longer be established in isolation, but must take account of corresponding factors in other countries. In short, we have moved far enough along the road from a national economy toward a world economy to compel some reasonable relationships, particularly among wage rates, in various countries of the world.

Changing Role of U.S. in World Trade

Immediately after World War II, the position of the United States in world economic affairs was unique. With the industrial capacity of both Europe and Japan destroyed, only the United States had the ability to produce the goods required to rebuild shattered economies and to meet the demands of peacetime.

Under these conditions, American goods could be sold relatively easily, regardless of the fact that their cost of production reflected substantially higher wage costs than then existed anywhere else in the world. This position of dominance in world trade continued for many years, notwithstanding the wage rate disadvantage, because the United States also enjoyed a substantial technological lead over the rest of the world. (If you know how to build a computer, and no one else does, it doesn't really matter whether you have the highest wage rates or not!) As a result of its position of dominance in world trade, the United States generated substantial favorable trade balances; in short, we sold a great deal more to other countries than we bought from them. The surplus funds generated were invested in overseas industries, particularly in Western Europe and Canada, thus balancing out the flow of money again.

From these overseas investments was born the multinational company. While an American company might never have shared its technology with, say, a French competitor, it was perfectly willing to share its technology with a French-based subsidiary. These and such other factors as the development of the European Economic Community resulted in a leveling of the competitive position of companies based in various parts of the world.

Without a monopoly in the marketplace, or at least a substantial technological lead, relative wage rates become a major factor in the competitive position of companies vying against each other in world trade. In this respect, American companies were at a significant disadvantage, particularly in industries requiring low technology or low labor skills.

For the first time in many years, the balance of trade of the United States has become an adverse one: Instead of generating a substantial surplus, we face substantial deficits — a situation which probably can be corrected only through a readjustment of relative wage rates between this country and other parts of the world.

Foreign Exchange Markets

The least painful way to adjust relative wage rates or other economic disparities between two countries is to adjust the rate of exchange between their currencies. Recent years have seen many such adjustments. In 1967, for example, the British pound was devalued 14%. In 1969, the French franc was devalued 10%. Also in 1969, the London Gold Pool was closed, and the free market in gold commenced; since that time, the convertibility of the U.S. dollar has been effectively suspended. In 1969, and again in early 1971, the Deutschmark was revalued by 10%. In 1970, the Canadian dollar was effectively revalued 8%. In December 1971, the Smithsonian agreement resulted in a general realignment of currencies, involving notably an 8% devaluation of the U.S. dollar against several major currencies and gold. And in June of 1972, the floating British pound touched off another monetary crisis. Each of these changes has been accompanied by periods of uncertainty, and each has affected financial markets throughout the world — sometimes favorably, sometimes unfavorably.

It can be predicted confidently that these changes are not the last in the series. The recent free market price of gold, exceeding $60 an ounce, is one clear indication of future trouble. The continued deficits of U.S. trade and payments balances is another. The basic problem is that the system devised at Bretton Woods in 1945 did not provide an appropriate method of accomplishing what is most needed today: a further devaluation of the U.S. dollar. Because most currencies are pegged in terms of the U.S. dollar (while the dollar is pegged in terms of gold), the U.S. has no effective control over the relative value of its own currency — a judgment which is in the hands of other countries which are understandably reluctant to concede their present trade advantages.

There is little doubt that the problem of over-valuation of the U.S. dollar must and will be solved, but it remains to be seen how much brinkmanship will be practiced in the course of the negotiations. There is general recognition that the most likely alternative is a world depression, and this knowledge virtually assures an eventual solution. A definite possibility is another general realignment of currencies, such as the one which took place last December, accompanied by a further increase in the value of gold.

Other solutions seem impractical. Unilateral revaluation of other currencies against the U.S. dollar — not accompanied by an increase in the gold price — would have the effect of substantially depleting central bank resources in other countries since, in terms of their own currencies, there would be a drop in value of both their gold reserves and their U.S. dollar reserves. In this international poker game, most of the cards are held by the other players; but the United States still retains the joker in the pack — the gold card — and it is clear from the decision not to restore dollar convertibility that the United States is determined to play this card for all it is worth.

In this connection, it is perhaps appropriate to remember the words of the Israeli foreign minister, Abba Eban, who said that "In the end, men and nations will do the reasonable thing — but only after they have exhausted all of the other alternatives."

Inflation and Interest Rates

Except for an extended period during the second half of the last century, and a few brief periods in this century, inflation has been a ubiquitous feature of the economic scene throughout modern history. What is new is the fact that inflation *at a much higher level* has been prevalent in the United States for several years. In the period from the end of World War II until perhaps 1965, inflation in other parts of the world continued at a substantially higher rate than in the U.S., which tended to help correct the disparity in wage rates and currency values between the United States and the other countries. But, in recent years, the rate of inflation in this country has caught up with (and in same cases surpassed) the rates prevailing elsewhere, thus aggravating the foreign exchange problem instead of helping to cure it.

The levels of interest rates which have prevailed recently show clearly that investors are now reflecting anticipated inflation in their yield demands, and that borrowers also are taking this factor into consideration in deciding whether and when to borrow funds. For many years, the U.S. enjoyed significantly lower interest rates than other parts of the world; today, however, interest rates prevailing in the U.S. are higher than those in several European countries.

What is the outlook for continued inflation? For many years, every government elected in every Western country has pledged itself to control inflation. But none really has succeeded, and most astute observers are skeptical as to whether any ever will. Inflation, of course, is nothing but a tax on capital — a redistribution of national income between capital-holders, wage-earners, and government. Without inflation, new sources of revenue and new methods of redistribution would have to be found; it is doubtful that any would be as palatable politically as the present indirect technique. Thus we must conclude that inflation is a permanent feature of the economic scene, and — considering the nature of its most proximate cause, our general expectation that next year's income will be higher than this year's — it is doubtful that any government will succeed in preventing inflation.

Social and Political Considerations

The U.S. is experiencing today a rate of unemployment which is quite high by historic standards. This unemployment, coupled with its near cousin, underemployment, is adding considerably to the social and political unrest that is so apparent in our society. To an important extent, the unemployment and underemployment problems in the U.S. are related closely to the questions of this country's competitive position with respect to wage rates. Quite simply, it is cheaper to manufacture certain products in countries where wage rates are lower, since the industries involved frequently require relatively low levels of skill.

The higher U.S. wage rates are in relation to world wage rates, the greater will be the extent of unemployment among the least-skilled members of the work force. Pressure for still higher wages is likely to lead to more widespread unemployment. And, in a country where high wage rates prevail, the cost of maintaining even a minimum standard of living increases correspondingly, and the financial plight of the unemployed — as well as that of the underemployed — becomes more serious.

In short, our system of relatively high wage rates (and living costs), by comparison with the rest of the world, would present no particular problem — if we were manufacturing products that could not be duplicated easily elsewhere, and *if* all the members of the work force were sufficiently skilled to participate in such a technological economy. But as long as there are members of society who are not able to participate — because they lack the education, the training, or the necessary intelligence — it is essential to provide jobs requiring relatively low levels of skills to occupy these people, and that will involve competition with workers in other countries. Moreover, it will be necessary to pay to these workers wages adequate to meet living cost requirements — and therein lies the dilemma.

The wave of consumerism which today is sweeping through this society and most parts of the world, coupled with closely related environmental concerns, also has significance with respect to future investment outlook. Both of these developments point, in different ways, to the same concern: Will companies be allowed to achieve a growth in profits which is commensurate with the foreseeable growth in sales? In this same vein, current political thought in certain quarters would support a substantial increase in corporate taxes — with similar consequences.

What are the probable effects of these several factors on the investment markets of the 1970s?

Fixed Interest

First, the prospect of continued inflation has clear-cut implications for the future level of long-term interest rates, the subject of greatest concern to long-term investors such as the managers of pension funds and life insurance companies. The implications of continued inflation, probably at a level which is high by historic standards in the U.S. but perhaps lower than that which has been experienced in the last three years, is that interest rates will also remain high. It will be surprising if interest rates on high-quality corporate securities fall below 7% for any extended period during the remainder of this decade.

In these days of higher inflation, you will hear more frequent talk about the "real rate of return" — the excess of the rate of interest over the rate of inflation. Historically, the real rate of return has ranged between 3% and 4% before taxes, and long-term interest rates have been fairly sensitive to inflationary expectations. As the rate of inflation rises, however, the real rate of return after taxes falls dramatically — and at rates of inflation of 5% or more, the real rate of return after taxes actually is *negative* for a taxpayer in the 50% bracket unless the nominal rate of interest is greater than 10%.

If recognition of the impact of inflation upon the real rate of return substantially alters the investment strategy of institutions and individuals, it is conceivable that long-term interest rates might rise into the area of 10% on first-class securities. Such very high rates of interest have prevailed even on government securities in both the U.K. and Japan at various times in recent years.

More than any other country, the U.S. is unaccustomed to high interest rates; thus political action to reduce interest rates is likely should very high interest rates prevail. A rate of 10% represents the psychological "two-digit barrier," which probably would be sufficiently potent to prevent interest rates from rising to or beyond this level for more than a short period of time.

In summary, the outlook for fixed-interest securities does not appear to be an optimistic one — since there exists the very real probability that investments made at today's price levels might show significant depreciation in value over the coming years.

Equities

This sector of the investment market is the most difficult of all to predict, because evenly balanced arguments run in each direction: On the one hand, continued inflation should lead to increased sales and profits, and should encourage investors to seek an inflation hedge through equity investments; on the other hand, profit margins are likely to be under serious pressure from such factors as consumerism, environmental protection, and taxes. The anticipated further devaluation of the U.S. dollar relative to other national currencies of Western Europe and Japan would be *very* bullish for the U.S. equity market in the long run. But balancing this is the fact that the current market level, approximately 20 times earnings as measured by Standard & Poor's index, is historically high — clearly in the upper 25% of the range as related to the Gross National Product, corporate profits, and other such factors.

Real Property

Real property may prove to be the best answer to the investment problem of the 1970s, because it represents a medium which provides inflationary protection without the likelihood of a profit squeeze. This assumes, of course, that rent controls are unlikely to be applied to commercial property for anything other than a short period of time; it also assumes that there will not be an unreasonable overbuilding of commercial properties, nor a fundamental change in the method of taxation of real estate income.

It is interesting to note that the trend of investment in the U.K. in recent years has shifted very much in the direction of property, and that pension funds have become particularly active in this field.

It is also worth nothing that the U.S. taxation system, as related to real property, tends to place a premium value on this type of investment when held by taxable corporations or individuals who are able to enjoy the special advantages afforded under the prevailing depreciation allowances. The boom in real estate investment trusts which has taken place in the past few years is probably related in part to recognition of this factor.

Actuarial Considerations

Several actuarial considerations are closely involved with this investment outlook for the 1970s:

The assumed rate of investment return for life insurance companies and pension funds clearly requires reexamination. The analysis suggests that the *nominal* rate of return (not the real rate of return) is likely to be higher in future years than it has been in past years.

The prospect of continued inflation suggests that the assumptions as to future salary increases should be reexamined for pension plans which provide benefits related to final average salary.

The prospect of continued inflation also suggests that plans providing benefits based on career-average salary may become even more inadequate than they are today. Similarly, the urgency of providing benefits to retired persons who are responsive to inflationary tendencies also is increased. These considerations have an important bearing on the design and the costs of appropriate pension packages.

The Actuary's Relationship to Investment Management

Presented to the Southeastern Life Insurance Bond Association, Atlanta, Georgia, May 31, 1979.

I want to say a few things this afternoon about the relationship of the actuary to the whole area of investment management.

My personal crystal ball has in it some visions of the future which suggest that, if the actuarial profession is to continue to be viable and growing, it is necessary to expand its areas of involvement beyond those that have been its traditional province. The actuarial discipline is very suitable for a variety of other types of involvements and notable among these is the whole field of investment management. In this context, I would note in passing that in the United Kingdom there are three "tracks" to achieving Fellowship in the Institute of Actuaries and one of these is investment management. If one looks down the road for the next ten years or so, it might well be that the Society of Actuaries will also have an investment track towards achieving Fellowship in that organization.

Some members of this profession see the role of the actuary in the investment activities of insurance companies or even in their financial reporting as it relates to assets as nil. Others see only a limited involvement — a participation in the fiduciary responsibilities of the insurance company to ensure that assets are suitably invested, but no responsibility beyond that.

I look upon the actuary's involvement in the investment aspects of insurance companies as going far beyond the fiduciary responsibility. I believe that the actuary can contribute substantially to the investment management function in a variety of ways. This afternoon I would like to discuss briefly five areas which illustrate ways in which the actuary can participate meaningfully in the investment management function:

- First, the *risk aspect* of investment management;
- Second, the *tax aspects;*
- Third, the application of investment expectations to *pricing and financial reporting;*
- Fourth, *liquidity problems;* and
- Fifth, certain actuarial aspects of *investment strategy.*

Let me now deal briefly with each of these topics.

Risk Aspects

I am impressed, to use a positive word for a negative reaction, by the lack of relationship between the investment risks insurance companies are prepared to assume and the mortality risks that those same companies are prepared to assume. It has always surprised me that companies were prepared to make sizable commitments of assets to particular types of investments, perhaps to various securities of one obligor, or to securities in one industry or one geographical area, in amounts that far exceed the retention limits of those companies on mortality risks.

If a company has a retention limit of $250,000, is it consistent that the company should be prepared to underwrite individual investment risks of $5 million? Those numbers are not at all disproportionate in my experience. There are many qualifications which need consideration: There is such a thing as a partial loss on an investment risk but there is no comparable such thing on a mortality risk; the probable loss on first class debt securities is obviously different from the probable loss on mortgages, particularly on special purpose properties; and so forth.

Another important factor affecting relative risk is the issue of tax. For some companies, a mortality loss will be tax deductible and would result in "coinsurance" by the government to the extent of either 23% or 46% of the loss. For other companies, within wide limits, a mortality loss does not result in a tax deduction and the entire loss is borne by the company out of after-tax dollars. In contrast, a capital loss on an asset might result in coinsurance by the government to the extent of 28% provided the capital loss could be offset by compensating gains. These are sizable adjustments and, obviously, individual companies should consider their probable tax positions when establishing limits on each of these types of risk.

There is also the issue of the mandatory securities valuation reserve which, in effect, permits investment losses to be written off without affecting statutory capital surplus. Thus, investment losses do not present the same threat to the statutory solvency of a company in quite the same fashion as mortality losses.

The most important qualification of all is that it is relatively infrequently that one has a massive coincidence of excess mortality on individual policies. In contrast, the realities of the marketplace clearly suggest that, if one investment turns sour, the probability is significantly increased that several other investments are also going to turn sour; in other words, if one company defaults on an obligation due to a general environmental cause such as high interest rates, tight credit, fuel shortages or inflation, the risk is increased that other companies will also default on their obligations for the same reasons. This clearly suggests a more conservative limit on investment risks than on mortality risks, which is quite contrary to industry practice.

Tax Aspects

Moving to the tax aspects of investment management, the actuary is well suited to advise management on the choice of investment alternatives. Life insurance companies, as most of this audience already know, are taxed under a unique and complex formula which can involve both taxable gain from operations and taxable investment income. Both of these items which can enter into the determination of taxable income are affected, differently, by the investment income and gains and losses arising on various types of investments. I have been surprised at how few companies, particularly medium and smaller sized companies, are fully aware of the tax impact of various types of investments.

The tax consequences of investing in fully taxable securities as distinguished from tax exempt and partially tax exempt securities are reasonably straightforward. It is necessary only to remember that only the company's share of tax exempt and partially tax exempt investment income escapes tax; the remainder, the policyholder's share, is fully taxable. Thus, so-called tax exempt investment income, in fact, bears tax, albeit at a reduced rate.

The subtleties arise when a given choice of investment alternatives leads to a change in the overall pretax investment yield. This affects the division of investment income between the taxable part (the company's share) and the nontaxable part (the policyholder's share). Recently, this has become more significant since the industry as a whole has reached the "peak of the parabola" — the point beyond which increases in investment earnings will produce even greater increases in taxable investment income. This is a large and complex subject which I will not attempt to discuss today. For those of you with an interest either in the subject or in needling your company's actuary, I would suggest that you ask your actuary to explain to you John Fraser's paper on the subject which is published in Volume XIV of the *Transactions of the Society of Actuaries.*

Pricing and Financial Reporting

In establishing investment expectations for pricing and financial reporting purposes, it is my strong view that those expectations should be based on no-risk investments. Various writers in the investment field, such as Ibbottson and Sinquefield, identify a risk premium that is attached to certain kinds of investments — for example, the difference in yield between Aaa bonds and Baa bonds. I have had clients ask me about the feasibility of pricing their products on the assumption that they were going to invest in medium grade utility securities which were going to yield 11%. It is important that one unscramble the risk premium associated with such investments from the pricing assumptions. Otherwise, there is a significant danger of double-counting. The same applies to assumptions selected for financial reporting under GAAP.

What do no-risk investment yields mean in this context? The classical answer to the question is that it means the yield either on Treasury bills or other government securities. But in the life insurance context, this may not be a satisfactory answer because the market in government securities is often artificially influenced by such extraneous factors as activities of foreign central banks, bank reserve requirements, etc. A better index of no-risk investment yields is, perhaps, Aaa corporate bonds or, for the more adventurous, Aa corporate bonds.

I am surprised at the number of companies that are pricing their products on the basis of pretax interest rates even though the industry as a whole is taxed in substantial part on its investment income only and not on its profits. For pricing purposes, it is necessary that after-tax interest rates should be used. This is clear for companies that are taxed on the basis of taxable investment income only, but it is also true for those companies that are taxed, wholly or partly, on the basis of taxable gains from operations.

Let us now consider the application of investment expectations to pricing. Typically, the starting point is the assumed new money rates. Under circumstances which have prevailed for the past twenty years, a declining new money rate would be assumed for nonparticipating products and a level new money rate would be assumed for participating products. It would be typical today for aggressive companies to assume a pretax new money rate of about 9.5%, declining to about 6% over a period of ten years in the case of nonparticipating products. Having established these assumptions, there are then two ways to proceed.

The traditional way works as follows: One assumes that the new money is invested, say, in fifteen-year noncallable bonds and determines an assumed portfolio yield based on cash-flow projections. On the assumptions quoted, a 9.5% new money rate declining to 6% over a period of ten years, this might develop a first year assumed yield of 9.5%, a fifth year rate of 8.8%, a tenth year rate of 7.9% and, finally, a rate in years 26 and subsequent of 6%.

The alternative approach, which I personally favor, gives us more understanding of what the investment process is all about. Assuming the same new money rates and assuming the same fifteen-year investments, one can then introduce this into the pricing assumption by making the following additional assumption: Assume that the cash flow for each year is invested at the available new money rate and at the end of each year the investments are sold and reinvested at the then available new money rate, realizing whatever capital gain or loss ensues. This produces a first year assumed interest rate of 12.2% — the 9.5% assumed new money rate plus 2.7% representing the capital gain on reinvestment. Similarly, the fifth year rate is 11.0% — the fifth year new money rate of 8.1% plus a capital gain of 2.9%. The tenth year rate is 11.6% and the rate for the eleventh and subsequent years is 6%. The effect of this approach is to mitigate somewhat the assumption of a declining new money rate by anticipating the capital gains which will arise if that expectation is realized.

Liquidity Problems

Except for a brief period in the 1930s and, for some companies, in the mid-1970s, the life insurance industry has not experienced significant cash-flow problems. Under today's conditions, with high interest rates and new classes of business, liquidity problems are potentially severe. The following classes of business are ones which are vulnerable: Flexible premium retirement annuities sold in the tax sheltered market are subject to rapid turnover; group deposit administration funds with limited penalties on withdrawal are also vulnerable; single premium deferred annuities, particularly when sold in large volumes relative to annual premium business and even more particularly when sold by stock brokers, are extremely vulnerable; the availability of low-interest policy loans caused negative cash flow in various companies in 1974–1975; nonparticipating permanent life insurance is vulnerable to replacement; and, finally, there are those contracts on which the issuing company intends to pay excess interest at a rate based more on portfolio rates than on new money rates.

All of these classes of business could give rise to liquidity problems. As was mentioned earlier, it is virtually universal to assume for pricing purposes a declining new money yield. But, when potential liquidity problems exist, it is necessary to consider the opposite hypothesis — the assumption of rising interest rates rather than declining interest rates. Beginning in 1974 in the United Kingdom and extending through 1976, a number of life insurance companies encountered serious financial difficulties. These related essentially to the problem caused by rapidly rising interest rates coupled with guaranteed surrender values. In the space of less than two years, interest rates on fifteen-year government securities increased from 8% to 17%, causing a market depreciation of more than 50%, leading to one liquidation, one reorganization involving a modification of policy benefits, and several rescues. Could that same result happen in this country? The answer is clearly yes and several companies can already be identified as seriously exposed.

In the early 1950s, the concept of immunization was developed by the British actuary F. M. Redington. He defined immunization as the situation where the assets held with respect to a given block of business are so invested that the expected receipts from the investments together with the future premiums would exactly meet the claims and expenses arising from the business in each and every subsequent interval of time. Under these circumstances, the financial position of the company is completely independent of future interest rates and market values because no investment or disinvestment of any funds relating to the business would be required at any subsequent date.

Immunization never became an important consideration in the investment policy of life insurance companies in Great Britain and had even less impact in North America. Nevertheless, the theory has received increasing attention in recent years, both in the United Kingdom and in North America, for various reasons: The wide movement in interest rates, the higher interest rate guarantees included in various new products, the increased volatility of fixed interest security markets, and the combined impact of high inflation and increasing lapse rates.

Perhaps a more practical approach to the problems which the theory of immunization tries to address is the preparation of cash-flow projections. Once again, this is an area in which the actuary's assistance is essential. Moreover, companies need to produce more than one cash-flow projection to illustrate the effect of different possible future environments. I cannot believe that a given company would have the same cash-flow outlook if new money rates went to 12% as it would if new money rates went to 5%. It is important for companies to know just what the consequences of these two hypotheses are.

Investment Strategy

An aspect of investment strategy that has some appeal to some people applies to classes of business where the liabilities are of a relatively short-term nature — for example, immediate annuities. The strategy is to commit funds received in a deliberately over-long position, thus committing the future cash flow at current investment rates. If the current investment rates are comfortably and substantially higher than the interest assumptions underlying pricing or GAAP or statutory accounting, this may be an attractive alternative. This is an example of how the application of actuarial concepts to the investment problem can involve strategy.

There are some implications of investment strategy that have an important bearing on the affairs of insurance companies, as viewed from the shareholder perspective. One example is that capital gains and losses are depreciated currency even though they are included in the bottom line — the investment community has a way of discounting the importance of capital gains and losses. This has considerable bearing on the issue of investment in equities such as real estate or common stocks because this type of investment generally involves a sacrifice of current yield in the expectation of ultimately higher returns. In my experience, capital gains are best used as a means of offsetting unrealized losses on fixed income investments and thereby improving overall yield.

There are a few areas where actuaries can make an important contribution to risk-limiting strategies of insurance companies and generally these risk-limiting strategies involve a trade of potential capital gains for current income. One is the options market that has become prominent in the U. S. in the last several years, and another is the convertible securities market that has been with us for some time. The anomalies which sometimes appear in markets for related securities lend themselves to the type of analysis an actuary is well equipped to perform.

Conclusion

I have attempted in these brief remarks to indicate to you those areas in which the role of the actuary interfaces with that of the investment manager. Too often, in my experience, the actuarial department and the investment department of insurance companies exist in splendid isolation from one another. May I suggest that, when you return to your respective home offices next Monday, you arrange to be introduced to the actuary of your company if you haven't already met him.

A Rational Basis for Taxation of the Life Insurance Industry and Its Policyholders

Presented as a treatise to the U.S. Treasury Department, March 10, 1982.

The taxation of life insurance companies and their policyholders has presented troublesome problems to Treasury Departments throughout most of the industrial world. The problems are generally caused because an attempt is often made to tax all or a portion of the investment earnings attributable to policyholders and all or a portion of the companies' earnings through a single tax law. This has been the case in the United States since Congress enacted the Life Insurance Company Income Tax Act of 1959.

Various systems of taxing life insurance companies and their policyholders have evolved in different countries. In the United Kingdom, for example, policyholders and companies are taxed only on their dealings with the outside world, not with each other; accordingly, their combined taxable income is equal to total investment income minus total expenses. In most of the rest of Western Europe, policyholders are not taxed (except on single premium business and short-term endowments) and companies are generally taxed on statutory net gain from operations with provision for the use of net level reserves for tax purposes. In Canada, three totally different tax systems have existed during the past 15 years and a fourth, aimed at taxing policyholders directly, is now before Parliament. In South Africa there is a flat tax on investment income at the rate of 7 1/2%. In Australia companies are taxed on total investment income (excluding dividends received from Australian companies) with a modest allowance for required interest on reserves (the allowance was successively reduced from 3% of reserves to 2% to 1% during the past 10 years). In New Zealand companies are taxed on the gross amount required before taxes to pay dividends to shareholders and policyholders alike. This oversimplified recitation is intended to illustrate the wide range of taxation systems on a worldwide basis — from the benign to the ridiculous.

Moreover, in the United Kingdom and several other countries, life insurance premiums, or a portion thereof, are deductible from personal taxable income. In effect, this represents a negative premium tax. This is somewhat comparable to the IRA program in the United States, but it applies generally to all normal types of life insurance, and the ultimate proceeds are generally not taxed in the policyholders' hands. In the United States and in Canada there is the opposite position — the various states and provinces levy taxes on life insurance premiums.

The time has arrived in the United States for a new basis of taxation of the industry and its policyholders, based on rational rather than revenue considerations.

Premises

For more than a century, the life insurance industry has been an important social and financial institution in the United States. The death benefits paid to beneficiaries have served a worthy social purpose and, indirectly, have increased tax revenues by concentrating premiums paid by many into the estates of the few who died prematurely. Traditionally, the life insurance industry has been a major provider of long-term debt capital, although this role is changing rapidly because of fundamental and major changes that are sweeping the industry and threaten its very survival in the savings market. The forces that are bringing about these fundamental changes have been called the Four Horsemen: with apologies to St. John the Divine and Grantland Rice, their names are Taxation, Expenses, Replacement and Inflation.

Because the life insurance industry and its policyholders represent a positive force to society as a whole, to the financial community and even to the Treasury, the method of taxation of the industry and its policyholders should not be disadvantageous by comparison with the taxation of other financial institutions and their customers. In various countries of the industrial world, preferential tax treatment applies. It is widely believed, particularly by Congress and the Treasury Department, that the present system of taxation is advantageous to the industry and its policyholders. This is not true, although the idea has been reinforced by the widespread use of modified coinsurance during the past three years; perhaps that phenomenon can be explained by the adage, traceable by the author to Professor G.S.A. Wheatcroft of the University of London, "An onerous tax system breathes through its loopholes." Furthermore, a rational method of taxation would be product neutral and neutral also with respect to the taxation of stock and mutual life insurance companies to preserve the competitive balance of the industry. Finally, the system of taxation should be understandable by laymen — and should be perceived by them to be fair. The present system of taxation meets none of these goals.

Proposal

It is proposed that, to the extent practical, the life insurance industry and its policyholders be taxed like any other financial institution and its customers. This easily can be accomplished by separately taxing the policyholders' earnings (net of policyholders' losses) and companies' earnings.

For practical and historical reasons, the tax imposed upon policyholders' earnings should be collectively assessed against all policyholders of a given company because they have entered into a collective risk-sharing agreement making it impractical if not impossible accurately to assess the gain or loss of each individual policyholder. Historically, this tax has been paid by the life insurance industry, particularly by mutual life insurance companies; to prevent yet another mountain of paper, it is proposed that each company should pay the tax on behalf of its policyholders. Obviously, some composite tax rate should be applied reflecting the average tax rate of life insurance policyholders generally. If the tax rate implicit in the All-Savers' Certificates offers any guideline, a rate of 30% is suggested.

The policyholder tax would apply only to nonqualified life and annuity business, although there are compelling reasons to grandfather existing annuities. Health insurance would obviously be excluded and possibly group life insurance should also be excluded because of its special status under Section 79.

The taxable income collectively attributable to policyholders would be:

1. All benefits paid, regardless of type, including policyholders' dividends, death benefits, surrender benefits, etc.; plus
2. The aggregate increase in cash values; minus
3. The sum of premiums paid.

Arguably, this taxable income might be "grossed-up" for the tax to be levied.

Since policyholders' earnings would be taxed fully from the operative date of the proposed legislation, it would no longer be necessary to tax any gains arising to policyholders upon surrender or maturity; the taxation of annuity benefits would need to be revised to avoid double taxation upon annuitization.

The taxation of company earnings is simpler. The policyholders' tax paid by the companies on behalf of their policyholders would, of course, be deductible by the companies as an excise tax. The entire body of tax legislation governing life insurance companies would then be repealed and they would be taxed as casualty insurance companies under existing statutes with two modifications required to insure an orderly transition and to avoid spurious amounts of taxable income arising for those companies previously taxed on an investment income basis but subsequently taxed on a gain from operations basis:

1. Existing policyholders' surplus accounts would be maintained with no further additions thereto and with withdrawals based on current law generating a tax equivalent to the current Phase III tax.
2. It would be desirable if not necessary to retain Section 818(c), permitting the use of net level reserves for tax purposes, to avoid reversals of tax deductions taken in earlier years which had no direct effect on taxable gain from operations; the alternative would be a "fresh start" reserve basis.

It should be noted this tax system would produce complete neutrality with respect to products be they participating, nonparticipating or pseudo-participating. There would also be neutrality as between stock and mutuals and parity with other savings institutions. In short, the playing field would be level.

It is difficult to estimate the amount of tax revenue that such a plan would generate because publically available data do not provide the answer. Perhaps it is better to consider the concept in abstract. It should be noted that the policyholders' total taxable income will not be as large as taxable investment income currently is because, while the entire investment income credited to policyholders becomes taxable, the amount of taxable income is reduced by the expenses which are charged to them. This is a right and proper result, consistent with the treatment of other savings instruments.

It should also be noted that the taxation of a life insurance company as a casualty insurance company would permit the full deduction of tax exempt investment income and the full allowance for intercorporate dividends. This latter point would answer some serious concerns within the industry that life insurance companies with subsidiaries, if the parent is taxed on the basis of taxable investment income, effectively pay double taxes on the earnings of their affiliates. This would level another playing field.

Conclusion

It was said at the outset that the time has arrived for a new basis of taxation of the industry and its policyholders, based on rational rather than revenue considerations. The principal flaw in the existing law (a flaw not present when it was enacted) is that it radically overtaxes the investment income attributable to policyholders because it does not allow as an offset the considerable expenses associated with purchasing and maintaining a life insurance policy. The result is a threat to the survival of the industry as it has existed for more than a century, because products which can be offered are at a competitive disadvantage with those offered by other savings institutions. A second flaw is that the tax levied on company earnings, which cannot be said conclusively to be either too high or too low, clearly is distributed irrationally among the companies which comprise the industry; in some cases, the policyholders pay the companies' tax, certain income is subject to double taxation and endless disputes and litigation have taken place or are pending regarding such questions as whether or not a company qualifies as a life insurance company, the treatment of deferred premiums, the treatment of tax-exempt investment income, what constitutes a dividend to policyholders and so forth. The proposal would moot many of these issues.

This proposal is being made in the interest of no client company. Neither is it being made in the interest of the firm with which the author is associated, several of whose members probably would not agree with this proposal. It is made, instead, from the personal perspective of one whose entire career has been spent in or providing services to the life insurance industry; it therefore cannot be characterized as wholly detached. The proposal, which is hardly more than a skeletal concept, is offered as a suggestion for a rational long-term basis of taxation for the industry and its policyholders. Obviously, many issues are not addressed — especially ones relating to prior years. The leading industry trade association currently is proposing stopgap legislation, which urgently is required to resolve major uncertainties of a magnitude sufficient to threaten the stability of the industry and even the national financial structure. The proposal described herein is in no way offered as a substitute for that temporary proposal.

Ownership and Control of Financial Institutions

Presented to the Life Office Management Association (LOMA) Financial Officers' Forum, Boston, Massachusetts, May 1, 1984. Reprinted with permission from LOMA.

I did not come here today to discuss with you the issue of whether or not deregulation and diversification is coming to the financial industries, and nor did I come here to discuss whether it should come. My premise this afternoon is that the movement toward deregulation and diversification is irreversible, and that the movement will profoundly affect the control of financial institutions.

What Is Control?

In developing this topic, let me spend a few moments discussing with you, first what control means, and second, what financial institutions are involved.

In my view, control of financial institutions can be viewed from three perspectives:

1. First, there is the issue of government regulation, including taxation. In the United States this means both state and federal regulation and taxation. This is the viewpoint of public policy.
2. Second is the viewpoint of ownership control of financial institutions; involved in this issue of ownership are organizations that are stock corporations, organizations that are mutual corporations and holding company systems of a wide variety of types.

3. The final viewpoint is that of management control, which is the perspective of officers and directors of the institutions involved.

Which Financial Institutions?

I spent a few minutes compiling a list of the financial institutions that are involved in this issue. I do not promise you that my list is complete, but I will be able to demonstrate in a moment that it is lengthy. One way to look at this is to look at specific industries. Another way to look at it is to try and dissect financial services into their various kinds. I propose to do both.

First, the specific industries that are involved. My list includes a dozen. There are life insurance companies, likely the central interest of this audience. There are general insurance companies. There are commercial banks, the thrift institutions, and the non-bank banks. There are pension funds. There are security dealers, both stock brokers and investment bankers. There are mutual funds. There are real estate brokers. There are credit unions and other consumer credit organizations, including credit card issuers. Finally, there are issuers of travelers checks; do you realize that issuing travelers' checks is essentially the right to print money? I am sure that each of you has had the experience, as you have traveled abroad, where it is actually easier to cash an American Express Travelers Check than it is to convert currency. If you have ever doubted that travelers checks are money, that experience should persuade you.

Looking at the matrix from the other viewpoint, the kinds of financial services that are involved in the activities of these various institutions might be classified this way: (1) First, there is the business of savings or investments. (2) Second, there is the business of risk transfer. (3) Third, there is the business of corporate and personal credit. (4) Fourth, there are the businesses involving real estate and associated mortgage lending. (5) Finally, there is the whole field of payment systems.

This is what I mean when I speak of the financial institutions and discuss their control.

Why Diversification and Deregulation?

I said I wasn't going to discuss whether or not, let alone should, the move toward diversification and deregulation happen. But I can't pass the opportunity to spend a few minutes on the issue of why it is happening. In my view, there are two engines of these forces of change — two engines that are driving the move toward diversification and deregulation: The first engine is distribution costs; the second is capital starvation.

Many of you may wonder why people in various financial industries feel that the grass is so green on the other side of the fence. Let me tell you something. It is not necessarily a case of the grass being greener on the other side of the fence; it is partly, at least, a case of the grass turning a little brown on this side of the fence!

Let me illustrate this with two of the industries. I will pick banks because they are, in my view, the most important of the financial institutions that are the subject of these remarks. I will pick life insurance companies because they are the ones that are of the most interest to this audience.

It may come as a surprise to some of you that banks have a serious problem with their distribution costs. Basically, their problem is that they are extensively involved in brick and mortar in the midst of an electronic age. If we were starting a bank from scratch today, as some of you might within the next few years, we would hardly place branches on every other corner in every major city that covered the territory that we intended to cover. A good friend and former colleague of mine, Mark A. Weinberg, the founder of Hambro Life in the U.K., is in the midst of launching an experiment which began last October, in which he is attempting to use a life insurance company as a springboard into the banking business. He intends to run a bank without branches. It is a very interesting idea. The bank's distribution cost problem is brick and mortar, and the other attendant costs.

The second problem the banks have is a scarcity of capital. If you will discuss with colleagues in the banking business some of their problems, you will find that they are definitely capital starved. Partly this has to do with the rules of banking, whereby each time a bank accepts deposits, it in effect commits a portion of its equity capital to support those deposits. Consequently, when it has an expanding volume of deposits it needs an ever-expanding volume of equity capital.

Let's look next at life insurance. Why is the grass turning a little brown on their side of the fence? Their problems are remarkably similar. They, too, have a distribution cost problem because their traditional distribution system is people-intensive in an age of automation. For the same reasons that there are fewer and fewer of us today who have milk delivered to our door in the morning, I think there are going to be fewer and fewer life insurance agents making person to person calls to sell their wares. It is simply a matter of the economic pressures involved in a people-intensive business — no different, for example, from the disappearance of elevator operators.

Life insurers are also facing a problem with respect to capital resources. Rates of inflation have been relatively high during most of the past decade, and simply to stand still in terms of new business has required considerable nominal growth in new business. Financing that stand-still growth has put a considerable strain on many companies. It is worth noting, too, the special case involved with mutual life insurers when it comes to capital resource issues — these institutions do not have access to capital markets to raise equity capital.

The Renegade Factor

These forces driving us toward diversification and deregulation have been contributed to in an important sense by what I call the "renegade factor." In the banking and thrift businesses particularly, the activities of money market funds and cash management accounts effectively led to the demise of Regulation Q. Regulation Q was the regulation that put a ceiling on the interest rates that banks could pay on small deposits. It protected the margins of the industries involved from the effects of price competition.

In the life insurance industry renegade forces have given us the replacement phenomenon. This, too, has placed great strains on the industry, and great strains on its distribution system, at least in the long run.

Partly as a result of these renegade factors, we have seen the breakdown of existing regulation within the financial service industries. It is predictable that the move towards deregulation and diversification is going to lead to meltdown. I mean meltdown in the terms of number of companies. And I also include the possible meltdown of whole industries now comprising part of the financial service sector.

Legitimate and Questionable Regulation

Let me turn now to the question of control. How should financial institutions be controlled? Let's look first from the viewpoint of public policy. I divide these remarks into two sections. The first section I call Areas of Legitimate Regulatory Concern, and the second sector I call Areas of Questionable Regulatory Concern (that is a euphemism, as you will recognize).

In the area of Legitimate Regulatory Concern, I think we must place in the forefront the issue of solvency of financial institutions, addressing the issue of consumer security. This gives rise to a whole host of legitimate regulatory matters dealing with such issues as capital requirements, financial reporting, investment restrictions, and so forth. The second Area of Legitimate Regulatory Concern I believe is the area of disclosure. Here, the issue of public policy involves that of consumer information. Disclosure can extend to a wide variety of topics. Some of them are product related: the disclosure, for example, of sales charges, premium rates, investment returns, benefits, subjects such as truth in lending, and so forth. Remember, we are not just talking about the life insurance industry. The second area of disclosure relates to investment matters — the nature of the underlying investment portfolio for a mutual fund, for instance, the historical performance of a fund, and so forth. This area also relates to information affecting the desirability of securities as investments — items such as profit history, solvency margin, the kind of information that you would find in a typical prospectus. So the second Area of Legitimate Regulatory Concern, I suggest, relates to disclosure and provision of consumer information.

The third area is that of fostering competition. Here, the public concern is to enhance value to the consumer of the products being offered. Fostering competition suggests that entry requirements into a given financial service business should not be prohibitive. It suggests, also, that there should be some anti-monopoly provisions, perhaps not necessarily unique to the financial business. Things to avoid are such items as price fixing, and so forth. There are also questions involving tax policy that are pertinent. There seems to be at least lip service paid to the concept that various financial institutions ought to compete on a somewhat "level playing field." I sometimes wonder how sincere those comments are.

Let me turn now to the other aspect of regulation — what I call the Areas of Questionable Regulatory Concern. It is my personal belief that the life insurance industry in this country has been ill served by having statutory reserve requirements. I think the statutory reserve requirements are basically wrong, basically counterproductive, and should never have been enacted in the first place. I question, too, whether statutory limitations on certain classes of investments are appropriate. These supposedly have been enacted to provide protection to the consumer, the policyholder in the case of a life insurance company. But I wonder if they have really done any real good. Are they, as some recent examples suggest, a license for mismanagement within arbitrary limits of technical compliance? I am thinking of things like arbitrary limits on the proportion of portfolios that could be invested in common stocks, real estate, associated companies, and so forth.

I was recently involved in an assignment in Australia. In that country, where life insurance companies are required to have 30% of their assets invested in government and near-government securities, I was amazed to find that 50% of the assets were invested in common stocks and real estate. It was easy to see on examination that that investment policy had been very beneficial to the policyholders in that country. The same is generally true of the U.K. life insurance industry.

Another area of questionable regulatory concern can be described as product related. I think that restrictions on product design are counterproductive. Why should we have waited so long to be able to market a very simple, almost self explanatory product such as the long-anticipated universal life variation of variable life? Why should it have taken three or four years, as it has already done? Why has the product still not received approval?

What about things like minimum required benefits? I think it could be argued that minimum cash value requirements of insurance policies are decidedly counterproductive from the viewpoint of policyholders. They have in fact hurt the very people they were intended to help.

What about the matter of restrictions on sales charges? What is the magic of 9% on a product classified as an investment product, when no limit applies to anything else? The logic escapes me, and I would question this as an area of legitimate regulatory concern.

There are factors that are competition related — things like minimum price and maximum benefit limitations. This was inherent in Regulation Q, which effectively legislated the maximum interest rate that could be paid by banks. It is inherent in an indirect way in the deficiency reserve requirements that are built into life insurance statutes. They tend to promote a minimum price level as a result of their existence.

Finally, in the area of regulation that I regard as questionable, we have restrictions that are designed to protect the status quo. Included are such things as legislation governing the replacements of life insurance policies, legislation prohibiting commission rebating, most statutes requiring licensing of agents and representatives, and so forth. Many examples can be found. These regulations are, for the most part, designed to protect the status quo.

A Critique of Existing Regulation

Let me critique the existing regulation of the United States. The first issue to address, I believe, is the question of whether regulation should be done at the state level or the federal, or whether a system of dual regulation should apply. Many people think that the issue of state versus federal regulation is a straightforward question which deals with the issue of whether one would sooner deal with fifty monkeys or one gorilla. I don't think it is quite that simple.

Today in the insurance industry we do have a dual system of regulation, and the overlaps are somewhat irrational. It is predictable that as the financial service industries consolidate there will be more overlap and the overlaps will become progressively more irrational. It is worth noting that, except for life insurance, most other financial services are mainly regulated at the federal level; if we are headed towards a world of consolidated financial service businesses, we are going to be dealing primarily with federal regulators and not state regulators in areas outside of insurance.

I raised the issue of federal regulation versus state regulation for another reason. I think it is entirely predictable within the next few years that either the public, or perhaps this industry will be asking for an insurance equivalent of the FDIC, the Federal Deposit Insurance Corporation. The standard answer to this is, "There are state guarantee funds," and indeed there are. There are state guarantee funds for life insurance in perhaps 35 states. Those state guarantee funds are currently being tested in one well-known circumstance, and it remains to be seen exactly how they will work, and the extent to which they will in fact protect the people who are involved as customers.

There is another problem with state guarantee funds. If the life insurance industry, for example, is to encounter serious problems, experience shows that the most likely area in which those problems may arise is the asset side of the balance sheets of the companies comprising the industry. Now, if problems arise on the asset side of the balance sheet, and if they are not aberrations of particular investment policy, it is quite likely that if one company is affected, many will be affected. Arguably, all of them will be affected.

State guarantee funds, which depend on mutual support within the life insurance industry, can be likened to three one-legged men holding each other up. When the leg is kicked out from under one of them, it is predictable that all three will collapse. For that reason I think that we may see not only regulatory pressure but also consumer and even industry pressure for an insurance industry FDIC at some time in the near future.

There is another reason why I would suggest that the case for federal regulation may indeed be stronger than we are traditionally apt to think. This has to do with taxes. Originally, states taxed premiums in lieu of taxing income of life insurance companies at the state level. I consulted the most recent edition of the *Life Insurance Fact Book*, and found that in 1982 the total industry bill for premium taxes was roughly equivalent to the total bill for federal income taxes. In most states, state income tax rates are about a tenth of federal income tax rates for corporations. It follows that the industry is getting a very bad deal by paying premium taxes in lieu of paying state income taxes. The order of magnitude may well be something like ten to one.

If the financial service industries are moving toward consolidation, and if there is going to be genuine competition among branches of the industry — for example, for savings dollars — I would suggest that in the end premium taxes are going to be a force with which the life insurance company will not be able to reckon. If one imagines, for example, that he is running a bank and that the tax mechanics applicable were that 2% tax was paid on all deposits into the bank, it is clear that his bank would be run out of business by banks that didn't have that tax. I would suggest to you that if the life insurance industry is going to compete effectively in the savings market, we have to begin immediately to lobby for an elimination of premium taxes.

Another critique of existing regulation has to do with the issue of form over substance. It appears that some people believe that umbrellas cause rain. Now given that belief, it is relatively easy to see how they could then believe that the way to control rain is to regulate umbrellas. I think that is exactly what we have all too often in the regulation of the insurance industries.

Much de facto deregulation has already happened. The non-bank banks, CMAs and so forth, are perhaps the easiest examples to cite.

Consumer interests obviously favor deregulation. Walter Wriston, then Chairman of Citibank, made a speech to the ACLI in October 1983. He called it "A String Bag and The Right Stuff." His reference to the string bag had to do with the public's preference for a supermarket rather than a string bag to carry around their purchases made from a number of specialty shops.

Lessons from Abroad

Lessons from abroad can be learned. If you look in the United Kingdom, and to a degree in Canada, you will find that there is much greater degree of discretionary regulation as opposed to the style of comprehensive and detailed regulation favored in this country. The whole concept of freedom of management with disclosure is well established and well tested, particularly in the United Kingdom.

It is interesting to note something that I call "The Tillinghast Paradox." It goes like this: If all the life insurance companies in the United States were subject to the regulatory requirements of the United Kingdom, they would all be insolvent, and if all the life insurance companies in the United Kingdom were subject to the regulatory requirements of the United States, they would all be insolvent. I told this to the Society of Actuaries in Ireland a few months ago, and I went on to observe that, at the risk of sounding like I was beginning a bad ethnic joke, that in Ireland both groups of companies would be solvent!

I think we have much to learn from abroad. It is fairly obvious to me that if the paradox be as I expressed, in a somewhat exaggerated form, one is left with these conclusions: Either the U.S. regulation is wrong, or the U.K. regulation is wrong, or they are both wrong; it does not admit the possibility that they are both right. But Ireland may be right!

Other Aspects of Control

What about ownership and management? What about the responsibility to the public and to consumer interests? There apparently are a lot of people in this industry who have the view that banks are unsatisfactory owners of insurance companies and that, for example, movie companies, bus lines, oil companies, and what not are better qualified than banks. This essentially was the force of Mr. Wriston's argument in the second part of his title, when he referred to the right stuff. He said that apparently banks don't have the right stuff to own insurance companies. Some of the arguments about this are ones with which you are all familiar. I would only observe that the particular argument about bad apples has a wide application — my view is that there are bad apples in every barrel.

What about accountability to owners? I think that in the insurance industry we are below average in our accountability to owners. There are a lot of reasons; they are complicated and it is not necessary to probe them here today. Mutual life insurance companies are a special case in this respect. The question of accountability to owners raises questions such as, "Is the profit motive the only motive?" Some will answer yes, some will answer no; it seems to work either way, but it helps to have a fairly clear idea which way the game is to be played.

In management skills I think the financial service industries are operating at a disadvantage. Partly it is because the regulation and control of these industries has kept them all one dimensional, by keeping them all in watertight compartments. This, however, is changing rapidly, and the life insurance industry and its management are going to have to change with it.

When the Gods Are Changing

In his book *Hawaii*, James Michener describes the movement of the early people from the island of Bora Bora in Polynesia, across the Pacific Ocean to the islands of Hawaii. His theory is that they made the trek as a result of religious persecution. It should be a familiar theme here in Boston. One of his characters in that section of the book says, "Times are always difficult when the gods are changing." I would suggest to you this afternoon that the gods are changing within the financial service industry generally, and within the life insurance industry in particular.

Times of change, as Michener's character observed, are not easy, but times of change are also opportunities. Each of us in our involvement in the financial service business over the next five to ten years will be faced with both problems and opportunities. It is up to us to decide which of those two things the same circumstances may be.

Mismatching for Fun and Profit

Presented to a Tillinghast Seminar, Chicago, Illinois, June 1, 1986. Reprinted from a video transcript with permission from Tillinghast - A Towers Perrin Company.

Good afternoon, ladies and gentlemen. I'm sure that this is a new experience for all of you to listen to a luncheon presentation that is beginning at 5:00 in the afternoon. If nothing else is memorable about the proceedings, perhaps at least you'll remember that. Mike Tuohy has told you the topic of these remarks, and depending on one's point of view, I suppose that my role this afternoon is either to add a touch of reality to what you've been talking about today or perhaps it's the reverse. Some of you may think that Mike is sitting over to my right simply because he was to make the introduction. That's not entirely true. Not all of my associates are entirely comfortable with some of the things I have to say, and Mike is there at the other microphone as their watchdog just in case my eccentricity crosses over the line into heresy.

About eight months ago, I was with Bob Winters of the Prudential at a social function and he and I got chatting about the state of the world, and during the course of that discussion, he made a statement that made quite an impact on me at the time. The statement was that the minimum size economic life insurance company is a lot larger than it used to be, and it caused me to do a considerable amount of thinking. And one of the conclusions that I was led to was an evaluation that since the days of Abbey Life that Mike referred to in the introduction, in my view the minimum size middle market life insurance company in the United States measured in new sales is five times as big as it used to be — five times as big as it used to be — and all that's inflation adjusted. That's a constant dollar evaluation. Now, many companies in the space of the last 15 years or so have grown at a rate that is significantly less than that. Even if they had maintained market share, they've grown at a rate that is significantly less than that which would produce a five times growth in sales, and consequently, many companies that in 1970 could have comfortably said to themselves that they were then viable, face the position that today they are not any longer viable, simply because the threshold or the hurdle bar has been raised.

This, in turn, led me to give some thought as to the reasons why this had happened and what might be done about it. My conclusion was that primarily it had happened because the life insurance industry had moved over the last 15 years from a business that used to be almost exclusively a distribution driven business into a business which, today, is very importantly financially driven, that all of this had taken place because the business had moved from the position of a high margin industry to a position where margins were significantly under pressure. Well, that being the analysis, my next question was what could be done about it? And, I concluded that there were certain strategies that companies could adopt for survival and success, specifically that there were four and most interestingly, there are only four. In your outline, these appear in the notes and I'd just like to touch on them in passing. They are as follows:

- Strategies for Survival and Success, First Reduction of Cost, and that simply means an absolute cost reduction — nothing to do with, for example, changing volumes of sales but simply programs intended to reduce cost.
- The second is Nothing to Do with Expense Reductions. It's programs intended to increase sales, and it's important to distinguish between those two.
- The third — Programs to Increase Margins. A good old fashioned price increase that is so characteristic of other businesses and is almost unknown in our particular business.
- And finally, Programs Intended to Increase Investment Income, and that's the topic that I intend to address this afternoon — Programs Intended to Increase Investment Income.

Now, the most interesting thing about these four strategies is that there are indeed four, and there are only four. If you would like to think about an example of the implementation of these strategies, I would refer you to Lee Iaccoca's success in rescuing Chrysler. You can see in his activities at Chrysler examples of each of these four strategies, so it's not a question of strategies that are particular to the life insurance business.

Now, programs to increase investment income basically are the centerpiece of what I'm going to be talking about this afternoon, and what I am going to suggest to you is that you reexamine the question of what business we are really in. What is the essential business of the life insurance industry? Back in the days when I was with ITT, that organization still owned Avis, and I can recall about 15 years ago being present at an ITT business planning conference which was a much vaunted activity around ITT in those days, took place in the friendly little confines of a specially built meeting room about the size of three basketball courts, and one of the presentations that I listened to was that given by the president of Avis. And he got up and he said, "The first thing you've got to understand is the business we are really in." And I thought to myself, boy, that's pretty silly. There isn't a person in this room who hasn't rented an Avis car at least once, and here he is saying he's going to tell us what business he's in. And after a pause for breath, he says, "You think we're in the business of renting automobiles." He said, "That's not true. Renting automobiles is simply a complicated way of manufacturing used cars." Well, this set me to thinking about various businesses.

Let me tell you about an example that applies to the life insurance industry. About 10 years ago, a life insurance company became the subject of a purchase, and after the transaction had been agreed, Tillinghast was asked by the buyer to come in and assist with the post acquisition financial rearrangement of this company's affairs. One of the things we had to do in order to restate its accounts to a purchase accounting basis was to appraise the company. So we went in and did our appraisal, reported back to our client and said, "Yes, our appraisal indicates the company is worth about $300 million, and that's what you paid for it, so that looks pretty good. Oh, by the way, we noticed in the context of our work that you are losing money on your new business." Well, ten years passed, ten years later, history repeated itself and the company was again sold. Once again, the new buyer came to us and said, "Will you assist us with the purchase accounting restatement?" And we said, "Yes, we'll be glad to do that," and the first thing we had to do was go in and appraise the company which we did, and we reported back to our client and said, "Yes, the appraisal looks like $600 million which is about what you paid for the company. Oh, by the way, we noticed you're still losing money on new business." Well then we stopped. And we said now how did this happen? How did that company in the space of ten years go in value from $300 million to $600 million while losing money on new business, and in the meantime, paying its first owners dividends that were something in excess of $100 million? Well, this caused me to take a look at the situation, and I discovered the following facts.

Prior to the original sale, the then president of the company decided that it was about time that this company built a new head office building, and he thought it would be a particularly splendid idea if the new office could be located near his home. He happened to know of a tract of land consisting of quite a few acres that was for sale, and he was a tennis buff and thought well, it would be a good idea to have all that land — we can put tennis courts on it and the employees can play tennis. So, they bought the property. They put up the head office building, built the tennis courts and you can guess the rest of the story. A very large highway was in the process of being constructed near this property. Today, it's a major office park in a major retailing center. And if you examine the facts, you'll find that about $100 million of the increase in value of this company is associated with this single real estate transaction. So I wonder. Just what business are we in?

It's made me wonder, too, about the banking business. One hears about the banking business and its problems which are closely allied to issues such as having expensive branch premises and yet, if you examine it, you might reach the conclusion that being in the business of banking was only a complicated way of speculating in branch office real estate because I think you will find that most banks have handsome profits on the branch premises that they own. Probably, those profits on the branch premises are worth more to them than any losses they might have incurred as a result of being overbranched, as it were.

So what business are we really in? I wonder if mismatching isn't the business of life insurance. Mismatching. It's interesting to note for the actuaries in the audience, and I assume there are quite a few here, that when we make assumptions that go into pricing, our assumptions do not contemplate in most cases the kinds of things that actually happen in real life. The pricing assumptions of that company I described 10 years ago took no account of the fact that it might make $100 million profit in a real estate investment. And similarly today, our pricing assumptions take little or no account of what might happen to the investments that we actually make in the course of our business in the real world. We tend to price on the assumption that the underwriting company will be investing its entire portfolio in something like AA bonds, and I wonder if the actuarial profession needs to take another look at this.

Let's look at some of the history from the investment world. I do this in the general spirit of asking whether we can read anything from footprints in the sand. Does the past offer us any guide as to the future? Well, I think that the past does offer some general guides as to the future, and I thought it would be appropriate to briefly discuss with you some of the history of the investment differentials involved in different kinds of investments. Begin, for example, with common stocks versus short-term government securities. Statistical work has shown that over time the yield differential between common stocks and short-term government securities (this is total yield differential — it includes both dividend yield and price changes) — works out to be the equivalent of 6% per annum compound. Yield differential between common stocks and short-term government securities is a very, very large differential. Would that our business was so simple that we could get 6% spreads. If it weren't for those terrible people in the insurance departments worrying about solvency and the press, and so on and so forth, it seems that we could turn this into a no-brainer business quite easily. We just collect lots of money, and we invest the whole thing in the stock market, and over time, we'd have a differential in yield of 6%, and that would be enough to make everyone happy. But unfortunately, we can't dismiss all these outside forces quite that easily, but that's a big yield differential, 6%. Covers a lot of sins, as I will get to in a few minutes.

One can find somewhat similar but less extreme yield differentials in terms of quality premiums on debt securities and also illiquidity premiums and debt securities. It's clear that less than prime debt securities pay substantially higher yields, and securities which are illiquid pay higher yields also. The differentials for both quality and illiquidity probably are more than 1% over the normal — whatever normal might be — pricing differential you would expect. For example, the quality premiums that are involved in debt securities clearly exceed the risk charge for default by something like 1% or more and similar conclusions can be reached on illiquidity.

For many years, the banking industry has played an investment strategy that should be of some interest to the insurance industry today. It's a classic in mismatching. I call it tobogganing down the yield curve. And here is how it works. Let's suppose that the yield on one-year government securities is 7%, and the yield on two-year government securities is 8%. And the question for the bank is how to invest their money. Well, the classic banking strategy has been to invest in two-year securities and then after one year to sell them. Now, the rationale for what they're doing is this. The 8% yield on two-year securities can be viewed as 7% for the first year and 9% for the second year. What they're essentially trying to do is to — what I've described as toboggan down the yield curve — by realizing not only the 8% yield in maturity that they capture on the purchase of the 2-year security but also a 1% premium when it's sold one year into the transaction. That's been a classic investment strategy for the banking industry, and it's noteworthy that the insurance industry's investment portfolios are moving in a direction which is very similar to that that historically has been occupied by the banking industry, so tobogganing down the yield curve is another possible investment strategy.

Real estate historically has been a very profitable investment for financial institutions in this country. In this country unlike elsewhere, real estate tends to be somewhat more volatile. Historically, real estate has always been importantly influenced by tax considerations which today are in considerable ferment. Real estate may not be as satisfactory a vehicle from this point forward as it has been in the past but nevertheless, historically, it has been a very satisfactory investment.

Can we read the future from the past? Well, I'm not sure. It's true that history does not necessarily repeat itself, but that's not the same as saying that it won't. Given the preference, it would be my inclination to expect that history would come closer to repeating itself than it would the reverse.

Now, how does one go about managing the risk involved in deliberate mismatching of investments? Let's look at the volatility and implied capital requirements that are inherent in certain types of investments. Common stocks, which (I mentioned earlier) have historically outperformed short-term government securities by a 6% yield differential per annum, tend to move in a channel where the bottom of the channel is approximately 1/2 of the top of the channel, so price movements of common stocks tend to move in that channel where the bottom is about 1/2 the top. Now, that means at any time since one does not really know where one is in the channel, at any time, it's conceivable that a common stock movement of –50% or +100% is possible, and so obviously, an investment policy which stresses common stocks has got to take account of a very high degree of volatility that exists on these investments.

Now, there's an offset to this, and the offset is time. Most of us are familiar with the rule of 72 which tells us that at a 6% yield, money will double in 12 years. Well, let's suppose that one is involved in a common stock investment program and that one is unlucky enough to buy at the top and sell at the bottom — buy at the top, sell at the bottom. If there's an intervening period of 12 years, during that 12 year period, the excess differential of common stock investments over short-term governments will have provided an extra yield of 6% which will have provided a doubling of the underlying investment over that same 12 year period. In other words, 12 years should pay for a round trip from the top to the bottom of the market. Fixed interest investments until the 1970s were characterized by relatively low volatility, but in the 1970s, at least for many of the 10 years involved in that period, the beta of fixed interest investments actually was greater than that of common stocks. There was actually greater volatility in the bond market than in the stock market during many of the years of the 1970s.

Real estate is another investment that is somewhat volatile, but there's a tremendous offset in real estate investments that ought to interest financial institutions like life insurance companies. There is a high degree of flexibility in the valuation of real estate investments. There are points in time when real estate really is illiquid and when its value really is susceptible to a wide range of opinion. Nevertheless, in real terms, it has become acceptable for real estate investments to be valued on a basis that reacts in only a minor way to what actually may be taking place in the marketplace, so real estate as it operates in practice with flexibility of valuation tends to be a fairly nonvolatile investment in practice. One of the disadvantages of a mismatched investment policy is that if it works, it's likely to lead to the profits that are gained by it, emerging as capital gains rather than ordinary income. For those of you who are associated with stock life insurance companies, you've got to keep in mind that the financial analysts, the investment community at large, does not view capital gains very kindly. They are treated as less than par in terms of earnings impact, and I don't expect that will change any time in the future, so even if the strategy works, it's got to be borne in mind that the extra profits that are going to emerge from a mismatched strategy may well emerge substantially as capital gains on common stocks, real estate and so forth.

Where does responsibility begin and end? How far can a financial institution go in mismatching its assets? How much mismatching is permissible and responsible? How much capital does it take for any given degree of mismatching? And the most interesting question, and the one in which I'm trying to focus this afternoon, what is the opportunity cost if you don't mismatch? What is the opportunity cost if you don't mismatch? And I'm suggesting to you it is probably substantial.

The random walk theory, or the efficient market theory, was much favored by Academia as a view of financial markets in this country, at least until the last few years. There have been some changing views of Academia with respect to whether or not the efficient market theory is really right or wrong. One of the persuasive ways of stating the case for the efficient market theory is to say that you can't beat the market. One of the persuasive ways of suggesting that the efficient market theory may be wrong is to say, well, then you can't underperform the market either, can you? And it's a very nice question, and it's an unsettled question in Academia as to whether or not the efficient market theory is correct. I think that our responsibility as people involved in the management of financial institutions is to try to optimize the risk reward trade that's involved in choosing investments of various classes. In other words, optimizing the risk reward trade that's involved in any degree of mismatching, and I'm suggesting to you that you do not optimize with a matched position.

That is not the optimum position in my opinion. I think the opportunity cost of a fully matched position is quite substantial, and the trick is to optimize the risk reward trade that's involved in any degree of mismatching. In a zero sum game, it is, of course, possible that there may be winners, but it's not possible that everyone can be a winner in that zero sum game regardless of whether the market is efficient or not. The real choice is to choose the degree of mismatching that's appropriate for a particular set of circumstances.

Let's look briefly at a few case studies. I'm sure that everyone in this room could put a name to junk bond life. In fact, the heard-on-the-street column from the *Wall Street Journal* of a week ago yesterday did just that. Some of you may have seen it, some of you may have missed it. I'd like to read a few paragraphs out of this article that appeared a week ago yesterday:

> First Executive and its Chairman, Fred Carr, seemed to have gotten respect and something more. How that happened is an interesting story. Only two years ago, shares of the Beverly Hills, California company were a target of short sellers. They thought First Executive was headed the way of Baldwin United, a fast growing annuity writer that wound up in bankruptcy law proceedings. E. F. Hutton's 1984 move to stop selling First Executive's annuity sent the stock reeling, but First Executive coped pretty well....
>
> Mr. Carr still has detractors because he buys so many junk bonds. At year-end, securities of three low rated companies, including Metro Media, Triangle Industries, equaled 40% of First Executive's net worth....
>
> For now, low interest rates have dispelled concerns about First Executive's junk bonds. Currently, it's investing money at 11% or more, roughly 2 percentage points higher than the money market rates it pays policyholders. Other insurers show a much lower spread. It's easy to see why some former skeptics now are believers. Formed in 1969, First Executive ranks among the top 25 U.S. insurers. Its assets over 5 years have grown almost 60% annually compounded. It's per-share operating earnings almost 40%. First Executive is better capitalized than most financial companies. Its assets of roughly $9 billion rests on about $1 billion of equity, and it has no debt.

Well, one can argue at some length about this case study. One can argue that it speaks for itself, that it's a demonstration that such an investment strategy works. One can argue that this is a case of being in the right market at the right time and that under different circumstances, the story would have a very different ending. I don't intend to suggest an answer to that question this afternoon, but I do suggest that you examine the issues that were involved in the investment strategy that was undertaken quite consciously by that company several years ago.

The Baldwin United story had a different ending, but there the facts were also different and they're not all that widely understood. Much of the activity at Baldwin United was tax driven. The company had an ingenious chief executive and it had a tax strategy for every season. Unfortunately, some of those tax strategies began to unravel and that unraveling played a major role in the precipitation of the financial crisis which is insuited Baldwin United. Meanwhile, the company had mismatched in the most extreme of ways. It had, in fact, used the funds backing certain of its liabilities in what one might describe as venture capital investments. Now, that is rather extreme mismatching. To use, for example, annuity reserves as the basis of the funds to mount a takeover bid is some kind of extreme in the panoply of possible mismatching strategies. And finally, what eventually precipitated the crisis was that all of this caused a cash-flow crunch, so Baldwin United is not a simple and a straightforward story. It clearly did have an unhappy ending, just as unhappy as the First Executive story was happy. The circumstances of the two companies are interestingly different, and they make a good twin study case.

Lessons can also be learned from what's going on abroad. In the United Kingdom and Australia, it is not at all unusual to find companies there that have very different liabilities by the way with well over 50% of their assets invested in equities and real estate, and that has given rise to a very successful industry in both of those countries, an industry that's been successful in large measure because it has actually delivered good value for money to its policyholders, and that was attributable to the success of its investment policy.

There are some sad stories abroad as well. Perhaps the saddest is Nation Life which set another record in mismatching. Nation Life during the property boom of the early 1970s in the United Kingdom which Mike Tuohy and I remember very well because we were trying to rent an office in London at that particular time and prime rental rates — this is twelve years ago — were about $200 a square foot at that time, as I recall. So there was an unrequited property boom in progress, and Nation Life managed to seize hold of a large single property located in Bornemouth on the south coast of England, and it bought this property at a very high price on the general theory that it could be developed. And it found that it was completely surrounded by properties that were protected by law in the U.K. This is rather like buying the Lincoln Memorial with the idea of putting a giant skyscraper on the site, and it came unglued in a very significant way, and I believe became the first life insurance company in the U.K. to actually go into liquidation for well over 100 years.

So the stories are mixed. There are some successes, there are some failures. Mismatched life is often a winner, but mismatched life needs adequate capital in order to be a sustained winner.

It's worth looking at the policyholders' viewpoints and also the shareholders' viewpoints in all of this. The policyholder expectations, when he buys a pooled investment, which is really what life insurance products are all about, policyholder expectations are that he gains a degree of liquidity by participating in this pooled investment, while meanwhile the underlying assets can be invested in a way that is not necessarily fully liquid, and on that basis, the policyholder expects to be able to enjoy a higher rate of return, and the financial institution sponsoring the pool expects to be able to make a reasonable spread. The policyholder who is investing for the long term and all of the permanent life insurance products that are sold in this country are sold from a long-term perspective really needs to consider investments other than AA type investments. There is, I think, a very important role for variable life insurance in the future because that product permits the policyholder to take advantage of that 6% yield differential that I mentioned available on common stock investments. Necessarily, all of this is importantly restrained by regulation in this country, more so than in most countries. The asset restrictions that are applicable in the United States to the investments of the life insurance industry are probably the toughest of any of the developed countries in the world. The shareholder's expectation also plays a role in all of this, and it would seem to me looking around the scene today that the shareholders generally expect a minimum return on equity of about 12%. If that doesn't happen, it's likely that the stock of a life insurance company earning less than 12% will sell at a discount in the marketplace. If that happens, the company will be worth more dead than alive, and this will invite the interest of a raider. So achieving acceptable rates of return is also important from the shareholder point of view.

My conclusions are pretty simple and straightforward. I think that the safety first investment strategy of full matching will not work. I do not think that the premium margins available on the life insurance industry today are adequate to support reasonable expectations of shareholders, of policyholders, or of anyone else. An AA investment strategy, in my opinion, will not work in today's circumstances. This is especially true if a company also attempts to match by term. I think that the fully matched investment position is fundamentally a losing game. The winning game, I would suggest, is rational risk taking, and this really brings us full circle to why you're here today. You're here to talk about matching, about examining the nature of the liabilities on contracts that are issued by the insurance industry. Well, what you're really doing is not trying to understand the nature of those liabilities in order to then turn around and exactly match them. I think that is a losing strategy. What is needed is to understand the nature and term of the liabilities for the purpose of establishing a baseline for the purpose of determining to what extent the company should then mismatch. I think that the winning play is in rational risk taking which seeks to optimize the relationship between the degree of mismatching and the potential risks and rewards involved in that degree of mismatching. And for this you need a par score card. And that really is the subject of this seminar.

The title talked about fun. Well, the fun of mismatching is mainly in the profit provided it works. Thank you very much.

Section 5
International

Employee Benefits and Risk Management: A Worldwide Perspective

Published in EMPHASIS, *December 1983. Reprinted with permission from Tillinghast - A Towers Perrin Company.*

This special issue of EMPHASIS is composed entirely of a speech made by James C. H. Anderson before the Association of Canadian Pension Management in Toronto, Canada, on November 22, 1983. Mr. Anderson is the managing principal of Tillinghast. He has been a senior executive of Georgia International Corporation, managing director of Abbey Life, and president of Abbey International Corporation.

Introduction

The interest of an audience of Canadian pension managers in such a wide ranging topic as indicated by the title of these remarks must lie in the desire to profit from new developments, be they successes or failures, occurring in other parts of the world which may have application to the situation in Canada. In preparing to deal with this topic, I have relied extensively upon a number of my associates, particularly Richard Lawrey of our London office and Charles T. Tagman, Jr. of our Boston office, who specialize in the international employee benefits and risk management fields, respectively.

Let me begin by defining the scope of this discussion of two seemingly unrelated topics:

1. Employee benefits are the various programs in all countries intended to provide sums of money payable either as lump sums or as a continuation of

income to employees unable to work because of old age, prolonged ill health or death; in some countries, privately sponsored programs which provide reimbursement for the cost of medical care are an important employee benefit which interrelates with similar government programs.

2. Risk management has been defined in many different ways but for the purpose of this discussion, risk management is the function which is responsible for identifying and evaluating property and liability risk hazards. The function then extends to minimizing risk through appropriate loss prevention procedures (such as sprinklers in buildings, product safety, employee safety, etc.) and to providing for the residual risks through either self-insurance or risk transfer, which is typically to an insurance company.

The two tangential points of these seemingly unrelated subjects are in the areas of loss control and funding by the employer, where self-insurance and insurance are the two alternative options and where the tax and cash-flow consequences of each are major considerations in determining the better choice.

Employee Benefits

Employee benefits payable on retirement, disability or death are generally provided in one of three ways: (1) via a social security program; (2) via an employer sponsored plan; and (3) via private provision made by the employee.

Worldwide differences tend to occur in the total level of provisions made for employee benefits and in the relative importance of each of these components. The Swiss refer to these components as the "three pillars of retirement income."

Let us begin by examining social security programs. In Canada, social security began in 1927, 19 years after the U.K. program was introduced and 38 years after the first social security system was originated in Germany by Bismark in 1889. The U.S. only began its program in 1935.

Social security programs initially provided income at a relatively low level in the event of sickness, disability, death or retirement. However, in some countries, notably in Europe, levels of social security benefits have grown over time to such a degree that there is need in some countries for supplementary employee plans for only the highly-paid employees. In Spain, for example, the social security benefits can reach 70% of earnings and the maximum benefit is equal to around two or more times national average earnings.

Since World War II, there has been a tendency for governments to respond to pressure to raise social security benefits and, during the post-war period, the demographic structure made it possible to do this without creating undue pressure on contribution rates because many workers supported few retirees. The short-term nature of a government's term of office has also been a major factor contributing to its willingness to increase social security benefits since associated tax increases are only required at a later stage! Now however, the tide has turned — falling birth rates and a rising population of pensioners, unforeseen by the experts in the 1960s based on fertility and longevity trends observed at that time, are starting to push social security contribution rates up. Improvements in health care, wide-spread contraception and increased divorce rates have also been contributing factors. This means that in the context of a pay as-you-go social security system, there will be fewer persons employed to pay the contribution needed to support benefits of a rising number of claimants. Although this demographic trend has not yet gathered full force in Canada, the same position will be reached a few years later than elsewhere.

To exacerbate the problem, high levels of unemployment are being experienced through the developed world; these seem unlikely to abate to their former level without fundamental future change in the way that we work. The presence of unemployment lends momentum to the concepts of job-sharing and earlier retirement both of which will have a greater impact on the burden of social security programs. In France, for example, the age at which full social security pensions can be claimed was recently reduced from age 65 to age 60, presumably to address the unemployment problem. The persons who made up the baby bulge at the end of World War I are now between the ages of 60 and 65 and, by the French government's latest move, many have been removed from the contributor category and have joined the beneficiary category. The results which will follow are self-evident.

Finally, to make matters even worse, people are living longer today and are likely to live even longer in the future. A 65-year-old male currently has around a 17-year life expectancy, and it is realistic to expect that figure to reach 20 years fairly soon.

Social security systems in their current forms seem unlikely to withstand these pressures. Ultimately, of course, a stable relationship between social security benefits and the salaries of active workers depends on there being sufficient growth in the economy to satisfy the needs of both categories of people. In the U.K. some of the burden of social security has recently been shifted to the private sector. A new component was added to social security in 1978 and employers with pension plans satisfying a minimum standard were allowed to opt out of the additional part and pay lower taxes. It is in some ways surprising that other countries have not followed this route to ensure that the objectives of social security (i.e., universal coverage and a minimum floor level of benefits) can be maintained in the face of growing pressures from demographic and economic forces.

The increasing number of social security benefit recipients and the decreasing numbers of contributors to those same programs will cause governments to choose among these three options:

1. to increase social security taxes and/or general taxation;
2. to decrease social security benefits; or
3. to do both.

Recent experience suggests that we should prepare for option 3!

In Europe and North America this has already started. For example, Germany and the U.K. have within the last four years reduced the extent to which their social security benefits are inflation-proof, and both have increased social security taxes substantially. In the United States, the most recent amendments to the social security program limited certain benefits and increased taxes; notably, the retirement age is now scheduled to rise gradually to 67. So far as social security is concerned, we must, therefore, expect to pay more and to receive less than is promised today.

Turning now to employer sponsored programs, company pensions began to gain popularity in Europe and North America in the 1930s and 1940s. Once corporate tax relief was introduced on employer contributions, growth was greatly stimulated. Contributing further to the growth in several countries was the period of price and wage controls during and after World War II, from which certain benefit programs were exempt. At this early stage, the impact of inflation had not yet been conceived let alone understood and the early plans tended to be of the career average benefit design.

Governments gave tax concessions to pension plans not only to encourage employers to take an interest in employee welfare but also to take pressure off social security systems. Over the interwar and post-war years, coverage of pension plans increased steadily with defined benefit pension plans becoming more popular than defined contribution plans primarily for three reasons:

1. past service credit was given to existing employees who may have been instrumental in founding the sponsoring company;
2. lower benefits, if any, were allocated to leavers before retirement age; any benefits were usually based on service and salary at the date of leaving with no allowance made for future pre- or post-retirement inflation; and
3. employers had almost total flexibility in the way that they financed the plan.

In the 1960s, inflation began to accelerate, earlier in Europe than in North America. With the advent of significant inflation came pressure from employees for a move away from average pay plans towards final pay plans. At a time of strong corporate profits (aided by accounting policies which did not recognize the effects of high inflation) projections then showed these final pay based benefits to be affordable — especially with long vesting periods, no minimum funding standards, increasing interest rates and no post-retirement inflation linking of pensions. Thus, employee pressure for improved benefits was generally difficult to resist, particularly in industries with strong labor organizations.

Today, pensioners, active members of company pension plans, the media, unions and politicians are applying pressure on employers to recognize the "inequity" of reduced pension benefits on early termination and retirement pensions which do not increase with inflation. They are seeking more regulations to close these so-called loopholes. Minimum vesting standards and minimum funding standards have already arrived in the U.S., the U.K. and most of Europe. Minimum benefit standards can be expected to become general. Companies are also being required to recognize the reduction in the real value of fixed pensions in times of inflation; in Germany and the United Kingdom there already are regulations in effect or pending on this subject.

The accountants are also attempting to limit companies' flexibility in the way in which they fund their pension plans. In particular they are seeking to standardize the amount of pension contribution that must be charged against corporate income each year; in the U.S. there have been standards of accounting practice in this area since 1968. Ultimately, this may also have an effect on the tax deductible contribution allowed the employer by the taxation authorities and the resultant loss of flexibility could be a further factor contributing to the reduction in popularity of defined benefit pension plans from the employer's viewpoint.

The problems suffered by social security have their counterparts affecting defined benefit pension plans sponsored by employers. There are, however, some significant differences. Most occupational pension plans are funded; thus, the retirement benefits paid to members are derived from contributions paid in the past during the working life of those members. In contrast, social security programs are unfunded; the benefits paid today come from today's contributions. Thus, the adverse trends in the numerical relationship of pensioners to contributors have a direct effect on required social security contributions but not generally on occupational pension plan costs.

There is, however, an indirect relationship. The funding schemes for occupational pensions require an appropriate investment return on capital in order to provide the benefits promised; generally, this requires a return in excess of the inflation rate. That return must be provided from the efforts of the collective economy in the form of an adequate real return on capital. Unless the present work force can sufficiently expand the economy, those who are employed in 20, 30 or 40 years time may not be prepared to see an ever increasing proportion of the total output of goods and services being expended to service the accumulated capital of those who have already retired and those about to retire. We may see them flexing their economic muscle in such a way that the capital set aside for retirement does not earn that real rate of return which was required. Signs of this are already apparent — for example, the demand that governments "do something about interest rates." Excess competition for goods and services within a static economy only produces inflation which, for those whose income is not inflation proofed, makes it difficult to compete and is likely to reduce the real return on capital.

If real rates of return decline then the cost of defined benefit plans will increase or benefits will decrease in real value. This is the counterpart to the demographically induced cost spiral in social insurance programs. This will reinforce the trend which is already well established in the United States toward defined contribution plans and away from defined benefit plans.

The two trends already outlined (i.e., financial pressure in social security programs and the trend away from defined benefit pension plans) can both be seen as part of a more general trend: the shift of responsibility and risk onto the individual and away from the state and the employer.

If this trend is to continue we can expect to see growth in the flexibility and choice provided in employee benefit programs — a move towards the so-called cafeteria plan and an increase in the opportunity for individuals to save for retirement in a tax effective manner. In case any of you are not familiar with cafeteria plans, I will quickly run through the menu. The principle is simple — every employee has a level of total remuneration, salary plus cost of benefits. He is then able to choose his own distribution of that remuneration among salary, death benefits, disability benefits, medical care costs, pension benefits, vacations and so on, in the particular mix that suits him. There are normally some limitations placed on the distribution of this remuneration either by taxation or other regulation, or by the employer or plan administrator for personnel reasons: an accountant who took six months vacation a year, in lieu of all other benefits, might not be too popular!

The trend by governments and employers towards providing opportunities for individuals to save tax effectively for retirement is evidenced in the U.S. by the emergence of 401(k) plans, designed to accommodate the cafeteria concept, which recently seem to have superseded Individual Retirement Accounts in their attractiveness. In the U.K. increasing use is made of tax-sheltering opportunities provided by so-called additional voluntary contributions or AVC schemes and by insured retirement annuity policies. In Canada, Registered Retirement Savings Plans have existed for many years and have expanded in scope over time. If individuals are to take greater responsibility for their own retirement benefit planning, they will expect to be assured of a fair return on the money they have set aside. They personally, rather than the sponsors of defined benefit pension plans, now will have a direct interest in ensuring that a real rate of return is earned on funds set aside for retirement;

they can be expected to share the traditional viewpoint of the capitalist, whose ranks they have joined!

Given the growing importance and political sensitivity of the issues involved, we should not expect any reduction in the way of regulations that govern pension plans; in particular, we can expect to see regulations reducing vesting periods in plans of all types and possibly also requiring some element of inflation proofing in those defined benefit plans that continue. Of one thing I am certain: governments will expend greater efforts in the field of employee benefits but they will not direct those efforts toward simplification but rather towards more regulation.

Because it aptly illustrates the link between employee benefits and risk management, let me touch now on one other major employee benefit in certain countries — the medical plan. There has been a tendency to design medical plans without concern for whether the risk assumed is or is not soundly insurable. This has led to plans being established where the benefit structure is quite liberal and where the claim levels are influenced by both the employee and by the medical profession. The plan itself often creates the situation where a patient's need for accurate diagnosis and treatment is no longer tempered by his ability to pay for the cost of medical techniques, which meanwhile have grown in both sophistication and cost.

In the United States a medical plan may cost more to operate on an annual basis than a pension plan. It is little wonder that in the United States there is in progress an extensive reexamination of the role of the employer in providing medical care for its employees. The same is true of government sponsored plans where, unfortunately, the "solution" has been to shift costs to the private sector! It is interesting to note that the techniques of loss control and alternative funding currently being developed in U.S. medical plans are totally consistent with risk management techniques developed originally in the property and liability field.

Risk Management

For many corporations, the name of the game is called "cash flow." There is increased interest on the part of senior financial management in making its risk management programs as cash-flow sensitive as possible. What does that mean to the corporation? Specifically, it means that the corporation is unwilling to allow insurance companies to hold its reserves for losses when the cash can be better utilized inside the corporation. I see, therefore, a continuing growth in self-insurance and captive insurance systems which essentially provide "pay as you go" coverage to the corporation. I also see a challenge to the insurance industry to develop innovative risk transfer programs with similar financial characteristics.

As an interesting statistic, in 1970 in the U.S., self-insurance and captives represented only 6% or $1 billion of the $15.6 billion commercial property and liability insurance market. By 1980, this same figure had grown to $14 billion or 22% of a $62.7 billion commercial property and casualty market. I suspect there are statistics which would demonstrate equivalent or greater growth of self-insurance in the employee benefits area during this same period.

I expect that, as the dollars involved continue to grow larger, the trend toward increased use of self-insurance and captives will continue, although the movement has recently slowed because the existing "soft" insurance market is offering bargain rates on many coverages.

Certainly on the worldwide front, astute financial managers are looking at captives and other financial mechanisms to attain optimum financial accounting and tax objectives while keeping the funds "in house." As a specific illustration, consider the growing number of captive insurance companies formed by multinational corporations not only to insure their property and liability programs but also to insure their worldwide employee benefit programs. Many multinational companies already have subsidiary insurance companies located normally in low tax areas such as Bermuda. Traditionally, these have been property and liability insurers but there is now a growing trend toward diversification into the insurance of employee benefit risks of international subsidiary and associated companies, particularly as related to third country nationals.

Spiralling insurance costs, unavailable coverages, growing exposures and governmentally mandated liability brought the issue of property and liability risk management to the forefront only in the last decade. Although some of these issues have been quieted, there are a number of social and economic forces that continue to impact the function. Although my comments might currently be most applicable to United States' corporations, a number of these factors impact any corporation doing business on a multinational level, without regard for country of origin.

Although the difficult insurance marketplace of the 1970s stimulated the growth of risk management function, the soft worldwide insurance market of the 1980s is providing it an opportunity to be refined. Because of the soft insurance market the risk manager is able to accomplish more in the design of the corporate insurance programs because underwriters are quite willing to improve terms and conditions and, frequently, reduce cost at the same time. Events like the MGM Grand fire, the Kansas City Hyatt collapse, and the asbestos litigation have forced the risk manager to look very closely at the structure and limits of existing insurance program. Many corporations have concluded that the traditional $50 million or $100 million level of umbrella coverage is inadequate and are now seeking limits in the $200 million, $500 million and even $1 billion range. These limits are available in today's marketplace; however, it is valid to question whether such capacity will be available should the insurance market return to more nearly normal conditions.

The trend towards the growth of service companies has resulted in the need to look at insurance protection requirements quite differently. Traditional insurance companies and banks are finding themselves in the position of owners or lessors of airplanes, owners and managers of civic arenas, hotels, and shopping centers. Computer consulting companies can be doing simulation studies on bridge stress, aerodynamics and water quality. Many financial institutions are selling stocks, giving investment advice, selling software systems and providing management services to other financial institutions. Certainly errors and omissions exposures and coverage needs have extended to a much greater sector of their business community than in the past where it was traditionally carried only by lawyers, engineers, accountants — and actuarial consultants!

I expect that high interest rates will prolong the soft insurance market and will foster continuing demands that insurance funding mechanisms for the large insurance buyer be more cash-flow effective. I also expect an increasing demand for safer products and working conditions which will provide a new emphasis on loss prevention activities. The design of cost effective employee benefit programs is one of these activities. In both the risk management and employee benefits area it is finally becoming recognized that the best way to control cost is to control losses. I believe the merging financial aspects of employee benefits and risk management will command growing attention of management in the coming years.

The Future

I believe it is no exaggeration to say that employee benefits, already a major social and political issue in many countries, will grow in significance and is likely to become the primary domestic political issue of the early 21st century throughout the developed world. Because of its magnitude, major efforts will be directed by both governments and employers towards the containment and control of costs, using techniques developed originally in the field of risk management.

The arguments favoring this view, which some may find startling, are overwhelming:

1. The demographics point clearly towards increased longevity and in many developed countries fertility rates are already below those required for Zero Population Growth. Even a significant increase in birth rates would not now alter the serious demographic problems which will arrive in the early part of the 21st century: the shape of the population curve is already substantially determined and the relationship indicated is that there will be no more than three active workers to support each retired worker plus all other dependent members of the population.
2. There is a widespread, nearly universal, lack of appreciation of the ultimate cost of "adequate" retirement benefits. Governments in particular have experienced years of unrealistically low costs for social security programs because it was not appreciated that a "Ponzi Scheme" was in progress as long as the work force expanded at least as rapidly as the retired population. This is no longer true and current estimates of the ultimate cost levels of existing social security programs are in the range of 20% to 30% of total income of active workers.
3. Further exacerbating the problem of an unrealistic appreciation of ultimate cost levels has been the effect on future expectations fostered by the rapid

growth in living standards experienced in most of the developed world during the period 1950–1970. Nowhere was this more apparent than in most of Europe and parts of Asia. Recently, from 1973 onwards, the growth of living standards has been disappointing and in many countries there actually occurred periods of decline since 1973. Contributing to the disappointing growth in living standards have been:

a. historically high unemployment, caused in no small measure by higher labor costs, including increasing retirement benefit costs;
b. historically high inflation;
c. competition from less developed countries, particularly in basic industries;
d. the energy cartel and the massive international wealth transfer generated by it; and
e. the rising cost of "involuntaries," those nongratifying elements of consumption including items such as medical care, insurance and the cost of crime.

These forces are requiring a reexamination of reasonable economic expectations throughout the Western World. In many countries, economic progress has often been measured by growth in numbers of the "middle class," usually defined in terms of income. Today, some commentators are describing a smaller "new middle class," defined in terms of those able to afford to own their own housing. Tomorrow's definition may be that still smaller group — those able to retire at the traditional age of 65 with an adequate and secure retirement income!

4. Social trends have also played an important role in altering the retirement income needs of the general population. The breakdown of traditional family units, manifested by rising divorce rates, marriage alternatives, two income families and increasing numbers of single householders, has led to the irrelevance of concepts which have long formed the framework of both social security plans and employer sponsored programs. Closely related are rising social concerns in the area of women's rights which have focused particularly on economic issues related to employment, including employee benefits. At least in the United States, this trend has been substantially reinforced by recent Supreme Court decisions which relate directly to

sex discrimination in employee benefit programs; in addition, legislation is now pending before Congress which would mandate unisex pricing of all insurance programs, notably life annuities, which relate closely to the field of employee benefits. The net result of all of these forces will be a further increase in demands on retirement programs of all types.

5. In political terms in the Western World, the ultimate reality is the ballot box. In areas such as Florida and Arizona, where the retired population is relatively large, the term "gray power" is already familiar at election time. The rising proportion of retired and soon-to-be-retired individuals in the voting age population is likely to ensure that issues of importance to that group will occupy center stage on the political scene. At least in the United States, and probably in most of the Western World where voting is not compulsory, retirees are more likely to vote than other members of the population, further increasing their potential political power.

As already indicated, government response to date has taken the form of increased taxation, arresting benefit escalation and cost shifting from the public to the private sector. Clearly, these trends will continue but will they go far enough and can the private sector absorb its increased cost? A former actuary of the Social Security Administration in the United States, A. Haeworth Robertson, published in 1981 a book entitled *The Coming Revolution in Social Security* which contains a lucid discussion of the many issues involved in the existing social security program in the United States, along with a proposal for its overhaul which he calls the "Freedom Plan." Interestingly, he suggests the substitution of a flat benefit for an income related benefit and further suggests funding from general revenues rather than specific payroll taxes. Among the more arresting of his observations is what he calls "The Impossible Dream" — his term for the popular concept of a universal program which provides adequate and secure retirement income. Rightly, he points out that ultimately there must be some rational relationship between the number of active workers and those who are retired or otherwise dependent. Without such a relationship, the goal of adequate retirement security is indeed "The Impossible Dream."

What clearly is needed is an increase in the age at which people expect to be able to retire. It is noteworthy that a change of retirement age from 65 to

70 would alter the ratio of active to retired workers from approximately three to one to approximately five to one, and the consequent cost of any retirement program, expressed as a fraction of the income of active workers, would reduce by approximately 40%.

The retirement age is the rational way to balance the equation. But there is an alternative fulcrum — the rate of inflation. If retirement programs have a cost in excess of what is tolerable by the active work force, including the cost of servicing capital accumulated by funded plans, that cost will be reduced through the manifestation of inflationary pressures caused by powerful and organized elements of the active work force with demands for a "larger piece of the pie." You may wonder, "Does not indexation eliminate this possibility?" My reply is "no" — if a 10% annual rate of inflation is required to balance the economic equation without indexation, and if generalized indexation is introduced with, say, monthly adjustments, it simply means that the equilibrium rate of inflation becomes, say, 10% a month instead of 10% a year. In fact, indexation applied on a widespread basis to an environment requiring an equilibrium rate of inflation simply sows the seeds of Weimar, where wages were paid twice a day and where the semi-daily rate of inflation reached 5%. The same phenomenon, which the OECD describes as "self-propelling hyper-inflation," can be observed in the current experience in many countries where indexation is quite general — such as Brazil, Argentina and Israel. The reverse of this phenomenon can be seen today in Iceland, where indexing was quite general until recently and where the annual inflation rate dropped from 130% (i.e. 7% per month) to an expected annual rate of less than 10%.

Recently, I was asked to speak by the Society of Actuaries in Ireland and, prompted by the recent spectacular collapse of a prominent auto insurer in that country, I decided to discuss the control of financial institutions. To this group, I would suggest that private pension plans are among the financial institutions that will be extensively controlled by governments to a greater degree in the future than has been the case in the past. The arguments already advanced suggest that pension funds may become the most important of financial institutions (if they are not already) and regulation should be expected in such areas as standards of benefit design, required funding and the control of investments. While further government intrusion into the affairs of private pension funds should rightly be regarded with considerable suspicion, it would be unrealistic not to expect it. This suggests that the efforts of those who are centrally involved in the issue of employee benefits should concentrate their efforts on channeling the inevitable incursions of government in constructive directions.

Let me illustrate with one example drawn from the area of pension fund investments. In the United States today one can observe a phenomenon which might be described as "asset stripping" which involves pension funds. Companies have been the subject of takeover bids which can largely be financed by releasing the accumulated surplus funds of their pension plans. At the other end of the spectrum, companies that have mounted takeovers or are involved in "leveraged buyouts" (a self-takeover by management and, sometimes, other employees financed by large borrowings) are sometimes using, in both cases, funds accumulated in existing retirement plans or funds to be accumulated in newly established retirement plans, such as Employee Stock Ownership Plans (ESOPs). I did not come here today to say whether or not any of these activities is right or wrong, but I am convinced that all will someday be regulated to a greater degree than is now the case — and not only in the United States. It is interesting to note the variance in investment regulation and philosophy in various countries — strict in the United States and Canada (particularly with respect to related party investments), permissive in the United Kingdom (but with disclosure), even more permissive in much of Europe (where the balance sheet liability approach to pension funding is quite common) and insular in South Africa, New Zealand and Australia (where pension funds are required to hold 30% of assets in government and near-government securities). In many if not most developed countries, pension funds are already the largest repository of long-term capital and it is clear that the investment of these substantial and growing funds does involve issues of public interest. The question is how best will the public interest be served?

Conclusion

My recent travels to a number of different countries have reinforced my view as to the growing importance and sensitivity of issues related to the fields of employee benefits and risk management. The subject of future regulation in the area of employee benefits must be one of central interest to this audience which is uniquely situated to influence the course of events in Canada. This will not be an easy process, particularly in Canada where special constitutional problems, relating to the relative roles of the Federal and Provincial governments, must be addressed.

Because the cost of employee benefits, whether publicly sponsored or privately sponsored, is certain to rise to very high levels, very soon, the importance of insuring that maximum benefit is achieved for each dollar expended obviously increases proportionately. In the future, those involved in the field of employee benefits profitably can draw upon the experience of their counterparts in the field of risk management, who are already addressing similar issues, albeit primarily in the area of property and liability risks.

The Changing Financial Services Scene

Presented to a Tillinghast Seminar, London, England, February 27, 1985.

Ladies and gentlemen, good afternoon. And, Michael, as for your introduction, the usual melange of flattery, some truth, the rest actionable! It's always a pleasure for me to have the opportunity to speak to people who are interested in or involved in the financial service business in various parts of the world and particularly, somewhat for the reasons that Mike mentioned — some of the true statements he mentioned — I'm particularly interested in having this opportunity to speak to you here today in London. My general topic is the changing financial services scene, and I am going to be discussing this from the perspective of several different countries because I think there is much to be learned about what's going on in each. The subject is a big one — the treatment will necessarily therefore be somewhat superficial.

Let me begin by talking briefly about the manifestations of change and I do so, I know, at the risk of preaching to the converted. I am familiar with what's going on in the financial services scene in five different countries — in Australia, in Canada, in South Africa, in the United States and here in the U.K. And in each of those countries there are great changes afoot. Let me give you just a few examples to put you in the mood.

First of all, I think you have to begin by asking what is the role of banks in each of these markets and how is the role of banks being redefined in the whole of the financial services world. Well, in Australia they are in the process of ending a long standing oligopoly in the banking business. You will get some disagreement from Australians when you ask them how many banks there are in their country — you get numbers ranging from three upwards. The government has announced that it will soon issue approximately six licenses; they are looking at about 40 applications and it is fairly clear that major changes are afoot in the banking world in Australia. In the U.S. we are probably going to see nationwide banking in the next few years and some of you may not appreciate just what that means. In the United States, believe it or not, there are 15,000 banks and, no, I did not get my decimal in the wrong place. There are 15,000 banks. These banks have essentially been forced into watertight compartments by the force of regulation in the U.S. I'll tell you one tale to give you an example of how this works. As you may know, drive-in banking has been with us for quite some time in the U.S. I expect you probably have it here as well where you simply drive your automobile up to an armoured glass cage, and you do your transaction without getting out of your car. Well, Texas has something called unitary banking, and under unitary banking law, the bank is allowed to have exactly one branch, one physical location. One of the major banks in Dallas decided that it would be a pretty good idea to put a drive-in window in the corner of their parking lot and they were immediately sued by their competitors and charged with opening another branch. So, nationwide banking will be a big step in the United States. It's already gone some distance. You will be not surprised, I am sure, to learn that it's already reached the Supreme Court which shows you just how far it's gone.

These changes in the banking business cause me to ask the question, "Are the sleeping giants going to wait?" And I think that's a question that has particular relevance here in the U.K. where you already have very concentrated nationwide banking. A few years ago back, during the Vietnam era, you will remember the folk song that had in it the line "Where have all the flowers gone?" Well, I have a question for you this afternoon: "Where have all the stockbrokers gone?" Ten years ago some changes happened in the United States, changes that are similar to those that are on the cards here in the U.K. today. These have to do with the whole subject of negotiated commissions on the stock exchange, and all of this has very much to do with the economics of the stockbroking business. All of that is, I think, pretty well known and pretty widely understood. What you may not understand as well is the fact that it is likely in my mind that you are going to see emerge here something that we in the States call the second, third and fourth markets. And these have reference to dealings in securities that take place off the national exchanges, where, essentially securities dealers act as principal in the sale of securities, and one of the things that happens when one moves into an environment where the second, third and fourth markets become important factors in addition to the auction market of the stock exchange is that the capital requirements of people engaged in the securities business increased quite dramatically. Suddenly they must maintain inventories of stocks. I think that the capital requirements of stockbroking have more than a little to do with what you are seeing happening here in the U.K. at this time with more and more financial institutions taking major interests in stockbroking firms, and obviously since these firms tended to be privately owned for the most part you can't explain it all by saying, "Well, these are unwelcome deals or unwelcome takeovers." Obviously, they have been takeovers that have been welcomed.

Further evidence of what's going on — one could speculate that perhaps in much of the western world, particularly in those countries that I name at the outset, we may be seeing the emergence of the new Anglicised zaibatsu. We're seeing, I believe, major change take place in the deployment of capital resources and I'd like to remind you on the way by of the relative magnitude of the capital resources involved in certain businesses. I'll use an analogy from the U.S. to illustrate the point. The largest life insurance company in the United States is the Prudential Insurance Company of America, capital funds approximately 3 billion dollars. That may surprise you as being as low as it is. The largest insurance organisation of any kind is State Farm, basically a general insurance company, capital resources around 8 billion. The largest bank is Citibank, capital resources around 5 billion. One of the interesting competitors in the financial services world today, an important competitor, is Sears, capital resources 10 billion. IBM earns almost that much in one year.

Recently there was an article in the *Wall Street Journal* that caught my eye. It had to do with General Motors and their strategic plan. Some of you may be generally aware of the fact that GM about a year ago acquired a very unusual company in Dallas called EDS. This is Ross Perot's operation and there has been an interesting recent book published about Ross Perot's personal organisation of a rescue mission for some of the EDS people that wound up in an Iranian jail. Mr. Carter should have let him run his operation! In any case GM acquired EDS and I am told that the cultural change at GM has been enormous. EDS basically is a computer operation; General Motors is in the process, deeply into the process, of moving its entire computer operation into EDS and it is not taking with it GM's culture. They are deliberately changing the culture of that aspect of GM's operation. They have recently made noises that suggest that a diversification into the financial service business is something that they have in mind too — the new zaibatsu.

Takeovers and mergers — the news has been very considerable on both sides of the Atlantic on this front, as well as in the other countries I have mentioned. Something that has not yet been in the news to any great extent but which I expect to be in the news increasingly in the future is the whole subject of demutualisation. One major demutualisation is in progress, involving a U.S. large insurance company. I would predict that several will happen here involving U.K. life insurance companies, and it is my understanding that legislation is now in place that permits the demutualisation of building societies. I think that's something we will also see. So, this is a very brief survey of some of the manifestations of change, and I suggest that this leads to the questions that I'm going to spend the rest of the time on, which are as follows.

First of all, the question is no longer "if" and the question is no longer even "when." The questions that I think are relevant now are "why," "how" and "who."

Let's look first at "why." Why has all of this been happening? Well, clearly some part of it, a large part in the United States and at variable parts elsewhere, has to do with the whole issue of deregulation of financial businesses. And that in turn has much to do with an almost worldwide shift that I see having taken place in government attitudes towards businesses of various types and towards taxation as well. So deregulation and government attitudes I think are major factors that are visible to some extent or other in all countries and in all sectors of the financial services world. For example, particularly in the U.S., there used to be the philosophy that big was necessarily bad. Major lawsuits were launched by the Department of Justice against IBM and against

AT&T for no other reason than that those companies were large — major anti-trust litigation launched by the Department of Justice — and the theory clearly was big is bad. All of that litigation interestingly has been settled in the last few years and the clear attitude, at least in Washington today, is that big is tolerable. Big is no longer bad, not good yet, but big is tolerable. We also are hearing, almost everywhere in the world, talk of so-called fiscal neutrality — that mythical level playing field on which all financial service companies will do battle. Well, I'd like to ask you a question — just who do you expect to be the surveyor of that level playing field? Just who do you expect to survey it? I think that there's far too much said that is not really meant about level playing fields. I think everyone wants his goal up on the highest possible hill and I think he wants his opponent's goal somewhere down in the valley and that all this talk about level playing fields is really quite an exercise in hypocrisy. But talk must have got through to certain places in government circles because I can tell you personally, from exposure to the Treasury Department under the current regime in Washington, that fiscal neutrality is indeed on their minds.

Another thing that is clearly on the minds of government is a reduction in marginal tax rates. You've had a major reduction in marginal tax rates here in the U.K. We have had a major reduction in marginal tax rates in the U.S. and that promises to go even further, both at the personal level and at the corporate level. Reduction in marginal tax rates — what does that mean? Well, it's very bad news for the tax avoidance business, that's what it means. I can recall back about 14 years ago when I was here in London with different responsibilities and we were coming up on this season of the year and the rumour of the year that year, which was 1971, was that there was going to be an increase in tax rates and I duly despatched my weekly report and earnings estimate to New York and in it I mentioned as one of the major developments of the week the fact that it was widely rumoured that we were going to have an increase in tax rates. The next sentence was "Therefore, that means we are going to have a boom in sales and an increase in after-tax earnings." Well, the telexes that arrived could be measured in yards! And of course the truth of the matter is that the company that was the subject of those remarks and many of the companies that are here in this room are extensively involved in the tax avoidance business in one way or another. And I am not saying this in any perjorative way, I am simply saying that that is the business of many of us in this room. So a reduction in marginal tax rates has quite a significant impact on the tax avoidance business. If, for example, the operative tax rate is reduced from 50%to 35% there is automatically a 30% reduction in the value of any tax shelter, even if nothing else happens to the whole of the tax system. Also on the deregulatory front we are seeing clearly loosening of restrictions, notably the banking business in Australia and the U.S., but also this is true in other industries as well. And, not surprisingly, the U.K. in my opinion has led the way in terms of deregulation of its financial businesses.

So deregulation — one of the reasons why — there is another reason why. That's what I call brown pasture versus green and what do I mean by that? Well, the reason why people are jumping out of one financial service industry into the other is not just that the grass is so green on the other side of the fence. The fact of the matter is that the grass is turning brown on their own side of the fence and many people recognise this. So the search for green pasture is partly an escape from brown pasture. Let me tell you some of the reasons. Retail financial service businesses of all kinds, in all parts of the world, are in trouble and basically they are in trouble because they are running in to a cost and margin squeeze. These businesses historically have been conducted on a people intensive basis, and people intensity is beginning to tell. There are limitations on the adaptation of technology as a substitute for people in the financial service businesses. We've had it in the administrative end but that has now more or less run its course, and the cost in margin squeeze is on for real in more or less all of these businesses. Now this has led all financial services businesses that are far thinking to look for one or two things. Either they are seeking a way to be more efficient, in other words a way to reduce their costs, or they are seeking to find protected — and read the word "captive" for "protected" if you want — markets, and the object of that is to increase their prices, i.e. their margins. So, forward thinking companies are doing one of two things — they are either trying for improved efficiency or they are trying for protected, i.e. captive, markets.

Let me talk about the kinds of brown grass that there are in various of the businesses. The banking business is fairly easy — their brown grass is too much brick and mortar, and brick and mortar has become quite expensive. It is interesting the exposure I had to ITT occurred at a time when they owned Avis and I heard the automobile rental business once described this way — it's a complicated way to manufacture used cars. Well, interesting, interesting. The banking business may be a complicated way to invest in bank properties. I wonder what the financial statements of banks would look like if you removed from them all of the impact of their property investments over the years. I suspect they wouldn't look too good. But brick and mortar is their problem. Its price has gone up on them and the ongoing cost of maintaining it is very high. They also face increased competition from the building societies who I think really have stolen a march in this country, from insurance bonds, from unit trusts. The life insurance business — that one's easy. Its brown grass is its distribution costs, and distribution costs have come into sharp focus as a result of the elimination of life assurance premium relief. The general insurance business — where's their brown grass? Well, I think it's in underwriting control. I think it's in the control of their underwriting results which really must begin at the fields and the general insurance companies, more or less worldwide with a few exceptions, are subject to a way of doing business in which they have relatively little control over their field representation. Therefore, they have relatively little control over their field underwriting, and I think if you contrast the underwriting results, for example, of State Farm with the results of many of its competitors, you can see the difference. I know that that is not the only factor but you can see a difference that I would attribute to that factor. What's the brown grass for the nonfinancial businesses? Well I think it's a retreat from shrinking margins caused mainly by third world labour costs. There's a commercial on television in the U.S. that shows the President of the company that owns Remington, and he does his own commercials. And he is quoted as saying, "If current trends continue everyone in the United States will be selling life insurance by the year 2000 and we won't be manufacturing anything." Well, this is a symptom that much of the manufacturing business of the world is shifting to third world countries because of their labour cost. Where are people looking for the green grass? One of the favourites on nearly everyone's list is the insurance business, and I suspect that that's a reason why most of you are here today, either as buyers or sellers, and the insurance business is a favourite because it's perceived to be traditionally a high margin business and this perception is particularly true in the case of life insurance. It's considered to be green grass by others because it is perceived as being a traditionally high margin business. Other people think that they are going to be able to improve the distribution costs in that business and therefore they think that the high margins available on the product will inure to them as profits. That's why the insurance business is viewed as green grass. How about banking? Well, that grass is not seen as too green — it's really seen as necessary for a full service financial operation because it is seen as the most important basis of customer control and ultimately customer control is expected to lead to higher prices. Therefore, banking is seen as a necessary piece of the puzzle more than as a desirable piece of the puzzle. How about the securities business? By which I mean the unit trust business, stockbroking, merchant banking and so forth. These are seen by other financial businesses as obviously synergistic. For example, on the investment side but there are others as well. Now there's an interesting analogy can be drawn between what's been happening in the financial service business and what's likely to happen and what has been happening in the United States in two other industries that have been extensively deregulated over the last few years. And any one of you in this audience that has travelled to the United States in the last few years has actually had personal exposure to both of these businesses.

The first is the airline business where deregulation began about six or seven years ago and what's happened? Well, we've had some very interesting things happen in terms of air fares — not all of them logical — but nevertheless it is clear that air fares have moved downwards over that period of time. The second thing that's happened is some extraordinary developments to organisations such as Braniff. On the first day of deregulation the then Civil Aeronautics Board announced that it would open for business at nine o'clock in the morning on such and such a date and that it would accept applications of filings on routes not in use and each of the airlines commissioned someone or other to go and stand in line and the line started about four days before the opening gun was to be fired. Well, who do you think was at the head of the line? It was Braniff and they filed on approximately the same number of routes that morning as they then served. They filed on a doubling of their route structure.

To their sorrow, because Braniff since has gone broke and has re-emerged, I stand here as a guest of Braniff Airways here in London today because, thanks to one of my colleagues, my wife and I were able to take advantage of their Frequent Flyer scheme which is usable on British Caledonian. The reason I was able to persuade him that he ought to give me his Frequent Flyer rights for a rather cheap price is that he expects that Braniff's going to go bust again! And other things have happened in the airline business, too. Continental, for example, has put paid to its unions as a result of airlines. Mike was telling me in the course of lunch that he's concerned about his travel schedule tomorrow because there's a rumour Pan Am is going on strike. I wonder if they'll emerge from a strike. And so on it goes. It has obviously reshaped the airline industry, deregulation has reshaped it because it has changed the margins, it has removed the previous culture in which the Civil Aeronautics Board would never have allowed Braniff to go broke. What they would have done is they would have regulated fare prices at whatever level was necessary to keep Braniff solvent — that's exactly what they would have done.

Telephone deregulation has been somewhat more complicated, a little less traumatic. The point of the telephone deregulation that I think has application to the financial business is its impact on personal telephone costs. Traditionally in the U.S. there's been a major subsidy between long distance service and residential service, and residential service has been extensively subsidised. Well, basically under the break-up of ATT, what happened was that the operating telephone companies, seven of them, were split off from ATT, and it's now called Snow White and the Seven Dwarfs, and each of these local telephone companies is responsible for the local service. ATT retains the long distance service, and hence this cross-subsidy is in the process of disappearing and residential telephone costs are going up. I would guess that in a deregulated financial services environment the retail customer is going to wind up paying higher prices in the end because probably he is now being subsidised.

Well, so much for why. Let me talk now about how. There are major strategic choices to be made by companies involved in the financial services business. Among other things I think they are going to have to do these things. I think they're going to have to define their business. I think they're going to have to define the markets they intend to serve and I think they're going to have to identify their real customers. Now you here in London get a fair menu of television fare from the U.S. but let me tell you that you are getting the expurgated edition of U.S. television. Those of you who travel to the States have probably seen it au naturelle, complete with its commercials taking up something like 25% of the total elapsed time. It's interesting how one hour of programmes in the U.S. tends to run in about 40 minutes over here. Well, there's a commercial that appears on television in the U.S. that is both an advertising slogan of its company and it's also a statement of its corporate mission. And it's nice and simple and it illustrates one approach to a company defining the business it's in. The company involved is the Ryder Corporation and the slogan says "Ryder rents trucks." That's all it does — Ryder rents trucks.

Now some of us in the financial service business might historically have been able to make similar statements about the kinds of business we're in. I doubt that's true today because I doubt that too many actually know what business they're in. Moreover I think that's probably a good idea because I think opportunism is going to have a lot to do with success over the next few years and I think that too great a preoccupation of the specifics of what business one is in may be counter-productive so I do not recommend you adopt the slogan " Ryder rents trucks." The basic choices are to be all things to some people or to be some things to all people. There are very few who will be brave enough or who have enough capital to undertake to be all things to all people. Some may have a go at it but I would be skeptical if they would be able to make it work. In other words, are you going to provide a wide variety of services to a defined market or are you going to provide a narrowly defined group of services to all comers? And that's the basic choice in deciding what business you're in and what market you're going to serve. This could broadly be defined as a choice between broad market participation which the banks, by definition, are going to become involved in. The banks are going to choose the broad market participation. They are definitely going to go for the "all things to some people" type of strategy. On the other hand, you can choose the boutique strategy — that is the "some things to all people, do it better strategy" if you like. And finally there's a variation of that that might be of interest to a number of people and that's the renegade strategy. Deliberately do it differently and preferably in a manner that exploits the weakness of the existing systems — the renegade strategy.

Whichever route is taken, I would forecast that efficient customer access is going to be the measure of whether it works or not. And how's that access going to work? Well some people think it's going to work through the medium of an individual that might be described as a financial account executive. A year ago we had a meeting in this very room on a subject that was somewhat similar to the topic of this seminar today, and Mark Weinberg spoke of the financial account executive as part of the future that he foresaw. Location selling is probably going to be another of the "hows" of getting to the customer — location selling. You can surely expect that banks will attempt to utilise their branch locations in this way. There are some experiments under way in the U.S. involving retailers using location selling. Telemarketing — this is the land of the futurist — this is the land where everyone has a personal computer and it's hooked up together with either cable television or with hard wired telephone lines — take your pick. And you sell and service and do everything else on everyone's personal computer. Telemarketing — that's probably something that is quite some time into the future but I expect that some parts of it will come. Point of employment access to the customer could be a big and a growing factor. The idea here is not unlike the basic idea of the home service business that most individuals, particularly unsophisticated individuals, need a great deal of servicing on their financial products and traditionally this servicing was provided in the home by the home service type companies. Well, some people think that that's still a good idea — you just change the venue from the home to the place of employment, so point of employment access to customers should be another large factor.

Most of the traditionalists are going to all crowd into one zone, and that's the zone that will be occupied by sophisticated intermediaries. Most traditional companies will probably crowd into this zone because it'll be the most familiar. I would predict that you would have a sharply reduced number of intermediaries and that price competition will be ferocious. Regardless of how the customer is accessed, it is clear that there will be major systems support requirements and, to the best of my knowledge, no integrated financial service system exists today. The closest I have seen to one is in San Antonio, Texas, and it's run by the United States Automobile Association. There's one aspect of strategy that's being pursued, among others, by Citibank in the U.S. It's a strategy that might be described as cherry picking in preferred market sectors. What Citibank is trying to do in certain test markets is to persuade people, and they are aiming definitely at the upper income class, hence the cherry picking, to persuade people that they ought to open a bank account with Citibank regardless of where in the United States that they might live and the whole thrust of the advertising is, "You don't need a branch bank down on the corner, what you need is a telephone and moreover our branches on the telephone never close, you can call us in the middle of the night and we're still open." So cherry picking in preferred market sectors is going to be a feature of the strategy of some companies. Now this could be fairly important because many financial businesses are still dependent on an important degree of cross-subsidy. If they were to lose even a small slice of their preferred markets it would dramatically change their economics. At one point in my career which, for understandable reasons, Mike did not mention, I worked for a company in Atlanta that was owned by funeral directors and on occasion I have attended one of their conventions which are really hilarious! That is not a facetious remark — they really are hilarious as long as they are 15 miles away from where they work. And they had a favourite toast after the statutory one which was "Who's your embalmer?" and the toast was "God bless my competitors — somebody's got to bury the poor people." Well, much the same idea applies in the financial service business.

Let me spend just a minute on the question of "who." Who are going to be the main players in this kind of game? Well I think you can identify five players — clearly the established banks are going to be major factors — the sleeping giants — I don't know how awake they're going to get but they sure are giants. And their activity is going to have a great deal to do with the whole shape of the market. And that applies to all of the countries that I've mentioned. Clearly the insurance companies have got a role to play in all this, too. I'm not sure exactly what that role will be — whether they are going to be the ancillary businesses or the central businesses I think remains to be seen. One of the disadvantages is that this industry is not particularly well capitalised and capital may be a major factor. Other financial organisations — you can think of merchant banks, you can think of organisations like Meryll Lynch that are extensively into the retail stockbroking business. You can think of American Express, companies with large credit card lists and so forth. You have the other consumer based organisations — organisations with large numbers of customers like retailers, Sears for example, Marks & Sparks for another. Regardless of who, I would forecast with some confidence that those who succeed are either going to be super-efficient or they're going to be renegades. Those are going to be the big success stories — the super-efficient and the renegades.

Finally, in determining who the winners and losers might be, I think it is important to keep in mind that the umpire of that particular question may well be the stock market. It's clear that there are going to be many many mergers and consolidations before all of this is over. It's clear that the number of such mergers and consolidations is such but cash alone cannot be the only medium of exchange that a lot of it is going to have to happen on the basis of swapping paper for paper. Now there's an axiom that applies to stock market deals and the axiom is that the companies with the highest P-E ratios or the highest market to book ratios are the survivors because their currency is the most favourably situated when it comes to current rates of exchange. It's rather like the pound and the dollar these days. It's clear that the market to book ratio of the dollar is higher and it's clear that the P-E ratio of the dollar is higher, maybe infinity for instance. Consequently the stock market may be the ultimate arbitrator of who wins the particular game.

The Consolidation of Financial Services: Its Implications for the Australian Insurance Industry

Presented to the Institute of Actuaries of Australia, Albury, NSW, Australia, October 2–4, 1985.

A major consolidation of the financial service industries is in progress in many developed countries. Australia is in the vanguard of this change, and its experience is likely to attract attention in other countries as a possible guide to what may happen elsewhere. The purpose of this paper is to analyze this development and to forecast its likely implications for the insurance industry in Australia. Necessarily, the analysis is speculative and the conclusions represent the personal view of the author.

Historical Background

For reasons related to both regulation and tradition, the major financial services industries have developed substantially in isolation from one another in most countries. The principal industries included in the group are banking and thrift, life insurance, general insurance and investment businesses of several types. Other financial services industries include consumer lending, credit cards, travelers checks and real estate brokerage, some of which are also involved in the trend towards consolidation. This paper will focus primarily on the banking and insurance industries.

Financial service industries are everywhere subject to extensive regulation. Among the regulatory provisions which have promoted the separate development of the banking and insurance industries, limitations on ownership and control are the most important. In some countries, banks and insurance companies have been barred from engaging in each other's or any unrelated business. Notwithstanding recent liberalization, there remain extensive restrictions on the ownership and control of trading banks in Australia and some restrictions on the ownership and control of other near-banking and insurance institutions. Restrictions of a somewhat similar nature are found in laws and administrative practices elsewhere; recently, these, too, have been relaxed in several countries.

Also contributing to the separate development of the banking and insurance industries has been the mutual form of corporate organization, which is a major factor in the life insurance industry and among the thrift institutions in Australia. A similar phenomenon exists in most other countries. The mutual form of organization is important to a lesser degree in the general insurance industry in Australia and elsewhere.

The largely separate development of the banking and insurance industries has resulted in substantial operational differences, including the pursuit of fundamentally different business strategies, the significance of which is a central theme of this paper.

Deregulation

Significant deregulation of the financial services industries has recently occurred in several countries and further deregulation is widely expected in some; these developments can be expected to alter the structure and competitive environment of the banking and insurance industries in several countries:

1. **Australia.** The banking industry in Australia has been conducted for many years as an oligopoly with four large domestic trading banks (one owned by the Commonwealth of Australia) operating throughout the country. In each state, one additional bank (owned by the state government) operates in its designated territory. This position has been transformed by the recent licensing of several additional domestic and foreign owned banks, two of which are joint ventures sponsored in each case by a major Australian life office and a major overseas bank. Three of the four established banks have since indicated an intention to enter the insurance business. Building societies, which are mutual co-operatives, and savings banks compete with the

trading banks in the thrift market. The Australian life insurance industry is dominated by Australian mutual offices, but there are a significant number of other companies, several of which are owned by large overseas insurers. The general insurance industry is dominated by government insurance offices and motor clubs in the retail sector of the industry and by overseas owned or controlled companies in the commercial sector. There have been no significant recent efforts to deregulate the insurance industry in Australia, but the business is relatively unrestricted and competitive; there are already a significant number of participants and new entrants to the market are permitted.

2. **United States of America.** The banking industry in the United States is widely fragmented among 15,000 banks, which operate within strictly defined geographical territories; these may be defined as a single branch location, a county, a metropolitan area or an entire state. This severe geographic restriction has characterized banking regulation in the United States for the past 50 years. In recent years, a progressive relaxation of this regulation has occurred within state boundaries and major bank holding companies have emerged. Regional interstate banking is now possible in the New England states and in the Southeastern states and it is widely expected that national bank networks will be permitted to operate within the next decade. Notwithstanding these and other recent liberalizations, banks are still restricted from engaging in many aspects of the insurance business, and this restriction applies to any organization which acquires a bank. This position is expected to change. The thrift industry, which includes mutual and stock savings and loan associations and consumer banks, is similarly fragmented among 15,000 separate institutions. Regulation applicable to these institutions is less restrictive, and some are engaged in the insurance business through subsidiaries. The insurance industry is only slightly less fragmented among 2,000 life insurance companies and 2,000 general insurance companies, most of which operate on a regional or national basis. Stock companies are more numerous but many large companies are mutuals. A major consolidation of the insurance industry is in progress, and there are today fewer than 1,000 independent groups, the largest of which has a market share of less than 5%.

3. **Canada.** The banking industry in Canada is highly concentrated among six large domestic banks, all of which operate nationally. Recently, the Canadian government has announced its intention to liberalize the banking laws in a way which would ease restrictions on entry into the banking business for both Canadian and foreign interests. The thrift industry in Canada, conducted through trust companies, is less concentrated than the banking industry but many of the largest trust companies are now affiliated with another financial institution or industrial group. The insurance industry in Canada is less fragmented than in the United States but more so than in Australia; the life insurance industry is dominated by approximately 10 companies, mainly domestic mutuals, each with market shares of less than 10%. The general insurance industry includes a significant number of foreign offices.
4. **United Kingdom.** The regulation of financial institutions in the United Kingdom does not include important restrictions on their ownership and control or their range of activities, but the banking and insurance industries in that country remain largely separate notwithstanding this. The banking industry is dominated by four large trading banks, but there are a large number of banks and near-banks active in at least parts of the banking business. As in Australia, mutual building societies are the dominant thrift institutions. The insurance industry, both life and general, is fragmented to a degree comparable to that in Canada. Pseudo-mutual and mutual life insurance companies are predominant; general insurance companies are overwhelmingly stock companies. Although there is some degree of cross ownership among banks and insurance companies in the U.K., there are no important examples of operational integration of these businesses.

The banking and insurance industries are also affected by regulation of a different kind which, in some cases, dictates the prices and availability of their services. In Australia, major changes are in progress which will impose price controls on workers' compensation insurance in New South Wales and will result in a government takeover of this business in Victoria. These are examples of expanded regulation rather than deregulation and their effects on the general insurance industry will be substantial. In the United States, the banking industry has been profoundly affected by the dismantling of Regulation Q, which imposed ceilings on interest rates which could be paid to various classes of depositors; this deregulation has effectively increased consumer benefits at the expense of the banking industry's operating margins. Also in the United States, rate regulation continues to be imposed by many state governments, and these are important in the health and automobile insurance fields. In several Canadian provinces, automobile insurance has been assumed by government agencies, and private health insurance in the medical field has been substantially displaced by government sponsored programs.

The common aim of these regulatory changes is to promote competition among purveyors of financial services and to assure that socially important services will be affordable, sometimes regardless of their actual cost.

It would be a mistake to identify deregulation as the cause of the trend towards the consolidation of the various branches of the financial services industry. Clearly, deregulation is a condition precedent but one must look elsewhere for the root causes.

The Forces of Consolidation

In the retail sector of the banking and insurance industries, traditional methods of doing business are leading to progressively higher cost levels. For competitive and other reasons, these increased cost levels have not been passed on to customers by price increases. The result is that both industries are experiencing margin pressures on their retail business and are seeking ways to improve those margins.

In the banking industry, the traditional method of doing business has involved widespread branch office networks and a correspondingly large staff. The increased cost of office accommodations and personnel, combined with competitive pressures on interest rate spreads, are responsible for the margin pressure in this industry.

In the life insurance industry, where two-thirds of the costs relate to the distribution process, productivity has not kept pace with the income requirements of a people-intensive distribution system. In some countries, the appeal of life insurance products has diminished due to changes in taxation; this is particularly the case in Australia and the United Kingdom, but the opposite change has recently occurred in the United States. Especially where consumer appeal has diminished, prices have come under competitive pressure and increased costs have not been supported by increased margins.

In the general insurance sector, margins have been affected everywhere by adverse claims experience. Social and government pressures have acted, in some countries, to arrest price increases necessary to support current experience.

In the commercial sector of the banking and insurance business, price competition has also intensified and claims experience has deteriorated, leading to margin pressure in these areas, too.

In response to these pressures, banks and insurance companies have attempted to reduce costs. Plastic bank cards, automated tellers and "telebanking" illustrate the response of the banking industry. Contracting and consolidated agency organizations illustrate the response of the life insurance industry. These developments can be observed in Australia and elsewhere.

Another response to margin pressures is based on the concept that unit expenses can be reduced if additional products are provided through the existing organization. This growth-oriented concept is very attractive and its logic is compelling. It is the basis of the strategic decision by many banks and insurance companies, in Australia and elsewhere, to diversify into each other's business and into various related businesses. In addition to its main attraction, this strategic plan has collateral advantages which are also attractive:

1. If a full range of financial services is offered, an exclusive customer base can be established which affords important insulation against price competition.
2. Additional products represent an opportunity to support the income needs of those involved in distributing financial products.

These are the forces of consolidation. Notably, the underlying motivation is not primarily the prospect of green pastures on the other side of the fence; rather it is the recognition that the pasture on this side of the fence is turning somewhat brown. These forces of consolidation are not altogether new: banks have already expanded into many new areas of service and the life and general insurance industries have long been engaged in cross consolidation. What is new is the prospect of significant cross-industry competition between banks and insurance companies.

A Contrast of Business Strategies

This prospect of significant competition across traditional boundaries between banks and insurance companies will involve a collision of two fundamentally different business strategies:

1. the consumer-driven strategy of banks, which stresses low cost consumer services provided directly and which is supported mainly by passive marketing efforts, such as consumer advertising; and
2. the distribution-driven strategy of insurance companies, which leads to cost levels which are decidedly high when compared with banks because it stresses commissions to intermediaries who provide aggressive marketing support.

The magnitude of the difference in cost levels as related to life insurance needs to be understood because banks and life insurance companies already compete, at least tangentially, in the savings market. Typically, banks offer savings accumulation products on a "no-load" basis and cover their costs by their interest spread which may involve an annual cost to the consumer of 2% to 3% of the accumulated funds; this cost is approximately equivalent to a "load" of 10% to 15% on the amount deposited. Typically, life insurance companies offer savings accumulation products in combination with insurance on a basis which involves an equivalent level annual "load" of 35% to 45%, considering both persisting and terminating policyholders; this does not include the risk charge, which is also subject to a similar "load." The figures cited relate to ordinary products and apply in Australia and elsewhere, subject to only minor differences. The comparison is quite different for other product lines, particularly single premium products and some in the superannuation field.

A substantial part of the large difference illustrated can be justified on various grounds:

1. Arguably, the risk charge should support loads higher than 35% to 45% — as an extreme example, airline trip insurance involves loads of perhaps 90% and is bought notwithstanding this; this might reduce the load effectively borne by the savings element to, say, 30% to 40%;
2. life insurance offers a different and potentially more rewarding investment alternative than bank deposits;

3. life insurance offers to some buyers tax advantages that are not available on bank deposits; and
4. life insurance requires more personalized service which is provided by intermediaries and represents "value added" for which the consumer is willing to pay.

Since life insurance products continue to be sold in competition with other savings alternatives notwithstanding their relatively high cost, well informed consumers must recognize and value these differences between life insurance products and other alternatives. If this is not true, it would be necessary to believe that life insurance products are only bought by consumers who are not well informed, which seems very unlikely.

The business strategies of banks and general insurance companies cannot as readily be compared because they are engaged in essentially different businesses which are tangential only in the case of credit-related insurance. Arguably, general insurance may be viewed by the public more as a "commodity" and may, therefore, be more price sensitive.

In summary, banks today offer savings products which compete at least tangentially with life insurance. These bank products are available at cost levels which are not more than one-third of the levels applicable to mainstream life insurance products. Life insurance products are nevertheless reasonably competitive in the eyes of the consumer because they offer values not available from bank products. Direct competition between banks and general insurance companies is practically nonexistent today.

The New Competitive Landscape

If, beginning in Australia as early as 1986, banks are offering insurance products and insurance companies are offering banking services, the competitive equilibrium between banks and life insurance companies will be altered and competition between banks and general insurance companies may begin. How will the competitive landscape then appear?

The primary competitive strength of the four major established banks is their large customer base and widespread branch networks; each would claim a relationship with 20% or more of the Australian households likely to need banking or insurance services. These banks have frequent contact with most of these customers. As confirmed by many surveys, these banks also enjoy a high degree of consumer confidence and name recognition; with sponsorship by any of these institutions, even a small new company would receive immediate acceptance and recognition by the consumer.

The primary competitive weakness of these banks is also related to their large customer base and widespread branch networks, which commits them to serve the large middle market and forecloses the possibility of selective marketing, at least for banking services. Another potential weakness is the lack of aggressive marketing skills, a shortcoming likely to be particularly important because it may not be acknowledged or even recognized. Capital may also be scarce resource and the price of entry into the insurance business could be very large.

The leading opportunity of the established banks is to market insurance products to existing customers on a basis which results in superior economic fundamentals. In the case of life insurance products, this translates into reduced distribution costs; in the case of general insurance products, this translates into superior claim experience as well as reduced costs. If banks can achieve superior expense fundamentals, they may be able economically to serve the lower income market, which has to a progressive degree been abandoned by the insurance industry.

The leading threat to the established banks is the possible loss of preferred customers to smaller and newer banks able to target selected market segments. Bank margins are inordinately dependent on these customers which represent only 20% of the total customer base.

The newer banks with no access to a customer base can be expected to capitalize on their flexibility by attempting to stake out a selected market niche. Those sponsored by organizations which have an established customer base in another business may attempt to wrest a share of the broad market for banking services from the established banks. Alliances and acquisitions involving building societies, retail and other organizations are a likely strategy for building a base of potential banking customers. Insurance services may feature prominently in the plans of those who pursue the strategy of offering "all things to some people."

The primary strength of established life offices, mostly mutual or pseudo-mutual, may be their large capital funds; most of this is undeclared surplus inside their life funds which could be used to finance a new venture without creating unmanageable strains on the emergence of declared surplus. These companies also have access to a large base of potential customers for banking and other financial services. Their existing agency forces might be either a major strength or a mayor weakness; this is likely to depend on the *perception* (not the reality) of the personal income opportunities available to existing agents under the new circumstances.

Established life offices with tied agents, like established banks, are committed to serve the large middle market unless they abandon their existing distribution system. This is their principal weakness, especially if it perpetuates their existing high-cost structure.

Smaller life offices, particularly those without tied agents, have the opportunity to concentrate on selected markets as boutiques or product wholesalers. A limited number may have the opportunity to affiliate with one of the newer banks and to develop a marketing strategy compatible with that of the affiliated bank.

General insurance offices which are not offshoots of established life offices already operate as boutiques or product wholesalers. Their primary strengths are technical knowledge and skills relating to products, underwriting and claims settlement. The probable initial strategy of banks in entering or expanding their activities in the general insurance market is not altogether clear; some may choose to further expand their existing underwriting activities while others may expand only their activities as distributors of general insurance products. The first possibility would threaten the market position of existing general insurance offices but the second would not. Most general insurance offices in Australia will not consider entry into the banking field because they do not have the necessary capital funds.

In summary, the initial strategy likely to be adopted by the principal competitors can be forecast with some degree of confidence. Except for differences attributable to regulation or to industry structure, the position in Australia is similar to that which applies elsewhere. The outcome of these strategies is not as clear. The central issue relates importantly to the ultimate efficiency of a consolidated banking and insurance industry. An editorial which appeared in the *New York Times* on June 27, 1985 asked (and answered) the question this way:

> Banks think they can sell insurance more cheaply and conveniently than insurance companies. Insurers apparently think so, too, for they are fighting an effort by banks in New York State to enter the business.

The author shares the view implied.

Conclusions

The author believes that banks, where they are allowed to engage in the insurance business, will capture a 10% to 20% share of the retail insurance market within five years following entry. If this assessment is correct, the traditional distribution-driven strategy of the insurance industry, particularly the life insurance sector, will cease to be economically viable and the existing distribution system, unless it is significantly changed, will implode.

This event is likely to happen in Australia before it happens elsewhere. This is partly because the consolidation of banking and insurance may develop in Australia before it does elsewhere and partly because the economics of life insurance distribution systems in Australia are already marginal or submarginal to a degree greater than observed elsewhere.

This conclusion should not be taken as a forecast of impending extinction for entrepreneur insurance agents. They are likely, even at the dawn of the Third Millenium, to be the dominant distributors of insurance products. But their numbers will have shrunk. A market share loss of even 10% to 20% is enough to drive out the marginal agents, perhaps 50% of the total. Reductions in rates of commission (or the equivalent) to the extent of 50% may be necessary to meet the new consumer-driven competition from bank-sponsored insurance operations; while this may be offset in part by income arising from other product lines, such as unit trusts, a further contraction of the distribution system is suggested. The surviving agents, while fewer in number, will be highly productive. They are likely to call themselves financial advisors.

The implications for life offices in Australia are quite serious. A few will spearhead the development of major financial groups offering a broad range of financial services; several will become members of such a group, spearheaded by another major financial or industrial organization, domestic or foreign. Some will survive as boutiques or product wholesalers catering to the product needs of the remaining intermediaries; the survivors in this group will have extremely low expense rates and an aggressive and successful investment record. The rest will be absorbed by the various survivors or will quietly wither away.

For the general insurance industry, fewer and less sweeping changes are indicated, at least initially, as a result of the consolidation of the banking and insurance industries; this industry may, however, face other problems of a serious nature.

The Third Millenium

There are also important implications for the actuarial profession in Australia and elsewhere. If its future remains tied to a significant degree to the life insurance industry and if that industry experiences the changes already described, the actuarial profession faces an extended period of decline. If, instead, the profession expands its horizon outward into new fields which lend themselves to mathematically based projection and forecasting techniques, for which actuaries are admirably suited, a different and brighter future beckons. Because Australia will be in the vanguard of change in the life insurance industry, its Institute of Actuaries could perform a major service for the profession worldwide by responding appropriately and promptly to the new circumstances. The separate education and examination process already operating in Australia could facilitate the adjustment of the training and qualification of actuaries necessary to lead the profession in new directions. The successful actuarial program at Macquarie University might also play a significant role.

The Third Millenium will begin for most people on 1st January, 2000, a Saturday; for purists, it will begin a year later, on 1st January, 2001, a Monday. When that day comes, whichever it is, will there be in Australia or elsewhere actuaries trained in new skills with no particular knowledge of Life Contingencies? The future of the profession may depend on it.

Acknowledgements

The author is indebted to his colleagues, G. L. Melville and John R. Trowbridge, for their review of this paper and their suggestions regarding its suitability for presentation to an Australian audience. The author is also indebted to the Institute of Actuaries of Australia for allowing a non-member who is not an Australian to present a speculative paper of this type.

The Changing Role of Life Insurance in a Modern Society

Presented to the Institute of Actuaries of Japan, Tokyo, Japan, June 6, 1986.

Life insurance was devised to solve a problem as old as mankind itself. The problem is the unfulfilled needs created by the premature death of an individual upon whom others are dependent. In the earliest and most primitive forms, the unfulfilled needs related to the actual survival of widows and orphaned children.

Early History

In some ancient societies, there emerged a "social contract" by which these needs were addressed, often reinforced by the prevailing religion. Remarriage and adoption were often the solutions. In other societies, such as in India until recent years, widows were expected to throw themselves on the funeral pyres of their dead husbands. With the invention of what is called money, other solutions became possible. For workers in the Industrial Age which began in the 19th Century, the need for protection became more urgent.

The earliest attempts to provide "pensions" for widows and orphaned children probably related to premature death in military combat. Later examples related to special hazards, such as voyages by sea. These arrangements were privately financed. In Roman times, certain fraternal and religious orders provided benefits to dependents of deceased members.

The risk transfer concept involved in insurance can be observed as early as 2000 B.C. among the Babylonians and the Phoenicians, who engaged in insurance-like transactions relating to the transport of goods by caravans or ship. During the fifteenth century in the city-states of Venice and Genoa, now part of modern Italy, insurance became a business, practiced by individuals called underwriters who had no other interest in the objects insured. Their activities in insuring ships and cargoes for specific voyages soon extended to insuring the lives of captains and crews. Gradually, the business of insurance spread to all important centers of maritime commerce in Europe, notably to London. It was mainly there that the business of insurance was extended into fields unrelated to maritime commerce; it was there, in the 17th century, that the first insurance companies were organized.

The earliest life insurance policies provided temporary insurance only. As such, they addressed only limited and specific needs, often related to periods of unusual hazards. The life insurance business existed then only as a minor branch of the wider insurance business. The business of annuities, based also on contingencies involving human life, was conducted mainly by private parties: this business was primarily responsible for early efforts to estimate human mortality which are recorded in the works of Sir Edmund Halley, Blaise Pascal and others.

The Modern Life Insurance Industry

In 1756, an English teacher of mathematics, James Dodson, conceived the idea of level premium whole life insurance. Using a table devised from the London Bills of Mortality, he painstakingly calculated premium rates and associated liabilities necessary to make such an idea financially sound; in the modern sense, he can be identified as the first actuary. Dodson's efforts to obtain a Royal Charter for a company to issue such policies were unsuccessful; such a concept, it was thought, was far too speculative. Although he did not live to see his idea become a reality, his associates, using his work, founded an organization in 1762 which exists today as the Old Equitable; for the first 100 years of its existence, it operated as a partnership among its policyholders because it had no charter.

The new product conceived by James Dodson, resulting in the formation of the Old Equitable, marks the beginning of the modern life insurance industry:

1. It separated the life insurance business from general insurance.
2. It made life insurance a long-term asset accumulation business.
3. Its high expense tolerance, especially in the early years of a policy with no surrender values, fostered the development of a commissioned-based agency system, initially composed of part-time agents.
4. Its technical nature created the need for the actuarial profession and for government supervision of the industry.

Four Transformations

The industry created by the invention of whole life insurance has since been transformed several times. In some countries, the transformations can be associated with the introduction of a major new product followed by an associated change in the distribution system of the industry. In the United States and other English-speaking countries, four developments of this kind can be identified:

1. Cash Values and Endowment Policies (mid 19th Century). The introduction of benefits payable to the insured himself transformed the principal activity of the industry into a savings business. The resulting increase in the appeal of life insurance made possible the development of the professional agent which led directly to the rapid growth of the industry.
2. Tax-avoidance Products (early 20th Century and currently). The introduction of significant income and estate taxes fostered the development of products aimed at politically acceptable forms of tax-avoidance; among these, pension products became the most important and led directly to the development of other products, such as group insurance, aimed at the employee/employer market. Concurrently, the emphasis of agents shifted towards financial planning.
3. Unit-linking (mid 20th Century and currently). The introduction of unit-linking transformed the industry in some countries (notably the United Kingdom and South Africa) into an investment business. The wider appeal and glamour associated with these products accelerated the growth of the industry and the development of its distribution system; life insurance selling

became a more professional and more desirable occupation in the eyes of many of the new recruits.

4. Unbundling (currently). The introduction of fully flexible unbundled products, such as universal life, was made possible by advanced computer technology and made necessary by environmental changes. Traditional products with fixed benefits and premiums no longer were well suited to the rapidly changing financial needs of a society experiencing high rates of inflation and fundamental changes in family structure; increasingly, the public in several English speaking countries rejected those products in favor of other alternatives. For the industry, the continuing implications of unbundled products are clearly profound; the expense tolerance of these transparent products is less than that of traditional products, and major changes in distribution and other costs will be required to support the price structure necessary to be competitive.

The Contemporary Transformation

In addition to the product revolution now in progress in the United States and several other English-speaking countries and the distribution system revolution required by that change, there is also in progress or impending important changes in the structure and ownership of financial institutions of all kinds. In several countries, financial industries are being deregulated and barriers between traditionally separate businesses, such as banking and insurance, have been weakened or removed. Inter-industry competition for the savings and other financial business of the public has become or is becoming as important as intra-industry competition. The focus of this new competition is on the control and efficiency of the distribution channels through which the market will be reached. Some of the possibilities could lead to significant reductions in insurance distribution costs which could support much lower prices. The life insurance industry, which has traditionally experienced relatively high distribution expenses, is particularly vulnerable to the possibility of severe price competition.

Change of another kind is also affecting the traditional role of life insurance as a politically acceptable form of tax-avoidance. In several English-speaking countries, dramatic reductions have recently occurred in the highest marginal income tax rates; in the United States, for example, the top marginal tax rate has fallen since 1980 from 72% to 50% and three proposals now under consideration by the Congress provide for maximum rates ranging from 27% to 38%. Clearly, the value of life insurance as a tax shelter has declined and a further decline is likely in the United States and elsewhere. This loss of tax-avoidance value by comparison with other financial products adds significantly to the pressure to reduce prices and increase value to the consumer in order to maintain a reasonably competitive position versus those other financial products, which traditionally have been offered with lower expense charges but without the tax-avoidance characteristics.

The Role of Life Insurance

What is the appropriate role of life insurance in a modern society? What needs can the industry serve as well as or better than competing financial businesses? What further changes in product, distribution systems and industry structure are called for?

The "core business" of the life insurance industry is income protection. The need for life insurance to replace income loss arising from premature death is stronger than ever notwithstanding the widespread phenomenon of the two-income family. As standards of living rise so do security expectations and so, disproportionately, does the ability to afford adequate life insurance protection. Considering the effects of inflation and taxation, younger workers with dependents often require as much coverage as ten times their after-tax income. Even in Japan, where life insurance protection relative to national income is the highest in the world, unmet needs are large.

This is a need which only the products of the life insurance industry can meet. The need requires a product which affords large amounts of effective coverage at younger ages and much smaller amounts later, a pattern which can be provided either by decreasing term insurance (indexed for inflation) or by unbundled products; orthodox endowment policies alone are not appropriate because the required asset accumulation and premiums are too large if the initial coverage and maturity values are equal.

This one aspect of the income protection business, even if it were expanded to its full potential, would not alone support the existing life insurance industry in most modern countries. If, for example, every employed individual were insured for four times his or her salary at an average one-year term premium rate of 4 per 1,000, the total premium income of the industry would be only 1.6% of national income. In most modern countries, total premium income is already larger than this. Just to maintain its present size, the industry in those countries must provide additional services beyond protection against income loss on premature death.

Traditionally, the main service provided by the industry has been its participation in the savings business oriented either towards tax avoidance or retirement. Although tax-avoidance may be a diminishing opportunity, the future of the retirement savings business seems promising and secure, its growth assured by the expanding needs of an aging population. Since retirement is another form of income loss, savings for this purpose can be viewed as another aspect of the income protection business. This view is helpful because it separates this service from short-term savings, which is traditionally the business of banks and other thrift institutions.

If protection against loss of income is to be the primary service to be provided by the life insurance industry, disability insurance is a necessary addition. In most modern countries, this need is dramatically under-served. Notwithstanding the considerable difficulty of underwriting this business on a sound basis, it is a necessary part of the core business.

The Role of the Life Insurance Industry

In all modern countries, these three branches of the income protection business offer sufficient scope to support a vigorous and expanding life insurance industry. Although other services may be offered, this should be the core business. External competition is a factor in only one of them — savings for retirement.

What must the industry do to compete successfully in this sector of its core business? The life insurance industry will be judged by the consumer in two primary ways:

1. Product Value. The products offered in the retirement savings sector of the income protection business must be perceived to be competitive with alternate products offered by banks, other thrift institutions and mutual funds.

Consumer perception will relate mainly to expense charges and long-term investment performance expectations.

2. Effective Distribution. The life insurance industry distribution system must be as attractive as competing channels of distribution based on such perceptions as trust, the quality of the advice provided, responsive service and convenience.

Today's Challenge

The challenge for the life insurance industry is to meet the competitive standards dictated by the consumer. The two primary issues can be expressed as follows:

1. The cost of the distribution system must be consistent with its perceived value. The traditional high cost distribution method of the life insurance industry cannot be expected to compete successfully with low cost alternatives unless a clear advantage is maintained in terms of value.
2. The security and investment expectations of the products offered must compare favorably or equally with those of other available products. The traditional emphasis on security, in terms of monetary guarantees, depreciates in value if inflation is regarded as a risk as great as default. Retirement savings should be protected, if possible, from inflation risks; as a practical matter, this requires increased emphasis on products linked to the results of inflation-sensitive investments such as common stocks and real estate.

The distribution issue raises the more difficult question: Can a high-cost, agent-based distribution system, offering only life insurance industry products (or some similarly limited range of products) but providing a high degree of personal service, compete successfully against alternative distribution systems which may offer cost advantages and a wider range of products but less personal service? This question is likely to be answered differently by different sectors of the consumer market. In some important sectors, the answer is likely to be "No." While some companies might operate successfully as specialists in the remaining market sectors, the industry as a whole will not prosper if it is confined to a market limited by its own distribution methods. At least some companies, including most of the largest, must meet this potential new competition by developing (or acquiring) more efficient distribution systems offering a wider range of financial products.

In many countries, the product and investment issue has already been addressed successfully by unit-linking. These countries may offer a prototype for study by others. In some countries, changes may be required in existing regulation to permit the introduction of the desired products and investments policies. To compete successfully in the retirement savings business, the industry must not be limited in the range of products offered.

The Future

The appropriate role of life insurance in a modern society is not difficult to identify. The needs identifiable in early history remain today. The role of life insurance is to address those needs.

The appropriate role of the life insurance industry in a modern society is much less clear. While the needs of the consumer remain, their form has changed and so has the appetite of the consumer. What has also changed, in some countries, is the willingness and ability of other financial service providers to meet those needs and satisfy those appetites in new ways. The result, at least in those countries, is likely to be a convergence of previously separate financial business, particularly insurance and banking. In those countries, the continued separate existence of the life insurance industry is not assured. In those countries, the role of the industry is likely to expand to encompass or be encompassed by other insurance services and other financial services of many types.

While some may mourn the demise of the old days and their old ways, the new challenges will be pregnant with opportunity. For those with vision of whatever age, but especially for the young, these are exciting times. The old and honorable business of life insurance then contributed for many years to the quality of life in Japan, in the English-speaking countries and elsewhere. Its future opportunity for continued and expanded service to modern society is clear. For actuaries and others who serve as stewards of this industry, there is a corresponding opportunity for personal growth.

Today's Response to the Challenge of Tomorrow

Presented to the Life Insurance Marketing and Research Association (LIMRA) European Region Members' Forum, London, England, November 25, 1986. Reprinted with permission from LIMRA International.

A month ago I was honored to participate in the program of the Annual Meeting of LIMRA, held in New Orleans. Today, I am honored again by your invitation. In New Orleans, where the audience was primarily North American, my assigned topic was "How We Got Where We Are Today," to which I took the liberty of appending "And Where Do We Go From Here." The theme of this meeting, "Today's Response to the Challenge of Tomorrow" is strikingly similar — but this time the audience is predominantly European and the primary interests are the life assurance markets in the United Kingdom and the Republic of Ireland.

I will not make the tempting mistake of assuming that the future direction of the industry is the same, world-wide; if it were, I could repeat what I had to say in New Orleans! Nor should you make the mistake of ignoring what is happening elsewhere on the grounds that the situation here is different — which it is; at least you may be able to learn cheaply from the mistakes of others or, as a prison newspaper put it, "Even the worst of us can serve as horrible examples."

In North America, I have been called The Cassandra of the Industry because my prophesies, like those of Cassandra, do not usually have happy endings. Some of you may be expecting more of the same this morning. You may be getting ready to say, as Ronald Reagan said to Jimmy Carter in the

1980 Presidential Debates, "There you go again!" It will be comforting to know that, unlike Cassandra, I am not always right! Sometimes I feel that, like Cassandra, I am never believed!

The New Realities

The life insurance industry, world-wide, is confronted today with three forces of change that are present in all the relevant countries, but in different strengths:

- Changes in regulation and taxation
- New technology
- Increased volatility of financial markets.

Regulation and Taxation

During the 1980s, governments under the leadership of Margaret Thatcher, Ronald Reagan, Brian Mulroney and others of a similar political persuasion have succeeded in their efforts to arrest or reverse the trend towards extensive government regulation of business and the associated high rates of personal and company taxation. (I accept that the Financial Services Bill may be an exception to this general rule!) This somewhat hesitant movement towards a market-driven economy has opened previously regulated and protected industries (such as airlines, banking and insurance) to new competition; at the same time, the elimination of many tax preferences, such as LAPR, and the reduction in marginal tax rates has affected particularly those industries extensively involved in the business of tax avoidance — notably property development and oil and gas exploration in America and life assurance in the United Kingdom and Australia.

The expected impact of the new forms of competition on consumer behavior has already appeared in America, Australia and Canada, where the popularity of low-margin term and annuity products has increased and alternative products, such as money funds and property trusts have grown rapidly. Its full fury may first be felt in Australia, where cross competition between insurance companies and banks is underway and where major companies in both industries are involved. It is important to recognize that only a small shift of market share — say 10% to 20%, in either direction — would have a substantial and adverse impact on the economics of either business, undercutting the viability of marginal agents and marginal branches more or less equivalently. A larger shift or a disproportionate shift either way would cause considerable damage.

The impact of tax law changes is already apparent in the level and mix of sales results of the life assurance industry in the United Kingdom. So far, increased sales of pension products have mitigated the impact of the decline in non-pension sales, but will this last? Will the pension market soon become the focus of new competition, initially from building societies, (as happened in Canada in the 1970s) or will these products be the target of the next move towards tax neutrality (as happened in America last month)?

These changes in regulation and taxation should be expected to lead some consumers to look elsewhere for some of the needs traditionally met by the life assurance industry. It is simply unrealistic to expect anything else in the United Kingdom, the Republic of Ireland or elsewhere.

Technology

We accept as commonplace today electronic marvels and other wizardry that would have confounded even the science fiction fanatics of a generation ago. To believe that we have already seen the best (or worst) is nonsense.

A few illustrations will reinforce the point: this afternoon, before this meeting adjourns, I will be in Washington; some of us in this room are carrying in our briefcases £100 calculators powered by flashlight batteries that rival computers which required whole buildings to house and cost £1 million 30 years ago (equivalent to £5 million or more in 1986); in America, an ordinary telephone can be used without human intervention to initiate banking transactions, such as paying bills or transferring balances between accounts; your next new car will probably be spraypainted and partly assembled by a robot; many of us have a mobile cellular telephone installed in our cars; and we boil the water to mix with our freeze-dried coffee in 30 seconds, using a microwave oven.

What's next? For specifics, I defer to the technocrats; but I have a clear idea of one of the likely common characteristics — many of the new wonders will continue the inexorable trend to substitute machine power for manpower and even for brainpower and some of them will provide alternatives to face-to-face and people-to-people contact.

The message is clear: the cost of labor and physical facilities continues to climb while the cost of alternatives continues to fall. The implications for people-intensive businesses (such as life assurance) and facilities-intensive businesses (such as banks) are profound. They are more easily recognized in businesses other than our own. Let me explain.

Suppose your company decided tomorrow to enter the banking business. Suppose, too, that it is impractical to buy an existing bank or similar institution. Faced with the need to start from scratch, would your business plan contemplate the opening of 1,000 or more branches? I am confident it would not!

Let me reverse the question. Suppose your were recruited by a bank to lead their entry into the insurance business. Suppose, again, that it is impractical to buy an existing insurance company or similar institution. Faced with the need to start from scratch, would your business plan contemplate the recruitment of 1,000 or more agents, trained and remunerated like the successful agents of today? I am not as confident that I can answer this question! Yet the answer should be the same. The same principles of cost effectiveness apply, but we see the problem more clearly when it is not our own.

Someday, soon perhaps, somewhere, here perhaps, someone, you perhaps, will devise a much more cost-effective way to distribute life assurance products. That way will probably involve, as it does now, the personal interface of an agent-like individual at the point of sale; the cost effectiveness will probably be based on a mechanized form of prospecting supported by a powerful customer information system; the cost savings will probably be realized by substituting fixed costs (like salaries) for variable costs (like commissions), thereby reaping the benefits of increased productivity. Among a hundred different experimenters searching for the right ingredients, only one may succeed, but that will be enough. The imitators will flock to the winning strategy.

This is not idle speculation. Within 15 years, at the dawn of the third millennium, the probability of this is 100% for all practical purposes; within 10 years, the probability is 75%; and within 5 years, the probability is 50%.

Volatility

The volatility of financial markets has become a regular feature of Wall Street on "triple witching hour" Fridays, when closing dates of various option and future contracts coincide. During the turbulent 1970s, the Beta of the gilt-edged market often exceeded that of common stocks — in London, in New York and elsewhere.

With increased volatility has come increased risk to financial intermediaries of all types. The risk of insolvency has been demonstrated to be real for both life and general insurance companies and for banks, on both sides of the Atlantic.

Increased risk has placed a large premium on size and capital for financial institutions of all kinds.

Financial instability has been accompanied by high and fluctuating rates of interest and high rates of inflation. The willingness of the consumer to save has eroded in some countries and the preferred choice among alternative savings products has changed almost everywhere. Here in the United Kingdom and also in Ireland the life assurance industry has responded well with timely new products, mainly of the unit-linked variety. Elsewhere, the industry has fared less well. In each affected market, agents and brokers were the first to feel the impact of changes in consumer preference — in their next commission check! In countries such as America, Australia and Canada, rates of commission and the cost of other benefits have increased because the industry responded to the need to protect the incomes of its only distribution system.

The Social Contract

In most countries, with an advanced life assurance market, there existed until recent years a stable social contract involving:

- the consumer, who tolerated high margin products (especially, high front-end loads);
- the agent, who remained loyal to his primary company and tolerated a commission cartel (New York Section 213 and the LOA Commission Agreement);
- the industry, which refrained from aggressive price and commission competition; and, in some countries,

- government, which subsidized the process, deliberately or inadvertently, through the tax system.

Collapse

Today, except in Japan, South Africa and the United Kingdom, that social contract has collapsed. The consumer has revolted; the loyal agent has become the demanding independent intermediary; the industry now engages in predatory price and commission competition (including raids on each other's business); and government, knowingly or unknowingly, has withdrawn its support.

Faced with the escalating expectations of consumers, increased commission demands and reduced government support, the profit margins of the industry have shrunk dramatically — often below zero on new business. Seeking to improve their cost fundamentals, many companies have elected to consolidate and become part of a larger group; others have engaged in major cost-cutting programs with major and adverse consequences to many of the affected employees, especially executives and middle managers.

In these countries, the Glory Years have been followed by the Troubled Years. Fortunately, the world-wide recovery of financial markets, which began in 1982, has strengthened the capital funds of the industry. This has provided breathing space, giving the industry time and resources to adapt to the New Realities. These are the Opportunity Years, but they will not last forever.

The Financial Services Bill

In the United Kingdom, the Social Contract is substantially intact — the one major exception is the withdrawal of government support for non-pension business. The fundamental ingredients for collapse are, however, present — consumer rejection, causing agent defection, causing commission escalation, etc.

The Financial Services Bill, by its requirement of polarization and its practical limitation on broker commissions (indirectly affecting agency commissions), affords some assurance that the Social Contract will continue — in some form — by promoting single company representation and by breaking the chain reaction at the point of commission escalation.

It does not, of course, guarantee consumer support for the high margin products offered by the industry. It does not guarantee that the current incomes of agents and brokers will continue. And it does not guarantee that new and more efficient distribution methods will not undercut the traditional system of agent and broker distribution. Mainly, it does reasonably assure that traditional offices will not become involved in an internal, self-destructive competitive battle on familiar terrain. It also reasonably assures that it will not be as easy, in the future, for an aggressive company to gain relative market share by offering commission inducements to brokers.

In summary, this legislation should work to the advantage of the industry, particularly the already established companies. One subtle threat is the possibility that it will also lead to complacency and increase vulnerability to an external threat — from banks or nontraditional competitors. Clearly it is a major step in the direction of re-regulation, contrary to contemporary political orthodoxy.

The Challenge of Tomorrow

The Challenge of Tomorrow is to deal effectively with the New Realities. The Financial Services Bill does not diminish that Challenge, even if it reasonably assures that the industry will not be called upon to meet it in a state of internal disarray caused by the progressive collapse of the Social Contract. How can this Challenge best be met?

Strategic Options

I suggest to you that most companies — nearly all, in fact — require a new, or revised, or better understood strategic initiative. The basic strategy of this industry needs re-examination. If it is sound, it should be reinforced; if it is found wanting it should be changed.

This discussion will be limited to strategic options aimed at continued independence and success; a discussion of the options involving sale to or merger with another company of larger or similar size must wait for another time and place.

Continued independence and success depends on establishing sustainable competitive viability. There are two and only two foundations for sustainable competitive viability:

- superior cost fundamentals and/or
- competitive avoidance.

Note the "and/or"; these two possible foundations are not mutually exclusive — on the contrary, they are mutually supportive and often, in the best managed companies, they are found together. Nevertheless, they are quite different and need separately to be understood.

Superior Cost Fundamentals

At the beginning, let's be sure we understand the objectives of the superior cost fundamentals strategy. The objective of this strategy is to establish competitive viability on the basis of low prices or high commissions, support that strategy by having superior cost fundamentals in other respects. Notice, low prices or high commissions. In our complex business, prices and commissions are interchangeably and inversely connected.

If this strategy to compete on the basis of low prices or high commissions is to be broadly based — in other words, if it is to cover many product lines, large sectors of the marketplace and so forth — you need to understand that critical mass is very large. My personal estimate is that, to compete in the broad middle market on the basis of superior cost fundamentals, a company requires individual new premium income of at least £25 million. Without that volume, it cannot in my view realistically aspire to achieve superior fundamentals in the broad marketplace.

It can, however, aspire to achieve superior cost fundamentals and compete successfully as a specialist company. It can decide that it is only going to do one thing or a few things and that it is going to do that one thing or those few things more efficiently than anyone else. It therefore expects to achieve superior cost fundamentals and compete successfully in its selected niche at a much smaller size. This is a realistic idea, but you should understand that the concept of traditional, primary company agency distribution system is inconsistent with this idea; it is unrealistic to expect agents to represent one company primarily and then restrict them to a narrow product line or market. In practical terms, in the United Kingdom, this strategy would be aimed at the broker market or supported by a nontraditional distribution system.

One of the problems with either strategy based on superior cost fundamentals is that the commitment to maintaining these superior fundamentals is permanent. This position is difficult to maintain. By definition, no more than 50% of the competitors can have superior cost fundamentals. The sensitive factors, in rough order of their importance, are as follows: the first is expenses, the second is investment returns, the third is persistency, and the fourth, a distant fourth, is mortality experience. It should also be noted that the life insurance industry, because of its high cost tradition, is not well positioned to compete on cost fundamentals with external competition from other industries, such as the banking industry or the investment industry, which enjoy a different historical cost position. In some plausible future scenarios, superior cost fundamentals become even more difficult to maintain in the face of new forms of competition.

Competitive Avoidance

Let me now discuss the other possible strategic options intended to provide continued independence and success. These are the strategies which are based on competitive avoidance. For most companies that aspire to independence, unless they are already large or well positioned to become specialists, these are the only realistic choices. Again, let's review the objective: the objective is to compete on the basis of higher prices or lower commissions than the price/commission leaders, avoiding price and commission competition by offering differentiated products or services, or by establishing a captive market or a captive distribution system. I repeat, the objective is to compete on the basis of higher prices or lower commissions, and to avoid competition by differentiation of product or service, or by establishing a captive market or a captive distribution system.

In our business, the product is money for future delivery and meaningful product differentiation is very difficult to achieve. There are also no significant patents, copyrights, or whatever in this industry; therefore, any product differentiation that is successful is likely soon to be imitated and the action of the imitators will probably undercut the success of the strategy by forcing prices down or commissions up. You can observe this phenomenon if you compare the initial and later experiences of the companies that first introduced unit-linked products, those that first attached the maximum tax avoidance market and those that first promoted income bonds.

Experience in other fields suggests, however, that product differentiation, if soundly conceived, will work. The public will indeed pay premium prices for premium benefits. Public acceptance is particularly noticeable when the premium benefits offered are aimed at their convenience, their comfort, their prestige, their self-confidence or their desire for personal service and recognition.

Some Examples

Let me give you some examples. Several years ago, many of you in this room received a mailing from the American Express Company which offered you the opportunity to carry a platinum American Express card. Some of you, when you received that mailing, may have remembered the unimpressive fellow in front of you in the checkout line the last time you were at a hotel had a green card just like yours. You may have felt the urge to accept the offer to acquire a platinum card to bolster your self-confidence. It cost you about £100 a year. The benefits you received were not really worth £100, but it did provide you with the confidence that you would impress the cashier the next time you checked out of a hotel! If you accepted the offer, you're not alone. On the first mailing, I am told that 50,000 people accepted the offer of the platinum card; as a result, almost £5 million dropped to the bottom line of the American Express Company's travel division! Self-confidence for sale at £100 per year!

Another example is a department store in America which also decided to offer a special charge card. One of my associates asked what benefits people received by paying $50 for the gold card when they could have regular card free. It was explained to him that when the gold card holders came into the store they had a special place to go in the store where they were given a free cup of coffee, and they got free gift wrapping — all of which didn't really add up to enough to make the price worthwhile. But the retailer went on to say, "But what they really like is what we call the 'gold gush'." The gold gush works like this: when a customer comes in with a gold card the salespeople are trained to react; they call to the sales person at the next cash register and say, "Look — I've got a gold card customer!" The other sales person is trained to come over and say, "My, my — A gold card!" By this time all of the other nearby customers are gathered around to see what all the fuss is about. They call this the "gold gush" and they train their sales personnel to do it! Personal attention for sale at $50 per year!

Not long ago I did a favor for some friends in Atlanta, and they thoughtfully gave me a memento. It was a glass paperweight, shaped like an oversized emerald, very nicely made. If K-mart sold them, I expect that they would offer them for about $1.50 each. However, this one has significant product differentiation. If you set this glass paperweight on the desk, without turning it over, you can read through the prism on the top of the paperweight what is stamped upside down on the bottom. What is stamped there is "Tiffany & Company." Now, I am sure that this particular paperweight did not cost $1.50, and I am also sure that the difference in price had nothing to do with the extra cost of stamping the bottom! This illustrates that people will pay for and appreciate prestige benefits. I am very fond of my Tiffany paperweight!

First class air travel is another example of a premium benefit for which the public will pay a substantial premium price. In this case, the product is comfort.

Realistic Possibilities

All of these are fairly exotic examples. What are some realistic possibilities for the life assurance industry? One of them is superior sales support; that's taking the view that the differentiation is the sales support that you give your intermediaries.The idea is to make it more convenient for them to do business with you; in the context of the Financial Services Bill, this is likely to attract more attention as related to the broker market. Another is exotic conventions. Again, the appeal is to the agent, based in recognition and ego-gratification. A third example is investment performance, a real potential differentiator between life assurance products which appeals both to intermediaries and to consumers; in this case, beauty is in the eye of the beholder!

Let me explain. When I was with Abbey Life, we had a fairly aggressive advertising program, which featured investment expertise. At that time our investment manager was Hambros Bank. Hambros Bank had and has an outstanding image and reputation, but some of our agents weren't satisfied with their actual investment performance at that time. They sometimes amused themselves by writing mock headlines for our advertising copy. One of them was, "Let Hambros Bank show you how to make a small fortune," and the subtitle said "First you start with a large fortune..." The lesson is that perceived investment performance is what counts, not actual investment performance!

The strategy of competitive avoidance might be targeted on the consumer or might more likely be targeted on the intermediary. But remember the objective. The objective is to charge higher prices or to pay lower commissions so that average cost fundamentals can be supported.

Captive Markets and Distribution

Another way of achieving competitive avoidance is through a captive market. This is a rarity, but it features very prominently in the strategy of banks that are interested in widening their involvement in financial service businesses.

Recently, I had the pleasure of speaking to a group of people from one of the Lutheran Fraternals in America (a type of Friendly Society); in the course of that discussion, I made the observation that they have something that is pretty close to a captive market, which is very, very rare in my experience in this industry. In fact, the only other example of a captive market that readily came to mind was the membership of the United States Automobile Association, all of whom are active or retired military officers. It was also very interesting to note that both the Lutheran Fraternal and USAA have a similar problem — their membership isn't expanding fast enough because soldiers and Lutherans are not being "manufactured" in sufficient numbers. I said to the Lutherans, "Now, USAA's problem could be solved with a small war; but your problem is going to take a second Reformation!"

Captive Distribution

Likewise, captive distribution is another effective method of competitive avoidance. That, in fact, has been the predominant strategy of this industry in the United Kingdom, Ireland and elsewhere. Today this is also quite rare in some countries and some cynics have said, "Ah yes, captive distribution — raising the question, 'Who is the captive?'"

Most companies represented here are likely to focus their efforts on building a captive distribution system. Through it, they expect to reach the agent's semi-captive market. In that market they will be able to realize higher margins through higher prices. This strategy is sound today. It could, however, be undercut by new competitive forces offering significantly lower prices supported by superior cost fundamentals. Even a small loss of market share could have a devastating effect on the economics and viability of such a distribution system. This strategy calls for a supporting or back-up plan to meet such an eventuality.

Conclusion

I believe that one of the important ingredients of success is self-understanding. Another is conviction — conviction that Business as Usual is not a winning strategy. I also hope and believe that most of those who dare to be different will be among the winners.

This aging prophet thanks you for your invitation.

Challenges and Opportunities for Life Insurance Companies in the Pacific Rim

Presented to the Life Office Management Association (LOMA), Singapore, September 23, 1990. Reprinted with permission from LOMA.

Today I will address the challenges and opportunities for life insurance companies in the Pacific Rim. Please don't "shoot the messenger"! I do not intend to present a country-by-country review, because I have neither the time nor the expertise to do justice to the topic on that basis. Instead, I intend to address the subject in a more generic sense and leave it to the audience to apply the principles which I will outline to the specific circumstances of each of the many and varied countries which comprise the vast region of the Pacific Rim.

Nature of the Business

Let me begin by reminding you of the nature of the business of life insurance. Its primary focus is on income protection relating to several contingencies affecting the lives of our customers:

- Premature death
- Disability
- Retirement

Cynics might add to the list the income protection of our agents! Even more cynically, ourselves!

For companies operating in some countries, notably the United States of America, the financing and administration of medical reimbursement plans is another important business but, since this applies to only a limited number of the members of this audience, I intend merely to note rather than to discuss this aspect of the life insurance business.

The future of the primary businesses of the life insurance industry is reasonably secure in most countries of the Pacific Rim. The need for income protection in each of its aspects is obvious and, as a practical matter, government is the only potential substitute provider.

Key Factors for a Viable Market

Many of you here today are involved or considering involvement in what might be described as emerging markets. The private life insurance industry can succeed only if certain key factors are present in a particular marketplace.

- Stable currency. Since benefits are denominated in monetary terms and extend over long periods of time, a stable currency is a necessary precondition for a viable market. Indexing and unit-linking are potential ways to overcome the lack of stable currency values, but these may involve unacceptably high risks to the insurance companies which act as financial intermediaries. There are historical examples of the demise and resurrection of the life insurance industry in countries which have experienced consistently high rates of inflation. Twenty-five years ago, one microcosmic example occurred in Iceland. There, the industry, which had reverted to an all-term status, was briefly resurrected by the introduction of unit-linked products based on overseas investments; these new products were then prohibited by the Landisbank Island, the National Central Bank, following which the industry again reverted to an all-term status.
- A market of reasonable size involving those with discretionary income. There can be no quantification of the necessary size since it is dependent upon the numbers of competitors and the relative margins available. Each situation must be evaluated on its own merits. But it is clear that a market, such as the Peoples Republic of China, which involves vast numbers of people who are living at near subsistence levels does not, despite their numbers, constitute a viable market.
- Availability of technical and management expertise. Technical and management expertise is required if a successful life insurance industry is to develop.

Some of the expertise may be imported from other countries but much of it, particularly in the sales area, will be required to have language skills and local knowledge particular to each market.

- Benevolent regulation. The life insurance industry, because of its fiduciary responsibility extending over long periods of time, prospers in a regulated environment as opposed to an unregulated environment. The reason for this is founded in the requirement for public confidence in institutions which trade in long-term future promises. But it is important that the regulation be of a benevolent nature, with particular concern for financial stability, rather than regulation of a restrictive type, which dictates terms and conditions under which the business is conducted, thereby suppressing innovation and healthy competition.
- Taxation. The life insurance industry, particularly as related to retirement income protection, is largely tax driven. The business prospers in those environments which provide tax incentives for savings through life insurance and which provide special tax incentives for the accumulation of retirement savings through pension plans. "Save now, pay taxes later" is the central theme.
- Availability of appropriate investments. The life insurance industry must have reasonably free access to investments which meet the needs of the industry and the nature of its liabilities. Investment in government securities is not an adequate answer. Privately issued debt securities, reasonably liquid property investments, a locally active stock exchange, and access to international securities markets are required to meet these needs.
- Political stability. The life insurance industry rarely can prosper absent political stability, not only currently but also prospectively and, since the nature of the business is long term, the time horizon of the anticipated political stability must match that of the business.
- Adequate capital. The life insurance business is capital intensive and requires an adequate capital base to be successful.

Competitive Forces

Unless prices, products and commission practices are extensively regulated, the life insurance industry everywhere faces intra-industry competition, which varies in intensity in different countries. In many countries, including Australia, Canada, New Zealand, and the United States, extra-industry competition has intensified in recent years and this is likely to be a continuing trend which will spread to other countries; this extra-industry competition tends to focus on the market for retirement savings plans and is not confined to life insurance products.

In various countries there is a marked trend towards the consolidation of financial service business of various types — life insurance, banking, general insurance, and investment businesses. This trend is likely to increase the extent of extra-industry competition, involving businesses with very different economics. Potentially, this may be damaging to the prospects of the life insurance industry, which generally operates as a high cost competitor and which may face strong price competition from other branches of the financial services industry with superior cost fundamentals.

The differences in the economics of the life insurance business, the banking businesses, and the investment business need to be understood. If each business were to express its margins as an "equivalent level load," using the parlance of the mutual fund/unit trust business, the cost structure of the life insurance industry would be in the range of 30%–40% of each and every premium; that of the banking business on long-term deposits would be 10%–15% of each deposit; and that of the mutual fund/unit-trust/investment industry would be 5%–10% of each investment. These are large differences. To some extent there are two major offsets: in some countries, life insurance products enjoy tax advantages not available on other financial products and in practically all countries, the life insurance industry offers the only "high-touch" distribution system, which customers obviously value highly. Nevertheless, the single greatest challenge to the life insurance industry is to reduce its expenses, two-thirds of which relate to the distribution process.

Markets of the Pacific Rim

The markets of the Pacific Rim are varied and diverse. Depending on exactly where the boundaries are drawn, this vast region encompasses 40% of the world's population, half of which is in the People's Republic of China. The countries which comprise this region include some of the most advanced and economically successful in the world, all with well developed life insurance markets, some of the most remarkable rapidly developing countries and some of the most primitive societies in the world.

The political situations which prevail are as mixed as the economic situations. The political stability of various countries and the region as a whole is threatened by a wide variety of potential problems:

- Last year's turmoil in the People's Republic of China suggests that that vast country is liable to undergo major political change — either revolution, or repression, or both.
- Notwithstanding the normalization of relationships between the Soviet Union and the People's Republic of China, there remains unresolved a border dispute along a frontier of more than 4,000 miles.
- Japan and the Soviet Union have an unresolved dispute involving the sovereignty of the Kurile Islands.
- The future of Hong Kong remains uncertain, more so now because of recent events in the People's Republic of China.
- Warfare continues in Indochina.
- The Philippines, following a remarkable bloodless revolution, has since had three attempted but unsuccessful coups d'état.
- The two Koreas remain at political odds.
- In Central and South America, which form most of the eastern boundary of the Pacific Rim, political and economic chaos are endemic.
- Even Fiji, which has long enjoyed stable government, has recently experienced a coup d'état.

The foregoing list, which is by no means complete, represents an imposing list of problems. While it is reasonable to suppose that time alone may cure some of the problems, it would be far too optimistic to assume that time alone will cure all of them. In the words of Abba Eban, the former Israeli Foreign Minister: "In the end, men and nations will do the reasonable thing, but only after they have exhausted all of the other alternatives."

The danger lies in the process of exhausting the other alternatives, which often becomes uncontrolled. Events in the Persian Gulf provide a current example.

It would also be a mistake to assume that over time the less developed countries will '"catch up" economically with the more developed countries. In fact, the opposite is more likely. Not every country can or will follow the example of Singapore. When the developed countries of the world, for admirable humanitarian reasons, decided to send penicillin, other wonder drugs, and medical assistance to the less-developed countries, it had the effect of increasing the survival rate of children to the reproductive age and has lit the fuse of a population time bomb which may have more severe eventual consequences than the original problem. If the reproductive rhythm in a particular country is based upon five children per family and if formerly only two lived to reproduce but now four live to reproduce, the consequence is that the population will double with each generation, say 25 years. This is precisely what is happening in many of the under-developed countries of the world, most notably in Kenya, which is experiencing an annual population growth rate of 3%, but also in certain countries of the Pacific Rim. In truth, the developed countries should have sent 100 condoms with each dose of penicillin!

When the population growth rate of any country equals or exceeds the growth rate of savings, it is likely that the economic progress of that country will either stagnate or suffer a reverse. In many less developed countries, the per-capita Gross National Product is constant or even declining. When this happens, the chronic disappointment of the populace will lead inevitably to political discontent and the most probable outcome is government repression, increased expenditure on police and military (exacerbating the problem), the advance of fanatical religious beliefs (a long established substitute for economic progress), the resort to international adventurism and even terrorism. It all sounds depressingly familiar — it sounds like modern-day Iran.

Iran is by no means an isolated example of this progression. Iraq is another. And we may soon witness another example in Argentina, which has recently suspended civil liberties, which is currently experiencing a rate of inflation of 50% per month (equivalent to a Weimar-like annual rate of 13,000%) and which last year elected a populist president on a platform of redistribution of wealth, renunciation of foreign debts, and a pledge to recover the Falklands/Malvinas. It takes little vision to imagine where this is likely to lead.

Opportunities and Problems

For companies already operating in the Pacific Rim and for companies considering entry to one or more of the markets of this region, there are both challenges and opportunities.

The opportunities are most likely to be found in those countries with rapidly developing economies, such as South Korea, the Republic of China (Taiwan), Hong Kong, and Singapore. But it must be recognized that in all but the last of these four countries, there are significant political risks which must be assessed in the light of a business that hardly can be expected to break even in less than twenty years. Exactly because these four markets stand out, they are also likely to become crowded unless entry is restrained by regulation; this raises the danger that capacity may expand even more rapidly than the markets themselves.

Countries with pre-emergent economies may also represent attractive markets, but only for investors with great patience. Nevertheless, a foothold development in these countries could prove to be very rewarding in the long term.

Countries with subsistence level economies and countries experiencing a decline in per-capita GNP appear to be very unattractive target markets except for investors with the patience of Job. Such an investment may, in fact, represent a bet favoring the establishment of a Worldwide Marshall Plan on an unimaginably grandiose scale designed to lift the economies of such countries closer to modern standards; this is a multigenerational bet since it necessarily implies very long-term progress involving education and training which cannot be achieved in a single generation.

The developed countries of the Pacific Rim present challenges and opportunities of an entirely different kind. In these markets, many of which are already overcrowded, the competitive situation is such that investors in a life insurance enterprise are unlikely to realize an adequate return on capital unless they are able to devise a "better mousetrap." Such an innovation, aimed at lowering costs and improving margins, is unlikely to be product-driven because imitation is relatively easy; for example, those who were first in the introduction of Universal Life in the U.S.A. enjoyed a first entrant advantage for only three to four years and even this short period was extended by important constraints placed upon the larger companies in the areas of systems and taxation. A service-based advantage, including sharp focus on particular market segments, could be much more long lived and might possibly be permanent. But the most dramatic advantage of all would be the development of a much more efficient system of distribution promising the possibility of a reduction in distribution costs of perhaps 50% and a reduction in overall costs of perhaps 33%; this is the possibility that has attracted the interest of certain banks in the life insurance industry and their operating plans are modeled along the lines suggested. An orthodox entry into the life insurance business of the developed countries of the Pacific Rim does not appear to be an attractive proposition. Many foreign-based companies have withdrawn from the Australian market.

The life insurance market in Japan deserves special mention. Clearly, it is the most successful in the world and, among the developed countries, it is one of the youngest. The Japanese life insurance industry is very large, very concentrated and capitalized at levels that are beyond the imagination of life insurance companies based elsewhere.

Let me give you some indication of what I mean by "capital resources":

- assets at market in excess of minimum statutory liabilities or realistic liabilities reflecting reasonable bonus expectations
- U.S. life industry capital resources are less than $100 billion, shared by 200 major companies (average $500 million, maximum $5 billion)
- Japanese life industry capital resources are estimated at $400 billion, shared by twenty major companies (average $20 billion, maximum $100 billion).

These companies are very formidable competitors for reasons of their size and their capital resources alone. For companies that aspire to enter the Japanese life insurance market, they present a major challenge. On the other hand, these companies, which for the most part have not yet expanded overseas, might decide to enter other markets where their capital resources could make them formidable competitors in a relatively short period of time. Potentially, the major Japanese life insurance companies, and even some of the minor ones, could have the most profound influence upon the future development of the life insurance markets of the Pacific Rim. These companies possess the resources either to buy their way or to burn their way into any market — including the U.S.A.

The Outlook

The outlook is for further rapid economic progress for most of the countries of the Pacific Rim, particularly those in Asia. This growing prosperity will probably spill over to some extent to neighboring countries, excepting those with population growth problems. Against this optimistic prognosis must be weighed the effects of some of the political problems already alluded to; these might either flare up in a serious way or, fueled by general prosperity, progress towards more stable societies. A mixed outcome to those political problems seems by far to be most likely.

In summary, there are reasons to be selectively optimistic in economic terms, but there are also reasons to be selectively cautious in political terms.

Section 6
The Actuarial Profession

Our Social Contract

Presented to a Tillinghast Officers Meeting, January 1, 1985.
Reprinted with permission from Tillinghast - A Towers Perrin Company.

I gave considerable thought to what to say today. Those of you who know me well will not be not surprised to learn that it's my custom to prepare remarks like this during the course of the meeting, and I do so partly out of my predilection for last-minute deadlines, but partly also to try to make them relevant to what is going on. One of the positive aspects of this arguably is that, therefore, there are never any slides. I was not unrewarded in this strategy this time around because yesterday at lunch our guest speaker, Jim Hayes, provided me with a theme. The theme basically is that organizations must have strategic plans and that those strategic plans must be communicated to the people who are involved in carrying them out. Now, Tillinghast does have and has long had a strategic plan. What it doesn't have is a book. We have talked about our strategic plans from many occasions in fragmentary groups, but I'm not certain that those strategic plans have been talked about to all of you at once, and that's what I propose to do this morning.

What is the strategic plan for us? Let me tell you what I think it is. I think our strategic plan is our joint commitment to a credible program to achieve an attainable goal to which we can collectively relate. I think that's what must be our strategic plan. Therefore, my remarks today are not going to be an epilogue; they're going to be a prologue. I want to talk to you about the future and not about the past. Issues I'm going to address are these — there are three: where have we been, where are we now, and where are we going?

Let's start with where have we been. In terms of our past strategic plan, it's clear from any outsider's point of view, if he stood back and looked at us, that our basic policy has been rational growth. That has been the strategic plan of Tillinghast for a long period of time, at least a decade. And it's worth inquiring why. First, rational growth has been pursued by us because of the belief that critical mass is a valid concept. It applies to each of our service areas separately. It applies even to the units through which we conduct our practice, the individual offices, if you like, or units within those offices. Critical mass has been one of the driving forces behind our strategic plan of rational growth. Our second motivation has been to achieve broad coverage of each of the three areas of service that are addressed by the actuarial profession. We, beginning as a firm of actuaries, were interested in covering each of those areas of service — the life insurance industry, the property/casualty industry, sponsors of employee benefit plans — the three traditional actuarial areas of service. We wanted to cover each of them. We wanted to be a full service actuarial firm at the outset, if you like.

Next, we were seeking stature. This policy of rational growth was partially an ego trip. We were seeking stature within the actuarial profession, and we were seeking stature outside. Next, we were seeking international stature. We were seeking this because an opportunity was presented to us in 1972 on which we have built since. In the process of that building, we have managed to replace what used to be called in this firm a Manitoba mafia with something that we call today the British mafia, and such are the consequences of this kind of expansion from time to time. I would suggest that we're going to have to start watching out for the Aussies as well. This firm is now a very international firm.

Our other reasons: If you look back on the time at which we embarked on this rational growth policy, we had a group of people in this firm who were young, they were ambitious and they were energetic. And they needed a mountain to climb. And growth was the mountain. Finally, growth carried with it financial attractions. The financial attractions were the prospect that it would lead to higher compensation for the individuals involved in the business of the firm and it would improve their security. Growth was our policy and those were the reasons why. And how was it achieved? Importantly, it was achieved via mergers and acquisitions. More than 25 firms make up the members of this audience today; 10 of them have joined us within the last 20 months. So mergers and acquisitions of other professional practices have been a prominent way of achieving the goal.

Second, we have attempted to create a culture which is conducive to internal growth and this, in fact, has been the most important element of our growth. What we have done importantly is to expand the beach heads that were established via the merger and acquisition group. Next, our growth has been opportunistically driven. We have been inclined to be interested in opportunities, almost any type, as long as they weren't misfits. Opportunistic growth has been a feature of where we have been. There's an exception to this. We have made one series of strategic acquisitions — these were done consciously and for a purpose. Those were the acquisitions that were made that took us into the risk management consulting business. This strategic decision was in response to the perception of what I call actuarial ground pasture. Now, we're going to come back to that in a few minutes.

Financial constraints have placed limitations on our growth in the past. These financial constraints have been in the form of the amount of equity capital we had inside the firm, but more importantly, our current income requirements for current distribution to employees. These have been important limitations for what we have been able to do. It has dictated the type of growth, it has dictated the limits on our growth. Let me repeat though that most growth has not come per se by the mergers and acquisition route. It basically has come from the recruiting which has followed those activities. And the growth has thus been internal. The beach head established the merger and acquisition route, the beach head exploited through appropriate recruiting.

What's the key challenge? The key challenge is having achieved all this — how did we achieve it? What was it that made us succeed where others might have failed? The key, in my opinion, was our ability to maintain what we call our culture, but if we were being a little more precise with our words, we might call it our social contract, in the midst of rapid expansion. We have been able to preserve that culture or social contract in the midst of rapid expansion. Let me tell you what I think the main provisions of our social contract are, and by social contract, I mean the relationship between me and each of you individually, between each of you individually and the others individually. I think that our social contract importantly includes a joint commitment to professional excellence. I think that is probably article one of our social contract. Second, it includes the concept that the emphasis should be on self discipline and self motivation. Third, it contains important provisions dealing with the fact that we share our fortunes with each other, good and bad. There is a strong element of sharing in our social contract, and I mean financial sharing. Contrasting to this and limiting it, the social contract also contains provisions that say, there must be adequate incentives within this organization to attract and retain capable people. If I were to describe our social contract in a few words, these are some that come to mind. I think it is tolerant but demanding. I think it is governed by the rule of reason. That's where I think we have been.

Where are we now? First, we have achieved critical mass, and stature is no longer a major concern in three of the four areas of our professional practice: casualty, life and risk management. But this is a continued concern in our employee benefits consulting operation, both critical mass and stature. Therefore, from this point forward, our growth in each of the areas of practice, should be strategically driven. We should seek to grow into areas that we specifically choose as targets of growth. That should apply to all of our areas of practice. Second, we should continue to be interested in opportunity growth as a means of achieving critical mass and stature in the employee benefits division and also as a means of entering other businesses that make strategic sense to us. Critical mass — that's our current position.

Next, we have to continue to defend our culture. I think it will require constant vigilance if we're to maintain that culture. That is the reason why we're all in this room today. It means that we have to continue to strive for the objectives that are involved in the program we call operation upgrade, and that operation upgrade basically means that each of us tries to hire people that are better than ourselves — better than ourselves — that's what operation upgrade means. We have to foster mutual trust, mutual confidence and good will. Within an expanding universe, there will be more than 300 people a year from now or within the next year constituting the professional staffs of Tillinghast, and as this universe expands, we're going to have to work harder to foster that mutual trust, mutual confidence and good will that is essential to our continuation as a successful organization. It's normal within an organization of this kind or any kind that from time to time there should be a certain amount of unhappiness — that is normal. If it didn't exist, the situation would not be normal, but what we must be careful of is that unhappiness does not become chronic and does not become concentrated in specific groups or pockets. For example, we've got to guard against the possibility that our U.S. and non-U.S. branches of the firm might, one or the other, become unhappy, collectively. We've got to guard against the possibility that the people who form the professional staff of one of our consulting divisions become collectively unhappy. We've got to be careful that people who occupy a certain status or income in the firm become collectively unhappy. Some unhappiness is normal — chronic concentrated unhappiness very dangerous indeed. We're going to have to confirm that social contract does indeed involve the sharing of fortune, good or bad. In 1985, they offer us a mild test of that clause in our social contract because the distributable earnings this year are running below our normal expectations. The July figures show 17% distributable profits against our goal of 20%. We're roughly a million dollars short. That million dollars is going to fall exactly into the hands of the people in this room. And that's going to be a subtract of one million from the 275 people in this room, and that is going to have to be dealt with and dealt with in a way that does not fracture our social contract.

Defending our culture, I think it also imposes considerable duty on each of us to behave in a certain way. If we are successful individually, if we are successful, I think we need to be tolerant of others, and if we are not as successful, I think we have to feel the pressure of our own self demands to improve. That's how I think this organization can progress and to realize all of its future potential. We have an inherent conflict in our operation that will always be present. The inherent conflict is that between professionalism and commercialism. If you like, it's a conflict between our soul and our bodies. It's always present; it always will be present. We could do something to ease that conflict. We can ease it and diminish its importance simply by better business practices which do not threaten our professionalism. Obviously, none of us wants to make, let's say, fee deals that are outrageous from a client's viewpoint even though they're commercially very attractive. We don't want to make arrangements commercially which threaten our professional standards. We don't want to undertake things that are very commendable professionally that threaten our financial results.

We're trying to resolve these conflicts all of the time. The things we can do that make it less necessary that we resolve the conflict is simply to sharpen up our business practices in those areas where there is no cause for action. For example, our billing practices, our practice with respect to how we deal with our expenses where each of us has a wide latitude, and our practice with respect to the staffing of our units. All of these are areas where we can bring closer together our professional objectives and our commercial objectives and avoid conflict.

We talk about leadership and organization. In 1985, as we have every year for a number of years, a new board of directors was elected by the principals of the firm. This year, that board involved a significant change. Significantly, we witnessed the younging of our governments. Two of the members of the board are under age 40. A new committee has recently been established to take yet another look at some of the refinements of the procedure whereby we deal with our governments. We've seen this year or within the last year the appointment of two new managing principals of divisions of the firm, and we have seen one managing principal transferred from one division to another. This has been change in our relationship and organization. These changes, I think, are important and necessary. They bring to our organization a vitality and a freshness that I see no other way to obtain.

There is a considerable lesson to be learned from the great cultural revolution of China. Chairman Mao who may well be recorded by history as one of the truly great men of the 20th century, regardless of what we think of his politics, did something quite unusual for a leader. When he recognized that his revolution had run out of steam, he knew that time had come to change things. That was an unusual insight on the part of leadership. He made a mistake by reintroducing in a new form the original revolution again, thinking that he had changed things, when in fact he simply had reinstituted the same thing. His successor has not made the same mistake.

One of the most compelling reasons for having new people involved in leadership roles in any kind of organization, be it a business like ours, be it a government, be it whatever, is to bring the freshness and the vitality that comes with new ideas from new people who aren't wedded to the past, who can look through the other end of the telescope and see things differently. Changes in leadership should apply throughout this organization. It's clear that it applies to the board, it's clear that it has applied to the division managing principals, and I have now decided that the time has come when it should apply to me as well.

At its December board meeting, the board of directors will be asked to designate my successor, and that successor will assume office at the time of our next annual meeting. At that time, in my opinion, we will have outgrown what I call our second generation management structure. We will have outgrown it in three years. The current structure was put in place at the beginning of 1984. My successor will be fortunate in that he will have the opportunity as he begins his term of office to introduce the third generation organizational structure in accordance with what he thinks are the best ideas of the time. Our current position is stronger than it has been in many years in one other important respect. The firm today has equity capital of about $7 million, and that represents approximately 14% of our revenues. This is a stronger capital position than we have enjoyed in quite some years.

Now, at last, let me talk about where we are going. It's my firm view that any strategic plan — name your organization, and I will apply the standard — any strategic plan is suspect if it is not propelled by natural forces. Now what does that mean? Well, that means simply that I would sooner walk down those stairs rather than up them. I would sooner swim with the current rather than against it. I'd sooner sail with the wind rather than against it. This is sound, sensible, common sense strategy. The opposite usually is not. When strategic plans are undertaken that involve walking uphill, swimming against the current, sailing into the wind, those strategic plans are suspect.

Well, what are the natural forces that relate to what we do, what we do as professionals? Well, with respect to a lot of us in this room, those who are actuaries, that's probably still more than 50% of this audience, natural forces are not moving in a direction which is favorable long-term for most traditional areas of actuarial practice. The exception to that is taking place in the casualty division. But in the life division and in the benefits division, natural forces are not going in a direction that is helpful to traditional areas of actuarial practice. Therefore, we, and this we I mean to apply to the actuaries among us, we, the actuaries, must seek outward expansion in our profession and in our professional activities. With respect to our professional organizations, if necessary, we must lead that outward expansion worldwide, because the problems are the same in practically every country. The actuarial profession is going to enter, in my view, an extended period of decline if it doesn't do something about this. We are an important enough force in that profession to have considerable voice in what is going to happen, and I am suggesting that we ought to raise our voices and lead the profession, if necessary, upward from its traditional center.

As a business, what does this mean to us? It means that the nonactuarial areas of our practice must become the focus of our strategic attention. Otherwise, we are not going to have a strategic plan that is propelled by natural forces. We must focus our strategic attention on the nonactuarial areas of our practice. What does this include? It includes risk management, it includes our activities in the merger and acquisition field, our activities as consultants in the strategic planning or financial institutions, activities in executive compensation, in benefits administration, computer software, investments, alternative health care systems, and so forth. These are examples of areas in which we are already involved, as least tangentially. And these should become the focus of our strategic attention. Growth in these areas can lead to necessary outward growth of our actuarial practice. Strategically, this is where we need to better our checks.

Next, our international practice must be strengthened and must be further expanded. Here, we would do so as part of our strategic plan in order to exploit our unique skills. There are no other firms quite like us in all of the world. We have unique skills in the international arena. We also can access the possibility of transplanting our skills from one country to another. And in doing so, we probably can extend the shelf life of our skills thereby. Ideas that may be out of favor in one environment may continue to have a viable existence in some other environment, so I think our international practice is another focus of our strategic plans.

Let me talk for a minute just to the actuaries in the audience. These remarks apply to a lesser extent to the rest of you, but they apply very sharply to the actuaries in the audience. At least 50% of you who are here today will embark on essentially new careers within five years — at least 50% of you here today, including myself, will embark on essentially new careers within five years. This is your next mountain to climb. And I ask if you're ready for the challenge and the commitment it demands. In particular, are you prepared to take the time that is going to be required to learn new applications of old skills and to learn altogether new skills. To the actuaries in this room, the next several years are going to be challenging ones. For the rest, they will also be challenging but not quite to the same dramatic extent.

Where are we going? I think it is clear that our future plans must include at least one and probably at least two major acquisitions or mergers. And I think I can identify the areas where those will take place. First, I think that a major acquisition or merger will take place in the employee benefits practice, the reason being to expand our existing range of services and our asides. In other words, to obtain the critical mass and stature that we enjoy elsewhere. The second major merger or acquisition I foresee is in some as yet unidentified new area of practice. The early line favors a foray into the banking industry consulting field as a possibility. Now, the financial reasons for both major acquisitions are compelling. The alternative to achieving this critical mass and status in the benefits field will be a long part and expensive slog to build up internally what we have now. It could be done, it will take a long time and it would be expensive. Similarly, a foray into some other new consulting practice would also likely prove to be long and expensive as an undertaking. So the financial reasons that suggest that two major acquisitions of the general type that I described are quite compelling. The available opportunities will probably dictate the choice of the new service area from a very large and very attractive menu of possibilities. I could stand here and list easily a dozen areas into which we might reasonably expand, and it will be from some one of those areas that the choice will be made. Probably on an opportunity basis. We're going to have to continue our vigilance in defending our culture, and we're going to have to continue our efforts to meet our financial goals in order to finance this ongoing transition.

Let me close by expressing to all of you my confidence in the future leadership of this firm, no matter who it might be or which group of individuals it might be. I am confident that the board will have the opportunity to make a choice among a number of different very attractive possibilities when it meets in December. Regardless of which choice they may make, I am confident in the future leadership of this firm. I have some advice today. It's not very long. The first suggestion I would make is that they dream daring dreams. Robert Browning said a man's reach should exceed his grasp or else what's ahead for him? I think they should dream daring dreams. Second, I think they should practice fiscal conservatism. I think their adventurism should be confined to their dreams and not their checkbooks. And my third and final piece of advice to them is this: Don't short sell youth. Napoleon became emperor of France at the age of 27, and Alexander the Great conquered the known world at age 18. Don't go short on youth.

My personal plans? I expect to have an interesting, continuing role within Tillinghast. It's not appropriate for any attempt to be made at this stage to define it. I have plenty of confidence that it will be interesting and challenging. I'm eager to be part of what I see to be an exciting future for this firm, and I expect to be able to continue to have the proud association I have today and what we together have accomplished. Thank you very much.

Which Future for the Actuarial Profession?

Presented to the New Fellows of the Society of Actuaries, St. Louis, Missouri, May 23, 1985. Reprinted with permission from Tillinghast - A Towers Perrin Company.

Words of welcome have already been spoken to those of you who are present as New Fellows of the Society of Actuaries. Like you, I, also, am attending my first New Fellows Luncheon. I would like to congratulate the members of the Organizing Committee for finding a very imaginative way to get me, an Associate of the Society, to a New Fellows Luncheon! I stand here today with feelings somewhat like those of the sergeant asked to welcome newcomers to the officers' mess. Perhaps the unorthodox arrangement presents us with the possibility of a memorable occasion — provided, of course, something memorable is said.

An Honorable and Rewarding Profession

Each of you is now a full-fledged member of an honorable and rewarding profession. I recall a discussion which occurred some years ago at Point Clear, Alabama, with John M. Bragg, a personal friend of many years standing and a former president of the Society of Actuaries; Jack observed that he did not know a single actuary unhappy with his selection of his profession. Being of a suspicious nature, believing that "All generalities are wrong including this one," I have tested Jack's view on many occasions and I must confess to you that so far his generalization remains valid: I, too, have yet to meet the actuary who expressed the wish that he had chosen another profession — accountancy, law or something else.

One of the advantages of membership in our profession is that we are among the most highly compensated people in the world, a subject to which I will return later in these remarks. Another of the advantages is that we are members of a profession now business oriented which has its deepest roots in the scientific community and which retains some of the important values consistent with that background. Thus, we have the opportunity to combine the economic rewards of a business-oriented profession with the intellectual values which spring from our scientific heritage.

I want to share with you today some of my views about the actuarial profession — where it began, how it grew, where it is today and where I see it going from here. In the course of these remarks, I will focus my attention importantly on your future as New Fellows of the Society, cognizant of the fact that some members of the Board of Governors of the Society are also listening to these remarks, some of which are aimed at them.

Our Profession's History

Early traces of the actuarial profession can be found in many places and some of our members have made it their hobby to explore this background. Perhaps the earliest activity that might be attributed to the actuarial profession was in the field of valuing annuities. The May 1985 edition of *The Actuary* contains information of this kind in a letter written by Jack Moorhead, another old friend and former president of the Society, who has become one of the leading historians of the profession. His letter concerns Edmund Halley, whose name is memorialized in the comet that will arrive in the vicinity of our planet later this year; in his letter, Jack reminds us that Halley authored a 1693 paper presented to the Royal Society entitled, "An Estimate of the Degrees of the Mortality of Mankind, drawn from curious Tables of the Births and Funerals of the city of Breslaw; with an Attempt to ascertain the Price of Annuities upon Lives."

I would date the beginnings of the actuarial profession we recognize and, also, the beginnings of the life insurance industry we recognize from an event which happened around 1760. At that time, a mathematician in the United Kingdom named James Dodson painstakingly calculated premium rates and related reserves for a scheme which he had conceived involving the issuance of level premium life insurance policies. He and certain associates applied for a Royal Charter to organize a company for the purpose of selling such policies to the public; in their wisdom, representatives of the Crown rejected his proposal as being far too speculative. Nevertheless, about 10 years later, an organization emerged that still exists today as the "Old Equitable"; interestingly, the organization began business as a partnership among its policyholders and continued to operate in that form for many years. I would identify James Dodgeson as the first actuary in the modern sense.

In the mid-nineteenth century, the Institute of Actuaries and the Faculty of Actuaries were organized in London and Edinburgh, respectively. In North America, the formal development of the profession began in the late nineteenth century with the formation of the Actuarial Society of America and we will celebrate the centenary of that event in 1989. Since its beginnings, the actuarial profession has developed along a path that parallels very closely the development of the life insurance industry in the United Kingdom, the United States of America and several other countries which make up what is sometimes called "The Old Commonwealth."

A second main branch of the profession later emerged as a result of the widespread development of public and private pension arrangements throughout much of the Western World. This development gathered considerable pace during the years that immediately followed World War II.

Beginning in 1914 with the organization of the Casualty Actuarial Society, a third major branch was established and has come of age particularly in the last 20 years. This branch of the profession has developed in parallel to the property and liability insurance industry. It is notable that, in North America, actuaries engaged in this area of practice are members of a separate professional organization, whereas in other parts of the world they are simply one branch of the wider profession.

The actuarial profession has also developed in other fields. Although these remain relatively minor in the overall context of the profession, their importance is growing rapidly and later in these remarks I will return to this subject. These fields include activities relating to health care financing, government, academia and the investment world.

Our Profession Today

It is helpful to review in quantitative terms the current status of the actuarial professional worldwide, a universe of perhaps 15,000 active professionals.

Approximately 50% of these are engaged in a field of activity that closely relates to the individual life and health insurance business. Mainly these people are employed by insurance companies that offer products of this type but some of them are consultants who deal with that industry and a few would be found in allied areas.

Approximately 30% of the members of the profession are engaged in fields relating to the areas of employee benefits, which include pension and other retirement plans, group life and health insurance, miscellaneous areas of employee benefits and closely allied subjects such as employee compensation. Mainly these people are employed by consulting firms, but there are significant numbers who are employed by manufacturers or distributors of products to meet these needs and a few who are employed by plan sponsors.

Approximately 10% of the members of our profession are engaged in a field of activity that closely relates to the property and liability insurance business. Mainly these people are employed by insurers who issue these products but there are a growing number of consultants in this field as well.

The remaining 10% of the members of the profession are widely scattered in other activities. It is worth noting that our sister organization in the United Kingdom, the Institute of Actuaries, offers one path to fellowship in the organization through the investment route. Perhaps for this reason, outside North America the investment field is much more important to the actuarial profession than it is in North America.

Our Profession in the Future

Let me turn now to the future development of the actuarial profession.

I am a great believer in what I call propulsion by natural forces. By this, I mean that I would sooner coast downhill rather than pedal uphill, sooner swim with the current rather than against it, or sooner sail before the wind rather than beat into it. Lord Byron said all this somewhat more entertainingly in "Don Juan":

Well — well, the world must turn upon its axis
And all mankind turn with it, heads or tails,
And live and die, make love and pay our taxes
And as the veering wind shifts, shift our sails;

Propulsion by natural forces is something to be enlisted if it is at all possible. To oppose such forces is an invitation to difficulty and, perhaps, failure.

For the actuarial profession, the natural forces that are abroad in our society today are moving in a direction which is not conducive to the continued growth of the two major traditional branches of our practice. Specifically, I refer to those professional activities which are closely tied to the individual life insurance business and defined benefit pension plans. In these two major areas of practice, we do not enjoy the benefit of propulsion by natural forces. The forces are against us: the path leads uphill, the current is flowing in the opposite direction and the wind is in our face.

In the individual life insurance business, great changes have taken place which are profoundly affecting that industry and the activities of our profession in serving that industry; these changes are continuing and are virtually certain to proceed further with continuing effects on our profession. The changes include the unbundling of products, the computer revolution, deregulation and, in the United States and elsewhere, possible tax threats to the industry's products. The widespread availability of affordable computers has made it possible to do such things as solving simultaneous equations without knowing the techniques for solving those equations. Similarly, many other mathematical problems can now be solved by brute force using computer power and some of these encroach upon territory that was previously the exclusive province of the actuary. As another example, deregulation is attended by the likelihood of meaningful cross industry competition between life insurance companies and providers of other financial services. I suggest to you that these forces are going to alter in a very fundamental way and in a very short period of time the traditional life insurance industry and the traditional role of actuaries providing services to that industry, whether as employees or as consultants.

Defined benefit pension plans, the mainstay of actuarial practice in the employee benefits field, are now on the wane because of such developments as the widespread interest in portable pensions more easily provided by defined contribution plans which involve fewer actuarial aspects. Defined benefit plans are also suffering a decrease in popularity because regulation now affords less flexibility in financing such plans. The high inflation rates of the 1970s have decreased the popularity of such plans among plan participants and have also decreased the willingness of sponsors to finance inflation protected plans with potentially high associated costs. These changes in the relative importance of defined benefit pension plans, resulting from social and economic change and associated government action, will affect the role of the actuary who provides service primarily in this area of practice.

These changes relating both to individual life insurance products and to defined benefit pension plans are a worldwide phenomenon, but the trend is particularly strong in the United States and it is also strong in Canada, the two countries in which most members of the Society of Actuaries practice. In my opinion, the actuarial profession, particularly its younger members such as the New Fellows who are here today, must look outside the traditional areas of practice for future viability and growth. It is unrealistic to expect that 80% of us will be employed in these two dominant areas of our practice in even five years time. Those of us whose professional activities are centered in these fields must prepare for change.

This implies the need for a strong commitment on the part of all of us, but particularly our younger members, in the area of continuing education.

This also means that there must be some new initiatives in the future education, training and qualification of actuaries undertaken by the Society of Actuaries. The Society is actively examining this whole subject. It is one in which I would encourage all of you to take an interest.

Yesterday, I received a release from the Conference of Actuaries in Public Practice, signed by its President, Mary Adams, which dealt with the issue of continuing professional education and the role that the Conference intends to play in this field. One of the sentences of the release is underscored and I think it is worth repeating: "The public is coming to expect professionals in all fields to be involved in a continuing education process."

New Areas of Practice

What are the promising new areas available to us if we choose to be members of an outward-reaching actuarial profession? If we believe that our traditional areas of activity are likely to shrink and if we decide that we are not going to be confined to those areas, where should we look for new fields of activity in which actuaries can function effectively? I have three ideas to suggest to you, but the list is surely much longer than this.

- First, I would look to those areas which lend themselves to applications of our existing skills in making financial projections and other calculations which involve probability and the time value of money — problems in fields such as the allocation of scarce resources, those associated with urban growth, demography and so forth. Similarly, in a field that is more closely related to the expertise of those with backgrounds in the employee benefits area, I would suggest the use of our existing expertise to develop imaginative employee incentive and compensation programs. Accordingly, my first suggestion relates to the application of our existing skills to new fields.
- Second, I would direct your attention to the field of investments. All of you are probably familiar with the so-called Random Walk Theory as it relates to investments. Boiled down, the theory holds that there is no such thing as a superior investment policy because everything is inherent in the current market price; thus, the behavior of financial markets is essentially random and it follows that no strategy can over-achieve (or under-achieve) the results produced by using a dart. The theory has many supporters and many detractors. If the theory is right, it makes nonsense of the entire field of investment management as practiced today. If the theory is wrong, investment management can be very profitable and is a key aspect of the functioning of our financial world. Either way, there is a role for actuaries. If the market is a random walk and if there is no such thing as superior investment policy, there remains the differential in probable results and price fluctuations between strategies involving higher or lower degrees of risk and price volatility. This is a suitable subject for the actuary. If, on the other hand, the market is not a random walk and there is something to the science of investment management, it is a science that surely lends itself to the skills that actuaries can provide if new skills are learned.
- Third, I would suggest that there are opportunities already available in the wider financial services scene, an area in which I find myself spending an increasing amount of time. There exists ample opportunity to apply to

businesses other than insurance the quantitative methods and measures which we have been trained to apply to the insurance industry's problems. Examples can be found in such areas as product pricing, financial projections and analysis and the development of quantitative management information. The scope for the involvement of actuaries in the wider financial services scene is likely to grow rapidly with the convergence of various financial services businesses which is clearly in progress. To exploit these opportunities, actuaries must master these wider fields of business.

Which future will we as individual professionals and collectively as a profession choose? One choice is business as usual, which I suggest to you in the strongest possible terms really means less business than usual. The second choice is for us as individuals and collectively as a profession to undertake new initiatives. These new initiatives might be quite radical. For example, I can well imagine that some 15 years from now, at the dawn of the Third Millennium, someone may stand where I stand today, addressing the New Fellows Luncheon of the Society of Actuaries, discussing a very different subject matter before a group of New Fellows who have no specialized expertise in the field of life contingencies. I can imagine that as a possibility, though my timetable may be too ambitious.

Your Personal Future

Let me turn now from the general to the specific. What does your personal future hold and what can you do today to influence that future? It is convenient for the purpose of the discussion to adopt a proxy for success and I will use personal income as such a proxy — not because I believe that it is the only or even the most important measure of success, but because it is a dramatic way to illustrate certain points I wish to make.

How does an actuary progress through four stages of his career which I will identify as early career, mid career, mature career and late career? At each stage there are differentiating factors between those who are successful and those who are less successful, using income as a proxy for success. What I will try to do is identify at each stage what those differentiating factors are.

Early Career

The first such factor, applicable to early career, is easy to identify: Clearly it is success with the examinations of the Society of Actuaries. There is a very high correlation between income levels and success rates in passing those examinations. All of you have just been through this process and I would like to raise in your minds a question: Do you think this, becoming a Fellow of the Society of Actuaries, is a completed phase of your career? I suggest that it is not necessarily a completed phase. I would point out to you that the examination taking process can still benefit your career if you now turn your attention to some other field. For example, I think that some of you should give serious consideration to undertaking the examinations of the Casualty Actuarial Society; I think that some of you should look at the CLU examinations; and I think that some of you should look at the CPCU examinations. In early career, examination success is clearly the dominant factor and it can still help you.

Mid Career

What happens when mid career begins, say, at age 30 and continues, perhaps, to age 40? If the experience of my own firm and that of other organizations to whose affairs I am privy are any guide, it is clear that a divergence begins among actuaries who like yourself have recently passed the examinations of the Society. It is clear to me that they then embark on two separate paths which can be measured in terms of income differences.

Usually, this is a time when a significant adjustment will occur in your personal income in recognition of the milestone you have just achieved and I hope that all of you have enjoyed or will soon enjoy such an adjustment in your personal incomes. After those adjustments have occurred, two groups of you will then embark on different paths. One will embark on a path where income in thousands of constant 1985 dollars is approximately equal to attained age plus 30; the second will embark on a path where income in thousands of dollars is approximately equal to 2.5 times attained age. At age 40 the difference is substantial: the first group will achieve an income level (in 1985 dollars) of approximately $70,000 and the second group will enjoy an income of approximately $100,000.

Why does this happen? I suggest to you that it is because the second group has found ways to expand the range of their skills; basically, they have moved outside the technical area and into the general area. To illustrate this in the context of those involved in the affairs of a life insurance company, the second group has moved from the area of product design (a technical area) into marketing (a more general area). This implies, of course, that the second group has a much higher degree of willingness to learn new skills.

A second differentiating factor is also easily observed: it is called ambition and effort. By my own observation, the members of the two groups I have described devote considerably different amounts of time to their profession. The first group probably devotes an average of approximately 35 hours a week and the second group devotes approximately 50. This is quite independent of the kind of organization with which they are associated, be it an insurance company, a consulting firm or some other kind of organization. There is a decided and discernible difference in the level of ambition and effort of the two groups.

There is a third difference as well and it is a difference that later on becomes even more important. By my observation, the two groups have very different levels of communication skills, both written and oral. The general rationale for the importance of this difference is quite simple: no concept, no product, no technical analysis is any better than the ability to communicate that concept, product or analysis. The second group clearly has an edge when it comes to communication skills. The Society of Actuaries offers to all of its members significant opportunity to improve their communications skills. I suggest to the New Fellows that they take full advantage of these opportunities by writing and presenting papers or articles of various types and by participating in programs of the Society. All of us can do a great deal to enhance our personal communication skills. The firm with which I am associated has a formal program to encourage its members to participate in full in the available programs of the Society.

Mature Career

Let me turn now to the mature career, where the divergence continues. The first group continues on course and their income level in thousands continues to be attained age plus 30. But the second group now subdivides. A large segment continues on its course with an income level of 2.5 times attained age. But a minority migrates towards a higher income level which may be four times attained age or even more. By age 50, the difference is very substantial: the first group has an income level of approximately \$80,000; the majority of the second group enjoys an income level of \$125,000; but a minority of the second group enjoys an income level of \$200,000 or more.

What are the distinguishing features of this third group which begins to emerge at about age 40? It retains the same distinguishing characteristics it had before with the addition of one important new ingredient — leadership skills. Again, the theory is simple: these exceptional people are able to multiply their own effectiveness by increasing the effectiveness of others. Again, the May issue of *The Actuary* includes a letter on point from David M. Gladstone which deals with actuarial education and which calls for an increase in the management content in that education. The letter prompted the Editor, Lambert Trowbridge, to include an editorial on the same subject. I agree that management skills is a subject that is sorely missing in actuarial education.

To a considerable extent, leadership skills can be acquired. For example, important aspects are described in two articles which appeared some years ago in the *Harvard Business Review*; both were written by J. Sterling Livingston, a professor at the Harvard Business School. One is entitled "Pygmalion in Management" and the other "The Myth of the Well-Educated Manager."

In the first article, Mr. Livingston's message is that subordinates respond to their superiors largely in accordance with the way their superiors view them. The article begins with a quotation from George Bernard Shaw's *Pygmalion*, in which Eliza Doolittle explains:

> You see, really and truly, apart from the things anyone can pick up (the dressing and the proper way of speaking, and so on), the difference between a lady and a flower girl is not how she behaves, but how she's treated. I shall always be a flower girl to Professor Higgins, because he always treats me as a flower girl, and always will, but I know I can be a lady to you, because you always treat me as a lady, and always will.

Mr. Livingston in this quotation identifies one important element in the effectiveness of managers in achieving better performance by their subordinates.

His second article addresses a closely related point. In it he analyzes the skills that are key to a successful manager and suggests that the successful manager wants success for his subordinates more than for himself. Management skills, I would suggest to you, are the key differentiating factor of the third group and can, to an extent, be learned.

Late Career

Let me turn next to the subject of late career, which may be of more immediate interest to the members of the Board of Governors who are present rather than to the New Fellows.

Early burnout is a problem in any professional activity and ours is no exception. The distinction between those who are subject to early burnout and those who continue their effectiveness into late career is quite dramatic; early burnout often leads to a radical income reduction to or below the age plus 30 level. I think that the risk of early burnout can be minimized or avoided in several ways. Periodically refreshing basic skills is one. The inspiration of others is another. When I say this, I can't help but think of my own associate, Thomas P. Bowles, Jr., another former president of the Society of Actuaries. Tom at age 68 is a remarkable example of someone who has stayed fresh and young and I believe it has a great deal to do with his willingness to learn new skills and his ability to inspire other people and, through this effort, himself to remain fresh and young in outlook.

We can learn much from Mao Tse Tung, a major historical figure of the twentieth century. Remarkably, Chairman Mao realized that his revolution in China had become a spent force and he attempted to undertake renewal; but he made a classic mistake by attempting to re-impose the original revolution under the label of the Great Cultural Revolution. While he recognized the need for something new, a rare perception, he erred by merely re-imposing old ideas in a new wrapper.

I believe that newness and freshness are the secrets to avoiding early burnout and to achieving continued effectiveness.

A Challenge

I ask each of you as New Fellows where you think you will fit in the spectrum of career possibilities that I have described. I suggest to you that your future is largely in your own hands. I suggest to you also that at least 50%, probably more, will within five years embark on what is essentially a new career. That does not necessarily mean that you will change employers. You can embark on a new career without changing employers and, conversely, you can change employers without embarking on a new career. I am talking about an actual change in the nature of your day-to-day activities and responsibilities. Most of you should now be preparing yourself for this change.

I believe the Society of Actuaries has an important role to play in this and I also believe that each of you has an important role to play in the Society. The Society needs your current interest and it needs your effort. In the future, it is going to need your leadership. In return, you are entitled to expect that the Society will effectively support the necessary changes that are occurring or impending within the actuarial profession.

You have just climbed one imposing mountain. How high are you prepared to climb the next mountain? In the next 40 years? In the next 20 years? In the next 10 years? In the next 12 months? How high will you climb during the remainder of 1985? How high between now and Labor Day, which is only three months away.

Here is a suggestion addressed specifically to that last short period between now and Labor Day. I would suggest to each of you, whether you are New Fellows or members of the Board of Governors, that between now and Labor Day you learn one major new skill; I would suggest to you that you start now and make this a summer project.

I suggest also to the New Fellows that now is a good time to take inventory, to make a realistic self-appraisal of the skills you now have and the ones that you will need to achieve the goals you have set for yourself in the next phase of your career. I suggest, for example, that you appraise your personal level of ambition and commitment. Do you sincerely want to succeed? Fifty hours a week or 35 hours worth? I think you should take inventory of your own communication skills because they will have much more to do with your future success than they have contributed to your past success. In the immediate future, the development of your communication skills will be as important to you as passing the examinations has been to your career to this point. I would also suggest that it is not too early to begin the development of your management and leadership skills, which really mean your ability to deal with people in an effective way.

About 150 years ago, Robert Browning wrote: "A man's reach should exceed his grasp, else what is a heaven for?"

The Challenge from Without

Published in the 1989 Centennial Celebration Proceedings of the Actuarial Profession in North America, *June 12–14, 1989, Washington, D.C., Vol. 1, pp. 245–261. Reprinted with permission from the Society of Actuaries.*

The actuarial profession in North America, whose centenary we celebrate this week, is neither old nor even middle-aged by comparison with other professions. We in North America are a middle child of a worldwide professional family: not as old as our siblings in the United Kingdom, but older than our siblings elsewhere. Like youth in all walks of life, the members of our worldwide professional family must ask ourselves what we intend to achieve when we grow up and how we intend to reach our goals.

The senior member of our worldwide professional family, the Institute of Actuaries, has adopted as its motto these words of Francis Bacon: "I hold every man a debtor to his profession."

In a similar vein, he might also have said: "I hold every profession a debtor to the society it serves."

In our search for purpose, we, the members of the actuarial profession in North America and worldwide, must respond to the challenges of the societies we serve if we are to remain a viable and respected profession. Let us now consider some of those challenges.

General Challenges

The general challenges of society which apply to our profession are the same as apply to other recognized professions. How do we compare, both absolutely and relative to other professions, with respect to some of the most important of these expectations?

- Personal Integrity. There have been remarkably few instances of personal dishonesty among members of the actuarial profession serious enough to warrant expulsion from or suspension of membership in the various professional bodies. We justifiably can be proud of this record.
- Professional Objectivity. Every profession is subject to tension among three competing and often conflicting interests: duty towards truth, duty towards the interests of clients/employers/communicants/patients and duty towards the interests of society. Every profession has its own bias; we in the actuarial profession, whose deepest roots are in the scientific community, place greater emphasis on our duty towards truth than do members of most other professions. Yet, since we deal routinely with the kaleidoscope of future possibilities, the opportunity exists to bend our views to suit the interests of our particular constituencies; this tendency can be seen in some of our work relating to the valuation of insurance companies for sale or purchase, some of our work relating to product pricing and some of our work relating to the funding of pension plans. Society has learned to expect from us an emphasis on duty towards truth; commercialism has weakened our stature in this regard particularly in recent years and particularly in North America.
- Professional Competence. In general terms, the actuarial profession worldwide can justly claim high marks for competence in its relatively narrow field. In this respect, actuaries in the United States of America suffer by comparison with those elsewhere since the profession is fragmented among several professional organizations with no common standards for membership.
- Professional Discipline. Society expects any recognized profession to have a strong disciplinary process to restrain or purge its membership. In North America particularly, but also elsewhere, the actuarial profession has strengthened its disciplinary process in recent years to a position of parity with most other recognized professions.

Specific Challenges

Besides the General Challenges which apply equally to all professions, the actuarial profession confronts several specific challenges particular to it alone.

- Professional Identification. If any profession is to receive lasting recognition and respect, society must know generally what it does and who its members are. The actuarial profession worldwide faces identification problems; what we do is not widely known. In the United States, these problems are compounded by the fragmentation of professional organizations which qualify its own members and which even compete with each other for relative status and recognition. We, the members of a small and obscure profession, whose members have nevertheless achieved notable success, must demand that our leadership take the steps necessary to receive more widespread recognition and respect, no matter how unpopular those steps may be among important but complacent segments of our membership.
- Fiduciary Responsibility. Actuaries not involved in the regulatory process must share with regulators the responsibility for the soundness of insurance companies, pension funds and other fiduciaries they serve. This broad responsibility is better recognized and more willingly accepted in some countries than in others. Among the laggards is the United States of America. Full acceptance of this responsibility may require some actuaries to develop skills not now part of our traditional scope.
- Public Issues. Actuaries have not participated as actively as might be expected in public issues within their areas of expertise. Proposals to socialize rates for certain insurance coverages and to finance in various ways retirement income needs, medical expenses and the cost of long-term care are major social and political issues. In the United States of America, most actuaries have been personally reluctant and most actuarial organizations have been even more reluctant to participate vigorously in the public debate concerning these and other public issues. Perhaps this is because many members of the profession are affiliated with insurance companies and other organizations having a vested interest in the outcome of these debates. Participation in these issues represent a major opportunity to increase the visibility and public respect of our profession.

The Outlook

Today, the actuarial profession, in North America and elsewhere, is flourishing. Its continued prosperity depends on its success in responding to the many, varied and constantly changing challenges it faces today and will continue to face. This is a never ending process. Our enemy is complacency.

We are members of a young profession that has already conferred upon its members both honor and personal achievement. We, the inheritors of that legacy, must bequeath it undiminished to our successors.

Focus 2000: Nontraditional Actuarial Practice in the Year 2000

Published in the Record of the Society of Actuaries *Vol. 16, No. 4A (1990): 2577–2581. Reprinted with permission from the Society of Actuaries.*

My fellow panelists and I, aided and abetted by our able moderator, have been asked to speculate about the future activities of our profession and the consequent implications for the education and training of actuaries who will practice in the year 2000. To address these issues, each of us has found it necessary first to develop a vision of the environment he expects at the close of this millennium, only ten years hence.

My colleagues have already described their respective visions. Each has elected to use the "close-up" technique, concentrating on areas in close proximity to the activities of our profession. Rather than presenting a third vision of this type, which would closely resemble the other two, I decided to step back one or two paces and present a "wide angle" vision representing my expectations for the year 2000.

Most, if not all, of the forces which will shape our civilization ten years from now already exist. What are those forces? What in the world is going on? I say "world" advisedly because we in the developed countries are a steadily diminishing fraction of a progressively more global civilization. I offer some suggestions:

- The outstanding demographic statistic is the continuing expansion of world population. In July, 1987, the World Population Organization of the United Nations reported that total world population exceeded 5 billion persons. Ten years from now, the total will already exceed 6 billion and most of the 7th billion will be aboard Spaceship Earth. Practically all of the increase will arise in countries which are already poor and which today account for more than 80% of world population. World population will not stabilize during the lifetime of anyone in this room and probably will not stabilize for at least 100 years. The outlook for the world population in the year 2000 will be as grim as, or grimmer than, it is today. Pressure on developed countries especially the U.S., to accept or tolerate large scale immigration will probably intensify.

- In most of the poorer countries, the rate of wealth creation is exceeded by that of population growth, leading to declining per-capita wealth and income. To achieve economic progress, these countries must export their labor to the developed countries and invest the proceeds. This has already occurred in Japan, Hong Kong, Korea, Singapore and Taiwan; notably these are countries with highly disciplined populations which share what others have called the "Chopsticks Culture" with emphasis on thrift, diligence, public education and limited expectations. Slow progress in this direction is likely to occur in China; but little can be expected within ten years beyond the establishment of a trend and some relaxation of the inhibiting political and economic system. Elsewhere, except in Eastern Europe and the Soviet Union, the outlook is bleak; restraining population growth and improving public education are multi-generation undertakings that may not even begin within ten years. The unfortunate people of these countries are likely to continue to fall victim to their own governments. Extreme nationalism and religious fanaticism will be offered as a substitute for economic progress. It all sounds depressingly familiar.
- The unexpectedly sudden changes in the political systems of Eastern Europe and the Soviet Union have transformed the geo-political landscape. The economic consequences are less easily predicted. The road from centrally planned to market-based economies will be long and rough. Nevertheless, major progress is likely within ten years. Population growth is not a problem and the people of these countries are reasonably well educated. These, too, may successfully emulate Japan, et al. Their appetite for foreign capital will be ravenous, suggesting that interest rates are likely to

remain high for many years. The relaxation of political tensions promises that military expenditures will decrease in both the West and, especially, the East, with substantial benefits to all.

- Throughout the developed world, but especially in the U.S., the general quality of credit — personal, corporate and government — has declined. This deterioration of credit quality undermines the validity of savings backed by the assets of the borrowers; the "real rate of savings," net of ultimate defaults, is not as high as it appears to be. To some extent, this result might be attributed to the "Knife and Fork Culture" with emphasis on credit, mediocrity, private education and unrealistic expectations.
- The activities of one notable creditor warrant special attention. From 1950 until 1980, the U.S. government was a reasonably prudent and conservative borrower. Government debt as a fraction of GNP declined and declined even more as a fraction of government revenues. In the past ten years that has changed. Unlike the governments of the Weimar Republic and Latin America, the U.S. government has not resorted to printing currency like newsprint rolling off the presses. That would be too obvious. Instead, they print government securities! The resultant borrowing creates illusory wealth. But in this case, the borrower is in control of the value of of the currency of repayment. In addition, the government has committed large chunks of future tax revenues to support promises made in the form of various social programs. The ongoing struggle in Washington today suggests that the unpleasant changes necessary to meet even the modest goals of Gramm-Rudman-Hollings will not enthusiastically be embraced by either political party. The ingredients of a major, extended, worldwide financial crisis are present in the deterioration of credit quality and political will. The crisis could occur at any time, or never. The potential risks to financial intermediaries (including sponsors of defined benefit pension plans) are enormous. No government policy, adopted now, will assuredly avert the potential crisis — it is already too late for sure things. No one can anticipate the event which might light the fuse. What will be the response of government? Among the various unpleasant options, one is likely to appeal more than others — a deliberate policy of high inflation intended to default on promises already made in a respectable way. In other words, the solution

would be a tax on monetized assets. Such a policy might even command covert bipartisan support, accompanied by a plethora of disclamatory rhetoric. The trick is to pull it off without triggering the crisis. Within ten years, the probability of crisis seems to this observer to be two-thirds, to the nearest third; and that of sustained inflation at an average rate of 10% per annum or more seems to be close to 100%, with or without the crisis.

If these predictions are realized, what then are the implications for the developed countries and their people, the employers and clients we serve and the actuarial profession?

- The world population problem, combined with the foreseen economic problems of the poorer countries will test the social conscience of the people and governments of the developed countries. A worldwide Marshall Plan on an unimaginably grandiose scale, already proposed by the Vatican, will be taken seriously and will sharpen the political differences which already exist. Consensus politics will be the likely loser.
- The geopolitical position of the next ten years will be based more on economics and less on ideology. The "haves" will be confronted by the insistent demands of the "have nots." Some political leaders will attempt to graft ideology onto economic self-interest. The likely result will be reduced military confrontation and increased terrorism.
- Financial intermediaries of all types will be threatened by potential crisis, whether or not it actually occurs. Those with limited capital resources relative to their size and risks underwritten will be especially vulnerable. Further consolidation involving all types of financial institutions seems inevitable. Some insolvencies among major insurance companies will occur if the possible (or probable) financial crisis occurs.
- Inflation at a sustained high rate, foreseen as a near certainty, will undercut the market appeal of traditional life insurance products. High interest rates, also foreseen, will exacerbate this trend and cause disintermediation problems akin to those of the 1970s.
- Surpluses now enjoyed by defined benefit pension plans will shrink and may become deficits. The trend towards the shelter of defined contribution plans will accelerate. The need for actuarial expertise will be supplanted by the need for administrative expertise.

- Actuaries thrive on crisis. At least for the next ten years there will be an abundance of opportunities of this type. But fewer career paths of the traditional type will be available.
- Successful actuaries in the year 2000 will need new or augmented skills in some areas. Actuaries have long concentrated on understanding the dynamics of the liabilities of their employers and clients; a similar understanding of the related assets, particularly including default and market risks, if needed. This can and should be included in current education programs and examinations. This should be viewed as part of the basic education and training of all actuaries, not as a specialized skill. Actuaries already qualified will also need this training. Future programs of the Society and other actuarial bodies need to feature this subject and to encourage papers on the subject.
- Opportunities for the actuaries will also emerge in areas outside the traditional practice of the profession. Asset management and risk assessment are portable to other financial businesses. The needs of government for skills possessed by actuaries will also increase the demand in that field.
- Above all, in a period which seems likely to strain public credibility of financial institutions, defined pension plan sponsors, government and their professional advisors, the need for integrity and objectivity is paramount. Actuaries may wince at their stodgy image, but ours is still widely regarded as an honorable profession. The blotches on our public reputation are few. That reputation must be guarded zealously. The guardians of our reputation are those in our professional organizations who are charged with the enforcement of professional discipline.

These remarks were prepared with considerable trepidation. They are intended to stimulate more than to inform. Necessarily, they are very subjective. One possibility haunts me. In at least one respect, actuaries of the future will not change; they will continue to mine the literature of our profession. I expect that some actuary of the year 2000, asked to participate in the program of the Society that year, may chance upon the record of this panel. No doubt, some of it will provide amusing quotations in the light of the affirmative certainty of what today is mere speculation.

Section 7
The Last Word

The Last Word

Published in Emphasis, *January 1985 – June 1991. Reprinted with permission from Tillinghast - A Towers Perrin Company.*

Prologue

For seven years, Jim Anderson shared his unique insights and perspectives on the insurance industry in “The Last Word” in *Emphasis* magazine.

Always incisive and often controversial, Jim has been dubbed the “Cassandra” of the insurance industry because his predictions, though frequently doubted, have often proved accurate.

Contents

1985/1 Reflections on the Professions

In this world of rapid change, it should be no surprise that the professions are re-examining their traditional roles and structures. Two examples will serve to illustrate the point:

1. Two of the "Big Eight" international public accounting firms have announced plans to merge their practices, and two others are reported to be conducting informal discussions towards the same end.
2. In the legal profession, the possibility of regional and even national amalgamation is receiving serious consideration.

What do these changes in long-established organizational patterns within two essentially conservative professions signal? The motivation appears to be a desire to expand client networks and to extend the range of professional skills and specialized expertise. At the same time, competition among law firms to recruit top graduates of leading law schools has intensified while graduates with lesser perceived potential compete for the remaining positions.

The Actuarial Profession. Not surprisingly, the actuarial profession is experiencing similar pressures.

The roots of the actuarial profession may be found in the scientific community and, somewhat later, in the life insurance industry. From those beginnings, the profession has expanded its membership and widened its focus gradually. With the expansion of the life insurance industry, which continued at a rapid rate until perhaps 15 years ago, the profession increased significantly in numbers. The growth of retirement plans, which gained impetus during and following World War II, created a significant new demand for actuarial services. More recently, particularly since 1970, demand for actuarial services by the property/liability insurance industry increased noticeably.

Will the actuarial profession continue to be dominated in the future, as it has been in the past, by members employed by the insurance industry, which is itself embroiled in a redefinition of its role in the wider financial services scene? Will it continue to concern itself primarily with the cost and funding of future payments which depend on such contingencies as the continuation or termination of life, property/liability hazards, medical costs and disability? Does the relative decline of actuarial employment within the insurance industry signal a major change? In a world of inexpensive, powerful computers and where many previously packaged benefits, such as life insurance and retirement guarantees, have been "unbundled," the unique ability of the actuary to provide the answers to these questions has been undermined. How can members of this specialized profession best apply their unique skills in this changing environment?

Broader Horizons. The actuarial profession must widen dramatically its horizons if it is to remain a viable and vibrant member of the professional community. Basic actuarial training also lends itself well to solving problems quite different in nature from the cost and funding calculations involved in insurance programs and pension benefits. For example, the actuary has skills which lend themselves to involvement in the fields of investment and economics; this has long been recognized in the U.K., where investments is one of three sub-specialties which can be chosen by those seeking to qualify as Fellows of the Institute of Actuaries. More generally, the training of an actuary is well suited to the development of solutions for problems involving long-range forecasting which are dependent upon contingencies of all kinds, not merely life, death, injury, accident, sickness, and so forth.

Changes Required. If the actuarial profession is to proceed in the indicated direction, following a wider path, the training of actuaries needs to be adjusted accordingly. Future training may involve a more generalized application of the theory of probability to the solutions of problems of many types. The intended purpose of such training would be to apply the techniques and expertise to a wide range of problems within society, suggesting the need for actuaries with a broad generalized knowledge of the subjects to which they would be asked to apply their special skills. Of these two conflicting forces, the second appears to be more powerful.

If change of this nature occurs, more actuaries are likely to be involved in public practice and new professional structures of a multidisciplined nature can be expected to evolve.

In Microcosm. Among my recent personal experiences was an assignment which involved a study of the retirement arrangements incorporated into the partnership agreement of a firm engaged in the legal profession. The problem to be solved clearly involved a projection of the probable and possible futures of the organization, to which actuarial techniques could be reasonably applied.

Also involved were numerous other interactive issues, such as the impact of contemplated changes on the basic economics and human aspects of the professional organization. This assignment included aspects of long-range planning, executive compensation, funded and unfunded retirement benefits and the "social contract" among the partners. It may, in microcosm, represent the actuarial practice of the future.

1985/2 Free Enterprise Needs a Tracheotomy

Strictly speaking, there is no likely system of taxation in a modern society which is wholly consistent with the concept of free enterprise. But some are more consistent than others. The system which now exists in the United States threatens to suffocate the concept of free enterprise.

Tax Reform. Recently, the Treasury Department has proposed a specific plan of tax reform. Other proposals have originated in Congress. The Treasury plan, like several-others, proposes the reduction of tax rates on personal income and corporate profits combined with the reduction or elimination of many tax preferences. Both changes, be it noted, move the tax system in a direction more consistent with the concept of free enterprise. Why, then, has the Treasury proposal been greeted with such hostility by the business community? The answer seems to be a mixture of widespread misunderstanding and specific, well-informed self-interest.

The Treasury plan would shift the apparent tax burden from individuals to corporations, mainly by eliminating investment tax credits and by modifying the Accelerated Cost Recovery method of depreciation. However, this would not necessarily lead to a reduction in aftertax profits; more likely, it would lead to an increase in prices and rents. Thus, to an important extent, the tax burden would actually shift to consumers rather than shareholders, and the result would resemble, at least partly, a sales tax or value-added tax. At the same time, taxes levied directly on profits would reduce. Very significantly, the Treasury also proposes to allow corporations to deduct 50% of dividends paid, thereby reducing substantially the confiscatory double taxation of corporate profits. An important result of these changes would be a shift in the capital structure of corporate America from debt to equity, a change which would lead to greater financial stability and reduced risk to investors. On balance, the Treasury plan must be good for business, notwithstanding the apparent increase in corporate taxes.

Certain changes in individual taxation proposed by the Treasury also have important implications for business. Tax neutrality is the prevailing theme. Among the proposals are:

1. taxation of certain employee benefits as income;
2. the elimination of the capital gains tax preference; and

3. taxation of interest credited under life insurance and annuity contracts as current income.

Threatened Industries. More substantial and better-grounded opposition to the Treasury plan is coming from those in the business community who now benefit substantially from existing tax preferences. In a few extreme instances, entire industries could become nonviable in a more neutral tax environment because existing tax subsidies are embedded in their price and cost structure. Among the more obvious examples of affected businesses are these:

1. Those who manufacture or distribute tax shelters and those engaged in the tax advice business would be damaged by both the reduction in tax rates and the simplification of the system.
2. Those involved in property development and investment would be damaged by changes in depreciation allowances and elimination of the capital gains tax preference; this dislocation would only be temporary since rents would ultimately rise, property prices would recover and development would resume.
3. Those involved in the manufacture, distribution and servicing of capital goods would be damaged to some extent by the elimination of the investment tax credit and the change in depreciation allowances; because the effect would be fairly uniform, there would be no relative change in their competitive position — all prices would effectively rise on capital goods.
4. Those involved in underwriting and distributing individual life insurance products at current expense loadings would be severely, if not fatally, damaged because permanent life insurance would become extremely unattractive to consumers; in this case, the Treasury plan is inconsistent with its own objective of neutrality because it allows no offset of expenses charged to policyholders against investment income credited to them — a flaw which can be corrected in various ways.

Worth the Price. Tax reform is never easy to achieve, particularly when the state of government finance requires at best a zero-sum game with equal winners and losers. Yet, the objective is worth a heavy price. The Treasury plan is a good beginning, deserving constructive criticism rather than hostility.

Little imagination is required to understand that a likely alternative is tax reform of a very different kind — enacted by a future government with different aims and a greater appetite for revenue, perhaps elected on a wave of public reaction to tax abuse — a plan which eliminates tax preferences without reducing tax rates.

Tracheotomy Now. Do we actually believe what we say about free enterprise? Are we really prepared for a free market environment without substantial tax subsidies? If so, how much longer must we labor to breathe through our loopholes? Why not a tracheotomy now?

1985/3 Outside the Nine Dots

Can the future be foretold with sufficient confidence to justify serious interest in the study and practice of futurism by business and professional organizations, by government and by academia?

The Practice of Futurism. At its most elementary level, futurism is a routine and accepted part of such short-term forecasting processes as budgeting and planning. At a somewhat more sophisticated level, it appears in longer-term forecasts, such as population projections. In both cases, the extrapolation of observable current trends is the primary basis for predicting the future. But even these limited attempts to forecast the future are subject to a disappointing degree of error — tolerated, perhaps, as "generally accepted" error.

At a considerably more creative level, futurism attempts to forecast the future on the basis of anticipated changes in observable current trends. Often, the forecasts relate to time periods extending beyond the responsibility or expectancy of those involved and sometimes beyond the scope of their imaginations. The degree of error, then, is quite high. Are these efforts mere speculation, worth only their value as entertainment? Or should they be viewed seriously as a basis for current decisions? Not surprisingly, it depends — on the time horizon, the purpose and the rationale supporting the forecast.

Commercial Value. Very long-term forecasts have limited commercial value, due mainly to the time value of money. It is said that some businessmen in London 200 years ago were undismayed by the American Revolution because they valued the West Indies more highly; in terms of present values, at commercial rates of interest, they almost certainly were right. Similar logic suggests that the Brooklyn Indians out-traded Peter Minuit when they sold Manhattan for $24 in 1626, equivalent to a price of $24 trillion today at only 8% interest. When the probable error of long-term forecasting is combined with the power of compound interest, the discount factor reduces the commercial value of most long-term forecasts to near zero for time periods beyond 20 years.

The Government Viewpoint. The viewpoint of government involves other factors. Even if cost-effectiveness is a major consideration, commercial rates of interest do not necessarily apply, and the real rate of interest may even be negative. If the relative values of the West Indies and the United States had been calculated on a political basis, the answer would likely have been different, even 200 years ago. The same applies to the Manhattan transaction. Very long-term forecasts are items of legitimate concern to government, particularly when it is recognized that commercial interests are likely to be unmoved by them. Forecasts of environmental problems illustrate the point.

Academic Concerns. The concerns of academia are quite different. These relate to the scientific validity of futurism and the need to distinguish serious, disciplined practitioners from lucky amateurs, inspired eccentrics and plausible charlatans. Because the time intervals are long, results cannot provide the basis of the evaluation. Even if futurism were validated and its serious practitioners identified, it would still remain unclear whether this represented a separate discipline or an aspect of other more recognized specialties, such as sociology, medicine or the physical sciences.

Futurism Today. Futurism today is at best a pseudoscience. It deals in probability, not certainty. Its practitioners are not clearly defined by background or training and seem bonded only by their common interest. Some critics detect a Cult of Pessimism, arguably with justification; as the paranoiac said, "I know I'm paranoid, but they really *are* following me!" Others suggest they operate *entirely* outside the nine dots. Yet these mainly able and mostly sincere individuals who call themselves futurists have much to offer to those of us accustomed mainly to the familiar ground inside the nine dots.

Some practical suggestions for the futurists:

1. Concentrate more on the near to intermediate-term future.
2. Forecast the timing; to do so may be as important as forecasting the event.
3. Think more in terms of probabilities with generous allowance for the unknown and the unexpected.
4. Think small; the micro-consequence may be more significant than the macro-event.

Connect the nine dots with a continuous drawing of four straightline segments. Hint: the solution requires the creative use of space outside the nine dots.

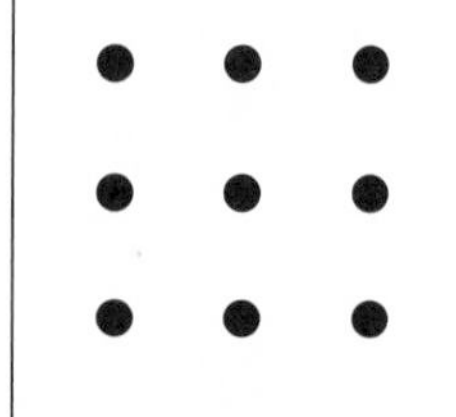

1985/4 The Solution Is a Proxy Tax

President Reagan's tax reform plan, "Treasury II," was launched with a powerful speech on May 28th. It promises to become the subject of an extended national debate, cutting across party lines and economic strata.

Like its predecessor, "Treasury I," the plan proposes to tax the "inside buildup" of life insurance cash values in the hands of policyholders; unlike the predecessor plan, this would apply only to newly issued policies.

Negative Response. The response from the life insurance industry to both plans has been extremely negative. The industry argues that taxation imposed on the inside buildup when no cash has been received is like taxing the appreciation of a home before it is sold. The Treasury argues that taxing the inside buildup is like taxing the interest on a bank deposit even if the interest is not withdrawn. Clearly, the truth lies somewhere between these points of view — life insurance policies are not houses and they are not bank deposits.

A Workable Compromise. Because Treasury II would only tax new policies, it affords the opportunity for a workable compromise which would involve the imposition of a "proxy tax" on life insurance companies; their newly issued policies would then be exempt from further taxation in the hands of policyholders. The proxy taxable income would be the aggregate net gain of policyholders, including the value of the death benefit, just as suggested by Treasury II. The proxy tax would be calculated at some composite rate, reflecting the probable average marginal tax rate of all policyholders, and the company would price its new products in a way that would include the cost (or benefit) of this tax. Very significantly, the aggregate net gain of policyholders would include those policyholders with a loss, which would cause an appropriate reduction in the proxy tax.

The Implications. What are the implications of this suggestion?

1. The principle of equity among types of financial instruments would be maintained, although there would be an element of averaging in the tax rate.
2. Policyholders would require no individual records for tax purposes with respect to individual policies and the "mountain of paper work" involved in other approaches would be avoided.

3. Life insurance products would offer a true aftertax return, calculated with a full offset of expenses charged to policyholders and profits retained by the company.
4. Early cash surrender values of this new generation of policies could be increased because, in the early years, the proxy tax would be negative (in other words, front-end expenses could be charged to policyholders on a net of tax basis).

Like Treasury II, this proposal would generate no consequential amount of tax for many years because it will take a long time before new policyholders have an aggregate net gain. Because life insurance cash value increases would, as a result, become effectively taxable, arguments about the deductibility of policy loan interest ought to disappear or at least reduce. While some adjustment would be required to the economics of the industry, such a plan would not threaten the vitality of the industry or its continued survival.

Remember the Customer. Financial intermediaries, particularly life insurance companies, were not pleased by either Treasury I or Treasury II. This is because the tax reform proposals may diminish the appeal of certain financial products being manufactured and distributed. Overlooked in the argument is the overall impact of tax reform on the individual customer, a point which should be of particular interest to mutual life insurance companies which exist for the benefit of their policyholders.

There is little doubt that almost any plan of tax reform involving a broadening of the tax base and a reduction in marginal tax rates would produce substantial benefits to the typical policyholder. Most of these individuals are not engaged in extreme forms of tax avoidance — life insurance is far too tame a tax avoidance device for seriously minded tax avoiders! By and large, policyholders are middle income, moderately affluent individuals, most of whom have "plain vanilla" tax returns. Tax reform would favor precisely these individuals.

* * *

The life insurance industry might be better served by separating itself from other special interests who will lobby vigorously for the preservation of more extreme tax shelters and by lending its considerable weight behind a plan which will bring material benefits to its customers.

1985/5 If You Can't Beat Them, Why Not Join Them?

A recent editorial in *The New York Times* said:

> Banks think they can sell insurance more cheaply and conveniently than insurance companies. Insurers apparently think so too, for they are fighting an effort by banks in New York State to enter the business.

The Central Question. Can insurance products be distributed through a bank to its customers more efficiently and more conveniently than through insurance agents to the public at large? If the intended distribution process makes extensive use of sales manpower, more efficient distribution requires an increase in sales frequency when compared to traditional distribution methods. The available evidence suggests that such a result is likely:

- Employer-sponsored programs, such as salary savings, are characterized by very high sales frequency, even when no price advantage is offered.
- At least one overseas savings bank, using a dedicated sales force, has achieved such a result.
- Experiments involving location selling in a retail environment have achieved much higher sales frequency than traditional distribution methods.

Other distribution techniques which are less manpower intensive may also prove to be as effective or even more effective, but these are largely untested for distributing mainstream insurance products.

The established customer base of a bank represents an opportunity to market insurance products with a high degree of confidence that the venture will succeed. The development of a dedicated sales force is one way to exploit the opportunity. Because this approach represents only a minor departure from existing distribution methods, the probability of success seems very high. If the expected economies are achieved, these could either be retained or be passed on to customers in the form of low-load, level-load or no-load products, increasing the likely sales frequency and the probability of success.

The Bank as Distributor. The question for the banking industry is how best to exploit its clear opportunity to distribute insurance products.

If the dominant motive is immediate financial benefit, the optimum strategy probably is to market reasonably competitive products offering relatively high commissions through either a dedicated or an independent agency-type distribution system. One way or another, as "rent" or whatever, the bank would share the immediate commission earnings.

If the dominant motive is to lock in the existing customer base by providing a superior service, the optimum strategy probably is to market products with a clear price advantage through a dedicated distribution system closely identified with the bank. Provided the expected economies are achieved, the bank would share the eventual financial benefits.

The Bank as Underwriter? The bank has no advantage as a potential insurance underwriter comparable to that which it enjoys as a potential distributor. If a bank becomes an underwriter, as and when allowed, it must provide the potentially large capital funds to support this activity; to most banks, there are more attractive ways to invest excess capital. There is, however, one important motive which may lead a bank to become an underwriter: It may consider doing so necessary to safeguard the investment of its customers' funds.

The Insurance Industry Perspective. The entry of banks as distributors of insurance products seems a near certainty and imminent, even under existing regulation. This event may transform the insurance industry by its disproportionate impact on the existing distribution system. Even a relatively small shift of market share to banks (say, 10% to 20%) would have a major impact on the already marginal economics of traditional agency systems.

To many insurers, this represents a threat; to some, it could represent an opportunity. Most banks are not, in several respects, well placed to exploit their potential:

- For regulatory reasons, a partner is needed today; the obvious possibilities are an insurer or an insurance broker.
- Recruiting, training, motivating and managing a sales organization require skills not usually found in a bank.
- Product knowledge and administrative skills of a special kind are needed to support the venture.
- Capital is a scarce resource needed to consolidate positions within the banking industry.

Joint Ventures. Joint ventures between banks and insurance companies are feasible today. But their eventual outcome is difficult to predict because the future regulatory climate is unknown. In a fully deregulated environment, a likely outcome would be total consolidation, a possibility which should be addressed at the outset. A stable, well-conceived joint venture offers important advantages to both parties. Banks can gain time, expertise and capital. Insurers can convert a threat to an opportunity: If you can't beat them, why not join them?

1985/6 Mutual Company Mergers: The 160% Solution

Mutual life insurance companies with modest capital funds are an endangered species. Among the 130 U.S. mutual life insurers, clearly one-third, probably two-thirds and possibly more are either sub-viable today or are likely to be so by 1990. Generally, this is because many of these companies do not have an effective distribution system and cannot afford to build one at today's high and rising cost levels. Short of demutualization, there is no practical way for these companies to raise additional capital.

The Obvious Solution. The obvious solution is the consolidation of these companies into fewer and larger units, either by merger with each other or by merger with a stronger organization, most likely another mutual. The aim would be to reach critical mass in terms of capital funds, distribution capacity and other key elements. Why, then, have very few mergers occurred between mutual companies?

The Equally Obvious Difficulties. Control of a mutual life insurance company by its policyholders is largely theoretical. As a result, its directors and senior management enjoy a degree of independence not often found in other business organizations. In a merger of mutual companies, this independence is at least diluted and may even be lost altogether by one of the parties, usually the smaller. Often, local pride and local employment considerations are factors contributing to the reluctance to be absorbed by merger. Members of the agency organization may also view merger as threatening to their livelihood, perhaps because of loss of territorial exclusivity or because less generous commissions may be a result. Is there a way to overcome these difficulties?

The 160% Solution. It is surprisingly easy for Mighty Mutual to acquire Miniature Mutual on terms which should be attractive to policyholders, directors, management, other employees and agents of both companies. The merger agreement would simply provide:

1. that policyholders of Miniature would receive a special distribution of a substantial amount, which might even be *equal to or greater than* the entire surplus of Miniature;
2. that "golden parachutes" would be provided to directors, management and other employees of either company who are dislocated by the merger;

3. that agents of either company, if adversely affected by the merger, would be entitled to appropriate compensation; and
4. that the cost of (1), (2) and (3) would not exceed 160% of the surplus of Miniature.

How does Mighty finance the acquisition on these terms? Since each of the special distributions will be tax deductible, the aftertax cost of "The 160% Solution" is equal to the surplus of Miniature. Assuming the available tax benefits are immediately realized, the surplus of Mighty is unchanged, although it must now support the combined business. Prior to 1984, this result could not have been achieved under tax laws then applicable to life insurance companies.

The immediate benefits to the policyholders of Miniature are clear. Directors, management and other employees of either company, if adversely affected by the merger, are compensated for "loss of office." Agents of both companies are also appropriately protected. If the merger is well conceived, the long-term benefits to policyholders of both companies, the selectively strengthened surviving management and the expanded field force should be substantial. In summary, everyone should win.

Hostile Tender Offers? An unwelcomed offer by Mighty Black Knight to Miniature is barely conceivable but would be unlikely to succeed. The directors and management of Miniature could probably thwart such an offer, at least temporarily, but might be compelled to seek a merger with Mighty White Knight instead.

Opportunity Knocks. There is a clear opportunity for a well financed mutual company to play the role of Mighty Mutual. Success depends on adequate surplus and taxable income, sound planning and an understanding of and empathy for the likely goals of Miniature. There is also a clear opportunity for Miniature to now seek a compatible partner of its own choosing for what eventually could become a compulsory marriage.

There are many possible variations on this theme. A similar strategy could be designed for the acquisition of Miniature by a stock life insurance company. The strategy also applies to fraternal benefit societies and mutual casualty companies, which face different problems of viability and capital starvation.

The need for many mutual insurance companies to reexamine their fundamental position and direction is clear. A compatible merger which protects the interests of the concerned parties may be preferable to other solutions, such as demutualization, or default alternatives, such as a slow decline. The 160% Solution is a practical alternative.

1986/1 Strategies for Survival and Success

"There is no doubt that the economic minimum-size life insurance company is a lot larger than it used to be."

The foregoing statement, made recently by a senior executive of a large insurer, is valid beyond doubt and pregnant with implications.

1985 vs. 1970. As recently as 15 years ago, the author was associated with a group of companies, all in the developmental stage, operating in various parts of the world. One of the common denominators which connected the activities of these companies was the observation that the minimum level of new business required for financial viability was approximately 100 sales per week or 5,000 per year with an average premium per sale of $300; thus, the required level of new business then was approximately $1.5 million.

Based on recent personal observations, the author believes that a similar level of viability today for a mainstream middle-market company is 500 sales per week or 25,000 sales per year with an average premium per sale of $600; thus, the required level of new business today is approximately $15 million.

The indicated conclusion is that the minimum-size company has a required sales level which is ten times what it was 15 years ago in current dollars and five times what it was in constant dollars. While these figures might be argued over a wide range and while they do not apply to companies of every type, they do present a reasonable indication of what has happened since 1970. It is worth noting that industry sales, measured by the number of new ordinary policies, have increased by approximately 80% during the same period.

Using the figures cited, which are subject to important qualifications, it is clear that many life insurance companies that were viable 15 years ago are no longer viable today, even though they may have grown at a pace corresponding to industry averages. A similar conclusion applies to many casualty insurers. For these companies, strategies for survival and success have become an urgent priority. What opportunities are available to them?

Four Programs. Programs of four types, all aimed at achieving viability, are available:

1. *Programs to reduce absolute costs* are intended to downsize the company so that it may achieve an acceptable level of unit expenses at a lower volume

of business. These programs include zero-based budgeting, the development of alternate and more efficient distribution systems and the concentration of a company's efforts on a narrow specialty.

2. *Programs intended to spread overhead over an increased base of business* include both internal and external growth strategies. These programs can be implemented by increasing the size of the distribution system, by the addition of product lines which do not correspondingly increase overheads and, externally, by acquisitions and mergers. All of these programs are subject to important capital constraints and the company undertaking them must have the resources necessary to support them.
3. *Programs intended to increase available margins* include selective price increases and the search for competitive "voids," the delivery of improved services to support higher prices, the containment of benefits costs through risk selection, claim administration and product design and the conservation of existing business to preserve the margins it contributes.
4. *Programs intended to increase investment return*, either for policyholders or for shareholders, can operate through aggressive investment programs designed to exploit the historic yield differentials which favor investments in common stocks, real estate, speculative and illiquid securities. These programs, responsibly implemented, imply the need for substantial capital funds and may lead to problems with the quality of reported earnings; nevertheless, these programs can contribute importantly to viability.

Learning From Lee. Lee Iacocca has been widely acclaimed for the management skills he exhibited in rescuing Chrysler Corporation. From the record, it is clear that one of his major strategies was the downsizing of Chrysler to permit it to show a profit at a lower aggregate sales volume. In addition, he succeeded in increasing sales to spread overhead, increased margins through product selection and pricing and, since Chrysler is primarily a borrower rather than an investor, his efforts to improve the terms of their borrowing correspond to the investment strategy described. His success illustrates each of the four suggested programs, applied in combination.

Conclusion. Not every company is well positioned to undertake all of the four possibilities described. A particular company may lack the necessary expertise or market position to undertake one or more of the suggested programs.

But for a company now operating at a submarginal level of business, it is important to recognize that inaction is a high-risk strategy. Managements of these companies require a clear vision of themselves and the environment and the conviction to dare to undertake new initiatives designed to address this most fundamental management problem.

1986/2 Playing "Chicken" with Credited Interest Rates

Interest-sensitive products now represent more than 50% of individual life insurance sales. These products, introduced in 1979 and widely offered since 1982, were developed in a period of high short-term interest rates. High interest rates accelerated the rapid acceptance of interest-sensitive products by distributors and consumers alike and influenced the initial investment policy of most companies offering these products.

Declining Interest Rates. This initial policy, geared to short-term investments, insulated companies from market risks associated with fluctuations in interest rates. Implicit in the policy was the presumption that credited interest rates would be responsive to changes in the level of short-term interest rates, thereby preserving the "spread." In the intervening years, interest rates have declined substantially and the decline has been greatest for short-term interest rates. The traditional positive yield curve has returned and is unusually steep; a differential of at least 200 basis points exists between short-term and long-term interest rates on government securities, with even larger spreads on other debt instruments. Under these market conditions, credited interest rates should have fallen to a level of perhaps 7%. In fact, this has not happened and most companies continue to credit interest rates of 10% or higher. Just what is going on? The possibilities include:

- Companies are incurring a "negative spread," which they are willing to sustain to protect their competitive position and market share.
- Companies have shifted their investment policy to an emphasis on longer-term or more speculative investments which offer higher yields, in order to support the credited interest rates.

The truth is that both of the possibilities are prevalent in practically all companies, in varying degrees. Both involve significant risks.

Playing "Chicken" with the Competition. There is an obvious reluctance on the part of all companies to reduce credited interest rates on what has become their top-selling product. Most companies would be prepared to follow a downward movement in credited interest rates but none, apparently, is prepared to lead it. This game of "chicken" is growing more expensive by the day.

For the life insurance industry, these products represent a new experience in visible competition. The insurance executive is reluctant to respond to the need for a price increase. It represents, perhaps, his first experience with this need. What should he do? It may be useful to look elsewhere for guidance.

For example, how does the banking industry deal with the need for a price increase, such as an increase in the prime rate of interest or a reduction in rates credited on certificates of deposit and other savings instruments? The pattern is clear. A major bank initiates the move in the expectation that its competitors will follow. While the leader is not always followed, usually he is and an industrywide transition to the new price basis is accomplished within a week.

Further afield, in the airline industry, fare increases are almost always led by major carriers. If the initial move is followed immediately by most other major carriers, the announced increase occurs. If other carriers do not follow, the originating airline usually withdraws or modifies the increase, usually within a few days.

The lesson for the life insurance industry is clear. A reduction in credited interest rates must be led by one of the major carriers. If the industry fails to follow the lead quickly, the leader can always rescind its action.

Playing "Chicken" with the Market. The risks associated with a shift in investment policy towards longer-term maturities and lower quality securities are a different form of the same game of "chicken."

By investing in longer-term maturities, companies can achieve higher rates of return but incur the risk of possible capital loss in the event of an upward move of interest rates. A similar result can be achieved by investing in lower-grade securities. Is the risk worth the reward? Is it responsible?

Using yields on government securities as a guide, a move from 30-day to one-year maturities affords a yield improvement of approximately 100 basis points. Two-year maturities offer an additional yield over one-year securities of approximately 30 basis points per year, which can be viewed as a premium of 160 basis points for the second year. Thereafter, the year-by-year segmentation shows only small increases in yield; each additional year, however, increases the exposure to market volatility.

Yields also may be improved by moving down the quality scale. On both short-term and long-term maturities, Aaa corporate obligations afford a premium of approximately 100 basis points over government securities with corresponding maturities. By moving from Aaa to Baa securities, yields on long-term securities can increase by up to 150 additional basis points.

It is clear that some shift of investment policy is warranted under today's circumstances. Cash values of interest-sensitive life insurance products may actually prove to be less volatile than some would expect. It can be argued that orthodox life insurance cash values are at least as subject to liquidity demands because of their policy loan provisions. In a diversified portfolio, some quality risk is also appropriate. On balance, the market risk associated with changes in interest rates is probably greater than the risk associated with investment grade securities of lower quality.

Leaders and Followers. There is clear need for price leadership within the life industry — just as there was until recently in the casualty industry. When this leadership's need is met, the next need will be for followers. The temptation to exploit a temporary marketing advantage by holding back could become a costly mistake.

1986/3 The Fourth Freedom

In a message to Congress delivered on January 6, 1941, President Franklin Delano Roosevelt articulated the goals since known as the Four Freedoms:

- Freedom of Speech;
- Freedom of Religion;
- Freedom from Want; and
- Freedom from Fear.

A Progress Report. From the perspective of 1986, it is clear that these goals have influenced the modern history of the United States.

Freedom of Speech, magnified many times by modern communications, is alive and robust in America. Its trophy case contains the scalps of two recent incumbent presidents.

Freedom of Religion has been extended to embrace equally religious convictions both familiar and unfamiliar, involving both belief and non-belief. Among the controversial results is a country in which the legality of abortion and prayer in public schools has been reversed.

Freedom from Want has yet to touch all segments of American society; want is still particularly prevalent among single parents and their children, the untrained and undereducated, the mentally or physically handicapped and the very old. Yet even among the disadvantaged 15% of the population, significant progress has been made since 1941 in such areas as health care, nutrition, housing and education. For the fortunate 85% of the population, Freedom from Want is a reality, even measured against a rising standard of expectation.

Fourth Freedom Lost? The Fourth Freedom, Freedom from Fear, has fared less will since 1941. Consider these questions:

- Are most Americans more or less concerned for their personal safety today than they were 45 years ago? On the streets? In their homes? When they travel?
- Are most Americans more or less subject today than they were 45 years ago to harassment, intimidation or punitive action by government agencies of all kinds? The Internal Revenue Service? The local police? The Environmental Protection Agency? The Occupational Safety and Health Administration?
- Are most Americans more or less threatened than they were 45 years ago by financial ruin arising from civil liability for wrongs, real or imagined?

Serving liquor to guests? Actions by minor children? Honest mistakes, or even careless ones?

It is clear that in several important respects the anxiety level of many or even most Americans has increased substantially since 1941. In part, this reflects today's more complex world; in part, it is the consequence of efforts to redress other wrongs, but at high cost in terms of Freedom from Fear.

Fourth Freedom Regained? Freedom from Fear is a worthy national goal. It is not beyond the wit of political leaders and opinion makers to devise the means to progress towards this goal without compromising other worthy objectives:

- Public safety can be improved without risking the creation of a police state.
- Government intimidation can be diminished without a corresponding loss of responsible personal and corporate behavior.
- Civil liability can be restrained without encroachment on the reasonable rights of legitimate claimants — but not without major loss of income to the legal establishment and some others.

The last of these is of particular interest to readers of this column.

The National Casino. The civil liability system of the United States operates as a national casino. Legislators and courts play the role of Gaming Commission. Players compete against each other, not against the House; participation by all players is compulsory. The House is operated by the legal establishment, which charges both players at the combined rate of 40% of the amount won or lost. Subject only to rules laid down by the Gaming Commission, each wager is settled by popular vote of spectator-players called juries.

Most winnings are tax-free but business losses are tax-deductible, assuring that government loses continuously, eventually charging its loss to all players. Some understandably frightened players have entered into loss-sharing agreements with each other, operated by insurers, who incur costs of 40% of all members' losses; the insurers may win or lose in any year, but the subsequent cost to join the agreement is then adjusted. This loss-sharing arrangement and government participation create the illusion that there are few substantial losers.

For 1984, it is estimated* that the aggregate losses of the losing players was $68.2 billion. From the same source, it is estimated that the amount won by

* See *The Cost of the U.S. Tort System,* by Robert W. Sturgis, Tillinghast, Nelson & Warren, Inc., 1986.

the winning players is only 25% of the aggregate losses. The remaining 75% represents amounts paid to the legal establishment and to agents, employees and service providers of the insurance industry. Clearly, the National Casino does not operate primarily for the benefit of the players themselves.

This madness can and must be stopped. The Gaming Commission must change these silly rules if Freedom from Fear is ever to be achieved. Unfortunately, most members of the Gaming Commission also are members of the legal establishment and more than a few are insurance agents. At what cost to society in money and anxiety must they be supported?

One-Eyed Justice? While the civil rights of criminal defendants are rigorously guarded, those of civil defendants are freely abused. The contrast is stark:

- Statutes of limitation are strictly applied in one case but nearly disregarded in the other.
- Unreasonable (and even reasonable) search and seizure is prohibited but unlimited self-incriminating discovery is not.
- Proof beyond reasonable doubt applies to one but the balance of evidence (and sympathy) governs the other.
- One system is engineered to exonerate anyone who might be innocent but the other to punish anyone who might be guilty.

Was Freedom from Fear intended to be enjoyed only by criminal defendants, not civil ones? Is Justice peeking — with one eye only?

1986/4 Will Old Banks Learn New Tricks?

The arrival of banks as distributors and, eventually, as underwriters of insurance products has been widely expected and loudly ballyhooed. Proponents and opponents alike have exchanged the customary pre-fight insults to the delight of the financial press, reveling in the prospect of a punch-up among the gentry. In the early betting, banks were the heavy favorites.

Thus far, the event has fallen as far short of expectations as the arrival of Halley's Comet: visible low on the horizon only on a clear night in an unpopulated area, through binoculars. As with the comet, the best viewing spot is probably Australia.

The Early Experiments. In the United States, most banks are constrained by applicable regulation from direct entry into the distribution or underwriting of most types of insurance. The exceptions include 16 grandfathered banks with long-established insurance agencies, banks chartered by certain states and some credit-related insurance coverages. With these exceptions, the insurance experiments undertaken by banks have been confined to distribution of insurance products in partnership with another organization — usually an established agency or an established insurance company. The examples include:

- Bank of America/Capital Holding;
- NCNB/Johnson & Higgins;
- Citibank/AIG;
- BancOne/Nationwide;
- Bank of Virginia/Equitable;
- First Interstate/Safeco;
- Marine Midland/Colonial Penn; and
- First Tennessee/Craddock.

These experiments have involved a variety of distribution and product strategies, all aimed at the established customer base of the sponsoring bank. The distribution strategies include direct response marketing, on-site independent agents, captive agents, lead-generating systems, cross-training of bank personnel and more — all in a dazzling array of combinations. The product strategies range from conventional to simplified to price differentiated. No dominant distribution strategy nor any dominant product strategy has yet emerged.

An Appraisal. Some of the experiments have been in progress long enough to appraise and the results to date range from unexciting to disappointing. Moreover, the newer experiments do not seem sufficiently different to justify significantly more optimistic expectations. No doubt a case-by-case analysis would reveal reasons, particular to each experiment, which would explain, in part, each disappointment. Clearly, that is beyond the scope of this appraisal, which searches for common threads which may explain the results. Some are visible; they involve a clash of cultures.

A Clash of Cultures. Banks and insurance companies have traditionally pursued fundamentally different business strategies which have left an indelible imprint on their respective cultures:

- *Banks are consumer driven.* They advertise and passively market easily understood commodity-type products to a broad market segment. Competition focuses primarily on convenience (location, hours and automatic tellers) but not price or product (which are practically uniform). The bank is more visible to the consumer than the banker.
- *Insurance companies are distribution driven.* They aggressively market complex products of widely varied real and perceived value (i.e., price) through a sales-driven network of independent or semi-independent distributors who select the market sectors addressed. Competition focuses primarily on commissions, which vary inversely with product value, creating a conflict of interest between the intermediary and the consumer. The intermediary is more visible to the consumer than the insurer.

Most of the insurance experiments by banks, involving established agencies and insurance companies, have not clearly resolved this clash of cultures. Neither culture can be applied unchanged with any reasonable expectation of success. The fundamental business strategy of a consolidated financial service organization needs to be different from that of both banks and insurance companies.

The Issues for Banks. Because theirs is the customer base to be addressed, banks are in control of any joint venture. Later, if regulation is changed, they may proceed independently. Either way, certain issues must be resolved:

- Many insurance products, unlike banking services, do not "sell themselves." Sales-driven intermediaries will be required and will, to some degree, always relate to the alien insurance culture.

- Many insurance products are not commodities and a wide variation of real and apparent prices is possible. The low-priced strategy is not necessarily the best strategy.
- Some insurance products are substitutes for certain products now offered by banks. In some cases, but not all, the insurance products are superior for the consumer but in most cases the insurance products are potentially more profitable. The potentially conflicting goals of the bank towards its customers must be clearly defined and the system of rewards and recognition applicable to its personnel must reflect its goals.
- Insurance products have much higher margins than banking products and traditionally bear much higher expenses, especially for distribution. The main opportunity for banks is the possibility of reduced distribution costs, not the opportunity for underwriting profits per se. To seize the opportunity, banks must adopt the more aggressive marketing approach of traditional insurance distribution systems, but without adopting the associated economics; this is the single most important management challenge.

These and other issues will create conflict with the established culture of banks that aspire to engage in the insurance business. Will old banks learn new tricks? Probably, especially after there are successful prototypes to imitate. The earliest examples may emerge outside the United States. Australia, where major banks and insurers are plunging into each other's business, is one of the likely places to watch.

1986/5 Who Owns Mutual Insurance Companies?

The ownership of mutual insurance companies is a subject of considerable debate, within the legal and actuarial professions and elsewhere. For whose benefit do these companies exist? Towards what end should they be managed? How should the success of their managers be measured and rewarded? These are substantial issues which relate directly to the way in which these companies operate. Are there no clear answers?

The Legal Theory. The legal theory of ownership holds that mutual insurance companies belong to their policyholders, but their ownership interest is not clearly defined. Which policyholders own the company? What is the amount of their individual interest? Does the sum of those interests equal the value of the whole company? If so, by logic or by definition? If not, who owns the rest? It is precisely because these fundamental questions of ownership are often unanswered that the operational issues are often unanswerable.

The widely accepted legal theory of ownership by some class of existing policyholders, possibly including some recent former policyholders, is not convincing; "[it] simply melts when held up to the flame of history" (*Time*, August 11, 1986). If operations were conducted according to this theory, for the benefit of current "owners," many mutual insurance companies would adopt some plan of reorganization or liquidation, most likely demutualization or sale to or assumption by another insurer. Failure by many companies to adopt such a plan is a clear denial of the theory. It is not the basis on which these companies are actually managed.

The Equitable Theory. The equitable theory of ownership apportions to each policyholder an interest defined either by the past contribution or the reasonable future expectation of each, determined on some reasonable and consistently applied basis. That interest, however calculated, might be positive (a likely result for older generations of business) or negative (a likely result for newer ones). Future surplus distributions, if made on the same basis, will reflect that ownership interest. The sum of the parts will not equal the whole and, typically, there will be a large remainder "belonging" to no one; in the case of mutual casualty companies, the remainder is a very large proportion of the whole. In the United States, the remainder is sometimes called "orphan surplus"; in some other countries, it is called the "free estate."

This theory of ownership is much more convincing, no matter what its legal standing. It squares with the observed acts; it avoids potential windfall gains by some policyholders; and it is generally consistent with the aspirations of management. Depending on what follows, it may also best serve the collective interest of all the parties involved.

Managing the "Free Estate." The equitable theory of ownership introduces an important new element, the management of the free estate. For whose benefit, if not the current "owners," does it exist? What are the legitimate and responsible uses of the free estate? Or the opposite? There are many possibilities:

1. *Absorbing Fluctuations.* This is the textbook purpose of the free estate. One desirable variation, which is fundamentally important in several countries, is the use of the free estate to support large holdings of mismatched investments, such as common stock and real estate, for the purpose of enhancing policyholders' long-term investment returns.
2. *Growth.* Growth to maintain or to achieve continuing viability is a legitimate goal, provided its cost is within reasonable bounds; growth in response to the "territorial imperative" in the executive suite or board room is at least questionable, especially if it is also uneconomic.
3. *Diversification.* Diversification to achieve economies of scale or to extend the services offered to policyholders on attractive terms is defensible, but diversification into unrelated businesses, unless viewed primarily as an investment, may be another manifestation of the territorial imperative.
4. *Subsidies.* Use of the income generated by the free estate to reduce costs borne by all current and future "owners," perhaps by marginal costing, is clearly legitimate, but subsidizing the indefinite continuation of an inefficient operation is clearly not.
5. *Public and Private Interests.* Use of the free estate to support public interests, such as charities or investments in worthy but uneconomic projects, or private interests, such as continued employment, is at least controversial and may be inappropriate.

Taxation of mutual insurance companies has a significant impact on the management opportunities and affects the relative desirability of various uses of the free estate. The taxation of mutual life insurance companies in the United States now includes an additional tax which is approximately related to the visible portion of the free estate.

A Unique Strength. The free estate is a unique strength of mutual insurance companies. Its potential operational and competitive advantages are considerable. In North America, this advantage is often under-recognized and under-exploited. Sometimes the advantage is dissipated for purposes that would not be allowed as part of an explicit policy.

Most mutual insurance companies in North America do not have clearly defined goals for the management of the free estate. Most could not even quantify it. Yet, by their actions, they are "managing" this vital element of their companies, every day.

This management process can and should be made explicit. It can also be linked to a system of rewards to align the personal interests of management with the general corporate interests. Boards of directors of mutual insurance companies should insist on an explicit policy and should be prepared appropriately to compensate those who successfully implement it. The management that addresses these questions and thereby defines its goals is likely to perform in a superior fashion, to the benefit of both their "owners" and themselves.

Who owns mutual insurance companies? Superior performance for the benefit of "owners" provides the economic justification of the equitable theory of ownership. The legal theory is most likely to apply to companies whose continued operations do not provide ownership benefits which compare favorably with the windfall gains offered by reorganization or liquidation. The quality of management is the real determining factor.

1986/6 Control the Process Before It Controls You!

A period of market-driven consolidation within the banking and insurance businesses has already begun. Eventually, consolidation *between* these businesses should also be expected. Other financial businesses, some of which have themselves already consolidated, can expect continued involvement. Major industrial organizations are likely to play an expanded role in this process, either as sponsors or as catalysts.

The Forces of Change. The underlying forces of change are deregulation and technology; these have been translated into market forces by the combined reactions of consumers and investors.

Deregulation, intentional and de facto, has intensified competition by removing cross-industry, geographic and minimum pricing barriers. Technology has accelerated the obsolescence of traditional business methods by creating new, but capital-intensive alternatives; the cost of the retooling required to compete is beyond the capital resources of many financial companies. Individual and corporate consumers have responded by choosing lower margin products and services. As a result of lower margins, the values of many independent providers of financial products and services have fallen well below their values in a consolidation and sometimes even below their breakup values. Individual and corporate investors, seeking to maximize the value of their investments in these companies, have supported takeovers and mergers, and some managements, responding to investor pressure, have supported and even sought friendly transactions.

The Shape of the Future. This process of consolidation is still in its early stages. In the United States, there are today thousands of independent banks and near-banks, several hundred independent insurance companies and hundreds if not thousands of other significant independent financial companies. The universe, however defined, consists of several thousand independent companies. How many of these will remain independent in 2000 A.D.?

Consider the banking and near-banking business. Each major metropolitan area of the country today supports 25 or more significant institutions of this type; some of these operate only locally, some statewide and a few regionally. If national or even regional banking becomes the norm, it is difficult to imagine that there will be more than 200 large national or regional banks; the experience in other countries would suggest 100 or fewer such institutions. On average, each of these survivors is likely to absorb 25 to 50 similar organizations as they progress to national or regional status, suggesting that 5,000 now independent banks and near-banks will be absorbed. It would be easier to argue for an even larger number of consolidations than for a smaller number.

Among insurance companies, considerations relating to necessary critical mass suggest that the number of mainstream competitors is limited to perhaps 100 life insurance companies and 100 casualty companies; this would allow a minimum market share of .5% if the smallest viable company was half as large as the average company. Not all of these 200 survivors will be independent of each other and some will be part of a wider financial group.

Among other financial companies, the analysis is similar. In fact, a major consolidation has already occurred among securities dealers and other branches of the investment community. Many more of these companies are likely to be absorbed within a group led by a bank or an insurance company.

This does not mean that, at most, 200 independent banks, 200 independent insurance companies and a handful of other independent financial companies will be the only survivors. It does mean that these companies, probably combined into 300 or fewer groups, are likely to control 80% or more of the entire financial services market. The remaining market will still support a significant number of specialized and geographically concentrated companies which remain independent. But, there will be many fewer than today's numbers and the nature of their operations will be much more narrowly focused.

The Message. The message is clear: Fewer than half, perhaps substantially fewer, of the now independent financial companies will remain independent in 2000 A.D. For most of these companies, perhaps a substantial majority, the relevant issue is not continued independence versus takeover; the relevant issues are the identity of the new parent and the terms of the transaction. Managements of most financial companies can reward their owners and profit personally by taking control of this process before it takes control of them.

1987/1 Pro Bono Publico

The fastest growing segment of the population of the United States is the over 65 age group. Today, these Senior Citizens represent 12% of the population; by 2020, they will represent 17% of the population. The expected annual growth rate is approximately four times that of the rest of the population.

A Market Opportunity. Besides this rapid growth, Senior Citizens are an attractive market segment for other reasons:

- Except for the elderly old, most Senior Citizens are reasonably affluent.
- Their financial security needs are easily identified and substantial.
- Many of those needs can be met with packaged products specifically designed for the market.

Financial service providers of all kinds are aware of these attractions and many providers have responded to the market opportunity in various ways, including reduced bank service charges and other concessions.

Insurance Industry Response. The response by the insurance industry leaves much to be desired. High margin products widely outnumber high value products. In too many cases, the products offered seem quite inappropriate to the real needs of most people in this age group. In a few cases, media advertising is blatantly misleading, even to the point of suggesting that the purchase of life insurance for $5 per month guarantees that the buyers "will not become a burden to their children!" These activities seem destined inevitably to lead to trouble. This age group is viewed sympathetically by both the public and the press and anything that smacks of exploitation is likely to cause a public outcry which may reflect adversely on the industry as a whole. This unhappy result is quite unnecessary. A better response to the market opportunity is required.

Addressing the Real Needs. What are the real financial security needs of a typical Senior Citizen who has an income adequate to meet his or (more often) her normal needs? What are the possible enhancements of the financial position of such a person? How can insurance products address these needs?

- If income arises from investment earnings and withdrawal of principal from savings, there is a risk of outliving the savings and a risk of mismanaging the investments. A life annuity addresses both risks.

- The financial risk associated with inflation is substantial, particularly for those who live to a very advanced age. In part, this risk can be addressed by an increasing annuity or by a variable annuity.
- The financial consequences of extended confinement in a hospital or nursing home can be devastating; often the quality of life which results is dictated by the available resources. An annuity which provided increased benefits under such circumstances would address this need.
- Income from sources other than savings, such as Social Security and pensions, may be adequate without the supplement that an annuity would provide. In that case, available savings are likely to be earmarked for a financial emergency or to provide an inheritance. Single premium life insurance which also provides income benefits while confined to a hospital or nursing home would address these circumstances; such a product would be more practical if the income benefits paid reduced the face amount of the life insurance provided, perhaps using the familiar $10 per $1,000 relationship between monthly income and face amount.

Life insurance products, notably annuities and ones which provide confinement-type disability benefits, can be designed to address in a constructive way the needs of most Senior Citizens. Annuity products, even with enhanced benefits during confinement, probably could be offered with few or even no underwriting requirements. Life insurance and annuity products also provide a measure of tax avoidance or tax deferment, which further increases their attractiveness. These financial security benefits, well designed and well packaged, would be valued highly by the buyer, who would likely be willing to pay an appropriate price for the reassurance and simplicity they would provide.

Affordability. The cost of an annuity which increases by 3% annually exceeds the cost of a level annuity by 30% at age 65 and 10% at age 85. Depending on the applicable restrictions, the added cost of a "double indemnity" hospital or nursing home confinement benefit superimposed on a life annuity might be ten times the additional monthly benefit; the same benefit, if superimposed on a standard underwritten life insurance policy as suggested, would cost less because of the offset to the face amount. Many Senior Citizens can afford the substantial single premium necessary to provide meaningful benefits; many more could afford the premium if concurrent arrangements were offered which permitted them to realize their home equity during their lifetime while retaining a life tenancy or similar interest.

Pro Bono Publico. The life insurance industry has the opportunity to perform a public service by designing products which address the real needs of this already important and growing market sector. At the same time, it can serve its own needs for profitable growth without the public approbation to which some current product offerings are vulnerable.

1987/2 The Search for Competitive Advantage

All economic activity is essentially competitive — a zero sum game with winners and losers. Success or failure in the game can be measured by the following fundamental equation:

$$\text{Return on Capital} = \frac{\text{Return Price Realized} - \text{Cost Incurred}}{\text{Capital Employed}}$$

A satisfactory return to the investor equals success; an unsatisfactory return equals failure. Different investors may have different requirements.

Competitive Advantage. The players who are likely to succeed are those which enjoy a sustainable competitive advantage which can be used to increase price realization, reduce costs or reduce the required capital. An investor with a lower required return on capital also has a competitive advantage. The search for competitive advantage is central to the strategic planning process.

Survival and Success. Survival and success in any economic activity depend on sound strategic planning and professional implementation. The process involves four steps:

- understanding the competitive environment;
- identifying existing and potential competitive advantages and disadvantages;
- developing a strategic plan which magnifies competitive advantages and diminishes competitive disadvantages; and
- implementing the plan in a professional manner, which requires information to manage the process.

Where to Look. In the financial services business, competitive advantage may be found in many forms. Price realization can be enhanced by product or service differentiation, by a captive customer base or by captive distribution. Cost advantages can be realized through economies of scale, superior investment performance, superior systems or distribution efficiencies (such as "piggybacking"). Required capital and required rates of return can be reduced by different capital structures (perhaps involving debt) and funding sources (such as reinsurance).

Confusion of Strategies. Once the competitive advantages have been identified, a sharply focused plan is required to magnify them. One serious error is lack of focus. For example, a cost advantage can be used successfully to compete on the basis of low prices or high commissions; but if the strategic plan also includes costly product or service enhancements, the competitive advantage of low cost is likely to be dissipated or even lost completely. An even more serious error is overreaching. For example, if a high-cost competitor offers low prices or high commissions, the strategy is certain to fail unless there is a more workable concurrent program to achieve superior cost fundamentals; a more realistic strategy might be one that aims to achieve higher price realization.

And When There is None? If a meaningful competitive advantage cannot be found, what then? One possible strategy is a merger, joint venture or strategic acquisition intended to create a competitive advantage through economies of scale, through access to captive customers or captive distribution, or by providing a differentiated product or service.

Deregulation. Deregulation, because it lowers the barriers to entry, disturbs the existing competitive advantage. Similar disturbance can be caused by new technology, tax reform, foreign competition, changes in consumer attitudes and many other developments. The accompanying chart traces the effects of the disturbance, which culminate in a new competitive equilibrium following a period of extensive rationalization. This process can be observed in an advanced stage

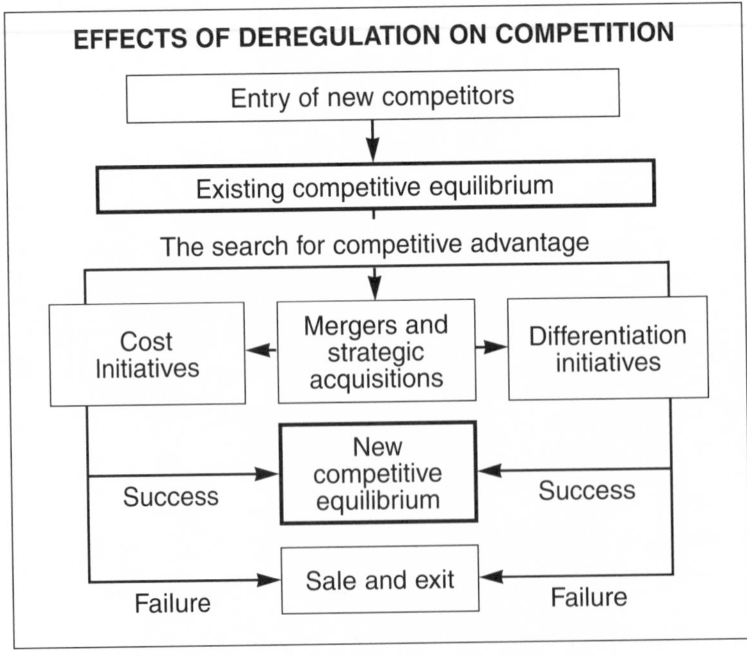

in the airline industry, in the securities industry and elsewhere; the early stages are already visible in the banking and insurance industries.

The Hard Reality. If no competitive advantage exists and if none can be acquired at a price consistent with the required return on capital, the business will probably not be successful and its sale or discontinuance is indicated. Many banks and insurance companies now face this hard reality and must effectively deal with it.

1987/3 The Rebating Debate

Rebating of insurance commissions to persons not licensed as agents is prohibited by state law throughout the U.S. and by provincial law in Canada. These laws are uniquely North American. Elsewhere, the little regulation that exists either imposes maximum rates of commission or requires disclosure of commission.

Last year, a United States District Court held that the Florida antirebating statute was an unconstitutional restraint of interstate commerce; that decision was later affirmed by the U.S. Court of Appeals and a further appeal to the U.S. Supreme Court is now pending. Two similar challenges to state laws were filed in Georgia and California. The Georgia case recently was dismissed on technical grounds relating to the qualification of the plaintiff to initiate the action. The California case is expected to be heard later this year. The battle has been joined.

The Issues. The rebating controversy involves three major issues:

- legal questions;
- matters of public policy; and
- established commercial interests.

Legal Issues. The constitutionality of various state laws is not the only legal issue. If the states cannot restrict interstate commerce, the United States clearly can. But a national statute which prohibited rebating would represent a major departure from the tradition of state regulation of the business of insurance. Such a departure would be viewed by many as more important than the issue of rebating. Moreover, would the United States Congress, starting afresh, enact such a law? This leads directly to the matters of public policy.

Public Policy Issues. Are insurance buyers in the United States and Canada better served because rebating of insurance commissions is prohibited?

Within the insurance industry, the answer is loudly affirmative. It is argued that rebating would undercut the professionalism of insurance agents by eroding their income and promoting unfair competition from "discount insurance brokers," who would merely execute transactions and provide no meaningful advice. It is also argued that rebating would lead to undesirable commission-splitting with finders and even to illegal or unethical "kickbacks" to those who control insurance-buying decisions of corporations, government agencies and others.

Among consumer advocates, the answer is loudly negative. A somewhat imprecise but relevant parallel is drawn with negotiated commissions on securities transactions. It is also argued that consumers should be able to choose the level of advice and service needed and to negotiate a suitable price for that advice and service. It is claimed that the prevailing price for such advice and service is too high and contributes to the "affordability" and "availability" problems prominent in the news.

These are not the only arguments and there are counter-arguments to each. These arguments are cited to serve only a limited purpose — to establish the clear conclusion that some consumers are better served by one system and some by the other.

It is instructive to ask: If there were no anti-rebating statutes in effect, is it likely that such statutes would be enacted today? When these statutes were widely enacted, following the adoption of model legislation by the NAIC in 1947, the prevailing relationships among consumers, insurance agents and companies were quite different; insurance pricing and commission practices were more standardized and more regulated; consumers were not as well informed; and self insurance, captive insurers and the direct marketing of insurance had not been conceived.

Given these significant changes and the general trend towards deregulation, it seems very unlikely that this type of legislation would be adopted de novo today. Whether or not it should be retained is a somewhat different question, because long-established commercial interests of most insurance agents and some companies are now involved. The commercial issues have affected the intellectual quality of the arguments advanced by some whose established interests may be threatened if these laws are overturned and by others who might benefit from that result.

Commercial Issues. An overwhelming majority of insurance agents and most companies believe they would be damaged if rebating were permitted. Are they right?

The fears of insurance agents are probably well grounded. Commercial buyers of insurance would be quick to demand discounts; this would expand a practice that already exists — in various forms, above and below the table. Sophisticated individual buyers would do the same, particularly on high-volume purchases of commodity like products (such as auto, homeowners and term life insurance) and investment-like products (such as single premium life insurance). In effect, agents' commissions would be set by market forces, probably at overall levels lower than those prevailing today. In this respect, agents and consumer advocates are in agreement! Many agents would regard the fee alternative as a more attractive possibility than they do today, especially if it were also perceived as enhancing their professional status.

The impact on insurance companies is not nearly as clear. In general, a market disturbance of any type threatens those with established market positions and those with the weakest cost fundamentals. In an environment which already demands industry rationalization, that process is likely to be accelerated by a disturbance of this type. For the eventual survivors and for the nimble opportunists, such an outcome may be an improvement upon the slow and painful rationalization now in progress. In the end, a new relationship among consumers, agents and companies may emerge — one that is more favorable from the company viewpoint. This may be the only practical way to achieve an actual reduction in distribution costs, which the industry needs to compete with alternate providers of financial products and self-insurance. One suspects that this possibility is recognized by many within the industry and that some companies, fearing backlash from their agents, support the defense of the status quo for the same reason that Bulgaria always supports the Soviet Union within the United Nations!

The Outlook. The attack on statutes which prohibit rebating appears to have at least an even chance of success. Many observers would rate the chance much higher; few would rate it lower. If the attack succeeds, fundamental changes seem likely to follow. Pitfalls and opportunities will abound. Old strategies will be found wanting. Markets lost to self-insurance might be recaptured. The ready will enjoy a large advantage. Insurance agents and companies need a contingency plan now. If individual companies are not prepared to lead their distribution systems in new directions, they will have no alternative except to follow in directions others choose.

A Footnote for Canadian Readers. If rebating becomes an accepted practice in the U.S.A., it will be hard to resist in Canada, even though the validity of these laws is not an issue there. In Canada, any change will come by legislative rather than judicial action. Because many companies and some large agencies operate on a coordinated basis in both countries, dikes along the St. Lawrence Seaway and the 49th Parallel are bound to leak. Already in Canada, de facto rebating has become the norm in commercial property and casualty insurance, achieved through premium discounts supported by commission reductions.

1987/4 Another Modest Proposal: Pay "Death Claims" to Living Policyholders

The value of a life insurance policy is not necessarily its cash surrender value. If the life insured is in seriously impaired health, the value is much greater. This principle applies equally to individual term policies and even to group life insurance certificates, which do not provide cash surrender values.

The Policyholders' Dilemma. Many of these same policyholders are in serious financial difficulties, most likely because of expenses associated with their impairment. Often, they need the proceeds of their policies more than their beneficiaries. To them, their life insurance policies may even represent an additional financial burden if it is necessary to continue the payment of premiums. If they could realize the actual value of their policies, not just the cash surrender value, many would choose to do so.

A Secondary Market? The obvious need is for a secondary market where life insurance policies could be sold (or borrowed upon) at a negotiated value. There is a precedent for this idea. In 19th century Britain, life insurance policies generally did not include provisions allowing encashment. As a result, policies were sold at auction by those policyholders wanting to raise cash. This practice continued into the early years of this century.

Notwithstanding the precedent, a secondary market would not be easy to organize. Besides possible legal challenges based on public policy or other grounds, the tasks of assembling and evaluating medical evidence ("negative underwriting"), reviewing policies, documenting the transfers and assuring timely payment of future premiums are formidable and likely to be expensive. Nevertheless, a few organizations might be prepared to offer such a service. Part of the needed capital could be obtained by exercising the policy loan provisions of the policies purchased.

A Better Alternative. A better alternative would be for the service to be provided by the life insurance industry itself. The problems of assembling and evaluating medical evidence would remain, but many of the other problems would be simplified or even eliminated if companies dealt only in their own policies.

For many well-capitalized life insurance companies this is a feasible suggestion. A current loss would be incurred to avoid a larger future loss. This concept may appeal particularly to mutual life insurance companies seeking to provide a valuable service to their owner-customers and to shrink their taxable surplus.

The Potential Demand. The potential demand for this facility is very large. Among the 30 million Americans over age 65, perhaps 3 million are seriously impaired; among the estimated 1 million Americans already infected by the AIDS virus, more than half are expected to develop the fatal disease. There are many other less obvious but potentially interested groups. In total, there may be 5 million seriously impaired Americans, 2 million of whom have life insurance policies. Among these, 1 million might be suitable candidates for such a program.

Some Practical Considerations. If a life insurance policy were cancelled by payment of a negotiated surrender value, the policyholder would be likely to have a large taxable gain. If equally large tax deductions for medical expenses are also available, this may not present a problem. Under other circumstances, a loan larger than the cash surrender value, secured by the policy but outside its policy loan provisions, might provide a better tax result for the policyholder, but not for the company.

The statutory surplus requirements of such a program are potentially very large and the availability of the facility could not be guaranteed. As a practical matter, it might only be offered to a narrowly defined group.

For stock companies, there are GAAP accounting problems associated with the alteration of the timing of losses.

The risk evaluation problem is analogous to that involved in underwriting substandard annuities. Only a few companies offer such contracts and, historically, their underwriting results often have been disappointing.

The problem of lost renewal commissions is sure to arise but is not likely to be significant in financial terms.

A Modest Proposal. In 1729, the Irish social satirist and clergyman, Jonathan Swift, composed a letter from an imaginary public spirited citizen with the abbreviated title, *A Modest Proposal.* Its ironic and grim suggestion was that the twin Irish problems of famine and overpopulation could be solved if Irish children were used for food by their parents. Some readers may view this Modest Proposal, involving the payment of "death claims" to living policyholders, as the ultimate ironic and grim variation of Cannibal Life!

Notwithstanding the many practical problems, this unconventional proposal is made quite seriously. It aims to serve a worthy social purpose at no real cost to the industry. Its potential for favorable public relations may alone offer sufficient reward. The industry needs new friends in influential places to achieve the regulatory climate necessary to protect the risk selection process on which private insurance of all types is founded. This proposal is an example of risk selection used to achieve positive social benefits.

1988/1 The Crash of 1987: Could It Have Been Foreseen?

Does the total return on common stock investments, year by year, represent a random walk around some mean expected return? In other words, is the expected return of each year independent of the returns of prior years, or is the expected return of each year influenced by the preceding experience?

Random Walk or Central Tendency? The prevailing opinion, in academic and actuarial literature, supports the random walk theory on the basis of a considerable body of statistical evidence. Notwithstanding that persuasive evidence, the instincts and observed actions of many informed investors support a different view; these contrarians believe that there exists some central anchor which prevents common stock prices from walking randomly, in either direction, beyond some limit.

Intuitive support for the central tendency theory is provided by such concepts as the necessity of a relationship between the market price of common stocks and the underlying net asset values of the issuing corporations, which do not exhibit the same volatility as stock market prices. Accordingly, at some high share price, the company will issue more shares, thereby arresting or reversing any further increase; and at some low share price, the company will be acquired, will buy its own shares in the open market or will liquidate, thereby arresting or reversing any further decline.

Such a central tendency, if it exists, would be significant because its potential impact on the *range* of possible results at any given level of confidence could be quite substantial. If, for example, it could be established that after a market loss of some amount had been sustained in a given period, a similar consecutive loss in the ensuing period was less likely, the long-term risks associated with common stock investments would be considerably lower than would be suggested by the random walk thesis. The impact on reserves required to support long-term guarantees included in equity-linked contracts would be very substantial.

Such a central tendency also would be important because it would validate the concept of market timing, at least under extreme circumstances. Market booms and crashes would be foreseeable events, at least in theory; random-walkers reject this possibility.

The Statistical Evidence. How can these competing theories be tested statistically? One test involves serial correlation, an investigation of the relationship of each observation (such as the total return for one year) to the observation for the preceding period. Positive correlation supports the thesis that good years are more likely to follow good years and bad years to follow bad years; this result would suggest that actual volatility is greater than that suggested by the random walk thesis. Zero correlation supports the random walk thesis. Negative correlation supports the central tendency thesis. Results of tests of this nature generally show near-zero serial correlation and such results are the major statistical underpinning of the random walk thesis. This test may, however, fail to detect "wave patterns" over longer periods; the serial correlation of a sine curve, for example, can be positive, zero or negative, depending on the choice of the intervals measured.

Another Statistical Test. A different test can be designed to examine the relationships among common stock returns and variances for time periods of different length. If, for example, annual rates of return are randomly and normally distributed on a logarithmic basis, expected rates of return and variances for periods of N consecutive years are mathematically related to the expected annual rate of return and its variance for periods of one year.

Such a test, based on the 60-year period 1925–1955 (subdivided into consecutive year periods of different length) develops the following results (expressed as antilogarithms of the two statistical measures for both nominal and inflation-adjusted rates of return):

Investment Period (Years)	Number of Periods	Mean Return	Standard Deviation	
			Actual	Expected
		Nominal Rates of Return		
1	60	9.8%	22.8%	22.8%
2	30	20.6	33.0	33.6
3	20	32.5	41.4	42.6
4	15	45.5	44.3	50.7
5	12	59.8	36.3	58.2
6	10	75.5	50.2	65.2
10	6	155.4	58.8	91.3
12	5	208.1	84.4	103.5
		Inflation-Adjusted Rates of Return		
1	60	6.5%	23.2%	23.2%
2	30	13.5	33.6	34.3
3	20	20.9	39.7	43.4
4	15	28.8	42.2	51.7
5	12	37.3	38.0	59.3
6	10	46.3	49.1	66.6
10	6	88.4	60.9	93.2
12	5	113.9	80.0	105.7

The results are unmistakable: On both value bases, as the investment period lengthens, the actual standard deviation is, in general, progressively less than the expected deviation. In other words, actual market prices did *not* vary as much as expected according to the random walk thesis. This pattern of results supports the concept that stock market returns *are* influenced by the preceding experience and that stock price variations *are* cyclical, as suggested by the central tendency thesis.

Conclusion. If the central tendency theory is valid, as suggested by intuition and supported by the foregoing analysis, there is validity to the concept of market timing, but perhaps only under extreme and rare conditions. Major stock market booms and crashes based on the reversal of excess speculation are, therefore, foreseeable.

On October 19, 1987, investors in most of the world simultaneously realized, as suggested by the fable of Hans Christian Andersen, that "the Emperor has no clothes." Will investors in Japan and the rest of the world soon discover that the Mikado also has no clothes?

(Note: This article was written Thursday, January 14, 1988, on which date the Nikkei Index of share prices in Japan was 22603.65.)

1988/2 AIDS: A Competitive Advantage for Smaller Companies?

Small and medium-sized life insurance companies are struggling to find a strategy which allows them successfully to compete with companies which enjoy the potential cost and other advantages of their larger scale. How might smaller companies succeed in this inherently uneven contest?

The Advantages of Scale. The primary advantage of scale relates to the allocation of fixed overhead expenses across a larger base of business. Economies of scale vary significantly among different classes of business. Other advantages of larger scale relate to the ability to afford leading-edge expertise and technology. These are powerful advantages, not easily answered by smaller competitors.

The Advantages of Focus. The main opportunity for smaller companies to counter the advantages of scale is to exploit the equally powerful advantages of focus. Focus may be market directed, service directed, distribution directed or product directed. The objective is to achieve either a cost advantage or higher price realization by concentrating on one or only a few areas. These powerful advantages cannot easily be imitated by larger companies, whose existing widespread operations cannot correspondingly be focused.

Focus on AIDS. The AIDS epidemic, with its serious implications for the life and health insurance industry, offers smaller companies a new way to exploit the advantages of focus. The objective would be to achieve a cost advantage by reducing benefit costs, not unit expenses.

The incidence of AIDS and HIV infection is not uniformly distributed throughout the United States. Concentrations are present in major metropolitan areas such as New York, San Francisco, Los Angeles, Washington, Houston, New Orleans, Miami and Atlanta. A smaller company, by withdrawing from such markets, could reasonably expect to reduce its mortality costs by a significant amount — probably 10% or more at male ages 20 to 50. For some products, such as term life insurance, this cost advantage would be significant enough to offset the advantages of scale enjoyed by larger companies. The mortality cost advantage would also be significant for other individual life insurance products, such as universal life. An even greater morbidity cost advantage might apply to individual health insurance products, but these products are often area rated and area rating dilutes the competitive advantage of geographic focus.

Larger companies would be hard-pressed to respond to this strategy of market-directed geographic focus. Larger companies operate nationally; for life insurance products, geographically differentiated pricing is probably not practical and almost certainly not permissible within a given state; on average, their mortality costs would surely be higher than those of their focused competitors.

Other Issues. Some smaller companies are already at least partially focused on markets outside the most affected metropolitan areas. Others could achieve a practically similar result by targeting their future recruitment efforts in other communities. It may not be necessary explicitly to withdraw from the markets to be avoided since attrition alone would likely achieve that result in a reasonably short period of time.

There may be other equally persuasive reasons which argue that smaller companies should adopt a geographic focus aimed at smaller communities. Consumer sophistication and price sensitivity are probably less pervasive in this market sector; the personal service and personal relationships of agents are likely to be more highly valued; persistency may be better. These probable advantages, combined with the clear advantage of lower mortality costs, are sufficient to establish sustainable competitive viability, even for a company with the disadvantages of smaller scale.

Nothing New Under the Sun? Some may view the suggested strategy as an appalling example of social irresponsibility — a "beggar thy competitor" exercise. The suggested strategy is not, in fact, a novel one. Geographic focus has long been a feature of the successful strategy of several prominent property and liability insurers. This has been particularly notable in the automobile insurance field. Some of the most successful ideas are transplants from another environment!

The Challenge for Smaller Companies. Smaller companies can exploit their potential advantages of focus only by eliminating some of their current activities. They must, to survive, do fewer things better. The reluctance of managements of smaller companies to undertake the necessary downsizing of their existing marginal activities is understandable and aptly described in William Shakespeare's *Hamlet:* "Thus conscience does make cowards of us all."

1988/3 Group Insurers: A Breed Apart?

Striking and fundamental changes have occurred and are occurring in the corporate group insurance business:

- The competitive focus of this cost-plus business has shifted towards "cost" and away from "plus."
- The role of the insurers is increasingly administrative and expertise-based rather than risk finance-oriented.
- Many smaller companies and a few prominent ones have withdrawn or announced plans to withdraw from this business.
- The business has experienced rapid growth, driven primarily by medical cost inflation, government policy and the aging of the population.

Cost vs. Plus. Corporate buyers of group insurance have awakened to the fact that their overall outlay for employee medical, life and disability insurance is mainly a function of the benefit cost rather than the insurer's retention. To compete successfully in this environment, the insurer requires detailed local knowledge to monitor claims settlements, relationships with an extensive network of preferred providers, skills in benefit design supported by an extensive statistical base and more.

Administration vs. Risk Financing. The contemporary corporate group insurance business rewards administrative skills and expertise more than the willingness to assume risk. In many respects, the skills and knowledge required to succeed are quite different from those required in other branches of the life and health insurance industry. In particular, marketing and distribution methods are very different; the agent does not occupy the same vital position.

The Implications of Consolidation. The changing competitive focus and the emergence of administrative skills and expertise as key elements in what is essentially a national market have raised the threshold of critical mass very significantly. Some have estimated that the minimum required volume of "premium equivalents" for a broadly based operation is now $1 billion. This has led many small companies and a few prominent ones to withdraw from this business, which now is largely concentrated among 20 or fewer companies, most of which have experienced growing market shares. Clearly, the threshold of critical mass is not the same for all companies; specialization, geographic concentration and other factors can act to reduce that threshold.

The Implications of Growth. The rapid growth of corporate group insurance and its concentration among fewer competitors, combined with the slow growth of individual life insurance, are factors that are changing quite dramatically the profile and culture of many of the dominant 20 companies. If the established trends continue, which seems likely, corporate group insurance will soon become the primary line of business for many or most of these companies (it already is for some). When this occurs, changes can be expected in the leadership of these companies, resulting in less tolerant attitudes towards other lines of business with marginal or submarginal economics or excessive distribution costs.

A Breed Apart? The dominant 20 companies may shrink in number further, accelerating the consolidation of this business. The surviving members are likely to evolve as a separately identifiable group, as different from the rest of the life insurance industry as multiline insurers are today. Many may acquire or be acquired by commercial lines property/liability insurers, which serve the same market; some probable survivors have already positioned themselves in this way. These companies, whatever their number, are likely to be "A Breed Apart."

1988/4 Preserving the "High-Touch" Distribution System

The individual personal insurance industry in North America — life, health, pension, auto and homeowners — is both blessed and cursed by its established agency distribution system.

The Blessing. The industry is the beneficiary of the only "high-touch" distribution system among all of its current or likely future competitors. This is an advantage not to be underestimated. Survey after survey confirms that most buyers of financial products prefer to deal with a qualified personal intermediary whom they trust.

The Curse. The curse of the system is its inherently high cost. Primarily, this relates to the man-hours of effort devoted to prospecting: how to find a potential buyer who needs the service offered *now*, not later. This "'prospecting time" is estimated to be as high as 80% of total agency effort for some lines of business, suggesting that the associated cost may be 50% of total distribution costs, or 33% of total expenses. The high failure rate of new agents is often blamed on their inability effectively to prospect.

Possible Solutions. The overriding objective is to retain the "high-touch" of the established distribution system while reducing the downtime associated with ineffective prospecting. How can this be accomplished? Some suggestions:

- information-based prospecting;
- multiproduct distribution;
- direct response prospecting; and
- seminars.

Information-Based Prospecting. Information-based prospecting is not new to the insurance industry. Individual agents have long been accumulating birth dates, expiration dates and so forth. Yet few insurance companies have undertaken a companywide initiative of this kind.

Some organizations, such as banks, thrifts and credit card sponsors, possess customer information that can be used to identify likely prospects and may take advantage of preferred access to their customers. Insurance companies also have useful information relating to existing policyholders, but have been reluctant to use that information directly, presumably for fear of offending their own agents.

A few insurers have actively sought to build an information base by offering "free" accident insurance to those willing to complete a comprehensive application form, which provides data useful to identify prospects for other products.

Multiproduct Distribution. All other things being equal, it is obvious that prospecting for someone who needs the service offered now will be twice as efficient (i.e., half as costly) if two services are offered rather than one. This obvious strategy has not worked in practice as well as the theory would suggest, but there are some notable successes and many partial successes. This strategy is better suited to larger organizations than to smaller ones, because it implies the need to develop and support additional products, each of which has its own separate "critical mass" requirement.

Direct Response Prospecting. The use of direct mail to identify likely prospects is extensive, both by companies and by individual agents. The techniques and the results vary widely. Clearly, the proliferation of "junk mail" has led to "list fatigue" and the cost effectiveness of this strategy has diminished. Greater selectivity, with respect to the mailing lists selected and to the products offered, is one way to counter the deteriorating economics.

The use of direct telephone as a prospecting method has also experienced increasing consumer resistance and deteriorating economics.

Advertising, in print and electronic media, is another form of direct response prospecting. Only the largest companies, with widespread market coverage, can afford to use the costly general media; other companies must be very selective in their choice of media. Both groups must be very selective in the products advertised because results vary widely according to the product appeal. It is difficult to measure the cost-effectiveness of this technique because the prospect cannot easily be identified as one motivated by a specific advertisement (except for such features as return coupons).

Seminars. The use of seminars as a prospecting strategy changes the process from one stage to two. The first stage involves the identification of prospects to attend the seminar; the second involves converting the attendees into prospects for the product. The strategies for each stage can be optimized separately.

The Outlook. If the manpower-intensive distribution system of the insurance industry is to continue in its current form and size, some strategy must be found to improve its economics. This is especially true with respect to the distribution of regular premium savings accumulation products, the backbone of most life insurance companies, because these products face increasing competition from outside the life insurance industry. Without a successful strategy to improve the economics of the insurance industry's current distribution system for individual products, the most probable alternative is slow decline accompanied by:

- the emergence of alternative "low-touch" distribution systems from outside the insurance industry;
- a large increase in the number of part-time agents less qualified to give the trusted advice that most buyers of insurance products seek; and
- increasing consumer reliance on employer-sponsored products for their life, health, pension, auto and homeowners coverages.

1989/1 Universal Life Ten Years Later

The first widespread offering of Universal Life was made in January 1979 by Life Insurance Company of California (late named E.F. Hutton Life). What has happened in the ten ensuing years? And why? And what next?

The Original Concept. Universal Life was conceived as a product intended to achieve three major goals:

- *Greater Flexibility.* Free-form family arrangements, more frequent divorce and change of employment, higher rates of inflation and other social and economic trends characterized the decade of the 1970s. These trends depreciated the value of long-term, fixed-dollar future promises, such as those offered by traditional life insurance products. The market demanded a more flexible alternative to achieve this goal, it was necessary to unbundle the product components and, consequently, to expose the cost of each.
- *More Competitive Investment Returns.* Most traditional life insurance products in 1979 were subject to a "proxy tax," paid by life insurance companies, which reduced the investment returns of policyholders by up to 3%. In addition, new money investment rates exceeded average portfolio returns by up to 3%, and traditional products were generally priced on the portfolio average basis. The emergence of money market funds and the subsequent dismantling of Regulation Q focused consumer attention on these differentials and the market demanded a higher return. Universal Life was designed to sidestep the proxy tax and to offer new money investment returns.
- *Reduced Distribution Costs.* Among the competitors in the retirement savings business, the life insurance industry experienced the highest costs, due primarily to its manpower-intensive distribution system. As cross-industry competition assumed greater importance, it became necessary to reduce distribution costs by offering a more appealing product, sold in greater volume at lower distribution costs.

The Realization. Some, but not all, of the goals have been achieved. Moreover, there have been unforeseen problems:

- *Flexibility.* From the consumer viewpoint, this goal has largely been achieved, but at some cost to the life insurance industry. The absence of a fixed-premium commitment, while addressing consumer needs, has presented new cash management problems to insurers.

- *Investment Returns.* Tax law changes in 1984 affecting life insurance companies have eliminated the proxy tax for most life insurance products. Meanwhile, as interest rates declined, beginning in 1982, new money and portfolio rates of return have converged. Thus, the initial advantages of Universal Life over traditional products have, in this respect, vanished.
- *Distribution Costs.* Beginning around 1983, new versions of Universal Life began to emerge. These products featured a return to traditional commission rates coupled with "concealed loads" of various types. This change represented a return by the life insurance industry to its traditional distribution-based philosophy and a rejection of the consumer-based philosophy which Universal Life was intended to promote.
- *Profitability.* In its original form, Universal Life was more profitable than concurrently issued traditional products. This was due to the reduced acquisition costs which then prevailed. The subsequent rise in distribution costs, high administrative costs and the greater price competition fostered by an unbundled product have significantly eroded profit margins for all but the most efficient competitors.
- *Replacement.* The original investment differentials fostered replacement activity of unprecedented dimensions, benefiting policyholders and agents at the expense of the life insurers.

What Next? Universal Life is here to stay. The challenge for the life insurance industry is to learn either to manage this product or to manage without it:

- *Distribution.* It may not be possible to distribute an unbundled product in the conventional, high-cost way. Universal Life may become the product of nonconventional distributors, while others offer it only as the product of last resort.
- *Investment.* The cash management problems of a product without fixed premiums are inherently different from those of traditional products. When the next interest rate spike occurs, consumer demand for new money investment returns on in-force Universal Life policies may give rise to significant new financial problems for the insurers. Variable Universal Life effectively addresses this problem by passing the investment risk back to the policyholder.

- *Administration.* The current administrative costs of Universal Life for most companies seem unreasonably high. This reflects, in fact, the relatively low in-force volume of most companies.
- *Competition.* An unbundled product fosters price competition, which is essentially cost competition. Universal Life will accelerate the demise of those high-cost competitors which continue to offer this product. They will face the distasteful alternatives of pricing their policies uncompetitively in order to recover their costs, or pricing them competitively by reducing premium rates to a level at which they cannot recover their costs.

1989/2 The Socialization of Private Insurance

Legislators, regulators and, recently in California, the public at large have contrived to use the system of private insurance to promote "social justice." The primary focus of these efforts has been on automobile and health insurance, the secondary focus on life and homeowners insurance.

"Social Justice." The actual cost of risk for most personal lines of business exhibits strong negative correlation with the economic means of the insureds. Thus, in a market-based — but not a group — environment, the poor likely will pay more than the rich for equivalent coverage. Accordingly, a system of private insurance, artificially restricted, affords the politically attractive opportunity for the rich to subsidize the poor without new government programs or visible additional taxes. This is the temptation to those in government who favor social engineering.

Artificial Restrictions. The artificial restrictions designed to achieve political goals include:

- *Socialization of Rate Classifications.* Restrictions on the variation of premium rates by geographic area, sex of the insured and other factors apply or have been suggested in various jurisdictions, notwithstanding large and demonstrable differences in the cost of risk among classes of insureds.
- *Limitations on Risk Selection.* Mandatory participation of insurers in Joint Underwriting Associations "to insure the uninsurable" is a widespread practice. Several jurisdictions have imposed limits on the right of life and health insurers to test for HIV infection. Auto insurers in many states are restricted on renewal options and several states have imposed mandatory offer requirements on new business.
- *Suppression of Rate Levels.* In Blue Cross hearings, state regulators sometimes push affordability over adequacy or solvency. Even more extremes exist in casualty insurance with some regulators setting rate levels, or with the public interposing its will (e.g., the 20% rate rollback via Proposition 103).

Attempts to repeal the laws of economics by restricting risk classification and/or underwriting standards, coupled with rate restraints, are reminiscent of King Canute's demonstration that even he could not control the tide.

Will It Work? Can unaffordable risks be insured at affordable rates? The Socialization of Private Insurance is really only feasible for types of insurance that are compulsory and noncompetitive. Even for monopolistic but voluntary coverages, feasibility is a question of degree; at some point, the better risks will withdraw from the arrangement and the entire scheme may collapse.

Is It Fair? Social Justice and Fairness are not necessarily synonymous. Social Justice relates primarily to the issue of who benefits; Fairness widens the issue to include the question of who pays. To achieve one goal at the expense of the other is a dubious exchange. If, to achieve social purposes relevant to a few, the result is the destruction of the private insurance system, which has served well the needs of the many, the efforts of the social engineers are a failure.

The Alternatives. Cross-subsidy among insurance classes with different risk profiles is not the answer to the problem of affordability. The objective is to reduce cost, not merely to transfer it. There are better alternatives:

- *Tort Reform.* Reducing the actual cost of the tort system by encouraging alternatives to litigation, by limiting damages for pain and suffering, by restricting punitive damages and by eliminating "double dipping" would reduce appreciably the cost of both automobile and health insurance. Contrary to popular belief and even the propaganda of the insurance industry, such a change would be in the public interest and not in the long-term interest of the industry; tort reform would actually diminish the market for insurance by reducing its cost.
- *Limitations on Medical Costs.* Health care providers operate on a cost-plus basis. For most people, there is the illusion that health care is "free." That illusion is understandable — employers and government finance most of the direct costs, and the indirect costs are not very visible. Some controls must be imposed.
- *Loss Prevention.* Insurance rating systems don't create high risks; they identify them. To that extent, they isolate areas for greater loss prevention, instead of mere risk transfer.

The Politics. Many varied constituencies have an important vested interest in the issues related to the Socialization of Private Insurance: politicians seeking reelection; the legal profession; the medical establishment; the insurance industry; employers; government; and, last and least, the general public, rich and poor.

The time has come to recognize that the public — not employers, government or insurers — pays the cost of this folly in higher premiums, higher prices for goods and services and higher taxes. The integrity of insurers is a legitimate concern of government; holding back the tide and legislating equivalent life expectancies for men and women are not.

1989/3 How Mighty Are the Fallen?

In August 1945, Japan was ruined: its population decimated; its cities devastated; and its national treasure depleted. In less than two generations, there has emerged from the ashes of 1945 a nation admired for its economic success, its social and political stability and its culture.

The Key Ingredients. Japan's economic success has provided the foundation for its other achievements. That success has many key ingredients:

- *Self-Discipline; Self-Denial.* The Japanese people have consistently accepted a lower standard of living than their economy would have supported. Contemporary American society has often been characterized as the "Now Generation"; Japanese society might similarly be characterized as the "Later Generation."

  Modest wage demands have allowed businesses to realize, to retain and to reinvest large profits; this and a very high personal savings rate have fueled the accumulation of wealth in Japan.
- *Education.* Education in Japan is achievement oriented and highly competitive. The aim is to provide an educational experience, not a social experience. School years are much longer than those in the U.S. and somewhat longer than those in other developed countries. The children of Japan are not exempt from the demands of their society.
- *Work Ethic.* The Protestant work ethic, by another name, is alive and well in Japan. A traveller arriving at Narita Airport in Tokyo can confirm this simply by observing the energy of baggage handlers.
- *Cooperation between Business and Government.* "Japan, Incorporated" is not a myth. Business and government are partners, not adversaries.
- *Defense Spending.* Since 1945, defense spending in Japan has been very low, while other countries have impoverished their societies through military expenditures aimed more at preserving existing regimes than meeting real defense needs.

Three Phases of the Economic Miracle. Since 1945, Japan's economy has passed through three phases:

- *Reindustrialization.* The early phase saw the reestablishment of basic industries, such as steel making and shipbuilding. Success was based on low wages and a highly motivated work force.

- *Technology.* The middle phase was characterized by the application of modern technology to the manufacturing process. Examples include the motorcycle, automobile and electronics industries.
- *Financial.* The latest phase is financial. High rates of personal savings and retained profits have provided a source of low-cost capital to finance the economic recovery and development of Japan. These engines of wealth accumulation have now exceeded the investment capacity of the Japanese economy and are affecting investment markets worldwide.

The Financial Phase. The Tokyo Stock Exchange is now the largest in the world. Japan's net foreign investments are the largest in the world. The value of Japanese real estate is stupendous by world standards. Most of the leading international banks are Japanese as are many of the world's leading life insurance companies. These are all well-known facts. What is not well known is the magnitude of the capital funds of various Japanese financial institutions, particularly the life insurance companies.

In the U.S., the aggregate capital of all life insurance companies is less than $100 billion. Capital is defined as the excess of market value of assets over the larger of minimum statutory liabilities or a realistic valuation of liabilities, including provision for future policyholder dividends. Perhaps 95% of this capital is shared by 200 companies; the largest has approximately $5 billion and the average, $500 million.

In Japan, the corresponding amounts can be estimated only within a wide range, perhaps plus or minus 50%. Published financial statements do not provide a realistic measure of capital, primarily because assets are valued at the lower of cost or market. A reasonable estimate is $500 billion. Perhaps 99% of this capital is shared by 20 private companies; the largest probably has more than $100 billion and the average, $25 billion.

Implications. In terms of capital, the private life insurance industry in Japan is probably larger than the private life insurance industries of the rest of the world combined. Moreover, the industry in Japan is very concentrated and its largely mutual composition allows it a long-term investment perspective.

Thus far, Japanese life insurers have only an incidental involvement in foreign markets, except as passive investors. But given their financial resources, they have the capacity to buy or burn their way into any market they choose.

Their future actions could alter the landscape of financial businesses worldwide.

Epilogue. The operational success of the life insurance industry in Japan is based primarily on the hunger of the Japanese people for trusted savings products; the financial success of the industry is based primarily on its investment strategy, driven by rising share prices and real estate values. Thus have the Fallen become Mighty.

1989/4 A Functional View of Insurer Performance

The insurance industry is not a homogeneous business. Most often, it is analyzed by lines of business — property, liability, health, life and so forth. An alternative way to analyze the industry is to examine its functions. To a considerable extent, these overlap its lines of business.

Among the several diverse functions provided by the insurance industry, three stand out: risk transfer, administration and financial intermediation.

How well has the industry performed on a functional basis?

Risk Transfer. The risk transfer function is the origin of the insurance business and continues to be its distinguishing purpose. In general, the industry has performed this function well, but there are some major shortcomings.

In the personal property and liability insurance sector, the service provided by the industry has become part of the social fabric of modern civilization. Without homeowners' insurance, would the private residential mortgage system exist? Who, other than the indigent or the reckless, would dare to own or drive an automobile without liability insurance? Or own or fly a private airplane? In these and related areas, the industry clearly has performed a socially valid and valuable service at reasonable cost.

Industry performance in the life and health insurance areas is not as favorable. In part, this is because major portions of these coverages often are employer provided and, hence, come and go with employment. Lapse rates on individual coverage are scandalously high; continuity of coverage is correspondingly low; and costs are quite high. Life and disability insurance benefits tend to be too low for younger persons with dependents and too high for older persons, with or without dependents; the tendency is to sell based on the ability to pay rather than on need. Moreover, inflation has caused the value of permanent life and long-term disability insurance to depreciate rapidly, and what was ostensibly level coverage, level premium insurance became decreasing coverage, decreasing premium insurance.

In all personal lines — property, liability, life and health — the industry is susceptible to the criticism that it often insures trivial risks that do not provide realistic social value but are quite expensive. First-dollar coverage may be appealing in the marketplace, but it may also displace more urgently needed coverage on the grounds of affordability.

In the commercial insurance sector, the service provided by the industry is suffering from adverse trends in capacity relative to the needs of those insured. One wonders what value there is if an insurer, capitalized at $1 billion or less, insures an industrial organization with capital funds of $10 billion, or $100 billion. Of course, through reinsurance, the risk-taking capacity of an individual insurer can be magnified. Nevertheless, the entire capital of the industry is less than the risk exposures of some major industrial corporations. Accordingly, one can foresee that major industrial organizations will insure each other through some risk-sharing operation and that the role of the insurance industry may become that of the facilitator of such arrangements.

Administration. Group medical insurance has become primarily a cost-plus administrative business for the insurance industry. In terms of dollar throughput, this is already or will soon be the largest branch of the industry.

Formerly, the competitive focus of this branch of the industry was on the "plus" of cost-plus. Today, it is more related to the ability of the administrator to contain the "cost." This requires sophisticated systems and detailed information. One major result has been a quantum leap in the necessary scale of claim management, evidenced by the recent withdrawal from this market of several prominent carriers.

Performance of this function is generally good and has consistently improved, but public perception of the industry's performance in this service area is quite mixed. The medical establishment claims it inhibits their clinical practice. The general public is upset by the administrative hassle which is the essence of effective cost control.

Financial Intermediation. Financial intermediation has become a large and growing function of the insurance industry. But the insurance industry's record as financial intermediator is negative or mixed. Substantial amounts have been lost upon the discovery that cash and loan values under individual life insurance contracts were, in fact, demand deposits. Sponsors of group pension plans have exercised one-way options in their favor, causing large and sometimes spectacular losses to the carrier involved. In the property/liability area, the results have been better, probably because the policyholders did not have the same discretion to select against the insurance companies to their benefit.

Conclusion. Viewed functionally, the insurance industry scores reasonably well on risk transfer and administration, and rather poorly on financial intermediation. This scorecard suggests two possible strategies: avoid the problem areas or capitalize on the mistakes of others.

1990/1 The Cost of Catastrophe

Within a period of eight weeks, four major disasters occurred in the United States:

- Hurricane Hugo, which struck the South Carolina coast at Charleston and moved inland as far as Charlotte, North Carolina;
- the Earthquake, centered at Santa Cruz, which radiated throughout the San Francisco Bay area;
- the Explosion and Fire which destroyed the Phillips Petroleum plant in Pasadena, Texas; and
- the Tornadoes which devastated Huntsville, Alabama and then skipped along the East Coast as far north as Newburgh, New York.

What are the implications of this series of events for individuals, business, the public sector and the insurance industry?

What Was the Cost? The cost in terms of lives lost and personal injuries sustained was remarkably small considering the severity of these four nearly concurrent catastrophes. Nevertheless, these must be counted as the main cost in human terms.

In financial terms, it is difficult at this stage to assess the cost of the overall damage and its distribution. A rough estimate among a wide range of possibilities is that the total damage will amount to $20 billion, and an equally rough estimate of the distribution of that cost is:

- individual, $5 billion;
- business, $3 billion;
- the public sector, $2 billion; and
- the insurance industry, $10 billion.

These estimates are quite crude and will doubtless later prove to be inaccurate. Nevertheless, they are useful as a foundation for an analysis of how the ultimate cost is allocated after transfers.

Transfers. Several important secondary transfers of the cost will occur among the various parties:

- Individual losses will give rise to tax deductions which may result in a transfer to the public sector of $1 billion.
- Business losses will generally be tax deductible, creating a transfer to the public sector of approximately $1 billion.

- Disaster relief provided by the public sector mainly to individuals may give rise to a transfer of $1 billion.
- The insurance industry will have tax-deductible losses of $10 billion, which may give rise to a transfer from the insurance industry to the public sector of $3 billion, considering the likely utilization of these tax losses and the timing of their use.

Additional transfers may occur depending upon the ingenuity of litigants in attempting to pursue liability claims against various parties — the public sector, contractors, etc. Some of these costs may then transfer to the public sector and the insurance industry.

The Ultimate Cost. After considering the major predictable transfers, the cost breakdown may be:

- individual, $3 billion;
- business, $2 billion;
- the public sector, $8 billion; and
- the insurance industry, $7 billion.

Catastrophe Reserves. Even after adjusting for these transfers, the property/casualty insurance industry's operating results will be hurt severely by this series of major catastrophes. And since the industry is not allowed to build up catastrophe reserves during the good years, the estimated $7 billion net cost will be funded directly from the current earnings and surplus of the industry.

A justifiable claim can be made that the property/casualty insurance industry should be allowed to establish tax-deductible catastrophe reserves, making contributions to the reserve in good years and drawing upon the reserve in years like 1989. There are many ways to structure such a reserve, but the need is clear. The cooperation not only of government but of the accounting profession would be required to produce rational results.

One example might serve as a model. It is derived from the mortgage guaranty insurance industry, where companies are allowed to establish tax-deductible contingency reserves but are then required to invest the amount of those reserves in non-interest-bearing government securities. Other alternatives may be more appropriate.

Nevertheless, in the context of an industry with a statutory capitalization of only $130 billion, the concept of a reserve for catastrophes clearly is warranted.

For several years, the Risk and Insurance Management Society has argued that non-insurance businesses should also be allowed to establish similar tax-deductible reserves for uninsured losses. Such provisions are allowed in Denmark and in Sweden. The Exxon Valdez episode illustrates the need. Clearly, such a provision would enhance the social accountability of business, probably to the ultimate benefit of the individual and public sectors.

1990/2 Eastern Europe: An Essay

Western leaders, members of the media and, one suspects, the Western Intelligence Community appeared to be as astonished as the general public by the swiftly moving events which have swept across Eastern Europe during the past year.

These events could not have developed without the acquiescence of the Soviet Union. President Gorbachev, after consolidating his power, introduced the policies of glasnost and perestroika. Whether his motives were philosophical or pragmatic will long be debated.

Eastern Europe. The first breach in the Iron Curtain occurred in Poland, where the government agreed to hold free elections, with the proviso that it would retain control of key ministries. The result was a resounding defeat for the Communist Party. When it became clear that the Soviet Union would not interfere, the rest of Eastern Europe was emboldened and other governments were forced to agree to power-sharing arrangements, pending even freer and less conditional elections. In some countries, the Communist Party was dissolved, or at least renamed. The reaction in Romania included the summary trial and execution of the longtime leader and his wife. The two Germanys are moving rapidly towards reunification. In Yugoslavia and Albania, which remain Communist but are not tied to Moscow, similar forces are stirring.

Western Euphoria. These changes and the promise of more have created euphoria among the peoples of the West. Their governments are more cautious. The prevailing public mood is that democratic governments and a partial return to a market-based economy will produce immediate benefits for the 100 million people of Eastern Europe.

The Darker Realities. Potential territorial and ethnic disputes smolder throughout the region. The average gross national product per capita of the countries of Eastern Europe and the Soviet Union was reported by the U.N. as approximately $2,000 in 1984. The same source reported the average GNP per capita of the Western developed nations at approximately $10,000. Although comparisons of this type are notoriously unreliable, the gap is too wide to be explained away as a statistical aberration.

The solutions to the potential political problems and the obvious economic problems are related. Most of these countries are already overburdened with international debts that almost certainly cannot be repaid. To placate popular expectations, immediate funding will be required to provide more consumer goods and, to modernize these economies, long-term capital investment will be needed.

A second Marshall Plan, even more ambitious than the first but with more participants, is required if the democratic and economic reforms under way are to succeed. Long-term investment capital from the private sector is also needed. The alternative is a return to some form of totalitarian rule.

Implications for Western Business. For private industrial companies, the possibility of exporting capital and technology to build or rebuild the industries of Eastern Europe is clearly present for those who are convinced that the investment rewards and risks correspond. Many of these opportunities will take the form of joint ventures with local partners. For such programs to attract capital from the private sector, funding to bolster the availability of consumer goods must come in the form of international grants for which no repayment can be expected.

In the financial services sector, the international banks will have unlimited opportunities to lend funds, but the lessons learned from previous loans to less developed countries will promote caution. The January 29, 1990 Life edition of the *National Underwriter* published an article relating to insurance opportunities in Eastern Europe, including a brief report of the activities of the American International Group in these markets. The article implies that most of the activities has to do with the export/import trade, although AIG expresses optimism that domestic opportunities will be found in areas involving short-term risks and administrative systems. The factors required for a viable savings-oriented life insurance industry are generally not present in these countries. Among the requirements are a stable currency, confidence in long-term political stability and reasonable amounts of discretionary income.

Conclusion. The recent events in Eastern Europe, if properly managed, can lead to extraordinary long-term benefits for the peoples of Eastern Europe and the world. These benefits are probably a generation away and, in the meantime, progress is likely to be disappointingly slow, with attendant political risks.

1990/3 Junk Bonds: Have We Learned Too Much?

The junk bond phenomenon of the late 1980s, which turned into calamity in 1990, has left a lasting imprint on Corporate America, financial intermediaries, pension fund administrators and investors. Whoever coined the term "junk bond" was both pundit and prophet. Socrates is credited with saying, "The first step in learning truth is to call a thing by its right name." Nevertheless, calamity may now become opportunity for some investors.

The Concept. The concept of using high-yield debt to replace equity capital is straightforward:

- Borrowers can afford high rates because interest is tax deductible.
- Investors can achieve higher net yields if the risk premium exceeds the net default rate.

The concept achieved growing acceptance and intermediaries received substantial fees for arranging such transactions. The result was the issuance of $200 billion of these securities. The main use of the proceeds was to finance corporate takeovers, often at very high prices.

The Problem. The concept was and still is valid. The problem was the indiscriminate use of junk bonds by borrowers and lenders, encouraged by promoters of these arrangements.

Borrowers responded to the availability of cheap capital by overreaching. Acquisition prices soared and daredevil financing became routine. No doubt personal egos contributed to the eagerness to acquire. Perhaps some borrowers were encouraged to make speculative or overpriced acquisitions on the basis of Ruin Theory: Their maximum loss was 100% of their often modest equity interest, whereas the potential gain might be much larger.

Investors evaluated these securities by comparing the risk premium to *historical* default rates, not recognizing that the new breed of leveraged buyouts involved significantly higher risk. Eagerly, they provided capital to finance deals that would never have been done at appropriate interest rates.

Promoters of these transactions were motivated more by the feasibility of the deal than by its soundness. They operated in an Alice-in-Wonderland environment which, simultaneously, was both a buyers' and a sellers' market.

Calamity. Late in 1989, the calamity began. Disappointing post-acquisition results, belated recognition of the default risk and scattered defaults and "restructurings" (with rumors of many more to come) resulted in a sharp drop in market values. Dealers who had promoted junk bonds were subject to SEC capital requirements based on market values. They faced the prospect of forced liquidation of their inventories at depressed prices. The most prominent dealer, Drexel Burnham Lambert, filed for bankruptcy holding a reported $1 billion inventory of these securities.

The junk bond market collapsed. Many issues declined to 50% of their original value; at these prices, yields to maturity were quoted at 20% to 30%.

The Insurance Industry. Some insurance companies invested significant amounts in junk bonds to support yields on certain products, notably single-premium annuities and Guaranteed Investment Contracts. Others purchased junk bonds for more general reasons. A follow-the-leader mentality developed. As long as these securities could be valued at amortized cost, no immediate threat to earnings or solvency was present. But forced liquidation or actual default would require the reporting of substantial losses. This possibility added to the concerns of an already panicky market.

The Current Situation. New issue activity in junk bonds is not likely to reappear soon. But existing junk bonds will remain outstanding for many years. Many issues are potentially attractive investments at current prices. The available risk premium on a number of junk bonds advanced from 3% or 5% to 10% or 20%. Just as the original risk premium was inadequate, at least on some issues, the current premium may be excessive.

An investment in junk bonds, when priced substantially below par, involves a number of special considerations:

- The default risk is not always a total loss; a *gain* is possible if default accelerates maturity and the payoff in bankruptcy is above the current investment value.
- The default risk with respect to each payment increases over time and warrants a more complex analysis than a simple comparison of yields to maturity and perceived quality.
- Assuming no default, market volatility and automatic reinvestment to maturity are comparable to deep discount bonds.

Out of the Ashes. Out of the ashes of the junk bond calamity, an unusual investment opportunity may have emerged for those with staying power and strong nerves. Some will be dismayed by this unfashionable suggestion and will argue, "We should learn from our mistakes." The reply might be, "Yes, but sometimes we learn too much."

1990/4 Honesty, Prudence and Competence

Regulators, legislators and insurance executives are expressing serious concerns about the solvency of all major branches of the insurance industry. Some suggestions, aimed at prevention or containment, have already been advanced.

The Hazards. There is general agreement as to the underlying hazards facing the industry as well as a recognition that these apply unevenly to its various branches and still more unevenly to individual companies. What are the major hazards?

- The underwriting risk most affects the property/casualty and health insurance branches.
- Mismatching of assets and liabilities affects all branches to some degree but is particularly important to life insurance.
- Speculative or inappropriate investments affect all branches.
- Rapid growth in risky lines of business and inadequate capitalization exacerbate all hazards.
- Mismanagement fosters irrational competition and often leads to industry-wide financial losses which, at a minimum, deplete the capital of all companies, even the better-managed ones.
- External guarantees encourage such reckless management practices as "betting the company."
- Regulatory inadequacy applies to all branches.
- Financial reinsurance can threaten both the ceding company and the reinsurer; certain other corporate transactions also provide current surplus relief at the expense of future profits. Some transactions resemble the issuance of "junk bonds" by the company seeking surplus relief.

These hazards are real and menacing, especially when combined, which often is the case. What steps might be taken to minimize the hazards or to contain their effects?

Prevention. The capital requirements to obtain and to maintain an insurance license vary among the states and range from absurdly low to modest. A significant increase in the minimums clearly is needed. At the same time, capital requirements should be made elastic to recognize different levels of risk exposure. This action can be taken on a state-by-state basis; once a significant number of important states have enacted more stringent requirements, the operations of undercapitalized companies would be limited geographically.

More frequent review and more vigilant enforcement of financial requirements by the various states would detect some problems at an earlier stage. The NAIC continues to support this concept and has recently required actuarial certification of property/casualty insurance reserves in all states for virtually all companies. Improved enforcement will require the authorization of additional funding by state legislatures which may, in many cases, be reluctant to "reward" departments with which they already are dissatisfied. The most likely alternative to effective state regulation is federal intervention leading to a system of dual regulation.

Containment. State guarantee associations traditionally have provided financial underpinning to policyholders. This self-insurance system generally has dealt effectively with scattered insolvencies among smaller companies but has not been tested with respect to widespread insolvencies or those involving large companies. Some hazards might simultaneously affect a large number of companies, leading to the possibility of industrywide collapse. State guarantee associations do not provide uniform coverage and do not always coordinate. The system is rightly seen by many to discourage prudence.

If proposed, a federally guaranteed system is likely to be viewed without enthusiasm by a Congress still smarting from the S&L debacle and worried about possible losses in the banking industry. A dual system of regulation and guarantees would invite the type of antiselection which occurred between the FSLIC and the FDIC, when stronger thrifts elected to become banks due to the insurance costs.

One suggested containment measure deals with the punishment of transgressors. The record in the S&L industry is not encouraging. Civil law may be a more effective deterrent than criminal law.

A Different Focus. It seems incongruous that the issue of solvency has become a real and widespread concern in a mature industry with a very good history of keeping its promises. The same might have been said a decade ago about the thrift and banking industries. Financial intermediaries of all types are feeling the pressure of reduced margins and the associated temptation to seek profits by assuming greater risks without an appropriate added charge.

The often failed attempts to enhance the security of those who rely on the promises of others are a reminder that there are no substitutes for honesty, prudence and competence. If this goal is to be the focus of future public policy, regulators need wider discretionary powers. Legislators should grant those powers and insist that they be wisely used.

1991/1 Internationalization: A Capital Issue

International operations have long been an important aspect of the financial services industry, particularly in such "wholesale" business sectors as institutional lending, reinsurance and securities underwriting. Initially, financial companies based in countries with well-developed financial markets exported their skills and capital to countries with less developed markets, many of which shared a common language and compatible legal traditions. The flow in this direction continues, noticeably in Europe, but a reverse current is also running and is likely to strengthen.

The New Invaders. In recent years, financial institutions from previously invaded countries have become invaders or potential invaders. Almost without exception, these New Invaders are well capitalized; in many cases, their available capital has outstripped the growth potential of their home markets, in which they already hold dominant shares. Lacking more attractive alternatives, some have decided to enter long-established markets, usually by acquisition of one or more existing companies. Nowhere is this new trend more apparent than in the life insurance industry in the United States.

Why U.S.A.? The attractions of the American life insurance business to foreign investors relate to the size of the market, its lack of concentration, the political and financial stability of the country and especially the ease of entry. As a result, foreign investors now own, control or have significant positions in a large number of U.S. life insurance companies, including some prominent ones.

Foreign investors have been generally aggressive in pricing their acquisitions, leading the market as a whole to higher prices and adding "hope value" to the share prices of quoted companies.

A Contrast of Capital. The capital-generating capacity of most life insurance companies follows one of two models:

- The North American model emphasizes products with meaningful monetary guarantees and fixed interest investments. Profits are driven mainly by investment spreads and underwriting gains, which generally are fully taxed as they accrue.
- The European model places less emphasis on products with meaningful monetary guarantees and more emphasis on equity investments in shares

and property; if the investment strategy succeeds, the resultant increase in capital allows even more focus on equity investments. Profits are driven mainly by capital gains, which generally are not taxed until realized.

Clearly, during the second half of the 20th century, the second model has outperformed the first by a very wide margin. Companies of the second type command capital resources which typically are five to 20 times those of operationally similar companies of the first type.

The Future. Will the reverse current continue to flow? And will the aggressive acquisition strategy of foreign investors be successful financially?

The first question is more easily answered than the second. The reverse flow of capital from younger markets to older will continue. The capital-rich companies of Japan have not yet invested heavily in the U.S. life insurance industry. Eventually, they will. Behind them stand other potentially major investors in Korea, Taiwan and Singapore. A severe and prolonged fall in share prices and property values in their home markets could interrupt the flow, but would not end it.

The financial success of the aggressively priced acquisitions by foreign investors will not be determined by the entry price, but by the subsequent operational success of their new subsidiaries. In general, the new owners have pursued a laissez-faire policy. But those who decided to sell had a reason and not necessarily just the attractive price. Some had doubts relating to their own prospects. Some of the newly acquired companies, now given a well-capitalized parent in a far-away country, may continue yesterday's strategy while their competitors, driven by more demanding owners, regroup into new configurations which cross traditional lines between various financial services and eventually lead to greater efficiency. Time alone will answer this question.

1991/2 Valedictory

Since 1985, I have had the privilege of writing "The Last Word" in *Emphasis.* My longtime colleague and dear friend, Thomas P. Bowles, Jr., was the creative force behind both the much-enhanced version of this publication and the concept of this column. For three and a half years, Tom served as the Editor-in-Chief of *Emphasis.* He and his able successor, Michael A. Walters, have been my constant and often needed prod, while Julius Vogel and several others have served always to monitor and sometimes to modify the intellectual content. For their collective and constructive efforts, I thank them all.

A Retrospective. As I look back across the years since this column began, certain key issues stand out:

- the need for the life insurance industry to contain its distribution costs;
- the probability that new competitors, most likely from the banking industry, will intrude into the insurance scene;
- the likelihood of massive consolidation of financial services businesses of all types, both domestically and internationally;
- the need for a more rational basis of taxation for the life insurance industry and its policyholders;
- the irrational costs associated with the property/casualty system of private insurance;
- the growing importance of non-U.S.-based financial institutions;
- the implications and results of various investment strategies; and
- the capital needs and future structure of mutual insurance companies.

Most of these issues remain outstanding today. Among them, only the question of taxation involving life insurance in the U.S. has been resolved — at least for now.

New Leadership. Recently, another longtime colleague and friend, Michael R. Tuohy, became managing director of Tillinghast. In my view, his appointment involves more than the assumption of the managerial responsibilities of a professional organization with which I am proud to have been associated; it entails the guardianship of its intellectual tradition. I am confident that this valued tradition will endure and prosper under his leadership.

The aim of this column always has been to stimulate more than to inform, and I expect this tradition also will continue. The readers of *Emphasis* can look forward in the months ahead to many provocative, challenging ideas from the thought leaders of this firm.

Valedictory. Some 30 years ago, my wife and I built a home. In the process, we consulted an interior designer at Rich's, Atlanta's leading department store. We explained to him our all-too-elaborate decorating schemes. He replied with advice I shall never forget: "The most important thing is to know when to stop." That time has now come with respect to my authorship of this column.

With great confidence, I hand over my quill to Michael R. Tuohy and his colleagues. I wish them well.

Finally, I want to express my appreciation to those amongst the readers who at times have complimented my efforts and to offer my regrets to those whom I may sometimes have offended.

Farewell.